College Counseling and Student Development

Theory, Practice, and Campus Collaboration

edited and written by
Derrick A. Paladino, Laura M. Gonzalez,
and Joshua C. Watson

AMERICAN COUNSELING
ASSOCIATION
6101 Stevenson Avenue, Suite 600
Alexandria, VA 22304
www.counseling.org

College Counseling and Student Development

American Counseling Association
6101 Stevenson Avenue, Suite 600
Alexandria, VA 22304

Associate Publisher Carolyn C. Baker

Digital and Print Development Editor Nancy Driver

Senior Production Manager Bonny E. Gaston

Copy Editor Regina Gregory

Cover and text design by Bonny E. Gaston

Library of Congress Cataloging-in-Publication Data

Names: Paladino, Derrick A., editor, author. | Gonzalez, Laura M., editor, author. | Watson, Joshua C., editor, author. | American Counseling Association.
Title: College counseling and student development : theory, practice, and campus collaboration / written and edited by Derrick A. Paladino, Laura M. Gonzalez, and Joshua C. Watson.
Description: Alexandria, VA : American Counseling Association, 2020. | Includes bibliographical references and index. |
Identifiers: LCCN 2019053886 | ISBN 9781556203800 (Paperback)
Subjects: LCSH: Counseling in higher education—United States. | College student development programs—United States.
Classification: LCC LB2343 .C6125 2020 | DDC 378.1/97—dc23
LC record available at https://lccn.loc.gov/2019053886

Dedication

To the best four-legged writing buddies in the universe:
Ernie, Sammy, and Iggy Stardust. Your unconditional love
always barks up the right tree.

—Derrick A. Paladino

To my children, future college students Julian, Javier, and Evelyn Gonzalez. You
inspire me and give me abundant hope for a future in which
every young person is honored, valued, and nurtured
to the fullest expression of self.

—Laura M. Gonzalez

To my friends and colleagues whose infectious enthusiasm for helping others
motivates and inspires me every day. Each of you help
to make the world a better place for us all.

—Joshua C. Watson

■ ■ ■

We would also like to dedicate this text to young (and young-at-heart) adults who are striving to reach their goals as college students and also to the passionate college counselors and student affairs professionals whose mission is to nurture the development, safety, and success of college students.

Table of Contents

Preface ix
About the Editors xv
About the Contributors xvii
Acknowledgments xxiii

Part I
The College Counseling Profession

Chapter 1
History and Evolution of College Counseling
Derrick A. Paladino, Kathryn P. (Tina) Alessandria, and David J. Denino 3

Chapter 2
Roles and Responsibilities
Joshua C. Watson and Derrick A. Paladino 27

Chapter 3
College Counseling Through a Multicultural and Social Justice Lens
Derrick A. Paladino and Michael M. Kocet 43

Chapter 4
Legal and Ethical Issues in College Counseling
Perry C. Francis 77

Part II
Collaborative Services in College Counseling

Chapter 5
Understanding the Student Affairs Context
Alan M. Schwitzer and Dana Burnett 101

Chapter 6
Building Collaborative Campus Relationships
Elizabeth Likis-Werle, Laura M. Gonzalez, Carolyn Rifkin, Alan M. Schwitzer, and Dana Burnett 125

Chapter 7
Outreach and Preventative Services
Derrick A. Paladino 141

Chapter 8
Crisis and Emergency Management
Brian Van Brunt, Amy Murphy, and Jeff Solomon 163

Part III
Student Development Theory, Student Learning, and Developmental Considerations

Chapter 9
Understanding Student Development Theory
Derrick A. Paladino 185

Chapter 10
Neuro-Informed College Counseling
Samuel Sanabria 201

Chapter 11
Psychosocial Theories of Student Development
Joshua C. Watson and Benjamin Robertson 217

Chapter 12
Cognitive and Moral Theories of Student Development
Joshua C. Watson, Laura M. Gonzalez, and Rachel Shakin 233

Chapter 13
Experiential Theories of Student Development
Laura M. Gonzalez and Steven Mencarini 249

Chapter 14
Social Constructivism and Identity in Student Development
Laura M. Gonzalez and Christopher C. Graham 261

Part IV
Clinical Issues in the College Context

Chapter 15
Family and Relationships
Lesley Casarez, Amy Murphy, and Brian Van Brunt 279

Chapter 16
Academic and Career Issues
Mark B. Scholl, Christy M. Buchanan, and Esther Suess 299

Chapter 17
Substance Use and Addiction
Elizabeth Likis-Werle 317

Chapter 18
Stress and Anxiety
Joshua C. Watson and Amanda Faucher 331

Chapter 19
Depression and Suicide
Joshua C. Watson and Amanda Faucher 353

Chapter 20
Continuum of Disordered Eating in College
Natalie Arce Indelicato and Brianna Kane 373

Chapter 21
Understanding and Responding to Self-Injury
Julia L. Whisenhunt 391

Chapter 22
Sexual Issues and Concerns
Meghan K. Root 413

Chapter 23
Sexual Victimization
Kristin Bruns 431

Index 443

Preface

The college counseling landscape has evolved quite a bit. Over the past decade, we have witnessed 2-year and 4-year colleges being shaped by increased attention to mental health issues, crisis response and triage procedures, and students coming to campus already taking prescribed psychotropic medication. In addition, social media and electronic communication have changed our society in important and indelible ways that we have only started to describe and respond to as scholars and practitioners. Also, greater access to college by a more diverse student population is an important gain that requires greater understanding of students working part-time or full-time while in school, having dependents themselves, being first-generation students, seeking online education, and being returning and/or nontraditional-age students. Indeed, in data drawn from 2016, the National Center for Education Statistics (2018) reflected that one in five college students is at least 30 years old, two in five attend a community college, and almost half attend college part-time at some juncture. Adding to this list of considerations is the context of community, national, global, and political events, which are experienced by students in ways that are both personal and career oriented. This list is by no means exhaustive but rather a dusting of the contemporary college student's ecology. We contend that these changes necessitate a greater understanding of college student mental health and well-being across campus support offices to facilitate the academic, social, and personal/emotional success of all students.

So, who are the key players in this important task of supporting college student development, well-being, and success? We have written this text for all individuals who are preparing themselves to serve students in the web of clinical and support services on a college campus. Thus, our audience could include graduate students in counseling programs who wish to work with college students and need perspective on what makes this clientele and this setting unique. Our audience could also include graduate students in student affairs who want to supplement their training with a greater understanding of mental health issues. We are also aware that some professional staff find their way to working on campus without a background in either of those training programs and thus find that they need some additional resources to fill in gaps in their preparation. We would like to speak with all of you, future and current professionals who care about and want to support today's college students. Too often, the work of college counselors occurs in silos and lacks perspective on how others on campus are approaching their work to promote college student wellness. In fact, we believe that promoting greater understanding and exchange between the worlds of college counseling and student development will lead to greater teamwork and collaboration. We welcome all readers who want to promote college student development in a holistic way.

This is important because today's students need support in some critically important ways. In recent years, college counseling center staff have experienced increases in the following:

- counseling center provision of direct services over indirect services
- counseling center utilization (i.e., increased by an average of 30%–40%, whereas enrollment increased by only 5%)
- the frequency of students with a lifetime prevalence of threat-to-self (TTS) indicators (TTS includes nonsuicidal self-injury, serious suicidal ideation, and suicide attempts)
- students with TTS indicators using more services than students without TTS indicators (i.e., 20%–30% more services)
- depression, general anxiety, and social anxiety as clinical issues
- resources being diverted to crisis and triage appointments rather than traditional individual counseling services
- the student rate of prior counseling
- the percentage of 18- to 24-year-olds enrolled in college (i.e., 2- and 4-year colleges and universities)
- students graduating in 6 years (Association for University and College Counseling Center Directors [AUCCCD], 2017; Center for Collegiate Mental Health, 2019; Musu-Gillette et al., 2017).

These changes are important to reflect on as they bring light to the experiences that shape a student's development, academic success, and campus climate. In addition, when thinking about the college as an ecological system, one must recognize the implications of this environment for clients with the abovementioned experiences who have just visited the counseling center and are now walking back to their residence halls and classes. The interaction of clinical issues, personal and social development, and academic progress makes for a very interesting community of which college counselors and student affairs professionals must gain a stronger understanding.

Research does inform us that college counseling services are working for students in some spaces. There are reports of counseling having a positive impact on academic performance and retention of students who take advantage of the services (e.g., counseling services have helped students stay in school; AUCCCD, 2017). In addition, college counseling was shown to be effective in reducing mental health distress (Center for Collegiate Mental Health, 2019). With the knowledge that clients utilizing services overall has increased approximately 46% from the 2010–2011 (82, 611) to the 2017–2018 (179, 964) academic years, it is great to see that the passion and work are helping student wellness (Center for Collegiate Mental Health, 2019). However, we, as counselors, must not lose sight of the students for whom utilization of counseling centers calls up stigma and shame or students who fear they will be misunderstood by counselors who "don't look like me" or "don't share my lived experience." Where will these students go to seek assistance? Each campus needs to keep a careful eye on the data that reflect students for whom counseling is working, students for whom it is less effective, and students who are not opting to engage with the counseling center. In some ways, these data can also encourage us to think outside the box as we consider the best ways to deliver services to today's college population. Counseling centers need to partner with student affairs in our common goal to support students, now more than ever.

The International Association of Counseling Services (IACS), the accrediting body for university, 4-year college, and 2-year community college counseling services, suggests four essential roles in serving the university and college community:

> 1) provide counseling to students experiencing personal adjustment, vocational, developmental and/or psychological problems that require professional attention; 2) play a preventive role assisting students in identifying and learning skills which will assist them to effectively meet their educational and life goals; 3) support and enhance the healthy growth and development of students through consultation and outreach to the campus community; and 4) play a role in contributing to campus safety. (IACS, 2016, p. 4)

More than ever, we find these roles increasingly important. There have been several college counseling scholars before us (Archer & Cooper, 1998; Davis & Humphrey, 2000; Sharkin, 2012) who have done wonderful work in these areas. Their accomplishments provide a platform of knowledge that inspired us to focus our work on better serving the campus community. We also hope that you, the reader, will continue to consider innovative ways that all campus service providers can work together to address new and emerging health and wellness issues in contemporary college students. Recent developments such as behavioral intervention teams and satellite counseling are examples of how college counseling and student affairs will need to adapt and respond to changing needs.

Throughout this text you will see the professional terms: college counselor, counselor, therapist, mental health professional, student affairs professional, and student development professional. These terms are used throughout the literature and across campuses nationwide when referencing the individuals often tasked with addressing student mental health and wellness. Although there are some similarities among terms, they are not completely interchangeable. First, college counselor, counselor, therapist, and mental health professional will refer to those professionals who are providing mental health services through direct service in the counseling center or outreach and prevention from the center. Second, student affairs professional, student support services, and student development professional refer to college staff who work in functional units on a college campus (e.g., the office of multicultural affairs, career services, accessibility services, residential life, Title IX, community standards, community engagement). This interchange and mention of both college counseling and student affairs is an important aspect of the intersecting audience of this text. We want readers to fully understand that college work should emerge from a rich collaboration between both mental health and student development camps. It's wise to combine efforts for the betterment of campus climate and student experience.

Thus, our purpose is to add college counseling and student development perspective to what you are learning in existing training programs; we are not trying to replicate or replace core courses (e.g., diagnosis and treatment) in preprofessional master's programs.

All chapters in this book begin with a personal reflection exercise. These exercises are included to provide readers with a way to deepen their experience of each topic.

This text is organized through four sections: Part I: The College Counseling Profession; Part II: Collaborative Services in College Counseling; Part III: Student Development Theory, Student Learning, and Developmental Considerations; and Part IV: Clinical Issues in the College Context. Part I of the book begins with Chapter 1, which provides an understanding of how the history and evolution of college counseling have influenced the landscape of this profession, including student populations. Chapter 2 invites readers to learn about the roles college counselors hold at the counseling center and in the greater campus community. Next, Chapter 3 discusses how culture, social location, and campus climate affect the student population. A multicultural orientation is introduced that gives the reader a sociocultural and social justice perspective with which to explore the remainder of the text. Finally, in Chapter 4, legal and ethical issues round out this part of the book with a discussion of relevant ethical issues (e.g., considerations that arise when college students are minors or when counselors hold multiple campus roles).

Part II begins with an understanding of the student affairs context in which we as counselors all work. In Chapter 5 readers will learn about the functions of student affairs on campus and how they support the student and campus. The important connection and collaborative functions that can happen among the counseling center and student affairs units are discussed in Chapter 6. Outreach is the focus of Chapter 7. The discussion of the importance and need for campus services over and above direct client service are discussed with examples from around the nation. Finally, in Chapter 8 we discuss emergency services on campus with a focus on crisis issues and the evolution of campus models of emergency response.

Part III moves readers to an understanding of how student development and student development theory impact and inform practice across all student support services on campus. Chapter 9 provides the reader with a broad understanding of the development of theory as well as how to use it in practice. In addition, the reader will be introduced to "The Case of Lina Miller" (see pages 186–187). Lina is examined in this chapter and through every theory in the remaining five chapters in this section. This will assist readers to consider how each theoretical vantage point has utility and limits. Neuro-informed college counseling is the focus of Chapter 10. Considering advances in understanding brain development, this chapter provides insight on the integration of neuroscience and college counseling along with an overview of the brain and neural networks. Chapters 11 through 14 introduce the reader to major student development theories that are used in conceptualizing college students. In addition, these theories also provide a blueprint for creating and delivering student services. Readers will learn about the following main areas in student development theory: psychosocial, cognitive/moral, experiential, and social constructivist. Applications to Lina as well as other cases will encourage readers to make the theory-to-practice connection in each chapter.

Part IV focuses on clinical issues connected to the college student population. These issues are discussed through a multicultural, sociocultural, and social justice lens using case studies with diverse student populations. It is our hope that the reflection exercises in these chapters will help the reader to (a) build empathy for the population and deepen awareness of the issue, (b) look at any preconceived notions about the population/issue, and (c) explore what the reader already knows. Chapters in this section have been handpicked to allow the novice and practiced college counselor and student affairs professional to develop additional awareness, knowledge, and skills to understand and attend to these student populations. The following chapters examine adjustment and clinical issues from a college student and campus perspective: Chapter 15, "Family and Relationships"; Chapter 16, "Academic and Career Issues"; Chapter 17, "Substance Use and Addiction"; Chapter 18, "Stress and Anxiety"; Chapter 19, "Depression and Suicide"; Chapter 20, "Continuum of Disordered Eating in College"; Chapter 21, "Understanding and Responding to Self-Injury"; Chapter 22, "Sexual Issues and Concerns"; and Chapter 23, "Sexual Victimization."

We hope you enjoy reading and referencing *College Counseling and Student Development: Theory, Practice, and Campus Collaboration* as you begin or continue your career in college counseling. We welcome you to this magnificent profession and thank those who are already assisting college students.

References

Archer, J. A., Jr., & Cooper, S. (1998). *Counseling and mental health services on campus.* San Francisco, CA: Jossey-Bass.

Association for University and College Counseling Center Directors. (2017). *The Association for University and College Counseling Center Directors annual survey.* Retrieved from https://www.aucccd.org/assets/documents/Governance/2017%20aucccd%20surveypublic-apr26.pdf

Center for Collegiate Mental Health. (2019, January). *2018 annual report* (Publication No. STA 19-180). Retrieved from https://ccmh.psu.edu/files/2019/09/2018-Annual-Report9.27.19-FINAL.pdf

Davis, D. C., & Humphrey K. M. (2000). *College counseling: Issues and strategies for a new millennium.* Alexandria, VA: American Counseling Association.

International Accreditation of Counseling Services. (2016). *IACS standards for university and college counseling services*. Alexandria, VA: Author.

Musu-Gillette, L., de Brey, C., McFarland, J., Hussar, W., Sonnenberg, W., & Wilkinson-Flicker, S. (2017). *Status and trends in the education of racial and ethnic groups 2017.* U.S. Department of Education, National Center for Education Statistics. Washington, DC. Retrieved from: http://nces.ed.gov/pubsearch

National Center for Education Statistics. (2018). *Undergraduate enrollment.* Retrieved from: https://nces.ed.gov/programs/coe/indicator_cha.asp

Sharkin, B. S. (2012). *Being a college counselor on today's campus: Roles, contributions, and special challenges.* New York, NY: Routledge.

About the Editors

Derrick A. Paladino, PhD

After growing up in a small town in Connecticut, I followed my parents to Florida for no other reason than to attend college because "that's what people did." I entered the University of Florida in the spring semester of 1995 as an adrift out-of-state and first-generation student with the desire to become an aerospace engineer. I was dropped off on campus (student population close to 50,000 around that time) with a less than novice understanding of what the college experience should be like. I entered with the reality that since my parents did not attend college, I was somewhat on my own to navigate this experience. I struggled academically early on and went through five different majors, finally resting on psychology with an education minor. Socially, I had left all my high school friends in Connecticut and had to figure out how to make new connections, which did happen, and I entered into some incredible friendships that last to this day. Another significant struggle was with my racial identity. Growing up half Latino and half White, but with darker skin, in a majority-White town invited much explicit and covert discrimination. It was the opposite in Florida, where I physically fit in but did not speak Spanish, therefore feeling isolated for a different reason. Racial identity was a consistent struggle for me during these 4 years until I entered my graduate work. It was a combination of my multicultural class and the 2000 U.S. Census (i.e., the first time individuals could check more than one racial category) that allowed me to begin to safely explore my identity. In all, acclimating to college was a struggle in some areas. I did not know how to reach nor utilize resources for most of my undergraduate years. I essentially hoped for the best and discovered which classes would grant me a decent grade. As I reflect on all that colleges offer in terms of assistance and development, there was much rich support available to me. I wish I had the awareness to tap into it. I look back on my time fondly and admire how it has shaped me. It was an enormous growth experience—one of emerging into adulthood, creating wonderful connections with people, learning about who I am, and figuring out the world one semester at a time.

I am currently a professor at Rollins College in the Graduate Studies in Counseling Program, where I oversee the Certificate in College and University Counseling.

■ ■ ■

Laura M. Gonzalez, PhD

I started my undergraduate career at Penn State University, on that enormous main campus with more than 40,000 other students. For a small-town youth like me, that was pretty overwhelming, and I never found a sense of belonging. Upon transferring to the small liberal arts campus of Colgate University, however, my inner scholar started to bloom. I was thrilled to be pushed by my peers and professors to bring forth all of my hidden talents, and to feel valued and accepted as one "smart girl" among many. I think the word *transformation* is used quite appropriately to describe the changes I felt as an undergraduate student, and the seed for my graduate degrees was definitely planted there. As a human being, I found the social milieu of Colgate to be challenging to me, but thankfully there were corners where I could find "my people"—in the Women's Studies House; the Peace Studies House; and many student organizations related to culture, identity, and inclusion. Although I didn't belong everywhere, I belonged somewhere, and that was enough. Later, I received my PhD in counselor education from North Carolina State University. Those experiences formed the basis for my lifelong interest in working with college students to promote holistic and healthy development, attainment of goals and aspirations, and personal transformation. Whether working on the college counseling or student affairs side of the house, I have always attempted to listen carefully to students' experiences and help them find their way forward. Even as a faculty member now, this central task remains the same.

I am currently an associate professor in the Teacher Education and Higher Education Department at the University of North Carolina at Greensboro (UNCG).

■ ■ ■

Joshua C. Watson, PhD

In 1997 I was about to graduate with a degree in psychology from the University of Connecticut. At the time, future career plans were "hazy" at best, as I figured an interesting opportunity eventually would come my way. About a month or so before graduation I was asked to meet with our associate director of residence life. I had been involved with student government and residence life throughout my time as an undergraduate, and I naturally figured he had called the meeting to offer me a job at the university. Long story short, that was not the case at all. Instead, he talked to me about advancing my education. He believed I would be a good candidate for student affairs positions and encouraged me to look at programs where I could get the training needed to work on campus. Inspired by his confidence in my potential, and without any promising job prospects, I decided to continue my education and enrolled in the counseling master's program at Clemson University for the upcoming semester. As a graduate counseling student, I completed my internship experiences at the university's Counseling and Psychological Services. Working with college students was a tremendous experience and ignited my passion for this specialized field. Throughout my doctoral training and into my career as a counselor educator, an emphasis on college students and their unique needs has directed my scholarly work and service to the profession. I currently work as a counselor educator at Texas A&M University-Corpus Christi, a federally designated Hispanic-serving institution where most students identify as being members of an underrepresented population and/or the first in their families to attend college. Researching the first-year college adjustment experience and working with these students has helped me appreciate the importance of a college education to individuals and their families. Further, I have come to see the many issues and challenges students face today, and I believe the services college counselors and student affairs personnel are providing to be vitally important to student success. I am glad you have chosen to work in this field and believe you will enjoy working with college students as much as I have. Best of luck in your journey!

About the Contributors

Kathryn P. (Tina) Alessandria, PhD, is a professor in the Department of Counselor Education at West Chester University in Pennsylvania, where she serves as coordinator of the Higher Education Counseling/Student Affairs Program. She served as member-at-large for the American College Counseling Association (ACCA) from 2006 to 2009 and has represented ACCA on the Higher Education Mental Health Alliance since its inception in 2008. Dr. Alessandria has been recognized by the ACCA with the College Counseling Advocacy Award (2013) and Professional Leadership Award (2018).

Kristin Bruns, PhD, is an assistant professor at Youngstown State University in the Counseling program. She is a Licensed Professional Counselor in the State of Ohio. Her professional counseling experiences have been in college counseling centers, as well as community agencies and a private practice. Her research interests include college student mental health, suicidality, and protective factors.

Christy M. Buchanan, PhD, is a professor of psychology at Wake Forest University. From 2012 to 2019, she served as associate dean for Academic Advising. She received her BA from Seattle Pacific University and her PhD in developmental psychology from the University of Michigan. Her research and teaching address adolescent and young adult development, especially the impact of beliefs and expectations about adolescence, family, and culture. Her administrative responsibilities included the orientation of new students and academic support for undergraduates.

Dana Burnett, PhD, is professor of practice emeritus, Department of Foundations and Leadership, at Old Dominion University. His research focus is in the area of student affairs, especially leadership for future leaders of postsecondary institutions and leadership development programs for undergraduates. Professor Burnett has served as a department chair and in several administrative positions, including vice president for student affairs and dean of students.

Lesley Casarez, PhD, is associate professor at Angelo State University, where she oversees the master's degrees in Professional School Counseling and Guidance and Counseling. She has previous experience as a graduate programs adviser and public school counselor and educator. She is actively involved in the Texas Counseling Association, Texas School Counseling Association, Three Rivers Counseling Association, and Phi Kappa Phi. Her accomplishments include numerous scholarly presentations and publications, with specific interests in school counseling issues, mental health, online learning, accessibility, and leadership.

David J. Denino, PhD, is director emeritus of Counseling Services and adjunct professor in the Clinical Mental Health program at Southern Connecticut State University (SCSU). He served as secretary and treasurer for the American College Counseling Association for several years and is an emeritus member of the Association for University and College Counseling Center Directors. David has been a recipient of the Connecticut Counseling Association's Distinguished Professional Award, Outstanding Teaching Award/SCSU, and the American Red Cross Hero's Award for his work as a disaster mental health responder.

Amanda Faucher, MA, is a licensed professional and a current doctoral student at Texas A&M University–Corpus Christi. She graduated Capella University with a master's degree in psychology and, later, Walden University with a master's degree in clinical mental health counseling. She formerly had a private practice where she specialized in transcranial magnetic stimulation. She has worked in various settings, including inpatient psychiatric facilities, outpatient rehabilitation, and community agencies. Her professional research interests include holistic approaches and mind-body work.

Perry C. Francis, PhD, is a professor of counseling and the coordinator of the Counseling Training Clinic at Eastern Michigan University. He has been an active leader in the American College Counseling Association for over 25 years, serving in various roles including president and governing council representative to the American Counseling Association. Additionally, Professor Francis chaired the Ethics Revision Task Force that produced the American Counseling Association's 2014 *ACA Code of Ethics*. He has written numerous articles and book chapters on ethics in the profession and presented on college counseling ethics nationally and internationally.

Christopher C. Graham, MA, completed a master's degree in college counseling and student development at the University of North Carolina at Greensboro in 2014 and has since been working at Florida State University in the Office of Fraternity and Sorority Life (currently as its director). His goal in working with college students is to ensure that each one has the chance to maximize his or her potential.

Natalie Arce Indelicato, PhD, is an assistant professor and the clinical director in the Jacksonville University Clinical Mental Health Counseling program. She is a Licensed Mental Health Counselor and Qualified Supervisor in the State of Florida. Her professional counseling experiences include working at college counseling centers and community agencies in Northeast Florida, and her research interests include college student mental health, community-engaged learning, and the mental health of girls and women.

Brianna Kane, MA, is currently a counselor education doctoral student at the University of Florida. She graduated from Jacksonville University with a master's degree in clinical mental health counseling. Ms. Kane has been a counselor and instructor within university settings and appreciates the diversity and complexities of students' lives. She takes a holistic approach with her students, seeking to understand the unique meaning systems that they each possess. Her professional and research interests include emerging adulthood and college students' wellness and success.

Michael M. Kocet, PhD, is professor and department chair of counselor education at The Chicago School of Professional Psychology. Professor Kocet earned his PhD in counselor education and is a licensed mental health counselor, a board-certified counselor, and an Approved Clinical Supervisor. His professional areas of interest include ethics; lesbian, gay, bisexual, transgender, and queer/questioning issues; and grief counseling. He is the editor of the book *Counseling Gay Men, Adolescents, and Boys: A Strengths-Based Guide for Helping Professionals and Educators*, published by Routledge, and is coauthor of the text *Ethical Decision Making for the 21st Century Counselor*, published by Sage. He is past president of the Association for Lesbian, Gay, Bisexual, and Transgender Issues in Counseling.

Elizabeth Likis-Werle, PhD, is an assistant professor of counseling at Western Carolina University. Previously, she taught counseling at East Tennessee State University and directed the Community Counseling Clinic. She earned her PhD in counseling and counselor education from the University of North Carolina at Greensboro and her master's in community counseling from Western Carolina University. Her work experience includes working in university counseling centers, mental health centers, school-based therapy, foster/adoption services, intensive outpatient programs, and wilderness therapy. Her specialties are college student identity, addiction, sexual trauma, and mood issues.

Steven Mencarini, PhD, is the dean of students at Guilford College and has served in various capacities within higher education institutions over the past 18 years. He received his PhD in higher education from the University of North Carolina at Greensboro, his master's in college student personnel from the University of Maryland, College Park, and his bachelor's degree in biology from the College of William & Mary. His research interests involve college student development and leadership development theories, as well as understanding the impact of college environments.

Amy Murphy, PhD, is assistant professor in the Department of Curriculum and Instruction at Angelo State University and program adviser for the MEd in student development and leadership in higher education as well as an academic advising certificate. She was formerly the dean of students at Texas Tech University and has more than 20 years of student affairs administrative experiences, including work related to behavioral intervention, student transitions, student activities, parent programming, and prevention and wellness. She is president of the National Behavioral Intervention Team Association, has authored two books, and writes and presents regularly on current issues in education related to safety and wellness.

Carolyn Rifkin, MA, graduated with her master's in college counseling and student development from the University of North Carolina at Greensboro in 2015. She has additional training in eye-movement desensitization and reprocessing and in motivational interviewing. Her work experiences include campus-based service-learning programming and community-based work as a therapist/addictions specialist.

Benjamin Robertson, MA, is currently a counselor education doctoral student at Texas A&M University–Corpus Christi. He graduated from the University of Texas Rio Grande Valley with a master's degree in counseling and guidance. Mr. Robertson has worked in various roles as a youth care worker, case manager, and counselor serving diverse populations in different settings. He emphasizes the importance of a humanistic approach in his work with individuals and invites persons to embrace a collaborative stance in making meaningful, positive changes. His professional and research interests include emotional intelligence and burnout in mental health workers.

Meghan K. Root, MA, has earned degrees from St. John Fisher College (NY), Lesley University (MA), and Widener University (PA). She specializes in sexual violence trauma and response and has experience in mobile crisis and sexual addictions and has worked at a small public college psychological health clinic. Since 2014, she has worked for the U.S. Air Force (AF) in the Washington, DC, area providing advocacy for survivors of sexual violence. She currently serves in the AF Integrated Resilience office as the education and training manager.

Samuel Sanabria, PhD, is an associate professor of counseling at Rollins College and specializes in multicultural, social justice, and sexuality issues in counseling with a focus on lesbian, gay, bisexual, and transgender communities. He began his career working as a clinician in substance abuse, anger management, and domestic violence programs. Since then, he has provided counseling and clinical evaluations for Wellstar Health System, Atlanta's largest not-for-profit health care provider, and dedicated 8 years to private practice, providing therapeutic and psychological assessment services for sexual minority, ethnic, and Latinx immigrant populations. He currently teaches a course on neuroscience for counselors.

Mark B. Scholl, PhD, is an associate professor in the Department of Counseling at Wake Forest University. He is an active member of several American Counseling Association (ACA) divisions, including the Association for Humanistic Counseling (AHC), the National Career Development Association, and the American College Counseling Association. He is a past president of AHC, past two-term editor of *The Journal of Humanistic Counseling,* and former chair of the ACA Council of Journal Editors. He is a member of the ACA Governing Council, representing the AHC division. His research interests include culturally responsive counseling and constructivist approaches to career counseling.

Alan M. Schwitzer, PhD, is a licensed psychologist and professor of counseling at Old Dominion University, where he is a faculty member in college counseling, higher education administration, and community college leadership. Prior to faculty work, he was involved in residence life, academic advising, and psychological services at Virginia Commonwealth University, The University of Texas at Austin, Tulane University, and James Madison University. He is a past editor of the *Journal of College Counseling* and currently works with the *Journal of American College Health,* the *Journal of College Student Development,* and *About Campus Magazine.*

Rachel Shakin, MA, is currently a counselor education doctoral student at Texas A&M University–Corpus Christi. Her master's degree in counseling with an emphasis in clinical mental health is also from Texas A&M–Corpus Christi. She has extensive experience with crisis/disaster mental health, sexual and domestic violence, and nontraditional students. Her strong humanistic foundation is the impetus wherein she assists others through holistic and creative means. Her professional and research interests include counseling professional identity and counseling supervision.

Jeff Solomon has been in law enforcement for 27 years and has an extensive background in the complex field of public safety in the school environment with 6 years serving as chief of police for a K–12 school district. He is a nationally recognized expert in school safety and has spoken at various events such as the Wisconsin School Resource Officers Conference and the Department of Justice Conference, presenting on "Missing and Abducted Children" in Texas. He recently met with U.S. Secretary of Education Betsy DeVos to discuss K–12 responses to active-shooter events. In 2019, he was invited to the Office of Juvenile Justice and Delinquency Prevention in Washington, DC, to cofacilitate a listening group of school safety experts to create a set of national standards for K–12 school safety.

Esther Suess, MA, is a mental health counselor at the Mood Treatment Center in Winston-Salem, North Carolina, with a specialty in the treatment of eating disorders and obsessive-compulsive disorder. She graduated with an undergraduate degree in psychology from University College Dublin in 2016 and received her MA in clinical mental health counseling from Wake Forest University in 2018. Her research interests include career counseling, cultural diversity in counseling, and eating disorders.

Brian Van Brunt, PhD, is a partner with the NCHERM (National Center for Higher Education Risk Management) Group, USA. Professor Van Brunt has worked in the counseling field for more than 20 years and specializes in educational counseling, behavioral intervention and support, and issues related to mental health and alcohol/substance abuse by students. He served as director of counseling at New England College from 2001 to 2007 and as director of counseling and testing at Western Kentucky University from 2007 to 2013. Professor Van Brunt is also a prolific writer, having authored numerous books, book chapters, and articles.

Julia L. Whisenhunt, PhD, is an associate professor of counselor education in the Department of Communication Sciences and Professional Counseling at the University of West Georgia. Dr. Whisenhunt earned her MA in psychology and EdS in guidance and counseling from the University of West Georgia and her PhD in counselor education and practice from Georgia State University. She is a Licensed Professional Counselor in the State of Georgia, a National Certified Counselor, and a Certified Professional Counseling Supervisor in Georgia. She is trained as an Applied Suicide Intervention Skills Training facilitator. Professor Whisenhunt has published and presented on the topics of suicide and self-injury at the international, national, regional, and state levels.

Acknowledgments

Derrick, Laura, and Josh thank the American Counseling Association's Publications Department and the wonderful Carolyn C. Baker and Nancy Driver for providing this opportunity to add our integrated perspectives to the field of counseling and college counseling and assisting us on this journey with their expertise. Additionally, we thank the college student, college counseling, and student affairs practitioner populations. It is our interactions with them that continually inspires our work in this area. Our individual appreciations follow.

Derrick: I first thank my wonderful coeditors Laura and Josh for entering this project and sharing the vision of providing vital education in the field of college counseling and student development. Next, I give thanks to my marvelous and brilliant wife, Amanda, who in many ways has taken on this project with me. Finally, I thank my son, Myles, who provided me with loving and fun distractions during my writing days.

Laura: I thank my faculty and student affairs colleagues, who are great models of scholar-practitioners and of dedication to student success. I also want to acknowledge the many dedicated, talented, and world-changing graduate students I have known at UNCG. Some of you are now my coauthors (Elizabeth, Steve, Chris, and Carolyn), but all of you were continually in my mind as I was working on this book. I have learned and continue to learn from you about what it means to be a 21st-century student in development and how to promote wellness in the most equitable way possible. Finally, I thank my husband and partner, Jesús Gonzalez, for being beside me every step of the way.

Joshua: I thank my advisers, mentors, and role models who helped me become the person and professional I am today. Each of you saw something in me that was worth encouraging, and I am forever grateful. Next, I thank Mikaela for being a constant source of support. You continually amaze me, and I count myself blessed to share life's journey with you. Finally, to those individuals working on the thousands of college and university campuses nationwide, thank you for all you do to help students succeed. Your work does not go unnoticed.

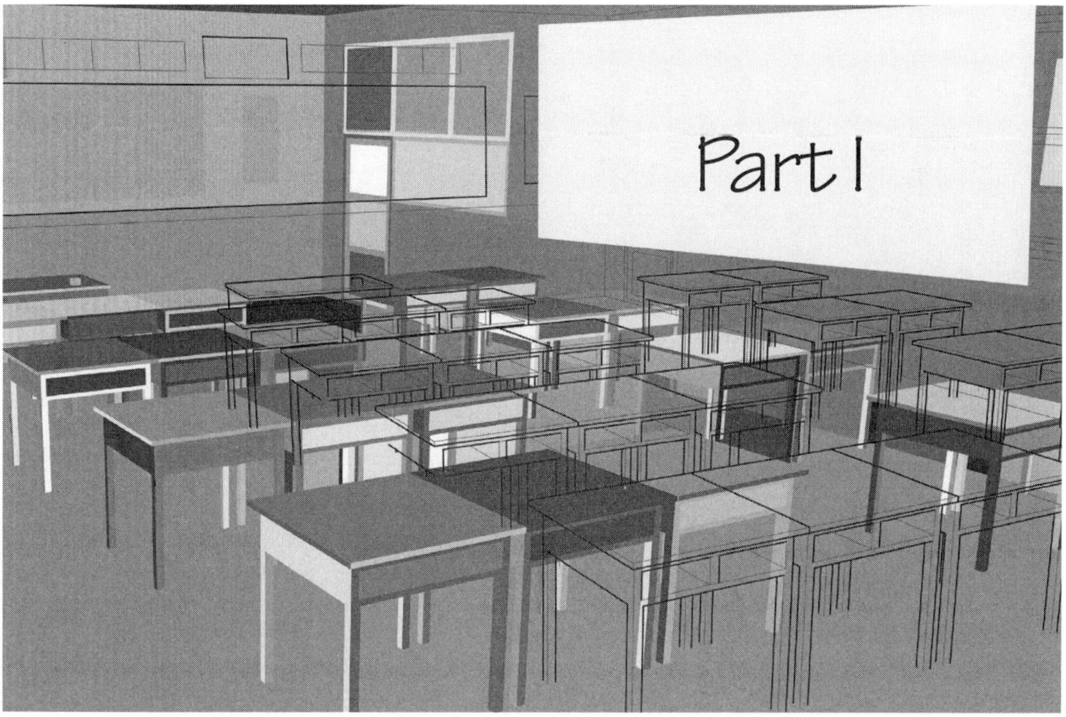

The College Counseling Profession

Chapter 1

History and Evolution of College Counseling

Derrick A. Paladino, Kathryn P. (Tina) Alessandria, and David J. Denino

We are not makers of history. We are made by history.

—Martin Luther King Jr.

■ ■ ■

Reflection Exercise

Your college experience is unique and specific to you. It is affected by many factors from both the personal and the societal levels and was indeed shaped by history. Before beginning this chapter, we would like you to reflect on your undergraduate college experience and with someone who attended college at a different time than you. Try to pick someone who is at least one generation apart from you.

Compare and discuss the following issues:

- Generally, how were your experiences different?
- Compare campus life.
- Compare classes and professor expectations.
- Compare demographics of professors, students, and staff.
- Compare family involvement.
- Compare campus resources used, knowledge of them, and their availability.
- Compare technology and communication.
- Compare cost.
- Compare community amenities (e.g., restaurants, services, development).
- Compare campus amenities (e.g., residence halls, food services, development).
- Compare political and social events and their influence on campus and on students.
- Compare course content delivery methods.
- Compare number of years spent in college.
- Compare common student concerns (e.g., adjustment issues like homesickness vs. diagnosed mental disorders).
- Compare campus climate.

■ ■ ■

College counseling is rooted in the traditional educational and vocational guidance movements of the 1930s. Throughout the decades, those origins have been amplified as the fundamental needs, demographics, and societal demands on college students have evolved. Marginalized and minority populations and reduced stigma associated with counseling coupled with an increased use of campus counseling services and increased levels of mental health crises all have played roles in the development of college counseling. Additionally, major events such as school shootings and evolving world events such as wars, civil rights movements, politics, and economic crises are a few of the reasons for counseling centers changing dramatically over the decades.

To gain insight into what college counseling is today, it is wise to consider the history of the profession and reflect upon its development. This chapter will begin with a focus on the early beginnings of college counseling. Throughout this journey, scholars have learned and compiled information about all that surrounds this profession. Therefore, this chapter will also discuss the development of professional associations, professional preparation standards, student definitions and generational influences, and brief mental health trends. It is our hope that this chapter will offer an increased understanding of the origins of the contemporary counseling center. We offer a similar glimpse of the origins of the student affairs context in Chapter 5.

Historical Development of College Counseling

Dean and Meadows (1995) stated that "college counseling can best be understood as the intersection of a professional activity and an environment" that has "developed from the merging of several movements: vocational guidance, mental health, and student personnel work" (p. 139). The influence of these three student-centered areas is evident when one considers the historical development of the college counseling center. Although the college counseling center progressed for the most part post–World War II, its evolvement has links to historical, political, and social situations of the more distant past (Archer & Cooper, 1998; Dean & Meadows, 1995; LaFollette, 2009; Prescott, 2008). We will begin this chapter by taking a brief look at its earlier developments.

The 1800s

The first college health program is recognized to have begun at Amherst College in 1861. It is during this time that colleges and universities began developing student health services with a focus on physical illness and an emphasis on healthy exercise to prevent emotional problems (Kraft, 2011). The appointment of Dr. Edward Hitchcock at Amherst College is noted to have led to the concept of "leading the psychological life," which is also believed to be the forerunner to the wellness movement (Reifler, 1990). His use of physical training for the body and mind and his philosophy of *mens sana in corpore sano* (a sound mind and body) resonated well with academic leaders of the time (Sweet, 2011).

From the earliest beginnings, in loco parentis (Latin for "in the place of the parent") described the "caretaker" relationship between American universities and their students (Dungy & Gordon, 2011; Lee, 2011). In fact, Lee (2011) stated, "Until the 1960s, American universities have been deemed by courts to be acting in loco parentis with respect to their students" (p. 66). Colleges were able to exercise great discretion and discipline, without due process, in developing the "character" of their students, without respect to their students' constitutional rights, and to regulate their personal lives (e.g., speech, association, and movement). We will discuss the end of in loco parentis later in this chapter. As you read through this chapter, we hope you hold an awareness of what was going on for college students while national and world events emerge.

The Early 1900s

The year 1910 brought a contribution to college mental health by Princeton University: the appointment of a psychiatrist, Stewart Paton, MD, to offer the first campus mental health clinic devoted to students with "personality development" problems (Barreira & Snider, 2010; Kraft, 2011). In the early 1920s, Yale University also validated the importance of mental health with the appointments of a psychologist as their president along with the first university psychiatrist (Archer & Cooper, 1998; Reifler, 1990). In addition, 1920 found the inaugural meeting of the American Student Health Association (later renamed the American College Health Association [ACHA] in 1948), where Frankwood Williams, MD, discussed the importance of a college's position in establishing student mental health programs (Kraft, 2011). As colleges and universities began to view the student as "more than academics," in the 1920s and 1930s, we begin to see a few dozen institutions start introducing mental health philosophies and professionals into their campuses.

In the 1930s two influential documents that supported the role of the institution in promoting college student mental health were introduced: *The Student Personnel Point of View* (SPPV; American Council on Education, 1937) and E. G. Williamson's (1939) *How to Counsel Students: A Manual of Techniques for Clinical Counselors*. The SPPV (American Council on Education, 1937, 1949) has been a pivotal influence in the field of college counseling, student affairs, and student development theory (the latter of which you will learn about in Chapter 9). The SPPV was a foundational document for student personnel services that is still referenced today. Both the 1937 document and the later revised 1949 document speak to the importance of viewing the student as a holistic individual. The student is made up of more than academic and vocational drives. The SPPV takes the position that students are intellectual, social, and emotional beings who have aptitudes, morals, and values that have an impact on who they are. Also included in this perspective is the emotional well-being of the student. Together, these form the common ground from which college counseling and student affairs can work together today.

Throughout his *How to Counsel Students: A Manual of Techniques for Clinical Counselors*, Williamson (1939) differentiated counseling techniques and student personnel work from instructional endeavors. Perhaps an early philosophical departure from the in loco parentis approach of the times was his statement that the institution should recognize that counselors and educators do not share the same set of skills (e.g., clinical vs. pedagogical). This manual, which discusses and supports the role of clinical counseling in student personnel work, was written with high school and college counselors in mind. It presents information on clinical techniques, diagnosis, counselor preparation, college counselor responsibilities, and specific student population issues (e.g., scholastic achievement, study habits, reading disabilities, overachievement, problems of the superior students, occupational and vocational choices). This document serves as an important step in allowing colleges to remove the responsibility of in loco parentis from administration and faculty and allow trained college mental health professionals to step in and assist students in need.

The 1940s and 1950s: The Influence of World War II

The influx of veterans enrolling in higher education institutions after World War II had a significant impact on college mental health services. The inflow of veterans was partly due to the Servicemen's Readjustment Act of 1944 (also known as the G.I. Bill), which gave veterans the opportunity to enroll in colleges, universities, junior and community colleges, and specialty schools (Hodges, 2017; Kraft, 2011; Prescott, 2008; Sharkin, 2012). The Veterans Administration lacked the resources to serve the millions of returning veterans so in turn they contracted with colleges and universities that were able to provide these services

(Barreira & Snider, 2010; McCarthy, 2014; Meadows, 2000). This new student population arrived in need of vocational guidance and educational counseling. It is important to note that prior to this time the majority of students were single, White males, usually between the ages of 18 and 22, who benefited from the in loco parentis function fulfilled by higher education institutions of the day (Hodges, 2017). The emergence of the experienced adult college student pressed colleges to examine how they addressed student needs. As a result, the G.I. Bill became a catalyst for increasing campus counseling services and gave rise to a debate about the education, qualifications, and training necessary to deliver counseling services (Hodges, 2017).

In 1947, President Harry S. Truman's Commission on Higher Education published a report that offered additional support for mental health services on campus (United States, President's Commission on Higher Education, 1947). Truman created the commission to reexamine postsecondary education post–World War II and to reinforce education as a necessity and a foundation of democratic liberties. This report suggested that colleges and universities should emphasize the emotional growth and personal/social adjustment of students while at college. Because of the abovementioned developments, we see an emergence of the need to serve more students. Kraft (2011) also noted that during this time there was a rise in the need for trained mental health practitioners to address the increased demand for counseling services.

Finally, it is important to note that, in 1945, Carl Rogers founded the first college counseling center at the University of Chicago. This particular counseling center was an inspiration to many mental health professionals and introduced a more developmental and humanistic way of assisting college students with "typical" life issues (McCarthy, 2014). McCarthy (2014) noted that this movement established merit in the creation of counseling centers that could combine educational, vocational, and personal adjustment counseling, thus beginning to explore a new approach for college counseling.

The 1960s and 1970s: Bringing Change

The 1960s and 1970s revealed significant developments in campus mental health services (Archer & Cooper, 1998; Barreira & Snider, 2010; Meadows, 2000). "By the 1960s, nearly all of America's colleges and universities offered counseling services to their students" (McCarthy, 2014, p. 14). In addition, these counseling programs began offering a wide range of services to their students (Dean & Meadows, 1995; Oetting, Ivey, & Weigel, 1970). Furthermore, the termination of in loco parentis and institutions' ability to regulate students without respect to their constitutional rights was a significant development. Below we will discuss the case of *Dixon v. Alabama State Board of Education* (1961) and its impact on ending in loco parentis.

In the 1960s colleges began noticing a shift in the relationships between the institution and the student. The ruling in *Dixon v. Alabama State Board of Education* (1961) is noted as the moment that colleges could no longer constitutionally regulate student rights (Lee, 2011, 2014). In the case of *Dixon v. Alabama State Board of Education* (1961), six Black Alabama State College students were expelled, without due process, after participating in a civil rights demonstration. Following the expulsion, Alabama State's college president wrote that the college had the power to remove these students for various offenses (e.g., Conduct Prejudicial to the School; Insubordination and Insurrection; Hoover, 2008). The 1961 court ruling now offered students in higher education protections from being disciplined without due process. Colleges were required to provide notification to students regarding their alleged violation(s), and students were given the right to have a voice and be heard regarding said violation(s). One should examine *Dixon v. Alabama State Board of*

Education (1961) within the larger civil rights movement as it provides a valuable illustration of how society has shifted the college landscape.

Several developments occurred during this time that fostered this growth and spoke to student need, thus giving students a voice (Kraft, 2011; Lee, 2011, 2014; Prescott, 2008):

- Students began demanding freedom from "institutionalized paternalism" (i.e., institutionalized paternalism permitted campus counseling centers to release confidential client information to campus officials, parents, and prospective employers).
- Student health services began creating student advisory committees to better understand and serve student needs.
- The ACHA published *Recommended Standards and Practices for a College Health Program* in 1961 (Committee on Standards for College Health, 1961).
- There was an increase in student activism on college campuses (e.g., the civil rights movement).
- In 1961 in loco parentis was no longer deemed legal.

In the 1970s we find the college counseling field being faced with budget cuts (Sharkin, 2012). Despite this, the field still gained strength through student voices, legislation, and advocacy from college counseling professionals. Below are several significant events that have affected the field of college counseling (Kraft, 2011; Prescott, 2008; Stone & Archer, 1990):

- Student movements of the 1960s contributed to the passing of the U.S. Family Educational and Privacy Act of 1974.
- In 1970 the ACHA created the Task Force on Students and College Health. This task force consisted of students (i.e., the consumer) assisting with insight into student health services.
- College counselors began viewing their role as larger than direct client service and began understanding their need to care for the campus.
- The roles of consultation, outreach, and training began to emerge as campus need grew.
- Morrill, Oetting, and Hurst (1974) created and introduced the "Cube," which offered a descriptive model of the dimensions of implementing counseling interventions. The three dimensions are (a) the target of the intervention (i.e., individual, primary group, associational group, or institution or community), (b) the purpose of the intervention (i.e., remediation, prevention, or development), and (c) the method of intervention (i.e., media, consultation, or direct service).
- In the late 1970s the American Psychiatric Association worked to refine diagnostic criteria that were more applicable to college students for the *Diagnostic and Statistical Manual of Mental Disorders* (3rd ed., American Psychiatric Association, 1980).

In these events we see the strength and advocacy of college counselors, as well as the developing voice of the students they serve in the field of mental health on campus. Privacy for students, an expanding scope for the counseling center, and intention of practice continued to emerge.

The 1980s and 1990s: Serving Minority and Marginalized Student Populations

From the 1970s into the early 1980s, college and university counseling centers began to broaden their scope of practice. In the 1980s higher education began to be shaped by an increase in enrollment of "female, older, ethnic minority, part-time, commuter, and other students" (Meadows, 2000, p. 28). With this population shift, the scope of college counseling needed to adjust to meet the needs of these student populations.

The 1990s brought along research to demonstrate an increase in the complexity and severity of student-client issues on the basis of the perceptions of counseling center staff (Sharkin, 2012). Stone and Archer (1990) suggested that this was a period of "increasing pathology, violence, the need for outreach and prevention and limiting services" (p. 8) due to increased numbers of students attending with more serious psychological concerns. Sharkin (1997) conducted a review of the research and data on this increase. He suggested that the surge in pathology may be a "perception among counseling center administrators and practitioners that problems presented by students have become more severe" (p. 579). Sharkin (1997) believed that there may be validity to the claim but did not find the empirical evidence to support it. In addition, the generalizability of these findings was limited because samples did not always account for 2-year colleges, small colleges, or institutions that simply did not have counseling center directors who completed surveys (Meadows, 2000). The perceived rise in severity could have been due to destigmatization of counseling that increased demand for services. Regardless of sample size, timelines, or other empirical issues, studies of this nature did bring more awareness to the plight of the college student to universities, communities, and the nation. A platform for advocacy was being built.

In 1990 the Americans With Disabilities Act (ADA) was introduced. The ADA prevented discrimination against students with chronic mental illnesses and increased access to college for students with disabilities. With this rise in student population, we potentially see an increase in demands on college health services professionals to understand and provide services for these students (Prescott, 2008). In addition, 1991 brought the ADA's *Accessibility Guidelines for Buildings and Facilities* (1991). These guidelines directed colleges to make buildings and the greater campus more accessible for students living with physical disabilities. In this era there was an increase in marginalized and minority college students. With this evolution, college counselors needed to increase their awareness of populations and clinical competence with these populations, as well as review their accessibility for students living with visible and invisible disabilities, to provide effective services.

The 2000s: A New Millennium

Hunt and Eisenberg (2010) suggested that college student mental health issues of today are of significant concern and present a great challenge for campuses. The days of "homesickness" and basic "adjustment" are long gone. In some respects, the college counseling center is very similar to a community agency under the guise of managed care. Many college counseling texts are teaching beyond the basics for clinical issues (e.g., academics, financial issues, family issues, and adjustment). Counseling students are now learning about crisis counseling, major depression, personality disorders, disordered eating, identity development, nonsuicidal self-injury, grief and loss, sexual victimization, panic attacks, psychosis, and substance use, to name a few. In addition, counselors must consider the comorbidity of these clinical issues with the understanding that many of these college students live in the same residence halls, attend the same classes, eat in the same campus dining halls, and walk the same campus. In addition to facing potential discrimination, these students "also have the additional burden of proving how activities such as concentrating, forming relationships with others, following schedules, regulating emotions, and managing disability symptoms are major life activities common to most people rather than specifically to a student with a psychiatric disability" (Gammon, 2013, p. 32). The broadening presenting problems of student clients and the complexity of their needs have raised issues regarding counselor training, expertise, and clinical readiness to provide direct services to students related to their interactions on campus.

College counseling center and client service surveys have indicated an increase in the utilization of counseling services, in centers offering direct service, and increases in student-reported clinical issues (Association for University and College Counseling Center Directors [AUCCCD], 2017; Center for Collegiate Mental Health [CCMH], 2019). Increased access to higher education is one reason we are seeing an increase in students' need for services. Reflecting on the field's history, developments such as the ADA, civil rights movement, destigmatization of mental illness, and an increase in students utilizing counseling services before attending college have all had a unique impact on today's college counseling center functions.

In a span of 6 years ending in 2015, counseling center utilization increased by an average of 30% to 40%, whereas enrollment increased by only 5% (AUCCCD, 2017). This increase in demand was motivated by the increase in students living with a lifetime prevalence of threat-to-self indicators who utilized 20% to 30% more services than students without these indicators. Around this same time, counseling centers reported increasing their services devoted to "rapid access" by 28% whereas "routine treatment" decreased by 7.6% (CCMH, 2019). With these shifts, over 30% of counseling centers now have a waiting list for first appointments (e.g., average wait = 17.3 business days). As you will read in Chapter 7, "Outreach and Preventative Services," counseling centers have started increasing their outreach services to attempt to reduce the demand for direct services and reach a larger area of the campus community. Another strategy for increasing the reach of services is to collaborate with student affairs staff, as suggested in Chapter 6. This is congruent with the emphasis in both the counseling field and student affairs on prevention and promoting healthy development.

The college counseling center has also seen a shift in organizational structure and an increase in what is known as "integrated care," where clinical (or behavioral) services and student health care (or physical) services work together in the same space (ACHA, 2010; AUCCCD, 2017; Brown, Perez, & Reeder, 2007; Mitchell, Oakley, & Dunkle, 2019). Integrated care can sometimes be found under the moniker of "Wellness Center" and may also include health educator and promotions staff. Mitchell et al. (2019) suggested that even though this is not a new concept, the "strong call for integrating mental health and physical health services on college campuses is a fairly recent phenomenon" (p. 91). There are some thoughts around why this convergence is occurring for the betterment of services. Some examples are better collaboration and communication between mental health and health professionals, provision of services from a centralized campus location, budget flexibility, a multidisciplinary staff, improved treatment planning, and reduction in costs (Brown et al., 2007). In addition, mergers may represent "a philosophical desire to provide holistic care, a wish to emphasize wellness, as well as a thrust to streamline resources" and interest in continuity of care (ACHA, 2010). Finally, in-house collaboration can be beneficial in other ways that allow both health and clinical staff to be on the same page regarding campus issues and how to work with specific areas of student concern. Many times, wellness centers will find medical staff walking students over to clinical resources because of medical diagnosis and vice versa. Along with the benefits of this merger, some have found potential costs to moving forward, including reduced confidentiality, compliance with standards connected to a different discipline, increased departmental stress during the merger, and increased vulnerability of records. Regardless of the recent increase in organizational restructuring, not all institutions have shifted in this direction. This is an area that will continue to be an important topic of discussion in the coming years.

The 2000s ushered in a digital industrial revolution. High-speed internet, text messaging, email, social media, Wi-Fi, and the smartphone have changed how students communicate with each other and how often they stay in touch with their families off campus; they have also increased students' access to information about mental health and the ways they can access services (online vs. face-to-face, via apps; Reif & Much, 2017; Seemiller & Grace, 2017; Wiedmer, 2015). Some authors have attributed some of the anxiety among the college student population to a lack of in-person interactions, fear of missing out, and self-worth connected to getting enough "likes" on their posts (Elhai, Levine, Dvorak, & Hall, 2016; Seabrook, Kern, & Rickard, 2016; Vannucci, Flannery, & Ohannessian, 2017).

Finally, an additional influence on campus mental health services comes from community and national events, such as terrorism, natural and human-made disasters, and other tragedies. Students not only hear about these events but also are inundated with a steady news stream breaking down every aspect and displaying videos and pictures of scenes that can be initially traumatizing and retraumatizing. Some of these events are close to home and have an impact on the entire campus community, including students, faculty, and staff, as well as parents/guardians. College shootings that injure and kill students, faculty, and staff take a toll on campuses. Recent examples include Dawson College (2006), Virginia Tech (2007), Northern Illinois University (2008), Azerbaijan State Oil Academy (2009), Hainan Institute of Science and Technology (2010), Youngstown State University (2011), Lone Star College-CyFair (2013), University of California, Santa Barbara (2014), Umpqua Community College shooting (2015), and Kerch Polytechnic College (2018), to name a few. In addition, community and national events like 9/11 (2001), the Sandy Hook Elementary School shootings (2012), the Orlando Pulse Nightclub shootings (2016), the Sutherland Springs church shootings (2017), the Las Vegas shootings (2017), the Tree of Life Synagogue shootings in Pittsburgh (2018), and the mosque shootings in New Zealand (2019) all had an impact on the college community and the staff and counselors who must care for students. In addition to these large-scale tragedies, campuses may experience localized issues such as a student death, campus hate crimes, and so forth. When one is reviewing these events, it is easy to imagine how a campus community experiences profound wounding and devastation. Colleges must heal as they experience student difficulty in returning to campus and classes and making sense of everything. The role of providing time-limited services to help students function in their educational environment has shifted as the decades pass. College counselors in some ways are expected to do more with less because of the increased demand for services and student reports of major clinical presenting issues.

Professional Organizations and Associations

It is important for students studying college counseling and student affairs to be familiar with professional organizations relevant to the practice of counseling in higher education. There are practitioners from a variety of disciplines who collaborate to serve the counseling needs of college students. The two oldest professional organizations that focus on student personnel issues are the National Association of Student Personnel Administrators-Student Affairs Administrators in Higher Education (NASPA) and the American College Personnel Association–College Student Educators International (ACPA). Both organizations were seminal to the growth of college counseling centers. In the years following the establishment of these organizations, the field has seen the rise of additional organizations that provide support, resources, and a professional identity to college counselors and student affairs personnel.

Currently, there are several overarching associations that recognize college counseling as a profession in higher education. Organizations, in counseling and student affairs, that have embraced the work and future of college counselors are as follows:

- American College Counseling Association (ACCA), an association for individuals who have a counseling professional identity and work in higher education settings, including colleges, universities, and community and technical colleges, whose purpose is fostering students' development;
- Association for University and College Counseling Center Directors (AUCCCD), a professional community that advocates for collegiate mental health;
- American College Personnel Association's Commission for Counseling and Psychological Services (CCAPS), which provides a home to both professionals and graduate students interested in working in counseling and psychological services in higher education;
- American Psychological Association Division 17, Society of Counseling Psychology, which is a home for all counseling psychology professionals;
- American College Health Association (ACHA), which serves as the voice for student health and wellness through advocacy, research, and education;
- National Association of Student Personnel Administrators Mental Health Focus Area and Knowledge Community, which addresses the mental health issues that students face;
- Higher Education Mental Health Alliance (HEMHA), a partnership of organizations that collaborate to advance college student mental health through an interdisciplinary lens.

These organizations provide community, research, data, resources, and trends for college counseling centers and counselors that contribute to best practices and future planning for the profession of college counseling. In addition, many provide academic journals that support the college counseling and student affairs fields. The following are some resources provided by several of these influential organizations related to college counseling and student affairs:

- *About Campus* (ACPA)
- *Clinical Psychology: Science and Practice* (American Psychological Association)
- *Journal of American College Health* (ACHA)
- *Journal of College Counseling* (ACCA)
- *Journal of College Student Development* (ACPA)
- *Journal of College Student Psychotherapy* (AUCCCD)
- *Journal of Counseling & Development* (American Counseling Association [ACA])
- *Journal of Counseling Psychology* (American Psychological Association)
- *Journal of Student Affairs Research and Practice* (NASPA)

ACCA, a division of the ACA, was founded in 1991 for individuals "whose professional identity is counseling and whose purpose is fostering students' development" (ACCA, 2009, para. 1). These professionally diverse mental health professionals find their home in higher education including colleges, universities, and community and technical college settings and come from the fields of counseling, psychology, and social work. ACCA's mission "is to be the interdisciplinary and inclusive professional home that supports emerging and state of the art knowledge and resources for counseling professionals in higher education" (ACCA, 2018, p. 1). In addition, ACCA (2009) strives to do the following:

1. support and enhance the practice of college counseling;
2. promote ethical and responsible professional practice;

3. promote communication and exchange among college counselors across service areas and institutional settings;
4. encourage cooperation with other organizations related to higher education and college student development;
5. provide leadership and advocacy for the profession of counseling in higher education. (p. x)

Resources for college counselors are abundant and include the *Journal of College Counseling*, an annual conference, webinars, research and leadership grants, college and community college surveys, and advocacy materials.

Association of University and College Counseling Center Directors

Established in 1950, AUCCCD (https://www.aucccd.org/) is the professional home to international college and university counseling center directors from the United States and its territories, Armenia, Australia, Bahamas, Canada, France, Japan, Oman, Qatar, St. Kitts, Nevis, Anguilla, United Arab Emirates, and the United Kingdom (AUCCCD, 2017). These institutions include 2- and 4-year public and private colleges. According to their mission statement, "we are a professional community that fosters director development and success. To advance the mission of higher education, we innovate, educate and advocate for collegiate mental health. We are committed to inclusive excellence and the promotion of social justice" (AUCCCD, 2018, "Mission," para. 1).

In addition to promoting awareness of student mental health, the association provides significant resources for college counseling centers. Since 2007, AUCCCD has administrated the Director's Survey (https://www.aucccd.org/director-surveys-public). These surveys were created "as a means to increase the objective understanding of factors critical to the functioning of college and university counseling centers" (AUCCCD, 2017, p. 2). It contains valuable information such as center demographics, budgets, responses to divisive social and political events, crisis and triage services, counseling modalities and service delivery, and client information (e.g., demographics, presenting problems, and clinical issues), session limits, and waiting lists. In addition, AUCCCD hosts an annual conference, creates position papers on college campus issues, and publishes the *Journal of College Student Psychotherapy*.

American College Personnel Association–College Student Educators International

The mission of ACPA (http://www.myacpa.org/), which was founded in 1924, "is to support and foster college student learning through the generation and dissemination of knowledge, which informs policies, practices, and programs, for student affairs and student services professionals and the higher and tertiary education community" (ACPA, 2018, para. 2). ACPA is made up of higher education and student affairs professionals and students. As an organization, it offers several publications that foster student development and support the higher education community: the *Journal of College Student Development*, *About Campus*, the *Developments* newsletter, and many position statements and resources on a variety of topics (e.g., undocumented students, campus safety, disabilities, social justice, mental health, freedom of speech).

In addition, it has created 19 commissions that offer specialized groups a way to connect. CCAPS (www.myacpa.org/commcaps) is one and focuses on college students' mental health. Its mission is to "maintain the voice of helping professionals focused on serving college and university students in a mental health setting" (CCAPS, n.d., "Mission and Goals," para. 1). CCAPS has put together a free and comprehensive college counseling and psychological services database of literature in the areas of college counseling, counseling psychology, college health, college student development, and professional counseling literatures. Literature in these five areas spans the years from 1998 to 2013.

National Association of Student Personnel Administrators—Student Affairs Administrators in Higher Education

NASPA (https://www.naspa.org/) was founded in 1918 with a focus on the advancement, health, and sustainability of the student affairs profession (NASPA, 2018). Their mission is "to be the principal source of leadership, scholarship, professional development, and advocacy for student affairs" (NASPA, 2018, "Our Mission," para. 1), which is accomplished through four guiding principles: integrity, innovation, inclusion, and inquiry. Members of NASPA are employed in a wide variety of functions and roles, including counseling and career services. Like ACPA, NASPA also identifies specialization groups in student affairs. Among the 10 focus areas is Mental Health (https://www.naspa.org/focus-areas/mental-health), which is composed of three constituent groups: Wellness and Health Promotion, Alcohol and Other Drug, and Disability Knowledge Community. The Mental Health focus area "supports ongoing efforts to address the mental health issues that students face" (NASPA, n.d., "Mental Health," para. 1).

American College Health Association

ACHA (https://www.acha.org/), founded in 1920, provides a voice for student health and wellness (ACHA, 2019). Through advocacy, education, and research, ACHA's mission is to advance the health of college students and campus communities. ACHA offers nine "sections" to reflect the range of professions that focus on college students' health and provide members with opportunities to network with others who share their scope of practice or expertise. Sections focus on providing resources and support relevant to their members; one of these sections is titled Mental Health.

The ACHA is the home of the *Journal of American College Health*; it offers opportunities for continuing education and an annual survey. The ACHA-National College Health Assessment is a nationally recognized research survey that provides precise data about college students' health habits, behaviors, and perceptions of health. The survey reports on nine areas: General Health of College Students; Disease and Injury Prevention; Academic Impacts; Violence, Abusive Relationships and Personal Safety; Tobacco, Alcohol, and Marijuana Use; Sexual Behavior; Nutrition and Exercise; Mental Health; and Sleep (ACHA, 2018a, 2018b).

Higher Education Mental Health Alliance

HEMHA (https://hemha.org/), created in 2008, is a partnership of organizations that collaborate to advance college student mental health through an interdisciplinary lens; it asserts that the issue of mental health is central to college student success and therefore is the responsibility of higher education (HEMHA, 2019). The members of this alliance include the following:

- American Academy of Child & Adolescent Psychiatry
- American College Counseling Association

- American College Health Association
- American College Personnel Association–College Student Educators International
- American Psychiatric Association
- American Psychological Association
- Association for University and College Counseling Center Directors
- The Jed Foundation
- National Association of Student Personnel Administrators–Student Affairs Administrators in Higher Education

HEMHA provides leadership to (a) think about college mental health issues at a strategic level, (b) identify and share mental health resources, (c) promote full community engagement in the mental health continuum of care, (d) define the role of advocacy in mental health, and (e) support and disseminate evidence-based practice across the mental health continuum (education, prevention, intervention, treatment, and aftercare). HEMHA is committed to advancing mental health throughout the realm of higher education and improving student recruitment, retention, and learning outcomes through efforts in multiple areas: advocacy, policy, practice, and research (see Figure 1.1). In addition, HEMHA provides leadership in the area of legislative advocacy.

HEMHA has published three resources on current mental health issues and trends facing campuses: *College Counseling from a Distance: Deciding Whether and When to Engage in Telemental Health Services* (2018), *Postvention: A Guide for Response to Suicide on College Campuses* (2014), and *Balancing Safety and Support on Campus: A Guide for Campus Teams* (2012). All resources are free and available at hemha.org and are written to appeal to all of the alliance's constituencies.

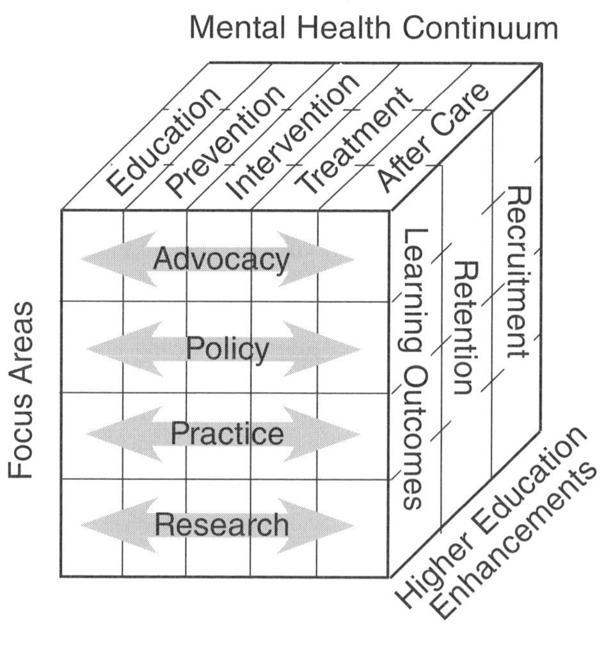

FIGURE 1.1

Higher Education Mental Health Alliance (HEMHA) Conceptual Framework

Note. From the Higher Education Mental Health Alliance website at https://hemha.org/about-hemha.

Professional Standards and Accreditation

There are several professional bodies that are responsible for identifying current standards of practice and education requirements related to counseling in higher education settings. The following sections introduce the Council for the Advancement of Standards in Higher Education (CAS) and the International Association of Counseling Services (IACS). Accreditation in higher education and college counseling services typically requires a period of self-study to meet standards, peer review of the self-study, and confirmation through a site visit. All accrediting bodies regularly review and update standards regarding best practices and higher education trends.

Council for the Advancement of Standards in Higher Education

Since 1979, CAS (https://www.cas.edu/) has been a consortium of professional associations in higher education (CAS, 2019). Through professional standards, CAS created standards and guidelines designed for the "development, assessment, and improvement of quality student learning, programs, and services" across 45 functional areas of student affairs (CAS, 2014, p. 1). There are 12 general standards for all functional areas, and all functional area standards are composed of specialty standards and guidelines. Among these 45 functional areas is Counseling Services. It is important to note that CAS does not offer certifications or accredit programs. Rather they provide "vetted and agreed upon" standards that allow functional units and professionals in higher education to "inform practice, management of programs, delivery of services, and assessment processes" (CAS, 2014, p. 2). CAS encourages interdisciplinary collaboration among professional associations to create standards representative of the profession. In addition, CAS can reduce silos by urging functional units to make use of other functional units on the same campus to assist with the self-study (e.g., the counseling center may have members from community engagement on the self-study committee). Increasing knowledge between student affairs units about what they do has the potential to build stronger bonds and advocacy when assistance is sought from the administration.

International Association of Counseling Services

Established in 1971, IACS (http://iacsinc.org/home.html) is the international accreditation association for university, 4-year college, and 2-year community college counseling services (IACS, 2017). Its purpose is to encourage and aid these counseling services in meeting high professional standards and advocating for the profession and its services. According to IACS's (2017) bylaws, it holds five main objectives:

1. To advance the professional development of counseling centers by establishing and encouraging high standards of professional performance and conduct.
2. To develop standards, policies, procedures, and principles for evaluating and accrediting counseling centers, not the counseling staff of those agencies.
3. To provide methods or procedures for assisting centers to meet established IACS Standards.
4. To build public goodwill, confidence, and knowledge of the counseling profession by educating the consumer and the public in the advancement, improvement, and uses of counseling centers.
5. To foster professional cooperation and communication among counseling centers operating in a variety of settings by providing opportunity for exchange of experience and opinions through discussion, study, and publications. However, it is not an objective of . . . [IACS] to handle consumer or staff complaints against a specific center or centers. (p. 1)

Unlike CAS, IACS accredits counseling centers along with providing professional standards. Centers are required to be reevaluated every 8 years along with submitting annual reports (IACS, 2017). There are five main areas of standards for university and college counseling services. These include Relationship of the Counseling Center to the University Community, Counseling Services Roles and Functions, Ethical Standards, Counseling Service Personnel, and Related Guidelines (e.g., Professional Development, Staff Diversity, Physical Facilities; IACS, 2016).

College Counselor Preparation

A clinical license is necessary to provide mental health counseling as a college counselor. This equates to a minimum of a master's degree that leads to licensure in social work, psychiatric nursing, marriage and family therapy, mental health counseling, or psychology. Having a variety of clinical orientations in the counseling center can create well-rounded service delivery and perspective. There is no specific degree in college counseling; however, master's- and doctoral-level students can specialize through coursework and clinical practicums and internships. Some programs provide specializations by way of certificate programs and specialty areas through counselor education accreditation. As preparation programs vary, college counselors trained in programs accredited by the American Psychological Association and/or the Council for Accreditation of Counseling and Related Educational Programs (CACREP) that meet industry standards are most often sought by employers. Nonaccredited training programs should be researched carefully because students need to be certain that training will result in licensure to provide clinical services.

In this section we specifically focus on college counseling over student affairs. There are currently no certifications, licenses, academic program accreditations, or specific credentials required to work in student affairs. Entry-level student affairs positions typically require a graduate degree in higher education, student affairs, counseling, educational administration, or a related area. Experience working in higher education as a student (e.g., working as a resident assistant, working as a peer adviser, working or volunteering in any functional unit) is also helpful to enter this profession. In addition, a desire to want to work with student personal growth, identity, development, and cocurricular student success is a great mind-set for those who want to work as a student affairs professional.

Credentials

Most counselors who work in higher education counseling centers earn state licensure as a counselor, psychologist, social worker, or psychiatrist. However, in other counseling-related offices licensure may or may not be required (e.g., in disability services, student and family care, career counseling, health and wellness promotion, and academic advising). This will vary by institution type. Individuals who hold licensure will be required to earn continuing education units to maintain these credentials. In addition, there are several voluntary certifications that can be added to licensure and meet the growing needs of the counseling center. Acquiring such certifications will make one's counseling and professional skills more desirable when applying for jobs. Below is one example per category; however, it is important to know that there are numerous certifications and specializations in each category:

- Addictions: Master Addictions Counselor
- Board Certified-TeleMental Health Provider

- Crisis: American Association of Suicidology Crisis Worker Certification
- Disordered eating: Eating Disorder Intuitive Therapy
- Sex therapy: American Association of Sexuality Educators, Counselors and Therapists Certified Sex Therapists
- Trauma: International Association of Trauma Professionals

In addition, counselors can acquire training in helpful approaches—for example, eye movement desensitization and reprocessing (trauma), and dialectical behavior therapy (personality disorders). One should always do due diligence to research professional and vetted certifications and trainings.

Council for Accreditation of Counseling and Related Educational Programs

Shifting from counseling center standards and accreditation, we find CACREP (https://www.cacrep.org/), an accrediting body that develops counselor education preparation standards and procedures that reflect the needs of a dynamic, diverse, and complex society. A program's achievement of CACREP accreditation is a reflection of their excellence in achieving these standards. Established in 1981, CACREP accredits master's and doctoral degree counseling programs offered by colleges and universities. General standards are outlined for the institution, common core content areas, field experiences, and specialty standards. Specialty areas relevant to college counseling include College Counseling and Student Affairs, Addictions Counseling, Clinical Mental Health Counseling, Career Counseling, and Counselor Education and Supervision. Of note for those interested in becoming a college counselor, Section 5, Standard E (College Counseling and Student Affairs) of the 2016 Council for Accreditation of Counseling and Related Educational Programs Standards (CACREP, 2015) states, "Students who are preparing to specialize as college counselors and student affairs professionals will demonstrate the knowledge and skills necessary to promote the academic, career, personal, and social development of individuals in higher education settings."

The Definitions and Evolution of the College Population

Defining characteristics of students have changed over the years and continue to evolve. Below we introduce some of the most common definitions of the types and generations of students we encounter on campus.

Student Populations

With increasing diversity among students, it is critical for college counselors to stay current with demographic trends and issues facing today's college students. This allows college counseling professionals to determine how the institution affects marginalized and minority students' experiences and success. Three main groups that are typically discussed are traditional students, nontraditional students, and first-generation students.

Traditional students are typically defined as a postsecondary attendee between the ages of 18 and 24. They are generally characterized as an undergraduate student "who earns a high school diploma, enrolls full time immediately after finishing high school, depends on parents for financial support, and either does not work during the school year or works part time" (U.S. Department of Education, National Center for Education Statistics, 2002, p. 1). Today, they are viewed as the exception more than the rule.

Nontraditional students or *adult students* are mostly viewed by the defining characteristic of being over the age of 24 and delaying college post–high school graduation. However, there are additional variables that have been incorporated into contemporary definitions. Working full-time, returning to school after a career or being in the military, commuting to campus, having family responsibilities, attending school part-time, and being a single parent all are potential characteristics of this population (U.S. Department of Education, National Center for Education Statistics, 2002; Terenzini, & Pascarella, 1998). Terenzini and Pascarella (1998) suggested that these students have rates of educational progress that are as varied as themselves. In addition, whereas traditional students can direct a significant portion of their energy toward academics, nontraditional students can be found in a competition between life and college for their time, energy, and financial resources (U.S. Department of Education, National Center for Education Statistics, 2002).

First-generation students are described as college students "who come from families in which neither parent attained any level of postsecondary education" (Lippincott & German, 2007, p. 89). These students are an important population to target because of the lack of college experience families can pass on. This information can include the usefulness of the counseling center and other campus services; what college classes are like; how one traverses campus, including navigating roommates; and overall identity. Some first-generation students have difficulty connecting their experience back to their families or asking for advice out of fear that they will not be understood or get the answer they are looking for.

Colleges today also observe the following populations on campus: undocumented students, international students, student athletes, graduate students, transfer students, and returning students. In addition, we see diversity within these populations across the following characteristics: gender, sexual orientation, race, spirituality, ethnicity, ability/disability, and mental health issues. As professionals, we must recognize that "whatever our ethnic or cultural identity, we should never assume that—even with extensive study and exposure—we can ever be fully knowledgeable about people whose culture and beliefs are different than ours" (Hoff, Hallisey, & Hoff, 2009, pp. 19–20). Intertwined is an understanding of how historical, systemic, and sociocultural influences have shaped students' lives as well as the institution and community in which they are embedded. As you move through this text, it is important to connect what you are learning regarding the history of the field and society, from this chapter, with Chapter 3: "College Counseling Through a Multicultural and Social Justice Lens." Understanding how current practices are influenced by the past is useful in developing awareness of how the past has had an impact on students and the campus community.

Generational Influences on Students

During the 20th and 21st centuries colleges have observed the impact of social and historical context on student generations. From the Baby Boomers to the iGens, college counselors, faculty, and staff have witnessed distances between themselves and students. In addition, counselors must be cognizant that students do differ in generations from their parents/guardians. In many cases colleges will have a set of generations connected to every student. They will need to understand not only their client's generation but also the interaction of that student with his or her family's generation, the faculty's generation, and their own generation. With some individuals holding opinions regarding different generations (e.g., resentment, contempt, jealousy, admiration, dismissal, beliefs of unearned entitlement) it will be important for college counselors to bring to awareness any bias they may possess. Because generations include events and experiences that have an impact on how students learn about and view the world, counselors must also take on the challenge of learning how to be effective with new generations as they enter college.

Below we will briefly describe college student generations to allow some perspective between current students, faculty, staff, and college counselors. It is important to keep in mind that students will not possess all characteristics of each generation; however, for those providing counseling services, familiarity with these general descriptions can assist with outreach, treatment, and service for both students and families (Girard, 2010):

- *Baby Boomers (Born 1946–1964).* Now 78 million strong, this generation was born because of a "baby boom" post–World War II as the world began to improve and become more stable (Girard, 2010; Seemiller & Grace, 2016; Wiedmer, 2015). Boomers are driven by a philosophy that working hard will lead to success and fulfilled ambition (Seemiller & Grace, 2016). Defining moments for this generation were the civil rights movement, the Vietnam War, the women's movement, President John F. Kennedy's assassination, space exploration, Woodstock, and Watergate. Their approximate age in 2020 is 56 to 74.
- *Generation X (Born 1965–1979).* This generation of approximately 47 million are the children of early Baby Boomers (Girard, 2010). Generation X (also known as *latchkey kids, MTV generation*; Whitehouse & Flippin, 2017) saw a 25% increase in married women entering the workforce, making it more common for both parents to work (Seemiller & Grace, 2016). They were the first generation to experience increases in divorce and daycare (Wiedmer, 2015). They are somewhat cynical, skeptical, and practical while maintaining priorities that include balancing work and family. In addition, this generation was more tech savvy, independent, ambitious, and self-reliant than their predecessors. Defining moments for this generation were the Space Shuttle Challenger explosion, Operation Desert Storm, the fall of the Berlin Wall, cable TV/MTV, AIDS, video games, disco, grunge, hip-hop culture, and personal computers. Their approximate age in 2020 is 41 to 55.
- *Microgenerations.* Some individuals recognize microgenerations as they end up being close to the end or the beginning of a generation. For example, individuals born between the late 1970s and early 1980s have called themselves Xennials (also known as the Oregon Trail Generation and Generation Catalano; Garvey, 2015; Stankorb & Oelbaum, 2014). This crossover generation (between the disaffection of Gen X and the optimism of Millennials) came of age just as communication was experiencing a shift, offering an experience that is half analog and half digital (Garvey, 2015; Stankorb & Oelbaum, 2014). This generation was in their adolescent years when computers, access to dial-up internet, and Napster became mainstream; they had no social media. In addition, many did not get cell phones until their 20s.
- *Millennials/Generation Y (Born 1980–1994).* Millennials, monikered the "Me Generation," are criticized for being entitled and having the expectation of being handed opportunities (Seemiller & Grace, 2016). Standing 71 million strong and optimistic, this generation is also web savvy and very connected to social media (Wiedmer, 2015). In addition, Millennials experienced constant information about world events through technology, the internet, and mobile phones (Wiedmer, 2015). With "hands-on" families offering financial and emotional support, they became the most educated generation in history and not as independent as Generation X (Seemiller & Grace, 2016). Defining moments for this generation were 9/11; the wars in Iraq and Afghanistan; the 2008 economic crisis; the prison release of Nelson Mandela; the Columbine school shooting; the Oklahoma City bombing; Hurricane Katrina; the Indian Ocean tsunami of 2004; the death of Princess Diana; Y2K; email and texting; Google; participation trophies; and video games, smartphones, and high-speed internet. Their approximate age in 2020 is 26 to 40.

It is during this generation that the term *helicopter parenting* emerged. If you worked at a school or college, at some point you probably encountered this parenting style. Just as it sounds, the helicopter parents are known to hover over their children like a helicopter. This may entail characteristics of overprotection, excessive interest, close attention to their child's positive and negative experiences, and filling in for a lack of resilience.

- *iGen/Generation Z (Born 1995–2012).* Starting and ending birth years for iGens vary; however, most agree with the earliest birth year of 1995. The final birth year for this generation has fallen in the range of 2010 to 2016. Seemiller and Grace (2017) reported that "the oldest of this post-Millennial generation arrived to college in 2013, and more than 4 years later, Generation Z students fill our classrooms, campus programs, and residence halls" (p. 21). They constitute 25% of the U.S. population, making them a larger cohort than the Baby Boomers and Millennials (Seemiller & Grace, 2017; Twenge, 2017). In addition, they are characterized as being loyal, compassionate, thoughtful, open-minded, flexible, responsible, socially conscious, and determined.

  This generation has experienced a lifelong use of the internet and digital communication and technology. They require less direction because of having access to digital tools and immediate access to and gratification from answers. They may have changing or deficient social skills due to advancing technology (Twenge, 2017; Wiedmer, 2015). iGen is the first generation to spend their entire adolescence with smartphones and broadband internet access at home and college (Seemiller & Grace, 2017; Twenge, 2017). Twenge (2017) suggested that this generation is less mature than previous generations because they are delaying experiences that promote autonomous decision-making such as learning to drive, getting a part-time job, engaging in sexual intimacy, and experimenting with alcohol. For many, the smartphone has taken over as the primary camera and is central in social interactions (i.e., use as a text device and through social media apps), computer use, and use as a music player, while being used less as an actual phone. Defining moments for this generation include marriage equality, the first Black president (President Barack Obama), the Sandy Hook Elementary School shooting, the war against ISIS, the election of President Donald Trump, and a significant increase in technological devices. Their approximate age in 2020 is 8 to 25.

  Another parenting approach emerged during this time, *lawnmower parenting* (also known as *snowplow parenting*), which describes parents who "mow a path" for their children. They are known to plow ahead, interfering and micromanaging to safeguard their children from failure and disappointment (Long, 2018). Parents with this approach have also been known to check their child's work and sometimes complete it for them. Ask any undergraduate college professor, and he or she will be able to give you some examples of lawnmower parents coming in to talk to them about their syllabus, assignments, and even a change in their child's grade. Another term for this type of parenting was coined in 2004 by Danish psychologist Bent Hougaard: *curling parent* (Bremberg, 2006). Like lawnmower parents, curling parents take the role of the "sweepers," and it is their role to sweep in front of the stone (their child) to create a path that reduces interference and negative experiences. Sweeping reduces friction between the stone and the ice in order for the stone to travel farther with nothing getting in its way.
- *Born on the heels of the iGen is a generation dubbed "Generation Google," "Generation Alpha," and "Generation α."* This generation typically contains the children of the Xennials and Millennials. Not much is known about this generation, yet they are believed to have been born during an increase of only children. They will likely continue to be more tech savvy and educated than past generations. It is speculated that they have an approximate beginning birth year of 2010.

Contemporary Mental Health Issues and Trends

The demand for mental health services on campus is growing faster than institutional enrollment (CCMH, 2019). Locke, Wallace, and Brunner (2016) cited research indicating that the most common presenting concerns among students seeking psychological services in recent decades continue to be depression and anxiety, and counseling center researchers agree (AUCCCD, 2017; CCMH, 2019). Along with this, students are reporting presenting problems that include an emphasis on relationships and academics with additional comorbid and overlapping concerns (Locke et al., 2016). Among the concerns that college counseling centers are witnessing are nonsuicidal self-injury, abuse of alcohol and other drugs, students with threat-to-self characteristics, student hospitalization, stress, disordered eating, sexual assaults, hate crimes, and problematic interpersonal functioning (AUCCCD, 2017; CCMH, 2019; Locke et al., 2016). In addition, the ACHA (2018a) reported that college students continue to be feeling overwhelmed (86.5%), exhausted (not from physical activity; 83.4%), very sad (67.3%), very lonely (63.1%), and hopeless (57.7%).

Trend data are gathered through individual research; however, several professional organizations have been monitoring the pulse of college student mental health issues. In addition, they report data on trends within college counseling centers (e.g., staff demographics, the distribution of services on campus, service delivery roles and percentages, waiting lists, and responses to community and national events). These yearly studies provide the most up-to-date statistics on who works in and who visits today's counseling centers. The following is a list of these annual and semi-annual studies and reports:

- The Association of University and College Counseling Center Directors (AUCCCD) Annual Survey. Since 2006, AUCCCD has administered an annual survey to increase understanding of "factors critical to the functioning of college and university counseling centers" (AUCCCD, 2017). The AUCCCD survey contains the largest sampling of counseling center directors in the world, and free reports are provided (https://www.aucccd.org/public).
- The Center for Collegiate Mental Health Annual Report. Since 2009, using Titanium Software, CCMH has provided data describing college students receiving mental health direct services provided by college counseling centers (http://ccmh.psu.edu/publications/).
- The ACHA-National College Health Assessment II. Since 2015, the ACHA-National College Health Assessment II has provided data on the health of college students. It has assisted "college health service providers, health educators, counselors, and administrators in collecting data about their students' habits, behaviors, and perceptions on the most prevalent health topics" (ACHA, 2018b, p. 2; https://www.acha.org/NCHA/ACHA-NCHA_Data/Publications_and_Reports/NCHA/Data/Reports_ACHA-NCHAIIc.aspx).
- The American College Counseling Association's Community College Task Force. The Community College Task Force has conducted an annual survey to gather benchmark data about common practices for personal/mental health counseling in community/2-year colleges since 2011. Although the ACCA website holds surveys only through 2015 (http://www.collegecounseling.org/page-18283), Edwards and Lenhart (2017) have continued to conduct this survey, which is available upon request from ACCA.

You will find these resources being used throughout this book's chapters. It is essential that college counselors examine the most up-to-date surveys along with studying what is occurring at their own center and campus. Maintaining knowledge and awareness around issues that have an impact on the counseling center and greater campus can lead to more intentional prevention, outreach, and direct service interventions.

Conclusion

History, in a social, political, systemic, and ecological sense, has significantly shaped college counseling. As we move through this century, the field will continue to evolve with each generation, their parents, and accompanying defining moments. A lot can be learned from studying the past and the journey of college counseling. With influences like national events, professional organizations, professional standards, and generational makeups, we have witnessed an amazing adaptation of college counseling centers. It will be more important than ever to continue current research and advocacy for the field. Finally, collaboration within higher education will assist all student affairs professionals in joining together to provide best practice, with consideration for unique student characteristics, while caring for the campus community.

Final Case Study

For this case study we want you to examine yourself during your undergraduate college experience. Reflect on your demographics and social locations during this time. Examples might include the following:

- Generation
- Age
- Relationship status
- Social and family support
- Family/personal socioeconomic status
- Traditional/nontraditional/adult student
- First-generation student
- International student
- Student athlete
- Full-time/part-time work activity
- Residence (on campus/off campus/with family)
- Transfer student
- Veteran
- Gender
- Sexual orientation
- Race
- Spirituality/religion
- Ethnicity
- Ability/disability
- Mental health

Case Exploration Questions

After spending time with this list, please answer the following questions as they relate to your different social locations.

How have historical, generational, systemic, and sociocultural influences

1. affected you and your collegiate experience?
2. enriched, assisted, or been a source of privilege during your college experience?

3. been an obstacle or ignored during your time in higher education?
4. influenced your social interactions, including involvement in student organizations and the development of your support systems on campus, during your higher education experience?
5. What was your access to technology in your college experience and how did that influence your college experience?

References

American College Counseling Association. (2009). Mission statement. Retrieved from http://www.collegecounseling.org/Mission-Statement

American College Counseling Association. (2018). Bylaws. Retrieved from http://www.collegecounseling.org/resources/About%20Tab/Bylaws/ACCA%20Bylaws%202018%20current%20version.pdf

American College Health Association. (2010). Considerations for integration of counseling and health services on college and university campuses. *Journal of American College Health, 58*, 583–596.

American College Health Association. (2018a). American College Health Association–National College Health Assessment II: Reference group executive summary Fall 2017. Retrieved from https://www.acha.org/documents/ncha/NCHA-II_Spring_2018_Reference_Group_Executive_Summary.pdf

American College Health Association. (2018b). American College Health Association–National College Health Assessment II: Reference group executive summary Spring 2018. Retrieved from https://www.acha.org/documents/ncha/NCHA-II_Spring_2018_Reference_Group_Executive_Summary.pdf

American College Health Association. (2019). About ACHA. Retrieved from https://www.acha.org/ACHA/About/About_ACHA/ACHA/About/About_ACHA.aspx?hkey=9deff142-0898-4f21-8a69-f5e0621eb59c

American College Personnel Association. (2018). Mission, vision, and values. Retrieved from http://foundation.myacpa.org/transform/association-priorities/

American Council on Education. (1937). *The student personnel point of view* (American Council on Education Studies, Series 1, Vol. 1, No. 3). Washington, DC: Author.

American Council on Education, Committee on Student Personnel Work. (1949). *The student personnel point of view* (Rev. ed.; American Council on Education Studies, Series 6, Vol. 13, No. 13). Washington, DC: Author.

American Psychiatric Association. (1980). *Diagnostic and statistical manual of mental disorders* (3rd ed.). Washington, DC: Author.

Americans With Disabilities Act of 1990, 42 U.S.C.A. § 12101 *et seq.* (West 1993).

Americans With Disabilities Act. (1991). *Accessibility guidelines for buildings and facilities.* Retrieved from https://www.ada.gov/1991standards/adastd94-archive.pdf

Archer, J., & Cooper, S. (1998). *Counseling and mental health services on campus: A handbook of contemporary practices and challenges.* San Francisco, CA: Jossey-Bass.

Association for University and College Counseling Center Directors. (2017). *The Association for University and College Counseling Center Directors annual survey.* Retrieved from https://www.aucccd.org/assets/documents/Governance/2017%20aucccd%20survey-public-apr26.pdf

Association for University and College Counseling Center Directors. (2018). Mission statement. Retrieved from https://www.aucccd.org/strategic-plan

Barreira, P., & Snider, M. (2010). History of college counseling and mental health services and role of the community mental health model. In J. Kay & V. Schwartz (Eds.), *Mental health care in the college community* (pp. 21–31). Hoboken, NJ: Wiley-Blackwell.

Bremberg, S. (2006). *New tools for parents: Proposals for new forms of parent support.* Stockholm, Sweden: Swedish National Institute of Public Health. Retrieved from https://www.academia.edu/15374211/New_tools_for_parents_Proposals_for_new_forms_of_parent_support

Brown, S. D., Perez, R. M., & Reeder, B. L. (2007). The costs and benefits of merging counseling centers with student health services: Perceptions of the experienced. *Journal of College Student Psychotherapy, 22,* 3–16.

Center for Collegiate Mental Health. (2019, January). *2018 annual report* (Publication No. STA 19-180). Retrieved from https://ccmh.psu.edu/files/2019/09/2018-Annual-Report-9.27.19-FINAL.pdf

Commission for Counseling and Psychological Services. (n.d.). Home page. Retrieved from http://www.myacpa.org/commcaps

Committee on Standards for College Health. (1961). *Recommended standards and practices for a college health program.* Rockville, MD: American College Health Association.

Council for Accreditation of Counseling and Related Educational Programs. (2015). *2016 CACREP standards.* Alexandria, VA: Author.

Council for the Advancement of Standards in Higher Education. (2014). CAS general standards. Retrieved from http://standards.cas.edu/getpdf.cfm?PDF=E868395C-F784-2293-129ED7842334B22A

Council for the Advancement of Standards in Higher Education. (2019). About CAS. Retrieved from https://www.cas.edu/about

Dean, L. A., & Meadows, M. E. (1995). College counseling: Union and intersection. *Journal of Counseling & Development, 74,* 139–142.

Dixon v. Alabama State Board of Education, 294 F.2d 150 (5th Cir. 1961).

Dungy, G., & Gordon, S. A. (2011). The development of student affairs. In J. H. Schuh, S. R. Jones, S. R. Harper, & Associates (Eds.), *Student services: A handbook for the profession* (5th ed., pp. 61–79). San Francisco, CA: Jossey-Bass.

Edwards, J., & Lenhart, A. (2017). *Survey of Community/Two-Year College Counseling Services, 2016–2017.* Alexandria, VA: American College Counseling Association.

Elhai, J., Levine, J., Dvorak, R., & Hall, B. (2016). Fear of missing out, need for touch, anxiety and depression are related to problematic smartphone use. *Computers in Human Behavior, 63,* 509–516.

Gammon, H. L. (2013). *The student perspective: An exploration of the experiences and needs of university students with mental illness.* Retrieved from https://corescholar.libraries.wright.edu/etd_all/768

Garvey, A. (2015). The Oregon Trail Generation: Life before and after mainstream tech. Retrieved from https://web.archive.org/web/20171113081411/https://socialmediaweek.org/blog/2015/04/oregon-trail-generation/

Girard, K. A. (2010). Working with parents and families of young adults. In J. Kay & V. Schwartz (Eds.), *Mental health care in the college community* (pp. 179–202). Hoboken, NJ: Wiley-Blackwell.

Higher Education Mental Health Alliance. (2012). *Balancing safety and support on campus: A guide for campus teams.* Retrieved from http://hemha.org/wp-content/uploads/2019/01/campus-teams-balancing-safety-support-campus-jed-guide.pdf

Higher Education Mental Health Alliance. (2014). *Postvention: A guide for response to suicide on college campuses.* Retrieved from http://hemha.org/wp-content/uploads/2018/06/jed-hemha-postvention-guide.pdf

Higher Education Mental Health Alliance. (2018). *College counseling from a distance: Deciding whether and when to engage in telemental health services.* Retrieved from http://hemha.org/wp-content/uploads/2019/01/HEMHA-Distance-Counseling_FINAL2019.pdf

Higher Education Mental Health Alliance. (2019). About HEMHA. Retrieved from https://hemha.org/about-hemha

Hodges, S. J. (2017). College counseling: Past, present, and future. In S. J. Hodges, K. Shelton, & M. M. King Lyn (Eds.), *The college and university counseling manual* (pp. 1–12). New York, NY: Springer.

Hoff, L. A., Hallisey, B. J., & Hoff, M. (2009). *People in crisis: Clinical and diversity perspectives* (6th ed.). New York, NY: Routledge.

Hoover, E. (2008). "Animal House" at 30: O Bluto, where art thou? *The Chronicle of Higher Education, 55,* p. A1.

Hunt, J., & Eisenberg, D. (2010). Mental health problems and help-seeking behavior among college students. *Journal of Adolescent Health, 46,* 3–10.

International Association of Counseling Services. (2016). *Standards for university and college counseling services.* Retrieved from https://0201.nccdn.net/1_2/000/000/195/93c/STANDARDS-Sec.-IV.-Amended-10-22-2016--edited-12-2016--edited-10-13-2018.pdf

International Association of Counseling Services. (2017). *Bylaws of the International Association of Counseling Services.* Retrieved from https://0201.nccdn.net/1_2/000/000/0a3/3fa/IACS-BYLAWS-10-5-17.pdf

Kraft, D. P. (2011). One hundred years of college mental health. *Journal of American College Health, 59,* 477–481.

LaFollette, A. M. (2009). The evolution of university counseling: From educational guidance to multicultural competence, severe mental illnesses and crisis planning. *Graduate Journal of Counseling Psychology, 1,* 1–7.

Lee, P. (2011). The curious life of in loco parentis in American universities. *Higher Education in Review, 8,* 65–90.

Lee, P. (2014). The case of Dixon v. Alabama State Board of Education: From civil rights to students' rights and back again. *Teachers College Record, 116,* 1–18.

Lippincott, J. A., & German, N. (2007). From blue collar to ivory tower: Counseling first-generation, working-class students. In J. A. Lippincott & R. B. Lippincott (Eds.), *Special populations in college counseling* (pp. 89–98). Alexandria, VA: American Counseling Association.

Locke, B., Wallace, D., & Brunner, J. (2016). Emerging issues and models in college mental health services. *New Directions for Student Services, 156,* 19–30.

Long, C. (2018). Educators weigh in on lawnmower parents. Retrieved from http://neatoday.org/2018/10/12/lawnmower-parents/

McCarthy, T. (2014). Great aspirations: The postwar American college counseling center. *History of Psychology, 17,* 1–18.

Meadows, M. E. (2000). The evolution of college counseling. In D. C. Davis & K. M. Humphrey (Eds.), *College counseling: Issues and strategies for a new millennium* (pp. 15–40). Alexandria, VA: American Counseling Association.

Mitchell, S. L., Oakley, D. R., & Dunkle, J. H. (2019). White paper: A multidimensional understanding of effective university and college counseling center organizational structures. *Journal of College Student Psychotherapy, 33,* 89–106.

Morrill, W. H., Oetting, E. R., & Hurst, J. C. (1974). Dimensions of counselor functioning. *The Personnel and Guidance Journal, 52,* 354–359.

National Association of Student Personnel Administrators. (n.d.). Mental health. Retrieved from https://www.naspa.org/focus-areas/mental-health

National Association of Student Personnel Administrators. (2018). About NASPA. Retrieved from https://www.naspa.org/about

Oetting, E. R., Ivey, A. E., & Weigel, R. G. (1970). *The college and university counseling center* (ACPA Monograph No. 11). Washington, DC: American Personnel and Guidance Association.

Prescott, H. (2008). College mental health since the early twentieth century. *Harvard Review of Psychiatry, 16,* 258–266.
Reif, C., & Much, K. (2017). #Socialmedia: A preliminary report of social networking use among university and college counseling center mental health providers. *Journal of College Student Psychotherapy, 31,* 257–264.
Reifler, C. B. (1990). Clements Fry, if you could see us now: The Robert L. Arnstein Retirement Lecture. *Journal of College Student Psychotherapy, 5,* 3–18.
Seabrook, E. M., Kern, M. L., & Rickard, N. S. (2016). Social networking sites, depression, and anxiety: A systematic review. *JMIR Mental Health, 3,* 1–19.
Seemiller, C., & Grace, M. (2016). *Generation Z goes to college.* San Francisco, CA: Jossey-Bass.
Seemiller, C., & Grace, M. (2017). Generation Z: Educating and engaging the next generation of students. *About Campus: Enriching the Student Learning Experience, 22,* 21–26.
Servicemen's Readjustment Act of 1944, 38 U.S.C. § 4101 *et seq.* (1944).
Sharkin, B. S. (1997). Increased severity of presenting problems at college counseling centers: A closer look. *Journal of Counseling & Development, 75,* 275–281. doi:10.1002/j.1556-6676.1997.tb02342.x
Sharkin, B. S. (2012). *Being a college counselor on today's campus: Roles, contributions, and special challenges.* New York, NY: Routledge.
Stankorb, S., & Oelbaum, J. (2014). Reasonable people disagree about the post-gen X, pre-millennial generation. Retrieved from https://web.archive.org/web/20171122214323/https://www.good.is/articles/generation-xennials
Stone, G. L., & Archer, J., Jr. (1990). College and university counseling centers in the 1990s: Challenges and limits. *Counseling Psychologist, 18,* 539–607.
Sweet, W. (2011). 150 years ago: Amherst established nation's first college health program. Amherst College News Archive. Retrieved from https://www.amherst.edu/news/news_releases/2011/08/node/337711/
Terenzini, P., & Pascarella, E. (1998). Studying college students in the 21st century: Meeting new challenges. *The Review of Higher Education, 21,* 151–165.
Twenge, J. M. (2017). *iGen: Why today's super-connected kids are growing up less rebellious, more tolerant, less happy—And completely unprepared for adulthood (and what this means for the rest of us).* New York, NY: Atria Books.
United States. President's Commission on Higher Education. (1947). *Higher education for American democracy: A report of the President's Commission on Higher Education.* Washington, DC: U.S. Government Printing Office.
U.S. Department of Education, National Center for Education Statistics. (2002). *Nontraditional undergraduates.* Retrieved from https://nces.ed.gov/pubs2002/2002012.pdf
Vannucci, A., Flannery, K., & Ohannessian, C. (2017). Social media use and anxiety in emerging adults. *Journal of Affective Disorders, 207,* 163–166.
Whitehouse, P., & Flippin, C. (2017). From diversity to intergenerativity: Addressing the mystery and opportunities of Generation X. *Generations, 41,* 6–11.
Wiedmer, T. (2015). Generations do differ: Best practices in leading Traditionalists, Boomers, and Generations X, Y, and Z. *Delta Kappa Gamma Bulletin, 82,* 51–58.
Williamson, E. G. (1939). *How to counsel students: A manual of techniques for clinical counselors.* New York, NY: McGraw-Hill.

Chapter 2

Roles and Responsibilities

Joshua C. Watson and Derrick A. Paladino

College students, by their nature, are a transient population. Their needs change. We can't be assuming that today's college students have the same needs as college students 10 years ago.

—Sarah Lipson, college student mental health researcher

Reflection Exercise

When you think about a college counselor, what do you envision that person's day-to-day activities as being? Perhaps seeing a full schedule of students in 50-minute session blocks? What about the types of issues they can expect to face? Are college students mainly presenting for help to address issues related to academic stress, relationship issues, career preparation, and homesickness? Yes, they are, but today's students also present with many other chief complaints or issues. As a result, the role of the college counselor has expanded greatly over time. Today, college counselors and the facilities they work in serve an integral function on college campuses. Their work is multifaceted and affects students' lives in many ways, not just in individual sessions in a counselor's office. To prepare you for what you will learn in this chapter, take a few moments to reflect on the following questions:

1. Have you ever worked with a college counselor?
2. If so, what were some of the reasons you sought help from a college counselor?
3. How do college counselors improve the overall campus culture for all students?
4. What are some of the goals you may have for yourself as a future college counselor in terms of contributing to student well-being?

The role of today's college counseling center (CCC) is extensive and comprehensive. Its functions have evolved in response to "social needs, political environment, national economy, and changing demographics" (Council for the Advancement of Standards in Higher Education [CAS], 2014, p. 1). Changes also occur as a result of internal factors unique to each campus environment, such as the existence as a standalone center versus counselors working in combination with health services or a wellness center or overseeing other areas such as accessibility services and career services (CAS, 2014). Also, CCCs may differ in makeup and services on the basis of institutional size (e.g., small and large schools), type (e.g., 4-year, community, and 2-year colleges), and mission of the host institution. Just like each institution has its own unique culture and mission, so too do CCCs (Brunner, Wallace, Reymann, Sellers, & McCabe, 2014). As student demographics change, and new campus issues emerge, the benefits of establishing and maintaining a fully comprehensive college counseling delivery center will become far more pronounced (Brunner, Wallace, Keyes, & Polychronis, 2017).

In this chapter we will highlight the makeup of the counseling center, focusing primarily on the roles and responsibilities of CCCs and their staff as well as the services they provide to the campus community. Two central services we will not discuss in this chapter are outreach and preventative programming and consultation services, because they are discussed in depth in subsequent chapters. Specifically, Chapter 7 addresses outreach and preventative services, and Chapters 5 and 6 encompass the student affairs context and building collaborative campus relationships, respectively. We do encourage you, the reader, to think about your strengths as a counselor-in-training, your preferences about work setting and scope, and the contributions you want to make in the future as you contemplate working with college students.

Today's CCCs are more structured than centers in the past. Many are either accredited by external bodies (i.e., the International Association of Counseling Services [IACS]) or have chosen to follow certain predetermined standards of practice (i.e., CAS). Both accreditation and standards (which you have learned about in Chapter 1) discuss the roles and responsibilities of the college and university counseling center. For example, IACS (2017) assesses counseling centers through five primary areas with an additional sixth area focusing on issues that have an impact on international CCCs. Each area holds specific standards that either "should" or "must" be met for the CCC to earn accreditation (IACS, 2017). The five main areas with examples of standards are as follows:

1. Relationship of the Counseling Center to the University Community (e.g., I.B. University and Community Relationships, I.C. Reporting Structure)
2. Counseling Services Roles and Functions (e.g., II.A. Individual and Group Counseling, II.C. Outreach Interventions, II.G. Program Evaluation, II.I. Training Programs)
3. Ethical Standards (e.g., III.B. Confidentiality of Counseling, III.C. Imminent Danger, III.F. Case Records, III.I. Shared Electronic Records Systems, III.K. Technology)
4. Counseling Service Personnel (e.g., IV.A. Director, IV.B. Professional Staff, IV.D. Trainees, IV.E. Support Staff)
5. Related Guidelines (e.g., V.A. Professional Development, V.B. Staff Diversity, V.D. Workload, V.F. Physical Facilities, V.G. Malpractice/Liability Insurance)

As one can see, for accreditation, the CCC must not only attend to clinical services provided but also explore staff composition and their interaction with the larger college community.

CAS (2011) is like IACS in that it provides vetted standards that "inform practice, management of programs, delivery of services, and assessment processes" for student affairs units (CAS, 2014, p. 2). Unlike IACS, it does not provide certifications or accreditations for the counseling center or any of the additional 44 functional units for which it has developed standards. The CAS Counseling Services Standards and Guidelines "provide college counselors with criteria to develop, enhance, evaluate, and judge the quality of campus counseling services" (CAS, 2014, p. 2). CCCs can either use the standards as guidelines to develop their programs or ask CAS to conduct a site visit to determine whether they are on par with standards. However, even with a successful site visit, no certifications or accreditations are provided, because CAS is primarily associated with the student affairs field, which does not typically require a license to practice.

Counseling Center Roles and Services

Counseling Center Roles

It is essential for any new clinical staff, intern, and student affairs professional to be familiar with the blueprint of their CCC's roles and services to better understand how they aid the campus. IACS (2017) and CAS (2014) agree that the counseling center is required to employ a director and clinical staff that must have minimum qualifications of a master's degree, from a regionally accredited institution, in relevant disciplines such as counselor education, mental health counseling, counseling or clinical psychology, social work, or marriage and family counseling. To provide clinical service, they should hold, or be eligible for, or be under supervision for state/provincial licensure or certification (CAS, 2014). Regardless of degree or licensure, all CCC clinical staff are referred to as "college counselors." Finally, guidelines require that clinical staff have completed a supervised practicum and internship during their program(s) of study. CAS (2014) recommends that these clinical experiences be conducted in CCCs to have a better understanding of the scope of responsibilities.

Counseling Center Director

Each year, the Association for University and College Counseling Center Directors (AUCCCD) pulls together a survey of counseling centers to give an idea of the trend in makeup and roles, student concerns, and other emergent issues on campuses nationwide. This past year, they surveyed 621 counseling centers, and you will find some demographic information from their findings in this chapter to better give a picture of the field. In general, directors oversee the entire workings of the CCC. It is their responsibility to view the center holistically, assess campus mental health needs, pledge to have the CCC run well, and ensure the center fulfills its mission and goals (Grayson, 2010). Missions and goals are the foundations of CCC services, which directors must maintain or revisit and revise if they are not being met. Following are a few examples of missions. Hold these in your mind as you continue this chapter:

- "The CWC's mission is to foster human development in all of its diversity through compassion, empowerment, advocacy, hope, and heart. At the CWC, we embrace differences and help nurture a healthy and healing campus environment for all" (University of Florida Counseling and Wellness Center, 2019).
- "Counseling and Psychological Service's mission is to provide compassionate mental health care for the emotional and developmental needs of all students in support of their success at Colgate" (Colgate University Counseling and Psychological Services, n.d.).
- "The mission of Counseling and Mental Health Services is to provide the highest quality clinical services to promote the emotional, relational, and academic potential of all students. We are committed to the core values of respect, responsiveness, in-

novation, and quality to enhance the unique experience of each individual at the University of Connecticut" (University of Connecticut Student Health and Wellness, n.d.).

Directors should have the ability to establish working relationships across campus. These relationships include administrators, faculty and staff members, students, colleagues, and community members (CAS, 2014). CCC director responsibilities include, but are not limited to, the following:

- General administration
- Provision of direct counseling services
- Coordination of services
- Strategic planning
- Budget and annual reports
- Program and staff evaluation
- Membership on divisional and campus-wide committees (e.g., behavioral intervention team [BIT], Campus Assessment Response and Education team)
- Participation in campus mental health policy formation
- Education of staff members regarding legal issues in mental health, medicine, and higher education, as well as those governing the delivery of counseling services (CAS, 2014; IACS, 2017).

After reading this list, you may be wondering how directors find time to handle their administrative duties and remain active clinicians. We admit, the responsibilities of a CCC director can be numerous. However, you should keep in mind that actual duties performed are based on the size of the counseling center. At a one-person center the director is required to do everything, at a three-person center the director's time is mainly devoted to direct service, and at mid/large centers, the director's administrative responsibilities become his or her primary workload (Grayson, 2010). At larger institutions, with greater operating budgets supporting the CCC, staff may be available to decentralize some of the tasks and responsibilities associated with managing the day-to-day operations of a CCC.

Besides the activities mentioned earlier, CCC directors also serve as the spokesperson and representative for the counseling center to the college and administration. Educating others about their role and services not only debunks any myths about what the counseling center does or why they are "so confidential" but also advocates for their needs (e.g., budget adjustments, hiring of additional clinical staff to meet the needs of students). Regarding hiring clinical staff, IACS (2017) suggests that CCCs should work to "maintain minimum staffing ratios in the range of one FTE professional staff member (excluding trainees) for every 1,000 to 1,500 students, depending on services offered and other campus mental health agencies" (p. 13). Finally, in some cases when the CCC is housed alongside medical/health services, we may see a "director of wellness" tasked with overseeing the administrative responsibilities of both service centers. In 2017 AUCCCD reported the following in their annual survey of director demographics (AUCCCD, 2017). The gender of directors was 66.2% female, 33.7% male, and 0.07% nonbinary/nonforming/fluid. For terminal degrees the majority (69.0%) had doctoral degrees, 28.7% had master's degrees, 0.8% were MDs, and 1.5% reported "other." For racial identity, 82.6% reported as White and 20.7% reported as non-White. Because respondents were asked to check all options that apply, the total percentage exceeds 100%. Most (61.7%) were licensed as psychologists, with 19.9% professional counselors, 11.4% social workers, 1.5% marriage and family therapists, 1.0% mental health counselors, 1.0% nurses or medical doctors, 1.0% other, and

0.5% psychiatrists. The remaining 2% chose not to respond to this item. Sexual orientation was reported as 86.4% heterosexual, 5.0% gay men, 4.2% lesbian, 2.8% bisexual, 0.8% queer, and 0.8% self-identified. Professional identity was listed as clinical psychology for 28.8%, counseling psychology for 35.6%, counseling for 20.4%, social work for 10.6%, and other for 4.6%.

Counseling Center Clinical Staff

Clinical staff generally provide most of the direct counseling services to students. Dean (2000) suggested that they are working from several levels at once: "They are assisting students with specific needs that interfere with successful functioning, providing students with opportunities for growth and development, and offering their expertise through consultation with others on campus" (p. 45).

They also come from a wide range of mental health professions. In addition, they provide outreach; orientations (e.g., resident assistant training, first-year student programming); consultation with students, faculty, and staff; evaluation; training and supervision; participation on campus-wide committees; management of crises; teaching; as well as provision of assistance with some of the director's role (CAS, 2014; Grayson, 2010; IACS, 2017; Sharkin, 2012). Depending on the size of the center and the institution, some CCCs will require clinical staff to take on additional coordination roles. Examples include outreach and community relations coordinator, assistant/associate director, clinical director, training coordinator, suicide prevention and crisis coordinator, testing coordinator, group coordinator, technology coordinator, and multicultural services coordinator. Some clinicians may even take on specialization roles in the areas of substance use, disordered eating, sexual assault and trauma, and outreach to underrepresented and marginalized student populations (Grayson, 2010).

Clinical staff may also find themselves serving as liaisons to residence halls, fraternities and sororities, and affinity and other campus groups. At some universities, the administration embeds clinical staff offices in residence halls, in athletic departments, or at satellite campuses. For example, the School of Veterinary Medicine at the University of California, Davis, and the John Marshall Law School have in-house counseling centers providing specific services to students in their programs. It is also suggested that clinical staff take leadership roles in "representing the center to other campus units" for reasons similar to those of the director (IACS, 2017, p. 11).

According to the 2016 and 2017 AUCCCD annual survey on clinical staff demographics, gender was reported as 72.6% female, 27.1% male, and 0.03% transgender, and race was reported as 69.6% White and 30.3% non-White. Sexual orientation was reported as 86.2% heterosexual, 5.1% gay, 6.0% lesbian, and 2.7% bisexual. Professional staffing (FTE) was reported as clinical psychologist (M = 2.02, sum = 1,000.48), counseling psychologist (M = 1.84, sum = 910.92), professional counselor (M = 1.41, sum = 697.74), social worker (MSW, LCSW) (M = 1.10, sum = 542.43), psychiatrist (M = 0.33, sum = 165.21), marriage and family therapist (M = 021, sum = 103.64), and psychiatric nurse practitioner (M = 0.08, sum = 41.33).

Additional Counseling Center Staff

Depending on the size and budget of the CCC, there also may be additional staff including psychiatrists and psychiatric nurses, accessibility service providers, learning disability evaluators, case managers, trainees, and student peer counselors. At each institution, campus needs should be assessed to determine the positions required to adequately address student needs and run an effective CCC. The type of staff members employed directly relates to the types of services a CCC can offer.

College Counseling Services

CCCs have become more innovative in recent years and have increased the variety of services offered to meet the diversified needs of a growing client base. The following represent brief descriptions of some of the more salient services offered.

Direct Counseling

Counseling services remain the most utilized treatment approach at CCCs. On average, approximately 60% of a college counselor's time is spent delivering direct client services (Barr, Rando, Krylowicz, & Winfield, 2010). Services are provided either individually or in a group format. Individual sessions are typically offered on weekly or bi-weekly schedules, depending on the student's presenting issue and symptom severity. The average session lasts 50 to 60 minutes. Although most CCCs do not have specific session limits for students, the average number of visits per student remains relatively low. In 2014, the national average was six visits per student (Gallagher, 2015). In lieu of extended therapeutic relationships, college counselors are more often called upon to triage issues and identify appropriate levels of care for students on the basis of their presenting issues. Increased demand for services and limited staffing have shifted the way services are provided on many campuses. Today, brief, same-day appointments; teletherapy; and community referrals are accepted practices.

Although individual counseling is by far the predominant service delivered, group counseling has been increasing in popularity. According to the 2017 AUCCCD survey, the average number of groups offered across institutions, regardless of size, was 10, with a high of 50 (AUCCCD, 2018). In addition to group counseling being more efficient and cost-effective, most college counselors report it to be an effective treatment option for students (Sharkin, 2012). Groups vary in terms of purpose and size. CCCs may offer psychoeducational, psychotherapeutic, or process-oriented support groups. Most groups seem to function best when membership is managed and the number of participants does not exceed eight to 10 members. Because of space constraints, this text does not address the topic of preparation to run a counseling group; however, many master's programs offer at least one course in group counseling.

Internet-based treatment options are becoming more ubiquitous as technology continues to shape how we communicate and function daily. Teletherapy, be it by phone, webcam, email, or text message, has existed in one form or another for 20 plus years (Novotney, 2017). Telehealth was initially viewed as a niche service; however, research is emerging to suggest it is equivalent to face-to-face care in various settings and is becoming a more accepted treatment alternative among providers and those seeking services (Andersson, 2016; Barak & Grohol, 2011). Among CCCs, the use of telehealth services remains limited. According to the 2017 AUCCCD survey, only 10% of CCC directors reported their facilities were using such services (AUCCCD, 2018). This percentage is up from previous surveys, indicating greater acceptance of this emerging treatment modality. Despite the noted utility of telehealth as a supplement to more traditional counseling services, there needs to be more development before this technology can stand alone as the primary service delivery mechanism on college campuses (Wu, 2017).

As part of the telehealth movement, many colleges and universities have begun implementing web-based services to supplement in-person counseling services, especially after hours or on weekends when traditional servicers may not be available. One such recent innovation is a product called Therapist Assisted Online (TAO; https://www.taoconnect.org/). TAO is an online platform that provides college students with mobile-friendly help to assist with everyday life challenges. Through a collection of evidence-based, interactive self-help modules, students can learn strategies and techniques to manage many of life's challenges (Benton, Heesacker, Snowden, & Lee, 2016; Rachyla et al., 2018; Shaw, Lee, & Benton, 2017). These modules are available 24 hours a day and are delivered in a self-paced format, allowing students to access help when CCC staff may be unavailable or a needed service is not offered. Some of the modules students access through TAO include stress management, mindfulness skills, problem-solving strategies, and resiliency training. In addition to addressing understaffing issues many CCCs face, these types of services also normalize mental health issues and promote their discussion among students who otherwise might not seek help (Novotney, 2017). Students can access the interactive features of TAO through a variety of devices including desktop, laptop, and tablet computers as well as many brands of smartphones. TAO, and services like it, do not promote themselves to be a substitute for counseling services, but they do seem to function as an effective supplemental treatment option. A growing number of colleges and universities nationwide are contracting with TAO to support the increasing need for mental health services among their student populations.

Across these service-delivery modalities, counselors have multiple approaches they can apply. In all counseling settings, CCCs included, the current trend is toward the use of evidence-based practices. The approaches counselors use should have empirical research backing their efficacy and effectiveness within the college student population. Examples of evidence-based practices frequently used in CCCs include cognitive behavioral therapies such as dialectical behavior therapy, acceptance and commitment therapy, trauma-focused cognitive behavior therapy, and certain forms of narrative therapy. As always, the decision as to which approach to use should be dictated by the individual client and presenting problem. Adherence to a single theoretical framework or treatment model may result in diminished results and less satisfied clients, especially with the diversity present in today's college student populations. Counselors need to be flexible and culturally responsive, understanding that any counselor-client pairing is likely to have a relevant dimension of difference embedded within it.

Triage

To help meet the growing mental health needs of students, some CCCs have begun implementing triage services to better direct students to appropriate levels of care on the basis of the severity of their presenting issues. According to Shaffer et al. (2017), mental health triage services come in a variety of forms, including phone screenings, in-person scheduled appointments, or walk-in services. In each of these variations, a counselor, usually a senior staff member, is assigned to conduct a risk assessment. This brief risk assessment, lasting 15 to 20 minutes in length, is meant to determine whether a student is an imminent risk to self or others and better understand the student's current mental state. On the basis of the student's responses, the case is assigned a level of urgency and dispositioned. Rockland-Miller and Eells (2006) developed a triage model specifically for CCCs. In their model, students were classified as either emergent, urgent, or routine in determining the level of care necessary at the time. Triage services often represent a more efficient use of staff time as two to three initial contacts can be made during a usual intake slot, saving intake/crisis time for appropriate student concerns (Hardy, Weatherford, Locke, DePalma, & D'luso, 2011). As Hardy et al. noted, triage services have both advantages and disadvantages, so CCCs must determine what is best for their student population. In Chapter 6, "Building Collaborative Campus Relationships," you will find additional information and discussion on a clinical triage framework model from the perspective of full campus collaboration (Hardy et al., 2011).

Psychiatry and Medication Services

Historically, psychiatrists have held ancillary roles in college mental health systems (Schwartz, 2011). Today, shifts in student demographics and mental health concerns are causing CCCs to reevaluate the role psychiatrists play. According to Kirsch, Doerfler, and Truong (2015), the number of students being prescribed psychiatric medications on college campuses has grown exponentially in recent years. In 2014, more than one in four students across college campuses nationwide currently were taking psychiatric medications (Gallagher, 2015). As a result, psychiatrist positions have become more common at CCCs. The AUCCCD study indicated half of all CCCs surveyed employed either a full- or part-time psychiatrist. Nearly two-thirds of the directors surveyed (64.7%) expressed a need for more service hours than they currently were able to offer (AUCCCD, 2017).

Severe mental illness has been documented to be growing in incidence on college campuses. Nearly all CCC directors (94%) report an increase in the number of students arriving on campus with serious psychological problems (Gallagher, 2015). With demand for services outpacing providers' capacity to help, CCCs must find new ways to treat students in more efficient and cost-effective ways. Psychiatric services might be a way to bridge this gap. Among students referred to a psychiatrist, either on campus or through community referral, the most common issues for which a psychopharmacological evaluation was sought were depression, anxiety, and attention-deficit/hyperactivity disorder, with half of these students already having active prescriptions (Kirsch et al., 2015). Over time, the inclusion of psychiatric services as a standard treatment option offered through CCCs is likely to increase, necessitating that clinicians develop a foundational knowledge of psychopharmacology to effectively work with student clients and communicate with prescribing physicians.

Psychological Testing

Some colleges and universities offer psychological testing and assessment services through their CCCs. Psychological evaluations, when conducted, interpreted, and reported in an appropriate manner, can be invaluable tools in understanding and addressing the learning, behavioral, or mental health needs of students. Types of psychological assessments provided by CCC staff are listed below. These assessments are conducted in many areas, including academic problems, learning disabilities, emotional or behavioral problems, relationship issues, personality problems, learning disabilities, or intelligence/giftedness evaluations. However, these services are frequently cost prohibitive. CCCs do not have budgets to support the purchase, administration, and scoring of many commercial instruments, and student fees or private insurance plans often do not cover the costs of such treatment options (Lyn, 2017). Some CCCs may offer career assessments because of university size and center oversight of campus services.

Researchers have begun developing low-cost, standardized, efficient, and psychometrically sound instruments designed to assess a range of psychological symptoms specifically for use with college students (Locke et al., 2012). Examples of such instruments include the 62-item Counseling Center Assessment of Psychological Symptoms (CCAPS-62; Locke et al., 2011) and the revised short form, the CCAPS-34 (Locke et al., 2012). The CCAPS-34 assesses symptom severity across seven domains: depression, generalized anxiety, social anxiety, academic distress, eating concerns, hostility, and alcohol use. An overall distress index also is provided. Supported by data collected from over 235,000 students nationwide, the CCAPS-34 scales demonstrate fair to above-average internal consistency, evidencing their reliability as a useful clinical tool.

Types of psychological assessments provided by CCCs follow:

- *General psychological evaluation.* Used to assess students' current mood and behavioral function, onset of mood or personality disorders, way of viewing the world, and current strengths and weaknesses. Examples include the CCAPS (34 or 62; Locke et al., 2011, 2012) and the Outcome Questionnaire-45 (Lambert, Gregersen, & Burlingame, 2004).

- *Psychoeducational evaluation.* Used to assess students' current levels of cognitive and academic functioning to evaluate the presence of potential learning differences, problems, and disorders. Examples include the Woodcock-Johnson Tests of Cognitive Abilities (Braden & Alfonso, 2003) and the Adult ADHD [attention-deficit/hyperactivity disorder] Self-Report Scale (ASRS-V.1.1; Daigre et al., 2009).
- *Neuropsychological evaluation.* Used to assess how brain abnormalities may be affecting students' cognitive, motor, behavioral, linguistic, and executive functioning skills. Examples include the Conners Continuous Performance Test (Conners, 1995) and the Mini-Mental State Examination (Folstein, Folstein, & McHugh, 1975).
- *Giftedness evaluation.* Used to assess students' overall and specific cognitive abilities and achievement to determine eligibility for placement in giftedness programs or other accelerated academic pathways. Examples include the Wechsler Adult Intelligence Scale–IV (Wechsler, 2008) and the Naglieri Nonverbal Ability Test (Naglieri, 2008).

Outreach Roles

As mentioned earlier, outreach initiatives are discussed further in Chapter 7. Here we want to briefly highlight the importance of outreach efforts. As CCC missions expand, increased emphasis is being placed on campus-wide service delivery. This requires CCC directors and staff to think outside the box and look at how they can interact with the campus community, not just those individuals who come to the center seeking services. Outreach efforts came into fashion in the 1970s as researchers and practitioners began noticing the impact environmental factors had on counseling outcomes (see Morrill & Hurst, 1971). Today, CCC staff recognize the value of outreach efforts as a cost-effective way to reach a large audience as the community mental health model is embraced. In fact, many CCCs have been urged to broaden their scope and offer services benefiting the entire campus community. Examples of outreach initiatives include campus-wide workshops (e.g., managing stress, recognizing intimate partner violence); screening booths at campus and community events (e.g., orientation, homecoming); and consultative services with faculty, staff, and parents. An example of a promising outreach initiative is Pathways, an acceptance and commitment therapy–based therapeutic skills seminar (Mull, Cleveland, Robinette, & Dixon, 2018). According to its developers, this innovative approach was designed to provide efficient and effective services to help address the issues caused by understaffing and extended waiting lists found at most CCCs. The increased popularity of these services prompted our inclusion of a separate chapter devoted to this topic.

Consultation Roles

Engaging in consultation is a common practice among college counselors. Consulting services are typically offered to help faculty, staff, administrators, and parents better understand developmental and mental health issues, especially as they relate to student well-being (Van Brunt & ACCA PAPA Committee, 2010). When consulting, the client is the individual who brings an issue to the counselor, not the student of concern (Mier, Boone, & Shropshire, 2009). The counselor first must assess the situation on the basis of the information provided. When an imminent threat does not exist, the counselor works with the client to identify solutions that can be applied with the student of concern. The IACS (2017) Standards delineate the ethical considerations for counselors engaging in the consultation process. Most notably, it is important to maintain confidentiality when consulting, so the identity of the student of concern is not revealed as part of the consulting process (Van Brunt & ACCA PAPA Committee, 2010). Counselors may also consult and collaborate with campus partners for the benefit of students, as described in Chapter 6.

Training and Supervision Roles

Most CCCs accept graduate-level students into training programs. Trainees are mainly involved in direct counseling services and outreach programming. Full-time clinical staff or postdoctoral interns, the latter of whom are themselves working under supervision, closely supervise their work (IACS, 2017). Some trainees are fully incorporated into the day-to-day work of the counseling center and can be highly involved in clinical case conferences and training. Trainees come from diverse mental health disciplines and are at various educational levels. Some of them may have had the benefit of completing a class on college student development, but some have come from a purely clinical training model that may not have underscored the normative developmental issues that can be common (and stressful) for college students. Thus, training to work in a CCC may include the need to use a textbook such as this to help orient trainees to the unique aspects of working with college students as clients or theories that can be relevant and helpful. Some examples of trainee backgrounds include practicum, advanced practicum or internship at the master's and doctoral levels, externs, postdoctoral residents, and peer educators who may be at the bachelor's level.

Peer counselors are typically either earning their bachelor's degree or have completed it and are in a master's program at the institution where they are volunteering. Per their name, they work as peers with other students. Some may offer career assessment and services while others may offer wellness or health education (e.g., Wellness ambassadors) and outreach programming. There are even peer counselors staffing nonclinical help lines for some CCCs. Many peer counselors receive training in active listening, resourcing, and referral skills. However, because of their level of clinical training and experience working with mental health issues, they do not work with moderate or severe mental health issues and will know when to make a referral.

Crisis and Behavioral Intervention Team Roles

College campus BITs are interdisciplinary groups of campus agencies and providers who respond in collaboration when students are in apparent or potential distress. Chapter 8 will provide further perspective on working with students in crisis. The purpose of BIT is to provide safe and secure campus environments for all students, so they can continue to function and fulfill their academic and personal goals. Examples of the concerning or distressing behaviors for which a BIT team may be called to action include depression, anxiety, psychosis, vandalism, alcohol/drug use, physical assault, sexual assault, suicidal ideation or attempt, and online or social media threats (Polychronis, 2018; Van Brunt & Lewis, 2014). The key to the success of these groups is their ability to be proactive and respond to threats early (Deisinger & Randazzo, 2014). Furthermore, counselors, as well as other campus personnel (e.g., residence life staff, student affairs personnel) who work closely with students, can participate in the threat assessment process and help funnel students to the level of care needed (McLean & Swanbrow Becker, 2018).

Core BIT team members on most campuses include case managers, law enforcement officials, counselors, health services or wellness staff, student affairs personnel, and representatives from campus offices such as academic affairs, residence life, disability services, veteran affairs, and international student services. These individuals receive highly specialized, regular training, allowing them to work effectively and efficiently in times of crisis when immediate action is needed. By way of their knowledge and training, counselors can play an important role on these response teams, although they must maintain confidentiality if CCC clients are discussed. When reports are received, the BIT team engages in a comprehensive process in which the identified threat is investigated and assessed. This process includes examining current threat level, mitigating continued or future risk of violence, responding to student concerns, initiating interventions to manage the situation, and coordinating resources for both short- and long-term follow-up.

Institution-Specific Roles and Responsibilities

In this chapter we have discussed the idea that the roles and responsibilities of CCCs and their staff vary across institutions. Each college and university, because of a multitude of factors, has its own challenges and unique complexities to address in providing quality mental health services to its students. Traditionally, the college counseling research literature has focused extensively on CCCs situated on traditional 4-year college campuses. However, a growing number of students are matriculating at community and 2-year colleges. In 2014, 42% of all undergraduate students were enrolled in community colleges (Bailey, Jaggars, & Jenkins, 2015). Assisting these students, often with far fewer resources than found on 4-year college campuses, are the counselors working at community and 2-year CCCs. Because of the unique complexities counselors at these institutions face, we thought it helpful to add the following information about community and 2-year colleges.

The mission of community colleges is to serve the local community of students (e.g., some attending directly from high school, and others reentry students; Epstein, 2015). Community and 2-year colleges' CCCs typically share the workload of the entire institution. We will discuss both roles and responsibilities of the community college CCC in this section. In many cases, these centers will execute much more than direct clinical service with a small staff and fewer resources. Epstein (2015) suggested that "work at community college counseling centers typically involves an exaggerated version of the challenges found at university counseling centers" (p. 289). CCC counselors may find themselves providing academic and admissions advising; assisting with students transferring to 4-year colleges; teaching; fulfilling administrative duties and committee work; and offering career counseling, accessibility services, and learning assistance (Dean, 2000; Edwards & Lenhart, 2017). Although community college counselors may wish to provide greater access to mental health services to students on their campuses, a host of logistical and financial constraints pose challenges (Conrad, 2010).

Community college counselors are typically seen in the roles of providing holistic support to students with academic, mental health, and career needs (Edwards & Lenhart, 2017). In addition, because of the demographics of today's community college, counselors "are in the position to assist with students who may be the first in their family to attend college, have academic challenges, and who face mental health challenges and career indecision" (Edwards & Lenhart, 2017, p. 1). In comparison to 4-year institutions, community college counselors may work with a greater proportion of students who are from "a lower socioeconomic bracket, first-generation, ethnically diverse, work many hours, tend to be older, and are parents" (Epstein, 2015, p. 292). Regardless of size in comparison to 4-year institutions, community colleges, overall, provide all mental health services, including suicide prevention and BITs (Edwards & Lenhart, 2017).

Since 2013, a community college counseling survey pioneered by Amy Lenhart and Jon Edwards has been distributed through the American College Counseling Association (ACCA; www.collegecounseling.org). Past surveys can be found on ACCA's website and have been distributed through the ACCA electronic mailing list. In addition, ACCA has a community college counseling task force that is a great resource for counselors at these institutions. Their role is to build a community among professionals and provide professional development opportunities; conference presentations and resources are also provided at the ACCA national conference. Their 2017 survey (n = 142) reported some significant differences for community/2-year colleges compared with 4-year colleges. For example, 73% provide mental health counseling and other services in the same office (Edwards & Lenhart,

2017). Community college counseling centers surveyed reported taking on additional roles over and above clinical services that include academic advising, career counseling, admissions advising, disabilities services, and teaching (Edwards & Lenhart, 2017). With respect to 4-year institutions many have separate student affairs offices that specifically work within areas. Another significant difference is that community and 2-year colleges typically have fewer full-time counselors/therapists than do 4-year institutions (AUCCCD, 2018; Edwards & Lenhart, 2017). Finally, another discrepancy between 2- and 4-year institutions is in psychiatric services offered on campus; 9.1% of 2-year and community colleges reported having these services as compared with 46.6% at 4-year institutions. When examining these differences, one must keep in mind that, among other demographic and logistical differences between these types of institutions, only 21.6% of community colleges surveyed reported that their college has on-campus housing (Edwards & Lenhart, 2017). This makes a direct comparison difficult, but it does bring up a reality. Different types of schools have different needs based on their infrastructure. A 2-year school with no residential housing may have fewer students utilizing services, but it also makes it more difficult to provide outreach to the student body, whereas a 4-year school may have more students using the center because of roommate conflicts, and the counseling center is doing much more orientation and training for campus staff. Despite these differences, all institutions are working towards campus wellness.

As you decide where you would like to work, it will be vital to examine the specific responsibilities your college counseling center has as directly connected to the campus framework, climate, and needs. The community and 2-year colleges' counseling centers provide a wealth of services to their students, and their staff wear many hats. Their role is vital and must be proactive because campuses typically do not have residential students. Working at a community college as a counselor provides great experience in clinical and student services.

Conclusion

In summary, CCCs are a critically important part of the web of psychological support that exists for college students. They provide necessary services that assist students in meeting the demands of multiple issues associated with attending college and managing all other life demands and challenges. As such, college counselors have unique roles and responsibilities, as described in this chapter and in related chapters in Part II of this book. They also are tasked with forging strong working relationships with various offices and departments across campus to provide a continuum of care to students.

Our hope is that you are reading this book because you value this mission and are contemplating working in a CCC or in a supportive capacity on a college campus. As you read through this book, and throughout your academic training, we encourage you to continue exploring what roles and responsibilities would be meaningful for you in your future as a professional.

Final Case Studies

Case 1

You recently accepted a position as CCC director at a small, private, liberal arts college in the northeast. Upon arrival on campus, you begin taking inventory of the services provided by the CCC and the resources available. Furthermore, you notice there has been an ongoing trend related to an increased demand for services over the past 5 years. In the past year, the number of students presenting for services increased 15%, resulting in many students being placed on a waiting list or referred elsewhere. Your staff is small, two full-time counselors besides yourself.

Case 1 Exploration Questions

Think about the many services provided by CCC staff that you have learned about in this chapter:

1. What would you identify as the most important functions and services to offer at your CCC?
2. How could you leverage partnerships with other campus or community resources to best meet the mental health needs of the student body?
3. How would you advertise and promote these services to attract students and help them obtain access to the services they need?

Case 2

Robert has recently experienced an intimate relationship breakup with his partner of nearly 3 years and has not been dealing well with the loss. He has begun skipping classes and is not socializing with his friends like he had been doing previously. Even though Robert has a history of depression and saw a counselor when he was a sophomore in high school, he is not currently taking any medications or practicing any self-care strategies. During his freshman year, Robert was cited for an alcohol-related incident (underage drinking) in the residence hall. He was referred for counseling and mentioned drinking becoming a bigger part of his social life since coming to college. Because of his recent relationship issues, Robert is currently experiencing thoughts of suicide and has increased his alcohol use. His friends are worried, and they alerted their resident assistant, who contacted the CCC for help.

Case 2 Exploration Questions

1. What type of services could be used to help assess Robert's current state of mind?
2. How would you triage Robert and determine the appropriate level of care needed?
3. What resources would you look to mobilize in helping Robert?

References

Andersson, G. (2016). Internet-delivered psychological treatments. *Annual Review of Clinical Psychology, 12*, 157–179.

Association for University and College Counseling Center Directors. (2016). *The Association for University and College Counseling Center Directors annual survey*. Retrieved from https://www.aucccd.org/assets/documents/aucccd%202016%20monograph%20-%20public.pdf

Association for University and College Counseling Center Directors. (2017). *The Association for University and College Counseling Center Directors annual survey*. Retrieved from https://www.aucccd.org/assets/documents/Governance/2017%20aucccd%20survey-public-apr26.pdf

Association for University and College Counseling Center Directors. (2018). *The Association for University and College Counseling Center Directors annual survey*. Retrieved from https://www.aucccd.org/assets/documents/Survey/2018%20AUCCCD%20Survey-Public-June%2012-FINAL.pdf

Bailey, T., Jaggars, S. S., & Jenkins, D. (2015). *Redesigning America's community colleges: A clearer path to student success.* Cambridge, MA: Harvard University Press.

Barak, A., & Grohol, J. M. (2011). Current and future trends in internet-supported mental health interventions. *Journal of Technology in Human Services, 29,* 155–196. doi:10.1080/15228835.2011.616939

Barr, V., Rando, R., Krylowicz, B., & Winfield, E. (2010). The Association for University and College Counseling Center Directors Annual Survey. 2010. Retrieved from http://files.cmcglobal.com/aucccd_directors_survey_monograph_2010_public.pdf

Benton, S. A., Heesacker, M., Snowden, S. J., & Lee, G. (2016). Therapist-assisted, online (TAO) intervention for anxiety in college students: TAO outperformed treatment as usual. *Professional Psychology: Research and Practice, 47,* 363–371. doi:10.1037/pro0000097

Braden, J. P., & Alfonso, V. C. (2003). The Woodcock-Johnson III Tests of Cognitive Abilities in cognitive assessment courses. In F. A. Schrank & D. P. Flanagan (Eds.), *WJ III clinical use and interpretation: Scientist-practitioner perspectives* (pp. 377–401). San Diego, CA: Academic Press. doi:10.1016/B978-012628982-4/50013-1

Brunner, J. L., Wallace, D., Keyes, L. N., & Polychronis, P. D. (2017). The comprehensive counseling center model. *Journal of College Student Psychotherapy, 31,* 297–305. doi:10.1080/875682225.2017.1366167

Brunner, J. L., Wallace, D. L., Reymann, L. S., Sellers, J. J., & McCabe, A. G. (2014). College counseling today: Contemporary students and how counseling centers meet their needs. *Journal of College Student Psychotherapy, 28,* 257–324. doi:10.1080/87568225.2014.948770

Colgate University Counseling and Psychological Services. (n.d.). Mission statement. Retrieved from https://www.colgate.edu/student-life/health-safety-wellness/counseling-and-psychological-services

Conners, C. K. (1995). *Conners' continuous performance test computer program: User's manual.* Toronto, Ontario, Canada: Multi-Health Systems.

Conrad, G. J. (2010). *A survey of mental health practices in the California community colleges.* [Unpublished doctoral dissertation]. San Diego State University, San Diego, CA.

Council for the Advancement of Standards in Higher Education. (2011). The role of counseling services. Retrieved from http://collegecounseling.org/CAS-Standards

Council for the Advancement of Standards in Higher Education. (2014). *CAS professional standards for higher education* (9th ed.). Washington, DC: Author.

Daigre, C., Ramos-Quiroga, J. A., Valero, S., Bosch, R., Roncero, C., Gonzalvo, B., . . . Casas, M. (2009). Adult ADHD Self-Report Scale (ASRS-v1.1) symptom checklist in patients with substance use disorders. *Actas Españolas de Psiquiatría, 37,* 299–305.

Dean, L. A. (2000). College counseling today: Changing roles and definitions. In D. C. Davis & K. M. Humphrey (Eds.), *College counseling: Issues and strategies for a new millennium* (pp. 41–56). Alexandria, VA: American Counseling Association.

Deisinger, G., & Randazzo, M. (2014). Targeted violence in schools: Understanding mental health and managing the risks. *The Police Chief, 81,* 42–46.

Edwards, J., & Lenhart, A. (2017). *Survey of Community/Two-Year College Counseling Services, 2016–2017.* Alexandria, VA: American College Counseling Association.

Epstein, B. (2015). Providing psychological counseling in community colleges: Even greater challenges and fewer resources. *Journal of College Student Psychotherapy, 29,* 289–295. doi:10.1080/87568225.2015.1074020

Folstein, M., Folstein, S., & McHugh, P. (1975). Mini-mental state: A practical method for grading the cognitive state of patients for the clinician. *Journal of Psychiatry Research, 12,* 189–198. doi:10.1016/0022-3956(75)90026-6

Gallagher, R. P. (2015). National survey of college counseling centers 2014. Retrieved from http://d-scholarship.pitt.edu/28178/1/survey_2014.pdf

Grayson, P. (2010). The counseling center team. In J. Kay & V. Schwartz (Eds.), *Mental health care in the college community* (pp. 95–112). Hoboken, NJ: Wiley-Blackwell.

Hardy, J. A., Weatherford, R. D., Locke, B. D., DePalma, N. H., & D'luso, N. T. (2011). Meeting the demand for college student concerns in college counseling centers: Evaluating a clinical triage system. *Journal of College Student Psychotherapy, 25,* 220–240. doi:10.1080/87568225.2011.581929

International Association of Counseling Services. (2017). *Standards for university and college counseling services.* Retrieved from https://0201.nccdn.net/4_2/000/000/053/0e8/2017-STANDARDS-10-5-17.pdf

Kirsch, D. J., Doerfler, L. A., & Truong, D. (2015). Mental health issues among college students: Who gets referred for psychopharmacology evaluation? *Journal of American College Health, 63,* 50–56.

Lambert, M. J., Gregersen, A. T., & Burlingame, G. M. (2004). The Outcome Questionnaire-45. In M. E. Maruish (Ed.), *The use of psychological testing for treatment planning and outcomes assessment: Instruments for adults* (pp. 191–234). Mahwah, NJ: Erlbaum.

Locke, B. D., Buzolitz, J. S., Lei, P. W., Boswell, J. F., McAleavey, A. A., Sevig, T. D., . . . Hayes, J. A. (2011). Development of the Counseling Center Assessment of Psychological Symptoms-62 (CCAPS-62). *Journal of Counseling Psychology, 58,* 97–109. doi:10.1037/ a0021282

Locke, B. D., McAleavey, A. A., Zhao, Y., Lei, P. W., Hayes, J. A., Castonguay, L. G., . . . Lin, Y. C. (2012). Development and initial validation of the Counseling Center Assessment of Psychological Symptoms-34 (CCAPS-34). *Measurement and Evaluation in Counseling and Development, 45,* 151–169. doi:10.1177/ 0748175611432642

Lyn, M. M. K. (2017). Essential services in college counseling. In S. J. Hodges, K. Shelton, & M. M. K. Lyn (Eds.), *The college and university counseling manual* (pp. 41–64). New York, NY: Springer.

McLean, K., & Swanbrow Becker, M. A. (2018). Bridging the gap: Connecting resident assistants and suicidal residents through gatekeeper training. *Suicide and Life-Threatening Behavior, 48,* 218–229. doi:10.1111/sltb.12348

Mier, S., Boone, M., & Shropshire, S. (2009). Community consultation and intervention: Supporting students who do not access counseling services. *Journal of College Student Psychotherapy, 23,* 16–29. doi:10.1080/87568220802367602

Morrill, W. H., & Hurst, J. C. (1971). A preventative and developmental role for the college counselor. *The Counseling Psychologist, 2,* 90–95. doi:10.1177/001100007100200405

Mull, A. A., Cleveland, C., Robinette, R., & Dixon, L. H. (2018). Pathways: An innovation in the delivery of college counseling services. *Journal of College Student Psychotherapy.* doi: 10.1080/87568225.2018.1523698

Naglieri, J. A. (2008). Naglieri Nonverbal Ability Test (2nd ed.). San Antonio, TX: NCS Pearson.

Novotney, A. (2017). A growing wave of online therapy. *Monitor on Psychology, 48,* 48.

Polychronis, P. D. (2018). A case for routine involvement of threat assessment and management teams with college students at risk for suicide. *Journal of College Student Psychotherapy, 33,* 290–298. doi:10.1080/87568225.2018.1492359

Rachyla, I., Pérez-Ana, M., Molés, M., Campos, D., Mira, A., Botella, C., & Quero, S. (2018). An internet-based intervention for adjustment disorder (TAO): Study protocol for a randomized controlled trial. *BMC Psychiatry, 18,* 161. doi:10.1186/s12888-018-1751-6

Rockland-Miller, H. S., & Eells, G. T. (2006). The implementation of mental health clinical triage systems in university health services. *Journal of College Student Psychotherapy, 20,* 39–51. doi:10.1300/J035v20n04_05

Schwartz, V. I. (2011). College mental health: How to provide care for students in need. *Current Psychiatry, 10,* 23–29.

Shaffer, K. S., Love, M. M., Chapman, K. M., Horn, A. J., Haak, P. P., & Shen, C. Y. W. (2017). Walk-in triage systems in university counseling centers. *Journal of College Student Psychotherapy, 31*, 71–89. doi:10.1080/87568225.2016.1254005

Sharkin, B. S. (2012). *Being a college counselor on today's campus: Roles, contributions, and special challenges*. New York, NY: Routledge.

Shaw, B. M., Lee, G., & Benton, S. (2017). Work smarter, not harder: Expanding the treatment capacity of a university counseling center using therapist-assisted online treatment for anxiety. In M. Maheu, K. Drude, & S. Wright (Eds.), *Career paths in telemental health* (pp. 197–204). New York, NY: Springer.

University of Connecticut Student and Health Wellness. (n.d.). Mission statement. Retrieved from https://counseling.uconn.edu/

University of Florida Counseling and Wellness Center. (2019). Our mission. Retrieved from https://counseling.ufl.edu/about/

Van Brunt, B., & ACCA PAPA Committee. (2010). *The preparation and role of college counselors* (ACAPCD-36). Alexandria, VA: American Counseling Association.

Van Brunt, B., & Lewis, S. (2014). *A faculty guide to addressing disruptive and dangerous behaviors*. New York, NY: Routledge.

Wechsler, D. (2008). Wechsler Adult Intelligence Scale (4th ed.). San Antonio, TX: Psychological Corporation.

Wu, M. S. (2017). *The application of telemedicine to college health at a four-year university and community college* (Honors thesis). Union College, Schenectady, NY. Retrieved from https://digitalworks.union.edu/theses/103

Chapter 3

College Counseling Through a Multicultural and Social Justice Lens

Derrick A. Paladino and Michael M. Kocet

> *All of us in the academy and in the culture as a whole*
> *are called to renew our minds if we are to transform*
> *educational institutions—and society—so that the way we live,*
> *teach, and work can reflect our joy in cultural diversity,*
> *our passion for justice, and our love of freedom.*
>
> —bell hooks

■ ■ ■

Reflection Exercise

The placement of this chapter holds purpose. We would like you to carry this multicultural, intersectional, and social justice lens in your mind's eye. As you read the remaining chapters, we hope you will continually ponder, "How does multiculturalism, diversity, social justice, and advocacy work affect my client, the student populations, our services, and the greater campus community?" Also, "How do oppression and privilege affect students on my campus?" Thinking about the majority populations and privileges that students, faculty, and staff hold on your campus is essential to determining what student populations may need assistance and what areas of social justice and advocacy the counseling center needs to focus on to increase and maintain equality and a safe cultural climate. In addition, this chapter should be used as the framework for deepening your understanding of Part IV, "Clinical Issues in the College Context." Finally, as you read this chapter, we would like you to insert yourself as the case study. We believe that the first step toward practicing from a multicultural and social justice orientation is to spend time with self-reflection and personal connection to this material. Before beginning, write down answers to the following five questions:

1. What are my cultural identities, and how do I define them?
2. How do my cultural identities overlap and affect each other?
3. How does society define my cultural identities?

4. What cultural and/or societal privileges (i.e., opposite of marginalized identities) do I hold?
5. Historically and currently, how have these privileges affected the lived experiences of marginalized populations (which may include you)?

As you continue through this chapter, you should pause at the end of each section to reflect on your answers. This experience will provide you with a better understanding of the self, how you are with other people, with clients different than you, and with the world. In addition, it will bring up awareness of the impact the world has on you and people who are different than you to assist you in exploring your practice with clients who hold social locations different from yours.

Finally, as you read through this chapter, please understand that not all marginalized and underrepresented students attend counseling because of their identity and not all behaviors, feelings, and thoughts are directly connected to their identity. It is important for college counselors to do their part to build a strong therapeutic relationship with their clients to make this distinction as they form a clinical strategy.

■ ■ ■

Practicing college counseling through a multicultural and social justice lens takes intention. By using this lens to view the student population, community, and college environment, we, as counselors, bring an inclusive perspective to the forefront when enacting any counseling center activity. From direct service to outreach and prevention, creating a center that is inviting, affirming, inclusive, and safe is vital.

This chapter focuses on underrepresented and marginalized student populations and their experiences in college. Chapter 3 starts off by defining multicultural concepts on campus and examining counseling center utilization of underrepresented and marginalized groups on campus. In this chapter the terms *multicultural* and *diversity* will be used interchangeably. We then discuss cultural and ethical competence in higher education. Finally, we review pertinent theoretical models and practice when working with underrepresented, marginalized, and oppressed student populations to increase equity and inclusion on campus.

The University of Hawai'i at Hilo's A'oa'o Pili Ola Counseling Services

We begin this chapter by presenting an example of stellar multicultural and social justice work done by the University of Hawai'i at Hilo's (UHH's) A´oa´o Pili Ola Counseling Services. While reviewing this case, please pay close attention to UHH's intentional and active role in identifying their target population, developing resources, and providing culturally appropriate services. As you will learn in this chapter, multicultural and social justice work, on the college campus, takes more than just awareness. It is the collaboration and passion of many individuals that make a campus—its staff, faculty, and students—move toward culturally inclusive practice. In all, it takes a community.

With an approximately 30% Native Hawaiian and Pacific Islander student population, UHH discovered that only 5% of this population was using counseling services. This discovery was brought on by several factors. First, Titanium (an electronic medical records system developed for college counseling centers) became a new tool for the counseling center that allowed staff to analyze the center's impact and whether they were meeting the needs of UHH's indigenous populations. Second, the development of a Student Health and Wellness Programs (SHWP) office with a new director who came from an institution that served Native Hawaiians brought in additional perspectives. Third, Asian American and Native American Pacific Islander–Serving Institutions grants provided funding for new programs out of the UHH Pacific Island Student Center and the Kīpuka Native Hawaiian Student Center. These offices became rich partners in their work to reach Native Hawaiians and Pacific Islanders. Finally, UHH's (2011) strategic plan generated a goal and actions through the lens of the institution's connection to their indigenous heritage:

> *Goal 4*: Cultivate, sustain and reflect a diverse, multicultural university that is rooted in the indigenous history of Hawai'i. We value diversity as central to our mission and essential for effective participation in an increasingly global society. We seek to cultivate an inclusive community of people with varied characteristics, ideas, cultures, and worldviews where our students, faculty, and staff celebrate difference and respect tradition. We especially embrace our responsibilities to the indigenous people of Hawai'i. We root our identity in this indigenous heritage and reflect the rich mix of Native Hawaiian, Asia-Pacific, local, national, and international cultures that embody the diversity of Hawai'i. We will foster cross-cultural awareness to promote an intellectual and social environment that challenges all of us to learn and grow. (p. 9)

For additional context, the SHWP encompasses Student Medical Services, Counseling Services, and Prevention. During the creation of SHWP's new mission, vision, and values, staff were intentional about serving the indigenous populations. In addition, further actions were taken during this time period:

- A Native Hawaiian author was invited to lead a session during the SHWP retreat to begin the work on building a knowledge base on how to integrate Native Hawaiian practices into the unit's work.
- Staff started seeking and participating in local and university-related professional development to build their knowledge base.
- Staff started integrating mo'olelo Hawaii (Hawaiian stories that have moral messages, idioms, adages, proverbs, etc.) into presentations, outreach material, and counseling work.
- The UHH campus went through signage transformation, as a result of Strategic Plan Goal 4. This included having office names in Hawaiian.
- Relationships were developed with trusted community and campus partners that can authenticate the counseling center and refer students to counselors by name.
- "Talk Story" was introduced as a counseling service over and above group and individual counseling.
- Western psychology–created assumptions about counseling (e.g., counseling goals, self-disclosure, duration of sessions, making appointments) were examined.

Additional information on types of counseling services can be found online (https://hilo.hawaii.edu/studentaffairs/counseling/).

After 2½ years of collaboration and outreach with vital partnerships, the Native Hawaiian and Pacific Islander student population use of counseling services rose to 20%. This increase is due to many moving campus and community parts but also included dedication, passion, and desire to become an active institution that reaches out to target populations. Communication and transparency were key during this journey. UHH's A´oa´o Pili Ola Counseling Services teaches us much about intention and 2-way collaboration to do both macro- and microwork that increases safety, trust, and inclusiveness on campus. On their web page, in big, bold letters, it reads, "Aloha & E Komo Mai! Hello and welcome!"—

a greeting that both provides an invitation and comfort and is a testament to and reminder of their active role and dedication to building a welcoming space.

Through a combination of counseling center staff awareness, access to resources (i.e., Titanium), a dedicated university focus, the creation of two new cultural centers, and the development of a new student affairs unit (SHWP), the UHH's A´oa´o Pili Ola Counseling Services was able to begin to successfully connect to their target population.

UHH Counseling Services was very invested in creating this environment for their Native Hawaiian and Pacific Islander students. Whereas they had resources and good relationships with collaborative offices at hand, some institutions may have limited means to foster culturally affirming resources on their campus. In addition, some campuses may not have the funding to bring in national or international guest speakers. Searching for the right consultation and resources may mean searching for speakers and other campuses that agree to speak virtually for students, faculty, or staff via digital platforms. Consultation is the way of student affairs and higher education. In Chapter 6, "Building Collaborative Campus Relationships," and Chapter 7, "Outreach and Preventative Services," you will be provided with additional information and discussion on how to find collaborations that can assist any counseling center in this mission.

Understanding Multiculturalism on College Campuses

College counseling centers can be a beacon of multiculturalism, social justice, and advocacy. Having an environment that is viewed as an inclusive space for underrepresented and marginalized students adds to a campus climate that invites comfort, safety, and bravery. Furthermore, it communicates to students, faculty, and staff that the center is a place of support when social injustice is present, on campus and in the community, and center staff are trained in becoming allies and engaging in explicit social justice work (Shelton, 2017). "Counseling centers that are leaders in diversity work will likely be a sought-after resource by other campus groups such as housing, Greek life, faculty members, parents and/or student groups, and organizations" (Shelton, 2017, p. 34). Many college counseling centers across the nation have successfully taken on this call to action (e.g., UHH) and operate through a multicultural and social justice lens. For instance, Paul Quinn College (a small historically Black college in Dallas, TX) is one example of an institution that examined their student needs to implement a wellness initiative that addresses mental health disparities in an African American student population (Moore et al., 2018). In the world of social justice and advocacy, if there is no intention, then there will be no result.

Although there are centers already providing this brave space for students, it is important that counseling students and staff look inward to reinforce their part in this process. Continuity within vision is vital. Finally, it is important to note that although the counseling center and all counseling center staff may have this continuity, other campus divisions, students, and community (i.e., faculty, staff, and administration) may not. Social justice work is constant, and centers and staff should revisit their mission and work in an ongoing manner. In addition, it is vital to understand that diversity, privilege, microagression, and so forth may look different at different types of institutions. This includes predominantly White institutions (PWIs), historically Black colleges and universities (HBCUs), and Hispanic/Latinx-serving colleges and universities. Size, location, public versus private, 2-year versus 4-year institutions variables will also have an impact. College counselors will want to understand their current campus cultural climate to develop and/or maintain support for target populations. This section will cover some definitions to carry with you as you continue through the chapter as well as statistics demonstrating utilization of counseling services by underrepresented student groups.

Diversity

Multiculturalism and diversity and their respective definitions have undergone an evolution in recent years. There is a prevailing perception that the term *multiculturalism* focuses primarily on race and ethnicity, whereas *diversity* is a broader, more encompassing term that includes race, ethnicity, religion/spirituality, gender, gender identity, sexual orientation, culture, socioeconomic status, age, and physical and mental ability. In the context of higher education, diversity can also speak to demarcations such as first-generation college students and nontraditional or adult learners. Sometimes the terms *multiculturalism* and *diversity* are positioned side by side and used interchangeably depending on individual staff member and even divisions across campus. This lack of clarity in terms can lead to greater confusion about the goals of generating a more just campus environment. Ambiguous definitions between college counselors, student affairs professionals, and academic affairs professionals can lead to dissimilar worldviews of campus climate.

Griffin (2017) indicated that diversity can include structural diversity (actual number of individuals from different racial, ethnic, and cultural groups on campus), diversity-related initiatives (activities in the classroom and also cocurricular experiences that center on marginalized populations or that foster cultural competency), and diverse interactions (which is engagement with individuals from different backgrounds). For the purposes of this chapter we are staying away from the term *diverse student* and will use *underrepresented and marginalized student*. We believe this terminology better defines the experiences of multicultural and nonprivileged populations on campus. Finally, any marginalized student can still hold majority status at their institution. For example, Black students attending an HBCU can still be affected by the marginalization from both community and society. They can also experience marginalization and microagression at their own institution.

Privilege

Privileged status can exist in several cultural social locations (Peters, 2017), including gender, race, sex, religious affiliation, nationality, age, physical ability (being able-bodied), body type, and social class privilege. Privilege is viewed as an identity (from the abovementioned examples) that offers advantages and benefits to a person or group population over another. It also exists between institutions. For example, this is seen in the disparity of government and state funding and contracts between PWIs and HBCUs, where HBCUs, who serve a vital role in educating low-income, first-generation, sometimes more financial aid–dependent college students in our nation, receive less (Jones, 2016; Sav, 2010; Toldson, 2016). In addition, in examining the role that intersectionality plays in the lives of clients/students, we must also consider that individuals may hold certain cultural privileges while at the same time concurrently being in a marginalized status due to lacking privilege with respect to other aspects of their identity or social situatedness. *Intersectionality* refers to the complex and cumulative way in which the effects of multiple forms of discrimination combine, overlap, or intersect in the experiences of marginalized individuals or groups (Merriam-Webster, 2019). For example, a White male student may be afforded cultural privilege due to his male status and his racial status but may not have able-bodied privilege because of a physical disability (e.g., one that necessitates using a wheelchair). On the other hand, a gay, non-Christian, Latinx female student will not hold racial, gender, religious, and sexual identity privileges. The White male student's privileged status and nonprivileged status may be salient in different social and cultural contexts and the ability to use his agency for the gaining of power and access to resources (Linder, 2016).

There are many instances of privilege in higher education. For example, the 2019 college admissions scandal dubbed "Operation Varsity Blues" by the FBI offers a clear illustration of financial and socioeconomic status privilege. It was reported that parents were using their wealth to find illegal assistance for their children's admittance to colleges and universities (Jaschik, 2019). Additional examples may include the following: a student of color being followed or questioned by campus security because of dress or phenotype; campuses that are still not in compliance with the Americans With Disabilities Act of 1990 and make it difficult for students with physical disabilities to reach certain areas or buildings on campus; a single faith space being designated for multiple religions when a majority religion is given an entire chapel or building; women in male-dominated majors being ignored by faculty and male students; professors not having course materials ready for visually or hearing-impaired students; campus not providing all-gender facilities for trans students; religion or race left off of demographic forms; and students with English as a second language taking an exam that privileges students with English as a first language.

In her seminal work on White privilege, McIntosh (1989) explored the phenomenon of both White and male privilege, and the fact that cultural privilege, especially by the holder, is often invisible and unrecognized. An important note about Peggy McIntosh is that she is a White woman speaking about White privilege. This is important to consider because most underrepresented and marginalized students already know or have a sense that they are living with a lack of privilege in some areas. This knowledge derives directly from their lived experiences and has been experienced in both direct and covert ways. Holding a privileged status comes with the responsibility to recognize how that privilege has offered the individual or population benefits while it has denied others the same or similar benefits (e.g., one has the responsibility to ask how privilege has advantaged oneself or others). In addition, from understanding we should see action and advocacy. Institutions, college counselors, and student affairs professionals must acknowledge that privilege is on every campus and how it has historically and currently affected underrepresented and marginalized students. From this awareness and deliberate acknowledgement, privilege can move toward equity and inclusion. All college staff should recognize their own privilege and how that may have an impact on an underrepresented and marginalized student. Staff may hold a level of competence, but that in and of itself may not initially allow a student to feel comfortable and brave with them.

McIntosh (1989) posited that the interlocking oppression of cultural privileges can take both active and embedded forms, with racism viewed as an individual act, rather than an invisible system designed to promote racial dominance by the majority culture. McIntosh defined White privilege as "an invisible package of unearned assets that I can count on cashing in each day, but about which I was 'meant' to remain oblivious. White privilege is like an invisible weightless knapsack of special provisions, maps, passports, codebooks, visas, clothes, tools, and blank checks" (p. 1). Considering race, gender, and other statuses, it is critical for college counselors and practitioners to unpack the ways that privilege has affected their lived experiences and to get beyond the privilege silos (Chan, Cor, & Band, 2018; Linder, 2016; Peters, 2017). Campus programming offered by counseling center staff should actively integrate discussion of privilege and its impact on the mental health and well-being of students, especially when navigating microaggressions (Lee, 2019) on campus by those who hold multiple cultural privileges.

Multicultural and diversity scholars have stated that campus leaders must engage in difficult but necessary dialogues about power and privilege and the impact that the "isms" have on the embedded cultural imbalance within the organizational and academic structure at the institution (Cuyjet, Linder, Howard-Hamilton, & Cooper, 2016; Harris & BrckaLorenz, 2017; Lee, 2019; Lo, McCallum, Hughes, Smith, & McKnight, 2017; Watt, Fairchild, & Goodman, 2009). According to the privileges identity exploration model, unraveling the notion of privilege is a lifelong undertaking (Watt et al., 2009). The privileges identity exploration model examines eight categories of defenses that students may show when expressing their political or social positions in and out of the classroom. Examples of the eight categories include denial, deflection, rationalization, intellectualization, false envy, principium, benevolence, and minimization. The privileges identity exploration model can serve as a useful tool for college counselors when they are helping students learn to dismantle internalized systems of privilege (Watt, 2009). The model normalizes that dissonance, as well as the defensiveness that takes place when deeply rooted systems of oppression (both external and internal) are challenged. For counseling center and other campus administrators, being intentional about creating dissonant moments on campus can help those in the majority or privileged statuses to deflect, react, and then challenge old norms and beliefs and make way for new information and knowledge about oppressed groups. This process can be difficult, depending on the professionals' awareness and acceptance of their own privilege. Dissonant moments can assist students, staff, professionals, and faculty to grow in their understanding of how privilege has assisted them as well as hindered underrepresented and marginalized groups. This is one step toward empathy, but the larger step is when empathy becomes social justice and advocacy.

Microaggressions

According to Lee (2019), microaggressions can constitute both intentional and unintentional verbal or nonverbal communication, gestures, or behaviors that communicate hostility and racism but, over time, are conducted with a more subtle or passive undertone. Aggressions can even be conveyed in more modern ways, such as through social media on campus, whereby those posting comments or statements of a microaggressive nature can be masked under veiled profiles that are not easily traceable and sent out anonymously (Armstrong, Smith, & Thomas, 2017; Gin, Martinez-Aleman, Rowan-Kenyon, & Hottell, 2017). Subcategories of microaggressions can include microinvalidations, microinsults, and microassaults (Sue & Capodilupo, 2008). Implicit bias and continual exposure to microaggressions on campus by fellow students, faculty, staff, and/or administrators can have long-term implications for the mental well-being of racial minorities and other underrepresented populations (e.g., lesbian, gay, bisexual, transgender, queer or questioning, intersex, and asexual or allied and those related to gender, ability, socioeconomic status, religion, and culture). Behavioral health specialists are especially encouraged to examine their own words, actions, and belief systems and how these play out in unintended consequences. It is also important to understand that microaggressions happen at every type of institution. Microaggressions do not discriminate. Even if one is in what he or she perceives as a safe college and peer group environment, microaggressions are experienced from both community and society. One's lack of privilege in our society does not disappear just because one is surrounded by those who share and understand that same lack of privilege.

Microaggressions (e.g., insensitive speech and behavior), whether they are about race, affectional orientation, class, religion, (dis)ability, or other identity markers, can arise in the counseling relationship and may be evoked by the mental health professional (Lo et al., 2017). "Conceptually, microaggressions can be thought of as a special case of ruptures in therapy, wherein experiences of discrimination and oppression from the larger society are recapitulated, which places the therapeutic relationship under duress and strain" (Owen, Tao, Imel, Wampold, & Rodolfa, 2014, p. 287). These "cultural ruptures" can cause minority clients to lose trust in their therapist, and the negative instance may convey the message that therapy is emotionally or psychologically unsafe. The experience of being on the receiving end of a microaggression can cause a rift in the therapeutic relationship that can, in turn, lead to a weaker working alliance, contributing to poor clinical outcomes (Owen,

Imel, et al., 2011; Salvatore & Shelton, 2007; Soloranzo, Ceja, & Yosso, 2000). When found to have unintentionally engaged in a microaggression, a microinvalidation, or a microinsult, the college counselor must take immediate steps to build a culturally affirming therapeutic environment to attempt to repair the cultural infraction that caused a potential cultural misunderstanding between clinician and client.

College students can experience a variety of microaggressions both in and out of the classroom. Students of color being ignored by a White professor when raising their hand; a professor not calling out a microaggression from another student; use of videos and materials only from the dominant culture, race, or gender; or a heterosexual student tweeting a homophobic comment with a photo of a gay student on social media are some examples of microaggression. These behaviors can contribute to marginalized students experiencing oppression, prejudice, and discrimination. Over time, repeated microaggressions can contribute to students feeling anxiety, depression, and fear. One way to mitigate this effect is to help educate students with majority and privileged identities to understand the blatant and subtle impacts that microaggressions have in fostering a hostile campus environment.

Utilization of Counseling Services

Promoting racial and multicultural justice in higher education and college counseling is vital to allow underrepresented students to feel a level of cultural congruence with their campus. Privilege and microaggressions can have an impact on marginalized students' campus comfort, so it is important to have an understanding of their usage of the counseling center for support. With colleges seeing an increase in mental health concerns, besides the increasing diversity of student populations, "there is a need to devote greater attention to the use and effectiveness of counseling services for racial/ethnic minority students" (Kim, Park, La, Chang, & Zane, 2016, p. 300). Studies have shown that underrepresented and marginalized students not only attend fewer counseling sessions than their majority student counterparts but also showed higher levels of distress at intake and termination (Han & Pong, 2015; Kearney, Draper, & Barón, 2005; Kim et al., 2016; Turner, Camarillo, Daniel, Otero, & Parker, 2017). National surveys of counseling centers have shown similar results regarding underrepresented and marginalized students when it comes to utilization (Association for University and College Counseling Center Directors [AUCCCD], 2017; Center for Collegiate Mental Health, 2019; see Table 3.1). In contrast, there have been findings that suggest counseling service utilization for students is consistent with the ethnic composition of the general student body (Hayes et al., 2011). In addition, the higher percentage of counselors of color (e.g., African American, Latinx, Asian American) saw a higher percentage of clients of color, respectively (Hayes et al., 2011). Finally, when reviewing client concerns around topics connected to marginalized identity, studies showed they were reported lower than other client issues—that is, AUCCCD: identity development, 9.3%; discrimination, 3.6%; race, 3.2%; sexual orientation, 3.0%; Center for Collegiate Mental Health: racial, ethnic or cultural, 2.9%; sexual orientation concerns, 2.4%; religion/spirituality, 1.4%; gender identity, 1.1%; discrimination, 0.7% (AUCCCD, 2017; Center for Collegiate Mental Health, 2019).

When one reviews the numbers, it seems as if college counseling centers are largely working with majority students. However, it is important to keep in mind that the lower number of minority students could be a result of the campus and counseling center demographics or a result of how culture interplays with the lack of utilization of counseling. Kearney et al. (2005) suggested that "minority students may be still having greater difficulty acclimating to university campuses because of specific concerns, such as social alienation and concomitant lack of social support, in addition to the racial discrimination they face, which their Caucasian counterparts do not" (p. 281). For each counseling center it will be important to look at its specific statistics and campus climate to best answer this question.

TABLE 3.1

Client and Counselor Demographics

Demographic	*Center Client %*	*Center Staff %*
White[a]	55.6	69.6
American Indian/Native American	0.6	0.5
Arab/Arab American	0.5	—
Asian/Asian American	10.5	8.3
Black/African American	10.1	11.2
Latino/Latina	10.0	6.9
Multiracial	6.9	2.3
Other race/ethnicity	5.8	1.1
Heterosexual/straight[b]	78.9	86.2
Transgender	0.6	0.3
First-generation student	22.5	—

Note. From Association for University and College Counseling Directors (2017).
[a]Center for Collegiate Mental Health (2019) listed White center clients at 65.4% and clinical staff at 71.7%. [b]Center for Collegiate Mental Health (2019) listed heterosexual/straight center clients at 86.7% and clinical staff at 86.2%.

Turner et al. (2017) stated that when students use outreach programs, it often mitigates against reticence to obtain mental health care. They argued that there are mental health disparities among underrepresented and marginalized students due to misperceptions about treatment. Turner and colleagues recommended better training for counseling center staff in promoting and valuing diversity and intersectionality, including a commitment to social justice interventions. Campus counseling centers need to partner with affinity groups and student networks to ensure that students are being given information that is timely and culturally sensitive and helps reduce stigma surrounding seeking out mental health services on campus. Regardless of the reason, there has been a response to these numbers in that we are seeing a reported increase in services for certain target populations (e.g., outreach for students who do not identify as the majority culture on campus; AUCCCD, 2017).

Although there is a need for more work to be done in creating college counseling students who are multiculturally affirming, it is important to note that campus counseling centers are taking critical steps to create welcoming spaces. Examples include the hiring of a more diverse and representative counseling center staff that mirrors the diversity that exists on many campuses and the intentional creation of inclusive outreach programming in areas such as racism; lesbian, gay, bisexual, transgender, and queer/questioning issues; hosting of religious events; and addressing the mental health needs of international students. Counseling centers are creating support groups for marginalized populations and are taking steps to ensure that the center environment is multiculturally inclusive, such as through pamphlets and lobby reading material for underrepresented students, ensuring office decor is inclusive and affirming. In addition, counseling centers need to be intentional with the continuity of reassessing their steps to ensure that they are maintaining the brave and inclusive space they have or intend to create.

Multicultural Competence and Ethical Practice

Cultural competence is a term that has been infused throughout the mental health and higher education professions for some time. With research suggesting that clients are capable of experiencing microaggressions in any therapeutic dyad (i.e., regardless of the ethnicity of the client or the therapist; Owen, Imel, et al., 2011), it is vital that all clinicians and student affairs professionals aim to understand their impact, the impact of the college environment, and how that plays into servicing students. In this section we will review the development of multicultural competence and multicultural orientation (MCO) in the college counseling and student affairs professions. The *ACA Code of Ethics* of the American Counseling Association (ACA, 2014) mandates that to be ethical practitioners, counselors must integrate multicultural and diversity competence into their work with clients and students (ACA, 2014, Standard A.2.c.). This includes being multiculturally competent regarding handling confidentiality (ACA, 2014, Standard B.1.a.), not condoning or engaging in discrimination (ACA, 2014, Standard C.5.), and demonstrating cultural sensitivity when providing a clinical diagnosis to clients (ACA, 2014, Standard E.5.b.). Developing multicultural competency is not something a clinician achieves by completing a single multicultural course, by attending a specific number of conferences or workshops, or by reading a particular volume of journal articles or multicultural books. Rather, development of cross-cultural competencies is a lifelong process of engagement.

Prior to our discussion on multicultural competencies, which focuses on the individual, we would like you to keep in mind the responsibility of the larger campus in this active work. When a campus holds a collectivistic and transparent approach to multicultural and social justice work, there is a greater chance of professionals and college units working from the same page. The Campus Climate Framework is a useful tool to assist with this approach. Assessment through the Campus Climate Framework's domains can assist institutional leaders in shaping the cultural climate that enhances diversity across the institution (Griffin, 2017). The Campus Climate Framework's four domains are (a) structural diversity, (b) history/legacy of inclusion or exclusion, (c) psychological climate, and (d) behavioral climate (Hurtado, Milem, Clayton-Pedersen, & Allen, 1998, 1999). Griffin (2017) suggested that these four domains affect and intersect one another and influence the beliefs, behaviors, perceptions, and attitudes about minoritized populations within a specific higher education setting. For college counseling and student affairs practitioners, assessing current and historical campus climate is a critical step when examining the mental health and well-being of today's student population.

Multicultural Competency

In the mental health profession, the ACA Governing Council endorsed the Multicultural and Social Justice Counseling Competencies (MSJCC; Ratts, Singh, Nassar-McMillan, Butler, & McCullough, 2015)—a revision of the Multicultural Counseling Competencies developed by Sue, Arredondo, and McDavis (1992). The MSJCC calls for counselors to move toward multicultural and social justice developmental competency in four domains: "(1) counselor self-awareness, (2) client worldview, (3) counseling relationship, and (4) counseling and advocacy interventions" (Ratts et al., 2015, p. 3). Embedded within the first three developmental domains of the MSJCC are aspirational competencies: attitudes and beliefs, knowledge, skills, and action (Ratts et al., 2015). In addition, this revision focused on expanding "multicultural competence to include the intersection of identities" (Ratts, Singh, Nassar-McMillan, Butler, & McCullough, 2016, p. 31).

During the counselor's journey toward competency, privileged and marginalized counselors are expected to explore their personal "attitudes and beliefs" (Ratts et al., 2015, p. 5) by increasing awareness of how their "social identities, social group statuses, power, privilege, oppression, strengths, limitations, assumptions, attitudes, values, beliefs, and biases" (Ratts et al., 2015, p. 5) have an impact on their practice and their privileged or marginalized clients (see Figure 3.1).

In addition to the MSJCC, ACA has endorsed several multicultural competencies to provide counselors with a resource and framework for assisting specific marginalized clients. They can be found in the Knowledge Center section of the ACA website (https://www.counseling.org/knowledge-center/competencies):

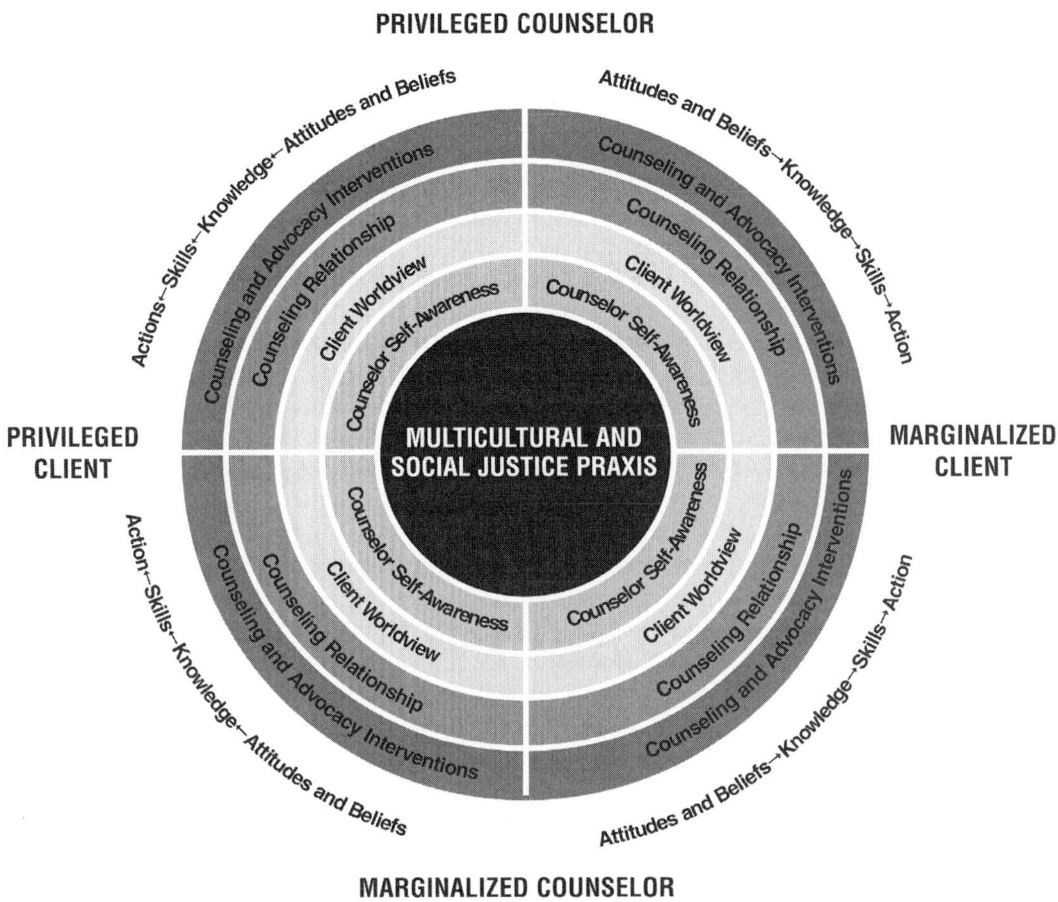

FIGURE 3.1

Multicultural and Social Justice Counseling Competencies

Note. From *Multicultural and Social Justice Counseling Competencies* (p. 4), by M. J. Ratts, A. A. Singh, S. Nassar-McMillan, S. K. Butler, and J. R. McCullough, 2015. Retrieved from https://www.counseling.org/docs/default-source/competencies/multicultural-and-social-justice-counseling-competencies.pdf?sfvrsn=20. Copyright 2015 by M. J. Ratts, A. A. Singh, S. Nassar-McMillan, S. K. Butler, and J. R. McCullough. Reprinted with permission.

- ALGBTIC Competencies for Counseling LGBQQIA Individuals (2012)
- ALGBTIC Competencies for Counseling Transgender Clients (2009)
- Competencies for Addressing Spiritual and Religious Issues in Counseling (2009)
- Competencies for Counseling the Multiracial Population (2015)
- Multicultural Career Counseling Competencies (2009)

Similarly, in 2017, the American Psychological Association (APA) adopted the document *Multicultural Guidelines: An Ecological Approach to Context, Identity, and Intersectionality* to increase cultural competency and awareness among psychologists (APA, 2017). This document was "conceptualized from a need to reconsider diversity and multicultural practice within professional psychology . . . with intersectionality as its primary purview" and with "considerations within practice, research, consultation, and education (including supervision) to directly address how development unfolds across time and intersectional experiences and identities" (p. 6). Included are 10 guidelines that discuss how psychologists can maintain multicultural competency in their clinical practice. Guidelines include, but are not limited to, an understanding that identity and self-definition is fluid; how personal bias, beliefs, and attitudes can affect their work; the importance of social, developmental, and cultural roles in a client's lived experience; understanding the influence of power, privilege, and oppression; and the use of a strength-based approach to build client resiliency and decrease trauma within the sociocultural context (APA, 2017).

As you have been reading, counseling professionals should be intentionally creating inclusive environments, strengthening their diversity knowledge, and adopting approaches and skills that appropriately attend to marginalized populations. In fact, it has been suggested that mental health professionals "who are more culturally competent may conceptualize clients' presenting problems and approach intervention decisions in culturally sensitive ways and do so consistently across their clients" (Owen, Leach, Wampold, & Rodolfa, 2011, p. 2).

Within the student affairs profession, diversity competencies can be found in *The Professional Competency Areas for Student Affairs Educators* document codeveloped by the American College Personnel Association (ACPA) and the National Association of Student Personnel Administrators (NASPA; ACPA & NASPA, 2015). This document includes a "Social Justice and Inclusion" competency that calls for professionals to "engage in critical reflection in order to identify one's own prejudices and biases" in addition to understanding "how one is affected by and participates in maintaining systems of oppression, privilege, and power" (ACPA & NASPA, 2015, p. 30).

In addition, professionals in the field have added to the literature on multicultural competency. One example is Kocet and Stewart's (2011) proposed student affairs competency model for addressing spirituality, secularism, religious pluralism, and interfaith cooperation. The 12 competencies focus on the areas of counselor awareness and respect, knowledge seeking, the impact on identity development, religious privilege, counselor values and bias, creation of safe campus spaces, limitation of knowledge, creation of meaningful dialogues, provision of student support/resources, understanding of intersectional impact, student needs assessment, and enhancement of own religious and spiritual development. It is evident that there has been movement in the fields of mental health and student affairs. In conjunction and if used, this allows better service for the multicultural college student population.

Multicultural Orientation

Throughout the literature, it has been discovered that "cultural competence has multiple levels," which include interventions and service, professional awareness, and the development of knowledge (Owen, Leach, et al., 2011, p. 6). In addition, the term *competency* has been used within most documents. Developing complete multicultural and social justice competency is quite the task for any professional. In this area it's safe to say that no one is ever fully competent, but rather that one is on a lifetime journey toward competency. One perspective that aligns with this is Owen, Leach, et al.'s (2011) MCO.

They propose that whereas multicultural competencies may assess a clinician's mastery, engagement, and implementation of her or his multicultural awareness and knowledge while counseling (i.e., way of "doing"), the MCO may assess a clinician's way of "being" (Hook, Davis, Owen, Worthington, & Utsey, 2013; Owen, Leach, et al., 2011). The perspective of "being" speaks to how we relate to and interpersonally complement our clients. It is "guided by the therapist's philosophy or values about the salience of cultural factors in the lives of therapists and clients" (Hook et al., 2013). The MCO model consists of three interconnected aspects that allow counselors to examine competence: (a) cultural humility, (b) cultural opportunity (as well as missed opportunities), and (c) cultural comfort (Owen, 2013; Owen, Leach, et al., 2011).

Cultural Humility

Hook et al. (2013) suggested that developing strong working relationships and conducting effective counseling with a client who is culturally different requires the clinician to "overcome the natural tendency to view one's own beliefs, values, and worldview as superior" (p. 354). Conversely, a counselor who invites cultural humility approaches underrepresented and marginalized clients with an openness to their worldview and lived experiences. Counselors with strong levels of cultural humility rarely assume competence. They do not allow "prior experience and even expertise [to] lead to overconfidence" when working with clients of different social locations (Hook et al., 2013, p. 354). Culturally humble counselors collaboratively explore cultural identities; are culturally validating; have a genuine openness to understanding all intersections of clients' cultural identities; and hold an interpersonal stance that is other-oriented, which encompasses respect, lack of superiority, and attunement (Hook et al., 2013; Owen, 2013; Owen et al., 2016).

Without this aspect counselors may struggle to connect and have meaningful experiences with their clients. Through their work, Hook et al. (2013) suggested the importance of "developing an interpersonal stance of humility when engaging with a client about his or her cultural background" (p. 361). In fact, Owen, Jordan, et al. (2014) found that "client perceptions of their therapists' cultural humility have been associated with positive therapy outcomes" (p. 91). Conversely, for clients who believed their counselor was less culturally humble, "there was a negative association between missed opportunities and outcomes" (Owen et al., 2016, p. 31).

Cultural Opportunity

Owen, Jordan, et al. (2014) described cultural opportunity, the second pillar of MCO, as the counselor's "ability [to] create opportunities to discuss and integrate clients' cultural heritage into the therapy process" (p. 92). These moments occur in the here and now as a result of the counselor's deep listening and attention. In a way this is a co-engagement whereupon the counselor and client can directly attend to the client's cultural identity (if warranted and related to the session topic) with a purposeful and meaningful dialogue (Owen, 2013; Owen et al., 2016). For example, Owen et al. (2016) discovered that clients whose counselors took appropriate opportunities to hold cultural discussions reported better treatment outcomes. In addition, their study also pointed "to the relationship between therapists attending to what a client identifies as salient regarding their identity statuses versus what counselors assume is relevant" (Owen et al., 2016, p. 34). Awareness and intention are key to entering a successful cultural opportunity.

Like cultural humility, a counselor can explicitly or implicitly ignore any engagement toward exploring and integrating a client's social location into a session. Owen (2013) suggested that there are multiple issues that can impede cultural opportunities in session such as the counselor's capacity to join a conversation about clients' culture and diversity, clients' variability in the desired degree of cultural discussions, and the level of a client's distress (e.g., resulting from severity of issue, lack of therapeutic relationship, and/or counselor's missteps).

Cultural Comfort

The third pillar of MCO, cultural comfort, is depicted as a counselor's comfort, ease, calmness, and authenticity when engaging in discussions about a client's salient cultural identities (Owen, 2013). Owen (2013) suggested that this pillar "influences the probability that psychotherapists initiate cultural conversations (e.g., opportunities) as well as the overall quality of the discussion" (p. 499). Moreover, counselors who are "more culturally comfortable will likely elicit direct or indirect conversations regarding clients' cultural heritage, resulting in a platform or an invitation for clients to explore their cultural identity and experiences in a positive therapeutic environment" (p. 499). A counselor who possesses humility, comfort with initiating relevant multicultural discussions, and an awareness of when opportunity and intention intersect can provide any multicultural client with a safe and trustworthy environment to do meaningful work. Multicultural competence can be viewed in the same way we look at self-actualization. Competence is an aspirational goal that counselors must persistently strive for. It may never be obtainable, but we must maintain this course, and never rest, to provide underrepresented and marginalized clients with the finest possible experience.

Multicultural Ethical Considerations

Practicing in a culturally competent way also concurrently promotes ethical professional practice. The ability to make ethically relevant decisions that affirm the dignity and welfare of multicultural student populations is critical. Student affairs professionals, especially college counselors, have a dual obligation of being knowledgeable of and integrating both the ethical standards within professional counseling (*ACA Code of Ethics*; ACA, 2014) and the ethical standards within student affairs (ACPA, 2006). When considering sound ethical practice, college counselors should consider five domains regarding professional responsibility: (a) student welfare, (b) the institution, (c) the profession, (d) the community, and (e) personal conscience (Dalton, Crosby, Valente, & Eberhardt, 2016). Both the *ACA Code of Ethics* and the standards of the College Student Educators International (ACPA) promote the use of shared ethical principles: autonomy, nonmalefeasance, beneficence, justice, fidelity, veracity, and affiliation. Being multiculturally competent is an ethical imperative, and cross-culturally competent counselors must recognize their own limitations. Whether they be related to lack of knowledge, challenges with cultural awareness, or the inability to adapt counseling skills to cross-cultural counseling relationships, counselors must understand the impact that their limitations have on the counseling relationship (Kocet, 2009).

Ethical issues in college counseling may involve both cultural and contextual circumstances (Chapter 4 further focuses on legal and ethical issues in college counseling). For example, if a client seeing a clinician at the counseling center habitually comes to his or her counseling session a few minutes late, the counselor, if from a majority worldview, may see that lateness as a sign of disrespect and lack of courtesy. However, if the student is a member of a cultural/racial group that views time as more fluid and less rigid, this lateness may not be an intentional sign of disrespect but rather may be a cultural disconnection or misunderstanding between the counselor and client. Time is one example, but any cultural difference between counselor and client can have an impact on the client's trust in the counselor and therapeutic process. When counselors do suspect that potential differences in cross-cultural experiences may have such an impact, they are encouraged to engage in dialogue with the client to better understand how culture reflects and shapes their lived experience. Ethically, the counselor needs to gather additional information to be better informed about the dynamics that are at play in the cross-cultural relationship. Of course, this should only occur when the intention is to better the session or therapeutic relationship, not to alleviate curiosity. Another example involves confidentiality. In some cultures, the notion of discussing personal issues with a stranger (in this case, a counselor) may be antithetical to the cultural traditions or viewpoints from within the student's community, yet different students may hold a worldview that sees confidentiality in a more open way and welcomes the counselor to discuss any issues raised in the counseling relationship with the client's parents, siblings, or other relatives without formal permission. They may not see the necessity of signing a formal release of information but rather view it as culturally appropriate to openly share information with those in their collectivist tradition.

Applying a Multicultural Lens to Practice

Cultural Theory

In this section we discuss three interconnected areas that we believe will be of assistance in understanding college students through a multicultural and sociocultural lens. They are (a) Bronfenbrenner's (1979) ecological systems theory, (b) identity development models, and (c) relational-cultural theory (RCT). As you read, you should discover the intersection between ecological systems theory and identity as development occurs for college students. It is both the personal worldview and the sociocultural narrative that creates how we behave, feel, and think about ourselves and the world. Finally, RCT will be discussed as a philosophy and means to connect with underrepresented students while understanding the weight of oppression, societal and historical influences, identity, and environment that stems from the two aforementioned areas. To inform your reading of this section, it is important to note that applying a multicultural lens is needed for any counselor-client combination (e.g., gender, religion, socioeconomic status, ability, race). In addition, as counselors, our having an acute awareness of how the client across from us may affect our ability to provide quality service should be a constant. For example, this may include a majority and privileged counselor working with an underrepresented and marginalized student as well as an underrepresented and marginalized counselor working with a majority and privileged student. Understanding who we are and what privileges we or the person across from us holds is vital to nurturing a deep and purposeful therapeutic relationship.

Bronfenbrenner's Ecological Systems Theory

We are all influenced by our environment and external systems with varying levels of awareness. Moreover, this understanding can assist us to better understand our client's worldview and lens in a holistic and systemic manner. Bronfenbrenner's (1979) ecological systems theory provides us a good example of this perspective. His ecological theory works from the "assumption that development cannot be accounted for by individual attributes that can be studied outside the context of the developing individual" (Evans, Forney, Guido, & Renn, 2010, p. 160) and "the ecological environment is conceived as extending far beyond the immediate situation directly affecting the developing person" (Bronfenbrenner, 1979, p. 7). His theory emerged from Kurt Lewin's (1936) equation $B = f(P \times E)$, that is, behavior (B) is a function (*f*) of the interaction of the individual college student or person (P) and his or her environment (E), which you will spend more time with in Chapter 9, "Understanding Student Development Theory." Bronfenbrenner's theory also provides us with a "way to look inside the interactions between individuals and their environments to see how and why outcomes may occur as they do" (Evans et al., 2010, p. 161).

Underrepresented and marginalized students bring with them a unique perspective and lived experiences that have an impact on how they interact with and are influenced by their campus, community, and society. Understanding their ecological world alongside their current identity development awareness (which is discussed next) will allow counselors and staff not only to better understand them but also to create meaningful relationships and provide appropriate services. When exploring ecological systems' influence on college students, Bronfenbrenner's (1979) theory compartmentalizes environmental contexts into four systems: (a) microsystems, (b) mesosystems, (c) exosystems, and (d) macrosystems.

The first level, the *microsystem*, is viewed as the "complex interrelations within the immediate setting" (Bronfenbrenner, 1979, p. 7)—that is, what is in the direct and immediate setting of the student. Renn and Arnold (2003) suggested that traditional-age college students' microsystems might include roommates (e.g., in a residence hall or apartment), classes, student organizations, an athletic team, jobs, and friendship and peer groups. In addition, for adult students and commuter students, microsystems might include families, full-time jobs, and community involvement. They also suggested that an individual microsystem "provides physical, social, and symbolic features that promote or inhibit increasingly complex interactions between students and their environments" (p. 270). Viewing the microsystem chronologically, Bronfenbrenner (1979) also suggested that there will be differences between the home and student's institution. In fact, we will see these differences in each "-system" (i.e., micro, meso, exo, and macro). Finally, when one is exploring a student's microsystem, it is important to recognize that "microsystems are unique to individuals and cannot be subsumed under some global rubric of youth culture or college student culture" (Renn & Arnold, 2003, p. 270).

The *mesosystem* focuses on the relationships between microsystems. Bronfenbrenner (1993) specifically defined it as a system that "comprises linkages and processes taking place between two or more settings containing the developing person" (p. 22). Renn and Arnold (2003) suggested that college students are "embedded in interacting mesosystems of academic, social, family, and work life" (p. 270). These interactions allow attitudes and information to filter through each microsystem reinforcing or exhausting one another, thus affecting behavior and development and raising any contradictory processes and messages between microsystems (MacKinnon & Floyd, 2016; Renn & Arnold, 2003). Finally, Bronfenbrenner (1979) pointed out that this interconnectedness can occur whether the developing student actively participates or never enters these events. For example, campus culture can have a large impact on specific microsystems.

The *exosystem* "refers to one or more settings that do not involve the developing person as an active participant, but in which events occur that affect, or are affected by, what happens in the setting containing the developing person" (Bronfenbrenner, 1979, p. 25). These events exert influence on the individual's development in particular ways (MacKinnon & Floyd, 2016; Renn and Arnold, 2003). Renn and Arnold (2003) suggested that the college student exosystem may include the federal government (e.g., financial aid policies), parents' workplaces, and institutional policies and policy makers. Finally, Evans et al. (2010) suggested that considering the exosystem in student development is to consider factors that are often out of students' control. In terms of marginalized students, it is important for counselors and student affairs staff to explore how their decision-making or the decision-making above them affects individual student populations (e.g., any Title IX changes by the Department of Education, decreased budget for the office of multicultural affairs, vetting of religious student organizations on campus that actively discriminate against lesbian, gay, bisexual, and transgender [LGBT] students).

The *macrosystem* "consists of the overarching pattern of micro-, meso-, and exosystems characteristic of a given culture, subculture, or other extended social structure, with particular reference to the developmentally instigative belief systems, resources, hazards, lifestyles, opportunity structures, life course options, and patterns of social interchange that are embedded in such overarching systems" (Bronfenbrenner, 1993, p. 25). In all, it "provides the societal context for the individual's life space" whereupon "societal perspectives, biases, and stereotypes, that relate to race, ethnicity, disability, and other realities of life can be examined intentionally" (MacKinnon & Floyd, 2016, p. 319). The macrosystem holds within it historical trends and events, social forces, cultural expectations, and mediocratic notions (Renn & Arnold, 2003).

Bronfenbrenner's (1979, 1993) ecological systems theory is a paradigm that offers us "insight into the constellation of environments any individual adult lives in" (MacKinnon & Floyd, 2016, p. 318). Using this theory to explore marginalized students allows professionals to increase awareness of how all systems, over and above simply attending college, have an impact on students' experience—what allows them to have higher levels of cultural congruity with their college experience and what might provide variables that alienate them from connecting to their experience. It's a system that allows professionals to "understand and not take for granted the issues that trigger reflection and response as multicultural adults seek to manage their complex lives with dignity and grace" (MacKinnon & Floyd, 2016, p. 320). "What happens in one affects the others as well as the developing individual" (Evans et al., 2010, p. 165).

Finally, development cannot be examined without the influence of time—which is defined by the *chronosystem*. Renn and Arnold (2003) suggested that "the chronosystem conveys the element of time as manifest in changes in the larger cultural forces of the macrosystem" (p. 272). Understanding how time, era, and sociohistorical conditions influence and shape students' ecological environment is vital to fully understand how they are interacting with their systems (MacKinnon & Floyd, 2016; Renn & Arnold, 2003).

Racial and Cultural Identity Development Models

It is not a stretch to infer that individuals from diverse social locations experience personal development differently. Individual cultural identity development considers the development of a specific group (i.e., marginalized or majority populations). Cultural identity can include race, ethnicity, gender, sexual orientation, and spirituality, among others (Johnson & Quaye, 2017; Moore-Thomas, 2014). There have been several pioneers in the study of cultural identity development that have looked at specific populations. From this we have seen the evolution of identity development models. These models provide counselors and professionals with a sense of how marginalized populations develop their cultural self in the world. The following is a sample of identity development models:

- Gender identity: Scott and Robinson (2001)
- Sexual identity: Cass (1979, 1990); Troiden (1989); McCarn and Fassinger (1996); Weinberg, Williams, & Pryor (1994)
- Feminist identity: Downing and Roush (1985); Hoffman (2006)
- People of color, minority and ethnic identity: Helms (1995); Sue and Sue (1990, 1999); Phinney (1996)
- Black identity: Cross (1971, 1995)
- Asian American identity: Kim (1981)
- Latinx identity: Ruiz (1990)
- Multiracial and multiple heritage identity: Henriksen and Paladino (2009); Poston (1990); Root (1998); Renn (2000)
- Native American/First People identity: Garrett and Walking Stick Garrett (1994); Choney, Berryhill-Paapke, and Robbins (1995)
- Spirituality and faith identity: Fowler (1981); Parks (2000); Poll and Smith (2003)
- White identity: Hardiman (1982); Helms (1984, 1995); Ponterotto (1988)

However, with the great comes the not so great. On one hand, these models are essential in recognizing the lived experiences of multicultural populations and should be studied, understood, and reflected on. They allow counselors to have cultural conversations with their clients that increase the therapeutic relationship, empathy, and the ability to have brave and meaningful dialogues about race, gender, and so forth. In fact, Sue, Sue, Neville, and Smith (2019) suggested that racial/cultural identity development models allow counselors to intentionally assess their clients to offer appropriate cultural interventions and dialogue. An additional, "important contribution derived from racial identity models is their acknowledgement of sociopolitical influences shaping identity" (Sue et al., 2019, p. 359).

On the other hand, counselors and professionals should be careful not to use identity development models in a stereotypical way. Most models do not consider within-groups differences and unique lived experiences based on ecological environment and sociocultural influences. In addition, people hold more than one salient identity. The intersectionality of identities is an important aspect to respect when working with any multicultural population.

To encompass a broader population, Sue et al. (2019) created the racial/cultural identity development model. This model was developed to apply to all cultures including White identity development. The model is made up of five stages of minority development: conformity, dissonance and appreciating, resistance and immersion, introspection, and integrative awareness. At each of the five levels of development there are four corresponding beliefs and attitudes that can assist counselors in better understanding minority clients (Sue et al., 2019). They also suggested that "these attitudes/beliefs are an integral part of identity and are manifest in how a person views (a) the self, (b) others of the same minority, (c) others of another minority, and (d) majority individuals" (p. 366). The racial/cultural identity development model is a good universal tool to understand minority clients, and in combination with ecological systems theory it becomes an important addition to fully appreciate how identity development is affected by one's direct, local, national, and world environments.

This subsection and the previous one have focused on identity development as well as the ecological system that influences it. These are crucial concepts for understanding, assessing, and working with college students. "Who we are" and "where we are" can be ever-changing, and continual assessment of this interaction affords a holistic understanding of the client's "perception of the interconnected reality of life" (MacKinnon & Floyd, 2016, p. 318).

Relational-Cultural Theory

In this subsection we briefly introduce the therapeutic philosophy and approach of RCT. We believe that it not only allows a counselor to attend to his or her client from an MCO but allows intentional and brave spaces for cultural identity and ecological system discussions. In addition, RCT complements the multicultural and social justice movement in a few ways:

- It identifies "how contextual and sociocultural challenges impede individuals' ability to create, sustain, and participate in growth-fostering relationships in therapy and life" (Comstock et al., 2008, p. 279).
- It illuminates the "complexities of human development by offering an expansive examination of the development of relational competencies over the life span" (Comstock et al., 2008, p. 279).
- It serves "as an alternative theoretical framework from which mental health professionals can explore how issues related to sex role socialization, power, dominance, marginalization, and subordination affect the mental health and relational development of all people" (Comstock et al., 2008, p. 279).

Because of the inclusive framework of RCT, it is our hope that you will further investigate the tenets of this theory on your own. It is not a theory that is widely discussed in theory of personality textbooks but is one that can be used to attend to all clients.

RCT is a comprehensive theory and model of human development that places relational development across the life span over individuation and autonomy at the center of an individual's growth (Comstock et al., 2008; Duffy & Somody, 2011; Frey, 2013; Jordan, 2018). This connection goes beyond "basic" relationships and instead looks at societal connections and influences. In addition to individual development, personality is built in "response to societal marginalization and power imbalances" (Prochaska & Norcross, 2018, p. 324). Through this perspective, "RCT promotes a contextual and relational lens for understanding human development" (Duffy & Somody, 2011, p. 224). In addition, RCT's underlying principles developed from feminist underpinnings and social justice foci that acknowledged relational experiences of women and individuals from other devalued cultural groups (Comstock et al., 2008; Frey, 2013). This theory offers a great lens from which to understand underrepresented and marginalized college students and the relational impact of individuals, community, and society on their identity. As you can see, RCT fits very well with identity development and ecological systems theory to round out a multicultural understanding of the college population.

RCT is generally characterized by growth-fostering relationships (including counselor-client relationships), mutual empathy and engagement, relational competency, authenticity, and mutual empowerment (Duffy & Somody, 2011; Jordan, 2000, 2018). Jordan (2000, 2018) summarized these into core concepts of RCT:

1. "People grow through and toward relationship throughout the life span" (Jordan, 2000, p. 1007).
2. "Movement toward mutuality over separation characterizes mature functioning" (Jordan, 2000, p. 1007).
3. "Relationship differentiation and elaboration characterize growth" (Jordan, 2000, p. 1007).
4. "Mutual empathy and mutual empowerment are at the core of growth-fostering relationships" (Jordan, 2000, p. 1007).
5. "In growth-fostering relationships, all people contribute and grow or benefit. Development is not a one-way street" (Jordan, 2000, p. 1007).
6. "Authenticity is necessary for real engagement and full participation in growth fostering relationships and mutual empathy" (Jordan, 2018, p. 29).
7. "One of the goals of development from a relational perspective is the development of increased relational competence and capacities over the life span" (Jordan, 2018, p. 29).
8. "Mutual empathy is the primary means through which we grow" (Jordan, 2018, p. 29).

Mutual empathy is a vital function of counseling for change and growth to occur but also may have an impact on society. Jordan (2018) suggested, "Placing mutual empathy at the core of human development not only affects the individual but also contributes to the growth of a just society. Social justice is the outcome of the practice of mutuality in which the needs and experience of both people in any given interaction are respected and honored" (p. 29).

RCT has been used across populations and modes of counseling. Jordan (2018) reviewed many of these uses, including its use in couples' therapy and family therapy and with special issues such as race and marginalization, posttraumatic stress disorder, substance use, disordered eating, adolescence, resilience, hospice and grief work, and work with the effects of marginalization. Frey (2013) suggested that "the practice of RCT emphasizes the critical role of the counseling relationship and relational tools in healing" and "does not detail a list of specific techniques for implementing the framework, but instead provides an orienting rationale and structure for how relational tools can be applied" (p. 179). Because of this, counselors can use techniques that complement RCT and that can be used through the lens of RCT. The ecomap (Hartman, 1978) is one example of such a technique—and will be discussed in the next section.

Culturally Appropriate Counseling Interventions—The Ecomap

We are being intentional in not presenting you with a collection of social location- and population-specific interventions. Doing so is dicey, because just applying an intervention to an entire population does not mean that it is going to work with every client. In fact, counselors run the risk of overgeneralizing underrepresented populations and student cultures—thus reducing their cultural humility. In addition, "although culturally adapted treatments may be beneficial, they do not ensure that therapists will be competent in the delivery of the treatment" (Owen et al., 2016, p. 31). However, we do want to present you with a universal technique that fits within the three pillars of the MCO perspective—the ecomap (Hartman, 1978). The ecomap can apply to any target population and offers an ecological understanding of a client's culture and worldview as it interacts with his or her environment. Along with opening this dialogue, understanding the unique perspective of the client will allow the counselor to increase his or her cultural humility. In addition, the ecomap can reveal cultural opportunities for discussion and increase the counselor's cultural comfort in that it reduces guessing and allows for a more understanding and meaningful therapeutic relationship. Finally, the ecomap is a technique that connects quite well with RCT and Bronfenbrenner's (1979, 1993) ecological systems theory. Exploring a student's development or issues through a (a) relational and (b) ecological/environmental lens offers counselors a holistic understanding of their client and assists them in growing toward their most effective life.

The Ecomap

Ecological approaches to understanding human development provide a way to understand how interactions between people and their environments promote growth and development. This is especially evident in the lives of college students living on or off campus. Students are surrounded by intertwined ecological systems that can include campus friends, roommates, specific courses, professors/staff, college athletic teams (i.e., student athletes), volunteering, romantic relationships, campus extracurricular activities, recreation and self-care, study groups, college major, personal spirituality, and work. In addition, they also bring with them interactions with long-standing ecological systems. For example, while at college they may continually be influenced by parental and guardian relationships, precollege friends and relationships, nuclear and extended family, culture, racial identity, social location, health care, or any other system that still affects their interaction with the college environment and experience.

There has been much discussion on the use of the ecomap and ecological systems when exploring clients' issues (Cogan, 2017; Hartman, 1978, 1986; Hartman & Laird, 1983; Logan, Freeman, & McRoy, 1987; National Child Welfare Workforce Institute, 2013; Paladino, 2009; Paladino & Davis, 2006). An ecomap is like a genogram in that it is a pictorial display of systemic impact that informs the college student about his or her world while raising the counselor's awareness of the student's relationships with family and social support networks (Paladino, 2009). In addition, it offers insight into client themes, needs, and goals. An ecomap differs from a genogram in that although it can include family history, it largely focuses on an individual's—in this case, the student's—environment and external systems (see Figure 3.2).

Creating and processing an ecomap allows the student to become "aware of positive and supportive environments and people in one's life [and] can increase the probability of positive identity development and the space to build self-worth" (Paladino, 2009, p. 96). It is the understanding of these interactions between students and their external environments that promotes growth and development. For example, the bidirectional influence between student and ecological system can reveal how some environments favor an individual's development more than others (e.g., privileged environments holding marginalized student populations) and how ecological experiences affect how individuals genuinely navigate the world. In some instances, it can uncover a student's unconscious

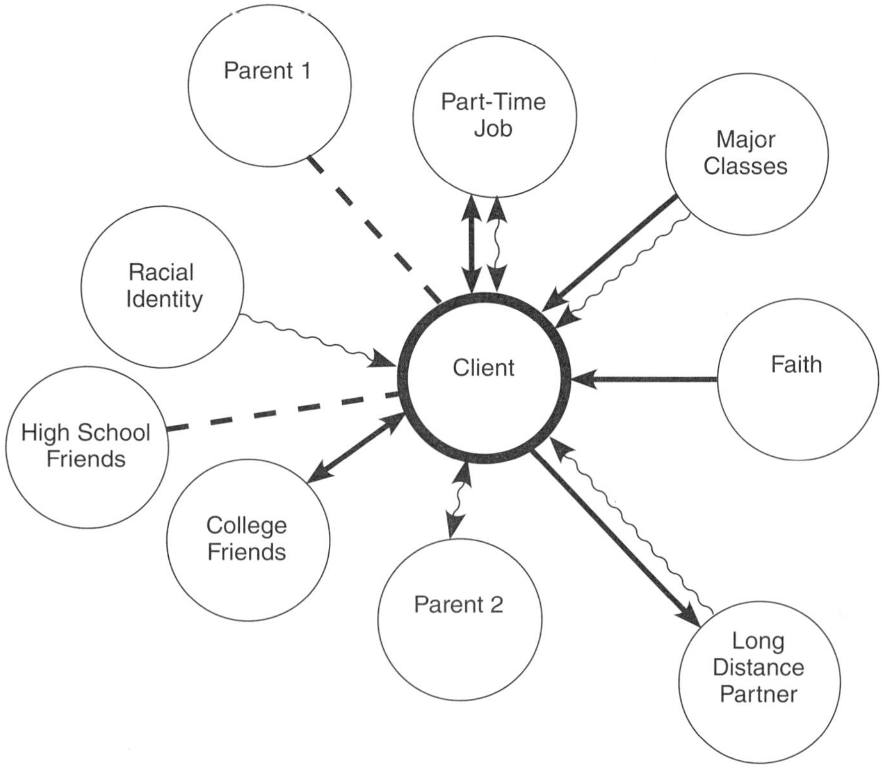

FIGURE 3.2
Example of an Ecomap

Note. Solid line indicates a strong/positive connection. Dashed line indicates a weak/tenuous connection. Wavy line indicates a stressful connection. Arrows indicate energy flow between client and systems.

interaction with certain systems (e.g., unknowingly contributing greater energy to a relationship than what is received). Cogan (2017) suggested several ways ecomaps can benefit the counseling process:

- "Identify sources of stress or anxiety" (Cogan, 2017, p. 80)
- Identify "the presence of, or lack of, support systems" (Cogan, 2017, p. 80)
- Reveal "where in a person's life they may want to focus to improve their overall wellness" (Cogan, 2017, p. 80)
- Identify personal support network and seek ways to expand or strengthen it (Cogan, 2017, p. 80)
- Shows "quality of connections as being either positive and nurturing or negative and stressful" (Cogan, 2017, p. 80)
- "Experience collaboration in a supportive forum" (e.g., counseling relationship) to "develop tools to reduce own stressors" (Cogan, 2017, p. 80)

In addition, ecomaps can assist with summarizing a client's strengths, reveal any immediate impact of sociocultural and political influences, and bring awareness to social location identity. The ecomap can also be used as a form of assessment by gaining initial information and measuring progress and change across time. As students learn how they currently influence their environments and vice versa, they can also create "aspirational" ecomaps that show their hopes for ecological relationships (e.g., a desire to have a more equal relationship with parents or discover time management so their major classes don't overtake their identity).

As a complementary technique to MCO, personal ecomaps can be created by counselors and student affairs staff to examine their level of cultural humility, comfort, and ability to use cultural opportunity. They "can allow counselors to reflect on how their ecological experience may impact their work in multicultural and cross-cultural counseling" (Cogan, 2017, p. 80).

Sometimes counselors may hold unknown blockades to connecting with their clients, and completing an ecomap can reveal those themes. In addition, ecomaps can shed light on potential countertransference issues with clients and help counselors to reflect on how their ecological experience and/or social identity may affect their work with clients. Finally, because college counselors will sometimes hold the role of supervisor of clinical interns, the ecomap can also be used as a tool in supervision in the same way. For example, both parties can create an ecomap to understand each other as part of the supervisory relationship.

Creating the Ecomap

As clients increase knowledge of their connection (e.g., positive, negative, strained, draining, weak, tiring, quality) to external networks, they can increase their awareness of impact, adjust the flow of their interactions, and discover safe and supportive environments (Hartman & Laird, 1983). The ecomapping process begins with the student being depicted in a large circle around which are smaller circles indicating connections with other ecological systems. There are many levels of complexity around creating ecomaps, with one example having the large circle containing a minigenogram. For the purpose of this text we will keep it simple to start. As you become more comfortable with the ecomap, you can add more or evolve what was created with your client. Shapiro, Meyers, and Toner (2011) suggested that "an ecomap resembles a diagram of a solar system" where the client—"the sun—is in the center, and other important people and institutions—planets orbiting the sun—are depicted as circles around the center" (p. 38). Once the systems are illustrated, the student will draw arrows between both the student and system and the system and student. The arrows indicate energy flow and which systems provide benefits and challenges for the student (Shapiro et al., 2011).

The ecomap can be developed in a way that is unique to the client and his or her experience. Systems can also be identities such as race, ethnicity, sexual orientation, and gender. Additional examples of making the ecomap specific to the client include distance of systems from the client, thickness of lines to show intensity, use of different colors, and addition of new symbols to the key. The idea is to create an experience that fully allows the client to understand and make meaning of his or her ecological world and worldview.

In Figure 3.2 the ecomap shows eight different examples (within nine systems) of energy flow and distance between systems and relationships through using standard ecomap symbols:

1. *Parent 1 and high school friends:* Both systems depicting a weak/tenuous relationship.
2. *Part-time job:* Client and system both giving positive energy and stress to each other.
3. *Major classes:* Client receiving both stress and positive energy from system.
4. *Faith:* Client deriving positive energy from system.
5. *Long-distance partner:* System stressing client while receiving positive energy from client.
6. *Parent 2:* Client and system are stressing each other.
7. *College friends:* Client and system giving positive energy to each other.
8. *Racial identity:* System stressing client.

When one is creating an ecomap, it is important to recognize that there are countless types of systems, relationships, distances, and energies. You should allow your client to get as specific as he or she likes when creating each system.

Interpreting the Ecomap

Reflecting on your student's ecomap is an intentional act. It has the power to reveal the client's perception of the value of each system and will depict a motivated, involved, supported, stressed, or drained student (Shapiro et al., 2011). For students the ecomap may highlight issues around diversity or at the least how their identity may be shaped by society. It can also reveal any impact stemming from campus climate. Through the lens of MCO, counselors may need to explore some of this with their clients. One way to do this is through broaching.

Day-Vines et al. (2007) defined *broaching behavior* as a "consistent and ongoing attitude of openness with a genuine commitment by the counselor to continually invite the client to explore issues of diversity" (p. 402). They stated that "the counseling relationship becomes the vehicle for navigating a discussion concerning issues of difference related to race, ethnicity, and culture" (p. 402). Broaching works quite well within the tenets of RCT as the relationship becomes the tool. Facilitative conditions such as "warmth, empathy, positive regard, openness, genuineness . . . counselor credibility" (p. 407) are vital aspects of this.

Broaching is not always a natural ability, so counselors should examine their current comfort and style. Day-Vines et al. (2007) created a framework for differentiating among five broaching styles:

- Avoidant counselors "maintain a race-neutral perspective, arguing that issues related to race and representation warrant little attention. They tend to minimize racial differences, contending instead that people are united by their humanity and that racial oppression should not exist." This results in "no attempt to broach cultural factors during the counseling process" (Day-Vines et al., 2007, p. 404).
- Isolating counselors do "broach issues of race and representation, albeit in a simplistic and superficial manner" (Day-Vines et al., 2007, p. 404).
- Continuing/incongruent counselors "invite clients to explore the relationship between their presenting problems and issues related to race and representation" (Day-Vines et al., 2007, p. 405).
- "Integrated/congruent counselors not only broach the subjects of race, ethnicity, and culture effectively during the counseling process, but they have integrated this behavior into their professional identity" (Day-Vines et al., 2007, p. 405).
- Infusing counselors are like integrated/congruent counselors with the primary difference being that "broaching represents a way of being and is not just incorporated into the counseling process as a professional obligation" (Day-Vines et al., 2007, p. 406).

Along with style are areas for *cultural opportunity*. Day-Vines, Booker Ammah, Steen, and Arnold (2018) described four domains of broaching counselors might use to initiate attention or respond to racial, ethnic, and cultural concerns:

- *Intracounseling dynamics:* "Interpersonal processes that govern the counseling relationship and permit counselor trainees to explore differences between the helper and the client, acknowledge that the counselor may not understand the client's experience completely, and invite the client to inform the counselor about her or his racial, ethnic, and cultural experience" (p. 97).
- *Intraindividual issues:* The counselor's "exploration of the client's multiple social identities (e.g., race, gender, class, religion, sexual orientation, immigration status, etc.) that shape the client's presenting concerns" (p. 97).

- *Intraracial, ethnic, and cultural issues:* "Sociocultural or within-groups issues that may arise between the client and people with whom he or she shares a common heritage . . . (e.g., bicultural socialization)" (p. 97).
- *Interracial, ethnic, and cultural issues:* "Efforts to assist the client negotiate cultural differences between herself or himself and people from other racial, ethnic, or cultural groups . . . including how the client negotiates encounters with the sociopolitical dynamics of racism, discrimination, oppression, and powerlessness" (p. 97).

These domains can be used as one assessment when processing the client's ecomap. In all, broaching serves as an important component of counseling work. It, rightfully so, "places the onus of responsibility on the counselor to initiate race-related dialogues" (Day-Vines et al., 2007, p. 402).

The National Child Welfare Workforce Institute (2013) also suggested areas for ecomap assessment: (a) hot spots, (b) bright spots, (c) missing spots, and (d) power differentials. Hot spots indicate "sources of pressure that take up much of your time and energy" (p. 1). They suggested that these are systems of pressure that need to change and relationships that require a lot of energy. Bright spots are "sources of positive energy where things work" (p. 2). Here we see balanced systems where energy is not overdrawn from each other but rather where energy is gained, fostering an increase in the student's functionality and overall life. Missing spots indicate the "relationships or experiences that are missing or need to be explored" (p. 2). And finally, power differentials reveal exactly that—they show whether "one party has more power than another" (p. 2).

From exploration of these four areas, goals, interventions, and refined clinical intention emerge. It is also important to work alongside the student's perception as the ecomap may open uncomfortable realizations about relationships, their racial identity, and ecological systems at college. What you see as value versus the student's perception of the value of the resource may significantly differ (Shapiro et al., 2011). Taking time to sit with each system and asking the student to give an overall feeling of his or her "solar system" is a good start to codetermining clinical intervention. In addition, through this process the client can develop a "growing capacity to discover, sustain, or alter its [the system's] properties" (Bronfenbrenner, 1979, p. 9).

Adapting the ecomap to explore and bring awareness to how different systems are impactful is beneficial for the client. Using Bronfenbrenner's (1979, 1993) ecological systems theory, ecomap systems can be discussed through the microsystem, mesosystem, exosystem, and macrosystem. For example, clients may look at financial aid issues, parental relationships, policy makers, historical events, and societal expectations in a way that allows them to understand their role in power within these systems and how oppression may have an impact on their ability to shift or change their relationship with that system. As you can see, this technique provides the level of awareness to understand and act from a multicultural and social justice perspective.

The Role of Social Justice and Advocacy in College Counseling

Social Justice in Action

Up to this point in the chapter, you have been learning about how to incorporate multicultural awareness and skill into your work as a college counselor. A counselor's understanding of underrepresented and marginalized college students, their identity, and environmental impact allows for inclusive dialogues and intentional treatment in session.

A broadened understanding of multiculturalism brings us to the philosophy and practice of social justice. Currently, the mental health (i.e., ACA, APA) and student affairs professions (i.e., ACPA, NASPA) are also supporting the elevation from competence to critical consciousness. Linder and Cooper (2016) suggested that student affairs educators (and we can loop in counselors) "must do more than become competent"; they "must engage in critical consciousness through an ongoing commitment to critical analysis and socially just education" (p. 381).

Social justice can be viewed as understanding the broad impact of oppression, power, privilege, discrimination, and unfairness from ecological systems on individuals. In addition, social justice is an act to correct these unjust systems and go to bat for marginalized groups from the micro- and macroperspectives. As an approach, social justice focuses on the understanding and acknowledgement of current and historical systematic societal inequities; the inequitable distribution of power, resources, and individuals' access to same; and that theory and practice are rooted in a sociocultural understanding of psychological functioning (Chang, Crethar, & Ratts, 2010; Smith, Baluch, Bernabei, Robohm, & Sheehy, 2003).

Likewise, Chang, Gnilka, and O'Hara (2014) stated that "the goal of social justice counseling is to promote access and equality to all persons, focusing particularly on those groups that have been disenfranchised based on their cultural/ethnic background (e.g., race/ethnicity, gender, age, socioeconomic status, sexual identity" (p. 59). When one is examining social justice work in a college setting, this might include the student, the institution and its policies, the local community, and the historical and current societal and sociopolitical narratives and influences. College counselors should also ponder how they will create social justice goals to develop relationships with the surrounding community and move to "eradicate oppression" on campus (p. 59). Some forms of oppression that have an impact on the campus are "racism, classism, sexism, and heterosexism," and these "clearly undermine emotional and interpersonal wellbeing and, thus, have the potential to result in psychological symptoms" (Smith et al., 2003, p. 7).

Within this work it is important for counselors to focus on the client without the presumption that change only occurs within the individual or his or her personal attributes (Chang et al., 2010). Rather, prevention and education are more effective when the counselor considers and interacts "with clients at the level in which they exist within their environments" (Chang et al., 2010, p. 85). Part of this process includes using tools for critical analysis that consider the role of power in the client's life (Linder & Cooper, 2016). Linder and Cooper (2016) suggested that this can start by asking questions that examine campus climate:

- Who is not represented?
- How does this policy impact X group?
- What are we not considering?
- What are the power implications of this decision? (p. 385)

Another step is acknowledging that social justice work does not have to be executed alone. Collaboration, partnerships, the sharing of budgets, the administration's support, and so forth better canvass the campus with this message (AUCCCD, 2017; Smith et al., 2003). The counseling center should not look at itself as an island or as a silo but rather should make connections with obvious partners such as the office of multicultural affairs, the LGBTQ campus center, and the student accessibility office. In addition, innovative connections to "not so obvious" constituents on campus help to spread the word and action of social justice with the hope that other functional units will join the advocacy movement to change the narrative of the campus.

Smith et al. (2003) suggested four areas to focus on when creating a social justice framework for the college counseling center: self-awareness, individual practice, practice within the college community, and relationship with the civic community. These areas can be experienced alone but are better managed as a counseling center group to increase collaboration, alliance, and consciousness. Self-awareness emphasizes a commitment to deliberate attention to one's own social awareness, critical consciousness, and unquestioned assumptions. In addition, a commitment to putting awareness into action with persistence despite the complexity of client or social issues is needed. Awareness can come from one's reflection, other counselors, clients, and even in supervision. Glosoff and Durham (2010) suggested that supervision can be used to create focused discussions around "issues of culture and power and privilege, examinations of culture, diversity, power, and advocacy" (p. 127). In addition, asking supervisees to focus beyond interventions and to consider issues of access, equity, and distribution of power is helpful.

The second area, individual practice, suggests that counselors and the college counseling center create commitments to study social justice issues, culture, and psychological development. This includes incorporating and implementing their understanding of oppression and contextual factors into culturally competent practice that is accessible to all students (Smith et al., 2003). The third area, practicing within the college community, invites a willingness to listen and partner with the college community to provide prevention, outreach, and other services (e.g., teaching, research, committee involvements) around relevant sociocultural, multicultural, and social justice issues. This approach also brings in missing voices and entails acquiring feedback from the campus community (e.g., underrepresented students, faculty, and staff). Finally, the fourth area, the counseling center's relationship with the civic community, allows the unit to broaden its scope to addressing "local situations that involve ensuring psychological well-being and social justice" (pp. 9–10).

Linder and Cooper (2016) also suggested strategies and resources for continually developing critical consciousness and inclusive campus environments:

- "Continually work to make the unconscious conscious" (e.g., inclusive spaces, the impact of policies on student groups, personal awareness; Linder & Cooper, 2016, p. 386).
- "Create identity-explicit, not identity exclusive, spaces" (Linder & Cooper, 2016, p. 386).
- "Approach work from a 'yes, and . . . ' perspective" (i.e., multiple groups can benefit from one opportunity; Linder & Cooper, 2016, p. 387).
- "Address racial battle fatigue, compassion fatigue, and vicarious trauma" (Linder & Cooper, 2016, p. 387).
- "Stay abreast of current issues" (Linder & Cooper, 2016, p. 388).
- "Seek out critically conscious committees" to "engage in activism and social change" (Linder & Cooper, 2016, p. 389).

Social justice on campus can present itself in many ways. By simply adding more inclusiveness to the intake form, offering alternative hours, and having a presence at social justice events, the counseling center can be viewed as inclusive and caring. In addition, the counseling center can assist with or create programming and discussions around social and political events that have an impact on marginalized populations (e.g., DACA [Deferred Action for Childhood Arrivals], the 2016 election, the Orlando shooting, and police shootings of Black citizens) and hire underrepresented counselors who not only represent the student body but hold a *cultural orientation model* perspective (AUCCCD, 2017). Finally, as you read in the example at UHH's A´oa´o Pili Ola Counseling Services, centers can work to increase services and create safe spaces for certain student populations.

Conclusion

Throughout this chapter you have not only been learning but also connecting yourself to how multicultural and social justice issues affect the college student population. As you have explored, one's identity within one's past, current, and societal ecological world gives a holistic understanding of worldview as well as an insight into a client's interaction with his or her presenting problem in counseling. Target student populations who live with microaggressions, discrimination, ism's, and little power or privilege, and who attend a campus environment that holds a majority perspective, need visibility and voice. Because of these experiences, college counselors need to recognize "the importance of providing culturally relevant services" (Kearney et al., 2005, p. 281).

As mentioned earlier, this chapter's placement holds significant intention. It is our hope that you will use the information you gained and your personal reflections as a filter from which you experience the remainder of this book. As you read about outreach and prevention, crisis management, student development theory, clinical issues, and so forth, think about how society, politics, history, and identity have an impact on these areas for college students.

Final Case Study

Alycia is a second-year African American student who identifies as pansexual. She is currently dating Marina, a first-year Latina student. Alycia comes to the counseling center reporting significant anxiety. Alycia has been anxious for several months because of a number of issues that have arisen on campus, as well as issues in the national news. When she meets with her assigned counselor, she is randomly assigned to a graduate intern, Steven, who is a doctoral psychology student at a nearby university. Steven is Caucasian and identifies as a heterosexual, Jewish male. Alycia is nervous on meeting Steven because he is White. She is unsure if he will understand her experiences on campus. Alycia begins to tell Steven that she is nervous because several students have indicated that they are attending the Straight Pride Rally downtown. Although the city disagrees with the organizers of the Straight Pride event, city ordinance permits individuals and groups from a variety of political and sociocultural perspectives to hold rallies and parades in the city, as long as the group is compliant with required zoning laws. Alycia also indicates that a number of White students in her residence hall have been talking about recent immigration policy and believe the president's policies about apprehending undocumented families is the right thing to do. Alycia says that she is hearing more hateful rhetoric coming from her peers than she ever has in her time at the university. Two weeks ago, she and her girlfriend were holding hands while walking back from the student union, and a group of college men were harassing and name calling them. They had to run into the safety of the dining hall to avoid further harassment. Alycia says that watching the news and reading the campus newspaper is causing her significant distress. She witnesses daily instances of her African American friends being questioned by university police when her White peers are not experiencing the same ill treatment by police. She also heard about an instance where a swastika was carved in a bathroom stall on the floor above her in her residence hall with the words "Jews will not replace us!" sprawled in the stall also. Although the police were called immediately to the scene to investigate it, Alycia has become more fearful and no longer feels safe on campus. She asks Steven for help managing her anxiety.

Case Exploration Questions

1. How is intersectionality playing a role in this scenario? What are the cross-cultural dynamics that exist between Alycia and Steven, her assigned counselor?
2. How should Steven respond to Alycia's anxiety? What is contributing to her feeling anxious and unsafe?
3. What counseling interventions might Steven consider using in his work with Alycia? What multicultural resources would be helpful for Steven as he conceptualizes this clinical case?

References

American College Personnel Association. (2006). *Statement of ethical principles and standards.* Retrieved from https://www.myacpa.org/ethics

American College Personnel Association & National Association of Student Personnel Administrators. (2015). *Professional competency areas for student affairs educators.* Washington, DC: Author.

American Counseling Association. (2014). *ACA code of ethics.* Alexandria, VA: Author.

American Psychological Association. (2017). Multicultural guidelines: An ecological approach to context, identity, and intersectionality. Retrieved from https://www.apa.org/about/policy/multicultural-guidelines.pdf

Americans With Disabilities Act of 1990, 42 U.S.C.A. § 12101 *et seq.* (West 1993).

Armstrong, A., Smith, M., & Thomas, J. (2017). College students' experiences with anonymous social media: Implications for campus racial climate. *Journal of College Student Development, 58,* 1101–1107.

Association for University and College Counseling Center Directors. (2017). *The Association for University and College Counseling Center Directors annual survey.* Retrieved from https://www.aucccd.org/assets/documents/Governance/2017%20aucccd%20survey-public-apr26.pdf

Bronfenbrenner, U. (1979). *The ecology of human development: Experiments by nature and design.* Cambridge, MA: Harvard University Press.

Bronfenbrenner, U. (1993). The ecology of cognitive development: Research models and fugitive findings. In R. H. Wozniak & K. W. Fischer (Eds.), *Development in context: Acting and thinking in specific environments* (pp. 3–44). Hillsdale, NJ: Erlbaum.

Cass, V. (1979). Homosexual identity formation: A theoretical model. *Journal of Homosexuality, 4,* 219–235.

Cass, V. C. (1990). The implications of homosexual identity formation for the Kinsey model and scale of sexual preference. In D. McWhirter, S. Sanders, & R. Reinisch (Eds.), *Heterosexuality-homosexuality: Concepts of sexual orientation* (pp. 239–266). New York, NY: Oxford Press.

Center for Collegiate Mental Health. (2019, January). *2018 annual report* (Publication No. STA 19–180). Retrieved from https://ccmh.psu.edu/files/2019/09/2018-Annual-Report-9.27.19-FINAL.pdf

Chan, C. D., Cor, D. N., & Band, M. P. (2018). Privilege and oppression in counselor education: An intersectionality framework. *Journal of Multicultural Counseling and Development, 46,* 58–73. doi:10.1002/jmcd.12092

Chang, C. Y., Crethar, H. C., & Ratts, M. J. (2010). Social justice: A national imperative for counselor education and supervision. *Counselor Education and Supervision, 50,* 82–87. doi:10.1002/j.1556-6978.2010.tb00110.x

Chang, C. Y., Gnilka, P. B., & O'Hara, C. (2014). Social justice counseling. In D. G. Hays & B. T. Erford (Eds.), *Developing multicultural counseling competence: A systems approach* (pp. 58–81). Boston, MA: Pearson.

Choney, S. K., Berryhill-Paapke, E., & Robbins, R. R. (1995). The acculturation of American Indians: Developing frameworks for research and practice. In J. G. Ponterotto, J. M. Casas, L. A. Suzuki, & C. M. Alexander (Eds.), *Handbook of multicultural counseling* (pp. 73–92). Thousand Oaks, CA: Sage.

Cogan, G. (2017). *The importance of teacher social and emotional competence to the development of prosocial classrooms: The role of teacher preparation*. Retrieved from https://core.ac.uk/download/pdf/84873046.pdf

Comstock, D. L., Hammer, T. R., Strentzsch, J., Cannon, K., Parsons, J., & Salazar, G., II. (2008). Relational-cultural theory: A framework for bridging relational, multicultural, and social justice competencies. *Journal of Counseling & Development, 86,* 279–287. doi:10.1002/j.1556-6678.2008.tb00510.x

Cross, W. E. (1971). The Negro-to-Black conversion experience: Towards a psychology of Black liberation. *Black World, 20,* 13–27.

Cross, W. E. (1995). The psychology of Nigrescence: Revising the Cross model. In J. G. Ponterotto, J. M. Casas, L. A. Suzuki, & C. M. Alexander (Eds.), *Handbook of multicultural counseling* (pp. 93–122). Thousand Oaks, CA: Sage.

Cuyjet, M. J., Linder, C., Howard-Hamilton, M. F., & Cooper, D. L. (Eds.). (2016). *Multiculturalism on campus: Theory, models, and practices for understanding diversity and creating inclusion* (2nd ed.). Sterling, VA: Stylus.

Dalton, J. C., Crosby, P. C., Valente, A., & Eberhardt, D. (2016). Maintaining and modeling everyday ethics in student affairs. In G. McClellan & J. Stringer (Eds.), *The handbook of student affairs administration* (4th ed., pp. 199–223). San Francisco, CA: Jossey-Bass.

Day-Vines, N., Booker Ammah, B., Steen, S., & Arnold, K. (2018). Getting comfortable with discomfort: Preparing counselor trainees to broach racial, ethnic, and cultural factors with clients during counseling. *International Journal for the Advancement of Counselling, 40,* 89–104.

Day-Vines, N. L., Wood, S. M., Grothaus, T., Craigen, L., Holman, A., Dotson-Blake, K., & Douglass, M. J. (2007). Broaching the subjects of race, ethnicity, and culture during the counseling process. *Journal of Counseling & Development, 85,* 401–409. doi:10.1002/j.1556-6678.2007.tb00608.x

Downing, N. E., & Roush, K. L. (1985). From passive acceptance to active commitment: A model of feminist identity development for women. *The Counseling Psychologist, 13,* 695–709.

Duffey, D., & Somody, C. (2011). The role of relational-cultural theory in mental health counseling. *Journal of Mental Health Counseling, 33,* 223–242.

Evans, N. J., Forney, D. S., Guido, F. M., & Renn, K. (2010). *Student development in college: Theory, research, and practice*. San Francisco, CA: Jossey-Bass.

Fowler, J. W. (1981). *Stages of faith: The psychology of human development and the quest for meaning*. San Francisco, CA: Harper & Row.

Frey, L. L. (2013). Relational-cultural therapy: Theory, research, and application to counseling competencies. *Professional Psychology: Research and Practice, 44,* 177–185.

Garrett, J. T., & Garrett, M. W. (1994). The path of good medicine: Understanding and counseling Native American Indians. *Journal of Multicultural Counseling and Development, 22,* 134–144. doi:10.1002/j.2161-1912.1994.tb00459.x

Gin, K., Martinez-Aleman, A., Rowan-Kenyon, H., & Hottell, D. (2017). Racialized aggressions and social media on campus. *Journal of College Student Development, 58,* 159–174.

Glosoff, H. L., & Durham, J. C. (2010). Using supervision to prepare social justice counseling advocates. *Counselor Education and Supervision, 50,* 116–129.

Griffin, K. (2017). Campus climate and diversity. In J. Schuh, S. Jones, & V. Torres (Eds.), *Student services: A handbook for the profession* (6th ed., pp. 73–88). San Francisco, CA: Jossey-Bass.

Han, M., & Pong, H. (2015). Mental health help-seeking behaviors among Asian American community college students: The effect of stigma, cultural barriers, and acculturation. *Journal of College Student Development, 56,* 1–14.

Hardiman, R. (1982). White identity development: A process oriented model for describing the racial consciousness of White Americans. *Dissertation Abstracts International, 43,* 104A. (University Microfilms No. 82-10330)

Harris, J. C., & BrckaLorenz, A. (2017). Black, White, and biracial students' engagement at different institutional types. *Journal of College Student Development, 58,* 783–789.

Hartman, A. (1978). Diagrammatic assessment of family relationships. *Social Casework, 59,* 465–476.

Hartman, A. (1986, April). *Families in theory and practice.* The 2nd National Symposium on Doctoral Research in Social Work, Ohio State University. Retrieved from https://kb.osu.edu/handle/1811/32365 and https://kb.osu.edu/bitstream/handle/1811/32365/2_title_paper.pdf?sequence=3&isAllowed=y

Hartman, A., & Laird, J. (1983). *Family-centered social work.* New York, NY: Free Press.

Hayes, J. A., Youn, S. J., Castonguay, L. G., Locke, B. D., McAleavey, A. A., & Nordberg, S. (2011). Rates and predictors of counseling center use among college students of color. *Journal of College Counseling, 14,* 105–116. doi:10.1002/j.2161-1882.2011.tb00266.x

Helms, J. E. (1984). Toward a theoretical explanation of the effects of race on counseling: A Black and White model. *The Counseling Psychologist, 12,* 153–165.

Helms, J. E. (1995). An update of Helm's White and people of color racial identity models. In J. G. Ponterotto, J. M. Casas, L. A. Suzuki, & C. M. Alexander (Eds.), *Handbook of multicultural counseling* (pp. 181–198). Thousand Oaks, CA: Sage.

Henriksen, R. C., Jr., & Paladino, D. A. (2009). *Counseling multiple heritage individuals, couples, and families.* Alexandria, VA: American Counseling Association.

Hoffman, R. M. (2006). Gender self-definition and gender self-acceptance in women: Intersections with feminist, womanist, and ethnic identities. *Journal of Counseling & Development, 84,* 358–372. doi:10.1002/j.1556-6678.2006.tb00415.x

Hook, J. N., Davis, D. E., Owen, J., Worthington, E. L., Jr., & Utsey, S. O. (2013). Cultural humility: Measuring openness to culturally diverse clients. *Journal of Counseling Psychology, 60,* 353–366.

Hurtado, S., Milem, J. F., Clayton-Pedersen, A., & Allen, W. R. (1998). Enhancing campus climates for racial/ethnic diversity: Educational policy and practice. *The Review of Higher Education, 21,* 279–302.

Hurtado, S., Milem, J. F., Clayton-Pedersen, A., & Allen, W. R. (1999). Enacting diverse learning environments: Improving the campus climate for racial/ethnic diversity in higher education. *ASHE-ERIC Higher Education Report, 26*(8). Retrieved from https://files.eric.ed.gov/fulltext/ED430514.pdf

Intersectionality. (2019). In *Merriam-Webster's online dictionary.* Retrieved from https://www.merriam-webster.com/dictionary/intersectionality

Jaschik, S. (2019). Dozens indicted in alleged massive case of admissions fraud. Retrieved from https://www.insidehighered.com/print/admissions/article/2019/03/13/dozens-indicted-alleged-massive-case-admissions-fraud

Johnson, A. A., & Quaye, S. J. (2017). Queering Black racial identity development. *Journal of College Student Development, 58,* 1135–1148.

Jones, T. (2016). A historical mission in the accountability era: A public HBCU and state performance funding. *Educational Policy, 30,* 999–1041.

Jordan, J. V. (2000). The role of mutual empathy in relational/cultural therapy. *Journal of Clinical Psychology, 56,* 1005–1016.
Jordan, J. V. (2018). *Relational-cultural therapy* (2nd ed.). Washington, DC: American Psychological Association.
Kearney, L., Draper, M., & Barón, A. (2005). Counseling utilization by ethnic minority college students. *Cultural Diversity and Ethnic Minority Psychology, 11,* 272–285.
Kim, J. (1981). The process of Asian American identity development: A study of Japanese American women's perceptions of their struggle to achieve personal identities as Americans of Asian ancestry. *Dissertation Abstracts International, 42,* 155 1A. (University Microfilms No. 81-18080)
Kim, J., Park, S., La, A., Chang, J., & Zane, N. (2016). Counseling services for Asian, Latino/a, and White American students: Initial severity, session attendance, and outcome. *Cultural Diversity and Ethnic Minority Psychology, 22,* 299–310.
Kocet, M. M. (2009). Multicultural ethical perspectives. In C. Lee, D. Burnhill, A. Butler, C. Hipolito-Delgado, M. Humphrey, O. Munoz, & H. J. Shin (Eds.), *Elements of culture in counseling: Theory and practice* (pp. 193–210). Boston, MA: Allyn & Bacon.
Kocet, M. M., & Stewart, D. L. (2011). Role of student affairs in promoting religious and secular pluralism and interfaith cooperation. *Journal of College and Character, 12,* 1–10.
Lee, C. (2019). *Multicultural issues in counseling: New approaches to diversity* (5th ed.). Alexandria, VA: American Counseling Association.
Lewin, K. (1936). *Principles of topological psychology.* New York, NY: McGraw-Hill.
Linder, C. (2016). An intersectional approach to supporting students. In M. J. Cuyjet, C. Linder, M. F. Howard-Hamilton, & D. L. Cooper (Eds.), *Multiculturalism on campus: Theory, models, and practices for understanding diversity and creating inclusion* (2nd ed., pp. 66–80). Sterling, VA: Stylus.
Linder, C., & Cooper, D. L. (2016). From cultural competence to critical consciousness. In M. J. Cuyjet, C. Linder, M. F. Howard-Hamilton, & D. L. Cooper (Eds.), *Multiculturalism on campus: Theory, models, and practices for understanding diversity and creating inclusion* (2nd ed., pp. 379–392). Sterling, VA: Stylus.
Lo, C., McCallum, D., Hughes, M., Smith, G., & McKnight, U. (2017). Racial differences in college students' assessments of campus race relations. *Journal of College Student Development, 58,* 247–263.
Logan, S., Freeman, E., & McRoy, R. (1987). Racial identity problems of biracial clients: Implications for social work practice. *Journal of Intergroup Relations, 15,* 11–23.
MacKinnon, F. J. D., & Floyd, R. D. (2016). Adult college students. In M. J. Cuyjet, C. Linder, M. F. Howard-Hamilton, & D. L. Cooper (Eds.), *Multiculturalism on campus: Theory, models, and practices for understanding diversity and creating inclusion* (2nd ed., pp. 309–327). Sterling, VA: Stylus.
McCarn, S. R., & Fassinger, R. E. (1996). Revisioning sexual minority identity formation: A new model of lesbian identity and its implications for counseling and research. *The Counseling Psychologist, 24,* 508–534.
McIntosh, P. (1989, July/August). White privilege: Unpacking the invisible knapsack. *Peace and Freedom,* 1–3.
Moore, J. R., Pollio, D. E., Hong, B. A., Valencia, C., Sorrell, M., & North, C. S. (2018). Pilot design and implementation of an innovative mental health and wellness clinic at a historically Black college/university. *Community Mental Health Journal, 54,* 371–375.
Moore-Thomas, C. (2014). Cultural identity development. In D. G. Hays & B. T. Erford (Eds.), *Developing multicultural counseling competence: A systems approach* (2nd ed., pp. 34–56). New York, NY: Pearson.

National Child Welfare Workforce Institute. (2013). *Two top-rated activities from the LAMM residential training: Ecomaps & logic models.* Retrieved from https://www.pdx.edu/ccf/sites/www.pdx.edu.ccf/files/TwoTopRatedLAMMActivities.pdf

Owen, J. (2013). Early career perspectives on psychotherapy research and practice: Psychotherapist effects, multicultural orientation, and couple interventions. *Psychotherapy, 50,* 496–502.

Owen, J., Imel, Z., Tao, K., Wampold, B., Smith, A., & Rodolfa, E. (2011). Cultural ruptures in short-term therapy: Working alliance as a mediator between clients' perceptions of microaggressions and therapy outcomes. *Counselling and Psychotherapy Research, 11,* 204–212.

Owen, J., Jordan, T. A., Turner, D., Davis, D. E., Hook, J. N., & Leach, M. M. (2014). Therapists' multicultural orientation: Client perceptions of cultural humility, spiritual/religious commitment, and therapy outcomes. *Journal of Psychology & Theology, 42,* 91–98.

Owen, J., Leach, M. M., Wampold, B., & Rodolfa, E. (2011). Client and therapist variability in clients' perceptions of their therapists' multicultural competencies. *Journal of Counseling Psychology, 58,* 1–9.

Owen, J., Tao, K. W., Drinane, J. M., Hook, J., Davis, D. E., & Kune, N. F. (2016). Client perceptions of therapists' multicultural orientation: Cultural (missed) opportunities and cultural humility. *Professional Psychology: Research and Practice, 47,* 30–37.

Owen, J., Tao, K., Imel, Z., Wampold, B., & Rodolfa, E. (2014). Addressing racial and ethnic microaggressions in therapy. *Professional Psychology: Research and Practice, 45,* 283–290.

Paladino, D. A. (2009). Counseling multiple heritage college students. In R. C. Henriksen & D. A. Paladino (Eds.), *Counseling individuals, couples, and families with multiple heritages* (pp. 83–100). Alexandria, VA: American Counseling Association.

Paladino, D. A., & Davis, H., Jr. (2006). Counseling and outreach strategies for multiracial college students. *Journal of College Student Psychotherapy, 20,* 19–31.

Parks, S. D. (2000). *Big questions, worthy dreams: Mentoring young adults in their search for meaning, purpose, and faith.* San Francisco, CA: Jossey-Bass.

Peters, H. C. (2017). Multicultural complexity: An intersectional lens for clinical supervision. *International Journal of Advanced Counselling, 39,* 176–187.

Phinney, J. S. (1996). Understanding ethnic diversity: The role of ethnic identity. *American Behavioral Scientist, 40,* 143–152.

Poll, J. P., & Smith, T. B. (2003). The spiritual self: Toward a conceptualization of spiritual identity development. *Journal of Psychology and Theology, 31,* 129–142.

Ponterotto, J. G. (1988). Racial consciousness development among White counselors' trainees: A stage model. *Journal of Multicultural Counseling and Development, 16,* 146–156. doi:10.1002/j.2161-1912.1988.tb00405.x

Poston, W. S. C. (1990). The biracial identity development model: A needed addition. *Journal of Counseling & Development, 69,* 152–155. doi:10.1002/j.1556-6676.1990.tb01477.x

Prochaska, J. O., & Norcross, J. C. (2018). *Systems of psychotherapy* (9th ed.). New York, NY: Oxford University Press.

Ratts, M., Singh, A., Nassar-McMillan, S., Butler, S., & McCullough, J. (2015). *Multicultural and social justice counseling competencies.* Retrieved from http://www.counseling.org/docs/default-source/competencies/multicultural-and-social-justice-counseling-competencies.pdf?sfvrsn=20

Ratts, M., Singh, A., Nassar-McMillan, S., Butler, S., & McCullough, J. (2016). Multicultural and social justice counseling competencies: Guidelines for the counseling profession. *Journal of Multicultural Counseling and Development, 44,* 28–48. doi:10.1002/jmcd.12035

Renn, K. A. (2000). Patterns of situational identity among biracial and multiracial college students. *The Review of Higher Education, 23,* 399–420.

Renn, K., & Arnold, K. (2003). Reconceptualizing research on college student peer culture. *The Journal of Higher Education, 74,* 261–291.

Root, M. P. P. (1998). Facilitating psychotherapy with Asian American clients. In D. R. Atkinson, G. Morten, & D. W. Sue (Eds.), *Counseling American minorities: A cross-cultural perspective* (pp. 214–234). Boston, MA: McGraw-Hill.

Ruiz, A. S. (1990). Ethnic identity: Crisis and resolution. *Journal of Multicultural Counseling and Development, 18,* 29–40. doi:10.1002/j.2161-1912.1990.tb00434.x

Salvatore, J., & Shelton, J. N. (2007). Cognitive costs of exposure to racial prejudice. *Psychological Science, 18,* 810–815.

Sav, G. T. (2010). Funding historically Black colleges and universities: Progress toward equality? *Journal of Education Finance, 35,* 295–307.

Scott, D. A., & Robinson, T. L. (2001). White male identity development: The key model. *Journal of Counseling & Development, 79,* 415–421. doi:10.1002/j.1556-6676.2001.tb01988.x

Shapiro, C., Meyers, A., & Toner, C. (2011). *Strength-based, family-focused practice: A clinical guide from Family Justice.* Retrieved from https://www.familiesoutside.org.uk/content/uploads/2011/02/family-justice-clinical-guide.pdf

Shelton, K. (2017). Multicultural counseling competency and diversity issues. In S. J. Hodges, K. Shelton, & M. M. King (Eds.), *The college and university counseling manual: Integrating essential services across the campus* (pp. 13–40). New York, NY: Springer.

Smith, L., Baluch, S., Bernabei, S., Robohm, J., & Sheehy, J. (2003). Applying a social justice framework to college counseling center practice. *Journal of College Counseling, 6,* 3–13. doi:10.1002/j.2161-1882.2003.tb00222.x

Soloranzo, D., Ceja, M., & Yosso, T. (2000). Critical race theory, racial microaggressions, and campus racial climate: The experiences of African American college students. *Journal of Negro Education, 69,* 60–73.

Sue, D., Arredondo, P., & McDavis, R. (1992). Multicultural counseling competencies and standards: A call to the profession. *Journal of Counseling & Development, 70,* 477–486. doi:10.1002/j.1556-6676.1992.tb01642.x

Sue, D. W., & Capodilupo, C. M. (2008). Racial, gender, and sexual orientation microaggressions: Implications for counseling and psychology. In D. W. Sue & D. Sue (Eds.), *Counseling the culturally diverse: Theory and practice* (5th ed., pp. 105–130). Hoboken, NJ: Wiley.

Sue, D. W., & Sue, D. (1990). *Counseling the culturally different: Theory and practice.* New York, NY: Wiley.

Sue, D. W., & Sue, D. (1999). *Counseling the culturally different: Theory and practice* (3rd ed.). New York, NY: Wiley.

Sue, D. W., Sue, D., Neville, H. A., & Smith, L. (2019). *Counseling the culturally diverse: Theory and practice* (8th ed.). Hoboken, NJ: Wiley.

Toldson, I. A. (2016). The funding gap between historically Black colleges and universities and traditionally White institutions needs to be addressed. *The Journal of Negro Education, 85,* 97–99.

Troiden, R. R. (1989). The formation of homosexual identities. *Journal of Homosexuality, 17,* 43–74.

Turner, E. A., Camarillo, J., Daniel, S., Otero, J., & Parker, A. (2017). Correlates of psychotherapy use among ethnically diverse college students. *Journal of College Student Development, 58,* 300–307.

University of Hawai'i at Hilo. (2011). *University of Hawai'i at Hilo: Strategic plan 2001–2015.* Retrieved from https://hilo.hawaii.edu/strategicplan/documents/2011-2015StrategicPlanWebVersionFINAL.pdf

Watt, S. K. (2009). Facilitating difficult dialogues at the intersections of religious privilege. In S. K. Watt, E. E. Fairchild, & K. M. Goodman (Eds.), *Intersections of religious privilege: Difficult dialogues and student affairs practice* (pp. 65–73). San Francisco, CA: Jossey-Bass.

Watt, S. K., Fairchild, E. E., & Goodman, K. M. (2009). *Intersections of religious privilege: Difficult dialogues and student affairs practice.* San Francisco, CA: Jossey-Bass.
Weinberg, M. S., Williams, C. J., & Pryor, D. W. (1994). *Dual attraction: Understanding bisexuality.* New York, NY: Oxford Press.

Chapter 4

Legal and Ethical Issues in College Counseling

Perry C. Francis

To be ethical counselors is not just to follow the standards of the profession, but to put your needs and motivations aside and enter the clients' world and walk with them as they learn new ways to be better and healthier than they were before.

—Perry C. Francis

■ ■ ■

Reflection Exercise

Ricardo is a first-generation college student from the U.S. territory of Puerto Rico attending State University in Florida. This is his first time away from his rural home, and he is having trouble acclimating to his new environment on the college campus. He hates dorm life and is having trouble connecting with his roommates. He is also struggling in his classes although he was a stellar student back home. He is depressed and anxious, something he has struggled with before coming to State. One of the ways Ricardo copes with his emotions is to drink . . . a lot. This has created some problems because he was caught with alcohol in his room and was sent to the dean of students for adjudication. He revealed his troubles to the dean and also talked about his fleeting suicidal ideation. On hearing about the suicidal ideation, the dean strongly recommended (mandated) that Ricardo be evaluated at Counseling and Psychological Services (CAPS). Ricardo is apprehensive about going to CAPS because he does not want anyone to think he is crazy. He is also concerned about what the counselor might tell the dean of students. The dean is also concerned about Ricardo and discusses the case with the Student Care Team to determine what other services State U. might offer Ricardo to help him be successful.

Ricardo does make an appointment at CAPS (he really didn't think he had a choice) and now presents himself to you for a first session. Consider each question below and record your answers. Keep the questions and your answers in mind as you read this chapter to see whether anything changes. At the end of the chapter, we will reflect on what you learned.

1. How might your informed consent be different given that Ricardo was essentially "mandated" because of his suicidal ideation?
2. What are the differences between a mandated assessment and mandated counseling?
3. What must you do to ensure that you are prepared and competent to see Ricardo, given his background as a first-generation student from Puerto Rico?
4. What advice would you offer to the Student Care Team if Ricardo had a previous mental health diagnosis and they recommended that he must withdraw from school?
5. What must you consider if Ricardo is a high school student (minor) taking classes at State University?
6. The dean of students wants you to be part of the discussion about Ricardo with the Student Care Team. How do you approach this task?
7. What was your impression of college counseling during your college career? After you have read this chapter, how might it evolve?

■ ■ ■

The range of practice for college counseling as a specialty in the counseling profession is as varied as the settings and practitioners in the field. There are counselors who work in technical and community colleges providing a myriad of student services including academic advising, career services, and personal counseling. There are others in the profession who work in large comprehensive universities whose only task is to provide psychotherapy either to help the student grow as an adult or, more likely, to remediate mental health concerns. In between the technical and community colleges and the large comprehensive universities are the many other institutions of higher education that employ counselors to provide counseling-related services to the student body. Finally, there are counseling professionals who work in a myriad of different student affairs offices (e.g., dean of students, disabilities services, wellness centers, and other offices) throughout various institutions whose role may not be to provide counseling but whose skills and abilities as counselors enable them to help students be successful learners and future citizens. In each of these settings, counselors apply the profession's code of ethics to their practice to ensure each student receives competent, caring, and appropriate services that reflect the values and best practices of the counseling profession (Francis & Dugger, 2014).

In this chapter I will apply the counseling profession's code of ethics—that is, the American Counseling Association's (ACA's) *ACA Code of Ethics* (ACA, 2014)—to the practice of college counseling. Many counseling specialties have their own code of ethics created by their corresponding professional association (e.g., American Mental Health Counselors Association, 2015; International Association of Marriage and Family Counselors, 2017). In the case of college counseling, the related professional association (viz., American College Counseling Association [ACCA]) has mandated as part of its bylaws that members will abide by the current version of the *ACA Code of Ethics* (ACCA, 2017a, Section 6). Additionally, the professionals who work in college counseling come from the four major mental health professions (i.e., professional counseling, social work, counseling/clinical psychology, and couples and family therapy; Sharkin, 2012) and are governed by their own professional association's codes of ethics. At this point in time, there has been no concerted effort to create a code of ethics that is specific to the college counseling setting, and therefore, for this chapter, I will apply the *ACA Code of Ethics* (ACA, 2014) to the college setting and population.

The following pages address the many ways counseling ethics are applied to specific issues in college counseling. They begin with the college student population and the many different people who cross the threshold of the counseling center. This includes how culture affects what we do as counseling professionals, the age of the student, the complexity of the case, and the limitations of settings and number of sessions. As noted earlier, college counselors do not only provide mental health services on campus but they also provide a myriad of different services, depending on the role of the counselor and function of the office. These roles and functions require a thoughtful application of the ethical standards. College counselors are asked to provide counseling and assessments for students mandated for services for various reasons. Mandated services such as these are ethically questionable, and their efficacy is often challenged. The information presented will help you puzzle through how you might want to respond to a request or demand for mandated services. Finally, I will examine the role of technology, social media, and telehealth as addressed by our ethics both in theory and practice. As you read through this chapter, keep in mind the opening case study and see if your answers to the questions change with additional information.

Ethics and the College Student Population

Diverse Student Populations

Colleges and universities across the nation are facing enrollment declines due to the decreasing population of high school students (National Student Clearinghouse Research Center, 2019). Yet, although enrollment is declining, the number of students from a variety of different racial and ethnic populations is increasing (National Center for Education Statistics, 2017). Add to this mix international students; lesbian, gay, bisexual, transgender, and queer/questioning students; and any number of other populations on campus, and you have a multicultural landscape that requires the college counselor to be willing to work with and knowledgeable about a diverse student population. As a reflection of the importance of diversity in our profession, the *ACA Code of Ethics* (ACA, 2014) identifies respecting diversity and multiculturalism as one of the core professional values of counseling: "honoring diversity and embracing a multicultural approach in support of the worth, dignity, potential, and uniqueness of people within their social and cultural contexts" (ACA, 2014, p. 3).

How does this affect the college counselor or even counselors who are not part of the college or university setting? Our code of ethics is infused with standards that direct all counselors to give due consideration to the many identities our clients (and students) bring into the consultation room. These values, *honoring diversity and embracing a multicultural approach*, can be seen in how our ethics address the life span of a counseling relationship:

- Providing information and facilitating informed consent that is both developmentally appropriate and culturally sensitive (see Standard A.2.c.).
- Managing the relationship and respecting the values of the client while also being aware of and not injecting one's own values into the relationship (see Standards A.4.a., A.4.b., and A.11.b.).
- Understanding personal and professional boundaries and their cultural significance in a client's life and the life of their family (see Standards A.6.b. and B.1.a.).
- Maintaining and expanding one's knowledge and awareness of working with a diverse client population (see Standard C.2.a.).

- Counselors are aware of how culture and cultural identity affect the choice and use of assessments and/or diagnosis. Additionally, the counselor should be aware of the history of misdiagnosis with groups and individuals who are not part of the majority culture (see Standards E.5.b. and E.5.c.).
- Counselors manage termination of services and referrals based on client readiness and need and not based on values conflict (see Standard A.11.b.).

All major mental health associations' codes of ethics address working with a diverse client population. Additionally, the educational accrediting bodies of these same professions (Council for Accreditation of Counseling and Related Educational Programs, American Psychological Association, National Association of Social Workers, and American Association for Marriage and Family Therapy) all mandate that understanding and having the ability to work with a diverse client population is a general expectation of all graduates. Beyond graduate school, professional counselors are to recognize that the truly educated never really graduate and are to work to maintain their competence not only in the advances in the art and science of counseling but also in their ability to work with a diverse client population (see *ACA Code of Ethics*, Standard C.2.f.; ACA, 2014).

The Minor Client

What does a counselor do if the student who is seeking services in the college counseling center happens to be under the age of 18? Although not a common issue, it is one that all college counselors must think through because not all students fit neatly in the 18- to 25-year-old age range.

The vast majority of college students are age 18 years and older. As such, they are considered adults and can consent for counseling services. On occasion, there are students who arrive on campus who have not reached the age of 18. This may be the result of any number of issues (for instance, dual enrollment programs, skipping a grade in K–12 setting, etc.). This presents an ethical and legal dilemma for college counselors. State laws vary on the age a minor may consent for treatment, the duration of the treatment, and the parent's right to review records (Boonstra & Nash, 2000). In the case of an inability to give consent because of minor status, the *ACA Code of Ethics* (ACA, 2014), Standard A.2.d., guides the counselor to

> seek the assent of clients to services and include them in decision making as appropriate . . . [and] recognize the need to balance the ethical rights of clients to make choices, their capacity to give consent or assent to receive services, and parental or familial legal rights and responsibilities to protect these clients and make decisions on their behalf.

When working with young children, the counselor will want to include them in the consent process by obtaining the children's assent for treatment. Assent for treatment involves sharing information with the children, who are the direct recipients of counseling, about the nature and boundaries of counseling; the different roles of the parent, the child, and the counselor; and the goals of treatment (Coffman & Barnett, 2015). When working with older children (12–17 years of age), the counselor will want to work with both the parents and the children to set up boundaries, so the children feel safe sharing in session. In most college situations, the minor college students are closer to the age of 17, and working with parents can be complicated because of distance, expectations, and a desire to balance the needs of an emerging adult (i.e., the college student) and the parents' desire to ensure their child is doing well in the higher education setting. Additionally, college students who are minors may not want the parents to know they are seeking mental health services.

It becomes incumbent upon the counselor and the counseling center to craft a policy concerning services to students who are minors that is both sensitive to the clients' needs and developmental readiness, the setting and context (e.g., local community college vs. a residential university), and the laws of the state where the counseling occurs. Many counseling centers do not provide services to minors that are part of an external program to the university (e.g., dual-credit students) for various legal and administrative reasons while at the same time providing services to students who are regularly enrolled at the institution.

Case Study

Background

State University is a medium sized institution in a suburban area that has long been known as an active member of the educational community and, as such, has created a program called the Early College Readiness School (ECR). The ECR is basically a school within a school. The students (ages 14–18) attend regular high school classes on campus as well as take college courses alongside the university's regular student body. They earn both high school and college academic credit and are considered members of the university's student body. Their school has its own school counselor, principal, and teaching staff. On occasion, some members of the ECR student body request or need counseling services that are beyond the capacity of the school counselor to provide. The principal of the ECR program has reached out to you, the counseling center director, to ask whether the ECR students can utilize the services of the counseling center. You have a small staff that is already operating at full capacity and a limited budget. Complete the following exercise as you work through this case:

- Determine what the laws are regarding providing counseling services to minors in your state.
- As you reflect on the laws and the *ACA Code of Ethics* (ACA, 2014), use an ethical decision-making model (see Cottone & Claus, 2000, for a review of decision-making models) and develop a list of reasons for either providing or denying services to the ECR students.
- Using those laws and the *ACA Code of Ethics* (ACA, 2014), create a policy that will either allow you to provide or deny services to the ECR students.

■ ■ ■

Complex Cases and Treatment Limitations

There is a mistaken impression among some that college students are seeking services for minor development issues such as relationship problems or struggles with individuation. Yet counseling center directors have long perceived that there are more students utilizing campus counseling services and presenting with more complex issues (Gallagher, 2014; Reetz, Krylowicz, & Mistler, 2014). Although the research on the rise of psychopathology in the college student population continues to be mixed (Kettmann et al., 2007; Much & Swanson, 2010), many more students are arriving on college campuses with increasing amounts of psychotropic medications (Caley, Webber, Kurland, & Holmes, 2010) and serious mental health issues that mirror those of their counterparts who are not attending college, and they are seeking counseling services (Francis & Horn, 2017). In many cases this has an effect on the level and amount of services that can be offered (Owen, Smith, & Rodolfa, 2009). These issues present many ethical dilemmas for the college counselor.

Session Limitations

In many cases the abovementioned increasing rate of utilization of counseling services reported by counseling center directors (Gallagher, 2014; Schwartz, 2016) has resulted in counseling centers imposing a limit on the number of sessions a student may use in a given academic year, with the average being 12 sessions (Owen et al., 2009; Schwartz, 2016). These session limits impose an additional ethical obligation on the counselor to fully inform the student prior to the initiation of services about the limits so that the student can make an informed decision about beginning counseling. The more complex decision for the counselor is whether or not to initiate services at all if the presenting issue will obviously require significantly more services than the session limits allow. As any seasoned counselor can tell you, the presenting issue is often not the only issue to be dealt with because, for example, a student may present with relationship problems that can quickly escalate into presentation of serious historical mental health issues, including abuse, personality disorders, or other concerns that require long-term mental health treatment. Because informed consent is "an ongoing part of the counseling process" (*ACA Code of Ethics*, Standard A.2.a.; ACA, 2014), as more complex issues arise, the counselor will need to review with the student the session limits and discuss the referral policy for continuing treatment.

Session limitations as an ethical issue is not as simple as creating policy and ensuring that the student has been duly informed of its existence. There are many other variables to consider that have an impact on client care. So, as you work with a student to manage a possible referral, you consider the following:

- whether the student has insurance or financial means to pay for off-campus counseling services (Iarussi & Shaw, 2016);
- whether the community has enough mental health providers who are willing to or have the training to work with college students (Owen, Devdas, & Rodolfa, 2007);
- the timing of the referral (e.g., at intake vs. termination of services); the types of issues or diagnosis that triggers the referral (Dewan, Steenbarger, & Greenberg, 2012);
- whether the student will follow through with the referral (Owen et al., 2007) and the issue of turning students away from services they may have paid for through their student fees.

As you work through these variables using an appropriate ethical decision-making model, you seek to ensure that students receive the most appropriate care within the limitations of the treatment models and settings you have at your disposal.

Setting Limitations

There are well over 4,700 colleges and universities in the United States (U.S. Department of Education, 2016). Many may not provide counseling services or only provide limited services as a part of a combined office (e.g., counseling, advising, and career services). Many small 4-year colleges and community colleges only provide short-term and crisis counseling services and do not have access to any psychiatric care if needed (Francis & Horn, 2017). As in the case of session limitations, the college counselor is obligated to fully inform any potential client of the setting limitation (i.e., range of services provided) and the referral policies if the student's issues exceed the mission of the center to provide services. Although the counselor in such a setting may be comprehensively trained to provide a wide range of psychotherapy services, if the setting does not have the support services necessary to provide extensive care involving a team approach (e.g., eating disorders, dual diagnosis), it is incumbent on the counselor to inform the student of the limitations and make an immediate referral. In the case of a crisis, stabilization of the client is required as well as an appropriate referral to competent care. In both the session- and setting-limitation environments, appropriate continuing communication about the boundaries of the services and initiation of continuing care through referral will avoid any accusation of abandonment or neglect. Yet, as previously noted, it is not a simple process of enforcing a policy or practice when the student in front of you is seeking your care.

Multiple Roles

Counseling centers and counseling center staff often carry out multiple roles on campus. As previously noted, the counseling offices may also house academic advising, career services, sexual assault prevention offices, disabilities resource services, and so forth (Hodges, 2017; Sharkin, 2012). Center staff may serve on various committees that range from threat assessment/behavioral intervention teams and crisis response teams to retention committees (Sharkin, 2012). At times, this places the counselor in situations in which students who are clients of counseling services or of that particular counselor are discussed.

Combined Offices and Roles

It is not uncommon for community college counseling centers to be combined with academic advising, career services, or disabilities services, among others (Edwards & Lenhart, 2015). The same can be said of small colleges and universities where resources are scarce (Sharkin, 2012). When a counseling center has multiple services, it is incumbent on the staff to ensure that students are made aware of how the different roles intersect and affect their records. This includes the legal and ethical boundaries of each service and becomes a complex task with each additional service added to the counseling center's duties.

For example, if a student is seeking advising services for course selection and registration or disabilities services for an accommodation in a course, those records (i.e., an educational record) are governed by the Family Educational Rights and Privacy Act of 1974 (FERPA). Those records can be accessed by an institutional employee (for instance, faculty, administrator, etc.) who has an educational need to know (FERPA Regulations, 2004). The student's conversation with an "academic adviser" is not considered confidential in the same way as a student's conversation with a licensed professional counselor providing psychotherapy. If the same student is seeking counseling services, those conversations and treatment records (i.e., case notes) are protected by state law and the ethics of the counseling profession and exempt from the educational record. They are considered ethically and legally confidential and cannot be accessed by anyone other than the counselor and the student without permission of the student, with some exceptions (for instance, harm to self or others, child or vulnerable adult abuse reporting, legal proceedings, etc.). Then only essential information can be provided to ensure continuity and quality of care (see *ACA Code of Ethics*, Standard B.2.e; ACA, 2014). The difference between a treatment record and an educational record has been defined in FERPA (1974). A *treatment record* is

> records on a student who is eighteen years of age or older, or is attending an institution of postsecondary education, which are made or maintained by a physician, psychiatrist, psychologist, or other recognized professional or paraprofessional acting in his professional or paraprofessional capacity, or assisting in that capacity, and which are made, maintained, or used only in connection with the provision of treatment to the student, and are not available to anyone other than persons providing such treatment, except that such records can be personally reviewed by a physician or other appropriate professional of the student's choice. (FERPA, 1974, 20 U.S.C. § 1232g(a)(4)(B)(iv))

An *educational record* is defined as follows:

> the term "education records" means . . . those records, files, documents, and other materials which—(i) contain information directly related to a student; and (ii) are maintained by an educational agency or institution or by a person acting for such agency or institution. (FERPA, 1974, 20 U.S.C.§ 1232g(a)(4)(A)(i)(ii))

It is the counselor's responsibility to make, maintain, and safeguard appropriate counseling records as they relate to the provision of counseling services (*ACA Code of Ethics*, Standard A.1.b.; ACA, 2014). This includes maintaining an appropriate boundary between students' counseling records and their educational records. Once a treatment record enters the educational record, it becomes a part of the educational record and is no longer governed by state mental health laws but by FERPA.

The simplest time for this discussion to occur is at the initial contact. The student and staff member can review the types of services available and offer the student the opportunity to give his or her informed consent (see *ACA Code of Ethics*, Standards A.2.a. and A.2.b.; ACA, 2014), especially if the services requested include psychotherapy. This becomes exceedingly difficult, if not impossible, during mass advising and registration events. It then becomes the responsibility of the counselor/adviser to evaluate whether informed consent is even possible or required given the circumstances. This does not mean the counselor/adviser cannot obtain informed consent at a later date should additional services be requested that involve counseling. Common sense and flexibility must be used in times when it is clear that the goal of the event is only to offer one service (advising/registration) and not provide for counseling.

There are those rare circumstances in which a student's treatment record can be accessed as an educational record. Although it did not take place in a combined office, such was the case in *Jane Doe v. University of Oregon, et al.* (2015). In 2015 Jane Doe (not her real name) accused three basketball players of gang raping her. She sued the university and the head coach of the basketball team when, according to the lawsuit, they mishandled the Title IX investigation into her claim. As a part of her lawsuit, she claimed emotional distress. Once she claimed emotional distress, her psychological state became relevant and opened the door for the university to review her treatment records once it learned it was being sued (Mangan, 2015). Although the action on the part of the university was both morally questionable and a public relations nightmare, FERPA allows a school to use a student's educational record if a student or parent initiates a legal action against the institution (FERPA Regulations, 2004, § 99.31). Although a school is allowed access to records, it should take into account the result such a disclosure will have with respect to the client-provider relationship as well as the effect it will have on the relationship between the students and the institution. Additionally, Oregon law allows a defendant in a lawsuit the ability to collect and review relevant documents when being sued (Mangan, 2015). Although rare, it is important for the college counselor to know and understand the workings of FERPA, their own state laws, and their intersection with the ethics in regard to records and their protection. It is also naive to believe that a client's records can never be accessed, as *Jane Doe v. University of Oregon* demonstrates. The *ACA Code of Ethics* (Standard A.2.B.; ACA, 2014) lists the types of information needed for an informed consent document and includes the clients' (students') right to confidentiality and an explanation of the limits of that confidentiality.

Multiple Roles in the College Community

Counseling center staff are part of the academic community that make up an institution of higher education. As such, they may be asked to serve on various committees, task forces, or panels. Additionally, they may work with other student affairs professionals in the creation of programs and seminars designed to support the educational, social, and emotional development of students. Finally, they may be involved in training university personnel who come into regular contact with students, such as teaching assistants, residence assistants, academic coaches and tutors, and others, on identifying mental health concerns (for instance, suicidal ideation, eating disorders, etc.) and making referrals (Sharkin, 2012). In each instance, the counseling professional has the opportunity to explain the role of the counseling center and help the community learn about the services provided and the boundaries that must be maintained for the center and the staff to maintain a positive reputation on campus (Lyn, 2017; Sharkin, 2012).

Many years ago I was asked to consult with a college concerning their search for a counseling center director. During my time on campus, I visited with select faculty members and many of the administrators who lead various offices within student affairs (housing, campus life, etc.). At each meeting, I was asked if it was acceptable for the counselors or the counseling center director to share basic information about a particular student who the administrators or faculty knew to be receiving counseling services. Each person noted that the previous director of the counseling center would share bits of general information about a student when asked. It was clear that the people asking for information were not simply curious but were taking seriously their responsibility to help students succeed and to maintain a safe and secure environment. Many served on the campus behavioral intervention team (BIT), as would the future counseling center director, and wanted to ensure they could tailor interventions to help a student succeed or to act appropriately if a student presented as a danger to self or others. It was obvious that the previous counseling center director was working hard to have a positive relationship with colleagues and, at the same time, maintain the confidentiality of the students receiving services. Yet sharing any information with others without the expressed permission of the student receiving services violates the student's right to privacy and confidentiality (see *ACA Code of Ethics*, Standards B.1.b. and B.1.c., ACA, 2014) and created an environment of expectations on the part of the faculty and administrators that would become a point of tension for the new counseling center director.

Behavioral Intervention Teams and the College Counselor

The Virginia Tech shootings on April 16, 2007, took the lives of 32 students and faculty and forever changed the impression of the college campus as a safe and serene environment. These shootings were followed by the Northern Illinois University shootings on February 14, 2008, where five students died and 17 were seriously injured. As a result of these acts of violence and others, colleges and universities have created BITs (Eells & Rockland-Miller, 2011). A BIT, according to the National Behavioral Intervention Team Association, is

> a multi-disciplinary group whose purpose is meeting regularly to support its target audience (students, employees, faculty, staff) via an established protocol. The team tracks "red flags" over time, detecting patterns, trends, and disturbances in individual or group behavior. The team receives reports of disruptive, problematic, or concerning behavior or misconduct (from coworkers, community members, friends, colleagues, etc.), conducts an investigation, performs a threat assessment, and determines the best mechanisms for support, intervention, warning/notification, and response. The team then deploys its resources, and the resources of the community, and coordinates follow-up. (National Behavioral Intervention Team Association, 2017, § 1)

College counselors have been a part of BITs since their inception and provide many necessary services including threat assessment, consultation, or direct intervention with students

(Deisinger, Ransazzo, O'Neill, & Savage, 2008; Van Brunt, Reese, & Lewis, 2015). It is important that the college counselor provide the BIT with an orientation about the laws and ethics surrounding the counseling profession, including confidentiality and privacy (see *ACA Code of Ethics*, Standards B.1.b. and B.1.c.; ACA, 2014) and how the counselor can best serve the BIT. Also included in this orientation are the laws and ethics about when a counselor is required to breach confidentiality (see *ACA Code of Ethics*, Standard B.2.; ACA, 2014) and share information in order to keep the student and campus community safe. What the college counselor does not provide is information on former or current clients who come to the attention of the BIT without the permission of those clients (see *ACA Code of Ethics*, Standards B.1.b. and B.1.c.; ACA, 2014) if the client's behavior does not meet the requirements of "serious and foreseeable harm" (see *ACA Code of Ethics*, Standard B.2.a.; ACA, 2014). The counselor can offer the BIT guidance on how to best serve the student, what interventions might be beneficial for students who struggle with the same issues, and possible behaviors one might expect from a student struggling with these same issues. In this way, the counselor can be a team member, help orient the BIT about the services the counseling center provides, and maintain the best practices of the profession for both the students utilizing counseling services and the safety of the institution.

Case Study

Jesse Gonzales has been the director of a small counseling center at Mid-State University for 7 years. He has developed a solid reputation on the small campus as professional, knowledgeable, and compassionate. As the director, he is a member of the school's Care Team (CT; also known as a BIT or a Student of Concern Team), whose task is to intervene with struggling students before their issues become so problematic that they put their academic progress at risk. At a recent meeting, there was a discussion concerning a student (Sam) who is a current client of the counseling center and of Jesse. Although Sam has made it known that he is attending counseling, his behavior has become more problematic and is raising concerns that he might hurt himself or others. Jesse recently evaluated Sam's behavior and determined he is a low risk for harming himself or others. The CT is discussing various interventions for Sam, many of which could be counterproductive to Sam's care. How would you answer the following questions?

- Given that Sam has already revealed that he is participating in counseling, should Jesse discuss his treatment with the CT in order to moderate their interventions with Sam?
- What should Jesse's role be with the CT? What boundaries should he maintain while participating in CT meetings?
- What would be required for Jesse to reveal information about clients to the CT?

Sam is free to share what he wants about his counseling with anyone he wants, and although it might be helpful to the CT to know more details about Sam's care and status, he has not given Jesse permission to share that information. To share information with the CT, Jesse would have to obtain a written release of information. Jesse would begin with a discussion with Sam about the need for such an action and how much and what type of information might be shared with the CT.

Without a written release of information, Jesse's role on the CT is that of consultant, offering insight on how students like Sam might react to different interventions implemented by the CT. At the same time, as Sam's counselor, he can help Sam address the issues presented in the CT meeting, using it as feedback if it is therapeutically appropriate.

■ ■ ■

Working With Student Affairs Colleagues and Title IX

One of the major goals of any institution of higher education is to provide a safe and secure environment where students can learn, professors can teach, and researchers can produce knowledge (Francis, 2000). This cannot take place if the college community is constantly battling sexual harassment and violence. Although such behavior has been an issue for decades, it was not until recently that the government and universities fully applied Title IX of the Education Code (Title IX, Education Amendments of 1972) to this persistent problem (Wies, 2015). As a result, many colleges and universities across the country have created positions (e.g., Title IX coordinator), policies, and procedures for handling complaints that fall under the Title IX umbrella. As a part of this increased compliance with the law, colleges and universities have designated all faculty and staff as mandatory reporters of sexual harassment of students in any form (including sexual assault; Holland & Cortina, 2017). Recognizing the unique role the college mental health provider has within the institution, the law does not require college counselors, when acting in their role as mental health providers, to be mandatory reporters (U.S. Department of Education, Office of Civil Rights, 2014). If college counselors are acting outside their role, for example attending a meeting when they are informed of a sexual assault, they become mandatory reporters (Wheeler & Bertram, 2019).

Advocacy and Care

The counseling center can have a positive impact once a Title IX report has been made by ensuring services are offered to both the reporting party (a preferred term for many who report sexual harassment or assaults; Sokolow, 2016) and the accused (Francis & Raleigh, 2017). This is especially relevant for the accused. There are not many secrets on a college campus, especially in the residence halls and related housing (e.g., fraternities and sororities). Once someone is accused of sexual harassment or assault, he (as the majority of sexual assaults on campus are perpetrated by men, the term "he" will be used throughout this section) may be labeled as a monster and often psychologically shunned, shamed, or isolated by various communities on campus. The reporting party can also suffer humiliation, accusations, and repercussions of initiating a report. The impact of this community reaction can range from confusion and self-sabotaging behavior to suicidal ideation (Francis & Raleigh, 2017). This situation can also be an opportunity for the counseling center to provide much needed psychotherapy to help the reporting party and accused understand what is taking place, how she or he got to that place, and what is necessary to move beyond that place. It may also require the college counselor to advocate (see *ACA Code of Ethics*, Standard A.7.a.; ACA, 2014) to ensure that services are offered and that equal treatment is given. Providing this type of care can give rise to conflictual feelings in the counselor concerning the accused. If this is the case, the ethics require the counselor to avoid imposing personal values (see *ACA Code of Ethics*, Standard A.4.b.; ACA, 2014) and to proactively act to deal with the counselor's issues to ensure the client is receiving appropriate care (Shiles, 2009).

Mandatory Assessment and Counseling

A bedrock principle in any codes of ethics in the medical and mental health fields is autonomy (Beauchamp & Childress, 2012). The *ACA Code of Ethics* (ACA, 2014) defines *autonomy* as "fostering the right to control the direction of one's life" (p. 3). Stated differently, autonomy is the right of the individual to choose whether to participate in treatment and have a say in the direction of that treatment. This principle challenges the practice of mandated assessment and counseling of college students. Yet mandated services have been a part of college counseling, as well as mental health work in general, for decades (Kiracofe & Wells, 2007). Most often used for alcohol abuse, concerns about violent behavior, use of illicit drugs and alcohol policy violations, and harassment (sexual, racial, speech; Consolvo & Dannells, 2000), it is important to note the difference between mandated assessment and mandated counseling.

Mandated Assessment

It is not uncommon for students to be brought to the counseling center for assessment because they have expressed some level of suicidal ideation. In fact, for many years colleges and universities have been working to train faculty and staff in identifying suicidal ideation among students, becoming comfortable in asking about suicidal ideation, and making successful referrals to the counseling center (Francis & Horn, 2017; Keyes, 2013) as well as providing decades of programming for the prevention of suicide on college campuses (Drum & Denmark, 2012; Francis & Horn, 2017; Joffe, 2008). In the end, all roads generally lead back to the counseling center, where the college counselor initiates an assessment to determine the level of suicidal ideation and make a determination concerning the next steps to take (entering treatment, hospitalization, etc.).

Violence against college students has been occurring for years both on and off campus (Hart & Miethe, 2011) and has only increased (Francis & Horn, 2017). Since the tragic and horrific events at Virginia Tech and Northern Illinois University, there has been increased vigilance with respect to identifying and evaluating those who express violent ideation or act in violent ways (Davenport, 2009). Once again, the college counselor is called in to make a determination of whether the student is safe as well as whether those around the student are safe (Van Brunt, 2012).

The use and misuse of alcohol and other drugs have also prompted mandatory assessments for college students. In the case of alcohol and other drugs, there are many programs that can be used by counseling center staff to provide both assessment and treatment, although the effects of the intervention are more short-term than long-term (Carey, Scott-Sheldon, Garey, Elliott, & Carey, 2016).

The purpose of an assessment is to "gather information regarding the client for a variety of purposes, including, but not limited to, client decision making, treatment planning, and forensic proceedings" (*ACA Code of Ethics*, Standard E.1.a.; ACA, 2014). When a student is "mandated" or "required" to participate in an assessment, it requires the counselor to take a slightly different approach in the session. This includes consideration of the following:

- *Client autonomy:* One of the foundational principles of all the mental health ethics is autonomy, the right to decide about the direction of one's life. Unless a client is unable to make an independent decision about his or her own care because of incapacity or age, the client has the right to accept or refuse treatment or assessment. Although refusing to participate in an assessment is diagnostic, the client has the right to refuse to participate or give permission to release the results from the assessment. Generally, most students who are a danger to themselves or others want help and are willing to cooperate (Suicide Prevention Resource Center & Education Development Center, 2014; Van Brunt, 2012).
- *Informed consent:* Prior to any assessment or evaluation, the student has a right to be fully informed as to the nature and purposes of what is taking place and why (see

ACA Code of Ethics, Standard E.3.a.; ACA, 2014). This includes being informed about who might have access to the data gathered during the session and the possible uses of those data.
- *Who is the client?* The student is the primary focus of the assessment and the counselor's care. Yet the counselor must take into account the institution that has mandated the assessment for the purposes of making decisions regarding the services that can or will be offered to the student or the student's continuing presence on campus, as in the case of a threat to others. An administrator will most likely receive the results of the assessment (with the student's permission or without permission in the case of incapacity). The counselor has a responsibility to produce a valid and reliable assessment that is understandable to the person reading the report, can be used to benefit the student, and, in many cases, can help ensure the safety of the student and others in the campus community (see *ACA Code of Ethics*, Standard E.3.b.; ACA, 2014).
- *Competence:* Should counselors use any assessment instruments beyond a clinical interview, they are obligated to ensure that they are competent to administer and interpret those assessments. Additionally, they must use only those assessments that are relevant to the situation at hand (see *ACA Code of Ethics*, Standards E.2.a. and E.2.b.; ACA, 2014).
- *Use of results:* Assessments and diagnoses have, in the past, been used in inappropriate ways to discriminate and oppress individuals and groups. Counselors are to be vigilant that the results of any assessments are only used in appropriate ways to the benefit of the client and the community (see *ACA Code of Ethics*, Standard E.5.d.; ACA, 2014). Counselors may refrain from making or reporting a diagnosis if they determine it would cause harm to the client, and they carefully consider the implications, both positive and negative, in making any diagnosis or assessment (see *ACA Code of Ethics*, Standard E.5.d.; ACA, 2014).

There are legal issues to consider when providing an assessment and recommendation that may lead to a student's involuntary removal or withdrawal from the institution. Federal law (i.e., the Americans with Disabilities Act [ADA]) prohibits discrimination against students with disabilities. One of the goals of the ADA is to protect individuals with disabilities from discrimination on the basis of preconceived notions, prejudice, stereotypes, and other unfounded fears (Lannon & Sanghavi, 2011). Implicit to this list are mental illnesses such as depression, anxiety, and bipolar disorders, three of the most common mental health issues presenting in the college population (Francis & Horn, 2017). A student in crisis (e.g., engaging in suicidal behavior) with a mental illness is afforded protection from discrimination due to the students' disability under the ADA to prevent the student's unwarranted removal from campus without proper evaluation, due process, and the consideration of reasonable accommodations (Martin, 2017). Ignoring the ADA places the counselor and college at risk for investigations by the federal government and lawsuits from students and their families (Wheeler & Bertram, 2019).

When a counselor is considering assessments of students with disabilities due to a threat of harm to self or others, it is important to make an objective determination based on the students' ability to safely participate in the regular activities of the institution (e.g., going to class, living in the residence halls, participating in university activities). It must be made on the basis of the most current medical knowledge and the best objective evidence available. In such a case, you are seeking to determine "1) the nature, duration, and severity of the risk; 2) the probability that the injury will occur; and 3) whether reasonable modifications of policies, practices or procedures can mitigate the risk" (Lannon & Sanghavi, 2011, p. 3). If a reasonable accommodation can be made to mitigate the risk, the university is required to implement it. For example, if a student's anxiety and depression, leading to chronic suicidal ideation, is exacerbated by living in the residence halls, removal from the university is an overreaction. The student may be removed from the halls and required to live off campus or in a different hall with less triggering stress (Lannon & Sanghavi, 2011; Martin, 2017).

When the college counselor is involved in the crafting of policies and procedures that govern mandatory or involuntary removal from the university, Lannon and Sanghavi (2011) recommended ensuring these policies include the following:

1. A focus on conduct and not disability. The policies need to be widely administered to all students and should not unfairly focus on those students with disabilities.
2. The practice of individualized assessments must be clear. The assessments include consultation with qualified medical and mental health personnel. Assessments and reports should not be based on any stereotypes or unfounded fears of those with disabilities.
3. Policies must ensure the consideration of reasonable accommodations. Any assessments must also take into consideration reasonable accommodations when necessary.
4. Due process must be offered and followed. Students may be removed from campus in times of immediate threat. Yet, before a final decision is rendered, the university must provide a timely opportunity for the student to be heard. This process must be applied equally to all students.

Finally, it is important to understand that these are hard decisions that have ramifications far beyond the immediate actions taken by both the students in question and the institution. Careful and competent assessments and evaluations must be made for the best possible outcome for the involved students; their classmates, professors, and staff of the university; and their families. It is also important to understand that involuntary withdrawals are relatively rare. It is the action of last resort and considered only in the most acute cases (Grayson & Meilman, 2012).

Mandated Counseling

The use and efficacy of mandated treatment has been debated within the profession for as long as the practice has been implemented (Kiracofe & Wells, 2007). People have been "sent" to counseling by families, spouses, courts, employers, and schools for various reasons and hopeful outcomes (Kiracofe & Buller, 2009). The efficacy of mandated counseling is varied and dependent on the type of treatment offered, the issue of concern, and the motivation of the "client" (Carey et al., 2016; Kiracofe & Buller, 2009).

As previously noted, the major ethical concern is that mandated counseling violates the autonomy rights of the student, especially if the student's continued enrollment is contingent on participating in counseling. Kiracofe and Wells (2007) outlined four problematic ethical and practice issues that arise when students are mandated to counseling through an administrative sanction:

1. Although the administration may see counseling as beneficial to the student, the student may perceive the requirement to attend counseling as onerous and unnecessary. Within the behavioral change process, the student may lack awareness of the impact of his or her actions on others and may not perceive a need to change (precontemplation; Prochaska, Norcross, & DiClemente, 2013). Consequently, the counseling center no longer serves as a place of nonjudgmental acceptance but as an arm of the institution enforcing sanctions on a resistant student.

2. The *ACA Code of Ethics* (ACA, 2014), Standard A.2.a., notes, "Clients have the freedom to choose whether to enter into or remain in a counseling relationship and need adequate information about the counseling process and the counselor." This standard implies that the client has the freedom to choose to enter into a counseling relationship without duress. Even though mandated into counseling, the student has the right to choose not to participate. Yet, by choosing not to enter into the counseling process, the student may be removed from housing, dining facilities, or even from campus. This is not a free choice and violates the principle of autonomy.
3. Counseling is not a panacea for disruptive behavior. Students may be in counseling, working on issues and concerns they have chosen in consultation with the counselor (see *ACA Code of Ethics*, Standard A.1.c.; ACA, 2014), and continue to be a disruptive force within the institution. By forcing the goals to change or mandating an agenda for the counseling sessions, the institution may be interfering with the therapeutic alliance for the sake of its own conduct demands.
4. Counseling centers may be placed in a situation where staff are required to report the student's attendance, his or her progress, or when the student had complied with treatment goals (Kiracofe & Buller, 2009). This undermines the confidential nature of counseling and leaves open the possibility that the counseling center is perceived as a judicial arm of the university. The counselor and the student lose the ability to choose what to share from session, leaving the counselor in the position of reporter rather than treatment provider.

Although mandated counseling has a long history in the mental health world, its success rate with college students for a variety of issues is at best mixed, with the preponderance of the evidence showing no support for its use (Kiracofe & Buller, 2009). Providing psychoeducational material in place of the standard 50-minute therapy session has shown the most promise and allows for fewer ethical conflicts (Van Brunt, Francis, & Raleigh, 2011).

Social Media and Telehealth or Distance Counseling

Social media has permeated our society. From Facebook to Snapchat, the public is using (and abusing) social networking sites (SNSs) at an increasing pace. Public and private companies, government entities, and colleges and universities have a presence on several SNSs. Clients are searching for information about their counselors through SNSs (Kolmes & Taube, 2016; Lehavot, Barnett, & Powers, 2010), and counselors are doing the same, despite ethical standards to the contrary (see *ACA Code of Ethics*, Standard H.6.c.; ACA, 2014; Kolmes & Taube, 2014). Recognizing the increasing use of SNSs and other technological advances, the authors of the *ACA Code of Ethics* expanded the guidance provided on technology and social media (*ACA Code of Ethics*, Section H; ACA, 2014).

College counselors and counseling centers are using SNSs for outreach, announcements, and information sharing (Golightly et al., 2017). Such usage requires that we, as counselors, pay close attention to our professional ethics, because social media and technology are quickly evolving, and the application of the ethics to this evolution is becoming increasingly complex.

Social Media and the Internet

The use of any electronic platform to share information about services, programs, and announcements requires periodic monitoring. Social media, by its very name, is often a give-and-take between two or more people. Yet those who direct counseling centers must realize that the flow of information should be in only one direction, from the counseling center out to the campus. Unless someone is monitoring the SNSs on a 24/7 basis, vital information could be missed, exposed to anyone viewing the site, or misunderstood by others. For example, if the Facebook account of the counseling center allows anyone to post his or her comments, a student may reach out to the center in a time of crisis when no one is monitoring the site (e.g., over the weekend). The crisis may escalate to dangerous levels and leave the student with no one to connect with for help. Another example is that a student could unknowingly announce to the campus that he or she is receiving services from the counseling center by simply posting a question about services on the SNSs.

Good practice and ethics require the leaders of the counseling center to do the following:

- Review any laws, regulations, and rules concerning the use of social media and technology prior to creating a website or SNS.
- Work with the college's information technology department to ensure the security of their site.
- Periodically review any electronic links to ensure they are working and lead to sites with accurate and relevant information.
- Periodically review the privacy settings for all SNSs used by the center, because privacy settings change periodically, leaving one open to settings changing without the knowledge of the account owner.

In general, all counselors who have personal information on an SNS should be aware that clients will search for them through electronic means (Kolmes & Taube, 2016). Increasingly, potential clients are searching for services through sites like *Psychology Today's* therapist finder (https://www.psychologytoday.com/us/therapists/) as well as consumer review sites (Yelp, Healthgrades.com, etc.). A Google search is not limited to a few sites but will encompass the vastness of the internet that includes SNSs. A counselor will want to review the privacy settings of his or her personal SNSs. It is recommended that you implement the highest settings for privacy so that your clients do not get to see you at your grandmother's birthday party or see those pictures from your last vacation. Additionally, many counselors include a statement within their informed consent that they are not available as a "friend" or "contact" via SNSs (see *ACA Code of Ethics*, Standards H.4.b. and H.6.b.; ACA, 2014; Ginory, Sabatier, & Eth, 2012). This helps to create an appropriate boundary between the counselor and the client and sends the message that counseling is a different and professional relationship that encompasses deeply personal sharing but within the confines of a therapeutic setting, not via the pages of someone's Facebook account.

Privacy is a two-way street. While counselors ask their clients to refrain from "friending" them on SNSs, counselors are also to refrain from searching for their clients on the web (see *ACA Code of Ethics*, Standard H.6.c.; ACA, 2014; Kolmes & Taube, 2014). This respect for clients' privacy allows clients the autonomy to decide what they want to share with counselors and what they choose to keep private.

Telehealth or Distance Counseling

Several years ago, a counseling center director I know shared with me her solution to a distance dilemma she faced when a student from her university who was on a 3-week study abroad trip with a group of fellow students suddenly died because of an accident. Her fellow students and the faculty sponsor were devastated. They were in a remote region of the country that they were visiting with little access to phones. With the university's permission, the counseling center director walked into her assistant director's office and asked if she had a valid passport. The next day the assistant director boarded an international flight to provide crisis counseling to the students and faculty sponsor.

Colleges and universities are increasingly sending students to different countries for a semester or more abroad. Additionally, these same institutions are venturing headlong into the world of online learning with many programs either partially or completely online. Finally, many students participate in internships that may take them across state lines to apply what they learned in the classroom to real-life settings. All these realities have at least two things in common: The students are not on campus, and some of them may need counseling services. In other situations, rural or underfunded campuses may not have access to psychiatric care and have utilized telehealth services that allow for real-time consultations via secure online platforms to bring the psychiatrist to campus. These same platforms can be used to provide counseling services that have been shown to be effective and beneficial to both local and far-flung students (Nobleza et al., 2018). This type of service is still in its infancy with only about 10% of counseling centers using this modality for service delivery (Association for University and College Counseling Center Directors, 2016).

This use of technology presents the counseling center with some unique legal, ethical, and practical challenges (Meilman & Weatherford, 2016; Menzano, Goodwin, Rockett, & Morris, 2011). These challenges include the following:

- Addressing the legal issues of providing counseling services across state and international borders.
- Ensuring a secure and confidential internet platform for the provision of counseling services.
- Modifying the informed consent and disclosure form to include the benefits and limitations of distance counseling.
- Limiting distance counseling services to only those issues that can be addressed in this modality.
- Assisting the student in identifying appropriate services if distance counseling cannot be used.
- Ensuring staff competence for working in this medium.
- Creating procedures for emergencies that cannot be addressed through distance counseling.

Distance counseling and telehealth have been shown to be effective for the treatment of anxiety, depression, and posttraumatic stress disorder (Olthuis et al., 2016; Rees & Maclaine, 2015; Thompson et al., 2015). With the continued growth of study abroad programs, internships, and online learning, distance counseling will increasingly be considered as one modality in the counseling center's toolbox (Meilman & Weatherford, 2016).

Advocacy Resources for College Counselors

There are two national membership organizations that focus on college counseling. They provide resources for continuing education, advocacy for our work as college counselors, and information for the public concerning the need for mental health services on the modern college campus. Although membership in professional organizations is not an ethical obligation, it is a good practice because it supports the work of college counselors everywhere.

American College Counseling Association

The ACCA (www.collegecounseling.org) is a division of the ACA and supports those professionals in higher education whose purpose is fostering students' development. It is an interdisciplinary association inclusive of all members of the mental health profession whose goal is to foster student growth through the use of counseling (ACCA, 2017b).

American College Personnel Association

The ACPA (www.myacpa.org) has several focus areas or commissions that encompass a broad range of student affairs practice and services. There are several areas that relate specifically to the practice of counseling in higher education (Counseling and Psychological Services) as well as areas where counselors work in support of college student development (e.g., Academic Support in Higher Education, Career Services, and Wellness; ACPA, 2017).

Conclusion

The college campus presents the mental health professional with many unique situations that are not present in other environments. The counselor may serve in multiple roles on campus; the center itself may not only house the counseling services but also include other related offices that may have different rules and laws governing their use of information; or the counselor may be asked to participate in services that have an impact on the safety and welfare of not just the individual student but also the entire campus community. The practice of counseling on a college campus requires the counselor to thoughtfully apply the ethics to the context of the campus and the best practices of our profession. College counseling is an exciting and challenging profession! You are privileged to be able to help the future of our society in ways that no one else can. Welcome to the profession.

Final Case Study

At the beginning of this chapter you were introduced to Ricardo from Puerto Rico. You were asked to record your answers to a series of questions and to keep those questions and your answers in mind as you read this chapter.

Case Exploration Questions

1. How would you modify any of your answers now that you have completed this chapter?
2. Did your answers become more complex and, if so, how?
3. Reflect on your own cultural development and awareness and how your education is affecting your development as a counselor.

References

American College Counseling Association. (2017a). Bylaws of the American College Counseling Association. Retrieved from www.collegecounseling.org/resources/Documents/ACCA%20Bylaws%202017%20proposed%20revisions%20without%20markings.pdf

American College Counseling Association. (2017b). Mission statement. Retrieved from http://www.collegecounseling.org/Mission-Statement

American College Personnel Association. (2017). Focus areas. Retrieved from http://www.myacpa.org/acpa-engagement#FocusAreas

American Counseling Association. (2014). *ACA code of ethics*. Alexandria, VA: Author.

American Mental Health Counselors Association. (2015). *AMHCA code of ethics*. Alexandria, VA: Author.

Association for University and College Counseling Center Directors. (2016). *The Association for University and College Counseling Directors annual survey*. Retrieved from http://www.auccd.org/public

Beauchamp, T. L., & Childress, J. F. (2012). *Principles of biomedical ethics* (7th ed.). New York, NY: Oxford University Press.

Boonstra, H. D., & Nash, E. (2000). *Minors and the right to consent to health care*. Retrieved from Guttmacher Institute website: https://www.guttmacher.org/gpr/2000/08/minors-and-right-consent-health-care

Caley, C. F., Webber, D., Kurland, M., & Holmes, P. (2010). The role of a psychiatric pharmacist in college health. *Journal of American College Health, 58,* 393–396. Retrieved from http://ezproxy.emich.edu/login?url=https://search.proquest.com/docview/744025042?accountid=10650

Carey, K. B., Scott-Sheldon, L. A. J., Garey, L., Elliott, J. C., & Carey, M. P. (2016). Alcohol interventions for mandated college students: A meta-analytic review. *Journal of Consulting and Clinical Psychology, 84,* 619–632. doi:10.1037/a0040275

Coffman, C., & Barnett, J. E. (2015, October). Informed consent with children and adolescents. Retrieved from http://www.societyforpsychotherapy.org/informed-consent-with-children-and-adolescents

Consolvo, C., & Dannells, M. (2000). Disciplinary counseling: Implications for policy and practice. *NASPA Journal, 38,* 44–57.

Cottone, R. R., & Claus, R. E. (2000). Ethical decision-making models: A review of the literature. *Journal of Counseling & Development, 78,* 275–283. doi:10.1002/j.1556-6676.2000.tb01908.x

Davenport, R. (2009). From college counselor to "risk manager": The evolving nature of college counseling on today's campuses. *Journal of American College Health, 58,* 181–183. doi:10.1080/07448480903221244

Deisinger, G., Ransazzo, M., O'Neill, D., & Savage, J. (2008). *The handbook for campus threat assessment and management teams*. Stoneham, MA: Applied Risk Management.

Dewan, M. J., Steenbarger, B. N., & Greenberg, R. P. (2012). *The art and science of brief psychotherapies: An illustrated guide*. Arlington, VA: American Psychiatric Press.

Drum, D. J., & Denmark, A. B. (2012). Campus suicide prevention: Bridging paradigms and forging partnerships. *Harvard Review of Psychiatry, 20,* 209–221. doi:10.3109/10673229.2012.712841

Edwards, J., & Lenhart, A. (2015). *ACCA Community College Survey (2015)*. Retrieved from American College Counseling Association website: http://www.collegecounseling.org/resources/Documents/ACCA-Community-College-Survey-2014-15-Final.pdf

Eells, G. T., & Rockland-Miller, H. S. (2011). Assessing and responding to disturbed and disturbing students: Understanding the role of administrative teams in institutions of higher education. *Journal of College Student Psychotherapy, 25,* 8–23. doi:10.1080/87568225.2011.532470

Family Educational Rights and Privacy Act of 1974, 20 U.S.C. § 1232g (1974).

Family Educational Rights and Privacy Act Regulations, 34 C.F.R. § Part 99 (2004).

Francis, P. C. (2000). Practicing ethically as a college counselor. In D. C. Davis & K. M. Humphrey (Eds.), *College counseling: Issues and strategies for a new millennium* (pp. 71–86). Alexandria, VA: American Counseling Association.

Francis, P. C., & Dugger, S. M. (2014). Professionalism, ethics, and value-based conflicts in counseling: An introduction to the special section. *Journal of Counseling & Development, 92,* 131–134. doi:10.1002/j.1556-6676.2014.00138.x

Francis, P. C., & Horn, A. S. (2017). Mental health issues and counseling services in U.S. higher education: An overview of recent research and recommended practices. *Higher Education Policy, 30,* 263–277.

Francis, P. C., & Raleigh, M. J. (2017, February). *Providing clinical care in ethically challenging times*. Paper presented at the meeting of the American College Counseling Association, Tampa, FL.

Gallagher, R. P. (2014). *National survey of college counseling center directors*. Retrieved from www.collegecounseling.org

Ginory, A., Sabatier, L. M., & Eth, S. (2012). Addressing therapeutic boundaries in social networking. *Psychiatry, 75,* 40–48. doi:10.1521/psyc.2012.75.1.40

Golightly, T., Thorne, K., Iglesias, A., Huebner, E., Michaelson-Chmelir, T., Yang, J., & Greco, K. (2017). Outreach as intervention: The evolution of outreach and preventive programming on college campuses. *Psychological Services, 14,* 451–460. doi:10.1037/ser0000198

Grayson, P., & Meilman, P. (2012). Mandatory leaves in limbo. *Journal of College Student Psychotherapy, 26,* 253–255. doi:10.1080/87568225.2012.711132

Hart, T. C., & Miethe, T. D. (2011). Violence against college students and its situational contexts: Prevalence, patterns, and policy implications. *Victims & Offenders, 6,* 157–180. doi:10.1080/15564886.2011.557324

Hodges, S. J. (2017). Career and academic counseling and auxiliary services. In S. J. Hodges, K. Shelton, & M. M. K. Lyn (Eds.), *The college and university counseling manual: Integrating essential services across the campus* (pp. 65–88). New York, NY: Springer.

Holland, K. J., & Cortina, L. M. (2017). The evolving landscape of Title IX: Predicting mandatory reporters' responses to sexual assault disclosures. *Law and Human Behavior, 41,* 429–439. doi:10.1037/lhb0000253

Iarussi, M. M., & Shaw, B. M. (2016). A collaborative process model for promoting successful referrals in college counseling. *Journal of College Counseling, 19,* 261–275. doi:10.1002/jocc.12048

International Association of Marriage and Family Counselors. (2017). *IAMFC code of ethics.* Alexandria, VA: Author.

Jane Doe v. University of Oregon, et al., Case No. 6:15-cv-00042-MC (D. Or. 2015).

Joffe, P. (2008). An empirically supported program to prevent suicide in a college student population. *Suicide & Life-Threatening Behavior, 38,* 87–103.

Kettmann, J. D. J., Schoen, E. G., Moel, J. E., Cochran, S. V., Greenberg, S. T., & Corkery, J. M. (2007). Increasing severity of psychopathology at counseling centers: A new look. *Professional Psychology: Research and Practice, 38,* 523–529. doi:10.1037/0735-7028.38.5.523

Keyes, L. (2013). Suicide and its prevention on college campuses. *Alabama Counseling Journal, 38,* 3–8.

Kiracofe, N. M., & Buller, A. E. (2009). Mandated disciplinary counseling: Working effectively with challenging clients. *Journal of College Counseling, 12,* 71–84. doi:10.1002/j.2161-1882.2009.tb00041.x

Kiracofe, N. M., & Wells, L. (2007). Mandated disciplinary counseling on campus: Problems and possibilites. *Journal of Counseling & Development, 85,* 259–268. doi:10.1002/j.1556-6678.2007.tb00473.x

Kolmes, K., & Taube, D. O. (2014). Seeking and finding our clients on the internet: Boundary considerations in cyberspace. *Professional Psychology: Research and Practice, 45,* 3–10. doi:10.1037/a0029958

Kolmes, K., & Taube, D. O. (2016). Client discovery of psychotherapist personal information online. *Professional Psychology: Research and Practice, 47,* 147–154. doi:10.1037/pro0000065

Lannon, P., & Sanghavi, E. (2011, November 1). New Title II regulations regarding direct threat: Do they change how colleges and universities should treat students who are threats to themselves? *NACUANOTES, 10(1).*

Lehavot, K., Barnett, J. E., & Powers, D. (2010). Psychotherapy, professional relationships, and ethical considerations in the myspace generation. *Professional Psychology: Research and Practice, 41,* 160–166. doi:10.1037/a0018709

Lyn, M. M. K. (2017). Integrating the counseling center into the broader campus. In S. J. Hodges, K. Shelton, & M. M. K. Lyn (Eds.), *The college and university counseling manual: Integrating essential services across the campus* (pp. 289–304). New York, NY: Springer.

Mangan, K. (2015, March 5). Just how private are college students' campus counseling records? *The Chronicle of Higher Education*. Retrieved from https://www.chronicle.com/article/Just-How-Private-Are-College/228229

Martin, D. (2017). Higher education institutions' treatment of students deemed a "direct threat" to themselves and the ADA. *Northwestern Journal of Law & Social Policy, 12*, 111–129.

Meilman, P. W., & Weatherford, R. D. (2016). "Wait! Can you do this too?!?": College counseling and distance education. *Journal of College Student Psychotherapy, 30*, 1–3. doi:10.1080/87568225.2016.1105636

Menzano, S., Goodwin, A., Rockett, G., & Morris, K. (2011). Practical, ethical, and legal considerations regarding videocounseling in college and university counseling centers: A response to Quarto's "Influencing college students' perceptions of videocounseling." *Journal of College Student Psychotherapy, 25*, 326–333. doi:10.1080/87568225.2011.605695

Much, K., & Swanson, A. L. (2010). The debate about increasing college student psychopathology: Are college students really getting "sicker?" *Journal of College Student Psychotherapy, 24*, 86–97. doi:10.1080/87568220903558570

National Behavioral Intervention Team Association. (2017). Behavioral intervention teams. Retrieved from nabita.org/behavioral-intervention-team/

National Center for Education Statistics. (2017). Fast facts: Enrollment. Retrieved from https://nces.ed.gov/fastfacts/display.asp?id=98

National Student Clearinghouse Research Center. (2019). *Current term enrollment estimates: Spring 2019*. Herndon, VA: Author. Retrieved from https://nscresearchcenter.org/currenttermenrollmentestimate-spring2019/

Nobleza, D., Hagenbaugh, J., Blue, S., Stepchin, A., Vergare, M., & Pohl, C. A. (2018). The use of telehealth by medical and other health professional students at a college counseling center. *Journal of College Student Psychotherapy, 33*, 275–289. doi:10.1080/87568225.2018.1491362

Olthuis, J. V., Wozney, L., Asmundson, G. J. G., Cramm, H., Lingley-Pottie, P., & McGrath, P. J. (2016). Distance-delivered interventions for PTSD: A systematic review and meta-analysis. *Journal of Anxiety Disorders, 44*, 9–26. doi:10.1016/j.janxdis.2016.09.010

Owen, J., Devdas, L., & Rodolfa, E. (2007). University counseling center off-campus referrals: An exploratory investigation. *Journal of College Student Psychotherapy, 22*, 13–29. doi:10.1300/J035v22n02_03

Owen, J., Smith, A., & Rodolfa, E. (2009). Clients' expected number of counseling sessions, treatment effectiveness, and termination status: Using empirical evidence to inform session limit policies. *Journal of College Student Psychotherapy, 23*, 118–134. doi:10.1080/87568220902743660

Prochaska, J. O., Norcross, J. C., & DiClemente, C. C. (2013). Applying the stages of change. In G. P. Koocher, J. C. Norcross, & B. A. Greene (Eds.), *Psychologists' desk reference* (3rd ed., pp. 176–181). New York, NY: Oxford University Press.

Rees, C. S., & Maclaine, E. (2015). A systematic review of videoconference-delivered psychological treatment for anxiety disorders. *Australian Psychologist, 50*, 259–264. doi:10.1111/ap.12122

Reetz, D. R., Krylowicz, B., & Mistler, B. (2014). *The Association for University and College Counseling Center Directors annual survey*. Retrieved from AUCCCD website: http://www.aucccd.org/assets/documents/2014%20aucccd%20monograph%20-%20public%20pdf.pdf

Schwartz, A. J. (2016). Session limits and the probability of the next visit. *Journal of College Student Psychotherapy, 30*, 238–251. doi:10.1080/87568225.2016.1219609

Sharkin, B. S. (2012). *Being a college counselor on today's campus: Roles, contributions, and special challenges*. New York, NY: Routledge.

Shiles, M. (2009). Discriminatory referrals: Uncovering a potential ethical dilemma facing practitioners. *Ethics & Behavior, 19,* 142–155. doi:10.1080/10508420902772777

Sokolow, B. A. (2016). Understand the rights of those impacted by discrimination under Title IX. In M. A. Paludi (Ed.), *Campus action against sexual assault: Needs, policies, procedures, and training programs* (pp. 3–7). Santa Barbara, CA: Praeger/ABC-CLIO.

Suicide Prevention Resource Center & Education Development Center. (2014). *Assessing and managing suicide risk: Core competencies for behavior health mental health professionals.* Washington, DC: Author.

Thompson, N. J., Patel, A. H., Selwa, L. M., Stoll, S. C., Begley, C. E., Johnson, E. K., & Fraser, R. T. (2015). Expanding the efficacy of Project UPLIFT: Distance delivery of mindfulness-based depression prevention to people with epilepsy. *Journal of Consulting and Clinical Psychology, 83,* 304–313. doi:10.1037/a0038404

Title IX, Education Amendments of 1972, 20 U.S.C. § 1681–1688 (1972).

U.S. Department of Education. (2016). *Digest of educational statistics, 2015.* Washington, DC: Author. Retrieved from https://nces.ed.gov/fastfacts/display.asp?id=84

U.S. Department of Education, Office of Civil Rights. (2014). *Questions and answers on Title IX and sexual violence.* Washington, DC: Author.

Van Brunt, B. (2012). *Ending campus violence: New approaches to prevention.* New York, NY: Routledge.

Van Brunt, B., Francis, P. C., & Raleigh, M. J. (2011, February). *Mandated educational programs: Suicide, aggression, and domestic violence.* Paper presented at the meeting of the Georgia College Counseling Association, St. Simon Island, GA.

Van Brunt, B., Reese, A., & Lewis, W. S. (2015). *The NaBITA 2015 Whitepaper: Who's on the team? Mission, membership, and motivation.* Berwyn, PA: Author.

Wheeler, A. M., & Bertram, B. (2019). *The counselor and the law: A guide to legal and ethical practice* (8th ed.). Alexandria, VA: American Counseling Association.

Wies, J. R. (2015). Title IX and the state of campus sexual violence in the United States: Power, policy, and local bodies. *Human Organization, 74,* 276–286.

Collaborative Services in College Counseling

Chapter 5

Understanding the Student Affairs Context

Alan M. Schwitzer and Dana Burnett

Ultimately student personnel workers are concerned that students become mature and competent persons. Student personnel work requires a comprehensive view of the development of the person.

—Knefelkamp, Widick, and Parker (1978), p. viii

■ ■ ■

Reflection Exercise

This chapter introduces 2- and 4-year college and university counseling in the campus student affairs context. Consider the following questions as you begin the chapter:

1. What were your own higher education experiences regarding your campus's student affairs professionals?
2. Did you reside on campus? Off campus? In Greek housing?
3. Did you participate in student activities? Were you a student leader?
4. Did you require the assistance of the counseling center or health center?
5. Did you engage in the activities of campus centers specifically focused on the experiences of female students? Students of color? Faith-based student groups?
6. Were you an athlete, military student, or nontraditional-age student?
7. How did your own experience of student affairs influence your decision to pursue a college counseling or student affairs career today?

■ ■ ■

College counseling is a specialized professional field providing services associated with mental health needs in a specific context: the higher education setting (Rudd, 2004; Sharkin, 2012). Furthermore, in this institutional setting, counseling centers usually operate within a specific organizational framework: divisions of student affairs. Student affairs divisions in American higher education provide services to address students' academic learning as well as their personal needs and life-span development. They work on campus in partnership with their institution's division of academic affairs, which focuses more closely on the primary objective of colleges and universities: academic education of students in their majors and disciplines (Schuh, Jones, Harper, & Associates, 2011). Understanding these parameters is essential to a successful college counseling career. Thus, building on our earlier chapters that described the foundations and history of college counseling, we will now address the student affairs context.

College counseling professionals—including professional counselors, along with psychologists, clinical social workers, psychiatrists, and others who work in counseling centers, mental health centers, health centers, and other student affairs and academic support offices across 2- and 4-year campuses—tend to be most visible during crises like the 1966 Texas Tower shooting at the University of Texas at Austin; the 2005 impact of Hurricane Katrina on Dillard, Loyola, Tulane, and other Gulf States campuses; and the 2007 Virginia Tech violence in Blacksburg; however, they serve student adjustment, development, and mental health needs every day (Schwitzer & Vaughn, 2017). An estimated 2,000,000 students nationwide visit their college counseling centers and millions more visit campus health centers and other student services annually (Gallagher, 2014; Turner & Keller, 2015). As a result, college counseling and student affairs professionals working in every corner of the campus—both inside and outside the counseling center walls—address the acute crisis as well as common adjustment and developmental issues affecting student wellness and success (Reynolds, 2011).

As we have said previously, the audience for this text is all future and current professionals who want to support the mental health and wellness of college students, whether as college counselors or student affairs professionals. This chapter is designed to increase all readers' understanding of the institutional setting in which they work—the campus. First, the chapter introduces divisions of student affairs, including the definition, purposes, and structures of such divisions. Next, the diverse array of higher education institutions in which counselors might be employed is described. Public and private, and small and large colleges and universities are considered. Campuses identified primarily by their population dynamics are reviewed, including historically Black colleges and universities (HBCUs), Hispanic-serving institutions (HSIs), predominantly White institutions (PWIs), and women's colleges. Furthermore, because community colleges educate about 44% of undergraduate students in the United States (American Association of Community Colleges, 2009), both 2-year and 4-year campuses are addressed. The chapter then outlines the scope of student support work in the college context. This scope includes supporting student adjustment, development, mental health, and wellness goals in the context of institutional academic missions. Finally, we offer an encouraging discussion of the ways counseling and student affairs professionals can adapt their skills for either setting or to work more effectively together.

College and University Division of Student Affairs: Background and Origins

In an address to the opening session of a 1987 joint conference of the American College Personnel Association (ACPA) and the National Association of Student Personnel Administrators (NASPA), outgoing ACPA president Judith Chambers remarked that "the intent of student affairs has always been to connect people who need with people who care" (as cited in Rhatigan, 2009). The 1987 joint conference was held in Chicago to celebrate the 50th anniversary of *The Student Personnel Point of View* (American Council on Education, 1937), which was described in Chapter 1. *The Student Personnel Point of View* document reflects a humanist perspective for the student affairs profession and captures a philosophy that has served as the foundation of the student development profession ever since it was written more than 80 years ago. In the words of the document that was published as the outcome of the Conference on the Philosophy and Development of Student Personnel Work in College and University, sponsored by the American Council on Education (1937),

> It is the task of colleges and universities . . . to assist the student in developing to the limits of his [sic] potentialities, and in making his contribution to the betterment of society. This philosophy imposes upon educational institutions the obligation to consider the student as a whole—his intellectual capacity and achievement, his social relationships, his vocational aptitudes and skills, his moral and religious values, his economic resources, and his aesthetic appreciation. [The philosophy] puts emphasis . . . upon the development of the student as a person rather than upon his intellectual training alone. (p. 1)

Twenty-first century American higher education evolved from 17th- and 18th-century colonial colleges, whose mission was to train future leaders and learned clergy, enrolling only a small percentage of the population—mostly White males of higher socioeconomic status. At these small, exclusive institutions faculty not only taught the classes and provided institutional leadership but they also provided whatever student support was available. President James Garfield, who graduated from Williams College when Mark Hopkins was the Williams president, described the ideal college of the era as "Mark Hopkins on one end of a log and a student on the other" (*American Authors 1600–1900*, Kunitz & Haycraft, 1977, p. 384). It was not until the middle of the 19th century and a new, pragmatic mission for American colleges—the training of students to engage in the "agricultural and mechanical arts" (Morrill Land-Grant College Act of 1862)—that the roots of the 21st-century student affairs organizations were planted. The evolution of colleges and universities continued with the second Morrill Act in 1890 (Agricultural College Act of 1890), which specified that public land-grant institutions for Black students should be established (given their exclusion from the predominantly White institutions of the day). Subsequently, the Higher Education Act of 1965 established the HBCU designation to include "any historically black college or university that was established prior to 1964, whose principal mission was, and is, the education of Black Americans, and that is accredited by a nationally recognized accrediting agency or associations" (U.S. Department of Education, 2019). Today's HBCUs are open to students regardless of race. Likewise, the Higher Education Act of 1965 included the category of Tribal Colleges for the first time. Subsequently, HSIs were formally recognized by Congress in 1992 (Espinosa, Turk, & Taylor, 2017).

The modern student affairs organization's lineage can be traced to three distinct origins: deans of men, deans of women, and personnel workers. Harvard University appointed the first dean of men in 1870 (Mueller, 1961). The primary function of the dean, in addition to teaching, was student discipline and enrollment of students. With the growth of land-grant and public universities came an increase in the number of enrolled women. Coeducation created the perceived need for deans of women to deal with the anticipated undesirable outcomes of the mixing of the sexes on college campuses. According to Horace Mann, who became president of Antioch College and an advocate for the enrollment of women in colleges, "The advantages of a joint education are great. The dangers of it are terrible" (Fley, 1966, p. 108). The third ancestor of current student affairs professionals was personnel workers whose job was to guide students into appropriate careers.

Modern Student Affairs Divisions: Definition and Purpose

During the latter half of the 20th century and especially in the current millennium, as the student profile in our colleges and universities has become more diverse, the philosophy embedded in the 1937 *Student Personnel Point of View* statement has served as the foundation for the development of specialized theories and practices that have provided support for women; students of color; adult students; students placed at risk by circumstances; students who are lesbian, gay, bisexual, transgender, queer, questioning, intersex, plus other identities; and others who were only marginally represented when the statement was crafted. Among the student affairs support that has evolved to serve 21st-century college students is that provided by counseling services.

The two major student affairs professional organizations are NASPA, Student Affairs Administrators in Higher Education; and ACPA, College Student Educators International. In 2010 these organizations appointed a joint task force to consider the future of student affairs as a profession. In its report, *Learning Reconsidered: A Campus-wide Focus on the Student Experience* (NASPA, 2004), the task force began by reviewing the work of similar groups that had gone before them. *The Student Personnel Point of View*—both the 1937 and 1949 versions—defined the role of student affairs as the delivery of services enhancing educational experiences of college students and defined the context of student affairs work in terms of institutional and societal values (American Council on Education, 1937). These early definitions of our roles in student affairs evolved as the student affairs profession evolved and began not only to base its work on the provision of services and support but also to base the nature of this support on theoretical concepts that govern the psychological and emotional development of college students. Then, during the early years of the new millennium, the focus of the student affairs profession shifted again to echo the statements contained in much earlier definitions of our profession. This professional evolution culminated in a landmark publication published jointly by ACPA and NASPA, *Learning Reconsidered* (2004), which argued for "the integration of all of higher education's resources in the education and preparation of the whole student" (p. 1).

Student Affairs and Its Relationship to Institutional Mission

Each degree-granting institution has a mission statement, which usually describes the unique goals of the institution. For example, the mission and goals of a community college will necessarily differ from those of a baccalaureate college, which will differ from the goals of a research university. Institutional goals, derived from an institution's mission, will influence the nature of the professional work for each student affairs organization, including the counseling center staff. Later in this chapter, some examples are provided of how institutional missions can vary significantly. See Box 5.1.

To accomplish the humanistic mission of a student affairs organization, a hierarchical and functional structure is needed (Kuk & Banning, 2009, p. 100). Depending on institutional size, the organization is led by a senior student affairs officer, usually at the vice-presidential level. On large campuses, there are often associate vice presidents heading multiple functional areas. In their study, Kuk and Banning (2009) found a marked diversity in the functional areas included within the student affairs organizations responding to their survey.The most frequent functions included were (in descending order) counseling services (97.4%), residence life (81.8%), career services (77.9%), health services (70.1%), student activities (70.1%), student centers (70.1%), campus recreation, (64.9%), judicial af-

BOX 5.1

Spotlight: The Community College Counseling Workplace

Like the college counseling and student affairs fields, this chapter focuses heavily on the 4-year college and university context. However, campus professionals should not overlook the critical role that community colleges, 2-year colleges, junior colleges, and other prebachelor's institutions fill in American higher education—or the important college counseling and student development work that happens on these campuses. Tracing their origins to 1902 as a division of the Joliet, Illinois, high school division, today there are more than 1,100 community colleges, and they enroll 45% of students seeking associate's, bachelor's, and graduate degrees in the United States (American Association of Community Colleges, 2014). Also, most of these campuses, 85%, employ counseling professionals to address student mental health needs and to fill other student affairs roles (American College Counseling Association [ACCA], 2013).

As with 4-year institutions, students with diagnosable disorders constitute the greatest source of demand for services on 2-year campuses, where 44% of counseling clients present severe psychological concerns—the most common of which are depressive disorders, anxiety and obsessive-compulsive disorders, bipolar disorder, attention-deficit/hyperactivity disorder, and posttraumatic stress disorder (ACCA, 2013; Gallagher, 2014; Jenks Kettmann et al., 2007). In turn, community college counselors commonly offer screening programs for depression, anxiety, and posttraumatic stress disorder (ACCA, 2013). At the same time, community college counseling roles are numerous and varied. College counselors on 2-year campuses can expect to go beyond traditional mental health counseling and work outside the counseling center walls. This aspect of community college counseling includes providing academic and career support, student development programming, and other services that contribute to the institution's goals and the needs of its learners (ACCA, 2013; Gallagher, 2014). In summary, "counseling professionals use a wide spectrum of skills and tools as they implement 2-year college missions and seek community college student outcomes" (Schwitzer, Pribesh, Ellis-O'Quinn, Huber, & Wilmer, 2016, p. 78).

fairs (62.3%), academic advising (58.4%), disability services (58.4%), multicultural services (58.4%), dean of students (58.4%), and enrollment services (50.7%).

The 21st century has created a new focus for student and academic affairs—student retention and graduation. As a result, some contemporary names of functional areas not found in most student affairs divisions at the beginning of the millennium include student success centers, offices of assessment and institutional effectiveness, and more expansive services for specialized populations on campus. Although the humanistic lens still predominates in the student affairs profession, those who manage institutional budgets and allocate increasingly scarce resources want to know what the demonstrated return on investment is for all student support services, including those allocated to counseling services.

Prototypical Division of Student Affairs on Today's Campuses

As we have been describing, divisions of student affairs usually provide the organizational home for college and university counseling centers, among many other services aimed at supporting the development and wellness of college students. On the one hand, the specific composition of a campus's division of student affairs depends on its student demographic makeup and other constituent characteristics as well as on its dynamics as a research university, 4-year college, liberal arts institution, or community college (Kuk & Banning, 2009). On the other hand, the prototypical student affairs division on an American college campus can be described (a) as being led by a senior student affairs office and (b) as comprising an array of common student services.

Senior Student Affairs Office

At the top of the student affairs organizational chart is the senior student affairs office. On specific campuses, this office might be described alternatively as a vice president's office (vice president of student affairs, associate vice president for student affairs, vice chancellor) or a dean's office (dean of students, dean of men or women). The function of the chief student affairs office's personnel is to provide leadership, management, and oversight for all of the institution's student affairs functions. In this office, the chief officer and the office's staff are responsible for organizational planning, assessment, and inter- and intra-organizational mediation and functioning, as well as professional development and support to enable student affairs personnel—including college counseling professionals—to perform their roles as student educators. Under its management function, this chief office is accountable for student affairs budgeting and resource procurement and management; personnel hiring; the evaluation process for staff members; the evaluation and creation of policy, especially those policies related to students; and communication with the president and other members of the executive staff to keep them informed about challenges and accomplishments of the division. Successful chief student affairs offices usually carry out their duties and make decisions and recommendations to members of the institution's executive staff using evidence-based data and with the collaboration of knowledgeable professionals—including counseling center directors and leaders—throughout the division.

Chief student affairs offices are essential partners for counseling centers and their directors in such critical areas as management of student demand for services (Schwartz, 2016); student help seeking and attrition (Marsh & Wilcoxon, 2015); mental health crisis management (J. B. Bishop, 2016); threat assessment and behavioral disturbances (Meilman, 2016; Pollard, Flynn, & Eells, 2015); recruitment, hiring, supervision, and evaluation of center staff (J. B. Bishop, 2016); and demonstration of counseling center outcomes with respect to institutional missions (Schwitzer, 2002).

Common Student Affairs Offices and Services

College counseling professionals are likely to partner with division of student affairs colleagues operating out of offices and services designed to promote and support student matriculation, manage the student living and student life experience, respond to student health and mental health needs, support student academic and career success, address the needs of specialized campus populations, and promote student development and campus engagement. Table 5.1 summarizes the student affairs offices and services that college counseling professionals are most likely to encounter (Kuk & Banning, 2009).

Faculty and Divisional Colleagues: Further Influences on the Work of College Counseling Professionals

In addition to the formal structures and processes comprising a student affairs division, on most college campuses, faculty have the most frequent contact with the broadest number of students. The focus on identifying students who may be experiencing academic or emotional difficulty, and doing so as early as possible, typically involves faculty and student

TABLE 5.1

Partial Sample of Most Common Student Affairs Division Offices and Services

Organizational Role and Student Affairs Office or Service	*% of Campuses*
Promote and support student matriculation	
Admissions	35
Financial aid	35
Orientation	34
First year/new student programs	31
Manage the student living and student life experience	
Resident life	81
Judicial affairs	62
Greek life	44
Respond to student health and mental health needs	
Counseling centers	97
Health centers	70
Disability services	58
Wellness programs	31
Alcohol and drug services	12
Support student academic and career success	
Career centers	78
Academic advising and support services	58
Learning centers	23
Student assessment services	19
Address the needs of specialized populations	
Multicultural student services	58
International student services	40
Women's centers	16
LGBTQ services	16
Adult student programs	12
Veterans services	12
Promote student development and campus engagement	
Student activities	70
Student centers	70
Student recreation	65
Athletics	27

Note. From "Designing Student Affairs Organizational Structures: Perceptions of Senior Student Affairs Officers," by L. Kuk and J. Banning, 2009, *NASPA Journal, 46*(1), 102–103. Copyright 2009 by National Association of Student Personnel Administrators. Reprinted with permission. LGBTQ = lesbian, gay, bisexual, transgender, and queer/questioning.

affairs staff, including representatives from counseling services. Informal means for assessing environmental factors that may pose impediments to student success are available through student affairs staff meetings and ad hoc meetings with other student affairs staff. Often those who directly provide support services and manage activities for students are in an optimum position to assess the institution's environmental obstacles that have an impact on student emotional wellness and the ultimate success of students (Shaffer, 2009). Thus, collaboration on campus is key, as will be explored further in Chapter 6.

Institutions, Their Characteristics, and Their Divisions of Student Affairs: Different Sizes and Shapes, Similar Issues

As college counselors, our employment experiences are influenced in part by the type of institution in which we work. Some of the most common distinctions are those made among 2- and 4-year; public and private; small and large; HBCUs, HSIs, PWIs, and Tribal colleges; and women's colleges.

The size and the shape of a student affairs division are largely determined by the institutional mission. But some issues that are foremost on the minds of student affairs leaders are similar from one campus to another and from one type of campus to another. Student affairs staff on 2-year, 4-year, public, private, small campus and large, HBCU, HSI, Tribal, or PWI colleges all are apparently focused on a similar set of issues. In the Spring 2016 issue of *New Directions for Student Services*, in an article entitled *What Troubles You? What Keeps You Up at Night?*, on the basis of surveys of student affairs leaders, Elizabeth Whitt and Larry Roper described the types of issues that are universal to campuses of all types, sizes, and student profiles (Roper & Whitt, 2016):

- *Affordability and access*—including the cost of attendance and access to the means for academic success (retention and completion)
- *Student health and well-being*—including student health and well-being, mental health and wellness, and campus and student safety
- *Diversity and inclusion*—increasing diversity doesn't necessarily mean greater inclusion; appropriate institutional responses to increasing diversity of our student bodies
- *Regulations and compliance*—issues of compliance and Title IX in particular
- *Technology and media*—the impact of digital and social media, the impact on campuses of the 24-hour news cycle
- *Student affairs leadership*—including the role and voice for issues affecting student affairs, evidence of the effectiveness of student affairs programs and services, and professional performance and identity

Along with the shared themes we have just discussed, student affairs divisions also vary according to their institutional context. For example, promoting diversity and inclusion for students at a PWI and at an HBCU would not look the same. Affordability and access are key to the mission of most community colleges, and the implementation of those ideas would be different at a highly selective private college. Appropriate responses to student health and well-being depend greatly on the profile of the students on each campus, including their relevant stressors and strengths. The following section describes some of the most common institutional types and some illustrations of how the different missions may influence student affairs and college counseling work.

The Carnegie Classification of Institutions of Higher Education

The Carnegie Classification of Institutions of Higher Education (Indiana University Center for Postsecondary Research, n.d.; http://carnegieclassifications.iu.edu/) is the standard framework for describing U.S. colleges and universities. The Carnegie basic framework includes research universities, comprehensive colleges/universities, liberal arts colleges, and community colleges. Although it is understandable that counseling services at each of these institutional types may be different, there is likely to be as much variation within each type as there is between types when we overlay considerations such as institutional size and whether the institution is private or public, secular or religious, predominantly residential or commuter, predominantly White or minority serving, ethnically diverse or homogeneous, and so forth. An examination of an institution's mission may provide a more accurate way of understanding the theoretical foundation that has guided the development and the provision of counseling services on a given campus. As an example, review the institutional and counseling center mission statements for the following campuses.

Hampton University, a well-known, historically Black private university, describes its mission as providing "an educational experience of exceptional quality at the undergraduate, graduate, and professional levels to students of high academic standing and potential with particular emphasis upon educational opportunities for Black students" (institutional website: http://www.hamptonu.edu/). Counseling services at this university describes its goals as follows: "University Counseling Services supports the mission of the University through the delivery of psychological services, crisis intervention, clinical training, testing, research, and alcohol/drug prevention and education. The goal of UCS is to help students maximize their personal development and navigate through their academic challenges."

Spartanburg Community College (institutional website: https://www.sccsc.edu/) describes its mission as providing "exceptional, accessible, learning centered education and workforce development programs and services." Counseling services on this 2-year campus "provides solution-focused, student-centered counseling services to enhance personal growth and development."

Mission statements for institutions and for counseling services are an excellent way to gauge what both are all about! See Box 5.2.

BOX 5.2

Spotlight: Community College Missions and College Counseling

Community college settings are likely to be a close fit for college counselors with a propensity for social justice goals. This is because, first, 2-year campuses maintain open-access enrollment practices that support a community college mission of providing students with equitable academic opportunity (Vaughan, 2006). In practical terms, as a result of the community college open enrollment, equitable-access mission, 2-year campuses typically serve a remarkably wide range of populations (Bulger & Watson, 2006). These populations include

> traditional-age late adolescent and young adult students, nontraditional-age learners across the adult life span, first-generation and underprepared college students, high-success university-bound learners, single parents and economically disadvantaged families, individuals with academic and social adjustment needs, midcareer dislocated workers, and culturally diverse communities (Schwitzer, Pribesh, Ellis-O'Quinn, Huber, & Wilmer, 2016, p. 77).

The second component of the community college mission is workforce development, with these campuses "serving as catalysts for economic transformation and workforce development in communities with high unemployment due to historical or prolonged economic depression . . . or large numbers of displaced workers due to recent, severe economic downturns (Schwitzer, Duggan, Laughlin, & Walker, 2011). Third, in comparison with 4-year institutions, the community college mission often includes extensive involvement with local K–12 school systems, whereby they offer "dual high school/college enrollment programs, GED and technical training programs, and associate degrees and prep programs leading from high school to 4-year institutions" (Schwitzer et al., 2016, p. 78). As a result, professionals in community college settings use not only their psychotherapeutic skills but also career, life-span, and academic tools to contribute to the open-access, workforce-development, and academic-opportunity missions their institutions fill in their local communities.

Following from the community college mission, a key organizational feature of 2-year colleges that positively influences the work life of college counselors and the roles they fill on campus is the extensive collaboration that usually exists between academic affairs and student affairs. Here, "the community college sector [leads] the way in the formation of strong, vibrant student and academic affairs partnerships as well as partnerships with external constituencies in the development and advancement of educational outcomes" (Bourassa & Kruger, 2002). In fact, many community colleges have combined responsibility for the two functions in one executive-level officer (McClellan, 2004).

College Adjustment, Student Development, Health and Mental Health Needs, and Wellness: Serving Students, Their Goals, and Their Institutions' Missions

So far in this chapter, we have reviewed the organizational context in which college counseling professionals conduct their work housed most often in divisions of student affairs and contributing specifically to the experiences of students and clients at higher educational institutions. These contexts have a direct influence on the scope and nature of the work college counselors provide, which is different than community mental health, hospitals, or K–12 schools as a setting. Campus offices such as counseling and mental health centers, health centers, and other student affairs support services are expected to effectively promote student well-being and the institutional mission (Schuh, 2011; Schwitzer, 1997, 2002, 2009).

Supporting Institutional Missions: Providing Effective Support

In fact, several different constituencies, in and surrounding the institution, have an investment in the outcomes that student support services produce in response to student needs (Schwitzer, 1997, 2002, 2009). First, institutional leaders such as presidents, provosts, and vice presidents of student affairs (or deans of students) tend to be most interested "in questions about academics, retention, and student success outcomes" (Schwitzer, 2002, p. 183). Accreditation bodies, state legislatures, and public scrutiny from parents and others all emphasize the importance of student services that promote student learning and success. Ideally, such services should demonstrate "the strongest resource-to-student-outcomes possible" (p. 183). Second, student affairs divisions tend to adopt a student-centered perspective that is informed by developmental theory (Evans, Forney, Guido, Patton, & Renn, 2010).

When counseling practitioners and student affairs professionals adopt a student-centered perspective, they hope to produce student experiences that are based on "conceptually derived relationships between (a) interventions, services, [and programs] provided and (b) the change they produce in students' health, functioning, or development" (Schwitzer, 2002, p. 183). Along with these contextual perspectives, counseling professional themselves are, of course, invested in providing support services that are an "accurate and sufficient" match with the diverse student populations they meet with every day (Schwitzer, 2009, p. 9). Those of us working on college campuses want to know that we are meeting the academic, developmental, and wellness needs of our various student-client audiences.

Making Decisions About Counseling Center Responses to Campus Needs: The Tripartite Model

As indicated, student affairs divisions on college campuses address students' academic learning as well as personal needs and life-span development. Counseling centers generally rely on a tripartite intervention model to decide the best strategy for addressing these needs on their campus. Using the tripartite intervention model, counseling centers decide among implementing (a) prevention programs aimed at students who might be susceptible to the development of a specific academic, adjustment, or other need; (b) intermediate services that address moderate and emerging counseling concerns; and (c) psychotherapeutic intervention for clearly entrenched and disruptive problems (Drum & Lawler, 1988; Schwitzer, 2005). Using this model, counseling centers' preventive interventions are a first line of defense and are intended to "forestall the onset of problems or personal-emotional needs" (Schwitzer & Thomas, 1998). Prevention programs are aimed at populations with no current need but that are susceptible or at risk for confronting an academic, adjustment, or personal need. The special challenge of prevention programs is that the target audiences, because they currently are experiencing no or very little distress or dysfunction, feel no urgency for change and low motivation for support. Correspondingly, counseling centers use prevention strategies that keep resistance low. This means relying on approaches that provide topical information, increase self-understanding, and promote healthier or more effective behavior. Next, counseling centers select intermediate services when a counseling-related problem "exists, is beginning to cause some difficulties for the individual, and its negative impact has the potential to grow, but currently falls short of causing clinically significant distress or dysfunction" in the student's daily life (Schwitzer, 2012, p. 283). At the intermediate level, the student's sense of urgency for assistance might be low to moderately high, and motivation for change might be low to moderate. Here, counseling centers set intervention goals of promoting the student's self-understanding and developing problem-solving strategies while keeping student engagement high and resistance low. This means relying on active service delivery modes such as problem assessment, limited individual counseling, theme- and skill-focused counseling and support groups, and interactive workshops. Finally according to the professional decision-making model, at the level of psychotherapeutic intervention, counseling centers select individual and group psychotherapy to address recurrent issues associated with entrenched needs and dysfunctional life patterns. At this level of difficulty, students ordinarily lean toward experiencing a higher sense of urgency and expressing higher motivation for change (Drum & Lawler, 1988; Schwitzer, 2005). See Box 5.3.

Supporting Student Adjustment

As can be seen in the illustration in Box 5.3, helping students meet the adjustment demands of college life is one critically important goal of college counseling and student affairs work. The mandated program in the illustration focused on the academic as well

BOX 5.3

Spotlight: Brief Mandatory Counseling Among Students Experiencing Risk

It might be helpful to consider an example applying these multiple contextual perspectives to college counseling work. Previously, Schwitzer and colleagues (Schwitzer, 2005; Schwitzer, Grogan, Kaddoura, & Ochoa, 1993) described programming strategies aimed at improving help seeking and, in turn, college success, among students who are most in need (e.g., entering with mental health stressors, adjusting to a new environment and responsibilities, living with an invisible or visible identity characteristic that departs from the institution's majority demographics, having deficits in their financial or academic resources, having fewer college role models).

A substantial accumulation of literature exists documenting the positive adjustment, developmental, and learning effects of student services—but the extensive literature also describes the challenges of reaching and engaging those students who could most benefit from these programs (Pascarella & Terenzini, 2005). These challenges exist because whereas students with social, family, and intrapersonal advantages tend to scan their environment for useful supports and then make use of these opportunities, students with fewer advantages tend to set unrealistically high self-expectations and in turn miscalculate their needs and avoid help seeking (Schwitzer, 2005). Unfortunately, one practical solution, mandated counseling, has produced only mixed results (both on college campuses and in other mental health settings; Schwitzer, 2005).

(Continued)

BOX 5.3 *(Continued)*

Turning to a real-life campus illustration, in an attempt to address these dynamics, the Tulane University Counseling and Testing Center was assigned to design an intervention program to improve retention among sophomores receiving financial aid whose cumulative first-year grade point average fell below 2.0 (Schwitzer, 2005; Schwitzer et al., 1993). From an institutional perspective, these learners were very much placed at risk for academic failure leading to suspension. However, in a division of student affairs context, these students were not aware of or engaged in the opportunities that could produce positive adjustment benefits. And from the counseling center's perspective, this unique population presented an identifiable population in need of positive impact. Following the tripartite professional decision-making model for counseling centers, Tulane's center assessed the target population's levels of need, urgency, and motivation—and decided on a preventive intervention strategy that would, as indicated by the model, emphasize providing topical information, increasing self-understanding, and promoting effective behavior while keeping resistance low.

Specifically, a program was developed in a collaboration between the counseling center and the financial aid office. Financial aid notified students of their status and referred them to a brief mandatory program in the counseling center. The mandatory part of the intervention consisted of two phases: Students first completed a written assessment of their academic attitudes and behaviors comprising the Survey of Student Habits and Attitudes (Brown & Holtzman, 1966) and Cooperative English Reading Comprehension Test (Educational Testing Service, 1960). They next attended one semistructured interview during which a counselor provided support, discussed the client's perceptions regarding academic experiences and difficulties, and reviewed the assessment results. The results provided stimuli for counselor queries; the counselor attempted to identify behavioral changes, emotional pressures, and other themes negatively influencing academic performance; psychological or developmental dynamics were explored; and practical suggestions were made. Then, depending on the situation, students were encouraged either to continue with regular counseling center sessions to address adjustment or development issues or to return periodically to address specific problems as they emerged.

As a result, return for counseling successfully increased for many students following the mandatory part of the program, and students were increasingly likely to bring up personal issues in the follow-up sessions. Furthermore, the greater the number of subsequent sessions attended, and the more often students returned at different times over their college career, the more likely they were to remain in school and graduate. In this illustration, institutional expectations for increased retention, student-centered student affairs hopes to positively affect student experiences, and counseling center goals of improving wellness and adjustment among their clientele all were accomplished: In other words, student clients and their needs were served from within the specialized institutional context that defines college counseling work (Schwitzer, 2005; Schwitzer et al., 1993).

as personal adjustment domains to identify important themes that were negatively influencing students' success. Generally speaking, a useful way to organize the many different types of adjustment needs that confront our students and clients is to associate them with four broad areas of demands: academic, social, personal-emotional, and institutional adjustment (Baker, McNeil, & Siryk, 1985; Baker & Siryk, 1984, 1989). These four areas of adjustment provide a guide that staff can follow to organize their targets for college student adjustment interventions.

Academic adjustment refers to a student's level of success in coping with the various educational demands characteristic of the college experience. Generally speaking, academic adjustment intervention goals focus not just narrowly on intellectual skill and study strategies but also on psychoemotional and contextual aspects of academic performance that often trip up college students' efforts more than ability does. These include motivation for pursuing academic achievements; knowledge of some tools for success and application to the tasks required; performance in the face of pressures (e.g., financial pressures, social pressures); and the learner's satisfaction, safety, and belonging within the academic environment.

Social adjustment refers to a student's level of success in coping with the interpersonal-societal demands inherent in the college experience. Social adjustment goals are wider than might be imagined at first. They emphasize the need to create and adapt to a range of new campus relationships, including relationships with peers and roommates, friendships and romantic relationships, relationships with faculty and academic staff, and relationships with other administrators and campus professionals. Of note, the creation of these key connections will look different for students who are in the numerical majority and find themselves bolstered by the institution as compared with students who have a minoritized identity on campus. Social adjustment also requires dealing with nostalgia, which can arise for students because of changing off-campus and precollege relationships. For example, traditional-age students must adapt to evolving relationships among family, high school friends, and so forth, as they progress into the college environment—while nontraditional-age adults must adapt to changing relationships in their own families and with coworkers during their transition to college student. The student's satisfaction, safety, and belonging in the campus social environment constitutes a third aspect of social adjustment.

Personal-emotional adjustment refers to a student's intrapersonal state during the college transition and the degree to which health or mental health problems arrive with the student or develop during the college transition. Personal-emotional adjustment has two components: psychological wellness and physical-health well-being. It is important to emphasize that all students bring both resources and challenges with them when they arrive on campus, and that learning about each student's unique personal-emotional experiences is a key goal.

Institutional adjustment has a dual focus and refers to (a) a student's degree of commitment to educational-institutional goals in general and (b) the degree of attachment a student develops to the institution in particular. Institutional adjustment sometimes is described as institutional attachment because the emphasis is on the quality of the relationship or bond that is established between the learner and the college or university. The responsibility for generating this bond lies with the institution as well, and requires attention to campus climate for students from varying backgrounds.

In the 2- and 4-year college and university context, meeting adjustment goals is an important emphasis because successful four-part adjustment is a prerequisite for college success (Sasso & DeVitis, 2015; Schuh, 2011). Likewise, adjustment goals are so critical to student affairs divisions that they usually weave adjustment-focused programming into almost every office's services and programs—from first-year orientation to residence hall programs and the like (Sasso & DeVitis, 2015; Schuh et al., 2011). For their part, college counseling professionals typically devote a lot of energy to supporting students' academic, social, personal-emotional, and institutional adjustment through individual and group counseling inside the counseling center and through preventive and supportive programming across the campus (Sharkin, 2012).

Naturally, like their counterparts in other mental health settings, college counseling professionals should use evidence-based practices (Schwitzer, 2009). In this light, Steenberger and Manchester (1996) emphasized the importance of clearly defining the population that a counseling or health center is targeting for attention. This can be especially important when providing counseling services and student affairs programming for adjustment. Generally, the abovementioned four aspects of college adjustment accurately capture the universal demands that just about all college and university students share in common (Beyers & Goossens, 2002). Still, these descriptions do not always capture the more specialized adjustment demands confronting unique campus populations. This matters to college counselors because, whereas some interventions might target widely defined campus groups (such as all undergraduate students), others might pertain to narrower populations (such as first-year African American women visiting counseling centers). For example, the College Counseling and Psychological Services Knowledge Base (American College Personnel Association, 2013) suggests that we pay attention to the specialized adjustment experiences of such campus populations as those defined by gender; those defined by race/ethnicity; lesbian, gay, bisexual, transgender, queer, questioning, intersex, plus other identities; first-generation students; academically defined populations such as those defined by college major or discipline; graduate students; community college learners; campus engagement groups such as student athletes, residential students, and Greek life members; and those populations, such as military and veteran students, that bring unique life experiences to their campus adjustment experiences. Students and clients also might present intersections of these identities. Therefore, although the four-part adjustment arrangement is a good guide, the specific approaches to providing adjustment services and programming that a center uses must be informed by understanding which aspects of adjustment apply to all students on campus, which aspects of adjustment apply to all students but seem insufficient for explaining some students' needs, and which apply accurately to some student populations but might be inaccurate for other students populations (Schwitzer, 2009). See Box 5.4.

Supporting Student Development

Although some of the work of campus professionals is aimed at alleviating mental health problems and achieving student adjustment goals—supporting student success

BOX 5.4

Spotlight: First-Year African American Student Peer Mentor Program

It might be helpful to consider an example of professional counseling work addressing student adjustment goals in the college context. Schwitzer (2009) described the importance of, and strategies for, designing services and programs that accurately meet the varied needs of diverse campus populations. In one of the first programming efforts along these lines (Schwitzer & Thomas, 1998), the James Madison University Counseling and Student Development Center was assigned to design a program to enhance first-year adjustment among African American students transitioning to this predominantly White institution. Institutional leaders had determined that programming was needed to support these matriculants because they did not always experience the same retention rates as their peers. The student affairs division's findings suggested that nonacademic factors, including the motivational and performance aspects of academic adjustment, and social adjustment, tended to be the most critical hurdles to success for this diverse group. In fact, their precollege academic characteristics (high school grade point average, SAT scores, etc.) suggested academics was less of a concern than the other aspects of college adjustment. Here again, from the counseling center's perspective, this population presented unique needs to be addressed (Schwitzer, 2009; Schwitzer & Thomas, 1998).

Following the tripartite professional decision-making model for counseling centers we introduced in the Making Decisions About Counseling Center Responses to Campus Needs: The Tripartite Model section, the James Madison University's center estimated the target population's levels of need, urgency and distress, and motivation for support—and decided that some prevention would be beneficial. Because students selecting the program could be characterized as having some clearly present needs, felt some urgency to address these needs, and were motivated for support, a program relying closely on intermediate intervention would be the strategy of choice.

(Continued)

BOX 5.4 *(Continued)*

In response, the counseling center relied on existing evidence that peer mentoring might be helpful for developing a comprehensive support program aimed at ameliorating motivational, performance, social, and personal-emotional aspects of first-year African American students' college adjustment (Schwitzer & Thomas, 1998). The program was developed in collaboration with the admissions office and the vice president for student affairs' office. During the summer, the admissions office invited incoming African American students to participate in a first-year peer mentoring program. Peer mentors, who were selected from among successful third- and fourth-year African American students, were extensively training as peer counselors using a model similar to resident assistant and peer health educator training; the division of student affairs provided mentors with a nominal stipend. Mentors met with assigned students on a regular schedule, kept records, and made referrals when needed. They were actively supervised by counseling center staff coordinators. More intense support was provided in the fall semester, with continuing but less contact in the spring, because the first semester presented the steepest adjustment curve. The counseling center staff also held several large-group activities, including an orientation and welcome meeting, periodic group meetings, and a dinner celebrating Kwanzaa. In summary, in keeping with the tripartite counseling center model, the program relied mostly on active service delivery, problem assessment, individual services by peer mentors, and supportive group experiences.

As a result,

> in contrast to the difficulty usually found when promoting help-seeking among under-represented students, participants were likely to raise typical first-year adjustment concerns in the presence of their mentors. Mentors provided empathic support or solution-focused suggestions . . . [and in turn] in contrast to the usual trend of declining adjustment over the first year, participants reported promising rates of problem resolution following mentor interventions [and] they had higher 2-year retention rates than [those students who declined the invitation to participate in the program]. (Schwitzer & Thomas, 1998, p. 31)

In this illustration, the counseling center staff's work included designing, providing training for, managing, and collaborating with other offices on a large-scale mentoring program that targeted goals in the specific area of college adjustment. Thinking contextually, meeting these goals benefited the institution, the student affairs division, and the students themselves. Further examples of collaboration and consultation will be provided in Chapter 6 for interested readers.

at meeting the demands of college life—college counselors and student affairs personnel also go beyond adjustment to promote student development (Reynolds, 2011; Sharkin, 2012). From their earliest modern inceptions, divisions of student affairs and counseling centers have been associated on college and university campuses with the higher educational mission of promoting students' psychosocial growth (Pascarella & Terenzini, 2005). In fact, from the institutional perspective, it is student affairs practitioners on campus who "act first and foremost . . . to actively assist students with the emotional and academic demands of college life"—and act as "educators and helpers" who "promote . . . [students'] personal development" (Reynolds, 2011, p. 399). That is, as viewed from the institutional context, ultimately it is student affairs professionals who embrace the goal of assisting students to become more advanced, mature, and competent persons by "attending to the needs of the whole student" (Knefelkamp et al., 1978; Reynolds, 2011, p. 399; Sharkin, 2012). In this context, college counseling professionals help individual students address their developmental issues when needed and simultaneously provide support for learners across campus as they attempt to makes gains in their *student development*, which has been described as

> a process in which an individual undergoes a number of changes toward more complex behavior, that result from mastering the increasingly complex challenges of life. These changes toward more complex behavior often culminate in the individual transforming to a higher developmental position that results in his or her viewing people, events, and things in fundamentally different ways (Drum, 1980, p. 23).

Goals are to help students advance in their autonomy, cognitive complexity, identity formation, ethical and moral development, gender-related and culturally related self-constructions, interpersonal dimensions, and other developmental domains that will contribute to adaptive functioning in the adult world (Evans et al., 2010).

Case Illustration: Fraternity Men, Alcohol Use, Social Desirability, and Expectations

Programming to promote more adaptive responses by fraternity men to the factors that promote excessive unhealthy alcohol use among this specialized campus population provides one relevant example of the work college counseling professionals perform to promote student development goals. Sasso and Schwitzer (2016) identified two important influences on some fraternity members' excessive alcohol use: social desirability orientation and alcohol use expectations. *Social desirability orientation* describes the tendency to conform to recognized social norms. College students, especially developmentally less advanced college students who are highly reliant on peer attitudes and have less fully formed self-identities, have especially strong social desirability orientations that lead them to support problematically high alcohol use, suppress expressing views that are counter to perceived norms, and avoid countervailing behaviors that appear to contradict social drinking messages—for fear of being negatively scrutinized and evaluated by their peers (Del Boca, Darkes, Greenbaum, & Goldman, 2004). *Alcohol use expectations* describe the tendency to have hopes and beliefs that excessive alcohol drinking will produce beneficial, positive, or salutary effects for the person who is drinking heavily (Borsari & Carey, 2003). The male identities influencing cultures such as those of fraternities, in turn, can result in high social desirability, especially among newer, less developmentally advanced members such as pledges and new members, and generally high positive expectations that alcohol will enhance one's social experience (Sasso & Schwitzer, 2016).

In response, Sasso and Schwitzer (2016) described developmental programming using educational formats that occur right in fraternity houses and Greek settings, using the tactics of group discussions, media presentations, and student self-assessments—all of which are hallmarks of developmental intervention. These programs use psychoeducation targeted at reducing conformity and building resiliency to social norms and pressures (in the identity formation developmental domain); replacing expectant thinking about alcohol use outcomes with accurate, more balanced beliefs (in the cognitive complexity developmental domain); and countering unhealthy male-culture ideals by replacing them with more balanced masculinity norms (in the gender-related construction domain of student development; Kilmartin, 2016; Sasso & Schwitzer, 2016). In this illustration, counseling center staff used evidence-based psychoeducation strategies, conducted in natural campus settings outside the office, to achieve young adult development goals in the special context of the college or university.

Supporting Student Health, Mental Health, and Wellness Needs

Finally, although the scope of work in the college context emphasizes the goals of addressing the common adjustment and developmental issues that can affect student wellness and success, the most significant aspect of college counseling comprises addressing student mental health needs (Reynolds, 2011; Sharkin, 2012). Although disruptions from student mental health needs may require the responses of professionals across student affairs, from residence life to deans of students or beyond, it is college counseling and psychological services professionals who are the campus specialists in this area. This clinical role is essential on today's campuses as today's mental health needs appear to be increasingly disruptive for the students who experience them, their peers, and the campus professionals and educators who work with them every day (Van Brunt, 2012). In fact, when Rudd (2004) compared "the mental health needs of adolescents and young adults in off-campus settings, [he] concluded that during the past decade, college counseling centers and university psychological services have essentially become community mental health clinics in a specialized institutional context" (Schwitzer & Van Brunt, 2015, p. 331). In other words, at the low end of the severity spectrum, large numbers of students seek counseling for moderate mental health needs emerging from normally expected adjustment, development, and other personal concerns; on the other hand, college practitioners simultaneously confront pressures to serve students with increasingly complex presenting concerns, clients with more severe psychological needs, and campus populations characterized by individual differences and diversity (K. K. Bishop, 2016; Gallagher, 2013, 2014; Schwitzer & Van Brunt, 2015). This is one place where the roles of counselors and student affairs staff members must be differentiated and scope of work duties should be respected.

College clients present a variety of mental health issues that arise from biological predispositions, psychological predispositions, precollege traumas, stressful circumstances during college, or some combination or interaction of these predispositions and circumstances (Rosenberg & Kosslyn, 2014). Among these, "the most pressing issues on today's campuses—due to their prevalence among contemporary student populations, their complexity and demandingness, or their potential for disruption" (Schwitzer & Van Brunt, 2015, p. 339; see also Gallagher, 2014; Turner & Keller, 2015)—are the following:

- Alcohol and other substance use
- Anxiety disorders and depressive disorders
- Dating and relationship violence and sexual violence
- Eating disorders
- Learning disabilities and attention deficit/hyperactivity disorder
- Nonsuicidal self-injury
- Severe psychological issues: bipolar disorder and schizophrenia

College students also seek services as the result of problems associated with individual differences that they may experience within the campus social environment, including acculturation difficulties adjusting to a new culture; social exclusion or rejection, which can include being targeted for intimidation, verbal abuse, or humiliation or being purposefully excluded from activities by their peers or other members of the campus community; or adverse discrimination or persecution based on being targeted because of characteristics such as gender or gender identity, race or ethnicity, sexual orientation, or physical appearance (American Psychiatric Association, 2013). See Box 5.5.

Outside the Center's Walls: Adapting College Counseling–Related Skills to Student Affairs Work Beyond the Office Domain

This chapter has highlighted the unique professional opportunities the college counseling field offers to work multidimensionally to address students' adjustment, developmental, learning, and mental health needs. As our case illustrations show, college counseling also offers engaging opportunities to work from multidisciplinary perspectives—not only with health centers but also with student affairs and academic affairs offices across the campus. Additionally, the field affords openings to meet student needs in student affairs roles outside the counseling center office (see Chapter 6 for more on campus collaboration). See Box 5.6.

BOX 5.5

Spotlight: Community College Students With Psychological Disorders

Here it may be useful to provide another illustration of college counseling work, this time on a 2-year campus. This example illustrates an effort to design an intervention for supporting the needs of community college distance learning students with psychological disorders. At first glance, such a population might seem like a very narrow audience for counseling center services. However, it is worth noting that 44% of clients seen by community college counseling staff present severe psychological concerns and 61% of these clients require crisis services (Gallagher, 2014). In fact, Francis and Abbassi (2010) reported that students with psychological disorders are most likely to choose community colleges and, more specifically, distance learning formats. From an institutional perspective, the colleges often rely on distance learning to deliver the college experience to students with psychological health needs because distance formats are seen as providing greater access, fewer interpersonal challenges, and a more "universally accessible" learning situation than can be found in traditional classrooms (Warren & Schwitzer, 2018). Even so, students with such needs still experience heightened risk of academic withdrawal and failure to achieve life goals even in 2-year distance learning (Jaggers & Xu, 2010; Xu & Jaggers, 2011). In response, Warren and Schwitzer (2018) described a project to identify the needs of students with psychological disorders and then, working in collaboration with their student services colleagues, academic affairs partners, and faculty, to develop responses to these learners' needs.

Once again following the tripartite counseling center services model introduced previously, Warren and Schwitzer (2018) conducted an evaluation with 2-year distance learners with attention-deficit/hyperactivity disorder, Bipolar I disorder, borderline personality disorder, dissociative identity disorder, obsessive-compulsive disorder, obsessive-compulsive personality disorder, and posttraumatic stress disorder (the students' diagnoses preceded the *Diagnostic and Statistical Manual of Mental Disorders*, 5th ed.; American Psychiatric Association, 2013). The assessment uncovered clearly present entrenched needs, distress and high urgency, and strong motivation for support and for change toward meeting academic and life goals. In turn, an approach that included psychotherapeutic intervention was suggested. However, at 2-year colleges, individual psychotherapy usually is narrowed, aimed at college success. Along these lines, the project produced guidelines for community college counselors to follow (Warren & Schwitzer, 2018): First, counseling should address with this population a "hurdle of self-disclosure," by which students have "uncomfortable, ambivalent feelings regarding exposure" or being made to feel "like I'm not very smart" (Warren & Schwitzer, 2018, p. 274) and, as a result, do not seek the accommodations or other supports to which they are entitled (and need). This component would be addressed in psychotherapy with counseling responses that offer "support with self-identity, self-beliefs, and self-disclosure"—to ameliorate "past or present experiences of, or anticipation of, humiliation or negative stigma from self-disclosure about mental health needs" (Warren & Schwitzer, 2018, p. 274). Second, counseling should address a "hurdle of personal connection," by which students experience inability in areas, of deeper interpersonal communication, including the wish for more one-on-one interpersonal success and better skills at preventing others from leading the student to "feel like a bad person" (Warren & Schwitzer, 2018, p. 274). This component is addressed in psychotherapy with counseling responses that offer "support with relationships in the institutional context" (Warren & Schwitzer, 2018, p. 274)—and cognitive-behavioral assistance developing successful strategies for directly and personally connecting with faculty and institutional service staff. Third, the project discovered that this population requires counseling support addressing time management hurdles. This component means including psychotherapy interventions to mitigate time management and distractibility problems, low frustration tolerance, difficulty with focusing, and other learning obstacles (Warren & Schwitzer, 2018). In this way, community college counselors working with students presenting diagnosable mental health disorders, especially at a distance, have a road map for successfully setting and reaching psychotherapy outcome goals.

BOX 5.6

Spotlight: Multiple Dimensions of Community College Counseling

A final note about college counseling in the community college context: As can be seen in this chapter's previous Spotlights, 2-year campuses probably offer professionals the greatest opportunity for multidimensional work in a higher education setting. Individual work with students not only focuses on addressing demanding psychotherapeutic needs but also includes advising plus academic and personal coaching. Beyond one-on-one engagement, community college counseling professionals are extensively involved with providing College 101 programs and classes, orientations, and workshops covering educational as well as life-span skills. Ideally, community college counselors offer these services preventively, to forestall the onset of difficulties, but they also provide responses at the intermediate and more entrenched levels of student need. Combining their counseling center services, their employment in student affairs and student development offices, their collaboration with school systems, and their workforce-development partnerships in their local communities, counselors in 2-year settings contribute comprehensively to their students' success (Schwitzer, Duggan, Laughlin, & Walker, 2011; Warren & Schwitzer, 2018).

Conclusion

This chapter introduced college counseling and student affairs work as a professional practice in a specialized context—and described this context from the broader perspective of 2- and 4-year college and university campuses. The chapter emphasized the ways in which such work is informed by the vision of college student development—an approach that emphasizes the college student experience in terms of adjustment, learning, development, and wellness and mental health. In this light, college counselors and their student affairs colleagues appear to articulate concern for and responses to the needs of students with the "strongest and most consistent voice" on campus (Knefelkamp et al., 1978, p. viii). Taken together, the chapter outlined the roles, outcomes, and rewards for counseling professionals who seek careers in higher education settings.

Final Case Study

Whyte and Guiffrida (2008) provided a real-life case study (in a *Journal of College Counseling* article) that vividly portrayed the challenges associated with consoling Deaf college students. As this chapter has explained, whereas, on the one hand, college counselors lead the way on their campuses when professional responses are needed to address student psychoemotional concerns, on the other hand, these counseling professionals do their work in combination with their colleagues across the student affairs context. Correspondingly, in Whyte and Guiffrida's case illustration, "one key to the success of Deaf college students at both Deaf and hearing institutions is to provide student support services that are geared to the developmental needs of Deaf students" (Whyte & Guiffrida, 2008, p. 185). In fact, in Whyte and Guiffrida's real-life case illustration, the client was a student at an institution whose mission focuses simultaneously on hearing and Deaf students, where Deaf students participate in classes with other Deaf students or in classes with sign language interpreters, and where a portion of the counseling center staff has special competencies in the area of Deaf student services.

The client is a student near the end of his degree program who, despite his academic progress so far, is

> considering dropping out of school as a result of relationship problems with some of his peers and health problems that have caused him to fall behind in his studies. . . . On his intake form, he indicated problems with anxiety, low self-esteem, depression, interpersonal conflicts and social withdrawal, and physical ailments including vertigo . . . [along with] several family problems. (p. 186)

He had decided to visit the counseling center following a conflict at a college party, after which, he said, he had become the target of rumors and gossip on campus, and his panic and social anxiety had increased.

Whyte and Guiffrida's (2008) case provides a good opportunity to reflect on an understanding of college counseling in the student affairs context. Few professionals have the benefits of working on a campus with so many resources for, and so many staff trained for, such a specialized population.

Case Exploration Questions

1. Identify the type of campus on which you would find your own ideal college counseling and student affairs job: 2- or 4-year college; large or small; PWI, HBCU, HSI, or Tribal college; or use other institutional characteristics.
2. On your campus of choice, how would you go about arranging and providing services at the counseling center? How would you prepare for your work with this client or help prepare your college counseling colleagues? Would you consider preventive, intermediate, and/or psychotherapeutic levels of intervention?
3. How might you professionally collaborate with the health center or disability services to address the client's different presenting needs?
4. What relationships might you establish with the advising center, student success center, or other academic supports?
5. What strategies might you engage in together with student affairs colleagues such as those in residence life, student life, or other offices?
6. Design a written plan whose goals, interventions, and outcomes all take advantage of the benefits that come from college counseling in the student affairs context.

References

Agricultural College Act of 1890, 26 Stat. 417 U.S.C. 321 *et seq.*

American Association of Community Colleges. (2009). Fast Facts. Retrieved from https://www.aacc.nche.edu/research-trends/fast-facts/

American Association of Community Colleges. (2014). Fast Facts. Retrieved from https://www.aacc.nche.edu/research-trends/fast-facts/

American College Counseling Association. (2013, Spring). *Community college task force survey of community/2 year college counseling services.* Retrieved from http://www.collegecounseling.org/wp-content/uploads/ACCA-CCTF-2013-Survey.pdf

American College Personnel Association. (2013). College Counseling & Psychological Services Knowledge Base. Retrieved from http://www.myacpa.org/ccaps-knowledge-base

American Council on Education. (1937). *The student personnel point of view.* (American Council on Education Studies, Series 1, Vol. 1, No. 3). Washington, DC: Author.

American Psychiatric Association. (2013). *Diagnostic and statistical manual of mental disorders* (5th ed.). Arlington, VA: Author.

Baker, R. W., McNeil, O. V., & Siryk, B. (1985). Expectation and reality in freshman adjustment to college. *Journal of Counseling Psychology, 32,* 94–103. doi:10.1037/0022-0167.32.1.94

Baker, R. W., & Siryk, B. (1984). Measuring adjustment to college. *Journal of Counseling Psychology, 31,* 179–189. doi:10.1037/0022-0167.31.2.179

Baker, R. W., & Siryk, B. (1989). *Student Adaptation to College Questionnaire manual.* Los Angeles, CA: Western Psychological Services.

Beyers, W., & Goossens, L. (2002). Concurrent and predictive validity of the Student Adaptation to College Questionnaire in a sample of European freshman students. *Educational and Psychological Measurement, 62,* 527–538. doi:10.1177/00164402062003009

Bishop, J. B. (2016). What they never told me about being a counseling center director. *Journal of College Student Psychotherapy, 30,* 226–231. doi:10.1080/87568225.2016.1219607

Bishop, K. K. (2016). The relationship between retention and college counseling for high-risk students. *Journal of College Counseling, 19,* 205–217. doi:10.1002/jocc.12044

Borsari, B., & Carey, K. B. (2003). Descriptive and injunctive norms in college drinking: A meta-analytic integration. *Journal of Studies on Alcohol, 64,* 331–341.

Bourassa, D. M., & Kruger, K. (2002). The national dialogue on academic and student affairs collaboration. *New Directions for Higher Education, 2001,* 9–38. doi:10.1002/he.31

Brown, W. F., & Holtzman, W. H. (1966). *Survey of Study Habits and Attitudes.* New York, NY: Psychological Corporation.

Bulger, S., & Watson, D. (2006). Broadening the definition of at-risk students. *The Community College Enterprise, 12,* 23–32.

Del Boca, F. K., Darkes, J., Greenbaum, P. E., & Goldman, M. S. (2004). Up close and personal: Temporal variability in the drinking of individual college students during their first year. *Journal of Consulting and Clinical Psychology, 72,* 155–164. doi:10.1037/0022-006X.72.2.155

Drum, D. (1980). Understanding student development. In W. Morrill, J. Hurst, & E. Oetting (Eds.), *Dimensions of intervention for student development* (pp. 14–38). New York, NY: Wiley.

Drum, D. J., & Lawler, A. C. (1988). *Developmental interventions: Theories, principles, and practice.* Columbus, OH: Merrill.

Educational Testing Service. (1960). *Cooperative English testing.* Monterey, CA: CTB/McGraw-Hill.

Espinosa, L. L., Turk, J. M., & Taylor, M. (2017). *Pulling back the curtain: Enrollment and outcomes at minority serving institutions.* Washington, DC: American Council on Education.

Evans, J. N., Forney, D. S., Guido, F. M., Patton, L. D., & Renn, K. A. (2010). *Student development in college: Theory, research, and practice* (2nd ed.). San Francisco, CA: Jossey-Bass.

Fley, J. (1966). An honorable tradition. *Journal of the National Association of Women Deans, Administrators and Counselors, 29,* 106–110.

Francis, P. C., & Abbassi, A. (2010). Ethical issues and considerations for working with community college students with severe and persistent mental disorders. *Community College Journal of Research and Practice, 34,* 423–437. doi:10.1080/10668920701382658

Gallagher, R. P. (2013). *National Survey of College Counseling Center Directors.* Alexandria, VA: International Association of Counseling Services.

Gallagher, R. P. (2014). *National survey of college counseling centers 2014.* American College Counseling Association [Monograph]. Retrieved from http://0201.nccdn.net/1_2/000/000/088/0b2/NCCCS2014_v2.pdf

Higher Education Act of 1965, 20 U.S.C. § 1001 *et seq.* (1965).
Indiana University Center for Postsecondary Research. (n.d.). *The Carnegie classification of institutions of higher education, 2015 edition*. Bloomington, IN: Author.
Jaggers, S., & Xu, D. (2010). *Online learning in the Virginia Community College System.* New York, NY: Columbia University, Community College Research Center.
Jenks Kettmann, J. D., Schoen, E. G., Moel, J. E., Cochran, S. V., Greenberg, S. T., & Corkery, J. M. (2007). Increasing severity of psychopathology at counseling centers: A new look. *Professional Psychology: Research and Practice, 38,* 523–529. doi:10.1037/0735-7028.38.5.523
Kilmartin, C. (2016, May–June). Being better and doing better: Men's health and mental health on campus. *About Campus Magazine, 22,* 12–20.
Knefelkamp, L., Widick, C., & Parker, C. A. (1978). *Applying new developmental findings: New directions for student services.* San Francisco, CA: Jossey-Bass.
Kuk, L., & Banning, J. H. (2009). Designing student affairs organizational structures: Perceptions of senior student affairs officers. *NASPA Journal, 46,* 94–117.
Kunitz, S. J., & Haycraft, H. (Eds.). (1977). *American authors 1600–1900.* Hackensack, NJ: Wilson.
Marsh, C. N., & Wilcoxon, S. A. (2015). Underutilization of mental health services among college students: An examination of system-related barriers. *Journal of College Student Psychotherapy, 29,* 227–243. doi:10.1080/87568225.1045783
McClellan, D. (2004). *The influence of organizational structure on the degree of adherence to the principles of a learning oriented student affairs division* (Doctoral dissertation). Retrieved from ProQuest Dissertations and Theses database. (Order No. 305108299)
Meilman, P. W. (2016). Conforming a voluntary medical leave of absence policy to recent interpretations of disability law. *Journal of College Student Psychotherapy, 30,* 54–63. doi:10.1080/87568225.2016.1105665
Morrill Land-Grant Act of 1862, 7 U.S.C. 321 *et seq.*
Mueller, K. H. (1961). *Student personnel work in higher education.* Cambridge, MA: Riverside Press.
National Association of Student Personnel Administrators. (2004). *Learning reconsidered: A campus-wide focus on the student experience.* Retrieved from https://www.naspa.org/images/uploads/main/Learning_Reconsidered_Report.pdf
Pascarella, E. T., & Terenzini, P. T. (2005). *How college affects students: A third decade of research* (Vol. 2). San Francisco, CA: Jossey-Bass.
Pollard, J. W., Flynn, C., & Eells, G. T. (2015). The role of threat assessment and management in college counseling: How's that net working? *Journal of College Student Psychotherapy, 29,* 248–256. doi:10.1080/87568225.2015.1072453
Reynolds, A. L. (2011). Counseling and helping skills. In J. H. Schuh, S. R. Jones, S. R. Harper, & Associates (Eds.), *Student services: A handbook for the profession* (5th ed., pp. 399–412). San Francisco, CA: Jossey-Bass.
Rhatigan, J. J. (2009). From the people, up: A brief history of student affairs. In G. McClellan, J. Stringer, & Associates (Eds.), *The handbook of student affairs administration* (3rd ed., pp. 3–18). San Francisco, CA: Jossey-Bass.
Roper, L. D., & Whitt, E. J. (2016). What troubles you? What keeps you up at night? *New Directions for Student Services, 153,* 19–37. doi:10.1002/ss.20166
Rosenberg, R., & Kosslyn, S. (2014). *Abnormal psychology* (2nd ed.). New York, NY: Worth.
Rudd, M. D. (2004). University counseling concerns: Looking more and more like community clinics. *Professional Psychology: Research and Practice, 35,* 316–317.
Sasso, P. A., & DeVitis, J. L. (Eds.). (2015). *Today's college students: A reader.* New York, NY: Peter Lang.
Sasso, P. A., & Schwitzer, A. M. (2016). Examining social desirability orientation and alcohol use expectations as factors in fraternity drinking. *Oracle: The Research Journal of the Association of Fraternity/Sorority Advisors, 11,* 17–35.

Schuh, J. H. (2011). Financing student affairs. In J. H. Schuh, S. R. Jones, S. R. Harper, & Associates (Eds.), *Student services: A handbook for the profession* (5th ed., pp. 303–320). San Francisco, CA: Jossey-Bass.

Schuh, J. H., Jones, S. R., Harper, S. R., & Associates. (2011). *Student services: A handbook for the profession* (5th ed.). San Francisco, CA: Jossey-Bass.

Schwartz, A. J. (2016). Session limits and the probability of the next visit. *Journal of College Student Psychotherapy, 30,* 238–251. doi:10.1080/87568225.2016.1219609

Schwitzer, A. M. (1997). Utilization-focused evaluation: Proposing a useful method of program evaluation for college counselors and student development professionals. *Measurement and Evaluation in Counseling and Development, 30,* 50–61.

Schwitzer, A. M. (2002). Using a chain-of-effects framework to meet institutional accountability demands. *Journal of American College Health, 50,* 183–186.

Schwitzer, A. (2005). Self-development, social support, and student help-seeking: Research summary and implications for college psychotherapists. *Journal of College Student Psychotherapy, 20,* 29–52.

Schwitzer, A. M. (2009). Adapting to students' social and health needs: Suggested framework for building inclusive models of practice. *Journal of American College Health, 58,* 5–10. doi:10.3200/JACH.58.1.5-11

Schwitzer, A. M. (2012). Diagnosing, conceptualizing, and treating eating disorders not otherwise specified: A comprehensive practice model. *Journal of Counseling & Development, 90,* 281–289. doi:10.1002/j.1556-6676.2012.00036.x

Schwitzer, A. M., Duggan, M. H., Laughlin, J. T., & Walker, M. A. (2011). Community college adjustment among dislocated workers. *Community College Journal of Research and Practice, 35,* 645–666. doi:10.1080/10668920801944068

Schwitzer, A. M., Grogan, K., Kaddoura, K., & Ochoa, L. (1993). Effects of brief mandatory counseling on help-seeking and academic success among at-risk college students. *Journal of College Student Development, 34,* 401–405.

Schwitzer, A. M., Pribesh, S., Ellis-O'Quinn, A., Huber, P. B., & Wilmer, E. C. (2016). Community college counseling: Why are research outcomes so elusive? *Journal of College Counseling, 19,* 76–95. doi:10.1002/jocc.12032

Schwitzer, A. M., & Thomas, C. (1998). Implementation, utilization, and outcomes of a minority freshman peer mentor program at a predominantly White institution. *Journal of the Freshman Year Experience and Students in Transition, 10,* 31–50.

Schwitzer, A. M., & Van Brunt, B. (2015). Student mental health issues on today's campuses. In P. Sasso & J. DeVitis (Eds.), *Today's college students: A reader* (pp. 331–345). New York, NY: Peter Lang.

Schwitzer, A. M., & Vaughn, J. A. (2017, May–June). Mental health, well-being, and learning: Supporting our students in times of need. *About Campus Magazine, 22,* 4–11.

Shaffer, J. L. (2009). *Role of residence hall staff in offering early warning academic intervention* (Doctoral dissertation). Retrieved from ProQuest Dissertations and Theses database. (Order No. 3392160)

Sharkin, B. S. (2012). *Being a college counselor on today's campus: Roles, contributions, and special challenges.* New York, NY: Routledge.

Steenberger, B. N., & Manchester, R. A. (1996). An introduction to the research process. *Journal of American College Health, 44,* 194–199.

Turner, J. C., & Keller, A. (2015). College Health Surveillance Network: Epidemiology and health care utilization of college students at US 4-year universities. *Journal of American College Health, 63,* 530–538. doi:10.1080/07448481.2015.1055567

U.S. Department of Education. (2019). *White House Initiative on Historically Black Colleges and Universities.* Retrieved from https://sites.ed.gov/whhbcu/one-hundred-and-five-historically-black-colleges-and-universities/

Van Brunt, B. (2012). *Ending campus violence: New approaches to prevention.* New York, NY: Routledge.

Vaughan, G. B. (2006). *The community college story* (3rd ed.). Washington, DC: American Association of Community Colleges.

Warren, G., & Schwitzer, A. M. (2018). Two-year college distance-learning students with psychological disorders: Counseling needs and responses. *Journal of College Student Psychotherapy, 32,* 270–281. doi:10.1080/87568225.2017.1396518

Whyte, A. K., & Guiffrida, D. A. (2008). Counseling deaf college students: The case of Shea. *Journal of College Counseling, 11,* 184–192. doi:10.1002/j.2161-1882.2008.tb00034.x

Xu, D., & Jaggers, S. (2011). *Online and hybrid course enrollment and performance in Washington State community college and technical colleges* (CCRC Working Paper No. 31). New York: NY: Columbia University, Community College Research Center.

Chapter 6

Building Collaborative Campus Relationships

Elizabeth Likis-Werle, Laura M. Gonzalez, Carolyn Rifkin, Alan M. Schwitzer, and Dana Burnett

We don't have to do all of it alone. We were never meant to.

—Brené Brown

■ ■ ■

Reflection Exercise

For a moment, think back to your own undergraduate days. Hopefully, there are memories that make you smile, but perhaps there are also some memories of difficult times and challenges. Who did you reach out to in those moments of pain or struggle? Was it a mental health professional in the campus counseling center, was it a trusted adult working in another place on campus who was not a counselor by training, or was it a family member or a friend? We don't have good data to help us understand where students start their help-seeking behaviors, and the most likely answer is "All of the above, depending." Therefore, we contend that building collaborations across campus support offices is the best strategy for ensuring that every student can find help when he or she needs it and can be referred to the right place within the network of help providers on the basis of their concerns.

■ ■ ■

College counselors and student affairs professionals without counseling degrees are all working toward the same goal, which is promoting the health, well-being, and development of college students so that they can reach their personal, academic, and career goals. As mentioned earlier, we do this in many different units on campus—from the counseling center to residence life to the dean of students office. Beyond the programmatic functions of such units, their underlying purpose is to create a sense of belonging and connection for students and to contribute to holistic student development and retention by generating an environment of caring or a meaningful relationship with campus staff (O'Keeffe, 2013). Even though our training backgrounds (counseling, student affairs, other) and the structure of where and how we work on campus may differ, this common goal should motivate us to move beyond our silos and form productive working relationships with each other. One example (further explained in Chapter 8) is the formation of behavioral intervention teams, which frequently pair counselors with the dean of students and other key frontline student affairs staff members in responding to students in crisis. However, we can formulate shared goals and collaborations in noncrisis situations as well. The goals of this chapter are to identify the benefits of building these collaborative campus relationships between counselors and student affairs personnel, describe how they could function for enhancing student experiences and campuses as a whole, outline some potential challenges in deciding how best to help students, and apply a triage model to help clarify the process of matching student needs to appropriate providers.

We have encouraged all campus helpers to consider consultation and collaboration, but what do we mean by those terms? Briefly, *consultation* as used in this chapter (client-centered consultation) represents the direct service provider asking other providers for additional perspective and advice on the details of the situation presented by the client/student (Archer & Cooper, 1998). Consultation is useful to establish a consensus about how a "reasonable person" would approach the situation and to improve the response to the student by including more than one professional perspective on the issue at hand. Consultants are advising the primary service provider but may not interact directly with the client; for example, a counselor and the dean of students might consult on how a student of concern could be approached on the basis of the student's needs and who has an established relationship with the student. *Collaboration*, on the other hand, is the act of working with a partner to coproduce something of value, such as a program, a service, a policy, a response, and so forth (Brunner, Wallace, Reymann, Sellers, & McCabe, 2014). Collaboration between counseling centers and other campus support offices can combine strengths and resources to be able to reach more students than either office could alone (e.g., the office of diversity, student activities, and the counseling center might develop an outreach program to support lesbian, gay, bisexual, transgender, and queer/questioning students).

Counseling and Student Affairs: Similarities and Differences

Although some current practitioners may not recall this, the professional organizations now known as the American Counseling Association (ACA) and the American College Personnel Association (ACPA), were once united as two constituent groups of the American Personnel and Guidance Association. It was 1992 when ACPA elected to withdraw from the ACA and chart a separate path (ACA, n.d.). However, ACPA has kept the competency category "advising/supporting/helping" in its professional statements, and ACA continues to support its interest in the mental health of college students through the American College Counseling Association, chartered in 1991. Thus, in the last 2 decades, this chasm between the two professional organizations has left practitioners in both arenas with missing links to bridge what used to be a natural connection (Protivnak, Paylo, & Mercer, 2013). Individuals seeking training to work with college students have been faced with a dilemma about the focus of their preparation—counseling or student affairs? We contend that continuing to separate these two disciplines could be doing a disservice to today's college students, and it is crucial for professionals in both areas to find innovative ways to collaborate.

There are similarities and differences in how college counselors and student affairs staff are trained and implement their training in daily work with college students (Reynolds, 2011). Understanding those similarities and differences can help us build respectful and functional professional alliances and know how to capitalize on each group's strengths.

Most (but not all) training programs diverge in the following ways. College counseling programs rely on counseling theories, helping skills, and counselor-supervised internships, whereas student affairs programs may focus on higher education administration, organization, and leadership. Additionally, many counseling programs do not have a college counseling track, and, consequently, the clinical mental health students interning and working at college counseling centers do not have exposure to student development theory and could benefit from this knowledge. Students in both student affairs and college counseling programs are frequently exposed to the student development theories that we will present in this book and are asked to think about ways to support positive developmental trajectories for college populations (through outreach programming, individual or group meetings, support structures, etc.) in the unique environment of a college campus.

In addition to having the capacity to create a therapeutic alliance and an effective short-term treatment plan, counselors working on college campuses are skilled in interpersonal communication, crisis intervention, multicultural competence, and outreach to promote wellness and development (Reynolds, 2009, 2011). This means that both counselors and student affairs staff may be engaged in the following tasks: advising, helping, learning, and development roles; student affairs equity, diversity, and inclusion roles; and leadership and assessment roles. It is important to note here that larger 4-year universities probably have more differentiation in their student support offices, and thus individual staff members may be responsible for different portions of this task list. However, on smaller campuses or at 2-year universities, staff members often wear more than one hat or work in a way that is cross-functional most of the time (Ethan & Seidel, 2013).

Counselors in Advising, Supporting, Learning, and Development Roles

Professionals with college counseling graduate training also are ideally prepared for other student affairs roles that support student success. Those with college counseling training are especially well-versed in the student affairs professional competency areas of Advising and Supporting, and Student Learning and Development. Advising and Supporting competencies comprise "the knowledge, skills, and dispositions related to providing advising and support to individuals and groups through direction, feedback, critique, referral, and guidance" (ACPA & National Association of Student Personnel Administrators [NASPA], 2015, p. 36). Those with college counseling training have strengths in this area's competencies, such as active listening and strategically pursuing objective student outcomes, identifying behavioral patterns, and effectively counseling individuals and groups. Student Learning and Development competencies comprise the "ability to apply theory to improve and inform student affairs and teaching practice" (ACPA & NASPA, 2015, p. 32). Those with college counseling training have strengths in this area's competencies, such as the ability to "articulate theories and models, . . . to facilitate holistic development," use "theory to create learning opportunities," and "inform divisional and institutional policy and practice" (ACPA & NASPA, 2015, p. 32). In addition, college counselors tend to be especially well-versed in student-centered, motivational, positive psychology–oriented approaches that are useful for advising and helping today's generational college cohorts (Wade, Marks, & Hetzel, 2015). In turn, as with their peers who are master's- or doctoral-level higher education practitioners, college counselors may find professional opportunities in settings such as academic advising, career centers, first-year student centers, student success centers, and so forth.

Student Affairs Equity, Diversity, and Inclusion Roles

Those working with college students in both clinical counseling and nonclinical student affairs settings should also be well-prepared for the student professional competency area of Social Justice and Inclusion, which comprises "the knowledge, skills, and dispositions needed to create learning environments that foster equitable participation of all groups and seeks to address issues of oppression, privilege, and power" (ACPA & NASPA, 2015, p. 30). Practitioners from both counseling and student affairs backgrounds have strengths in this area, such as integrating cultural knowledge with campus issues, designing inclusive programs, and creating culturally relevant policies and services (ACPA & NASPA, 2015). Additionally, both groups share the goals of facilitating others' learning and practice regarding social justice and ensuring institutional practices are responsive to the abilities, beliefs, and characteristics of the campus's diverse populations. In summary, we believe both college counseling and student affairs training can prepare professionals who value culture and inclusion in their practice with students—an essential skill on contemporary campuses (Teramoto Pedrotti, 2015).

Leadership and Assessment Roles

Finally, master's and doctoral training in college counseling or student affairs/higher education prepares practitioners for professional roles in campus leadership and assessment. The Leadership competency area in student affairs comprises the knowledge, skills, and attitudes required of a leader, whether it be a positional leader or member of a staff. "Leadership involves both the individual role of a leader and the leadership process of individuals working together to envision, plan, and affect change in organizations and respond to broad-based constituencies and issues" (ACPA & NASPA, 2015, p. 27). Some of these competencies involve being able to discern the appropriate leadership models for various situations on campus and motivate, inspire, and empower others to contribute toward the effectiveness of the organization (ACPA & NASPA, 2015). Student affairs leaders also must be competent at assessment and evaluation. The Assessment, Evaluation, and Research (AER) competency area focuses on "the ability to design, conduct, critique, and use various AER methodologies" to manage organizations using the results obtained from AER processes, and to shape the climate surrounding assessment on campus (ACPA & NASPA, 2015, p. 20). Although doctoral-level graduates may be more fully prepared for the assessment roles of student affairs leadership, both master's- and doctoral-level professionals should have the foundations for leading in staff roles or middle management. In fact, even though higher education training is more commonly associated with leadership positions, we also think college counselors are well-suited to modern demands for positive leadership skills including: "shifting the focus from the negative to the positive, developing a language of strengths, utilizing strategies that foster hope, and building emotional intelligence" (Durham Hynes, 2015, p. 281). For the right college counselor, these strengths can lead to positions directing student affairs offices and services, or positions in divisional leadership.

Rationale for Collaboration

Counselors are specifically trained to work with students experiencing mental health disorders, trauma, and crisis, but in some cases their clients present in the campus counseling center for services only because a student affairs staff member became aware of the problems and referred them (Rosenthal & Wilson, 2016). Counselors also are positioned to have a significant impact beyond the college counseling center by using their comprehensive skill set in collaboration with a variety of student development offices across campus. Student affairs offices (which number in the dozens at a typical campus) have much better access to and sustained connection with students across many situations, including those that are normative and typical (e.g., advising, living units, student activities) and those that are nonnormative or extreme (e.g., policy infractions, crisis response). However, student affairs offices are not structured to provide confidential mental health services, even if the staff members have sufficient background to do so. Of note, it is critical to the safety and well-being of students that support staff members not practice outside of their scope and understand the limits of their roles. Conversely, it is also true that most counseling centers are not staffed in such a way that they could serve the entire student body, whereas student affairs offices could conceivably touch the life of every student that passes through campus in some way. Thus, we need to consult, collaborate, and refer students to the office that can best serve their needs.

This alliance among campus helpers is important for the health and well-being of our students. Campus professionals have reported the presence of more severe mental health disorders among students on campus now than at any time in the past. Recently, the Association for University and College Counseling Center Directors reported that 48.2% of college students were living with anxiety, 34.5% reported depressive symptoms, and 25.2% of students reported suicidal thoughts (LeViness, Bershad, & Gorman, 2017), which represents similar or higher levels of symptomatology compared with what was reported previously in 2012—namely, 41%, 35%, and 16%, respectively (Mistler, Reetz, Krylowicz, & Barr, 2012). Many college students experience grief issues, as 30% of students in one study had experienced the loss of a close friend or family member (Balk, Walker, & Baker, 2010). In addition, the Association for University and College Counseling Center Directors survey reported that 25.5% of students were prescribed psychotropic medication. College student clients also reported significant addiction and relationship issues (LeViness et al., 2017). Students with weaker support systems and the tendency to conceal emotional distress from others are the very students who would benefit most from working with a professional counselor but may be less likely to present for help (Kahn & Williams, 2003). According to recent research, less than half of college students reporting symptoms of psychological distress seek treatment (Hunt & Eisenberg, 2010). Added to the increase in complex student issues, mental health needs, and crisis situations on college campuses in the last 12 years (Hollingsworth, Dunkle, & Douce, 2009; LeViness et al., 2017), the difficulty in getting college students into the counseling center creates a complicated challenge.

In addition to diagnosable mental health issues, traditional-age college students typically confront normative developmental stressors, such as separation and individuation from family of origin, identity issues, healthy or unhealthy relationships, academic/career decisions, the building of competence in a variety of tasks, and so forth (Chickering & Reisser, 1993). There are also moments at which unexpected crisis situations overwhelm the normal coping strategies of young adults and require special intervention. Therefore, college student mental health can often be a composite of coping with normative development, crises or stressors, and diagnosable mental health issues (Brunner et al., 2014). As was mentioned in Chapter 5, this reinforces that college student support services must function in a way that is preventative, developmental, and remedial (Dean, 2000). Because of our holistic view of college student needs, counselors must also embrace more comprehensive service models, where "counseling centers can take the lead in moving beyond the therapy room, becoming more visible on campus and developing initiatives and partnerships that focus on resilience, prevention, and early intervention" (Brunner et al., 2014, p. 281).

Student Needs and Service Utilization

Counseling center staff provide clinical responses to these student needs in the campus context and generally use a three-part service model that comprises preventive, intermediate/developmental, and psychotherapeutic interventions (Drum & Lawler, 1988; Schwitzer, 2012). Preventive strategies are used with the goal of reducing the likelihood of a mental health concern. Prevention is introduced when need for counseling currently does not exist, but susceptibility to a certain mental health problem is possible. Methods emphasize psychoeducational formats such as lectures and outreach programs, media presentations, written and web-based resources, and self-assessment. An example is Love Your Body Week as part of an eating disorders awareness campaign or a healthy relationships forum around Valentine's Day. Prevention strategies and outreach efforts are also typical of the work of student affairs professionals and thus represent an area with great potential for collaboration.

Next in the three-part model, intermediate or developmental strategies are used when a mental health need is emerging or is clearly present—when a psychological problem exists, causes difficulties, and has the potential to grow but currently falls short of severely impairing the student's everyday functioning, adjustment, or development. Intermediate intervention focuses on mitigating moderate symptoms, helping clients add new skills or dimensions to their daily functioning, and preventing current problems from derailing normally expected adjustment or development. An example would be a student who experiences extreme anxiety after a series of poor performances on exams and who needs to develop and implement breathing strategies, self-talk challenges, and relaxation techniques. Some developmental concerns with mental health roots are best addressed by counselors, but other developmental concerns that are normal and typical can be addressed in student affairs settings as well.

The model then turns to psychotherapeutic intervention when a student presents with issues that are disrupting daily life. When psychotherapeutic intervention is the appropriate goal, students may be experiencing acute suffering but sometimes are reluctant to receive help regardless of their distress (Chen, Romero, & Karver, 2016). Psychotherapeutic intervention requires more extensive individual and group psychotherapy; it also sometimes requires multidisciplinary approaches that integrate medication, hospitalization, off-campus referral, or separation from the institution for treatment. An example may be a student with little family support and a history of emotional dysregulation who becomes suicidal upon a relationship ending. The student may come to the attention of the student affairs staff through his or her resident adviser or the dean of students, or the student may present as a walk-in at the university counseling center. Students with more acute concerns should be seen by mental health counselors. Thus, any individuals operating as professionals in the student affairs context must have skills at preventive, intermediate/developmental, and psychotherapeutic intervention strategies (Drum & Lawler, 1988; Schwitzer, 2012) or know where to refer the student when the presenting issues are more severe than their training allows them to address.

The literature is not clear with respect to where college students might typically seek help for their existing mental health issues, daily stressors, or normative developmental problems, and whether that varies by population (Hunt & Eisenberg, 2010; Nordberg, Hayes, McAleavey, Castonguay, & Locke, 2013). As noted previously, campuses of various sizes and levels will have differing structures for their student support services. Certainly, the college counseling center is the best place for students with the most severe concerns. The reality is that counseling centers with limits in staff and session numbers (Shelesky, Weatherford, & Silbert, 2016) may not be able to provide support for students who are able to function on a daily basis but have stressors or normative concerns nonetheless.

It may be helpful to consider student concerns within a triage framework (Hardy, Weatherford, Locke, DePalma, & D'luso, 2011), in which a decision-making tree assists with the process of determining whether students need to be seen in the counseling center, given campus-based support services, or referred to the community (Schoen & McKelley, 2012). The levels of severity of student concerns fall on a continuum: On one end are the most serious cases of suicidality, safety, and other crises that require immediate triage with the university counseling center; on the opposite end are clearly developmental cases that can be handled by most student development professionals (e.g., roommate conflicts, homesickness). The gray area in between is perhaps the most elusive, in which both counselors and student support staff may be trained to assess, provide emotional support, and make referrals to other resources for specific needs.

In some ways, this suggestion of triage levels parallels the existing case management approach in counseling centers, wherein student needs are initially assessed, referrals are made if students cannot be seen for a variety of reasons, and follow-up is conducted to ensure that students' needs are being met (Shelesky et al., 2016). However, most existing case management models are pointing toward the more clinical end of the spectrum and not considering the utility of referring students with less severe concerns to campus partners. There are some exceptions—one is the case management in student affairs model provided by Adams, Hazelwood, and Hayden (2014), which starts with assessment of needs but then moves toward student advocacy and empowerment in referring students with less severe concerns toward appropriate campus-based services. Another exception is a new trend in offices of "student and family care," where students can be evaluated for nonclinical adjustment issues in an environment that does not promise confidentiality. Indeed, session notes can be entered into a shared computer system and accessed by the dean of students, by residence life staff, or by other staff members on the front lines who can keep an eye on potential behavioral issues. If students' concerns can be addressed by this initial care network, then they will be. If more concerns are raised, the student can be referred to confidential counseling. Once again, we would like to emphasize the ethics of providing appropriate services to students depending on the severity of their needs. Student safety must be a primary concern throughout this process.

Triage Model for Addressing College Student Needs (Likis-Werle and Gonzalez)

Students with Triage Level 1 developmental needs may be referred to appropriate campus student support services. Their needs are simple/mild, temporary, contained, individual, and recent. Problems are not disrupting daily function excessively. On a 10-point scale, these concerns are in the 1 to 3 range. Some examples include students who have failed a test or are falling behind in class and need to regain good standing, students with common or typical roommate disagreements, and students who are uncertain about future career options, exploring identity shifts.

Assessment strategies include answering questions such as the following: Is this concern commonly encountered and normal (such as career exploration or academic adjustment)? Is the student able to participate in the problem-solving process and reporting positive function in other areas of life? Are there existing resources and programs on campus that are set up to assist with these concerns?

Students with Level 2, middle-ground needs, must be assessed carefully for the most appropriate services. Their needs may be a mixture of the severity levels described in Levels 1 and 3, such as severe/acute, but more temporary, contained, and recent with good likelihood of resolving. Or mild, but pervasive, with historical precedent and systems involved. On a 10-point scale, these concerns are in the 4 to 6 range. Examples include a student who is grieving a loss in the family but is using support systems and an appropriate coping mechanism, a student who has dealt with anxiety for many years and is experiencing some flare-ups as part of college adjustment but has strategies for minimizing the impact; a relationship breakup. Pertinent assessment strategies include that a counselor should at least be consulted as part of the assessment of these issues to be sure that evaluation is holistic (across affective, behavioral, cognitive, and systemic areas, and including historical and current risk factors). Frequency, duration, and intensity of symptoms and behaviors should be included as well as assessing the necessity of and/or the student's ability to carry out a self-care plan and putting safety nets in place.

Students with Level 3, serious clinical and mental health needs, must be seen by a counseling clinical staff. Their needs are complex/severe, emerging as part of a crisis, pervasive, systemic, either with acute onset or with longer historical precedent, and potentially more permanent. Daily function is completely disrupted. On a 10-point scale, these concerns are in the 7 to 10 range. Examples include students expressing suicidal ideation, students with existing serious mental health diagnoses such as posttraumatic stress disorder or schizophrenia, and students with eating disorders. Common assessment strategies include answering questions such as the following: Is the student oriented to place and time (basic mental status evaluation), might the student be of harm to self or others, and is safety an immediate concern?

Let's work through some examples of each triage level and how it could look in the life of a college student. Key questions to ask oneself include the following: Is the concern being expressed (a) simple/mild or complex/severe, (b) temporary or more permanent, (c) pervasive or contained, (d) individual or systemic, and (e) recent or with longer historical precedent?

Level 1 Concerns

Level 1 are the least urgent, so they are more likely to be characterized as simple/mild, temporary, contained, individual, or recent. In terms of the amount of disruption the student is experiencing to daily life, Level 1 concerns would be minimal. That is not to say that these concerns are not real in the lives of students or do not cause discomfort. Rather, these concerns are part of the normal developmental transition to campus or into a new role and can be resolved using basic listening skills and attention to student development along cognitive, academic/career, social, and personal trajectories. The university setting offers many support resources for students, including but not limited to academic advising, career services, multicultural affairs, residence life, leadership development, campus activities, and wellness centers. Professionals in these offices can collaborate to help address nonclinical situations during this formative time period. Counselors and student affairs practitioners are alike in their background in student development theory. Both sets of support staff spend a great deal of time practicing active listening skills and creating a holistic picture of the clients' issues within their unique cultural and developmental context. An understanding of college student development theory (e.g., Chickering & Reisser, 1993; Perry, 1970; Schlossberg, 1984) coupled with a wellness approach to obstacles can elicit strengths-based interventions for normative stressors.

For example, a counselor or student affairs professional trained in Chickering and Reisser's (1993) developmental model (discussed in Chapter 11) could help a struggling student understand the psychosocial vectors of developing autonomy and managing relationships as typical developmental tasks for college. A prenursing student who did not get accepted to her program of choice may approach a resident assistant wanting to quit school, but a support person trained in Schlossberg's (1984) transition theory (see Chapter 13) could help the student understand the meaning of this "nonevent" transition and frame the resources needed to change directions and create a Plan B. Likewise, if a student confided during an advising appointment that she was feeling low after doing poorly in a class, a helper could normalize the experience, explore student strengths, assess for support networks, identify values, and set varied student-centered goals. In this way, the normative discouragement and lowered self-esteem that might result from a poor grade could be addressed before becoming a more serious mental health concern (e.g., depressed affect). These opportunities to promote growth and development could be implemented in a variety of campus settings.

Level 1 concerns might be evaluated as potential Level 2 concerns if they are multilayered (e.g., career questions that are causing significant conflict between the student and family members, who are threatening to stop paying tuition; or a roommate conflict that also involves discrimination around a social identity and the possibility of hate-based language or behavior). Consultation is always wise to gather together several perspectives on how to proceed.

Level 2 Concerns

Level 2 concerns are perhaps the most difficult to triage as they occupy the middle ground between clearly mild/simple concerns and clearly severe/complex concerns. That is to say, if the resolution is not immediately obvious, the concern is likely to be in this level. Along a 10-point scale of concerns, these are likely to be in the 4 to 6 range, although each layer of the student's story may create a more complete and complex picture and thus shift the rating. Concerns may involve more than one person (relational or systemic), they may have a longer history in the student's life (current normative grief tied to a past unresolved loss), or they may be causing a moderate level of disruption in the student's daily life (unable to attend class, not eating or sleeping well). If you are sitting in a counseling center and hearing these stories, you are well positioned to determine severity and decide whether this concern can be added to your current caseload (or is not rising to the level of distress that requires immediate response). If your caseload is full with more severe client concerns, then you will need to use judgment to decide whether the student should be referred to off-campus counseling or to other on-campus support resources. In truth, some students will not follow up on off-campus referrals (because of cost, inconvenience, or other doubts), so some thought should be given to collaborative support between student affairs and counseling on campus.

If you are sitting in a student development office, however, you should approach Level 2 concerns with great caution. Students may be discussing the concern with you as a person who they have come to trust and may resist your impulses to refer them to a counselor. However, if you have any concern at all about the student's well-being or ability to resolve the presenting issues, then consult with the counseling center or more seasoned professionals in your office while the student is still present. Referral can be done in a way that is kind, is caring, and preserves the good relationship you have with the student, but it must be clear to the student that his or her best interests will not be served by student affairs alone. Collaboration means partnering with others on campus for the good of the student. A person with solely administrative training may not be prepared to attend to serious concerns for students in the middle level of the triage system, and it is honest and ethical to state that clearly. However, in consultation with others, that staff person is bolstered by multiple perspectives on the problem at hand. Depending on the preferences of campus leaders, counselors working in student affairs offices could be listed on a triage document so that the campus could rely on them to make an initial assessment about Level 2 concerns and help refer students to the service best suited to their needs.

Level 3 Concerns

Level 3 concerns are usually clear in that they represent crisis, breakdown of coping, severe mental health symptomatology, and pervasive/complex issues (e.g., 7 to 10 on a 10-point scale). No matter where students with these concerns are first seen (for instance, diagnosable mental health disorder, danger to others, life-threatening conditions such as eating disorders, suicidal ideation, substance dependence, etc.), they should be referred to the counseling center at once. Because these complex issues often affect others in the campus environment as well (e.g., roommates, friends, classmates, faculty/staff), it is likely that collaboration with student affairs will be an important part of the resolution.

Guided Learning and Practice

The concepts of consultation and collaboration align well with professional identity among student affairs professionals and college counselors. Student development professionals with counseling degrees can provide topical consultation and training on campus regarding how to assess student needs, listen for underlying context and dynamics, and distinguish levels of concern. We would also like to offer a few ideas for ways that college counselors and student affairs staff members could collaborate, knowing that each campus environment is unique and that you will need to work out new arrangements that meet the needs of your future employers or avoid roadblocks and barriers to collaboration that may be specific to your campus. Recall the example of the behavioral intervention team that was mentioned earlier—these weekly meetings between student affairs and counseling staff are focused on providing needed supports to students who are being flagged around campus as having urgent needs. Working together eliminates some of the vulnerabilities in a system where staff are making important decisions in isolation.

For example, programs geared toward first-generation college students provide counseling and support to assist with the unique stressors this population may face, such as lower levels of family support, less knowledge about higher education, uncertain financial support, lower educational expectations, higher levels of adjustment stress, and in some cases higher levels of posttraumatic stress disorder–type symptomatology (Jenkins, Belanger, Connally, Boals, & Durón, 2013). Because they have fewer family role models in this regard, first-generation college students may not be aware of the types of support available to them in a campus environment and may feel isolated and thus less likely to present for services of any type. In addition, first-generation college students may have other social identities that make their daily life on campus more complicated (e.g., students of color at predominantly White institutions, immigrant students with undocumented family members, students who have been homeless). Addressing these complex sets of experiences may require both clinical and developmental support strategies (Level 2 or Level 3), and services could be implemented in a variety of campus settings in a collaborative way. In these "gray areas" in between the clearly clinical and clearly developmental needs, collaborations between student affairs professionals and counselors could make an important impact on first-generation students' well-being and academic retention and could mobilize other needed support services on behalf of students.

As we have discussed, today's college counseling and psychological services continue to develop responses to increasingly complex and demanding student mental health needs (Gallagher, 2015; Turner & Keller, 2015). One innovative strategy that has gained traction among U.S. campuses is the use of embedded or satellite counselors. With this strategy, university mental health practitioners "reach out to the campus community and decrease barriers to psychological care" through services that are coordinated with other student affairs (or occasionally academic affairs) offices such as residence life and student life centers; the goal is to put counseling professionals in places that "increase the availability and ease access to counseling services" (Orchowski, Castelino, Mei Ng, Cosio, & Heaton, 2011, p. 242; see also Mowbray et al., 2006). Using this approach, a trained professional is housed in an office in students' naturally occurring social environment to give them greater and more immediate access to an available counselor. Administratively, the counselor might report to the counseling center director, to the director of the office or service in which they are serving, or to the vice president of student affairs (or dean of students). Two examples include Central Michigan University, where counselors operating in satellite offices around campus provide staff consultation and student counseling services right in residence halls, and Eastern Michigan University, where counseling professionals housed in the First Year Center provide individual counseling, consult with residence staff, and support counseling center crisis staff (Orchowski et al., 2011). A similar model is the employment of counselors-in-residence, who are live-in counseling professionals in residence halls (Davis, Kocet, & Zozone, 2001). Another model of embedded services is Let's Talk (Boone et al., 2011), in which more informal assessment services are offered to underserved populations with less wait time and paperwork. Currently more than 50 campuses have adopted this model, setting up walk-in hours in multicultural centers, residence halls, and campus cafés for a few hours each week to improve accessibility, visibility, and trust.

Conclusion

Thus, to reiterate our central point, as college student mental health concerns become more prevalent and counseling centers are working at full capacity, student affairs professionals and counselors trained in college counseling and student development theory are positioned to collaborate in important ways to support student health and wellness (Watson, 2013). The majority of college students will not present for services in a counseling center but may be comfortable looking to student affairs offices for support when needed. The key is knowing which types of concerns are appropriately addressed in which setting (because of severity, complications, and duration of concerns). We advocate a developmentally focused triage model, developed by Likis-Werle and Gonzalez, for matching seriousness of student concerns with service providers (counselors or other professionals) in student development offices and encourage counselors and student affairs professionals to identify many ways to work together for the good of the students. To plan and implement such a triage system, college counselors and student affairs professionals must work together as a team, aligning their communication, strategies, and responses to students. We have offered multiple strategies for counselors and student affairs professionals to collaboratively address student success, well-being, and retention and have called for more research to be conducted regarding where college students go for help and barriers to help seeking. We underscore the point that adding experiential simulation exercises in counseling and student development courses could help illustrate the complex roles and responsibilities of a college student development professional (Schwitzer, Gonzalez, & Curl, 2001) and would add the evaluation of such exercises to a future research agenda for college counseling and student development.

Counselors are well prepared to assess, refer, and remediate student issues across a wide continuum from developmental to clinical and to offer training and consultation to professional staff and faculty. We have described several types of issues that trained counselors are equipped to navigate and made recommendations for how to ethically incorporate these services into various student office roles.

Final Case Studies

Many campuses have an office that serves students with documented disabilities (e.g., physical, psychological, learning, vision, hearing) who are in need of accommodation to achieve their goals as learners. In this case, we will describe a student who presents for services at such an office and will ask you to consider the students' needs and where those could most effectively be met (using the three levels in the triage model).

Guiding answers are included among the questions. However, prior to reading the answers, you are encouraged to pause and think about how you might conceptualize this case yourself, applying the material you have read in this chapter.

Case 1

A student comes to you stating he was accustomed to receiving accommodations in high school related to his diagnosis of mild autism and is advocating for those same supports on campus. You explain that there are eligibility criteria and that this is a multistep process, and the student gets confused.

Case 1 Exploration Questions

1. How would you assess his eligibility and his ability to complete the process independently and successfully?
2. Would you refer the student to counseling services and, if so, at what point?
3. What level of concern would this situation be in the triage model? Look back in the chapter to determine your answer before continuing with the next paragraph.

Students with disabilities span the continuum in terms of need, functioning, and co-occurring issues. When students register with the office for accommodations, it may be useful to refer the student to a counselor to discuss stress management, concurrent concerns, self-advocacy on campus, support groups, or other basic needs. This would be a Level 1 tier.

Case 2

Later in the semester, the student's name surfaces at a behavioral intervention team meeting because of a verbal altercation with his roommate. Residential life staff discovered the student was refusing to get out of bed and attend classes, and his roommate wants to move out. Upon further assessment, the resident director ascertains that the student was performing poorly in classes, reporting feeling down and irritable.

Case 2 Exploration Questions

1. What questions would you ask the student?
2. How would you go about consulting counseling center staff?
3. What level of the triage model would this situation represent? Be able to explain your answer before you move on.

Often a student with an outwardly visible disability experiences social stigma in the campus community and may not have consistent use of emotional coping skills under stress. Expressing feeling down or irritable may be a sign of depression or anxiety and, if not addressed, could develop into more serious issues. Social and emotional stressors as well as challenges in learning tasks most likely require a more comprehensive assessment through counseling services. The college counselors could determine the nature and risk level of the student's symptoms and underlying context and then follow up with individual or group interventions. This situation would fall into the middle ground of a Level 2 tier.

Case 3

Toward the end of the semester, the dean of students receives a call from a faculty member regarding the student. During a consultation about a failing grade, the student reported to the faculty that other students were bullying him. The student then said, "Don't worry, you won't see me anymore" and stormed out of his office. The student was in the lobby of the building acting bizarrely, and other students were trying to calm him down.

Case 3 Exploration Questions

1. What would be your first step in responding to the faculty member?
2. Is de-escalating the student appropriate and why?
3. What professionals would you involve immediately?
4. What safety concerns might you need to consider?
5. How would you collaborate with the counseling center in an urgent/emergent case? Be able to explain your answer before you move on.

This represents a crisis situation, Level 3, that would require the expertise of a trained counselor and collaboration among several student affairs professionals. The student may feel physically and emotionally traumatized and may be unable to engage in daily tasks. Helping the student from a trauma-informed supportive lens while gaining his trust would be key, as well as ensuring the safety of the student and others in the building. The counseling center staff would need to assess the student for homicidal or suicidal risk, find out the precipitating factors, make a plan for intervention and follow up, and communicate with the appropriate faculty and staff involved. In addition to collaborating in the abovementioned ways, a counselor can provide an in-service training or continued consultation for other staff members to update them on the most frequently diagnosed disabilities of current students (e.g., attention-deficit/hyperactivity disorder, posttraumatic stress disorder, severe anxiety in testing situations, autism, traumatic brain injury, visual impairment). Student affairs offices can aid students with disabilities through key transitions (e.g., initial social and academic adjustment to campus, job search strategies). Finally, both counselors and staff members can contribute to outreach programming for the rest of the campus to help raise awareness of the experiences of students with disabilities and dispel common myths and stereotypes.

References

Adams, S. D., Hazelwood, S., & Hayden, B. (2014). Student affairs case management: Merging social work theory with student affairs practice. *Journal of Student Affairs Research and Practice, 51,* 446–458.

American College Personnel Association and National Association of Student Personnel Administrators. (2015). *Professional competency areas for student affairs practitioners.* Retrieved from https://www.naspa.org/images/uploads/main/ACPA_NASPA_Professional_Competencies_FINAL.pdf

American Counseling Association. (n.d.). Our history. Retrieved from https://www.counseling.org/about-us/about-aca/our-history/aca-milestones

Archer, J., & Cooper, S. (1998). *Counseling and mental health services on campus: A handbook of contemporary practices and challenges.* San Francisco, CA: Jossey-Bass.

Balk, D. E., Walker, A. C., & Baker, A. (2010). Prevalence and severity of college student bereavement examined in a randomly selected sample. *Death Studies. 35,* 459–468.

Boone, M. S., Edwards, G. R., Haltom, M., Hill, J. S., Liang, Y., Mier, S. R., . . . Yau, T. Y. (2011). Let's talk: Getting out of the counseling center to serve hard-to-reach students. *Journal of Multicultural Counseling and Development, 39,* 194–205. doi:10.1002/j.2161-1912.2011.tb00634.x

Brunner, J. L., Wallace, D. L., Reymann, L. S., Sellers, J., & McCabe, A. G. (2014). College counseling today: Contemporary students and how counseling centers meet their needs. *Journal of College Student Psychotherapy, 28,* 257–324.

Chen, J. I., Romero, G. D., & Karver, M. S. (2016). The relationship of perceived campus culture to mental health help-seeking intentions. *Journal of Counseling Psychology, 63,* 677–684. doi:10.1037/cou0000095

Chickering, A. W., & Reisser, L. (1993). *Education and identity* (2nd ed.). San Francisco, CA: Jossey-Bass.

Davis, H., Jr., Kocet, M. M., & Zozone, M. S. (2001). Counselor-in-residence: A counseling service model for residential college students. *Journal of College Counseling, 4,* 190–192. doi:10.1002/j.2161-1882.2001.tb00200.x

Dean, L. A. (2000). College counseling today: Changing roles and definitions. In D. C. Davis & K. M. Humphrey (Eds.), *College counseling: Issues and strategies for a new millennium* (pp. 41–56). Alexandria, VA: American Counseling Association.

Drum, D. J., & Lawler, A. C. (1988). *Developmental interventions: Theories, principles, and practice.* Columbus, OH: Merrill.

Durham Hynes, S. (2015). The intersection of positive psychology and leadership development. In J. C. Wade, L. I. Marks, & R. D. Hetzel (Eds.), *Positive psychology on the college campus* (pp. 279–298). New York, NY: Oxford University Press.

Ethan, D., & Seidel, E. J. (2013). On the front lines of student crisis: Urban community college professors' experiences and perceived role in handling students in distress. *College Student Affairs Journal, 31,* 15–26.

Gallagher, R. P. (2015). *National survey of college counseling centers 2014.* Retrieved from http://d-scholarship.pitt.edu/28178/

Hardy, J. A., Weatherford, R. D., Locke, B. D., DePalma, N. H., & D'luso, N. T. (2011). Meeting the demand for college student concerns in college counseling centers: Evaluating a clinical triage system. *Journal of College Student Psychotherapy, 25,* 220–240.

Hollingsworth, K. R., Dunkle, J. H., &, Douce, L. (2009). The high-risk (disturbed and disturbing) college student. *New Directions for Student Services, 128,* 37–54.

Hunt, J., & Eisenberg, D. (2010). Mental health problems and help-seeking behavior among college students. *Journal of Adolescent Health, 46,* 3–10.

Jenkins, S. R., Belanger, A., Connally, M. L., Boals, A., & Durón, K. M. (2013). First-generation undergraduate students' social support, depression, and life satisfaction. *Journal of College Counseling, 16,* 129–142. doi:10.1002/j.2161-1882.2013.00032.x

Kahn, J. H., & Williams, M. N. (2003). The impact of prior counseling on predictors of college counseling center use. *Journal of College Counseling, 6,* 144–154. doi:10.1002/j.2161-1882.2003.tb00235.x

LeViness, P., Bershad, C., & Gorman, K. (2017). *The Association for University and College Counseling Center Directors annual survey.* Retrieved from https://www.aucccd.org/assets/documents/Governance/2017%20aucccd%20survey-public-apr26.pdf

Mistler, B. J., Reetz, D. R., Krylowicz, B., & Barr, V. (2012). *The Association for University and College Counseling Center Directors annual survey.* Retrieved from http://files.cmcglobal.com/Monograph_2012_AUCCCD_Public.pdf

Mowbray, C. T., Megivern, D., Mandiberg, J. M., Strauss, S., Stein, C. H., Collins, K., . . . & Lett, R. (2006). Campus mental health services: Recommendations for change. *American Journal of Orthopsychiatry, 76,* 226–237.

Nordberg, S. S., Hayes, J. A., McAleavey, A. A., Castonguay, L. G., & Locke, B. D. (2013). Treatment utilization on college campuses: Who seeks help for what? *Journal of College Counseling, 16,* 258–274. doi:10.1002/j.2161-1882.2013.00041.x

O'Keeffe, P. (2013). A sense of belonging: Improving student retention. *College Student Journal, 47,* 605–613.

Orchowski, L. M., Castelino, P., Mei Ng, H., Cosio, D., & Heaton, J. A. (2011). The design and implementation of a counselor-in-residence program. *Journal of College Student Psychotherapy, 25,* 241–258.

Perry, W. G. (1970). *Forms of intellectual and ethical development in the college years: A scheme.* New York, NY: Holt, Rinehart & Winston.

Protivnak, J. J., Paylo, M. J., & Mercer, J. C. (2013). The perceived value of counselor preparation for student affairs professionals. *Journal of Counselor Preparation and Supervision, 5,* 49–64.

Reynolds, A. L. (2009). *Helping college students: Developing essential skills for student affairs practice.* San Francisco, CA: Jossey-Bass.

Reynolds, A. L. (2011). Helping competencies of student affairs professionals: A Delphi study. *Journal of College Student Development, 52,* 362–369.

Rosenthal, B. S., & Wilson, W. C. (2016). Psychosocial dynamics of college students' use of mental health services. *Journal of College Counseling, 19,* 194–204. doi:10.1002/jocc.12043

Schlossberg, N. K. (1984). *Counseling adults in transition: Linking practice with theory.* New York, NY: Springer.

Schoen, E., & McKelley, R. (2012). Clinical assessment at college counseling centers: The consultant-on-duty model. *Journal of College Counseling, 15,* 274–288.

Schwitzer, A. M. (2012). Humanism in college and university counseling. In M. B. Scholl, A. S. McGowan, & J. T. Hansen (Eds.), *Humanistic perspectives on contemporary counseling issues* (pp. 227–252). New York, NY: Routledge.

Schwitzer, A. M., Gonzalez, T., & Curl, J. (2001). Preparing students for professional roles by simulating work settings in counselor education courses. *Counselor Education and Supervision, 40,* 308–319. doi:10.1002/j.1556-6978.2001.tb01262.x

Shelesky, K., Weatherford, R. D., & Silbert, J. (2016). Responding to the increased needs of college students: A case study of case management. *Journal of College Student Psychotherapy, 30,* 284–299.

Teramoto Pedrotti, J. (2015). Cultural competence in positive psychology: History, research, and practice. In J. C. Wade, L. I. Marks, & R. D. Hetzel (Eds.), *Positive psychology on the college campus* (pp. 81–98). New York, NY: Oxford University Press.

Turner, J. C., & Keller, A. (2015). College health surveillance network: Epidemiology and health care utilization of college students at U.S. 4-year universities. *Journal of American College Health, 63,* 530–538. doi:10.1080/07448481.2015.1055567

Wade, J. C., Marks, L. I., & Hetzel, R. D. (Eds.). (2015). *Positive psychology on the college campus.* New York, NY: Oxford University Press.

Watson, J. C. (2013). Rethinking the provision of counseling services: A paradigm shift for college counselors. *Journal of College Counseling, 16,* 3–5. doi:10.1002/j.2161-1882.2013.00022.x

Chapter 7

Outreach and Preventative Services

Derrick A. Paladino

When we have inner peace, we can be at peace with those around us. When our community is in a state of peace, it can share that peace with neighboring communities.

—Dalai Lama

■ ■ ■

Reflection Exercise

One assumes that if you are reading this chapter that (a) you are either in a graduate counseling, student affairs, or allied mental health program or (b) you have completed an undergraduate degree at some point. With this in mind, I am inviting you to reflect upon your undergraduate and/or community/2-year college experience:

1. List outreach programs you remember being a part of your experience. These programs may have been offered through your residence hall, an affinity group, fraternity and sorority life, fairs on campus, flyers, emails, and so forth.
2. Write what you remember about these programs. What kind of acute or lasting impact did they have on you? How did they grab your attention? Were they inclusive and accessible? What made you attend, not attend, leave early, or stay after? How was the title? What was the facilitative style like? Was it a single session, semipermanent, or freestanding program?
3. What types of programs would you have benefited from that were not offered?

Spend some time with what you wrote and hold these experiences in your mind as you continue through this chapter as well as Part IV, "Clinical Issues in the College Context."

■ ■ ■

In this chapter we explore the concept, design, and implementation of outreach and prevention programming. It will begin with an exploration of definitions and standards connected to outreach and primary prevention services. You will then learn about the need for these services on campus as well as their function within a college counseling center. Finally, the chapter will discuss how one goes about creating and implementing programs specific to your campus. To assist with your understanding of the material, throughout the chapter you will find examples of college counseling center outreach programs that are current and tested in the field (see Boxes 7.1 through 7.5). Your personal outreach experiences as a student may or may not fit into what is discussed. As you read on, think about what went right and what alteration would have had a better impact on your development and wellness during these years.

The Association for University and College Counseling Center Outreach (AUCCCO; 2015), in its bylaws, defined outreach services as activities that extend the expertise of counseling centers to the larger campus community. By reaching a greater percentage of the student population than individual counseling appointments could alone, outreach and prevention services support, educate, and embed wellness across campus. More specifically, they can address several stigmatizing and ecological issues associated with attending college.

The Impact of Outreach and Prevention on Campus

- Increases resiliency and coping (Parcover, Mays, & McCarthy, 2015)
- Fosters developmental and interpersonal growth (Archer & Cooper, 1998; Kern, 2000)
- Nurtures a holistic identity (Kern, 2000)
- Promotes positive mental and emotional health (Asidao & Sevig, 2014; Parcover et al., 2015)
- Minimizes maladaptive student behaviors and problems (Archer & Cooper, 1998; Kern, 2000; Parcover et al., 2015; Sanchez & King-Toler, 2007)
- Decreases societal and cultural stigma associated with mental health and seeking support (Parcover et al., 2015; Sanchez & King-Toler, 2007; Shelton, 2017)
- Positively impacts equality, inclusion, and campus community culture (Sanchez & King-Toler, 2007)
- Assesses and addresses campus-wide needs (Archer & Cooper, 1998; Sanchez & King-Toler, 2007)
- Increases counseling center visibility and services (Parcover et al., 2015)
- Supports the institution's curricular and the cocurricular experiences (Kern, 2000)
- Complements the educational mission of higher education (Archer & Cooper, 1998; Kern, 2000)

Outreach and prevention have also been found to assist with retention and increase graduation rates, which make college administrators very happy (AUCCCO, 2016). With outreach as a counseling center's central mission, it has the power to contribute to a campus-wide culture of health, caring, and student mattering (Asidao & Sevig, 2014). As you read through this chapter, please refer to your learnings from Chapter 3, "College Counseling Through a Multicultural and Social Justice Lens." Outreach and prevention work best when an intentional environment is created that (a) allows for trust, vulnerability, and compassion; (b) honors the lived experiences of students; (c) respects the systemic impact and influence on students; and (d) creates a brave space for those affected by the outreach topic.

Because of the steady rise of student mental health issues on campus, there has been need for counseling centers to "broaden their focus considerably and to serve the entire campus community" (Ferriero, 2014, p. vi). Outreach, both contributive and preventive, can effectively reduce stress on the counseling center while still providing meaningful student services (Golightly et al., 2017; Kern, 2000). In addition, as you learned in Chapters 5 and 6, collaboration within the campus context significantly contributes to caring for students and their experiences.

Currently, many of these interventions are "aimed toward reducing demand as opposed to promoting services and gathering potential clients" (Golighty et al., 2017, p. 451). This is immediately beneficial to the center because, for some students, outreach is sufficient to address their needs (Shelton, 2017). Students are also entering college with more mental health and counseling savvy. This, in combination with the increased accessibility to college for students living with mental health issues, warrants this approach to prevent growing waiting lists and counselor burnout. For example, outreach can provide psychoeducation for development, direct students to alternative campus resources (e.g., office of student and family care, office of multicultural affairs, career services) for assistance, and help progress personal resources and resiliency.

Finally, outreach provides solutions to addressing mental health within challenging budgetary environments (Hunt, Watkins, & Eisenberg, 2012). Outreach can be a cost-effective solution to remedial services or individual therapy (Ferriero, 2014). Less budget, time, and staff resources are needed for running a workshop for students versus seeing those same students in individual counseling sessions (Ferriero, 2014).

The metaphor of a carrier pigeon comes to mind. The carrier or homing pigeon was historically used to communicate with individuals by delivering messages (sometimes over long distances) before returning home. These messages were left with recipients to experience the message, reflect, increase awareness, and/or make choices. The same can be said about today's college counseling center. Outreach and preventive programming are "flown" into areas of the campus community with hopes that students will experience a message, reflect, increase awareness, and make deliberate choices—and in some cases not needing to return with the pigeon. These messages also can reach students before they experience crisis, thus reducing emergency triage (Parcover et al., 2015). This embedding of prevention and treatment continues students on their path of academic and wellness success (Hunt et al., 2012). See Box 7.1 (Rollins College outreach example).

BOX 7.1

Outreach Example: Rollins College

Rollins College Counseling and Psychological Services offers a program entitled Sex and Chocolate. Refined with the use of interns over the years, this program was designed to educate, address questions, open conversation, and decrease stigma regarding sexual health and wellness. It is structured around student questions: Prior to the event, students are encouraged to write down questions they may have pertaining to sexual health and wellness, anonymously, to increase comfort. The questions are reviewed by a team of facilitators at the Wellness Center, who then present their responses and engage in dialogue surrounding sexual health. The program has become a popular word-of-mouth event that various organizations request. Counseling and Psychological Services has worked with Fraternity and Sorority Life as well as with faculty who request the program for their first-year student classes. Sex and Chocolate allows students to attain knowledge about healthy practices that are both preventive and developmentally appropriate. Staff have reported that they love this program because it really opens students' eyes to the fact that multiple perspectives and practices exist when it comes to sexual wellness. It empowers students to use their knowledge and implement practices that align with their beliefs and values.

Outreach and Primary Prevention Services: Definitions and Standards

There are many definitions of outreach and prevention. In fact, institutional definitions of outreach can vary quite a bit because of specific needs and campus environment. Differences include available resources to provide outreach, center and campus leadership, institutional size, mission, and overall scope of practice (Golightly et al., 2017). Below are examples of definitions:

- Outreach is "any organized program, workshop, media effort, class, or systematic attempt to provide psychological education—includes systematic attempts to modify the campus environment" (Stone & Archer, 1990, p. 557).
- "Outreach services are defined as activities which extend the expertise of counseling centers to the larger campus community" (AUCCCO, 2015, bylaws).
- "Outreach programming is a series of intentionally planned presentations and interactional experiences provided to students by college counselors" (Kern, 2000, p. 206).

As the field evolves, current definitions of outreach are expanding. There is an increased focus on social justice and advocacy, large-scale programming, close-knit partnerships and liaison relationships across the campus, potential restructuring wherein staff work outside the center, postvention of events, and use of technology to connect with students (Golightly et al., 2017).

Outreach activities can be implemented in terms of developmental and/or preventive models. Activities can also be direct, by use of facilitators with certain groups on campus, or indirect (i.e., awareness campaigns using brochures or signage across campus, campus-wide emails, campus alerts). Archer and Cooper (1998) suggested that outreach, in and of itself, is the "method or process of the activity, while prevention and development refer to the goals of the activity" (p. 122). Developmental outreach concentrates on student growth and healthy change. Thus, developmental programming may focus on psychosocial, cognitive, moral, ethical, behavioral, and identity areas. Prevention focuses on obstructing negative behaviors and mental health issues before they become severe. It is all in the terminology: Prevention occurs pre-event, or before distress becomes dysfunction. Typically, prevention is categorized in three ways: primary, secondary, and tertiary. Hoff, Hallisey, and Hoff (2009) defined these three levels as follows:

1. "*Primary prevention*, in the form of education, consultation, and crisis intervention, is designed to reduce the occurrence of mental disability and promote growth development, and crisis resistance in a community" (p. 26).
2. "The term *secondary prevention* implies that some form of mental disability has already occurred because of the absence of primary activities or because a person is unable to profit from those activities. The aim of secondary prevention is to shorten the duration of disability, often by providing sustained support and easy access to crisis services" (p. 27).
3. "The goal of *tertiary prevention* is to reduce long-term disabling effects for those who are recovering from a mental disorder. Social and rehabilitation programs are an important means of helping these people return to former social and occupational roles or learn new ones" (p. 28).

Working with the word *prevention*, we can define these three areas as pre-event, event, and postevent. Although this concept was fostered through a public health perspective, it directly applies to how college counselors can increase wellness on campus. Primary prevention (pre-event) might occur through new student orientations, consent week education, health promotions, and general workshops on coping and stress reduction. Another example of primary prevention is assessing the campus using campus climate surveys to uncover student issues and themes for programming. Secondary prevention (event) may be facilitated through providing direct clinical service, debriefing the campus after a student death, working with student affairs offices to provide support to students currently in need, and participating in national depression and anxiety screening days. Finally, tertiary prevention (postevent) can occur through support groups, follow-up services, and even the provision of medical leaves for students. With campus collaborations at the heart of prevention, this programming has a higher rate of success (Owen & Rodolfa, 2009). Three key college counseling associations, described below, have weighed in on the role and function of outreach and prevention. You will see that throughout these organizations the consensus and perspectives are that outreach is a vital role of the college. In addition, the 2016 Council for Accreditation of Counseling and Related Educational Programs (CACREP) Standards (CACREP, 2015) also discussed evidence-based prevention as an important part of training. In all, student affairs and counseling centers view outreach and prevention as something required, fundamental, and to be done with intention. See Box 7.2 (Rowan University outreach example).

The International Association of Counseling Services

The International Association of Counseling Services (IACS) is the accreditation body for university, 4-year-college, and 2-year-community-college counseling services. IACS's standards stress the importance of outreach services and interventions. Counselors are expected to be intentionally "involved in consultation with faculty and staff, student needs, advocacy, program development, outreach programming, retention activities, research, and program evaluation that support the efforts of faculty and staff in enhancing the university environment" (IACS, 2017, p. 2). IACS (2017) suggested that outreach interventions should do the following:

- "Offer preventive programming focused on developmental needs of students";
- "maximize the potential [of students] to benefit from their academic experience";
- "help students acquire new knowledge, skills and behaviors";
- "encourage positive and realistic self-appraisal";
- "foster personal, academic and career choices";
- "enhance the ability to relate mutually and meaningfully with others";
- "increase the capacity to engage in a personally satisfying and effective style of living";
- "be responsive to sexual/relational orientation, gender identity, racial, cultural, disability and ethnic diversity among students, and reach students who are less likely to make use of traditional counseling services" (p. 5).

BOX 7.2

Outreach Example: Rowan University

Rowan University's Counseling and Psychological Services, in conjunction with the Wellness Center, created a program entitled Paws for a Break. They reached out to an area therapeutic animal program (Alliance of Therapy Dogs) to provide a space for students to relax, de-stress, and connect with one another while meeting with therapy dogs and their handlers. A successful onetime program turned into a partnership of Alliance of Therapy Dogs and Rowan University's Residential Learning and University Housing and is now an ongoing event. This program serves 100 to 300 students a month with about a 50% increase in usage since its origination. Program evaluation is now conducted through pre/post questions about student health/well-being and mood.

Council for the Advancement of Standards in Higher Education

The Council for the Advancement of Standards in Higher Education (CAS) has standards for 45 functional areas on campus including college counseling services. Outreach is a required role for the counseling center and must address "developmental needs and concerns of students" and provide "support for students from diverse backgrounds" (CAS, 2011, p. 9). In addition, programming should assist "students to maximize their potential to benefit from the academic environment and experience"; provide "consultative services to the institution to help foster an environment supportive of the intellectual, emotional, spiritual, and physical development of students"; and offer "advocacy for a healthy and diverse learning community" (CAS, 2011, p. 5).

CAS views outreach services through two missions: (a) developmental and (b) preventive. Developmental missions focus on students' personal growth (e.g., realistic self-appraisal, appropriate perennial and occupational choices, intellectual development) and acclimation to the academic environment (CAS, 2011). Preventive missions concentrate on anticipating conditions that may have a negative impact on students' well-being (i.e., environmental and developmental) and introducing programming to attend to those target issues and populations.

The Association for University and College Counseling Center Outreach

Developed in 2009, the AUCCCO is an organization that specifically focuses on assisting "professionals involved in the leadership of outreach, consultation, and campus community interventions . . . to provide opportunities for networking, professional identity development, idea exchange and creating standards for quality outreach services" (AUCCCO, 2018, http://www.auccco.com/Mission-Statement). AUCCCO (2018) agreed that outreach and prevention efforts are fundamental to counseling center work and intentional programming must be viewed through ecological factors that affect the student and campus community. The effect of national events, campus climate, and the evolution of college student cohorts is one primary lens to understand campus needs. Finally, outreach should address campus diversity and promote social justice, including the intersection of multiple social identities and social locations (AUCCCO, 2018).

Need for Services

With the frequency of college students living with mental health issues, there has been an influx of students utilizing the counseling center. This is a noteworthy increase in awareness and acceptance of mental health by college students. It also may be a symptom of students entering college with fewer coping skills or previously existing conditions—potentially a generational influence. Regardless of the reason, with 35.3% of centers gaining staff positions in 2017, and only 7.4% losing staff positions, the field has not seen a decrease in waiting lists (LeViness, Bershad, & Gorman, 2017; Rando, Krylowicz, & Reetz, 2010). The Association for University and College Counseling Center Directors (AUCCCD) Annual Survey has shown a slight increase in waiting lists (31.4% in 2010 to 34.1% in 2017) but no decreases since it was first studied (LeViness et al., 2017). In addition, "for counseling centers with a waiting list, the average wait for a first appointment was 17.3 business days" (LeViness et al., 2017). Overall, we have the good (reduced stigma or increased awareness of need) with the bad (not enough staff to provide direct service), thus creating the dilemma of need versus time versus staff size.

With the increase of students with mental health issues, the Campus Care and Counseling Act was passed as part of the Higher Education Act at the federal level. This act provided additional competitive grant opportunities for campus mental and behavioral health service centers "to ensure that college students have the support necessary to successfully complete their studies" (Campus Care and Counseling Act, 2003, p. 5). This was a gain for centers, but as noted in aforementioned studies, further assistance is crucial. Until that appears, outreach and prevention are viable and much needed options to care for and maintain campus well-being.

In 2011, The National Alliance on Mental Illness conducted a study that surveyed 765 college students (currently enrolled or enrolled in college within the past 5 years) diagnosed with a mental health condition (Gruttadaro & Crudo, 2012). The resulting document is entitled *College Students Speak: A Survey Report on Mental Health.* This survey explored areas such as student dropouts, clinical services and supports, and supportiveness of colleges on mental health. Of note, 64% of participants reported that they are no longer in college or are not attending because of a mental health–related reason (Gruttadaro & Crudo, 2012). Although respondents identified that campus-based accommodations and mental health services might have helped them stay in school, they also reported that "they were not aware of or did not access these supports while they were students" (Gruttadaro & Crudo, 2012, p. 5). Respondents were also asked about barriers to seeking services; 36% reported stigma as a barrier; 34%, busy schedule; 25%, hours of service; and 24%, lack of info (Gruttadaro & Crudo, 2012). In addition, respondents offered reasons why they found their colleges supportive or not supportive (see Table 7.1).

The "not supportive" reasons illustrate where outreach and prevention might be missing. This study also reinforces the important role colleges must play when it comes to mental health awareness and service. Sanchez and King-Toler (2007) agreed, stating that "consultation and outreach activities are an integral part of the services that counseling centers provide to the university community" (p. 286) that can both promote wellness and prevent maladaptive behaviors. Reducing stressors, supporting underrepresented groups, educating on consent, raising awareness on depression/suicide, and educating on drug/substance use is just a piece of the puzzle. However, this is a start to students believing their college is supportive of mental health. See Box 7.3 (George Washington University outreach example).

TABLE 7.1

Top Five Reasons Students Found Colleges Supportive or Not Supportive

Supportive	*Not Supportive*
There are advocates on campus who help students understand their rights and access services and supports.	The school does not educate faculty, staff, and students on mental health. Thus, stigma persists, and professors do not follow accommodations.
The school understands that college can be stressful, and that mental health is a priority. The college educates faculty, staff, and students on mental health.	They do not publicly acknowledge or discuss mental health issues with the campus community and the impact these issues can have on students.
The college links with community mental health services and supports if there are not enough available on campus.	There are not enough mental health staff members and/or care available to students. There is a lack of follow-up once students access help.
The college provides walk-in appointments, easy appointment scheduling, 24/7 care, unlimited counseling and support groups for students.	The college does not openly welcome students living with mental health conditions. Students are penalized for their mental health conditions.
All students are aware that help is available.	Mental health services and supports on campus are not publicized. Students have to seek them out.

Note. Reprinted from "College Students Speak: A Survey Report on Mental Health," by D. Gruttadaro and D. Crudo, 2012, National Alliance on Mental Illness, p. 19. Retrieved from https://www.nami.org/About-NAMI/Publications-Reports/Survey-Reports/College-Students-Speak_A-Survey-Report-on-Mental-H.pdf.

BOX 7.3

Outreach Example: The George Washington University

The George Washington University's (GW's) Counseling and Psychological Services (CAPS) created the Let's Talk series, which collaborates with two academically demanding professional school partners: the GW School of Medicine and Health Sciences and the GW Law School. Because these unique student populations struggle with finding time to utilize counseling services, CAPS brings services to students with this program. Let's Talk is an informal "consultation" hour that takes place weekly within both schools. A licensed clinician is present in the same room at the same time weekly for one-on-one 15-minute student consults that end with recommendations/referrals to CAPS or on-campus partners. Informal groups run on-site when students have similar issues or concerns. Student use is tracked on a weekly, monthly, and yearly basis. Assessment has shown an increase in the utilization of services by both medical school students and law school students. Successful collaboration between CAPS staff and the GW medical and law schools has been made possible by the designation of a liaison or CAPS point person for each school. Regular meetings occur to maintain communication, identify trends, get feedback on services, and sometimes develop additional specific professional school programming.

Outreach and Prevention as a Function of the Counseling Center

Outreach plays a large role in counseling center work with 87.2% of centers reporting that outreach is an integral part of their mission (AUCCCD, 2017). In addition, 89% reported providing psychoeducational groups and workshops (AUCCCD, 2017). With this high percentage, having a designated outreach coordinator can assist with structure, focus, and continuity. According to the AUCCCO (2016) survey, the professional title for this work is quite diverse and a large proportion of outreach coordinators (64.38%) have between 0 and 4 years of experience (see Table 7.2).

Regardless of title, Sharkin (2012) suggested several outreach coordinator responsibilities:

- "Fielding requests for presentations and programs" (Sharkin, 2012, p. 44).
- "Ensuring that each requested program is assigned" (Sharkin, 2012, p. 44).
- "Promoting outreach and programming as a key component of service delivery" (Sharkin, 2012, p. 44).

TABLE 7.2

Professional Titles for Outreach Coordinators as Reported by the Association for University and College Counseling Center Outreach Annual Study: 2016–2017

Professional Title	%
Outreach Coordinator	45.21
Associate or Assistant Director of Outreach	28.77
Staff Clinician	23.29
Outreach Director	5.48

Note. From Association for University and College Counseling Center Outreach, 2016, p. 6. Additional titles included Outreach and Training Coordinator, Outreach Specialist, and Education and Prevention Coordinator.

- "Explore opportunities for collaborative efforts with other offices and student groups on campus" (Sharkin, 2012, p. 44).
- "Compilation of materials to be used for outreach (e.g., handouts and pamphlets)" (Sharkin, 2012, p. 44).
- "Maintenance of a calendar for outreach programing during the academic year" (Sharkin, 2012, p. 44).
- "Collection of data from programs conducted (e.g., attendance, evaluations, etc.)" (Sharkin, 2012, p. 44).

In addition, some counseling centers that are housed within larger wellness centers on campus may do a large percentage of the outreach and prevention programming, which is created and disseminated by the health promotions office and staff who hold public health degrees. This is sometimes referred to as "wellness outreach."

Surveys have been conducted on 2-year and community colleges. According to the American College Counseling Association Survey of community/2-year college counseling services conducted by Edwards and Lenhart (2017), 68% of these institutions provide psychoeducational programming to students. With these institutions encompassing mostly commuter student bodies, outreach can be quite difficult. In fact, 78% of surveyed institutions reported not having on-campus housing (Edwards & Lenhart, 2017), and in another survey only 28% of public community colleges have on-campus housing (American Association of Community Colleges, 2018). Thus, outreach must occur where students are, which can sometimes require creative thinking and alternate campus environments such as classrooms, communal areas, and online environments.

A large percentage of these institutions (79%) use their center home page to reach students (Edwards & Lenhart, 2017). Facebook (36%) and online mental health screening tools (21.6%) are also means. Finally, it was reported that programs or classroom visits composed 36.1% of counseling center referrals. This suggests the necessity for campus collaboration to reach the remaining students—which is happening. A large percentage of referrals come from faculty, accessibility services, advising offices, and tutoring services (Edwards & Lenhart, 2017). There has been an increase in early programming in 2-year and community college to assist with students' first year in higher education. In a study conducted by Alamuddin and Bender (2018), it was found that 95% of 2-year institutions offer first-year orientations, 87% provide first-year seminars, and 71% offer proactive interventions based on early alerts. See Box 7.4 (Savannah College of Art and Design outreach example).

Creating Outreach and Prevention Programming

King Lyn (2017) suggested that counseling centers that have robust outreach, prevention, and consultation programs are "best equipped to lead the campus community in help-

BOX 7.4

Outreach Example: Savannah College of Art and Design

Savannah College of Art and Design's (SCAD's) Counseling and Support Services created a collaborative program, entitled the SCAD Pizza Fairy, where pizzas are delivered around campus to students quarterly. The purpose was to raise awareness of the availability of mental health services after it was learned that students did not have full knowledge of the center. Since 2004, this program has done much more than the original goal of raising awareness and continually conveys a message of care and support as it reaches about 1,000 students per quarter. Collaboration includes residence life, academic departments, and funding for pizzas from local psychiatrists and psychiatric hospitals. It has a Facebook page with over 2,500 followers.

ing students find appropriate treatment" (p. 300). Intention, preparation, and delivery are of great importance for this service. Considering that, this section will cover the nuts and bolts and practical side of creating and presenting outreach and prevention services. Many counseling centers are also finding themselves needing to develop strong programs because of outreach becoming a primary intervention on some campuses (Golightly et al., 2017). For example, in 2006 the University of Michigan Counseling and Psychological Services began examining new ways of promoting mental health on campus (Asidao & Sevig, 2014). They found they were relying too much on direct client services and offering presentations when they had available time. Through this awareness they partnered with campus staff to actively engage students in systematic ways that would strengthen a web of support and enact a community of caring (Asidao & Sevig, 2014, p. 134). Increasing campus awareness occurred through using educational programming; increasing Counseling and Psychological Services' presence on campus; and providing tools to faculty, staff, and students for self- and other assistance. This type of work not only increases targeted programming to foster wellness but it also opens dialogues with "faculty, student leaders, and administration" (Fauman & Hopkinson, 2010, p. 262).

There are several skills needed to provide successful programming and prevention. Asidao and Sevig (2014) suggested that these include identifying outreach needs; building multicultural competency; and training others in effective prevention, outreach, and evaluation. Additional competencies are interpersonal and facilitation skills, flexibility and structure, ability to generalize student comments or questions, and ability to create a safe space for vulnerability but knowing how to prevent a program from becoming counseling.

Outreach Mission and Goals

Alongside skills, two additional areas help shape programming: (a) creating an outreach mission statement and (b) setting outreach goals. These areas help further solidify a center's understanding of and commitment to outreach and prevention. Below are examples of outreach mission statements:

> It is our mission at CWC to go beyond the walls of our offices and reach out to the campus community to promote psychological and interpersonal wellness on campus. (University of Florida Counseling and Wellness Center, 2019)
>
> SHaW Outreach advocates for the balanced and integrated emotional, social, and academic functioning of our diverse community. Guided by our commitment to diversity and social justice, SHaW Outreach strives to create a safe and inclusive environment to enhance the quality of life on our campus. We aim to reach every member of our community through specialized training which raises awareness, reduces stigma, addresses barriers, and promotes holistic wellness. (University of Connecticut Student Health and Wellness, n.d.)
>
> The Counseling and Testing Center is committed to reaching out to the university community. Outreach and consultation services are a vital part of how the Counseling and Testing Center interacts with the university at large and promotes student development outside the physical space of the Counseling and Testing Center. . . . The outreach programs focus on meeting the developmental needs of students and on promoting their academic, personal, social and psychological growth. (Georgia State University Counseling and State University, 2019)

Outreach mission statements send the message of campus community and care as well as create a framework for program design.

Outreach and prevention goals provide for consistency across programs. Goals include collaboratively identifying widespread community health issues and providing education and access to prevention techniques and activities that reduce or eliminate risk before it becomes problematic (Manderscheid, 2007). Overall goals are great, but college counseling centers should adjust goals on the basis of the uniqueness of their campus and student populations. For example, a 2-year college will have different goals because of the commuter versus residential student populations. As an example, Loyola University created five outreach goals with a public health focus:

1. Promote awareness of core mental health concepts among both Counseling Center clients and the wider community, including universal delivery on topics that are widely applicable to our student community.
2. Increase the probability of referrals by students, faculty, and staff for concerning students.
3. Endeavor to consider the impact on various subpopulations and individuals of social and economic issues, access to resources, and physical and emotional safety concerns.
4. Continually re-assess and identify needs of the student population.
5. Promote a strengths-based framework rather than an illness-focused approach. (Parcover et al., 2015, pp. 201–202)

These goals create a consistent narrative. A center might also consider where outreach services and their mission statement are located on the center's website. A transparent wellness message is important for students, faculty, and staff.

Creating an outreach mission statement and outreach goals should be a collaborative experience organized by the outreach coordinator. Getting on the same page regarding outreach and prevention work will allow center staff to hold the same narrative when connecting with other student affairs staff, faculty, student organizations, and other campus entities. In addition, this collective narrative allows the center to distinguish itself. In beginning this process, the counseling center team should first ask themselves the questions, "Who do we want to be as participants in college outreach and prevention?" and "Who are we actually as participants in college outreach and prevention?" Comparing aspirational with actual is the first step to understanding this component of your counseling center. Next, you will want to explore your institutional characteristics regarding students, faculty, environment, and campus climate.

Using Campbell and Yeung's (1991) Ashridge mission model, centers can construct and rework their mission on the basis of four important mission statement parts (adjusted for the counseling center):

- *Purpose*—Does it say why the outreach and prevention arm of the counseling center exists and their responsibility to the campus community?
- *Strategy*—Does the statement give an impression of a distinctive competence in the area of outreach and prevention?
- *Values*—Does it convey what the counseling center believes in regarding outreach and prevention? Does this also convey staff values?
- *Policies and behavioral standards*—Are action standards evident that staff can compare their outreach creation and delivery with?

Finally, centers will want to make sure the statement is concise, reads well, and offers a snapshot of who they are in this area. Establishing goals is the next step. When the mission statement is used as an overall objective, goals should become action elements that, when combined, fulfill the mission.

Students and Outreach

There is a lot to consider when creating and conducting outreach and prevention programming, including barriers that impede students seeking help. Examples include one's culture, identity, social location, developmental level, and learning style. Thus, a lens of diversity is suggested when creating an outreach mission, goals, and programming. This lens can actively tailor programming "to the needs and challenges faced by underrepresented and marginalized communities on campus," and "advocate for underserved students, promote inclusion, reduce cultural barriers for help seeking, and increase access to students who might otherwise never seek counseling" (Golightly et al., 2017, p. 453). Others have concurred that increasing access and delivery of mental health can reduce psychological and cultural barriers that stand in the way of access to underrepresented students (Eichler & Schwartz, 2010; Sanchez & King-Toler, 2007).

It is vital to understand student developmental and learning styles as students are complex and unique. Kern (2000) suggested that theories provide direction and a sound basis for effective outreach programming. Staff should also examine student development theories through a multiculturally informed lens because many theories were developed on majority-White and higher socioeconomic students. Part III of this text ("Student Development Theory, Student Learning, and Developmental Considerations") goes further into how to use student development theory with a contemporary lens as well as discusses several theories. Also, student development theory is the language of student affairs, so understanding these theories fosters a common language across campus.

Types of Outreach and Prevention

From brochures to social media, outreach takes many forms. It includes "presenting to specific groups, such as academic classes, residence hall groups, and fraternities/sororities, or being present at campus wellness fairs or student services expos" (Marks & McLaughlin, 2005, p. 86). If programming meets the center's mission, has intention, is based on specific campus needs, and reaches specific target populations, then outreach format can vary. There are several focal areas for outreach and prevention. They will shift depending on need and environment; however, Owen and Rodolfa (2009) suggested three key areas to consider. The first, campus climate, focuses on ecological and systemic needs of the college. Examples may include wellness fairs and educational or social media campaigns that attend to mental health awareness on campus. The second, interpersonal relationships, focuses on fostering healthy, positive, and meaningful relationships. It also helps individuals make "relationship decisions to reduce and prevent psychological distress" (p. 29). The third and final area, intrapersonal functioning, focuses on raising personal awareness and "identifying warning signs of mental health distress" (p. 30).

Outreach and prevention programs can be simplified into people, places, and things. The *people* area focuses on determining the target population for programming; the *places* area is defined by the means, mode, and delivery system of programming; and the *things* area concentrates on the program topic and issues. Successful programming is possible when these three areas work in harmony.

People: Target Population

Target populations on campus include students (e.g., affinity groups, campus organizations, freshmen, athletic teams, nontraditional students, minority students, international students), faculty (e.g., tenure track and adjunct), staff (e.g., student affairs, academic affairs, resident assistants, facilities, coaches, clergy), and student families or guardians. Additional populations include advisers, teaching assistants, dining and housekeeping services, and campus safety and police staff (Fauman & Hopkinson, 2010). Selecting a target population should be based on assessment that yields empirical evidence of need, not informal theory. For example, a counseling center might offer intentional outreach or preventive programming to resident assistants for different reasons. As part of their responsibilities, resident assistants learn basic helping skills and crisis assessment. In addition, counseling center staff may approach resident assistants with preventive programming on burnout or reactive programming after a campus crisis in which they assisted. Outreach aimed toward faculty and staff occur because they are typically the first line to observing troubled students (e.g., psychological, medical, and career-oriented assistance; Cronin, 1991; Sharkin, 2012). Parents and guardians become a part of outreach programming at new student orientations, during family weekends, and through psychoeducation on college student adjustment.

Places: Means, Mode, and Delivery

Delivery systems are quite diverse and, as mentioned earlier, should be based on assessing for appropriate means to reach target populations. The laundry list of formats includes classic presentations (requested and offered), panels, social media campaigns, website messaging (AUCCCD, 2017), mobile-friendly website self-help, wellness fairs, general brochures, brochures specific to target populations (Poyrazli, 2015), flyers and other publications (Sharkin, 2012), counseling center open houses (Cronin, 1991), online screenings, student media (e.g., radio station broadcasts, podcasts, and newspapers), campus emails, animal-assisted therapy/therapy dogs (Daltry & Mehr, 2015), tabling, and SWAG ("stuff we all get"—typically, free items such as stress balls, pens, and t-shirts that have the counseling center logo or emergency hotline information). Choosing a method can feel overwhelming, but by understanding one's target population, the optimal method for connection will emerge. One example, *Starting the Conversation: College and Your Mental Health*, by the National Alliance on Mental Illness (NAMI) and the Jed Foundation, is a great example of a paper and web-based method to reach parents and guardians (NAMI & JED, 2016).

Things: Topics and Issues

Topics and issues enter a counseling center's radar for several reasons. Workshops can be requested; a campus climate survey might highlight student or campus environment issues; and a community, national, or global event may call for debriefing or education. Regardless of program topic, the outreach coordinator must assess for the need to prevent wasted resources (i.e., time and budget).

Although there are a myriad of topics and issues, Kern (2000) suggested three key areas of focus:

- ***Educational-career***: study skills, test taking, note taking, textbook reading, time management, learning styles, career decision making, the freshman experience, the senior experience, job hunting, resumes, and interviewing strategies;
- ***Personal-social:*** relationships, dating, financial wellness, date rape, depression, anxiety disorders, addictions, anger management, conflict management, understanding personality characteristics, personality styles, leadership skills, culture and identity, contemporary issues or "hot topics," and decision making;
- ***Health-related:*** drug and alcohol abuse, sexually transmitted diseases, HIV and AIDS, diet and exercise, and pregnancy concerns. (p. 211)

Additional topics include college adjustment, political and social climate, acculturation, privilege, discrimination and oppression, grief, suicide prevention and gatekeeper training, disordered eating/body image, parent orientation, self-injury, sex and intimacy, coping with holiday stress, sleep issues, and any other mental health awareness or wellness topic. In certain circumstances, topics may center around educating administration and university officials about the counseling center, scope of practice, limitations, and needs (Much, Wagener, & Hellenbrand, 2009).

Institutions are viewing outreach through a holistic wellness perspective. Originating at Ohio State University (Ohio State University Wellness Center, 2018), the "Nine Dimensions of Wellness" (see Table 7.3) were created to assess multiple areas of student development and balance lifestyles. Outreach and prevention programs can address these nine domains while creating a universal model that offers a consistent narrative (see Table 7.3).

In addition, it is useful to generate a list of potential concerns and issues. Many centers have created general and month-by-month lists not only to aid in creating a schedule for programming but also to be posted on their website for parents and students to be informed about what may come. Preparation can be prevention, and the Rockhurst University counseling center offers a great example of a month-to-month list (https://ww2.rockhurst.edu/counseling-center/parent-resources/college-transition).

Program Design

Sound program design is at the heart of any successful program. First and foremost, empirical need is essential to achieving a successful program. Parcover et al. (2015) suggested three key questions once the need is identified:

1. What are the issues that need to be addressed?
2. What resources do we want the community to be aware of?
3. How can we communicate our message to increase help-seeking and referrals? (p. 203)

In addition, counselors not only should understand the people, places, and things but also must deliberately explore areas such as collaboration, timing, advertising, accessibility, processing model, and assessment.

TABLE 7.3

Nine Dimensions of Wellness

Wellness Dimension	*Definition*
1. Emotional	The emotionally well person can identify, express and manage the entire range of feelings and would consider seeking assistance to address areas of concern.
2. Career	The professionally well person engages in work to gain personal satisfaction and enrichment, consistent with values, goals and lifestyle.
3. Social	The socially well person has a network of support based on interdependence, mutual trust, respect and has developed a sensitivity and awareness towards the feelings of others.
4. Spiritual	The spiritually well person seeks harmony and balance by openly exploring the depth of human purpose, meaning and connection through dialogue and self-reflection.
5. Physical	The physically well person gets an adequate amount of sleep, eats a balanced and nutritious diet, engages in exercise for 150 minutes per week, attends regular medical check-ups and practices safe and healthy sexual relations.
6. Financial	The financially well person is fully aware of financial state and budgets, saves and manages finances in order to achieve realistic goals.
7. Intellectual	The intellectually well person values lifelong learning and seeks to foster critical thinking, develop moral reasoning, expand worldviews and engage in education for the pursuit of knowledge.
8. Creative	The creatively well person values and actively participates in a diverse range of arts and cultural experiences as a means to understand and appreciate the surrounding world.
9. Environmental	The environmentally well person recognizes the responsibility to preserve, protect and improve the environment and appreciates the interconnectedness of nature and the individual.

Note. From the Ohio State University Wellness Center (2018) website at https://swc.osu.edu/about-us/nine-dimensions-of-wellness/.

Not Reinventing the Wheel

With lots to consider, spare time a premium, and trying to do more with less, counselors should take advantage of preexisting free and organizational membership materials. In addition, college counselors reaching out to college counseling centers will find a community that is willing to share materials. The college and university counseling communities are strong, collaborative, and willing to share resources.

Counseling Center Village, University of Buffalo

The Counseling Center Village (http://ccvillage.buffalo.edu/) is an online community resource created by college and university counseling centers nationally and globally. Resources include, but are not limited to, psychoeducational workshop outlines, manuals, handouts, readings and conference presentations, screening days and wellness fairs, and links to professional organizations.

AUCCCO

AUCCCO grew out of a passion and need to create community for counseling center outreach professionals because of the greater weight on outreach, education, and prevention. Their website lists many resources including outreach coordinator manuals, annual counseling center outreach survey and report, outreach mission statements, diversity resources, presentations resources on a myriad of topics, brochures, evaluation/tools resources, workshop design strategies, mental health smartphone applications, and a dedicated outreach electronic mailing list. Most colleges have an institutional membership that includes access to the abovementioned materials. In addition, membership includes mentorship programs, reduced conference fees, resource sharing, professional support, and formal connections to counseling center outreach professionals.

Therapist Aid

Therapist Aid (https://www.therapistaid.com/) provides free evidence-based education and therapy tools. Materials are created with the client in mind and avoid jargon. This resource is great for gathering ideas for specific topics to aid in outreach and prevention.

From Concept to Evaluation

There are many ways to design a program, but to ensure consistency and efficiency, outreach coordinators should create a structured outline. Cooper and Heenan (1980) suggested 11 "key elements in workshop design" that offer such a structure (pp. 107–109). These elements *are gathering information about participants, fun and/or engagement, time, appropriate sequencing, simplicity, variety, expectations, climate setting, pacing, flexibility,* and *assessment and evaluation*. In addition, there is significant research suggesting how certain elements impact design and presentation (Archer & Cooper, 1998; AUCCCO, 2016; Cooper & Heenan, 1980; IACS, 2017; Hunt et al., 2012; Kern, 2000; Marks & McLaughlin, 2005; Sanchez & King-Toler, 2007; Shelton, 2017). Table 7.4 combines additional suggestions, from the literature and the chapter author, using Cooper and Heenan's (1980) model as a foundation. Key elements have been increased to 13, with the addition of *advertising and promotion* and *processing and debriefing* (see Table 7.4).

Challenges to Outreach Programming

Even with resources, counseling centers still face roadblocks to delivering effective services. Factors such as staff size, time constraints, budgetary issues and cuts, and low attendance can affect programming (Marks & McLaughlin, 2005). Ferriero (2014) also discussed issues and challenges to outreach programming and offered additional issues:

TABLE 7.4
Fundamental Outreach and Prevention Program Design Elements

Key Element	*Action Example*
1. Gathering information about participants	Knowing the student target population and subject; size of the group; voluntary versus mandatory; familiarity of the participants with each other (Cooper & Heenan, 1980) Knowing student needs and concerns (Cooper & Heenan, 1980; Kern, 2000) Developing and conducting campus and target population needs assessments (Kern, 2000) Being mindful of "sexual/relational orientation, gender identity, racial, cultural, disability and ethnic diversity among students" (IACS, 2017, p. 5) and "power and political influence" (Archer & Cooper, 1998, p. 122)
2. Fun and/or engagement	Ensuring fun for the presenter as well as for students (Cooper & Heenan, 1980) Using creative experiences, activities, and information that maintain attention and deepen meaning
3. Time	Knowing time limits for program goals and if breaks are built in; allowing time for reflecting, integrating, and debriefing; allowing time for unanticipated issues (Cooper & Heenan, 1980) Knowing days and times that may be most appealing and convenient to students (Marks & McLaughlin, 2005) Avoiding conflicts with major or traditional campus events, student mealtimes, and weekend involvement (Kern, 2000)
4. Advertising and promotion	Using flyers, brochures, campus email, using counseling center staff; having faculty build outreach programming into their curriculum; advertising on the counseling center website and college calendar; collaborating with outside center staff, offices, and faculty; offering food and giveaways (Marks & McLaughlin, 2005) Generating program titles that are catchy and innovative (Marks & McLaughlin, 2005; Shelton, 2017) Generating program titles that keep cultural stigma in mind and that do not pathologize students and mental health concerns (Shelton, 2017) Creating simple and legible flyer designs
5. Appropriate sequencing	Using natural design flow with a beginning, middle, and end; following the principles of sequencing (Cooper & Heenan, 1980) Understanding the level of interaction needed for both structured and nonstructured experiences
6. Simplicity	Using easy-to-understand design for the presenter(s) and participants (Cooper & Heenan, 1980)
7. Variety	Appealing to the emotional, intellectual, physical, cultural, and spiritual parts of self (Cooper & Heenan, 1980)
8. Expectations	Knowing program expectations; offering transparency of expectations (Cooper & Heenan, 1980)
9. Climate setting	Considering locations, nontraditional therapeutic settings and students' natural environment (Kern, 2000; Sanchez & King-Toler, 2007) Considering size of physical space, furniture setup, comfort, lighting, temperature, and availability; ensuring setting is conducive to safe interpersonal exchanges, self-exploration (Cooper & Heenan, 1980)
10. Pacing	Keeping accessibility in mind when considering locations Paying attention to presenter's pacing and rate of speech; observing participants' pacing to absorb material and experiences; being mindful of packing in too much information and experiences (Cooper & Heenan, 1980)
11. Flexibility	Being flexible during the presentation and reworking the design for most impact (Cooper & Heenan, 1980)
12. Processing and debriefing	Asking questions for personal and group reflections; using here-and-now versus then-and-there questions; using horizontal versus vertical disclosure questions. Kolb's 4-step cycle—concrete experience, reflective observation, abstract conceptualization, and active experimentation (Kolb, 1984) SAGA: sharing, analyzing, generalizing, and applying (Ober, 1991)
13. Assessment and evaluation	Conducting ongoing evaluations for in vivo flexibility; concluding evaluations (Cooper & Heenan, 1980) Conducting evaluations shortly after the program is complete for accurate evaluation (Kern, 2000) Survey instrument modality examples: iPads, clickers, pencil and paper, online tools (e.g., Qualtrics, SurveyMonkey, QP scanners, Titanium) Immediate (e.g., program, presenter[s], educational material, attendee knowledge) and larger scope evaluations (e.g., counseling center and campus impact, related retention)

- Lack of time can limit the "amount or longevity of outreach initiatives" (p. 98).
- Individual students seeking help "take precedence over outreach" (p. 98).
- "Finding common ground or reasons for counseling centers to interact with student organizations" (p. 98).
- "Getting students to participate in programs or events is an issue" due to busy schedules (p. 99), campus climate (p. 100), students' attitudes toward campus events (p. 100), and "over programming in student affairs" (p. 100).

Assessing and predicting barriers is the best way to avoid pitfalls. Of course, students' lives are very busy, and attending any nonmandated program is a constant struggle.

Collaboration

Whether it is combining budgets or using captured student populations, when staff across campus assist with programming, barriers become minimized. Campus partnerships can be formed with professors, staff, students, and other campus and student organizations that support the infusion of mental health, wellness, and preventive principles within the college community (Ferriero, 2014; Golightly et al., 2017; Sanchez & King-Toler, 2007). The idea is to not address student mental health and wellness needs in isolation but rather extend the counseling center's reach through mutual support group systems to increase visibility and development (Golightly et al. 2017; Sanchez & King-Toler, 2007). Student organizations with a focus on mental health and prevention offer additional arms in this venture—for example, Active Minds (Sontag-Padilla et al., 2018) and student wellness ambassador programs (Parcover et al., 2015). Reaching out to individual offices or speaking about needs and campus issues in larger student affairs forums can foster connections. For example, the counseling center can work with the office of international students to create educational and supportive programming regarding the Deferred Action for Childhood Arrivals policy and its impact on campus. They can also connect with career services regarding job seeking and graduation stress. Finally, recruiting student affairs offices and student organizations to promote and advertise presentations is beneficial (Marks & McLaughlin, 2005). See Box 7.5 (Berkshire Community College outreach example).

Conclusion

With the increase of direct service to students, counseling centers must create inventive ways to care for the campus without overextending staff and elongating waiting lists. Outreach and prevention can be the channel to accomplish this. But programming should

BOX 7.5

Outreach Example: Berkshire Community College

Staff at Berkshire Community College Personal Counseling Center collaborate with Title IX, their Women's Center, and related community centers/partners to discuss sexual assault and domestic violence. Outreach programs include showing *The Hunting Ground* (Scully et al., 2015), followed by a panel discussion with a Sexual Assault Nurse Examiner, a district attorney, and a representative from a local women's resource center; a week-long event on Domestic Violence with a forum entitled Breaking the Cycle of Domestic Violence, as well as the Clothesline Project ("The Clothesline is made up of t-shirts created by survivors of violence, or created in honor of someone who has experienced violence"; Clothesline Project, 2016).

be current and specific, educational, preventive, and developmental as it serves as the impetus for change (Kern, 2000; Marks & McLaughlin, 2005; Sanchez & King-Toler, 2007). Looking forward, Golightly et al. (2017) suggested some areas for centers to reflect on. First, training and internship programs can include "specific training and supervision surrounding outreach service delivery" (p. 458). Second, counseling centers should explore creating outreach-specific standards and best practices in relation to professional ethics and empirical evidence. Third, acquiring and/or creating staff outreach coordinator positions is another area for centers to reflect on. Finally, assisting the field to increase the empirical support of outreach prevention programming is also an area for reflection. With intention, direction, and collaboration, outreach and prevention can increase healing and wellness on campus and reduce stress on the counseling center.

Final Case Study

You are a staff clinician at your institution. Your counseling center director asked you to create an outreach program on the topic "going home for the holidays." This evolved from an increased rate (in comparison with past fall semesters) of first-year students reporting elevated levels of distress from the combination of finals and especially leaving campus for the break. The director believes that with the semester's end fast approaching, and students not showing and/or canceling because of finals, it is important to reach out to them outside of the counseling center.

Case Exploration Questions

1. Knowing your campus environment and student population, what are your initial thoughts about why there might be an increase in student distress about leaving for winter break?
2. People: What do you know about your target population?
3. Places: What means, mode, and delivery system of programming would fit best?
4. Things: What program topics, subtopics, and issues are important to cover?
5. What "Dimensions of Wellness" does this outreach and prevention program cover?
6. Which campus offices might make good collaborators in this endeavor, and why?
7. What challenges might you, as a staff clinician, and this outreach program encounter?
8. More specifically, what does your program look like being walked through Table 7.4, "Fundamental Outreach and Prevention Program Design Elements."

References

Alamuddin, R., & Bender, M. (2018). *First-year student support: Supporting high-achieving first-year students at public two-year institutions.* Retrieved from https://www.jkcf.org/wp-content/uploads/2018/09/Supporting-First-Year-Students-Jack-Kent-Cooke-Foundation.pdf

American Association of Community Colleges. (2018). Fast Facts. Retrieved from https://www.aacc.nche.edu/research-trends/fast-facts/

Archer, J. A., Jr., & Cooper, S. (1998). *Counseling and mental health services on campus.* San Francisco, CA: Jossey-Bass.

Asidao, C., & Sevig, T. (2014). Reaching in to reach out: One counseling center's journey in developing a new outreach approach. *Journal of College Student Psychotherapy, 28,* 132–143.

Association for University and College Counseling Center Directors. (2017). *The Association for University and College Counseling Center Directors annual survey.* Retrieved from https://www.aucccd.org/assets/documents/Governance/2017%20aucccd%20survey-public-apr26.pdf

Association for University and College Counseling Center Outreach. (2015). *Bylaws: The Association for University and College Counseling Center Outreach.* Retrieved from http://www.auccco.com/resources/Documents/2015-auccco-bylaws-1.pdf

Association for University and College Counseling Center Outreach. (2016). *The Association for University and College Counseling Center Directors annual survey 2016–2017.* Retrieved from http://auccco.com/resources/Documents/Tools%20and%20Resources/The%20AUCCCO%20Annual%20Survey%20and%20Report%202016-2017%20Overview.pdf

Association for University and College Counseling Center Outreach. (2018). About section. Retrieved from http://www.auccco.com/

Campbell, A., & Yeung, S. (1991). Creating a sense of mission. *Long Range Plan, 24,* 10–20.

Campus Care and Counseling Act of 2003, H.R. 3593, 108th Cong. (2003).

Clothesline Project (2016). About the Clothesline Project. Retrieved from http://clotheslineproject.info/about.html

Cooper, S., & Heenan, C. (1980). *Preparing, designing, leading workshops: A humanistic approach.* Boston, MA: CBI.

Council for Accreditation of Counseling and Related Educational Programs. (2015). *2016 CACREP standards.* Alexandria, VA: Author.

Council for the Advancement of Standards in Higher Education–CAS. (2011). The role of counseling services. Retrieved from http://collegecounseling.org/CAS-Standards

Cronin, C. (1991). Counseling center outreach: A guide to simple inexpensive programming. *International Journal for the Advancement of Counselling, 14,* 253–261.

Daltry, R. M., & Mehr, K. E. (2015). Therapy dogs on campus: Recommendations for counseling center outreach. *Journal of College Student Psychotherapy, 29,* 72–78.

Edwards, J., & Lenhart, A. (2017). *Survey of Community/Two-Year College Counseling Services, 2016–2017.* Alexandria, VA: American College Counseling Association.

Eichler, R. J., & Schwartz, V. (2010). Essential services in college counseling. In J. Kay & V. Schwartz (Eds.), *Mental health in the college community* (pp. 57–93). Hoboken, NJ: Wiley.

Fauman, B. J., & Hopkinson, M. J. (2010). Special populations. In J. Kay & V. Schwartz (Eds.), *Mental health in the college community* (pp. 247–265). Hoboken, NJ: Wiley.

Ferriero, J. R. (2014). Outreach practices of a small college counseling center: A comprehensive model to serve the college community (Doctoral dissertation). *Doctoral Dissertations 2014–current.* (Paper 81)

Georgia State University Counseling and State University. (2019). Outreach and consultation. Retrieved from https://counselingcenter.gsu.edu/services/outreach-consultation/

Golightly, T., Thorne, K., Iglesias, A., Huebner, E., Michaelson-Chmelir, T., Yang, J., & Greco, K. (2017). Outreach as intervention: The evolution of outreach and preventive programming on college campuses. *Psychological Services, 14,* 451–460.

Gruttadaro, D., & Crudo, D. (2012). *College students speak: A survey report on mental health.* National Alliance on Mental Illness. Retrieved from https://www.nami.org/getattachment/About-NAMI/Publications-Reports/Survey-Reports/College-Students-Speak_A-Survey-Report-on-Mental-Health-NAMI-2012.pdf

Hoff, L. A., Hallisey, B. J., & Hoff, M. (2009). *People in crisis: Clinical and diversity perspectives* (6th ed.). New York, NY: Routledge.

Hunt, J. B., Watkins, D., & Eisenberg, D. (2012). How do college campuses make decisions about allocating resources for student mental health? Findings from key participant interviews. *Journal of College Student Development, 53,* 850–856.

International Association of Counseling Services. (2017). *Standards for university and college counseling services.* Retrieved from https://0201.nccdn.net/4_2/000/000/053/0e8/2017-STANDARDS-10-5-17.pdf

Kern, C. W. (2000). Outreach programming from the college counseling center. In D. C. Davis & K. M. Humphrey (Eds.), *College counseling: Issues and strategies for a new millennium* (pp. 205–219). Alexandria, VA: American Counseling Association.

King Lyn, M. M. (2017). Integrating the counseling center into the broader campus. In S. J. Hodges, K. Shelton, & M. M. King (Eds.), *The college and university counseling manual: Integrating essential services across the campus* (pp. 289–303). New York, NY: Springer.

Kolb, D. A. (1984). *Experiential learning: Experience as the source of learning and development.* Upper Saddle River, NJ: Prentice Hall.

LeViness, P., Bershad, C., & Gorman, K. (2017). *The Association for University and College Counseling Center Directors annual survey.* Retrieved from https://www.aucccd.org/assets/documents/Governance/2017%20aucccd%20survey-public-apr26.pdf

Manderscheid, R. (2007). Considering a public health approach: The public health framework might work well in addressing mental health and substance use problems. *Behavioral Healthcare, 27,* 45–46.

Marks, L. I., & McLaughlin, R. H. (2005). Outreach by college counselors: Increasing student attendance at presentations. *Journal of College Counseling, 8,* 86–96. doi:10.1002/j.2161-1882.2005.tb00075.x

Much, K., Wagener, A. M., & Hellenbrand, M. (2009). Practicing in the 21st century college counseling center. *Journal of College Student Psychotherapy, 24,* 32–38.

National Alliance on Mental Illness & the Jed Foundation. (2016). *Starting the conversation: College and your mental health.* Retrieved from https://www.nami.org/collegeguide/download

Ober, K. (1991). "Processing" questions for each level of "SAGA." Retrieved from https://ubwp.buffalo.edu/ccvillage/wp-content/uploads/sites/74/2017/06/Processing.pdf

Ohio State University Wellness Center. (2018). Nine dimensions of wellness. Retrieved from https://swc.osu.edu/about-us/nine-dimensions-of-wellness/

Owen, J., & Rodolfa, E. (2009). Prevention through connection: Creating a campus climate of care. *Society for College and University Planning* (January–March), 26–33.

Parcover, J., Mays, S., & McCarthy, A. (2015). Implementing a public health approach to addressing mental health needs in a university setting: Lessons and challenges. *Journal of College Student Psychotherapy, 29,* 197–210.

Poyrazli, S. (2015). Psychological symptoms and concerns experienced by international students: Outreach implications for counseling centers. *Journal of International Students, 5,* 306–312.

Rando, R., Krylowicz, B., & Reetz, D. (2010). *The Association for University and College Counseling Center Directors annual survey.* Retrieved from http://files.cmcglobal.com/aucccd_directors_survey_monograph_2010_public.pdf

Sanchez, D., & King-Toler, E. (2007). Addressing disparities: Consultation and outreach strategies for university settings. *Consulting Psychology Journal: Practice and Research, 59,* 286–295.

Scully, R. K., Blavin, P., Dick, K., Ziering, A., Wadleigh, T., Kopp, A., . . . Anchor Bay Entertainment. (2015). *The hunting ground* [Motion picture].

Sharkin, B. S. (2012). *Being a college counselor on today's campus: Roles, contributions, and special challenges.* New York, NY: Routledge.

Shelton, K. (2017). Multicultural counseling competency and diversity issues. In S. J. Hodges, K. Shelton, & M. M. King (Eds.), *The college and university counseling manual: Integrating essential services across the campus* (pp. 13–40). New York, NY: Springer.

Sontag-Padilla, L., Dunbar, M. S., Ye, F., Kase, C., Fein, R., Abelson, S., . . . Stein, B. D. (2018). Strengthening college students' mental health knowledge, awareness, and helping behaviors: The impact of Active Minds, a peer mental health organization. *Journal of the American Academy of Child & Adolescent Psychiatry, 57*, 500–507.

Stone, G. L., & Archer, J., Jr. (1990). College and university counseling centers in the 1990s: Challenges and limits. *The Counseling Psychologist, 18*, 539–607.

University of Connecticut Student Health and Wellness. (n.d.). SHaW outreach services. Retrieved from https://counseling.uconn.edu/outreach-services/

University of Florida Counseling and Wellness Center. (2019). Our outreach mission statement. Retrieved from https://counseling.ufl.edu/outreach/

Chapter 8

Crisis and Emergency Management

Brian Van Brunt, Amy Murphy, and Jeff Solomon

If you want to go fast, go alone. If you want to go far, go together.
—African Proverb

■ ■ ■

Reflection Exercise

Prior to reading this chapter, please write down answers to the following questions. Consider these as you continue through the chapter:

1. What crisis events and emergencies are likely in your work?
2. Have you experienced emergencies and crisis events before? What did you learn? How were you affected?
3. How prepared do you feel for responding to an emergency or crisis today? What about providing support and resources after the crisis?
4. What resources and information would help prepare you when a crisis strikes?

■ ■ ■

Whereas Chapter 7 outlined the importance of counselor roles in strategic outreach and prevention, Chapter 8 acknowledges that despite our best efforts the college campus is certainly not immune to crisis and emergency. When the inevitable crisis or disaster strikes the campus community, the college counselor may be involved in the initial intervention, ongoing management and clinical response, or "postvention" and/or recovery efforts. The counselor can offer expertise in understanding the impact of trauma as well as informing emergency management processes. This chapter will explore the nature of crisis events on the college campus, ranging from individual crises to natural disasters. Then we will discuss current models and essential principles in emergency management for the college counselor, sharing in detail one promising practice for the prevention and management of campus concerns, the Behavioral Intervention Team (BIT), or Concern, Assessment, Response, Evaluation (CARE) team (Deisinger, Randazzo, O'Neill, & Savage, 2008; Sokolow,

Lewis, Shuster, Swinton, & Van Brunt, 2014; Van Brunt, 2012). Behavioral Intervention Teams are collaborative, multidisciplinary teams actively identifying at-risk behaviors in the campus community, gathering data from multiple sources across the campus and community, and deploying interventions to prevent the escalation of behavior. The college counselor's role and expertise on the BIT is critically important to its effectiveness, so this chapter provides information on tools for the counselor to collaborate with the BIT, including performing violence risk assessments.

We have included three case examples at the start of the chapter to help the reader to better understand some of the range of crisis events counseling staff may be called in to assist with on campus. The case examples highlight the role of the counselor alongside other student affairs professionals and campus units responding to a crisis. You will notice we outline the scope of a counselor as it relates to crisis and emergency as including more than individual counseling and instead being a critical part of a crisis team. We expand on the opportunities for a collaborative relationship between college counselors, faculty and staff, the campus conduct office, campus safety, and others to better prevent and respond to campus crises. Crises and emergencies can feel daunting and scary even for the most prepared and experienced counseling professional. We hope this chapter can offer a framework and guidance to support counselors in their work preparing for and responding to crises and emergencies.

Case Examples

The Case of Daria

Daria has experienced chronic depression for most of her life. She tells her roommate, friends, and classmates of her plans to kill herself over the weekend. She has been struggling with feeling accepted at school and the surrounding conservative community in that she identifies as a lesbian. The community becomes worried about her and reports their concerns to the campus BIT, conduct office, and residential life. Daria disappears the night before she said she would kill herself, and no one is able to find her. Off-campus police are called in, and they search the woods surrounding the campus with a group of campus staff and resident advisers. Daria is found sitting in the woods with a backpack filled with knives, a rope tied into a noose, a supply of her medication, and a bottle of vodka. She is taken into custody and hospitalized.

Under what circumstances can Daria return to campus? What is the role of college counseling for Daria? How can college counseling be most helpful in Daria's situation? What is the impact to her friends and community resources related to the search and suicide attempt? Should there be a minimum standard of mental health stability for students to attend college? What can the college require versus suggest?

The Case of Carlos

Carlos is a 34-year-old war veteran returning to college after several active duty tours in Afghanistan. He does well in his classroom environments but is someone who likes order and consistency in his work and time. He begins to become increasingly anxious that his military paperwork and financial aid forms have not been processed correctly and shows up several times a day to ask the financial aid and Veterans Affairs office to check their records. The behavior is confusing to the staff, and, beyond checking their records, they are not quite sure how to help Carlos. What kind of services could have been offered to Carlos prior to his anxiety growing? What departments on campus would be the best to assist Carlos? Is a referral to counseling appropriate? What resources in the community could help? How could departments collaborate to support veteran and military students on campus? Should Carlos's disruptive behavior in the classroom skip the campus conduct process given his military service?

Group Cases

A White supremacist group on campus is scheduled to speak, and another group of students protests the event by showing up with signs calling them Nazis and fascists. Campus safety attempts to keep the groups apart throughout the day, but during the talk, students from the counterprotest throw eggs and baggies filled with red paint at the speaker and panel. Campus safety calls in off-campus police support, and several students are arrested. Clashes continue between groups on campus over social media and in heated arguments in the classroom. What are the limits of free speech on campus? How could college counseling be helpful in this scenario, prior to the incident, during, and after? How does the CARE/BIT team work with police and student conduct to address this behavior? When considering sanctions, what role do punitive sanctions (e.g., paying a fine), developmental sanctions (e.g., reflecting on behavior through an essay or counseling), and/or restorative justice (e.g., paying back those who have been injured or hurt in the community) play in addressing individual behaviors in this incident?

■ ■ ■

Types of Crisis: From Natural Disasters to Active Shooters

Crisis events on the college campus truly run the gamut. As Part IV will outline, there are several individual student crises that require the clinical expertise of the college counselor, and there are other crisis experiences present on the college campus ranging from intentional acts of harm against individuals and the community to natural disaster events. Consider for a moment the types of incidents that occur in the college environment. A student experiences chronic depression with suicidal thoughts. A student is bullied or assaulted by another student. Natural disasters such as earthquakes, tornados, hurricanes, and snowstorms affect the campus. An active shooter targets the campus to obtain revenge or hurt others whom he or she believes deserve retribution. Students yell and threaten financial aid and registrar staff over perceived frustrations with the campus bureaucracy. Campus police address incidents of drug sales and gang violence. Campus protests and counterprotests spin out of control and escalate into violence. The campus grieves the loss of members of their community.

Good crisis prevention starts with early identification of concerning behaviors. Most faculty and staff understand the importance of seeking assistance for an actively suicidal student, the need to call for police assistance during an active emergency, and the impact of natural disasters on the campus community. Unfortunately, less concerning behaviors or incidents occurring prior to a crisis can be overlooked, and campuses miss the opportunity to intervene with resources and assistance before situations escalate. College counselors and other student affairs staff are an important stakeholder in educating the campus community on the importance of prevention, early alerts, and referrals to campus services and to a BIT.

There are many opportunities to educate your populations on concerning behaviors and BIT services other than new student orientation. In this case, redundancy and the duplication of efforts are important and encouraged. Make sure your campus safety or campus police force are on the same sheet of music as your counseling staff, and even offer to train your campus law enforcement. This accomplishes two goals: First, it educates a population that may not understand all of the campus resources as they relate to BIT, and, second, it affords face time with campus law enforcement. It is essential to build a relationship with law enforcement prior to the crisis; the first time you meet your local law enforcement should not be in the middle of a crisis. It is always preferable to develop a working relationship with law enforcement and recognize a friendly face during times of stress and confusion.

Van Brunt and Lewis (2014) and Van Brunt and Murphy (2017) identified the types of behaviors faculty and staff should report to conduct offices or BITs to get in front of crisis and emergency situations. These are not behaviors being reported to get the student in trouble or remove the student from campus, but rather to better assess the risk of a given situation. As we will describe later in the chapter, BITs put together puzzle pieces of information from across campus and connect the student to care and support. These types of examples help a counselor to distinguish between different types of behaviors when consulting with faculty and staff and to recognize the types of behaviors important to report to a BIT. See Box 8.1 for some disruptive behavior examples and Box 8.2 for some dangerous behavior examples.

College counselors should also be trained in the identification of both disruptive and dangerous behaviors and how to use crisis de-escalation skills to redirect and calm upset

BOX 8.1

Disruptive Behaviors

Disruptive behaviors are those that interrupt the normal learning environment but do not create a threat for violence. Although many of these behaviors could be considered frequent activities students engage in given their developmental growth, the core of crisis de-escalation requires early identification and early intervention. The following are some examples of disruptive behaviors:

- Taking/making calls, texting, using smartphones for social media, and so forth, while waiting in line for assistance or in the classroom.
- Frequent interruption while talking and asking nonrelevant, off-topic questions.
- Inappropriate or overly revealing clothing, including extremely sexually provocative clothes, pajamas, or sleepwear.
- Engaging in cross talk or carrying on side conversations while you are trying to speak. May be to a friend or on a phone.
- Interruptions in conversation, frequent use of the restroom, smoke breaks, and so forth.
- Poor personal hygiene that makes it difficult to continue a conversation or teach class.
- Lack of focus or paying attention to conversation. Excessive sighs or eye rolls.
- Use of alcohol or other substances in your presence. Attending a meeting while under the influence of a substance. Being intoxicated in class.
- Entitled or disrespectful talk to staff or other students. Interrupting the professor.
- Arguing points of contention or asking for special treatment after the staff or faculty requests the student to stop.
- Eating or consuming beverages in meetings or class without permission (or against the office norms).
- Showing up to meetings or class in inappropriate or strange clothing (dressed in military gear, Halloween costumes when it is not Halloween, etc.).
- Reading magazines, newspapers, or books or studying for other classes/doing other homework during a conversation with you or during class.

BOX 8.2

Dangerous Behaviors

Dangerous behaviors are those that interrupt the normal learning environment and create a threat or risk of physical violence. Left unchecked, these behaviors typically escalate into arguments, fights, and potential police involvement. As with disruptive behaviors, early identification and intervention are critical to mitigate the crisis. The following are some examples of dangerous behaviors:

- Racist or otherwise exaggerated (not just expressed once to press a button) thoughts such as, "Women should be barefoot and pregnant," "Gays are an abomination to God and should be punished," "Muslims are all terrorists and should be wiped off the earth."
- Bullying behavior focused on students in the counseling center waiting room, outside the office, in the classroom, or in the residence halls.
- Directly communicated threat to staff, faculty, or another student, such as "I am going to kick your ass" or "If you say that again, I will end you."
- Prolonged nonverbal, passive-aggressive behavior such as sitting with arms crossed, glaring or staring at staff, and refusing to speak or respond to questions or directives.
- Self-injurious behavior such as cutting or burning self during a meeting or exposing previously unexposed self-injuries.
- Physical assault such as pushing, shoving, or punching.
- Throwing objects or slamming doors.
- Storming out of the office or room when upset.
- Engaging in conversations that are designed to upset other students or staff such as descriptions of weapons, killing, or death.
- Exhibiting psychotic or delusional speech.
- Engaging in arrogant or rude talk to staff or other students.
- Objectifying language that depersonalizes the staff or other students.

individuals. Counselors are often asked to consult with faculty and staff struggling with difficult student situations. In fact, each of the three case studies in this chapter provide examples of incidents wherein counselors may be tasked with consultation with campus community members. When offering insight and advice to those faculty and staff, it is important to stress this as a two-stage process. The first stage is calming the initial crisis, addressing the behavior, and de-escalating. The second stage is sharing the concern forward to the BIT or the conduct office if a BIT does not exist. There is a tendency to see the problem as finished after the initial crisis has been resolved. A better approach is understanding that although the initial crisis is resolved, perhaps there is risk of this problem expanding to other places and new behaviors. This early intervention helps prevent the escalation of incidents, allowing a focus instead on resources to help students succeed. College counselors can positively encourage BIT referrals by explaining the importance of faculty and staff recognition, response, and referrals in these situations.

College counselors should also be familiar with concepts central to violence risk assessments. Van Brunt's (2012) book *Ending Campus Violence* reviewed over 90 incidents of violence that took place in high schools and on college campuses. On the basis of that research, Van Brunt and Murphy (2017) developed 10 general concepts to attend to when it comes to what kind of behaviors or situations most commonly lead to violence. Although not an exhaustive list, this is a helpful starting place for faculty and staff to better understand the nature of more extreme violence. College counselors should recognize these as cautionary warning signs or red flags for further investigation by the BIT:

1. Attend to students who share with others details related to a planned campus attack (known as "leakage" in the threat assessment field).
2. Attend to work conflicts and terminations with fellow staff and academic failures and program dismissals with student.
3. Investigate and closely monitor unrequited romantic relationships that lead to isolated, irrational behavior.
4. Look for manifestos or large societal messages that indicate a deeper, entrenched view of the world or call to action.
5. Identify those who feel hopeless or are irrational in their logic.
6. Watch for all bullying behavior (perpetrator and victim), and attend specifically to bullying behavior that creates isolation and an environment where a smoldering individual grows more dangerous in his or her thinking.
7. Look for gaps in students who need mental health services on campus.
8. Although rare, be concerned about the sociopath and those that take pleasure in harming others and expressing obsession-filled hate and threats of violence toward individuals or groups.
9. Pay attention to small hints and dropped information. Those who engage in violence rarely just snap; violence is often the product of months (if not years) of planning.
10. Watch for the hopelessness and desperation to escape pain that occurs in suicidal individuals.

These risk factors are important to recognize as potential aggravating factors for targeted violence. In efforts to prevent violence, it is critical to look beyond the yelling student or the aggressive student making threats to others. Helping the community understand what risk factors to share and how these can be detected and reported forward in a moral and ethical manner is essential. Counselors need to educate students, faculty, and staff to be aware of these risk factors in the community. These concerns should be shared with the campus BIT or CARE team to act preventively and address the problem before it escalates.

Campus Models for Emergency Response

Counselors have traditionally been called on to assist with community response during or following a crisis, but they should also be involved in emergency preparedness activities and policy design as well as help to deploy trauma-informed campus systems well before a crisis ever occurs. Uhernik's (1998) text about counselors and disaster response emphasizes the importance of counselors understanding how their role and the function of behavioral health is part of a larger framework for emergency management. Many campuses train for emergencies using systems related to the U.S. National Response Framework such as the National Incident Management System (NIMS) and the Incident Command System (ICS) (www.fema.gov/national-incident-management-system). Uhernik suggested counselors should seek NIMS and ICS training to better coordinate with other emergency responders. It is likely your institution and outside agencies will follow NIMS/ICS during a crisis. This may include establishing a Unified Command, Emergency Operations Center, Incident Commander, and other positions found within ICS. As a counselor, it can be helpful to work with ICS, even as much as running a parallel ICS within your counseling functions and/or duties. This offers a better understanding of the larger operation, whom you will report to, and with whom you will coordinate and adjust the normal operating procedures in terms of ICS's during a crisis. Remember, this process typically is required for your institution under state and federal law.

Another aspect of emergency response might involve the establishment of a Family Assistance Center. In this setting, counselors are often tasked with providing crisis counseling and support for those affected by the emergency, including family members of students.

Minimally, counselors should be prepared with the following information and resources about their campus and unit's emergency response model:

- Does the campus have an emergency operations plan or emergency response plan? What types of incidents does it cover? What activities described in the plan relate to the function of counselors?
- Does the counseling unit have a communication plan for crisis situations? What is your role in the plan? How would you be notified about required duties and responsibilities? How will your unit communicate with other campus partners during the emergency?
- What roles and responsibilities are identified for your counseling unit during campus emergencies? What is the system or process for maintaining normal counseling services and activities during a campus emergency? Is there an alternative location to provide services should your facility be unavailable?
- Are there specific campus characteristics, populations, or attributes that influence the response to a campus crisis? Are you assisting more commuter students? Will you be consulting with more adjunct faculty? Are there special populations that will need additional assistance? Are certain issues and topics hot buttons for your campus and more difficult to manage?
- Does your campus participate in NIMS or ICS training? Are there opportunities for your participation or requirements to participate in trainings and exercises? Does your counseling unit train on emergency response and crisis?

When counselors are asked to assist in campus emergency response, it is important to recognize how the scope of services being provided is different from a counselor's typical mental health treatment services. The Department of Homeland Security and the Federal Emergency Management Agency have outlined key principles for crisis counseling that are different from other mental health treatment. Crisis counseling

> supports short-term interventions that involve the counseling goals of assisting disaster survivors in understanding their current situation and reactions, mitigating stress, assisting survivors in reviewing their disaster recovery options, promoting the use or development of coping strategies, providing emotional support, and encouraging linkages with other individuals and agencies who may help survivors in their recovery process (recover to their pre-disaster level of functioning). (Federal Emergency Management Agency, 2017)

Crisis counseling is thus more outreach-oriented and nontraditional. Services may be delivered in the campus community instead of in an office setting where students must actively seek out services, or they may be offered via group settings or telephone. We have mentioned the need for a coordinated response to large-scale campus emergencies, but counselors may also be asked to respond to residence halls, student organization meetings, or classrooms where students are struggling with grief and loss in specific populations. Providing services in these nontraditional settings is an important aspect of the role of a counselor responding to emergencies on the college campus. In the third example, the campus is affected by an event involving extremist violence. This may not feel like an incident requiring a counselor response, but counseling services are a critical contributor to the recovery processes of the campus. Outreach to affected students and group counseling can offer safe opportunities for dialogue during times of campus turmoil. Counselors should be ready to work alongside colleagues in other campus units when crisis strikes. These collaborative relationships are one of the most powerful ways to respond effectively and comprehensively to campus crisis.

Crisis Intervention

Responding to a crisis event requires counselors to switch from everyday life to the extraordinary situation in front of them. Identifying this point of transition allows counselors to establish the proper mindset to respond quickly and to appropriately address the behavior presenting in front of them. Counselors who are not able to transition from an everyday meeting and conversational skills into the skills required to intervene when disruptive or dangerous behavior occurs will not be as effective in achieving the desired outcome. Uhernik (1998) identified several models for immediate disaster behavioral health response, ranging from critical incident stress management (https://icisf.org) to psychological first aid (Everly & Lating, 2017) to cognitive behavioral therapies (Beck, 2011). Counselors should review the various evidence-based practices, discuss them with their supervising units, and determine the best techniques for their skills and campus needs.

There are also several practical skills that can be used during crisis interventions. These foundational techniques can be taught to faculty and staff by counseling units when training on managing disruptive and dangerous behavior around campus. A common challenge when training counselors is to have them attend to their surroundings. It does no good to be right and strive to win the argument but end up physically assaulted. These are the times when a counselor says, "Well, Dylan . . . I am sorry you are upset, but it clearly says right here in the informed consent—that you have had since the beginning of your treatment—that you cannot miss more than two appointments or you will be banned from making future appointments." Although the counselor is certainly correct making these statements to the student, he or she may be missing the subtle changes in the student's behavior such as clenched fists, shifting back and forth, and glaring eyes that signal an impending attack. Likewise, a key to preventing disruptive behavior from escalating requires counselors to bring their attention and focus to bear on the existing behavioral problem. Too often, behavior management becomes a nuisance and a frustration, and key questions are not considered in deference to getting back to the content of the rules or policy enforcement.

When staff members are working with Carlos, in the second case example, a natural reaction would be to return in kind his insulting behavior or to set a firm limit about his behavior. A successful intervention with Carlos begins with seeing him as overwhelmed and not interacting at his best. Counselors are well suited to apply their skills in rapport building, basic empathy, and avoiding lecturing or escalating, but they can also convey the importance of these concepts when assisting faculty and staff with difficult situations. When staff use these skills, they can conceptualize the problem in a manner that does not lend itself to internalizing Carlos's expressed frustrations or taking offense. Then staff are better able to respond with full use of their skills and abilities rather than in a reactive manner. The staff should remain calm and give the student an opportunity to tell his or her story. They should use active listening (a paraphrasing technique) and try to repeat back to the student what he or she has indicated is a concern. They should show empathy without committing to a change in regard to the decision. They should use phrases such as "It sounds like this has been a frustrating process for you," "I can understand being angry or scared trying to balance school after returning from combat," or "What I hear you saying . . ."

When one is confronted with crisis behavior, some questions to ponder include the following:

- Why is this student acting out right now? What might be some causes of his or her inappropriate behavior (interrupting, misuse of technology, rude or entitled response)?
- What are my goals for an intervention with this student? What is the desired outcome of my intervention?
- What kind of intervention with this student will bring about the desired effect?
- Is this a behavior I should address now or something I should address after the student finishes?

In terms of these basic attending skills, Miller and Rollnick (2002) shared some ideas on how to address a crisis event with an expression of empathy in their approach of motivational interviewing. This expression of empathy involves a conversation with the student that attempts to both understand the student's perspective (empathy) and communicate an understanding of that perspective (expression of empathy). This expression of empathy respects the student's point of view, freedom of choice, and ability to determine his or her own self-direction. Suggestions for change from the counselor, faculty, or staff member are subtle, and the ultimate change is left up to the student. Counselors skilled in crisis intervention techniques not only are more prepared to respond to individual incidents but also are better able to communicate to faculty and staff more effective ways to respond to difficult situations.

Crisis Recovery and Trauma-Informed Care

Most emergency response models include multiple stages: planning and preparedness, coordinated response activities, and recovery. Counselors can help ensure that campus processes and departments are prepared to work with students following crisis and trauma as part of a recovery phase of crisis and emergency management. For students returning to campus after a crisis or others who experience trauma while enrolled, counselors and other staff who are skilled in trauma-informed processes and care are more likely than those who lack such skills to be able to engage with these students and form the connections helpful to their future success. The suggested mindset is one that considers the previous experiences and perspectives of a student and how they affect the student's current behaviors and attitudes. Trauma-informed care (Treleaven, 2018) focuses on the strengths of each individual student, incorporates a goal of building resilience, and reminds the campus community that it is not about "what is wrong" with a student but is instead about considering "what happened" to the student.

Trauma-informed care is the idea of designing departmental processes and interactions in a manner that accounts for the impact of trauma on students and other members of the campus community. When we, as counselors, are thinking about our ongoing interactions with students who have previously experienced trauma, these are tools that we can use to increase the utilization of our services for students as well as their overall impact. Staff can use techniques and processes associated with trauma-informed care to help create environments better designed for students recovering from crisis and trauma. When we consider Carlos in the second case example, incorporating trauma-informed processes into work in financial aid and other campus units can make a difference for the experiences of students and can prevent additional crises from occurring. Counselors can collaborate with other departments such as Veteran and Military Affairs to inform units like financial aid on the impact of trauma for our military students and how to create more thoughtful environments in our service units. Counselors could consult with financial aid and help identify alternative ways to respond to Carlos's anxiety such as helping him to check the status of his paperwork online, giving him specific timelines for the completion of financial aid processes, or allowing him to choose how he would like communication about his financial aid status. In many ways, a trauma-informed approach enables counselors to deliver a level of service for students that improves rapport, reduces missed understandings, and supports the student's experience.

Trauma-informed processes have been used successfully in several settings, including medical and mental health care, substance abuse treatment and recovery, homeless and refugee populations, and military veteran services. In recent years, trauma-informed processes have reemerged as a critical component of effective and equitable responses to incidents of sexual violence. Being trauma-informed means

- recognizing situations and experiences that create trauma;
- acknowledging the array of responses and reactions to trauma in both the short term and the long term;
- considering campus environments and their impact on those who have experienced trauma;
- having an awareness of the causes and impact of retraumatization;
- understanding the impact of trauma on those indirectly involved such as friends and family;
- prioritizing student choice and decision-making related to traumatic events;
- focusing on student safety and building trust, and understanding the influences of cultural competence in relation to trauma (Office of Violence Against Women, 2013).

The nature of some crises and emergencies can also result in recovery periods on a campus where the risk of additional crises is high. An example is following a campus suicide. Suicide postvention efforts specifically consider the grieving process, risk factors for suicide, and high-risk behaviors and environments related to suicide prevention following the crisis event. Tailored postvention efforts such as those outlined by the Higher Education Mental Health Alliance (2014; https://hemha.org) consider the unique elements of a crisis and how to incorporate prevention activities into a community's recovery efforts. This work incorporates elements distinctive to the incident such as the presence of online and social media activity related to the student suicide and targeted communications to high-risk groups such as students who knew the deceased. These comprehensive plans consider elements of suicide recovery ranging from considering whether the student was a client of the counseling unit to protocols for memorials and campus events related to the student's death. If we consider Case Example 1, involving Daria, although she did not complete a suicide attempt, her behaviors were certainly disruptive to the campus community and required response and prevention efforts for those students affected by what occurred. Case management could assist her in feeling more supported around her sexual orientation through a counseling referral, connection to local resources, or a campus lesbian, gay, bisexual, transgender, and queer/questioning club. Counseling may also be involved in offering services to those who reported concerns about Daria. Recovery efforts that are tailored for an individual campus, sensitive to the needs of the campus community and individuals involved, and widely collaborative offer the best opportunities for a long-term, effective response to a community crisis.

Behavioral Intervention and CARE Teams

The good news for college counselors is that you aren't in this alone. Most colleges and universities have invested in developing a BIT or CARE team, whose purpose is to identify, assess, and manage threat and dangerousness on campus. The college counselor is an important part of the community and can help ensure the team knows about crisis events, however small, that occur within various departments, offices, or residence halls. In fact, the first stage of any BIT or CARE work is ensuring the community knows about their process and what to report forward to the team. The discussion early in the chapter on the recognition of disruptive and dangerous behaviors is a good starting point for reporting to the BIT.

Following the shooting tragedy at Virginia Tech in 2007, there has been a push to formalize teams of staff and faculty at institutes of higher education to assess potential threats to campus security. It is estimated that over 80% of 4-year colleges and universities have such teams (Eells & Rockland-Miller, 2011). More recent data from the Association of University and College Counseling Center Directors (LeViness, Bershad, & Gorman, 2017) showed that 91% of schools had these teams. Depending on the mission and purpose of the team, they also help identify at-risk students to provide services and connection among existing departments. Although teams were around prior to the shooting in 2007, they were more informal and focused on resolving immediate crisis events or on critical incident/emergency response following natural disasters, explosions, and fire. Teams existed in the forms of campus "mom and dad" administrators who were serving as de facto parents independently, and as ad hoc "student of concern" teams who operated without protocol or objective measurement. The evolution of knowledge and practices has led to more formalized, protocol-driven, objective teams.

Schools without residential housing and those that are community and technical colleges may struggle to obtain the resources needed to operate a BIT successfully. Schools with a large online presence are also challenged to translate the BIT work from the 4-year college model to better address community colleges. Further research is needed to collect and analyze data on the differences among BITs that are related to educational setting—colleges with residential life, 4-year schools, community colleges, for-profit colleges, technical colleges, online institutions, and so forth.

The National Behavioral Intervention Team Association (NaBITA) is the largest member organization in the United States dedicated to the development, implementation, and improvement of BIT and CARE teams. There are dozens of free white papers and peer-reviewed research articles available from this organization. They suggest a three-phase model that includes data gathering, analysis, and intervention. The first phase involves educating the community through a website, brochures, posters, videos, and in-person trainings to report concerns forward to the team. Once concerns are reported, the team then uses tools such as the NaBITA Risk Rubric (Sokolow et al., 2014), the Violence Risk Assessment of the Written Word: VRAW^2 (Van Brunt, 2015b, 2016), the Structured Interview for Violence Risk Assessment: SIVRA-35 (Van Brunt, 2012, 2015a), and the Extremist Risk Intervention Scale: ERIS (Van Brunt, Murphy, & Zedginidze, 2017) to better rate the potential risk. Once the analysis is complete, the team then moves on to intervention and addresses the behavior through counseling, law enforcement, case management, and the conduct process as appropriate.

Threat assessment teams focus primarily on identifying threats to campus safety. BITs focus on identifying behaviors of concern and providing intervention strategies and action plans to address the behavior. NaBITA describes a process wherein the BIT or CARE team operates as an umbrella, and underneath that umbrella several members of the BIT have an expertise in threat and violence risk assessment. This helps reduce siloing of information between the BIT/CARE and threat assessment team, removes the need for separate reporting and policy/procedure manuals for two teams, and avoids the need to create complicated referral processes between the BIT/CARE and the threat assessment team. It also allows for those who are doing the threat and violence risk assessments to be part of the process earlier, prior to a direct threat or a conditional ultimatum being made.

Counselors often act in various capacities on the campus BIT/CARE or threat assessment team. This may involve sitting as a regular core team member, conducting threat or violence risk assessments, consulting on mental health–involved cases, or assisting with intervention and support outreach for at-risk students. In the next sections, we discuss some of the challenges and opportunities that exist when a counselor is working as part of the BIT in a collaborative manner to prevent violence on campus.

The Role of the Counselor on the BIT

A frequent topic discussion at academic conferences in higher education centers on the role of counselors, psychologists, social workers, and marriage and family counselors on the BIT. In some states, including Texas and California, there have been efforts to expand the definition of a counselor to include non–mental health treatment staff. These staff may or may not have clinical degrees or licensure but are asked to perform some basic adjustment, personal crisis, and academic counseling. Although this work is valuable and important, the misuse of the name counselor often leads to confusion with the student population and the community. When one is looking at BIT communications, both internally and externally with other departments, state confidentiality laws and/or the Health Insurance Portability and Accountability Act of 1996 (HIPAA)—depending on whether your counseling center does third-party billing; most do not—govern clinical communications from licensed medical and mental health providers. This is one reason why it is not ideal to have a medical or mental health professional lead the team. Imagine that medical and mental health staff communication requirements are like a light that those staff members have attached to them. Wherever they go, that light follows. This light becomes the guiding principle for the team's communications rather than the Family Educational Rights and Privacy Act of 1974 (FERPA). When licensed, clinical individuals are hired to provide nonclinical services, it is often difficult for medical and mental health clinicians to make that shift from privileged communication to the more open format of FERPA, which is the standard by which BITs communicate. In summary, some colleges hire licensed clinical staff to work in a nonclinical capacity. This means their communications are governed by FERPA and not HIPAA or state confidentiality law.

Private information, in a higher education or school context, is information protected by FERPA. Private information can be shared internally when there is a legitimate educational interest, often referred to as a "need to know." Private information can be shared externally when an exception to FERPA is met, such as in cases of emergencies, dependency, and consent. FERPA protections extend only to records kept by college officials in a written or recorded medium. Information you learn of or know of from in-person interactions that is not made into a record is not protected by FERPA. A right to privacy has also been recognized by the courts outside of statute when there is public revelation of information in which an individual would have a reasonable expectation of privacy. A lawsuit, resulting financial damages, or loss of a professional license could occur from this kind of breach of privacy.

A more protective layer of legal insulation is confidentiality. Confidentiality, whether conferred by statute or by ethical codes, is the right of a client/patient to control how information he or she shares with a professional is protected. Because the client has the right of confidentiality, the professional has a commensurate duty to maintain that confidentiality. Confidentiality is most often conferred in the relationship between therapist and client or between a health care provider and patient. It can also be formed between advocates and victims, or in some states, between athletic trainers and athletes. Confidentiality is more protective than privacy, because there is no authorized need-to-know basis for breaching confidentiality. Instead, confidentiality is bounded by consent of the client or patient, by statute and exceptions to statutes, and by court-made doctrine as in situations of a duty to warn (e.g., Sokolow & Tarasoff v. Regents of University of California, 1976, case). Exceptions to confidentiality vary from state to state and can pertain to child abuse disclosures, HIV+ status, elder abuse, substance abuse, and other statutorily created health or safety risks. Additionally, confidential records may be subpoenaed and/or may be accessible by an employer in the event of litigation. A confidential relationship is often demarcated by the creation of an informed consent that explains the protections afforded by the relationship.

The most sacrosanct level of protection under the law is that of privilege. Privileged communication is secret and protected from disclosure, which can only be pierced by a court order or waiver of the owner of the privilege. Privilege is rarely in play for the BIT but would readily be found in the relationship of lawyer-client, spouses, journalist sources, and the confessional (although clergy may only have the protections of confidentiality in some jurisdictions). There are many nuances to what kind of communication, even within the relationships described as privileged, can actually be legally protected. There is also some bleed between categories. For example, courts recognize doctor-patient privilege in most jurisdictions, while statutes and ethical codes may also protect the doctor-patient relationship with confidentiality. Additionally, a medical records privacy act (HIPAA) also confers patient privacy. Privilege and confidentiality protect the relationship, whereas HIPAA (and FERPA in a college environment) protect only the records of that relationship.

The larger question plaguing many teams is this: How can counseling share more with the BIT given the limitations of their state confidentiality restrictions and privileged communication? First, it is important to understand that the term *counselor* is used broadly in the United States and may not always refer to a licensed mental health professional hired to provide mental health treatment. When these two conditions are not met, the "counselor" in question falls under FERPA and has a wider latitude to share with the BIT under FERPA's emergency exemption and the legitimate educational interest clause. Van Brunt and Sokolow (2019) published an article titled "The Role of the Counselor on the Behavioral Intervention Team." This article offered a detailed exploration of how licensed staff hired by the university to provide medical services can share information with the team.

The most straightforward way to approach the issue of sharing is to have the medical provider, the counselor, or the psychologist offer the student a release of information form, to be signed by the student, that allows the clinical staff to share whatever needs to be shared with the team. This release of information process is standard and well understood in the medical and counseling community and is a widely practiced way to share information about treatment with others. The second approach involves defining some exceptions to confidentiality in the informed consent document that allow for more free information sharing with the BIT as clients begin counseling. The traditional exceptions include imminent danger to self, imminent danger to others, or abuse of a minor/elder. This second approach often solves the problem, allowing more free communication, but may receive pushback from counselors or psychologists who are concerned about the erosion of their confidentiality with patients. More details on this approach are highlighted in *The Role of the Counselor on the Behavioral Intervention Team* (Van Brunt & Sokolow, 2018) and in Table 8.1.

The following are some frequently asked questions as they relate to this topic:

"This is a slippery slope. If we start down this path, won't we be sharing everything?" The answer here is that we are not arguing for full sharing of all information, merely the information that is needed for the team to help an individual of concern, and more important, not to do any harm to that individual. Also, we are looking at a limited release of information to the professionals on the BIT, not disclosure of private information to the entire university staff (e.g., resident advisers, custodial staff).

TABLE 8.1

Range of Positions for the Counselor When Working With BIT/CARE Teams

Approach	Description
1. Disconnected and silent	In this overly restrictive stance, the counselor will not attend the BIT meeting, consult on cases, or be involved in any way. Additionally, as a result of the limits of confidentiality, the counselor is not allowed to offer any information and therefore does not need to attend. Such counselors prefer to work in the confidential counseling center and view BIT work as outside their scope or role as a school employee. Alternatively, counselors attend the BIT meeting but refuse to participate actively. They acquiesce to attendance as it is a job requirement but share nothing and take nothing away from the meeting. Needless to say, this is not the most well-regarded approach.
2. Consulting counselor	This reasonable, middle-ground approach has counselors attending the meeting and speaking only in hypotheticals. They consult on cases and share information about general mental health topics (e.g., the risk of a suicidal student after an inpatient hospitalization, the best treatment approaches for eating disorders, or how autism spectrum disorder responds to medication). They do not talk about active or past clients with the BIT or make diagnoses of students being evaluated by the BIT.
3. Sharing helper	In an effective, but slightly more controversial approach, the counselor makes use of an EIC that students can choose to sign, allowing counselors to have a wider latitude to share information with the BIT when the counselor determines it would be in the best interests of the client. Sometimes, the counselor will inform the client of the decision to share before doing so. The counselor shares information as outlined in the informed consent to support the work of the BIT and keep the community safe, while also valuing the confidential nature of the relationship with clients. The counselor may go so far as to offer the team hypotheses about concerning behaviors related to mental health or share informal assessments about student subjects of the BIT who are not clients.
4. Out on a limb	The counselors may or may not use the EIC, knowing that they may risk censure, but probably not loss of licensure. If they use the EIC, they use it more expansively and share information with the team that is not just in the best interest of the client but also for the protection of the community. This professional speaks in hypotheticals that are obviously not hypothetical, uses the "cannot confirm or deny" code, "back channels" information, and is often willing to share confidential information about whether someone is known to the counseling center and is attentive to his or her treatment program. They may hear a road map for an intervention and simply signal assent or objection without offering much more. Alternatively, they may help to frame a road map for a student without letting the team know the student is a client. They mean well, trying to ensure their client is safe, but also share with the BIT in a way beyond which a typical client would likely be comfortable (regardless of the presence of an EIC).
5. Unconditionally open	In this extreme and unethical position, some counselors may not give their client a choice about an EIC, or don't create an EIC with the client, or act in violation of the terms of an informed consent. They share everything they know about a client with the BIT, usually without the knowledge of their client, without any deference to their license or state laws. They see job security as paramount and comply with whatever is required by the BIT, or they imaginatively view the BIT as a "treatment team" within the bounds of their confidentiality. Such counselors may earnestly believe that ethical rules were framed for private practitioners, not those in a campus context, where overzealous protection of information can get people killed. Or the counselors may have convinced themselves that their administrative role, governed by FERPA, supersedes their ethical duties as a therapist. Sometimes a clinical director who serves on the team uses the rationalization that they do.

Note. BIT = Behavioral Intervention Team; CARE = Concern, Assessment, Response, Evaluation; EIC = expanded informed consent; FERPA = Family Education Rights and Privacy Act.

"What if students won't come to counseling unless they feel that their information is safe and private?" That just has not been the case. Students continue to use counseling services in record numbers. In fact, counseling centers across the country remain inundated with requests for services and have difficulty meeting the need. It is essential to share the expectations with students prior to beginning counseling and obtain understanding from them about what is shared, with whom, and when.

"But, isn't confidentiality the cornerstone of the counseling relationship?" Yes, we agree that it is. However, there are numerous exceptions to this. They include abuse to minors and elders. Some states require domestic violence to be reported. Some centers require hazing to be reported as an exception to privileged communication between a student and a medical or mental health provider. When insurance is billed, there is often an exception when seeking approval for additional care. Plus, we are all familiar with the exception around immediate harm to self or others. Although confidentiality is important, there are exceptions. Counseling centers should use an informed consent document to create an exception around reporting at-risk student behavior to the team. For nonlicensed staff who have some counseling-like aspects of their job, these typically fall under FERPA and not the higher standard of privilege. As mentioned earlier, FERPA gives wide latitude to share concerning information forward with the BIT/CARE and parents/guardians.

One of the less controversial and more general ways a counselor can help the BIT/CARE team is by discussing the importance of helping faculty and staff understand the importance of reporting behaviors forward to the BIT. This is an active process that requires the BIT to educate the community about what they should be reporting forward to the team.

A Range of Positions for a Counselor

This leaves counseling staff in one of five positions when it comes to sharing information with the BIT or CARE team. These positions are shown in Table 8.1 and can be summarized as follows: First (Position 1), the counselor does not acknowledge anything about the meeting and does not attend; second (Position 2), the counselor attends the meeting but says and does nothing; third (Position 3), the counselor attends the meeting and speaks only in hypotheticals and never about anyone he or she is seeing in treatment; fourth (Position 4), the counselor uses an expanded informed consent document that allows sharing between the counselor and BIT at sub-Tarasoff and subimminent risk levels (Tarasoff is the law in most states that governs under what conditions privilege can be breached; in essence the counselor is defining in the informed consent a less stringent standard for information sharing with the BIT); or fifth (Position 5), the counselor shares whatever he or she likes with the team about his or her clients.

It is reasonable to assume that Positions 1, 2, and 5 are outside the norms of practice. Position 5 is unethical and would result in the counselors losing their license to practice. Position 1 is unhelpful, petty, and extreme. Position 2 is certainly ethical but is completely worthless and a waste of time both for the BIT and the counselor. This leaves most clinical staff debating between Positions 3 and 4. Position 3 is more conservative, allows for full protection for the counselor's privilege, and is helpful for the BIT/CARE. Position 4 is extremely helpful to the BIT/CARE team and gives counselors protection when they share information. The downside of Position 4 is a tendency for clinical staff to feel they are being deceptive toward their clients and are operating outside the bounds of what one might do in a private practice.

Counselors and Violence Risk Assessments

Another role of the counselor on the BIT or CARE team may be to conduct violence risk or threat assessments. These assessments are different than psychological assessments. Van Brunt (2015a) wrote,

> Psychological assessments often seek to diagnose and develop a treatment plan for an individual. Threat or violence assessments are designed to determine if the student is a risk to others on the basis of a structured interview that determines the presence of targeted violence risk factors. Clinical staff typically are asked to assess individuals with mental health disorders who pose a potential for risk to others. Examples include the individual experiencing a manic phase in his or her bipolar disorder or a patient who has a psychotic break and begins to act the commands issued by hallucinatory voices. "Harm to others," in other words, is focused more on mental health motivating causes that drive individuals to violence. (p. vii)

However, the problem lately has been that many of the individuals being dropped off at the counselor's office (particularly in K–12 and higher education settings) are making threats or posing a threat to others but have no indication of mental health problems. A student, upset at a friend, posts on Facebook that they are "coming over to your house with a knife to kill you." Another student threatens a college professor because of a poor grade on an assignment. Still another uses social media and tweets, "I'm going to bring a bomb to school tomorrow." Although mental illness may be an important contributing factor in any of these three examples, the core of any assessment must be based on threat assessment principles, not clinical pathology. An entire community of law enforcement, human resources, and federal agencies (Naval Criminal Investigative Service, Central Intelligence Agency, Federal Bureau of Investigation, Homeland Security) is exploring the assessment of threat and dangerousness.

A helpful resource to listen to is the American Counseling Association podcast entitled "Harm to Others" (https://www.counseling.org/knowledge-center/podcasts/docs/default-source/aca-podcasts/ht052---harm-to-others). This podcast explores Dr. Van Brunt's thoughts through an hour-long audio discussion on the topic of threat assessment.

Collaborative Care and Support

During a crisis and an emergency, a campus community relies on individual departments working in tandem to address all the elements of the crisis. This can involve counselors providing mental health treatment to those affected by the crisis, residential life staff supporting students in the halls through discussion and education, and campus safety/police increasing their presence around the community to provide reassurance and restore a sense of control and calm. In the case examples throughout this chapter, we offer three distinct crisis incidents. Case Examples 1 and 3 would clearly be reported to campus law enforcement or emergency services, but Case Example 2 might fly under the radar. All three should be shared with the campus BIT, and all three showcase the need for a collaborative response.

In the first case, we see the need for a coordinated plan upon Daria's release from the hospital, including referral to and follow-up from counseling services as well as a possible discussion with student conduct about the nature of her disruptive behavior. Although it would never be our suggestion to punish a student for a mental health concern, there should be a consistent and coordinated approach to reminding students of community conduct standards; and a discussion with Daria should take place concerning how her behaviors were disruptive to the campus community. This can be done in a balanced and caring manner, incorporating a trauma-informed approach with the student, and prioritizing her use of mental health resources. What is important is not to rely on an either/or response; both accountability through the conduct office and support through the counseling office are important. This is not about telling a student not to be suicidal or not to talk about suicidal thoughts—in fact, those restrictions create liability risks for the school. Instead, the conduct office will work to carefully reestablish expectations related to disruption and safety. Daria's case should also be referred to the BIT for review. In some cases, a violence risk or threat assessment as discussed in this chapter is needed in addition to a mental health assessment to adequately assess the risk associated with Daria's case. Furthermore, counseling units may partner with residence life and other departments to offer prevention and follow-up activities for the campus community related to recognizing suicidal ideation, how to make referrals and resource suggestions, and how to report concerning behavior. Oftentimes, the follow-up to suicide attempts gets restricted to one unit on campus; however, this case highlights the need for a coordinated, collaborative, and caring response.

In the second case, we discussed in the chapter how counselors can share basic crisis intervention techniques and skills during consultations with faculty and staff when dealing with situations like Carlos's. It could be helpful to discuss the potential impact of trauma Carlos experienced in his military experiences and how that may be influencing his ability to gain effective access to services in the financial aid and veteran services office. The more ideal scenario is that the counseling office is already working with other departments as well as community resources to offer training and education on how to best serve veteran and military student populations as well as how to coordinate resource referrals for the greatest effectiveness. Furthermore, this case, similar to the first case, again highlights the importance of a consistent conduct response to cases of disruption. Using the campus conduct process even when a student has previous military service or has experienced trauma from other incidents ensures that there is a consistent pattern of communication about campus expectations. This scenario should also be reported to the campus BIT to allow a broader assessment of risk factors associated with his behavior and a discussion of resource referrals and interventions helpful to Carlos's situation.

Finally, in the third case, we highlight the importance of the counselor role as a part of a larger prevention effort and response to campus incidents. As mentioned in Case Example 2, we hope that there is a proactive stance in the counseling unit participating prior to incidents in collaborative educational programs to help promote attitudes and skills that protect against violence. Examples of such programming include difficult dialogue trainings to help faculty lead discussions on divisive issues and to help students participate in a critical yet civil manner. Other activities can be created to promote empathy, cultural competency, resilience, and information literacy to enhance the campus community's resistance to more negative incidents. In response to the third case, the counselor may encounter individual students affected by the activities that occurred, may be tasked to support campus recovery efforts, or may be asked to assist with a violence risk assessment as part of a BIT response for one or more students involved. In the latter, the tools suggested in this chapter related to violence risk assessment would provide a framework for the counselor's work alongside the BIT team and campus law enforcement.

Conclusion

Throughout this chapter, we have highlighted the unique and important role of the counselor in crisis and emergency response. Each counseling function is part of a larger, collaborative student affairs and campus response to individual and campus incidents of crisis. The combined effort of counselors alongside other professionals creates a powerful system for responding to the most difficult situations occurring in campus communities. It's important to remember that you are not alone in planning for and responding to crisis. A crucial skill for counselors is the ability to understand the role of other departments and rely on them as partners in your service to the campus community.

Moving forward, it would be useful for counselors to attend trainings to better improve their skill set. More and more graduate schools are offering courses in threat assessment, crisis management, and emergency response. NaBITA (www.nabita.org) offers a full range of certification courses for counselors, administrators, conduct officers, and police. The Association of Threat Assessment Professionals (www.atapworldwide.org) also offers threat assessment trainings and a certification. Other large organizations serving colleges and universities also offer regional and topical trainings on these issues. These would include the Association for Student Conduct Administration (www.theasca.org); NASPA, Student Affairs Administrators in Higher Education (www.naspa.org); the American College Personnel Association, College Student Educators International (www.myacpa.org); and the

American College Counseling Association (www.collegecounseling.org). When looking at training, there always is a debate on cost, travel, time of year, and how best to spend limited resources. There is something quite useful about attending trainings outside of one's main area to expand one's knowledge of other areas. For example, having a counseling center director attend the conduct administrator conference can provide useful information that can increase collaboration among departments. Likewise, it is very helpful to training with your entire department or team, so bringing in a training organization like NaBITA to train at your college or university may be more useful and cost-effective.

Final Case Study

Nate posts on social media, "I'm tired of all of this. If one more person tells me that being gay is a 'lifestyle choice' or that I must be gay because something bad happened to me as a child, I will f-cking lose it and go all Columbine on this school."

Nate is a second-year student with good grades and is involved in student theater and the lesbian, gay, bisexual, transgender, queer, plus other identities support group on campus, and he is active with intermural soccer. The BIT team receives a report from another student about Nate's post, and he is asked to meet with a counselor to better assess his risk and need for support.

Case Exploration Questions

1. How does an individual's right to free speech balance against the potential risk?
2. What are some of the questions you might ask related to establishing the risk of violence?
3. Discuss how counselors may focus on increasing protective factors for Nate.
4. How might you address the privileged and confidential nature of the assessment and support offered by counseling against the desire to keep the larger community safe?

References

Beck, J. (2011). *Cognitive behavioral therapy: Basics and beyond* (2nd ed.). New York, NY: Guilford Press.

Deisinger, G., Randazzo, M., O'Neill, D., & Savage, J. (2008). *The handbook for campus threat assessment and management teams.* Stoneham, MA: Applied Risk Management.

Eells, G., & Rockland-Miller, H. (2011). Assessing and responding to disturbed and disturbing students: Understanding the role of administrative teams in institutions of higher education. *Journal of College Student Psychotherapy, 25,* 8–23.

Everly, G., & Lating, J. (2017). *Johns Hopkins guide to psychological first aid.* Baltimore, MD: Johns Hopkins Press.

Family Educational Rights and Privacy Act of 1974, 20 U.S.C. § 1232g (1974).

Federal Emergency Management Agency. (2017). Crisis Counseling Assistance & Training Program. Retrieved from https://www.fema.gov/recovery-directorate/crisis-counseling-assistance-training-program#1

Health Insurance Portability and Accountability Act of 1996. Pub. L. No. 104-191, 110 Stat. 1936 (1996).

Higher Education Mental Health Alliance. (2014). *Postvention: A guide for response to suicide on college campuses.* Retrieved from https://hemha.org/wp-content/uploads/2018/06/jed-hemha-postvention-guide.pdf
LeViness, P., Bershad, C., & Gorman, K. (2017). *The Association for University and College Counseling Center Directors annual survey*. Retrieved from https://www.aucccd.org/assets/documents/Governance/2017%20aucccd%20survey-public-apr26.pdf
Miller, W., & Rollnick, S. (2002). *Motivational interviewing: Preparing people for change* (2nd ed.). New York, NY: Guilford Press.
Office of Violence Against Women. (2013). *Building cultures of care: A guide for sexual assault services and programs.* United States Department of Justice. Retrieved from http://www.nsvrc.org
Sokolow, B., Lewis, S., Shuster, S., Swinton, D., & Van Brunt, B. (2014). *Threat assessment in the campus setting.* Berwyn, PA: The National Behavioral Intervention Team Association.
Sokolow, B., & Tarasoff v. Regents of University of California, 551 P.2d 334 (Cal. 1976).
Treleaven, D. (2018). *Trauma-sensitive mindfulness: Practices for safe and transformative healing.* New York, NY: Norton.
Uhernik, J. (1998). The counselor and the disaster response team: An emerging role. In G. R. Walz, J. C. Bleuer, & R. K. Yep (Eds.), *Compelling counseling interventions: Celebrating VISTAS' fifth anniversary* (pp. 313–321). Ann Arbor, MI: Counseling Outfitters.
Van Brunt, B. (2012). *Ending campus violence: New approaches to prevention.* New York, NY: Routledge.
Van Brunt, B. (2015a). *Harm to others: The assessment and treatment of dangerousness.* Alexandria, VA: American Counseling Association.
Van Brunt, B. (2015b). Violence Risk Assessment of the Written Word (VRAW^2). *Journal of Campus Behavioral Intervention, 3,* 12–25.
Van Brunt, B. (2016). Assessing threat in written communications, social media, and creative writing. *Journal of Gender and Violence, 3,* 78–88.
Van Brunt, B., & Lewis, W. (2014). *A faculty guide to addressing disruptive and dangerous behavior.* New York, NY: Routledge.
Van Brunt, B., & Murphy, A. (2017). *A staff guide to addressing disruptive and dangerous behavior on campus.* New York, NY: Routledge.
Van Brunt, B., Murphy, A., & Zedginidze, A. (2017). An exploration of the risk, protective, and mobilization factors related to violent extremism in college populations. *Violence and Gender, 4,* 81–101.
Van Brunt, B., & Sokolow, B. (2018). *The role of the counselor on the behavioral intervention team* (White paper). Berwyn, PA: National Behavioral Intervention Team Association.
Van Brunt, B., & Sokolow, B. (2019). The role of the counselor on the behavioral intervention team. *The Journal of Campus Behavioral Intervention, 7,* 1–11.

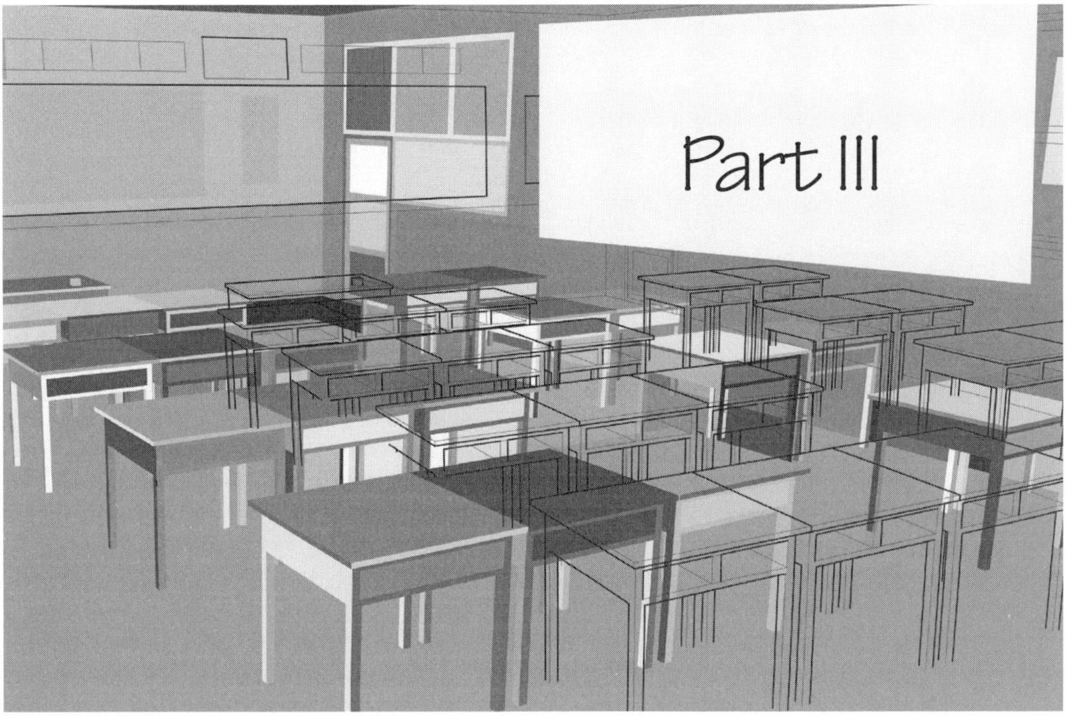

Student Development Theory, Student Learning, and Developmental Considerations

Chapter 9

Understanding Student Development Theory

Derrick A. Paladino

You come to nature with all your theories,
and she knocks them all flat.

—Renoir

■ ■ ■

Reflection Exercise

Theory is an aspect of several, if not all, components of your life. If not grounded in empirical theory, then most human decision-making is based on informal theory. Informal theory, a concept originated by Parker (1977), suggests that individuals make implicit connections among events and persons in their environment on the basis of a body of common knowledge and their own everyday experiences. It is a place of initial thought formulation prior to the introduction of grounded theory. In fact, it can allow the practitioner to start connecting with his or her client and even develop empathy.

Prior to reading beyond this section of the chapter, reflect on the college student descriptions below. For the purposes of this exercise you are to assume that these students are at your current institution. On the basis of these descriptions and knowing your institution, (a) what do you believe these students' experience is like; (b) what might their support system look like; and (c) if they were to struggle, what might some of their adversities be?

1. A first-generation freshman from out of state who is beginning college in the Spring semester.
2. A 20-year-old student of color who is taking part in fraternity/sorority rush.
3. A transgender student entering sophomore year.
4. A 22-year-old student athlete on the basketball team.
5. A full-time student (choose an academic major) who works full time and lives off campus.

To continue this exercise, you can imagine that these students are at different types of institutions—for example, community and 2-year schools, historically

Black and Latinx colleges and universities, vocational or technical colleges, small private liberal arts colleges, performing arts colleges, military colleges, and large land-grant universities. Remember that informal theory is only a start to your understanding. Formalized theory is the next required step for competent practice.

■ ■ ■

This chapter is the beginning of Part III, which emphasizes some of the theories that form the basis for both college counselors and student affairs professionals to work with students. Regardless of what your role will be, to provide holistic support to college students, you will need to understand some of the ways they might be thinking about themselves and their identities, how they fit or don't fit with others in their social environments, how they make sense of the world around them cognitively, and how their experiences and interactions shape their growth and development. In addition to providing this theoretical foundation, we want to present the case of Lina Miller as a tool you can use to deepen your understanding and ability to apply theory to student development. As always, it is essential to continually use a multicultural and social justice lens (as you learned in Chapter 3) when understanding and building empathy for her plight. We hope you will spend time in each student development theory chapter considering this brief narrative and comparing how each theory would highlight her struggles and experiences differently. The chapters that follow are Chapter 10, "Neuro-Informed College Counseling"; Chapter 11, "Psychosocial Theories of Student Development"; Chapter 12, "Cognitive and Moral Theories of Student Development"; Chapter 13, "Experiential Theories of Student Development"; and Chapter 14, "Social Constructivism and Identity in Student Development."

Chapter 9 starts off by presenting the case of Lina Miller, followed by introducing the importance of student development theory, including its emergence into the field. In addition, early theorists who have laid groundwork for the evolution of theory are discussed. Next, readers will learn about the importance of viewing theories through an inclusive and social justice lens. Finally, the chapter will begin your preparation to study student development theory to prime you for the next five chapters.

The Case of Lina Miller

Lina Miller is a first-generation college student with an Iraqi mom and a White American (U.S.) dad who served in the Army in the Gulf War. She has just completed new student orientation and moved into her residence hall room at Southwest State University, a midsize, public, predominantly White institution about 2 hours from her home. After her initial sense of excitement and freedom, Lina is starting to experience some worries as the first week of college gets underway. Her roommate seems very friendly, but Lina has also heard her telling others on the hall, "Oh yeah, my roommate is a Muslim from somewhere in the Middle East." Lina was born in California and has always felt herself to be American in her traditions and cultural upbringing. Her parents did not insist that she practice any religious tradition, so she does not identify with a particular faith, even though she understands Islam from observing her mother. She thinks her roommate's comments will alienate others before she even gets a chance to know them, so she feels discouraged and misunderstood.

Her academic transition is also off to a rocky start. Her Calculus I class contains 200 students and already feels much harder than her high school math classes. She can barely tell who the faculty member is from her seat in the back of the auditorium, and she has no intent to go ask her any questions. She had a general sense that she wanted to explore math- and science-related majors, so this early challenge is making her overgeneralize about her chances of getting into any of her desired areas of study. She wonders why she even thought it was a good idea to come to college, because she was mostly just trying to make her parents proud and show her younger brother that it was possible. When she calls her family at night, she tries hard not to let them know that she is overwhelmed and sad, minimizing any negative feelings she is experiencing, as she knows they have put a lot of their savings into her tuition bill and are excited that she will have this opportunity that they never had. She doesn't believe she can ask them for help with this new experience that is so different from their lives.

After Lina purchases her books and sees how expensive everything is going to be, she decides to get a job in the campus bookstore. It is not hard work, and it helps keep her worries away to some extent, but it has also made her time management more difficult as she tries to fit in homework and studies. She sees faculty members come into the bookstore from time to time, but they never seem to notice her, underscoring her perception that faculty are distant and don't really want to talk with students. The only person on campus whom she has felt comfortable with is her academic adviser, whom she met during orientation; he does remember her name and chats with her whenever he sees her on campus. She decides that she can trust him and makes an appointment to try to sort out her concerns. She is becoming so worried about fitting in socially, surviving academically, and not disappointing her parents that she has a difficult time sleeping at night and has begun to skip meals.

College is viewed by many scholars and practitioners as an exciting time of development and "coming into one's own," an experience where one develops into a competent educated adult and makes lifelong social connections. Instead, Lina's transition is clouded by struggle and stress, potentially affecting her physical and mental health functioning. Lina's experiences indicate several struggles in her first semester at Southwest State University. Her encounters include explicit and perceived discrimination, oppression, and microaggressions. In addition, she is encountering struggles with identity, academic challenges, financial difficulty, new living situations (i.e., residence hall life, roommates, distance from home, life without her immediate family), and perceived responsibility to her parents and sibling. Along with these new experiences and environment, she appears to be feeling discouraged, worried, misunderstood, invisible, and alone. At this point, Lina is merely surviving at Southwest State University and is nowhere near thriving. One hopes that her adviser, peers, coworkers, faculty, boss, family, and she will gain awareness with respect to her struggle. Lina would benefit from assistance, support, knowledge of campus resources, and a referral to the college counseling center. A college counselor could assess her current state of functioning and provide intervention and advocacy to support her adjustment.

■ ■ ■

The Importance of Developmental Theory

Counselors and other mental health professionals are taught counseling theory (e.g., cognitive behavioral, Adlerian, person-centered, narrative, psychodynamic, Gestalt, and rational emotive behavior therapy) to guide informed assessment, treatment planning, and counseling with clients. Although this education in counseling theory provides a foundation for conceptualization and intentional approaches, it is not enough to simply understand counseling theory when working with individuals. A competent mental health professional must also value any and all developmental theories that accompany the specific population they are working with. Counseling programs also require life-span development coursework—see, for example, the 2016 Council for Accreditation of Counseling and Related Educational Programs (CACREP); Standards (CACREP, 2015), Standard 2.F.3. This foundational knowledge assists counselors by offering a general understanding of how an individual grows, thinks, feels, and encounters normative transitions from birth onward.

For the imminent college counselor, only a portion of the life-span development course will typically focus on the traditional-age college student, leaving much to be learned for working with this population. Students will certainly read about Erik Erikson in such courses, as his theory spans many ages and stages of development. Erikson (1959, 1968, 1993) introduced eight psychosocial stages of development and transition that occur throughout one's life span and are influenced by the sociocultural demands of relationships (e.g., parents, caregivers, peers). Within these eight stages there are two that particularly connect to the traditional-age college population. According to Erikson's (1993) model, identity versus role confusion in adolescence (approximate ages: 12 to 19) and intimacy versus isolation in young adulthood (approximate ages: 20 to 25) are principally connected to the traditional college student period. Within these life-span stages, we witness individuals exploring identity (i.e., social and personal); developing a core sense of self, values, and goals; asking the question, "Who am I?"; discovering healthy versus unhealthy relationships; and learning about intimacy, commitment, safety, and care within friendships and partnerships (Erikson, 1993). These are logical elements to consider as you survey the typical college student experience. We see these factors in what Lina is encountering, and, most likely, you may be connecting to them as you reflect on your own time in college. Understanding these stages will illuminate the challenges and milestones that many college students face. For example, we see these two stages play out in that Lina is already wondering if she should remain in her present course of study and in that she is starting to feel isolated and invisible because of her living and classroom environments.

Fortunately, within the span of Erikson's (1993) identity versus role confusion and intimacy versus isolation stages, we find the field of college student development and college student development theory. Here lies a grouping of theories that attend to the experience, normative challenges, and development of the individual college student. In most counseling-related academic programs, college student development theory is not required nor provided as a learning experience. Some counseling programs house specialty areas such as CACREP's College Counseling and Student Affairs track (a list of currently accredited programs can be found at https://www.cacrep.org/directory/); offer certificate programs, such as the College and University Counseling Certificate at Rollins College; or have one-off electives or will have developed courses that provide these learning experiences. Students who do not have the ability to take such courses will find themselves entering into clinical experiences at counseling centers without having essential knowledge about the college student population, over and above their personal college experience or informal theory. Informal theory, a concept originated by Parker (1977), suggests that individuals make implicit connections among events and persons in their environment based on a body of common knowledge and their own everyday experiences. Although this is a reasonable place to begin with conceptualization, the ability to employ empirically informed and tested theories is required for competent practice.

Graduate programs focusing on higher education and student affairs have required the learning of college student development theory for a long time. Student development theories attempt to explain the process of human development in college students and, as such, serve as the educational foundation of the student affairs profession (Reason & Broido, 2011, p. 91). A student affairs practitioner's population is college students, so it is wise to study this particular set of developmental issues. College counselors should hold this same position if they are not formally taught these theories. This knowledge becomes even more important for counselors who work at community/2-year colleges because some hold multiple roles at their institution. The 2014–2015 American College Counseling Association Survey of Community/Two Year College Counseling Services found that many counselors are not only located in student affairs offices (70.2% of respondents) but are also performing duties in addition to providing personal/mental health counseling to college students (Edwards & Lenhart, 2015). These additional responsibilities include academic advising, career counseling, admissions advising, and disabilities services. Because "counselors generally wear many 'hats' at these institutions" (Edwards & Lenhart, 2015, p. 3), they should become acquainted with philosophy and theories connected to student affairs. We hope Part III of this text will offer a beginning to that education and will increase the use of this common language among all higher education professionals. College counseling professionals are strongly encouraged to continue their study of student development theory over and above this introduction as theories continue to evolve in our diverse society.

The Emergence of Student Development Theory

Student development theories sprouted from those in the student affairs profession discovering the need for creating guiding principles that emphasize understanding and fostering the development of the holistic student (Evans, Forney, Guido, Patton, & Renn, 2010; Jones & Stewart, 2016). One such document, *The Student Personnel Point of View* (SPPV; American Council on Education, 1937, 1949), was quite influential. The SPPV created a philosophy that encouraged institutions of higher education "to consider the student as a whole—his [sic] intellectual capacity and achievement, his emotional make up, his physical condition, his social relationships, his vocational aptitudes and skills, his moral and religious values, his economic resources, his aesthetic appreciations" (American Council on Education, 1937, p. 3). This document (and the revised 1949 statement) placed an emphasis on the development of the student as a complete person over intellectual training alone (American Council on Education, 1937, 1949). The SPPV's encouragement of the profession and professionals created a strong foundation for reflection and evolvement, thus assisting in the development of further literature following this area.

The student development field has created a rich body of literature regarding college students and their educational environments (Strange, 1999). On the basis of this literature, Carney Strange (1999) created a framework of 14 propositions "for the purposes of challenging practitioners and scholars to examine their relevance for what they practice and for how they come to inquire about and understand the college experience" (p. 573). Several of Strange's propositions focus specifically on the developing college student. The following is a list of eight of the 14 propositions from two of the content areas. These areas (a) Student in Developmental Terms and (b) The Nature of Development highlight the complexity of understanding the growth and development of the individual college student experience:

Proposition 1: Students differ in age-related developmental tasks that offer important agendas for "teachable moments" in their lives.

Proposition 2: Students differ in how they construct and interpret their experiences, and such differences offer important guides for structuring the education process.

> *Proposition 3*: Students differ in the styles with which they approach and resolve challenges of learning, growth and development, and such differences are important for understanding how and why students function in characteristic manners.
> *Proposition 4*: Students differ in the resolution of tasks of individuation according to their gender, culture-ethnicity, and sexual orientation: such differences offer important contexts for understanding the challenges students face in their search for personal identity.
> *Proposition 5*: Development occurs as individuals reach points of readiness and respond to timely and appropriate learning experiences.
> *Proposition 6*: Development occurs as individuals respond to novel situations and tasks that challenge their current level or capacity.
> *Proposition 7*: Development occurs as individuals evaluate a learning task to be sufficiently challenging to warrant change and sufficiently supportive to risk an unknown result.
> *Proposition 8*: Development occurs as an interactive and dynamic process between persons and their environment. (Strange, 1999, pp. 573–579)

These propositions underscore variables that affect psychosocial life, age-related developmental challenges, stages of maturity or resolution, and cognitive structures or patterns of meaning making that individuals bring to their educational experiences (Strange, 1999). They also describe the college student as someone who is constantly evolving within a "dynamic cultural context" (Strange, 1999, p. 577) and who is affected by a dynamic process that is a "result of the interactive mutual shaping of persons and environments" (p. 580).

Student Development and Environments

The notion of people interacting with environments as a theoretical base to understanding behavior has historically been a foundational part of student development work. Kurt Lewin (1936) created an equation that describes such an interaction. His equation $B = f(P \times E)$ states that a student's behavior (B) is a function (f) of the interaction of the individual college student or person (P) and his or her environment (E). This paradigm stresses the importance of both the individual and the educational environment in understanding growth and development of individual college students (Strange, 1999). Strange (1999) suggested there are two assumptions when considering this concept: (a) that "human development cannot be understood adequately by reference to individual human differences alone. Rather it must be examined within the context of environmental differences as well" (p. 579) and (b) that "it is assumed that although environments influence the characteristics of individuals, at the same time individuals influence the nature and characteristics of their environments" (p. 579).

Within Lina's case we see a student who is quite affected by her college environment. In her most recent equation, $B = f$ (Lina × Southwest State University), the environment of Southwest State University is quite different from her high school experience: $B = f$ (Lina × High School). The Southwest State University environment contains new living arrangements, much larger classes, financial dependence on her parents for tuition, and financial hardship as she pays for books and other basic needs. The interaction of who Lina is holistically/historically and her new college environment/ecology has introduced academic difficulties. In addition, she is now grappling with time management issues, as well as a self-minimization of her feelings while communicating with her support groups (e.g., her parents). Early in her first-year experience, Lina is already starting to show signs of struggle. If Lina or her environment does not evolve, she may develop additional behavioral characteristics such as sleep disturbance, poor appetite, social withdrawal, and missing class, which, if persistent, will eventually decrease her functioning. This interactionist perspective is an important aspect of student development work and thus serves as a basis of many foundational, as well as contemporary, student development theories.

Early Student Development Theories

In general, theories strive to explain the human condition, including behavior, reactions to events, and experiences. Through a review of the literature, Jones and Abes (2011) recognized theory as serving a minimum of six purposes. They suggested that theory is used to "describe, explain, predict, influence outcomes, assess practice and generate new knowledge and research" (p. 151). Theory also humanizes. If underscored with the idea that students are unique and holistic, it moves a practitioner from the mentality of treating or reacting to a symptom/behavior/incident toward a more compassionate and understanding attitude when deciphering issues. With this focus, theory can help practitioners understand and respond to students empathically (Knefelkamp, 1984, as cited in Evans et al., 2010, p. 26). In addition, theory gives counselors a blueprint. Counselors who operate without a theoretical structure are more vulnerable to the wealth of client information that can leave them directionless while trying to choose a clinical direction (Prochaska & Norcross, 2014). They become more apt to rely on informal theory.

As you have read, student development theories have shaped the nature and practice of student affairs work to a great extent, and college counseling to a somewhat lesser extent—although mostly due to limited opportunity from training programs. They have worked to create a cocurricular understanding of what happens at college, including "attention to both students' cognitive acquisition of knowledge and their development and maturation" (Dungy & Gordon, 2011, p. 67). There are several fundamental theories that have assisted this movement, including Sanford's (1962, 1966) psychosocial development model and theory of challenge and support.

Sanford (1962, 1966) believed that in order for development to occur, individual college students need a balance between challenge and support. In addition, he suggested that the student must possess a readiness for a particular task or challenge. His three concepts of challenge, support, and readiness make up this developmental model. Challenge assists students to progress through experiences and gain developmental competency; however, too much or too little can stifle development. When appropriate levels of support are provided, challenges can be taken on in such a way that healthy development is promoted. If students are presented with too much challenge, they may give up, whereas if too much support is offered, they may never become autonomous and grow as individuals. As in Lewin (1936), we see development as a function of one's environment.

Examining Lina's case, we immediately see a diverse set of challenges with little support. Lina plans on meeting with her adviser, which adds a support system and potential adjunct assistance. However, if her challenge and support do not balance out, then, according to Sanford's (1962, 1966) theory, we will see her continue to struggle. With Lina being a first-generation college student, her readiness for these new challenges is unknown. One must assess how she was prepared by her high school, teachers, family, and personal research for what to expect at college, specifically one with Southwest State University's ecological makeup.

General Groupings of Student Development Theories

Theories about college students, environments, and organizations have grown significantly over the past 50 years. A clear example of this depth and breadth can be found in a list of theories and theoretical perspectives originally developed by McEwen (2003) and revised by Jones, Abes, and Cilente (2011). This list includes both foundational and contemporary theories from "frameworks grounded in empirical research" (Schuh, Jones, Harper, & Associates, 2011, p. 136). Although not an exhaustive list, it does provide a very strong scope of student development theory and a great cheat sheet when deciding on what theories to use.

As noted in the aforementioned document (Jones et al., 2011; McEwen, 2003) and in Part III of this book, foundational student development theories were typically organized as discrete families of theories. Jones and Stewart (2016) categorized these foundational works into four main families (that you will further explore in Chapters 11, 12, 13, and 14): (a) psychosocial, (b) cognitive-structural, (c) person-environment, and (d) maturity. These foundational families fall within the "first wave" of three waves in the evolution of student development theory. The first wave is viewed as foundational and primarily psychological and developmental. In addition, it "tended to address singular developmental domains," moving away from a holistic understanding of the student (Jones & Stewart, 2016, p. 19). There was also an assumption that these theories viewed development to be similar for all individual college students (Jones & Stewart, 2016). The second wave of theories was an outgrowth of the singular-minded limitations in the first wave. It focused more on the holistic student by examining social identities and diverse populations. The second wave allowed for a sociocultural perspective of the college student experience and introduced the idea of self-authorship. In this wave we see a psychological perspective that focuses on a singular identity where the "self" precedes society (Winkle-Wagner, 2012). This is in direct contrast to the sociological perspective (that emerges in third-wave theories), which promotes the notion that "society comes before self," "self is located in social structures," and "identity stems from socialized roles" (Winkle-Wagner, 2012, p. 55).

Third-wave theories applied "critical and poststructural perspectives to an understanding of student development" (Jones & Stewart, 2016, p. 18). An example of a third-wave theory is critical race theory. Hernández (2016) discussed critical race theory as a shift in the way student development is theorized and researched. Critical race theory moves away from an individualized and individualistic focus, expanding to include an analysis of a student "in relation to her political, racialized, environment" (Hernández, 2016, p. 168). The third wave introduced a social justice perspective, which is also a current professional competency area for student affairs professionals (American College Personnel Association [ACPA] & National Association of Student Personnel Administrators [NASPA], 2015; Jones & Stewart, 2016) and counselors (Ratts, Singh, Nassar-McMillan, Butler, & McCullough, 2015). When a social justice perspective becomes foundational, a practitioner is able to examine how systems of oppression (e.g., racism, classism, heterosexism, ableism, genderism, sexism, and religious oppression) have an impact on the individual college student (Abes, 2016).

Although there is evolvement throughout each wave, this does not mean the earlier waves become obsolete. Winkle-Wagner (2012) suggested that both psychological and social perspectives guide student development theory and complement each other, allowing for the following:

1. multiple and singular notions of identity;
2. the study of individual and group development processes;
3. the influence of the social structure and cognitive processes on the self;
4. the study of roles, commitment, and identity salience alongside inquiry into traits and personality;
5. the exploration of reflection and cognition; and
6. generalizable, macro-level methodologies alongside more interpretative, micro-level research methods. (p. 49)

Thus, establishing an integrative approach from all three waves and two perspectives allows for a more comprehensive analysis of a student's experience and leads to intentional practice. An additional theoretical evolution now integrates an understanding of, and use of, biological development and neurodevelopment within theory—that is, using what we are learning about brain development to better inform our use of classic student development theory when conceptualizing and practicing. This increased attention to biology and neurodevelopment will truly allow the integrative theoretical approach to be viewed as more holistic.

Student Development Theory and the Profession

Student development theory assists in understanding (a) the complex intermingling of psychological, developmental, and cognitive variables; (b) the impact on "why," "what," and "how" students are behaving, thinking, and feeling; and (c) how situations and ecological influences affect an individual student's experience. Furthermore, "knowledge of student development theory enables student affairs professionals to identify and address student needs, design programs, develop policies, and create healthy college environments that encourage positive growth" (Evans et al., 2010, p. 7). Hubbard (2012) suggested that theories offer a road map to assist professionals in describing characteristics of student populations, demonstrating differences in student learning processes, and offering an understanding of campus environments. Finally, it is important to note that student development theory can assist with explaining both normative developmental issues and mental health crises, diagnoses, or nonnormative situations. With the growing prevalence of mental health issues on campus (Ferriero, 2014), student development theories are particularly needed to understand the interaction of both developmental and mental health issues. The importance of understanding and intentionally using college student development theory is evident.

Evans et al. (2010) stated that "student development theory provides the basis for the practice of student development" (p. 7). They urged that formal theories validated by research are needed. In fact, the student affairs profession agrees. ACPA (http://www.myacpa.org/) and NASPA (https://www.naspa.org/), in a united effort, created 10 professional competency areas that include an understanding and application of college student development theory (ACPA & NASPA, 2015). *The Professional Competency Areas for Student Affairs Educators* "document lay[s] out essential knowledge, skills, and dispositions expected of all student affairs educators, regardless of functional area or specialization within the field" (p. 7). In addition, it is organized in a way that provides outcome statements of proficiency in foundational, intermediate, and advanced levels. One of the 10 competency areas is Student Learning and Development. The Student Learning and Development competency addresses "concepts and principles of student development and learning theory" (p. 7), including theory application to inform student affairs practice. Student affairs practitioners are expected, at the foundational level, to harness a critical understanding of student development theories. This understanding includes the following:

- Articulating theories behind college student development and holistic development;
- understanding strengths and limitations of said theories;
- constructing learning outcomes for practice, training, and programing; and
- understanding how "race, ethnicity, nationality, class, gender, age, sexual orientation, gender identity, dis/ability, and religious belief can influence development during the college years" (ACPA & NASPA, 2015, p. 32).

Student development theory informs competent practice, and being that the college counseling center exists as a functional unit within student affairs, it too falls under these competency areas. College counselors may find themselves primarily connected to professional clinical organizations such as the American Counseling Association (https://www.counseling.org/), the American College Counseling Association (http://www.collegecounseling.org/), and the American Psychological Association, Division 17 (http://www.div17.org/). These are important parts of one's identity and continuing education; however, it is important for college counselors to infuse student development theory into their clinical and outreach practice. Having a common language of theory also allows the college counseling center to work alongside other functional areas, such as residence life, student and family care, and offices of diversity and inclusion to design training and outreach programming that attends to the specific needs of the college student population. A common theoretical understanding makes for a more cohesive and collaborative higher education entity.

Viewing Student Development Theory Through an Inclusive Lens

We witness a shift of inclusiveness in the second and third waves of student development theory evolution. Although foundational theories (i.e., first-wave theories) are important, there was much room to grow in developing an inclusive ecological and sociocultural perspective of the individual college student. Jones and Abes (2011) suggested that early theories viewed students through theoretical language over and above student stories and narratives. This theoretical language approaches students through a perspective of diagnosis and categorization rather than viewing their individuality and uniqueness. Overgeneralization through theory can lead to pathologizing students and essentially viewing them as their specific behavior or issue rather than seeing them as people. For example, in the counseling field and allied mental health professions we sometimes hear clinicians refer to their clients as their diagnosis. They may say, "My borderline client," "My depressed client," or "My bipolar client." This dehumanizes and generalizes individuals and begins the slippery slope to losing empathy. A more humanistic approach to viewing individuals is viewing them as people (students) who are "living with" and not "suffering from" ailments. Rather, we would prefer to hear, "My client living with anxiety."

When studying early foundational theories, one will discover that they were not developed from a wide scope. Most theories of that time were developed using majority White male college students from privileged socioeconomic backgrounds and did not acknowledge narratives of underrepresented students (Abes, 2016; Jones & Stewart, 2016; Torres & Lepeau, 2013; Winkle-Wagner, 2012). However, regardless of sample makeup, some practitioners still use these theories with general application to individual college students. Torres and Lepeau (2013) suggested that continuing to apply these theories to today's student populations can marginalize and alienate students. It is vital to hold a critical lens to understand how these theories were created prior to using them for professional practice or general knowledge. In addition, without adjustment, these foundational theories have limited application to our current college population and changing environments. Students identifying as first-generation, students returning to college later in life, international students, single parents, students working at full-time jobs, students in colleges with enormous populations, students enrolled in blended college programs, and so forth are not accounted for in the research samples.

There are solutions for using foundational theories. As long as practitioners are viewing stages, phases, concepts, student characteristics, and campus ecology through a lens of diversity and a sociocultural structure, a first-wave theory can be quite useful. It rests on the practitioner to evaluate and determine the value of a particular theory with a specific student, in a specific campus environment, at a specific time. For example, international students will have a different personal experience of safety and inclusiveness depending on the political climate and campus environment. If we, as counselors and student support providers, are to assist these students through a foundation of theory, many variables must be considered first. Jones and Stewart (2016) suggested that theory becomes healing, is liberating, and is a catalyst for social change when it is "centered on issues and questions that elevate larger historical, social, and cultural structures that pattern a diverse array of lived experiences" (p. 17). The hope is that with this focus, theories can increase one's ability to explore and make deeper meaning of the unique lived experiences of underrepresented college students in diverse environments (Pope, Reynolds, & Muller, 2004). Counselors who are able to have deep empathy and engage in accurate perspective taking have a greater chance of making solid connections with their clients compared with counselors who are not able to do so.

Theory is a tool, and tools cannot operate unaccompanied (at least until robots take over the world). The user—as a person—plays a large part in how theories are applied and students are viewed. Personal awareness is key because, as was discussed with respect to informal theory, one does not enter into experiences without reflecting on and sometimes filtering experiences through one's own past. Evaluating how our assumptions and biases, as counselors and student support providers, may interact with our evaluation of situations and students is vital. Jones and Abes (2011) suggested looking inward when thinking about identifying and applying theories to practice. Know your student population, the individual client's social locations and diverse lived experiences, and the sociocultural and sociopolitical campus environment first, and then apply theory in a culturally appropriate manner. For example, what would you need to ask Lina about her experience as a part of a bicultural family with varied languages and religious traditions to be able to understand her more fully and select a useful theory through which to view her concerns and campus-based experiences?

Preparing to Study Developmental Theory

Torres and Lepeau (2013) stated that "one of the important contributions developmental theories make to practice is that they allow the administrator to understand the experiences of students with completely different life stories and characteristics that influence their sense of self and worldview" (p. 16). Theories illuminate student narratives and bring forth richer understandings that foster competent practice. Counselors studying this language will find themselves holding a greater comprehension of the complexities surrounding how and why students develop. This will lead to intentional and developmentally appropriate clinical and outreach services and a "consistent and coherent approach" (Murdock, 2009, p. 2).

Determining whether a theory is sound is important as well. Murdock (2009) suggested that there are five qualities that support good theory—precision and testability, empirical validity, parsimony, stimulation, and practicality. Precision and testability refer to the ability of a theory to be easily operationalized and be testable. That is, it can provide sound predictions about clients' behavior that can be empirically put to the test. In addition to theories having sound empirical validity (based on how subjects were observed and surveyed/tested), good theory is characterized by parsimony. Parsimony denotes simplicity in choosing a noncomplex theory that describes or explains behavior in the simplest of forms. However, depending on the complexity of a case, a more multifaceted theory may be needed. The fourth quality, stimulation, describes the intellectual excitement and thought-provoking nature of the theory, which speaks to its usefulness and connection to a field or profession. Murdock (2009) cautioned about "fadlike" approaches in that they will possess this quality. Finally, practicality refers to applicability of the theory and its ability to hold "solid conceptual frameworks" (Murdock, 2009, p. 17).

As you have read, theory is essential to conducting intentional and professional practice. It provides an essential lens for the professional's roles, responsibilities, and decisions (Jones & Abes, 2011). Counselors who do not use theory may get lost in their genuine efforts to help their clients (Murdock, 2009). In addition, Evans et al. (2010) suggested potential challenges to using theory in higher education:

- "Time can be perceived as an issue when it comes to using theory" (p. 27) because of competing priorities.
- "Practitioners' lack of knowledge or failure to remember what they previously learned" (p. 27). This can be as a result of time, resources, and/or personal and professional investment in building and maintaining competency.
- "Practitioners may encounter less than supportive attitudes among other staff members who choose to dismiss the knowledge base" (p. 27). This may stem from colleagues who do not use student development theory as a foundation of practice, either from a lack of knowledge in situations in which there should be knowledge or an unwillingness to consider the importance of learning theory.
- "Some practitioners confuse a developmental perspective with permissiveness" (p. 27). They may believe that behavior backed by a student's developmental location gives the student, in a sense, an "out" and may lead to reduced sanctions.

One should reflect on these challenges to decipher whether they are roadblocks to one's work. An additional challenge is that some professionals view the use of a single theory as sufficient. This does not provide for a holistic and honest context for understanding development (Stage, 2012). Jones and Abes (2011) agreed and suggested that (a) it is rare that a single theory can carry enough explanation for practical application; (b) there are no formulas for determining which theories work best with which set of circumstances; and (c) although theories guide us toward potential interpretations, no one theory should ever be regarded as "the way" to understand a student's experience or struggle. As can be seen in the case of Lina (pages 186–187), the world is diverse and consists of individuals from diverse social locations who hold unique experiences. Theories should be made use of with such a lens.

Throughout the next five chapters you will be introduced to several classes of theories of college student development, starting with Chapter 10, "Neuroinformed College Counseling." Neuroscience allows us to further appreciate student experiences from a more holistic perspective by including biological influences throughout early, later adolescent, and young adult developmental ages and stages. Neuroscience or neuro-informed counseling is not a theory in and of itself. The knowledge that, as humans, our mind can be altered by way of our thoughts, emotions, and experiences (Makinson & Young, 2012) and that the "process of brain maturation extends well beyond adolescence" (Fine & Sung, 2014, p. 522) assists counselors and student affairs professionals in better understanding the current experience of clients and students. In addition, knowledge of neuroscience can lead to an enhanced understanding of what techniques and approaches can best assist students in and outside of session, including in planning campus outreach.

The following chapters are grouped as follows: Chapter 11, "Psychosocial Theories of Student Development" (Chickering, 1969; Chickering & Reisser, 1993; Marcia, 1967); Chapter 12, "Cognitive and Moral Theories of Development" (Belenky, Clinchy, Goldberger, & Tarule,

1986; Kohlberg, 1969; Perry, 1970); Chapter 13, "Experiential Theories of Student Development" (Baxter Magolda, 2001; Kolb, 1984; Schlossberg, 1984); and Chapter 14, "Social Constructivism and Identity in Student Development" (Abes, Jones, & McEwen, 2007; Renn, 2004). Although this is not an exhaustive list of student development theories, it does provide a solid foundation for understanding the college student experience.

Conclusion

At the conclusion of a recent student development theories class, one college counseling intern wrote that "this year put into perspective how important intentionality and theory-driven counseling is for clients. Thank you for helping me see how important being a life-long learner in this field is for clients and for my own personal development." Understanding and applying theoretical knowledge will better inform and increase intention in your clinical practice and outreach programming design and execution—which can also include programming for new student orientation. In addition, you will have connected to the common language used among student affairs and higher education professionals. This will assist with collaboration and communication. As you continue through this section, each chapter will connect theories and concepts to the case of Lina to describe phenomena through each perspective. As mentioned earlier, it is helpful to connect theories to your own unique college experience. I offer an assignment each week in my student development theory course in which students reflect on how certain student development theories and theory components directly relate to a critical point, experience, or college year in their life. When one is completing such an assignment, it is important to use the particular theory's language for full immersion. It is suggested that you use this additional learning component as you move through the following five chapters. In addition, it is recommended that you (a) critique each theory through a sociocultural lens and (b) view each theory through your institutional lens—where you are learning and training. Remember, "Theory should be applied in a critical way, with the recognition that other approaches exist and that theories contain biases that can be dangerous to clients" (Murdock, 2009, p. 5). In all, learn each theory. Socioculturally adapt each theory. Integrate theories.

Final Case Study

Dean Cresmas is a 25-year-old freshman in his first semester at a small liberal arts college in Pennsylvania. He recently completed 6 years of active duty in the Navy, where he served in the submarine electronics field. He is excited to begin his first year of college using the G.I. Bill to fund some of his education and plans to study engineering. Dean is the first of his family to attend college, and he is an only child. His dad is an officer in the Navy, and his mom works for the post office on base. They both live in Hawaii.

Dean was not the best student in high school. He did well enough that his grade point average and post–high school experience allowed him to gain acceptance to college. Over the years he has lost direct contact with his friends from high school although he still sees what they are up to through social media. He also does not have a lot of direct contact with his Navy peers. He was very close to many of them and looks fondly on their times and experiences together. He speaks to his mom a few times a week to check in to see how she is doing. His dad and mom have been in a rocky marriage since he graduated from high school and left home for the Navy.

Dean is currently living in the freshman residence hall in a triple. He has a campus work-study job with the office of accessibility. His typical day includes early morning running, going to classes, and his work-study job. In between these activities he typically studies, plays video games, and eats all his meals at the dining hall.

Case Exploration Questions

1. What is your informal theory of Dean?
2. What emotions and thoughts might Dean experience in his first year in college?
3. What transitions might Dean experience? What is their impact?
4. What internal and external factors can influence his success, failures, and development?
5. How might his learning style be affected?
6. What might reinforce and/or hinder Dean's involvement on campus?
7. What college services might Dean benefit from?
8. How does Dean fit into traditional student development models?

References

Abes, E. S. (2016). Situating paradigms in student development theory. *New Directions for Student Services, 154,* 9–16.

Abes, E. S., Jones, S. R., & McEwen, M. K. (2007). Reconceptualizing the model of multiple dimensions of identity: The role of meaning-making capacity in the construction of multiple identities. *Journal of College Student Development, 48,* 1–22.

American College Personnel Association & National Association of Student Personnel Administrators. (2015). *Professional competency areas for student affairs educators.* Washington, DC: Author.

American Council on Education. (1937). *The student personnel point of view* (American Council on Education Studies, Series 1, Vol. 1, No. 3). Washington, DC: Author.

American Council on Education, Committee on Student Personnel Work. (1949). *The student personnel point of view* (Rev. ed., American Council on Education Studies, Series 6, Vol. 13, No. 13). Washington, DC: Author.

Baxter Magolda, M. B. (2001). *Making their own way: Narratives for transforming higher education to promote self-development.* Sterling, VA: Stylus.

Belenky, M. F., Clinchy, B. M., Goldberger, N. R., & Tarule, J. M. (1986). *Women's ways of knowing: The development of self, voice, and mind.* New York, NY: Basic Books.

Chickering, A. W. (1969). *Education and identity.* San Francisco, CA: Jossey-Bass.

Chickering, A. W., & Reisser, L. (1993). *Education and identity* (2nd ed.). San Francisco, CA: Jossey-Bass.

Council for Accreditation of Counseling and Related Educational Programs. (2015). *2016 CACREP standards.* Alexandria, VA: Author.

Dungy, G., & Gordon, S. A. (2011). The development of student affairs. In J. H. Schuh, S. R. Jones, S. R. Harper, & Associates (Eds.), *Student services: A handbook for the profession* (pp. 61–79). San Francisco, CA: Jossey-Bass.

Edwards, J., & Lenhart, A. (2015). *ACCA Community College Survey (2015).* Retrieved from American College Counseling Association website: http://www.collegecounseling.org/resources/Documents/ACCA-Community-College-Survey-2014-15-Final.pdf

Erikson, E. H. (1959). *Identity and the life cycle.* New York, NY: Norton.

Erikson, E. H. (1968). *Identity: Youth and crisis.* New York, NY: Norton.

Erikson, E. H. (1993). *Childhood and society.* New York, NY: Norton.

Evans, N. J., Forney, D. S., Guido, F. M., Patton, L. D., & Renn, K. (2010). *Student development in college: Theory, research, and practice.* San Francisco, CA: Jossey-Bass.

Ferriero, J. R. (2014). Outreach practices of a small college counseling center: A comprehensive model to serve the college community (Doctoral dissertation). *Doctoral Dissertations 2014–current* (Paper 81).

Fine, J. G., & Sung, C. (2014). Neuroscience of child and adolescent health development. *Journal of Counseling Psychology, 61,* 521–527.

Hernández, E. (2016). Utilizing critical race theory to examine race/ethnicity, racism, and power in student development theory and research. *Journal of College Student Development, 57,* 168–180.

Hubbard, S. M. (2012). Theory and practice in student affairs. In F. K. Stage & S. M. Hubbard (Eds.), *Linking theory to practice: Case studies for working with college students* (pp. 1–11). New York, NY: Routledge.

Jones, S. R., & Abes, E. S. (2011). The nature and uses of theory. In J. H. Schuh, S. R. Jones, S. R. Harper, & Associates (Eds.), *Student services: A handbook for the profession* (5th ed., pp. 149–167). San Francisco, CA: Jossey-Bass.

Jones, S. R., Abes, E. S., & Cilente, K. (2011). Theories about college students, environments, and organizations. In J. H. Schuh, S. R. Jones, S. R. Harper, & Associates (Eds.), *Student services: A handbook for the profession* (5th ed., pp. 138–148). San Francisco, CA: Jossey-Bass.

Jones, S. R., & Stewart, D. L. (2016). Evolution of student development theory. *New Directions for Student Services, 156,* 17–28.

Kohlberg, L. (1969). Stage and sequence: The cognitive developmental approach to socialization. In D. A. Goslin (Ed.), *Handbook of socialization theory and research* (pp. 347–480). Chicago, IL: Rand McNally.

Kolb, D. (1984). *Experiential learning: Experience as the source of learning and development.* Englewood Cliffs, NJ: Prentice-Hall.

Lewin, K. (1936). *Principles of topological psychology.* New York, NY: McGraw-Hill.

Makinson, R. A., & Young, J. S. (2012). Cognitive behavioral therapy and the treatment of posttraumatic stress disorder: Where counseling and neuroscience meet. *Journal of Counseling & Development, 90,* 131–140. doi:10.1111/j.1556-6676.2012.00017.x

Marcia, J. E. (1967). Ego identity status: Relationship to change in self-esteem, "general maladjustment," and authoritarianism. *Journal of Personality, 35,* 118–133.

McEwen, M. (2003). The nature and uses of theory. In S. R. Komives, D. B. Woodard Jr., & Associates (Eds.), *Student services: A handbook for the profession* (4th ed., pp. 153–178). San Francisco, CA: Jossey-Bass.

Murdock, N. L. (2009). *Theories of counseling and psychotherapy: A case approach* (2nd ed.). Upper Saddle River, NJ: Pearson/Merrill.

Parker, C. A. (1977). On modeling reality. *Journal of College Student Personnel, 18,* 419–425.

Perry, W. G., Jr. (1970). *Forms of intellectual and ethical development in the college years: A scheme.* New York, NY: Holt, Rinehart & Winston.

Pope, R. L., Reynolds, A. L., & Muller, J. A. (2004). *Multicultural competence in student affairs.* San Francisco, CA: Jossey-Bass.

Prochaska, J. O., & Norcross, J. C. (2014). *Systems of psychotherapy: A transtheoretical analysis* (8th ed.). Stamford, CT: Cengage Learning.

Ratts, M. J., Singh, A. A., Nassar-McMillan, S., Butler, S. K., & McCullough, J. R. (2015). *Multicultural and social justice counseling competencies.* Retrieved from http://www.counseling.org/docs/default-source/competencies/multicultural-and-social-justice-counseling-competencies.pdf?sfvrsn=20

Reason, R. D., & Broido, E. M. (2011). Philosophies and values. In J. H. Schuh, S. R. Jones, S. R. Harper, & Associates (Eds.), *Student services: A handbook for the profession* (5th ed., pp. 80–95). San Francisco, CA: Jossey-Bass.

Renn, K. A., (2004). *Mixed race students in college: The ecology of race, identity, and community on campus.* Albany: State University of New York Press.

Sanford, N. (1962). *The American college.* New York, NY: Wiley.

Sanford, N. (1966). *Self and society: Social change and individual development.* New York, NY: Atherton Press.

Schlossberg, N. K. (1984). *Counseling adults in transition.* New York, NY: Springer.

Schuh, J. H., Jones, S. R., Harper, S. R., & Associates. (Eds.). (2011). *Student services: A handbook for the profession* (5th ed.). San Francisco, CA: Jossey-Bass.

Stage, F. K. (2012). The role of theory in a practical world. In F. K. Stage & S. M. Hubbard (Eds.), *Linking theory to practice: Case studies for working with college students* (pp. 1–11). New York, NY: Routledge.

Strange, C. (1999). Student development: The evolution and status of an essential idea. *Journal of College Student Development, 40,* 570–586.

Torres, V., & Lepeau, L. A. (2013). Making the connection: The use of student development theory in first-year and transition programs. *Journal of The First-Year Experience & Students in Transition, 25,* 13–26.

Winkle-Wagner, R. (2012). Self, college experiences, and society: Rethinking the theoretical foundations of student development theory. *College Student Affairs Journal, 30,* 45–60.

Chapter 10

Neuro-Informed College Counseling

Samuel Sanabria

One of the key practical lessons of modern neuroscience is that the power to direct our attention has within it the power to shape our brain's firing patterns, as well as the power to shape the architecture of the brain itself.

—Daniel J. Siegel,
Mindsight: The New Science of Personal Transformation

■ ■ ■

Reflection Exercise

Anyone who has ever had to cram for an exam or stay up all night to meet a project deadline knows what stress feels like. Some types of stress can be beneficial and are necessary for our overall well-being. They help our bodies stay sharp by keeping us active and help our brains stay alert by keeping us focused and motivated. However, chronic stress can lead to a variety of concerns including heart disease, high blood pressure, depression, and anxiety. You are invited to think of different situations in which you experienced a lot of stress (e.g., getting a speeding ticket, having to do a presentation in front of an audience, forgetting your partner's birthday) and spend some time reflecting on the following questions:

1. What were some examples of situations that you thought about that caused the most stress? Did you notice any running themes in your examples of situations?
2. What were some of your physical responses to this stress? Think about your energy level, appetite, body temperature, heart rate, muscle tone ,and breathing rate. On what part of your body did you feel the most tension?
3. Did your stress affect your ability to concentrate on tasks or be present with others? If so, how?

4. What are some of the ways you relieve stress (e.g., exercise, meditate, paint, spend time with friends)? What is it about these activities that helps you relax?

Keep these insights in mind as you read this chapter. Try to make personal connections to your understanding of how the brain and body respond to stress.

■ ■ ■

Contemporary college counseling theories have long recognized the importance of a biopsychosocial approach to the assessment, conceptualization, and treatment of college students (Sharkin, 2012). A biopsychosocial approach to college counseling considers biological, physiological, psychological, social, cultural, and environmental factors that affect students' development; however, trends in mental health have included an increased focus on specific biological and physiological factors (Matto & Strolin-Goltzman, 2010). This focus stems from advancements in the field of neuroscience that provide a conceptual and methodological framework for understanding how brain functioning can affect client experiences (Goncalves & Perrone-McGovern, 2014).

This chapter will begin by introducing neuroscience integration to college counseling followed by a brief overview of the brain and neural networks. Following will be an overview of the stages of brain development, which will be used to enhance our understanding of student development. Given the complexity of brain functioning throughout the life span, the focus of this chapter will be on college-age students, which is traditionally students 18 to 24 years of age. This is a crucial period because the brain continues to develop up to the mid- to late 20s. The chapter will conclude with practical directives to integrate neuroscience into your practice. To illustrate neuroscience integration, the case of Lina (see pages 186–187) will be used throughout the chapter.

Neuroscience: Advancements in Counseling

Advancements in mental health services have always relied on current scientifically based research (Goncalves & Perrone-McGovern, 2014). Although the field of neuroscience has been around for decades, it was not until the invention of functional magnetic resonance imaging—which can measure brain activity through the detection of blood flow—in 1990 that we began to see major advancements in the understanding of human cognitive, social, and emotional development (Badenoch, 2008). Compared with many other areas of scientific research, neuroscience is still in its infancy. The more that is discovered about the development, structure, and function of the brain, the more questions remain unanswered. For example, neuroscientists know that the brain is in constant use, even when we are asleep; however, the specific purpose for activity during sleep is still unknown (Caverzasio et al., 2018). Fortunately, we know enough about the brain today that this knowledge can be integrated to enhance our counseling services on college campuses. With the help of functional magnetic resonance imaging and other neuroimaging technologies (e.g., electroencephalography and positron-emission tomography) neuroscientists are rapidly expanding our knowledge of the human brain and will someday know the answers to our many questions.

Neuroscience and the Practitioner

Part of being an effective college counselor includes having an awareness of and being able to address, in session, the different experiences of college-age clients (Badenoch, 2008). These experiences include sociocultural, environmental, spiritual, biological, and now technological influences on clients' identities, thoughts, behaviors, and feelings. Neuroscience provides a basis for understanding each of these aspects as it relates to students and can be used to improve the effectiveness of mental health services. The integration of neuroscience into our approach to college counseling is often referred to as *neuro-informed counseling*. It is important to note, however, that neuroscience is not a distinct theoretical model of college counseling. Instead, it is a lens through which to better conceptualize students' experiences, so we can select the most effective therapeutic techniques that will enhance overall outcomes. Being neuro-informed does not imply that we, as counselors, are authorities in brain and neural functioning or can be called neuroscientists; it simply means that we understand basic brain and neural functioning in ways that inform our approach to therapy.

Overview of the Brain

The human brain is unquestionably the most intricate, versatile, and flexible system in human biology, yet it remains the least understood system when it comes to its complex structures and functions. The brain contains approximately 100 billion interconnected nerve cells called *neurons*. As human beings, our feelings, thoughts, and behaviors are regulated by the brain as impulses, which are transmitted from one neuron to up to 10,000 other neurons (Garrett, 2011). The rate in which information and impulses are transmitted is approximately 286 miles per hour, the fastest transmission of signals within the human body. Moreover, the brain expends 20% of our body's energy, yet, at a little over 3 pounds, makes up only 2% of our body weight. When we consider these details, we can understand why the brain remains one of the most mysterious and fascinating parts of the human body. The following sections will include a brief overview of three major structures that support neural functioning: the brain, neurons and neurotransmitters, and the nervous system. The Lina case study will be used at different points in the chapter to illustrate how the brain, neurons and neurotransmitters, and the nervous system can drive affective, cognitive, and behavioral responses.

Areas of the Brain

It is easy to view the brain as a monolithic organ that functions as the command center for all our thoughts, feelings, and behaviors; however, this is too simple an interpretation. In fact, the brain consists of many specialized parts with similar, yet distinct, functions that work in concert to regulate body functions (Kindsvatter & Geroski, 2014). It is these specialized parts of the brain that drive our intelligence, emotions, creativity, memory, speech, thoughts, and movements, as well as regulate all the organs in our bodies. The brain helps us make meaning of the world through information received from our senses. It also responds to stressful situations (e.g., test taking, a move to a new location, interpersonal conflict) by elevating our heart rate and breathing. To better understand how the brain can manage all of this, it is best to break down the parts of the brain, starting with the three evolutionary structures: the brain stem, the limbic system, and the cerebrum.

The Brain Stem

The *brain stem*, sometimes referred to as the *reptilian* or *primitive* brain, is the oldest part of the brain and first evolved 500 million years ago (LeDoux, 2003). It is located at the base of the brain, connecting the spinal cord to the other parts of the brain, and controls many of our basic survival and reflex functions (e.g., breathing, heart rate, digestion). The brain stem also transmits messages between the brain and the rest of the body. The brain stem is made up of several regions. The *midbrain*, the most complex region of the brain stem, is associated with vision, hearing, motor control, arousal, and body temperature regulation. The *pons* is located above the medulla oblongata; it serves as a message station between the cerebellum and the cerebrum. It also plays a key role in sleep and dreaming. The *medulla oblongata* is the lowest part of the brainstem; it is responsible for automatic functions such as breathing, sneezing, and digestion. The *cerebellum* is also known as the "little brain"; it is located at the rear of the brainstem and controls movement, balance, and spatial awareness. This was our evolutionary ancestors' main brain before the other two layers began evolving.

The Limbic System

The *limbic system*, sometimes referred to as the *mammalian brain*, is the second oldest part of the brain and evolved approximately 300 million years ago. It has perhaps the most central influence over our emotional responses to stressors (McEwen, 2000). The limbic system is located between the brain stem and the cerebrum and is responsible for regulating bodily functions (e.g., heart rate, blood pressure, body temperature), assisting in the formation of memories, and activating emotional responses. This is also the region of the brain that, when faced with a perceived threat, triggers the fight, flight, or freeze response. This is an evolutionary and involuntary response that is intended to ensure survival. The limbic system consists of the following main parts that work together to help protect humans from threatening events. The *amygdala* is responsible for the emotional response to stimuli, especially threatening stimuli, and then alerts the hypothalamus to respond. The *hypothalamus* is primarily responsible for maintaining homeostasis within the body (e.g., breathing, heart rate, body temperature) through the release of specific regulating hormones, including *cortisol*, a stress hormone that is released during threatening events (triggered by the amygdala) and activates the fight, flight, or freeze response in the body. The *hippocampus* is mainly associated with storing experiences, especially threats, as long-term memories that can then be used to compare new experiences with past events. This comparison process helps inform survival responses.

Let's now turn to some details about the case of Lina and examine how they are related to limbic functioning. This is Lina's first time away from the comforts of home, and she is learning to navigate new and different social rules that can often feel overwhelming. Situations she encounters are often stressful, which activates the amygdala, notifying the hypothalamus to release cortisol to prepare the body for "protective" actions. Lina's protective response is to "flee" from stressful experiences. We know this because Lina is avoiding facing her fears by socially withdrawing from others and keeping her feelings from her family. Instead of seeking emotional support, she is choosing to avoid her feelings with the hope that they will disappear or somehow resolve themselves. Unfortunately, Lina's avoidance and social isolation response have created a cycle of stress. By avoiding her problems, she is allowing herself to be in a constant state of alertness to threatening situations, which increases feelings of vulnerability. This constant state of alertness and vulnerability then motivates her further avoidance and social isolation. For example, Lina overheard her roommate refer to her as a Muslim, which triggered an automatic belief that others would reject her. Therefore, instead of facing the possibility of rejection, she has chosen to isolate herself. Without the opportunity to form meaningful and intimate relationships, Lina reinforces the belief that she is alone.

The Cerebrum

The most modern part of the brain, the *cerebrum*, evolved approximately 200 million years ago. It is the most superior (topmost) and anterior (front most) part of the brain and is responsible for human beings' most complex thoughts and behaviors. It is the area of the brain that allows us, as humans, to reason, plan, integrate multiple sensory modality inputs, regulate behavior, suppress unwanted emotional and sexual urges, and direct movement. The cerebrum is the "thinking" part of the brain and serves as a much-needed companion to the emotional response part of the brain, the amygdala (Stuss, 1992). The cerebrum is divided into four lobes:

- The *frontal lobe* is located in the front of the brain. This is a part of the brain that is associated with thinking, movement, and behavior. It is also referred to as the *executive functioning* part of the brain and is responsible for reasoning and problem-solving.
- The *occipital lobe* is located in the back of the brain. It primarily serves as the visual processing center. It allows us, as human beings, to understand what we are seeing. It is also the part of the brain that is most active while we are dreaming.
- The *parietal lobe* is located at the top of the brain and has two functions: (a) integration of sensory information that has to do with touch, taste, and temperature and (b) language processing.
- The *temporal lobe* is located at the bottom middle part of the cerebrum. This part of the brain is responsible for processing auditory information received through the ears. It also makes meaning out of sounds and speech.

The cerebrum is also divided into two hemispheres:

- The *left hemisphere* is responsible for controlling the right side of the body and is generally associated with creativity, intuition, insight, and abstract thinking.
- The *right hemisphere* is responsible for controlling the left side of the body and is generally associated with language, reasoning, science and math, and logical thinking.

Let's examine Lina's case study as it relates to the cerebrum. Lina reports that her motivation for being in college is born out of family obligation. She wants to honor her parents, especially because they have sacrificed so much to support her, and to be a role model for her younger brother. At this time, it is difficult to ascertain whether these feelings are the cause of her stress; however, it would be a reasonable assessment given her situation and what we know about stress and brain circuitry. Through evolutionary history, the brain has developed a survival-maximizing response to threatening situations, reducing or shutting off executive functioning in the frontal lobe area. Engaging our executive functioning could slow response time, especially when time and energy are used to cognitively process a threatening situation. This response occurs mainly during times of acute stress; however, Lina is experiencing prolonged stress that manifests a similar effect by blunting cognitive functioning, making the limbic system more active and susceptible to depression. Impaired cognitive functioning also interferes with self-motivation, learning, and the ability to retain information. It is possible that Lina is personalizing these experiences, believing that she is either uninterested in college, incapable of succeeding in college, or both!

One way she has chosen to avoid addressing her problems is to seek employment at the campus bookstore. This may have seemed like a good idea on the surface, especially given how expensive college is, but as a result, she is experiencing new difficulties with time management. She now has the added stress of trying to fit homework and studies around a work schedule. On top of this, she has placed herself in a situation in which she interacts with others on campus, such as faculty members, without the benefit of their knowing her. Unfortunately, this gives Lina the uneasy feeling of being unnoticed, further increasing her need for isolation.

Neurons and Neurotransmitters

The structure of a neuron includes the *cell body*, a nerve fiber called an *axon*, and branching filaments called *dendrites*. The function of a neuron is to receive, process, and communicate information within the brain and between the brain and the body through electrical and chemical signals. Information from one neuron is electrically transmitted through the axons and released as chemicals, called *neurotransmitters*, across a small gap called a *synapse*, which are then received by the dendrites of another neuron. This transaction is called *neurotransmission*. Each neuron is connected to approximately 10,000 other neurons, and communication between them occurs nearly instantaneously.

There are more than 50 identified neurotransmitters, which serve different purposes. They control major bodily functions including heart rate, breathing, digestion, and movement. They also regulate mood, sleep, and concentration. There are two broad types of neurotransmitters—*excitatory* and *inhibitory*. Excitatory neurotransmitters (e.g., dopamine, epinephrine, and glutamate) serve to stimulate brain activity whereas inhibitory neurotransmitters (e.g., serotonin, gamma-aminobutyric acid, and acetylcholine) help calm and balance the brain. These neurotransmitters work together to regulate the brain and body to enhance chances of survival. For example, as soon as real or perceived danger is detected, the amygdala releases the excitatory neurotransmitter norepinephrine to the adrenal glands, which signals the release of the hormone adrenaline. Once released, the hormone prepares the body for action by increasing heart rate, raising blood pressure, and increasing the amount of sugar in the blood (LeDoux, 2003; Stuss, 1992). After the real or perceived danger has subsided, the brain begins the process of restoring body homeostasis through the release of the inhibitory neurotransmitter gamma-aminobutyric acid, which lowers heart rate (etc.) back to normal levels.

There are three leading neurotransmitters related to Lina's experience: dopamine, epinephrine, and norepinephrine. Each of these affects her body in different ways. Adequate dopamine levels allow us, as human beings, to focus our attention in the moment and serve as our main regulator for pleasure and rewards, whereas lower dopamine levels occur during periods of chronic stress. It is likely that Lina is experiencing a depletion of dopamine as a result of her ongoing stress from school and social concerns. Dopamine depletion negatively affects learning, motivation, and memory and can lead to depression. Lina may also be experiencing high and prolonged levels of epinephrine excretion. Moderate increases in epinephrine excretion, best known as adrenaline, stimulate attention, mental focus, and cognition; however, high and prolonged levels of epinephrine excretion can lead to insomnia and cognitive decline as seen in Lina's case. Rapid and moderate bursts of norepinephrine may improve brain functioning as it prepares the body for fight, flight, or freeze response. Chronic low-level release of norepinephrine affects sleep, stress resilience, and concentration. It can also lead to apathy and a lack of motivation, all of which Lina is exhibiting.

Developmental Plasticity

All human brains have the capacity to adapt to changes in experiences, no matter how large or small (Pascual-Leone, Amedi, Fregni, & Merabet, 2005; Siegel, 2012). One way to look at the brain is to imagine it as a never-ending series of roadways that are constantly morphing into different paths. When we repeat thoughts or behaviors, we are reinforcing already established road connections. When we challenge these thoughts, or change our behaviors, we create new neural connections or pathways. By repeating these new thoughts and behaviors, we reinforce the newly developed pathways while the previous pathways are slowly extinguished. This is often referred to as *neuroplasticity*.

Chronic stress can severely impair neuroplasticity, especially while the brain is still forming, thus affecting mood and the ability to learn. Fortunately, this impairment is not always permanent (Frank, 2008; Pascual-Leone et al., 2005). The body and brain have an innate ability to heal themselves, especially in young adults. There are many ways to reverse damage to neuroplasticity and neural connections. Simply reducing chronic stress and learning new coping skills can lead to great results.

From a developmental perspective there are critical periods in which neural connections are formed more easily than at other times. For example, young children have an innate ability to learn new languages, including complex grammar rules, with ease. The period of time in which learning a new language comes easily for most children is before the age of 12; however, regardless of one's age, the brain continues to be adaptable to new experiences even if there is a functional decline in cognitive, motor, and social domains in old age. Through deliberate practice, one could experience structural reorganization and functional changes in response to new stimuli. Fortunately, typical college-age students are at a developmental stage in which the brain is still developing and many new neural connections are being made.

Stages of Brain Development

The brain undergoes developmental changes throughout the human life span. Understanding when and how the brain changes can provide the counselor with valuable insight into students' affective, cognitive, and behavioral experiences. The majority of brain development occurs by the age of 2, which underscores the importance of early childhood experiences like parent attachment, environmental stressors, and access to health care and nutrition. However, some aspects of the brain, specifically the frontal lobe, are not fully developed until late adolescence or early adulthood, which is important information for college counselors working with college-age students. The following is a summary of developmental changes occurring at different stages of life. The first three stages are important to understand as they are the building blocks to phenomenological experiences. This understanding may provide certain therapeutic insights and added empathy when working with students. What is specifically important to college counselors is the third stage (adolescence/young adulthood), which is the developmental focus of this chapter and the primary age range of students with whom college counselors work.

Stage 1: Early Childhood (Ages 0 to 5)

Neurons are rapidly making new connections. Repeated experiences strengthen neural connections whereas infrequent or inexistent experiences eliminate others. Healthy parent-child bonds are important at this stage of neural development.

Stage 2: School Age (Ages 6 to 12)

Neural connections continue to form while temporal lobes grow and reach maximum levels. Frontal, parietal, and temporal lobe connections are strengthened. As a result, the child begins to understand, process, and respond to social cues on a deeper level. By age 6 a child's brain is 95% the weight of an adult brain.

Stage 3: Adolescence/Young Adulthood (Ages 13 to 21)

Neural connections in frontal lobes continue to grow. Executive functioning skills, which affect emotional regulation and reasoning, are still developing. Axons sheathed with a fatty substance, called *myelin* or *white matter*, increase, contributing to faster electrical pulses that intensify emotions. The adolescent becomes more adept at learning how to manage emotions and develop reasoning skills.

As a young adult, Lina is at the third stage of her brain development. Her brain has just endured considerable growth, specifically in the frontal area of the cerebral cortex. Lina is at an age at which her frontal lobe is completing full development, which signifies an enhanced capacity to further develop emotional regulation and reasoning skills. It is important to note that regardless of whether her frontal lobe is fully developed, she is able to form new neural connections through developmental plasticity while gradually extinguishing old connections. Although her current mode of emotional regulation and reasoning was developed during earlier stages, she is still in her prime for learning new ways of thinking and behaving. Without the benefit of self-reflection, Lina is engaging in automatic and unconscious behaviors of avoidance and isolation. This is a hardwired and natural response to her stress. Maintaining this pattern not only prevents her from finding relief from her stress but also adds to her feelings of depression. Counseling would be most beneficial for Lina because it would help her to recognize and challenge unwanted cognitive thoughts and behaviors, creating new neural connections along the way. The use of expressive forms of therapy may provide better outcomes.

Stage 4: Adulthood (Age 22 to Late 30s)

The frontal lobe is fully developed, improving impulse control and decision-making skills. White matter connections continue to develop, improving the transmission of electrical pulses. The brain reaches peak performance at around 22 years of age, which is maintained for approximately 5 years.

Stage 5: Middle Age (40s and 50s)

Neural connections continue to be made. The brain is better able to integrate information and experiences. The rewiring of neural connections can occur with new experiences. The brain is able to engage in increasingly complex thinking, including developing and maintaining diverse social relationships.

Stage 6: Older Age (Age 60 and Older)

Some structures and regions of the brain begin to decline. White matter decreases, affecting processing speed. Brain cells are lost, affecting memory and time to accomplish complex tasks. Despite these declines, vocabulary and experience-based knowledge persist.

Neuroscience and Counseling

College counseling theories provide effective counseling frameworks that support student success. Neuroscience, however, provides additional insights into student experiences that can be used to enhance many aspects of the counseling process (e.g., assessment, client conceptualization, counselor's empathy, and treatment interventions). As stated earlier, neuroscience is meant to be used to complement established college counseling theories. Neuroscience research supports the effectiveness of traditional approaches including person-centered therapy, cognitive behavior therapy, and mindfulness (Cozolino, 2010). It also supports the importance and positive influence of the therapeutic relationship (Atkinson, 2005). Therefore, having a familiarity with neuroscience and an understanding of how it can be used to enhance counseling services is becoming increasingly important for college counselors. The following are examples of how the counseling process can improve students' brain functioning.

Hope and Empowerment

We know that the brain changes throughout a person's lifetime, and every new experience provides opportunities for new neural connection and stimulation. Consider what happens when a student who has been struggling with depression for an extended time can no longer cope with the impact of that depression. By making the decision to call for a counseling appointment, she has already experienced positive changes through a sense of hope and empowerment. These feelings trigger the release of endorphins that reduce the effects of stress and increase feelings of pleasure. Endorphins also help to modulate the physical pain associated with stress, similar to the "runner's high" experience.

So far, Lina's college experience has been filled with overwhelming feelings of uncertainty and doubt, feelings that have led to a sense of hopelessness. After realizing that taking the job at the bookstore is not helping her current situation, she decides to make an appointment with the one person on campus she feels she can trust, her academic adviser. Perhaps a part of her feels that her adviser could provide some insights that would have made a welcome difference in her experiences. After she made the appointment, her mental dialogue changed from "What am I doing here" and "I don't think I can make it" to "I wonder what I will learn from my adviser" and "Maybe there is something that's available to me." As a result of these thoughts, Lina noticed a slight change in her mood. She moved from a sense of hopelessness to one of possibility.

During their meeting, her adviser recommended that she see a counselor at the campus wellness center. At first, Lina was resistant. She was taught that counseling was intrusive and that personal affairs should only be discussed within the family system. Her adviser normalized her feelings by saying that many students have similar concerns but that many who decided to seek counseling ended up feeling better. He then suggested that she try it for a couple of sessions. This helped Lina open up to the idea of counseling, and together she and her adviser made an appointment with the wellness center. Lina continued to feel hopeful and empowered.

The Counseling Relationship

Just as we, as humans, have a basic need for food, we also have a basic need to be a part of a group and to have meaningful relationships. One of the defining aspects that distinguishes us from other vertebrates is the proportional size of our social brain (amygdala, frontal lobe, and temporal lobe), which is larger, in relation to the body, than in any other species. An elephant's brain may be larger than a human's brain, but it is proportionately smaller given the elephant's body size. This is significant because a larger social brain is linked to participation in larger social groups, social intelligence, and an overall need for meaningful relationships. Our brains experience a decline in memory and intellectual functioning when we are socially isolated. Social isolation also reduces dopamine production, thus reducing motivation and feelings of pleasure. When students begin counseling, they are entering a significant relationship that engages and strengthens their social brain. Although the therapeutic relationship is professional in nature, it is still an important experience for both the student and the counselor (Cozolino, 2010; Linden, 2006).

Lina attended her session with the wellness center college counselor and at first was nervous about what she would be asked. She thought the counselor would be stoic and ask her personal questions that she was uncomfortable answering; however, she was pleasantly surprised when she was approached in a warm and genuine manner. The counselor introduced herself and welcomed her to her office. The room was also safe and inviting. Lina felt comfortable with this environment and with her assigned counselor. During the first session, the counselor was friendly and did not pressure her to immediately share personal information, which helped Lina to relax and to take her time. After a few pleasant exchanges the counselor asked Lina what brought her to counseling. Lina began to share her feelings about being in college, her lack of motivation, the stress of juggling a job and schoolwork, her roommate's comment about being a Muslim, her feelings of isolation, and her fear about disappointing her parents. The counselor was engaged in empathetic listening, which made Lina feel heard and supported. Lina also felt like someone cared and finally understood her experiences. Her feelings of loneliness slowly decreased the more connected she felt with her counselor.

Lina's experience with counseling was beneficial and actually enjoyable, and she decided to schedule another appointment. This was the first time since coming to college that Lina felt she wasn't alone. Her sense of hope and empowerment was now accompanied by support. As a result, Lina developed new senses of optimism and motivation to continue with college.

Therapeutic Dialogue

Students seek counseling for a variety of reasons, but one experience that is shared by nearly everyone is the feeling of being stuck. Providing a safe space and freedom for students to examine their thoughts, feelings, and behaviors while exploring new and more congruent ones can reduce the feeling of being stuck and lead to a more desired life (Linden, 2006). Through reflective dialogue, students develop meaningful insights into self, others, their environment, and the world (Kounios & Beeman, 2010; Siegel, 2012). These insights help create new ways of thinking, which, in turn, create new neural pathways.

Counseling also promotes mental well-being through neurogenesis and epigenesis. *Neurogenesis* refers to the development of new neurons, as opposed to new neural connections. It was once believed that humans would lose the ability to create new neurons as they age. Fortunately, recent studies (Crosson et al., 2017; Ecapilla-Gonzalez, Eherranz-Pérez, & Egarcía-Verdugo, 2015; Frank, 2008; Iannitelli, Quartini, Tirassa, & Bersani, 2017) on neuroscience have revealed that the brain is capable of generating new neurons, which can occur during learning and the experiencing of new situations, regardless of age. *Epigenesis* refers to the process by which genes are activated and expressed through social interactions and environmental triggers. Our mental process, including how we, as human beings, understand ourselves in relation to our environment, serves to increase not only mental functioning but also our physical health. Contemplate the idea that as you read and reflect on the contents of this book you are gaining new knowledge and insights that will not only create and rewire neurons but also manipulate gene expression in a way that may improve your health. Amazing!

With the support of her counselor, Lina was able to identify and link together experiences that had a significant impact on her sense of worth and identity. She shared her experiences growing up in a multiheritage family and how post-9/11 social reactions toward Muslims have affected her ability to connect with her Islamic identity. She also shared how much pressure she felt from her parents to do well in school and to be a role model for her younger brother. Through continued therapeutic dialogue, Lina was able to develop new insights into her fears, lack of motivation, and decision to withdraw from others, especially from her parents.

As Lina developed new insights, she created neural pathways that altered her mood and thought processes. The more she was able to engage in therapeutic dialogue, the more she was able to gain deeper insights and strengthen her neocortical connections. As a result, Lina began to see her life circumstances differently. She noticed an improvement in her ability to respond to stress in a more productive manner.

Mental Wellness Versus Mental Illness

When there is a focus on negative issues and problems during therapy, unwanted neural connections are reinforced. Focusing on a student's problems activates the amygdala, leading to a more prominent influence of the amygdala during therapy. As a result, the student's frontal lobe may be impaired, which limits the student's ability to form rational thoughts and to identify potential solutions. Likewise, when a student dwells on the negative during counseling, it increases cortisol, a stress hormone, which has an effect on memory, mood, and overall physical health. A more solution-focused approach is recommended, especially with college-age clients who are at the developmental stage of brain growth completion. Positive-focused therapies, such as solution-focused therapy, narrative therapy, and other strength-based therapies, are effective with this population (Sobhy & Cavallaro, 2010).

Throughout the initial stages of counseling there was a focus on uncovering Lina's phenomenological experiences. Many of the experiences that were explored brought up painful feelings; however, her counselor was careful to also explore the strengths Lina exhibited throughout her life, especially during her difficult times. This helped Lina to view herself as a fighter and a survivor, which increased her self-esteem.

After a few counseling sessions, Lina had enough insight to clearly identify what she wanted to do with her college experience. With the help of her counselor, Lina was able to define specific goals for herself and enter the working stage of counseling. Her counselor decided to incorporate solution-focused therapy to help Lina strengthen positive neural connections and increase prefrontal cortex functioning.

Mindfulness Therapy

Mindfulness-based interventions (MBIs) have received a tremendous amount of attention over the past decade. Neuroresearchers have found that regular meditation and mindfulness practice has been linked to better mental health (Bohlmeijer, Prenger, Taal, & Cuijpers, 2010; Fjorback, Arendt, Ørnbøl, Fink, & Walach, 2011; Regehr, Glancy, & Pitts, 2013), especially reduced depression and anxiety. It has also been linked to enhanced interpersonal well-being. The basic tenets of MBI involve regulating focus; being curious and open to experiences; living in the "here and now"; and having nonjudgmental awareness of thoughts, emotions, sensations, and the environment (Kabat-Zinn, 2015). MBI strengthens the anterior cingulate cortex, which is located behind the frontal lobe and is associated with directing focus and attention, and self-regulation (Regehr et al., 2013). This strengthening of the anterior cingulate cortex could lead to better test scores and time management. In addition, the anterior cingulate cortex is associated with memory and learning from past experiences. MBI can lead to better decision-making skills (Fjorback et al., 2011). This is especially important for college students, given the constant and fast-changing pace of college life. Neuroscientists have also discovered that MBI strengthens the part of the brain related to perception, body awareness, emotional regulation, complex thinking, and sense of self (Bohlmeijer et al., 2010; Fjorback et al., 2011).

During therapy, Lina was introduced to the practice of mindfulness. Her counselor explained the benefits of living a mindful life and dedicating time each day to uninterrupted meditation. At first, Lina's counselor coached her in session on basic mindfulness practice, including deep breathing and body awareness. Her counselor then started and ended each counseling session with a brief practice on mindfulness. Lina immediately began to feel a difference as she was better able to relax and experience clarity of mind. She started to incorporate mindfulness in her daily life and noticed that she was more attuned to herself, her friends, and her environment. She also noticed her grades improving as she refocused her attention on her studies with minimal distractions. This change in her school performance gave her new purpose and a new outlook on college. She began to show more interest in her classes and even identified potential career paths.

Integrative Theory

As mentioned earlier, the brain is divided into two hemispheres: the left and the right. Although both sides of the brain are connected and work together on all issues, there are basic functions that are dominant to each side (Beeman & Bowden, 2000). The left hemisphere is considered to be the more logical side of the brain whereas the right hemisphere is more primitive or emotional. The left hemisphere is responsible for rational, methodological, language-based, and conscious knowledge. This is the part of the brain that is used to solve technical problems or understand details, and it is most active during therapeutic interventions that are cognitive based (Beeman & Bowden, 2000). The right hemisphere is responsible for unconscious, social, creative, and emotional knowledge. This is also the part of the brain that resolves problems through intuition and relates on an emotional level. The right hemisphere is activated during more emotive forms of therapeutic interventions (Beeman & Bowden, 2000).

Integrating the functions of the left and right hemispheres is important for mental health development (Siegel, 2006). When the left and right hemispheres work together to promote energy and information flow, there is an increase in mental functioning. In other words, the mind becomes more coherent and efficient. The mind is better able to experience and endure stress and to view problems from different perspectives, thus increasing options and motivation for problem-solving (Linden, 2006). The mind is also better able to negotiate different social situations and relationships, as well as balance mood (Siegel, 2012). Therapies that are flexible and incorporate a cognitive, affective, and insight approach are most effective with respect to linking the left and right hemispheres. Moreover, therapies that include a variety of therapeutic techniques, including those that stimulate creativity, are helpful in increasing brain integration (Badenoch, 2008; Cozolino, 2010).

Lina's counselor made sure to assess her progress throughout the therapeutic process. Lina reports feeling better and has already seen progress with her motivation and self-esteem. Lina made the decision to quit her job at the bookstore so she could focus on her studies and, as a result, her grades improved. Lina also feels more comfortable with her roommate and even attends a few campus social gatherings with her. Overall, Lina had positive outcomes from therapy and is ready to move into the termination stage of counseling.

During the termination phase, the counselor has Lina process her new approach to school and other stressors. Because the counselor understands the importance of integrating the left and right hemispheres of the brain, she makes sure to use therapeutic approaches that would facilitate this integration. The counselor starts by having Lina engage her brain's left hemisphere. Using affective and insight therapeutic approaches, the counselor has Lina describe her steps toward growth and identify learnings that had the most impact on change. Although this method reinforces Lina's newly developed schemas, it still uses just one side of the brain and is incomplete. In order for Lina to improve her overall mental health and cognitive functioning, both sides of her brain need to work in sync. Therefore, after each significant discovery, the counselor has Lina engage the right hemisphere by having her explore her feelings associated with each insight and schema. This cross-lateral approach links Lina's analytic side of the brain to her emotive side of the brain, which helps Lina feel more congruent.

Promoting Mental Wellness Through Outreach

There are many ways to increase brain health and, consequently, mental wellness. Noted neuroscientist David Rock and psychiatrist and neuroscientist Dan Siegal developed a model for brain fitness called the healthy mind platter (Rock & Siegel, 2011). This model could serve as a guide for assisting college counselors' work in developing and promoting campus-wide mental wellness programs. The key to a healthy brain lies in participating in a variety of activities that use different parts of the brain. By participating in these activities on a regular basis, a person is "exercising" and caring for the whole brain. The following is an overview of the healthy mind platter with suggestions on how to promote and integrate this model on college campuses.

Sleep Time

Regular and consistent sleep is vital for brain health. The average amount of sleep for optimal health is 8 hours; however, people's needs vary. Sleep helps refresh the mind and consolidate memory. One way to encourage good sleep habits is to have quiet hours in dorms, especially during exams week.

Physical Activity Time

Exercise strengthens the physical body and brain functioning, especially in later life (Cotman & Engesser-Cesar, 2002). Exercise increases heart rate, which boosts oxygen levels to the brain, improving memory and learning. Exercise also stimulates growth of new neural connections and reduces stress hormones, allowing for more frontal cortex functioning. Campus athletic facilities provide a place for students to exercise; however, there are many other ways to provide exercise opportunities. Creating student clubs in which specific physical activities are the focus (running, rowing, swimming, etc.) is another great way to get students moving.

Playtime

It's important that, as human beings, we make time to enjoy life through playful activities. This allows our brain to cultivate our creativity and adaptability. A good way to encourage playful behavior is to designate on-campus spaces for the purpose of play. The campus could also have weekly outdoor activities, like scavenger hunts, that encourage students to have fun.

Focus Time

Students are probably most familiar with this activity given the academic demands of college. Focus time allows students to strengthen their frontal lobes and is vital for working memory development. Exercising this region of the brain helps strengthen executive functioning skills, including decision making and rationalization. It also helps with emotional regulation. Colleges can designate several quiet areas around campus for studying and working on projects.

Time In

Reflection, mindfulness, and meditation are all examples of "time in" activities. This activity allows students to reduce stress and be attuned to themselves and their environment. College campuses can have quiet spaces throughout campus where students can meditate. If space is an issue, then perhaps an arrangement could be made to share one of the designated study areas (the abovementioned areas conducive to focus time) such that part of the day is dedicated for meditation time. Yoga classes are another good way to get some time in.

Connecting Time

Social support is necessary for optimal brain health, especially when the support comes from an intimate and stable relationship. As human beings, our brains have evolved to be social, and we can even experience physical pain when socially isolated (Eisenberger & Lieberman, 2004). Many long-term and significant relationships are established during the college years, and it is important that college campuses provide opportunities for students to engage with one another in meaningful ways.

Downtime

The brain needs time to disconnect from any activities that require brain power. This is not the same as leisure time, which involves activities. Instead, it means inactivity and doing nothing. From my experience this is perhaps the easiest to implement on campus. Just encourage downtime and let students go for it.

Conclusion

Neuroscience research is an instrumental part of counseling practice. It provides a biological foundation for understanding clients and the process of counseling. As college counselors, by increasing our understanding of neural systems and brain functioning, we can work toward a more informed approach to assessment, case conceptualization, and treatment planning and thus can improve cognitive, social, emotional, and vocational experiences for students. Every contact with students introduces new ideas, produces changes to memory, and increases learning. Likewise, the campus environment can provide the necessary stimulus to promote brain growth and development. Incorporating neuroscience into practice, college counselors can identify specific interventions in their counseling sessions and assist in creating outreach programs to enhance environmental stimuli that can provide longer lasting results. But remember, to effectively integrate neuroscience into your practice as college counselors, it is important that you keep up with advancements in research. What we are learning about the brain and neural systems is expanding every day.

Final Case Study

Sae is a 21-year-old transgender male seeking treatment at his college's counseling center for what he describes as "intense anxiety." This anxiety has affected his academic performance to the point that he is concerned about being "kicked out" of the architectural program at his college.

He reports feeling unmotivated to work on his project and spending a lot of time on social media, isolated from his friends and family. He remembers experiencing anxiety as far back as the age of 8, when he first experienced feeling different than other children his age. It was at this time that he began to develop insecurities about his body and feared that there was something "wrong" with his mind and body.

As he developed into adolescence, he began to feel more out of place within his own body and he even contemplated suicide to free himself from constant emotional pain. At the age of 14, Sae met another transgender male and finally understood what he was experiencing and, more important, that he was not alone. Sae decided to keep this secret from his family and friends out of fear of rejection. He was particularly concerned about hurting his mother, whom he was very close to.

It wasn't until he went away to college at the age of 19 that he decided to express his true self in public. This is his first time seeking counseling services, and he is hoping to find some relief from his anxiety so he can improve his academic performance.

Case Exploration Questions

1. How might the development of Sae's brain and neural networks have been affected by his early experiences with gender identity confusion?
2. In what ways could his recent decision to fully express his gender identity and his being away from his family exacerbate his anxiety?
3. From a neuroscience perspective, what therapeutic technique do you think would be most effective in helping him to manage his anxiety?

References

Atkinson, B. (2005). *Emotional intelligence in couples therapy: Advances from neurobiology and the science of intimate relationships.* New York, NY: Norton.

Badenoch, B. (2008). *Becoming a brain-wise therapist: A practical guide to interpersonal neurobiology.* New York, NY: Norton.

Beeman, M. J., & Bowden, E. M. (2000). The right hemisphere maintains solution-related activation for yet-to-be-solved insight problems. *Memory & Cognition, 28,* 1231–1241.

Bohlmeijer, E., Prenger, R., Taal, E., & Cuijpers, P. (2010). The effects of mindfulness-based stress reduction therapy on mental health of adults with a chronic medical disease: A meta-analysis. *Journal of Psychosomatic Research, 68,* 539–544.

Caverzasio, S., Amato, N., Manconi, M., Prosperetti, C., Kaelin-Lang, A., Hutchison, W. D., & Galati, S. (2018). Brain plasticity and sleep: Implication for movement disorders. *Neuroscience and Biobehavioral Reviews, 86,* 21–35.

Cotman, C. W., & Engesser-Cesar, C. (2002). Exercise enhances and protects brain function. *Exercise and Sport Sciences Reviews, 30,* 75–79.

Cozolino, L. (2010). *The neuroscience of psychotherapy: Healing the social brain.* New York, NY: Norton.

Crosson, B., Hampstead, B. M., Krishnamurthy, L. C., Krishnamurthy, V., McGregor, K. M., Nocera, J. R., . . . Tran, S. M. (2017). Advances in neurocognitive rehabilitation research from 1992 to 2017: The ascension of neural plasticity. *Neuropsychology, 31,* 900–920.

Ecapilla-Gonzalez, V., Eherranz-Pérez, V., & Egarcía-Verdugo, J. M. (2015). The aged brain: Genesis and fate of residual progenitor cells in the subventricular zone. *Frontiers in Cellular Neuroscience, 9,* 365.

Eisenberger, N. I., & Lieberman, M. D. (2004). Why rejection hurts: A common neural alarm system for physical and social pain. *Trends in Cognitive Sciences, 8,* 294–300.

Fjorback, L. O., Arendt, M., Ørnbøl, E., Fink, P., & Walach, H. (2011). Mindfulness-based stress reduction and mindfulness-based cognitive therapy: A systematic review of randomized controlled trials. *Acta Psychiatrica Scandinavica, 124,* 102–119.

Frank, D. L. (2008). Neuroplasticity: Bridging psychoanalysis and neuroscience. *Psychoanalytic Quarterly, LXXVII,* 921–938. doi:10.1002/j.2167-4086.2008.tb00370.x

Garrett, B. (2011). *Brain and behavior: An introduction to biological psychology* (3rd ed.). Thousand Oaks, CA: Sage.

Goncalves, O. F., & Perrone-McGovern, K. M. (2014). A neuroscience agenda for counseling psychology research. *Journal of Counseling Psychology, 61,* 507–512.

Iannitelli, A., Quartini, A., Tirassa, P., & Bersani, G. (2017). Schizophrenia and neurogenesis: A stem cell approach. *Neuroscience and Biobehavioral Reviews, 80,* 414–442.

Kabat-Zinn, J. (2015). Mindfulness. *Mindfulness, 6,* 1481–1483.

Kindsvatter, A., & Geroski, A. (2014). The impact of early life stress on the neurodevelopment of the stress response system. *Journal of Counseling & Development, 92,* 472–480. doi:10.1002/j.1556-6676.2014.00173.x

Kounios, J., & Beeman, M. (2010). The aha! moment: The cognitive neuroscience of insight. *Current Directions in Psychological Science, 18,* 210–216.

LeDoux, J. E. (2003). *Synaptic self: How our brains become who we are.* New York, NY: Penguin.

Linden, D. (2006). How psychotherapy changes the brain—The contribution of functional imaging. *Molecular Psychiatry, 11,* 528–538.

Matto, H. C., & Strolin-Goltzman, J. (2010). Integrating social neuroscience and social work: Innovations for advancing practice-based research. *Social Work, 55,* 147–156. Retrieved from https://doi-org.ezproxy.rollins.edu:9443/10.1093/sw/55.2.147

McEwen, B. (2000). The neurobiology of stress: From serendipity to clinical relevance. *Brain Resolution, 886,* 172–189.

Pascual-Leone, A., Amedi, A. Fregni, F., & Merabet, L. B. (2005). The plastic human brain cortex. *Annual Reviews of Neuroscience, 28,* 377–401.

Regehr, C., Glancy, D., & Pitts, A. (2013). Interventions to reduce stress in university students: A review and meta-analysis. *Journal of Affective Disorders, 148,* 1–11.

Rock, D., & Siegel, D. J. (2011). *The mind platter, for optimal brain matter.* Retrieved from https://www.drdansiegel.com/resources/healthy_mind_platter/

Sharkin, B. S. (2012). *Being a college counselor on today's campus: Roles, contributions, and special challenges.* New York, NY: Routledge.

Siegel, D. J. (2006). An interpersonal neurobiological approach to psychotherapy. *Psychiatric Annals, 36,* 248–256.

Siegel, D. J. (2012). *The developing mind: How relationships and the brain interact to shape who we are.* New York, NY: Guilford Press.

Sobhy, M., & Cavallaro, M. (2010). *Solution-focused brief counseling in schools: Theoretical perspectives and case application to an elementary school student.* Retrieved from https://www.counseling.org/resources/library/VISTAS/2010-V-Online/Article_81.pdf

Stuss, D. T. (1992). Biological and psychological development of executive functions. *Brain and Cognition, 20,* 8–23.

Chapter 11

Psychosocial Theories of Student Development

Joshua C. Watson and Benjamin Robertson

In the social jungle of human existence,
there is no feeling of being alive without a sense of identity.

—Erik Erikson

■ ■ ■

Reflection Exercise

First-time parents are fascinated with their baby's firsts. The first time the baby laughs. The baby's first word. The first time the baby walks. Each of these moments are memorable and represent an important developmental milestone. Although typically more celebrated among children, these developmental milestones continue throughout life. You may not remember saying your first word or taking your first step, but you probably remember driving a car for the first time, your first date, and your first day of college. In fact, next to your early childhood years, the early adulthood period, when most people go to college, is the most developmentally active period. Think back to your college experience. Reflect on your growth from your first year to your graduation:

1. What was it like being responsible for your learning and having to make your own decisions?
2. Did you change your major as you learned more about yourself?
3. Did your view of the world change as you met a diverse group of people across campus?
4. Were you more prepared for the future when you graduated college than you were when you first set foot on campus?

Your responses to these questions likely indicate you changed a lot throughout the years spent in college. This is the case for most people. In fact, the complexities of this developmental stage have captured the attention of numerous scholars. In this chapter, we will examine a collection of theories that focus on the psychosocial development that occurs in young adults, particularly related to their experiences in college.

■ ■ ■

Collectively, psychosocial theories of development, which can be applied to the development of identity in students, are popular lenses through which college counselors and student affairs professionals seek to understand student development. Based on Erikson's (1950, 1963) famous developmental stages, theories of psychosocial development allow us to conceptualize how individuals grow and develop over the course of their lives (Long, 2012) and qualitatively change their thinking, feeling, acting, and relation to self and others (Chickering & Reisser, 1993) because of their maturing identity. Conflict, independence, interdependence, and autonomy are underlying values of psychosocial theories of development (Long, 2012).

A hallmark of psychosocial theories is the notion that identity development is a process through which individuals learn to make sense of the world they live in, develop a stable sense of self, and begin the process of self-realization (Kim, 2012). This process typically occurs in a sequential manner and largely is shaped by the successful resolution of a series of specific age-related developmental tasks. Before one advances to subsequent stages of development, a mastering of skills must occur. As such, scholars have noted that identity development is the by-product of the accumulative effects of different states and experiences individuals encounter across the life span (Evans, Forney, Guido, Patton, & Renn, 2010).

Because psychosocial theories of development help frame counselors' and student affairs personnel's understanding of how students rationalize, behave, and develop as human beings, they provide great utility in working with a college-age population. For decades, counselors and student affairs personnel have successfully applied psychosocial theories in situations requiring them to assist students in developing autonomy, becoming independent, and resolving conflicts with others, as well as in framing discussions of various identity elements including gender, race, ethnicity, and sexual orientation (Long, 2012). Additionally, these theories are used to examine important issues students face in their lives as they develop a progressively more mature identity such as how they define themselves and their relationships with others and what direction they want to take in their lives vocationally. As such, a strong working knowledge of these theories will prove useful as you begin working with college students to address the variety of psychological, emotional, social, and interpersonal challenges they are likely to face during their time on campus.

In this chapter, we will focus on two specific psychosocial theories of student development: Chickering and Reisser's seven-vector model and Marcia's identity status model, using the case of Lina (see pages 186–187) as an example to illustrate how personal experiences are shaped by the process of learning who we are and how we fit into the world. Volumes of research on both Chickering's and Marcia's models exist, and their applications with a variety of student populations have been explored. The utility of each will be up to you to decide on the basis of the work you do. Our goal here is to provide you with an overview to better understand what these theories purport. As you read about each theory, begin thinking about how you can use it as a framework for the work you plan to do with students.

Chickering's Seven Vectors of Identity Development

One of the more prominent theories of psychosocial student development is Chickering's (1969) seven vectors of identity development theory. In fact, over the past 50 years, Arthur Chickering has had the most pronounced influence on theory, research, and practice in the study of student development (Chickering & Reisser, 1993), with his model generally recognized as the most widely known and applied theory of student development. Today, counselors and student affairs professionals use elements of his model at both the micro- (individual student) and macro- (campus-wide) levels (see Table 11.1).

TABLE 11.1

Seven Vectors of Identity Development

Vector	1969 Chickering Model	1993 Chickering and Reisser Model
1	Developing competence	Developing competence
2	Managing emotions	Managing emotions
3	Developing autonomy	Moving through autonomy toward interdependence
4	Establishing identity	Developing mature interpersonal relationships
5	Freeing interpersonal relationships	Establishing identity
6	Developing purpose	Developing purpose
7	Developing integrity	Developing integrity

Unlike other developmental theorists, Chickering designed his theory to specifically focus on identity development during the college years. In his initial theory, student identity development occurs through a series of stages known as *vectors*. The purpose of the seven vectors was to illustrate how a student's development in the college setting can affect him or her emotionally, socially, physically, and intellectually. These seven stages were referred to as vectors "because each seems to have direction and magnitude—even though the direction may be expressed more appropriately by a spiral or by steps than a straight line" (Chickering, 1969, p. 8). Within each vector, students must successfully accomplish a series of tasks dealing with their cognitive, emotional, and interpersonal maturity through a process involving differentiation and integration. This process allows individuals to experience meaningful achievement.

Chickering's original model was developed in the 1960s based on his research with students at Goddard College, a small, predominantly White, mostly female, private liberal arts school in northern Vermont (Chickering, 1969). Studying traditional-age college students in their sophomore and senior years, Chickering administered a series of achievement tests, personality inventories, and other instruments to identify the salient factors influencing their development. A revision to this initial theory appeared in the 1990s when Linda Reisser, dean of students at Rockland Community College, partnered with Chickering to update the model to reflect a more contemporary school of thought. In addition to revising and reordering the seven vectors on the basis of research emerging over the previous 25 years, Chickering and Reisser broadened application of the initial model to students of all ages and "tried to use language that is gender free and appropriate for persons of diverse backgrounds" (Chickering & Reisser, 1993, p. 44). These revisions were designed to make the model more inclusive and representative of the developmental processes of all students regardless of age, gender, ethnicity, or cultural background. The vector descriptions that follow represent the terminology and definitions used by Chickering and Reisser in their revised model.

Fundamentally speaking, there is no blueprint for how the seven vectors are to be navigated. The rate of progression from one stage to another varies by person, and regression to an early stage also is possible. However, Chickering and Reisser (1993) have noted the first four vectors are generally experienced by students in their first and second years of college, and the remaining three vectors are experienced throughout the third and fourth years of college. Although students typically address these stages in a linear fashion, the possibility exists for also experiencing multiple stages concurrently because they are not meant to be interpreted as existing in a hierarchy (Chickering & Reisser, 1993). Each of the seven vectors associated with this model are presented below.

Developing Competence

The first vector is called *developing competence*. In this vector, students begin building a vast array of intellectual, psychosocial, and physical skills (Chickering & Reisser, 1993). Many of these skills are in response to their new environments and circumstances encountered on the college campus. As skills develop, so too does students' confidence in their ability to competently perform in these new situations. During this first vector, students develop competence in three important areas. These areas include intellectual competence, interpersonal competence, and physical and manual skills competence. Examples of students in this first vector include those learning how to conduct research and write papers for class or how to balance a diet and maintain a healthy lifestyle while living on campus.

Although competence development is a critical aspect of this vector, it is important to note that the competence built in this initial stage can be stifled by previous negative experiences in one's life (Goldberg, 2016). Keep in mind that, although this is the first stage, students are coming into college not necessarily with a blank slate but rather with a conglomeration of experiences. Prior successes and failures have a significant impact on the rate at which new skills are mastered and competence developed. Nontraditional students who have had rich life experiences before returning to school may present far differently than an 18-year-old first-year student who is living away from home for the first time. Although they may be more skilled at taking care of themselves and making decisions, their time away from school may have them questioning their ability to succeed academically. In the case study of Lina, we see a student who begins to question her academic abilities and vocational goals after struggling in an introductory calculus course. As a counselor, how might you help students like Lina identify their strengths and begin building a sense of competence?

Managing Emotions

The second vector is called *managing emotions*. At this stage students learn the importance of context. Specifically, they begin to understand what types of emotions are acceptable and when these emotional reactions are appropriate to express. Not only do the students understand their emotions in a societal context but they are able to learn how to cope with their emotions in a more productive manner (Chickering & Reisser, 1993). Rather than ignoring or suppressing their feelings, students begin to recognize emotions as warning signs of greater issues. Feelings of guilt, shame, anger, fear, anxiety, and confusion are common experiences for students as they adapt to their new collegiate environment. Left unchecked, these negative emotions can be debilitating and result in several academic, social, and personal challenges for a student. However, positive emotions also present cause for increased self-awareness. Although far less research has focused on the management of positive emotions, the ideal situation is for the student to practice self-regulation in all situations.

From a counseling standpoint, the therapeutic goal in working with students in this second vector is to learn how to appropriately express emotions. This process includes finding safe outlets for emotional expression before negative feelings lead to immobilization and positive feelings lead to transcending boundaries. As students become more aware, and begin exploring their identity, worldview, and interpersonal relationships, they develop the ability to recognize emotions sooner and use strategies designed to help better regulate their self-expression. This prevents emotionally charged outbursts that could negatively affect the individual and potentially impede identity development. Learning to manage emotions is a complex process, with downregulation being a skill that is difficult to master. However, once this skill is mastered, students gain confidence in knowing their behaviors will be consistent. Working with her counselor, Lina can begin defining a way to process the feeling of being invisible, which she experiences when faculty and others on campus do not recognize or speak to her, that does not lead to a downward spiraling of negative emotions.

Moving Through Autonomy Toward Interdependence

The third vector, *moving through autonomy toward interdependence*, represents a key developmental stage for multiple reasons. First, it is the stage at which students begin learning how to function with a high degree of self-sufficiency. They assume greater control of their lives and become responsible for most decision-making. Progression through this stage marks the transition from childhood to adulthood. Unlike in high school, where the learning environment is completely structured, college allows for more autonomy in students. They can select classes fitting their schedules, decide when to study and when to socialize, and choose the campus activities or organizations in which they want to participate.

Second, this is the stage at which students learn that their newfound responsibilities and autonomy do not exist in a vacuum. Successful navigation through this stage requires students to develop the ability to achieve balance between their need and desire for connection with others and their own autonomy (Scholl, 2001). This perspective of transitioning from being students predominantly depending on themselves to accepting and understanding the interrelation between other members of a society is key for their development. Students start realizing their limitations and the acceptability of asking for help when needed. Furthermore, existing relationships may be reconceptualized and new relationships sought on the basis of new criteria. For example, students may now view their parents as a source of support and consult rather than solely as the authority figures in their lives. In Lina's case, her counselor might encourage her to share with her parents her feelings and how she doesn't want to disappoint them or let them know about her struggles. On the basis of the description of her family presented in the case study in Chapter 9, they more than likely would be supportive.

Third, as autonomy builds, so too does a sense of emotional maturity. Students in this stage become surer of themselves and stand by their convictions. They are less likely to be swayed by the opinions of others and to act in a manner that appeases others more than it benefits themselves. Existing relationships that do not support the student's beliefs or goals may be terminated as students become less reliant on external support and more willing to risk losing friends or status to pursue their own interests (Chickering & Reisser, 1993).

Developing Mature Interpersonal Relationships

In the fourth vector, *developing mature interpersonal relationships*, one's capacity for intimacy and one's appreciation of others' differences are two defining components of the stage (Chickering & Reisser, 1993). Students at this level might be more open and accepting of others because they have come to tolerate differences and appreciate how diversity in society can bring about different perspectives. Campus diversity helps students gain exposure to different cultures and breeds a sense of openness and curiosity. As students look to broaden their horizons and learn more about others, they begin refining first impressions, reducing biases, and enjoying the richness a diverse campus provides (Chickering & Reisser, 1993).

This stage is important for future growth. The interactions students have with others provide invaluable learning experiences resulting in a more defined sense of self. By accepting diversity, students expose themselves to individuals they previously may not have associated with or befriended. Mature interpersonal relationships are built on the basis of an openness to new ideas and perspectives. As Reisser (1995) noted, progression through this vector facilitates the complex interplay between autonomy, interdependence, and intimacy. Lina's identification of her academic adviser as someone she can trust and confide in exemplifies the integration of these developmental tasks.

Establishing Identity

The fifth stage, *establishing identity*, is shaped by progress made on each of the previous four vectors. The skills mastered and competencies gained across previous stages provide the pieces needed to begin formulating one's identity. Specifically, students at this stage begin identifying the people, places, and experiences they find safe and satisfying and seek to increase the presence of these elements in their lives. According to Chickering and Reisser (1993), identity development involves seven key components, including, first, comfort with body and appearance; second, comfort with gender and sexual orientation; third, sense of self in a social, historical, and cultural context; fourth, clarification of self-concept through roles and lifestyle; fifth, sense of self in response to feedback from valued others; sixth, self-acceptance and self-esteem; and seventh, personal stability and integration. Collectively, these contextual influences suggest individual development is a unique and personal experience that cannot be generalized. Counselors are advised to understand the worldview of their students as a way of giving depth and understanding to perceived issues and challenges as a matter of culturally competent practice.

Collectively, these seven components contribute to the development of a solid sense of self. Students who achieve such a perspective fully recognize themselves as the authors of their lives and the person responsible for how they relate to the world. Initially, this vector focused primarily on physical characteristics and personal appearance. However, you can see in the revised version of the theory attention is now paid to internal constructs such as identity and self-concept as well. What makes this stage so important to address in a counseling setting is that researchers have shown that the sense of identity students develop is positively correlated with the satisfaction they retain throughout college and negatively correlated with deleterious outcomes such as attrition and academic failure (Lounsbury, Huffstetler, Leong, & Gibson, 2005).

Developing Purpose

Developing purpose is the sixth stage and describes a period in which students begin preparing for their future professional endeavors, solidifying commitments to significant people in their lives, and identifying and committing to their own personal interests (Chickering & Reisser, 1993). Foubert, Nixon, Sisson, and Barnes (2005) noted that the sixth stage does not invariably happen toward the end of the college career of a student. Rather, they purported that most of a student's development of purpose in life occurs during the first year of college with continued revision and refinement occurring throughout the rest of the college experience. However, whether the student is developing purpose in the first or the last year, it is crucial to acknowledge that this stage is characterized by intentional preparation for the student's future.

As students gain conviction toward life goals, they become more intentional in what they do and with whom they associate. Additionally, they become more likely to persist in the face of many obstacles or challenges they might experience. As such, they can begin setting their priorities in terms of vocational plans, personal interests, and interpersonal and family commitments (Chickering & Reisser, 1993). Working with Lina, a counselor could help her see that her performance in a single class need not close off potential career paths. Rather, she can use this experience as an opportunity to further explore what she wants to do for her career and what aspects of that career appeal to her most.

Developing Integrity

The seventh and final vector, *developing integrity*, is where students develop a complete understanding of what is important and of value to them and how their values and identity can be used to facilitate interaction with the world around them (Goldman, 2017). This stage involves a consolidation of previously held ideas and beliefs. This consolidated set of beliefs provides a sense of consistency that guides future behavior and supports the revisiting of those life rules that they accepted on authority in the past and the exploration of how those rules fit with their new emerging identity (Chickering, 1969). Incongruent beliefs are discarded, and those beliefs consistent with the newly clarified set of beliefs are kept and integrated into the identity. In a way, the progression through this vector represents the merging of the ideal and real self. An example of this vector related to Lina involves her emerging cultural and religious identity. As stated in the case study, Lina is areligious, having not really been forced to critically examine her religious beliefs by her parents or others. The negative experiences she is having with others not being accepting of her faith could be mitigated if she were to take time to identify what is truly important to her and the role faith plays in her identity. The more secure she becomes in her identity, the less troubling comments from others will be for her.

Additionally, one can view this stage as students realizing that their own beliefs, morals, and ethics are guiding beacons for how they communicate with others in society. At this point, students may feel capable or confident in their abilities. They believe in themselves, accept themselves for who they are, and feel comfortable interacting with the world around them with a strong sense of assuredness. Furthermore, in this vector, students develop the ability to personalize humanizing values and begin applying them to their own behavior. This state provides students with the opportunity to express themselves in a personally satisfying and socially acceptable manner.

Theory in Review

In both the original (1969) and revised (1993) versions of the model, Chickering attempted to bridge the gap between knowledge and practice by promoting an explanation of holistic student development during the college years. By offering potential explanations for how and why college students progress the way they do, Chickering and Reisser's seven-vectors model helps counselors work with students to understand how they become increasingly complex in their thoughts, feelings, and emotions and to develop a mature and stable sense of self and purpose. When one is using this theory as a framework, it is important to keep in mind that the vectors do not represent a linear progression, and although students generally go through the vectors in the order described, regression and advancement can occur at any time (Evans et al., 2010).

Furthermore, identity develops at each of these vectors as a result of individuals' interactions with their surrounding environments. These interactions are shaped by previous beliefs, ideas, and cultural background. Because the model examines identity development in the context of the immediate environment, recognition of student background and worldview is an important and necessary consideration. As you read through the Identity Status Theory section later in this chapter, look to find ways in which these two theories—the seven vectors of identity development theory and the identity status theory—are similar and ways in which they differ.

Guided Learning Application: The Case of Lina

As you read in Chapter 9 (pg. 186), Lina is a biracial first-generation student who has recently enrolled at a local public university. In this section, we will look at how Lina's current situation would be conceptualized through the lens of Chickering and Reisser's (1993) seven-vector model of student development.

Although she has a wealth of life experiences behind her, going off to college represents a new challenge for Lina. In many ways, she probably falls into the developing competence vector. Despite previous experiences, the first few weeks of college appear to present her with several challenges she is having a hard time addressing. Coursework is more challenging than she remembered or expected, and finding a balance between work and school causes added stress. As a first-generation student, Lina likely has few close role models she can turn to for advice and guidance as she navigates the newness of college. She seems to want to ask for help but at the same time is turned off by the prospect of seeking help, instead fading into the crowd on campus. We also see in the case study that she is disheartened by the fact that faculty seem to pass by on campus without interacting with her, adding to her feelings of invisibility.

Because college represents a new challenge for Lina, one that she has no previous experience to pull from in understanding how she should cope, she struggles. Her struggles begin leading to emotional (feelings of sadness and hopelessness) and physical (poor sleep and eating habits) symptoms. For Lina to succeed, she will need to develop skills allowing her to succeed in the college environment. This requires activity and occurs over time. As skills develop and she is more acclimated to the expectations and rules of college, she will be able to formulate a new way of thinking and behaving that works for her. This new approach should allow her to address current and future stressors in a productive manner. The academic adviser in this case study would be wise to help Lina see her existing skills. Then, he can help her see how these existing strengths can be mobilized and effectively put to use in the new environment with novel challenges. If all goes well, Lina will begin developing a greater comfort with her situation and have a plan in place to successfully move forward.

Identity Status Theory

Identity status theory was developed in the 1960s by Canadian developmental psychologist James Marcia. The theory builds off the work of Erik Erikson (1950, 1963) and his popular theory of psychosocial development in which individuals must overcome or successfully resolve a series of normative conflicts sequentially ordered across eight stages. Unlike Erikson, who viewed psychosocial development across the life span, Marcia focused primarily on development occurring during the adolescent years. Whereas both theorists agree that the formation of an ego identity is a major event in the development of personality, they differ in their beliefs regarding how identity emerges during these critical formative years.

In Erikson's theory, the main task of adolescence is to solve the developmental crisis of identity versus identity confusion. As individuals begin transitioning from childhood to adulthood, they start to explore their independence and discover who they are as individuals. Those who successfully establish a stable sense of self and positive relationships with peers report better emotional and psychological well-being (Ragelienė, 2016). They also are more likely to remain true to their values and beliefs regardless of situations they find themselves in. Individuals who struggle to find their identity are more likely to conform to the beliefs of others and be confused about their future and what they should be doing. Feelings of uncertainty often lead to struggles finding themselves as adults.

Marcia adopted a different perspective. Whereas Erikson focused attention on the outcome of crises, Marica was more interested in the degree to which adolescents explored and committed to an identity across multiple life domains. For him, adolescence consisted of neither identity achievement nor identity confusion. Instead, the achievement of a strong sense of adolescent identity consists of two distinct components: exploration and commitment. *Exploration* (originally referred to as a *crisis*) represents a time when a situation or event challenges old values and beliefs and new alternatives are explored (Marcia, 1966). To illustrate, let's consider the case of Elizabeth. Elizabeth is a first-year student who arrives at college fully intending to major in premedicine and become a doctor like her father. However, during her first semester she struggles with several of her math and science courses. She finds the material difficult to comprehend and not very exciting. Conversely, she is fascinated by her communications courses. She relates to the material and can see herself with a fulfilling career in this field one day. Her experience causes her to reexamine her career goals and explore possible career alternatives. Elizabeth is unsure of what to do. For as long as she can remember she has talked of becoming a doctor. Now, confronted with her academic struggles and lack of passion for certain courses, Elizabeth is being forced to reexamine her beliefs.

Exploration is an important component of adolescence, especially for college students. However, exploration alone will not result in a fully formed identity. Equally important is the *commitment* to a role or value that emerges from experiencing a developmental crisis and the resulting exploration phase. In the case of Elizabeth, her experience leads her to believe a career in medicine might not be right for her, and she becomes more committed to exploring her options in the communications field, an area about which she has discovered she is passionate.

During adolescence, Marcia conceptualized individuals as progressing through a series of points along a continuum of identity development, calling these points identity statuses. According to Marcia (1964), the term *identity status* refers to the classification of an individual on the basis of the degree of exploration and commitment to the values, beliefs, and goals contributing to identity that person has made. In his model, Marcia introduces four distinct identity statuses: identity diffusion, identity foreclosure, moratorium, and identity achievement, depending on how high or how low the individual is in terms of exploration and commitment (see Figure 11.1). Collectively, identity statuses represent observable phenomena associated with the underlying ego growth processes described by Erikson (Kroger, Martinussen, & Marcia, 2010). Initially, these statuses were viewed as progressive extensions of one another; however, the contemporary understanding is that they are distinct categorical phases defined by a specific configuration of exploration and commitment. A description of each status follows.

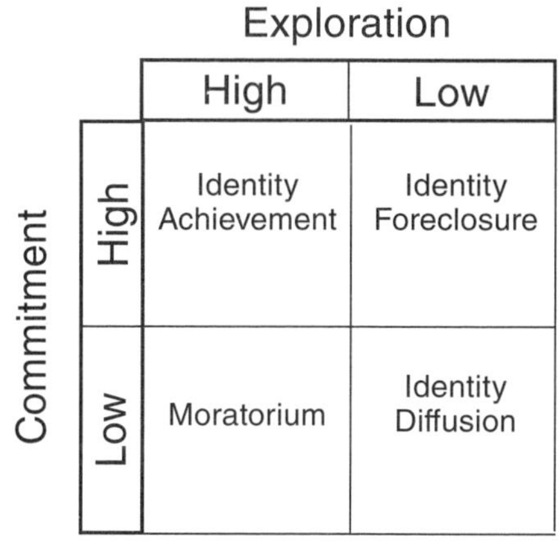

FIGURE 11.1
Marcia's (1980) Identity Status Model

Identity Diffusion

The first status, identity diffusion, is characterized by individuals having neither explored nor committed to an identity. Adolescents at this status often have few, if any, career goals or life aspirations. They are unsure of what they want to be and sometimes even of what some of the options available to them are. Instead, they tend to be more reactive and passively go through life addressing issues as they arise without any planning or foresight. This lack of drive and direction often results from the adolescent not having had to make many choices in the past. With little to no experience making their own choices, it is not surprising that individuals at this status have difficulty envisioning what they want to do or who they want to be. Individuals at this level are extremely impressionable and quick to follow the lead of others because they have yet to establish their own identity. Identity diffusion is the least complex and most immature of all the statuses (Côté & Levine, 2002) and includes low levels of both exploration and commitment.

To help illustrate this concept, let's look at an example. Our case study of Lina clearly fits in the identity diffusion status. For example, faith is a part of her identity that largely has gone unexplored. Her parents, practicing Muslims, did not pressure her to follow a doctrine, so she may not have taken the time to explore how she feels about various faiths. Because she was not forced to make a choice earlier in life, the process of gathering data needed to make an informed decision might not have happened. Now, confronted with negative comments and microaggressions by other students on campus, Lina might be swayed from ever possibly exploring her family's religious background and her thoughts about it, believing it the safe approach given how others are responding to her. Lacking a solid understanding of who she is and what she believes, Lina may be highly impressionable, thus making decisions regarding her identity to satisfy others more than herself.

Identity Foreclosure

The second status in Marcia's model is called identity foreclosure. At this status, individuals begin committing to relevant roles, causes, and belief systems in their life. This commitment is made without exploring alternatives. They think they know who they are even though they have not yet explored all their options. In many cases, these early commitments are made to values and belief systems held by parents and are accepted wholly without question (Marcia, 2010). Absent any identity crisis causing them to begin critically examining their values and beliefs, individuals in the foreclosure status experience no pressure to explore other options. What they have committed to seems to work for them and is not causing any identity distress. Their commitment to a belief system comes without questioning. In a sense, the identity assumed is fictitious, like wearing a mask.

An example of someone at this stage is the student who recently has turned 18 and is preparing to vote for the first time. Having not been eligible to participate in past elections, the student may not be familiar with the candidates, their platforms, or the ideological base of the parties they represent. In many cases, the student's opinions and commitment to a candidate often end up reflecting his or her parents' beliefs or what appears to be the predominant sentiment in social groups and across campus. The commitment is to something familiar and does not require going out on one's own. Often, following popular thought means sacrificing one's values and belief system. In this case, the student votes a certain way because his or her parents voted that way. This stage is characterized by a high degree of commitment and a lower degree of exploration.

Moratorium

Individuals in the moratorium stage are actively exploring various ideas and beliefs but have yet to make a commitment to any of them. This state of active exploration often is precipitated by the experience of an existential crisis. This crisis calls on the adolescent to make a choice and firmly commit to a value or belief, so the adolescent searches for an identity to adopt. To ensure they make informed choices, adolescents in this stage may experiment with a variety of lifestyles and belief systems as they search for their identity. Some of the choices they make may conflict with the values and beliefs of their parents or other authority figures. This exploration is healthy if it is done in a safe manner. Because this is the most common identity status for late adolescents and young adults, college counselors should recognize the increased need for support and guidance that students may experience during this formative life stage.

An example of the moratorium status would be a student deciding whether to pledge a fraternity on campus. Does this student value the friendship, comradery, and networking opportunities pledging may bring? Or is he apprehensive about joining a culture that is commonly perceived across campus as being characterized by excessive alcohol consumption? These competing values make it difficult to commit, and as a result, students may choose to experiment with different lifestyles to see what fits or what is most socially acceptable. For students exploring various commitments and looking to make a lasting decision, the absence of a strong commitment can be a positive or a negative experience. Positively speaking, a lack of commitment could lead to feelings of openness, wherein curiosity and experimentation are encouraged (Luyckx, Soenens, & Goossens, 2006). Negatively, indecisiveness has been associated with feelings of anxiety and depression (Schwartz, Zamboanga, Weisskirch, & Rodriguez, 2009). This stage is characterized by a high degree of exploration and a low degree of commitment.

Identity Achievement

Individuals who reach the identity achievement status have a well-developed sense of self and are fully committed to the values, beliefs, and life goals they have selected. Marcia referred to this status as the successful completion of the moratorium status (Marcia, 1966). At the identity achievement status, individuals choose their identities through an active selection process by which all available options have been carefully explored and considered. Through exploration, students can make informed commitments. The information they receive resonates with how they perceive themselves and is compelling enough to motivate action. This status is characterized by a high degree of both exploration and commitment. At an identity achievement status, individuals are confident in the values and goals they have chosen to live by and have a clear purpose directing them in life.

Theory in Review

As mentioned earlier in this chapter, the conceptualization of identity statuses has changed through the years. Our current understanding of these statuses is that they exist in a fluid state along a continuum. This contemporary perspective is based on a set of fundamental premises regarding identity formation. First, there is no uniformity in how individuals experience each of the identity statuses. There is no discussion of the degree to which each is experienced. The amount of exploration needed to make a secure commitment consistent with the identity achievement status varies across individuals. Understanding where individuals are in the model is based on their self-reported responses to a semistructured interview protocol.

Second, it is important for college counselors to understand that completion of one status is not a prerequisite for beginning another. Although the statuses do fit loosely in a sequential order based on the amount of exploration and commitment made, they are independent of one another. Unlike other developmental stage models, successful completion of a stage or developmentally appropriate task is not required. Individuals can move from one stage to another without necessarily achieving closure. Additionally, it is not required that an individual progress through all four statuses. Some individuals may be able to achieve a secure identity having experienced only a few of the statuses.

Third, an individual's status is not universal. Individuals can be at different statuses related to different aspects of their identity. For example, a student may have achieved a secure and stable career identity where she knows exactly what she wants to do and has researched her chosen field and mapped out a specific strategy for making her career goals a reality. However, this same student may be less decisive with respect to her sexual orientation. Since beginning college, she has begun questioning her beliefs and values and is not sure who she is nor to whom she is attracted. As a result, she begins experimenting and dating different people to figure it all out. When it comes to her career, this student would most likely be in the identity achievement status, but in terms of understanding her sexual orientation, she would probably be in the moratorium status.

Fourth, movement through the statuses is a bidirectional process. It is possible for a student to regress to a less mature status as new experiences and developmental crises may arise. A student may experience a traumatic event such as a relationship ending or a failing grade in a class that initiates a reevaluation of his or her current understanding of the world and associated value system.

Fifth, researchers have noted cultural limitations of the identity status model, arguing for an integration of racial identity development theory when applied to students from diverse cultural backgrounds (Sneed, Schwartz, & Cross, 2006). Assuming a narrative approach when working with students will allow the counselor to help students define their identity in relation to their context and surrounding environment.

Guided Learning Application: The Case of Lina

Now we will examine Lina and her situation in the context of Marcia's (1966) identity status model. As you recall, Lina's case included a wealth of information regarding her transition to college. Using Marcia's identity status model as the theoretical lens for conceptualizing this case, you could make the claim that she is in the moratorium status. As described earlier in this chapter, the moratorium status is a time when one is engaged in an acute crisis and exploring and actively searching for values to call one's own. Lina reports a difficult start to her college career both academically and socially. She thought she had a good idea as to what she wanted to major in, but her struggles with her calculus course have her doubting her choices and her ability to be successful academically. Additionally, she feels she may be excluded from social activities because her new roommate calls her a "Muslim from the Middle East" when talking with others even though Lina was born and raised in California. Although she has always identified more with American culture, these characterizations by others have her confused about how she is being perceived by others.

According to Kroger and Marcia (2011), individuals in the moratorium status often struggle in defining themselves in new contexts where previous beliefs and understandings are called into question by acute crises. To help alleviate some of the internal conflict they feel, students may convert internal struggles into external struggles. In Lina's case, she decides she can no longer keep her feelings bottled up as she is starting to feel depressed and overwhelmed by the college experience. She turns to her academic adviser whom she trusts and decides to vocalize what she is feeling and seek help.

Conclusion

The psychosocial developmental models, especially those specific to college students described in this chapter, have proven useful in understanding how individuals develop a mature identity. As a result, these theories are used frequently by college counselors and student affairs personnel in situations requiring students to resolve conflict with others or develop a sense of autonomy and independence. Despite volumes of research on each, there are some poignant critiques that should be noted when choosing to use such an approach. First, by their very nature, these theories are reductionist in nature. They attempt to consolidate the human experience into tightly packed and well-organized stages or statuses. However, individuals are unique and complex. Their developmental experiences are unique and may not fit well with some of the prescribed progression patterns of these models.

Second, these theories highlight the importance of context and worldview when understanding students. Several social, political, economic, cultural, ethnic, and gender-related factors need to be considered. These factors often are uniquely experienced by the individual, if at all. Although initially thought to assist in framing discussions around cultural identity, emerging research appears to indicate that psychosocial developmental models like Chickering and Reisser's may not adequately capture the development process of culturally diverse students. For example, the literature includes studies in which women (Foubert et al., 2005), students of color (Liversage, Naudé, & Botha, 2017), and sexual minority students (Zubernis, Snyder, & McCoy, 2011) have been found to differ in their progression through the seven vectors. As college campuses become increasingly diverse, theories or models based on a uniform approach to explaining student development may not work well in a pluralistic society.

Final Case Studies

Case 1

Fred is a 19-year-old student who recently arrived on campus for his freshman year. He is attending a school nearly 3,000 miles from his hometown, and this is his first time living away from home. Fred has been enjoying the college lifestyle and making several new friends. However, he seems to be having trouble with his academics. Specifically, Fred is finding it hard to make all his classes and budget his time for studying. His intentions are good, but he says he becomes easily distracted by other activities. For example, Fred states he has missed classes because he woke up too late, the weather was too nice outside, friends wanted to hang out, and he already knows the material that would be covered. At midsemester, Fred was informed that he was not passing his biology course. He states he knows it is because he is missing class so much, but he is unsure what to do. He mentions how much easier it was in high school where all the decisions were made for him. As he states, "All you need to do is show up, and they tell you where to go and when to be in a certain class." He adds, "Life would be much easier without me having options and decisions to make."

Case 1 Exploration Questions

1. As the counselor working with Fred, how would you go about understanding his situation on the basis of Chickering's seven vectors of identity development model?
2. What stage do you see him at?
3. What ideas might you have for helping Fred make better decisions when it comes to his academics?

Case 2

Esmerelda is a first-generation college student from a Hispanic family. She grew up in a low-income environment and watched her parents struggle financially to support her and her siblings. As a result, she dedicated herself to her schoolwork throughout high school. She was determined to get a job that would provide for her, so she would not have to experience the hardships her parents faced. For as long as she could remember, she wanted to be a doctor. She told friends and family she wanted to be a doctor because they were successful and earned a high salary. Her parents encouraged her and told Esmerelda that if she worked hard, she would one day become a doctor. When Esmerelda began college, she was set on becoming a doctor. She told her adviser that was what she wanted to do, so a schedule was created for her that included several science- and math-based courses. Esmerelda struggled in these courses. She tried her best to keep up, but it felt like her textbooks were written in a foreign language. She was able to finish the semester with a 1.9 grade point average, which left her on academic probation. Her adviser met with her and suggested she investigate a different major given her difficulty in the science and math classes, but Esmerelda would not hear of it. She said she had to become a doctor and there was no other option. "Becoming a doctor is all I have ever wanted," she said. "I want to be able to live comfortably and not worry about money or stuff like that."

Case 2 Exploration Questions

1. On the basis of what you have learned in this chapter, how would you describe Esmerelda's desire to become a doctor?
2. On the basis of Marcia's identity status model, what stage of development does Esmerelda appear to be in?
3. How would you assist Esmerelda in moving beyond this stage of development?

References

Chickering, A. W. (1969). *Education and identity*. San Francisco, CA: Jossey-Bass.

Chickering, A. W., & Reisser, L. (1993). *Education and identity* (2nd ed.). San Francisco, CA: Jossey-Bass.

Côté, J. E., & Levine, C. G. (2002). *Identity formation, agency, and culture: A social psychological synthesis*. Mahwah, NJ: Erlbaum.

Erikson, E. H. (1950). *Childhood and society*. New York, NY: Norton.

Erikson, E. H. (1963). *Childhood and society* (2nd ed.). New York, NY: Norton.

Evans, N. J., Forney, D. S., Guido, F. M., Patton, L. D., & Renn, K. A. (2010). *Student development in college: Theory, research, and practice* (2nd ed.). San Francisco, CA: Jossey-Bass.

Foubert, J. D., Nixon, M. L., Sisson, V. S., & Barnes, A. C. (2005). A longitudinal study of Chickering and Reisser's vectors: Exploring gender differences and implications for refining the theory. *Journal of College Student Development, 46,* 461–471. doi:10.1353/csd.2005.0047

Goldberg, D. B. (2016). Impact of childhood sexual abuse on college student development: A seven-vectors perspective. *Journal of College Counseling, 19,* 168–179. doi:10.1002/jocc.12039

Goldman, Z. W. (2017). Explaining doctoral students' relational maintenance with their advisor: A psychosocial development perspective. *Communication Education, 66,* 70–89.
Kim, E. (2012). An alternative theoretical model: Examining psychosocial identity development of international students in the United States. *College Student Journal, 46,* 99–113.
Kroger, J., & Marcia, J. E. (2011). The identity statuses: Origins, meanings, and interpretations. In S. J. Schwartz, K. Luyckx, & V. L. Vignoles (Eds.), *Handbook of identity theory and research* (pp. 31–53). New York, NY: Springer.
Kroger, J., Martinussen, M., & Marcia, J. E. (2010). Identity status change during adolescence and young adulthood: A meta-analysis. *Journal of Adolescence, 33,* 683–698. doi:10.1016/j.adolescence.2009.11.002
Liversage, L., Naudé, L., & Botha, A. (2017). Vectors of identity development during the first year: Black first-generation students' reflections. *Teaching in Higher Education, 23,* 63–83. doi:10.1080/13562517.1359159
Long, D. (2012). Theories and models of student development. In L. J. Hinchliffe & M. A. Wong (Eds.), *Environments for student growth and development: Librarians and student affairs in collaboration* (pp. 41–55). Chicago, IL: Association of College and Research Libraries.
Lounsbury, J. W., Huffstetler, B. C., Leong, F. T., & Gibson, L. W. (2005). Sense of identity and collegiate academic achievement. *Journal of College Student Development, 46,* 501–514. doi:10.1353/csd.2005.0051
Luyckx, K., Soenens, B., & Goossens, L. (2006). The personality-identity interplay in emerging adult women: Convergent findings from complementary analyses. *European Journal of Personality, 20,* 195–215. doi:10.1002/per.579
Marcia, J. E. (1964). *Determination and construct validity of ego identity status* (Unpublished doctoral dissertation). State University of New York, Buffalo.
Marcia, J. E. (1966). Development and validation of ego identity status. *Journal of Personality and Social Psychology, 3,* 551–558. doi:10.1037/h0023281
Marcia, J. E. (1980). Identity in adolescence. In J. Adelson (Ed.), *Handbook of adolescent psychology* (pp. 159–187). New York, NY: Wiley.
Marcia, J. E. (2010). Life transitions and stress in the context of psychosocial development. In T. W. Miller (Ed.), *Handbook of stressful transitions across the lifespan* (pp. 19–34). New York, NY: Springer.
Ragelienė, T. (2016). Links of adolescents' identity development and relationship with peers: A systematic literature review. *Journal of the Canadian Academy of Child and Adolescent Psychiatry, 25,* 97–105.
Reisser, L. (1995). Revisiting the seven vectors. *Journal of College Student Development, 36,* 505–511.
Scholl, M. B. (2001). Recommendations for a conceptual model of counseling supervision. *The Clinical Supervisor, 20,* 177–189. doi:10.1300/j001v20n02_13
Schwartz, S. J., Zamboanga, B. L., Weisskirch, R. S., & Rodriguez, L. (2009). The relationships of personal and ethnic identity exploration to indices of adaptive and maladaptive psychosocial functioning. *International Journal of Behavioral Development, 33,* 131–144. doi:10.1177/0165025408098018
Sneed, J. R., Schwartz, S. J., & Cross, W. E. (2006). A multicultural critique of identity status theory and research: A call for integration. *Identity: An International Journal of Theory and Research, 6,* 61–84. doi:10.1207/s1532706xid0601_5
Zubernis, L., Snyder, M., & McCoy, V. A. (2011). Counseling lesbian and gay college students through the lens of Cass's and Chickering's developmental models. *Journal of LGBT Issues in Counseling, 5,* 122–150. doi:10.1080/15538605.2011.578506

Chapter 12

Cognitive and Moral Theories of Student Development

Joshua C. Watson, Laura M. Gonzalez, and Rachel Shakin

We should attend to students' needs for challenges, to stretch their cognitive powers, and for supports, to reduce the threat of failure and the insecurity of not knowing something with certainty.

—Robert J. Kloss (1994)

■ ■ ■

Reflection Exercise

Think back to when you began college. I am sure a range of thoughts and emotions are stirred. Beginning life at college naturally generates feelings of excitement and anxiety for a host of reasons, including the physical move, increased academic responsibilities, and the forming of new friendships and social relationships. Additionally, if you were a traditional student, you likely were expected to be more independent, adventurous, and responsible than you might have been in high school. The new environment and situational demands may have challenged your view of the world and caused you to reconsider some personal beliefs. This process is completely normal and to be expected. To assist you in working with college students, think back to your time as a student and what the experience may have been like for you:

1. What were your beliefs about the world before you entered college?
2. Who were the sources of truth you turned to for information?
3. What were the situations in college that most challenged your ways of thinking?
4. How did your perspective change during your time in college?

With your responses to these questions in mind, we will begin exploring the cognitive and moral theories of student development. As we look at each theory, think about how your experiences relate to the developmental stages described, and how this knowledge might assist you in better understanding your clients from their point of view.

■ ■ ■

The cognitive and moral theories of student development derive from Piagetian psychology (Piaget, 1936) and provide a useful lens through which college counselors and student affairs personnel can examine how students interpret, rationalize, and make meaning out of their lived experiences. At the core of these theories is the premise that cognitive development, encompassing the ability to think and reason, is a progressive process beginning in childhood, continuing through adolescence, and culminating in adulthood. As individuals mature, they begin developing more complex thought processes providing them with a greater understanding of the world around them. These cognitive processes include such formal logical operations as the ability to think abstractly, reason from known principles, understand multiple points of view, and consider the process of thinking. Using these advanced processes, individuals acquire and consolidate knowledge, allowing them to function in an ever-changing world.

According to Piaget (1952, 1958), cognitive development centers around two key concepts: adaptation and equilibrium. *Adaptation* refers to the ability of individuals to evolve and meet the situational demands of a changing world. The process of adaptation occurs through both assimilation and accommodation. In *assimilation*, individuals use existing schemata to help process and understand new objects or situations. For example, a college student struggling with academic work may revert to prior study habits proven effective in previous semesters to help prepare for an upcoming examination. In contrast, *accommodation* occurs when an object or situation does not fit an existing schema, and the individual is forced to change said schema to fit the new object or situation. An example of accommodation would be that a student realizes that prior approaches to stress management no longer work with the increased stress associated with having adult responsibilities. In this case, the student must amend existing schemata and develop new coping strategies that work with the new stressors faced.

The process of adaptation, through assimilation and accommodation, continues as the individual strives for a state of equilibrium. In the *equilibrium* state, a balance between self and world emerges. It is at this point that one's adaptive functioning capabilities are effectively meeting situational demands. It is this quest for equilibrium that motivates the learning process and helps individuals persevere in the face of challenge and adversity.

Each of the theories discussed in this chapter views cognitive growth as a sequential process, with development occurring when cognitive structures are adapted to accommodate new information and existing perceptions of the world become altered. Rather than focusing on what students think, the authors of these cognitive and moral theories of development focus on the way students think (Evans, Forney, Guido, Patton, & Renn, 2010). Central to this class of theories is the particular emphasis placed on values such as teaching, learning, reflection, change, and empathy (Long, 2012). Additionally, attention is paid to the intersectionality of heredity and environment because both have been shown to contribute equally to intellectual development and offer an explanation as to why students cognitively develop as they do. In the following pages, we introduce you to three classic theories of cognitive and moral development: Perry's scheme of intellectual and ethical development; Belenky, Clinchy, Goldberger, and Tarule's women's ways of knowing; and Kohlberg's theory of moral development. In addition to describing the basic tenets of each theory, we demonstrate their usefulness for college counselors and student affairs professionals and use each to conceptualize our case study of Lina (see pages 186–187).

Perry's Scheme of Intellectual and Ethical Development

In 1968, William Perry introduced the first theory examining the intellectual development of college students to be used extensively in student affairs practice (Evans et al., 2010).

Perry's revisionist theory introduces readers to a structural model aimed at assisting college personnel in better understanding how college students "come to know the theories and beliefs they hold about knowing, and the manner in which such epistemological premises are a part of and an influence on the cognitive processes of thinking and reasoning" (Hofer & Pintrich, 1997, p. 88). This structural model, published in Perry's classic 1970 text *Forms of Intellectual and Ethical Development in the College Years: A Scheme*, posits a sequence of developmental stages that serves as a general framework into which students can fit various theories, philosophies, and value sets.

Based on data collected from the White males in his courses at Harvard University using observation, open-ended interviews, and measurement, Perry's model provides an interpretative structure to the experiences and transformations students recalled having during their college years. The model identifies nine distinct positions students experience concerning their intellectual and moral development. These positions, clustered into four stages, reference the perspective students take in viewing the world around them. At each position, what students learn is less important than how they learn. For Perry, the qualitative changes students make in terms of how they view the world, make sense of their experiences, and adapt their style of learning were vital. Essentially, each stage offers a unique way of describing how students view themselves in relation to what they believe knowledge to be (Kloss, 1994). The four stages in Perry's model include dualism, multiplicity, relativism, and commitment. A description of each, along with illustrative examples, follows.

Dualism

In this first stage, individuals have a naive view of the world and what is the truth. They operate from a bifurcated perspective in which there is either fact or fiction with no middle ground. Students new to college often operate from a scheme in which clearly defined roles exist. In this scheme, students view instructors as the definitive sources of truth and knowledge. Conversely, students are viewed as passive recipients of knowledge, absorbing whatever facts their instructors might be willing to share. The learning process consists, then, of attending class lectures, taking copious notes, memorizing key terms and concepts, and being able to regurgitate information on assignments and examinations. In the dualism stage, students are unable to consider the possibility that the information shared by their instructors may be biased or flawed. In describing this stage, Perry summed up new students' view of knowledge with the statement "When I came here I didn't think any question could have more than one answer" (Perry, 1970, p. 64).

Within the dualism stage, there are two positions. The first is *basic dualism* (Position 1). In this position, students view the world in terms of polar extremes of good/right/us and bad/wrong/them. They operate under the assumption that all problems are solvable, and their primary goal becomes finding the correct solution to the given problem. Learning entails figuring out the correct solutions to life's problems. Knowledge, then, becomes the accumulation of solutions a student can identify, remember, and recall. Students must listen to authorities (e.g., instructors), whose primary function is to teach them to become knowledgeable.

The second position is *full dualism* (Position 2). In this position, students begin recognizing that authorities disagree at times. These disagreements can occur between individuals, academic disciplines, and general schools of thought. Aware that disagreements can occur, students shift their learning strategies and begin decoding "facts" to determine which are correct and which are incorrect. In other words, students begin critically examining what they are taught, retaining information they deem reliable and useful and discarding information that is inconsistent or flawed. For example, during an instructor's lecture, facts and opinions may be shared. The student now consciously attends to these statements assessing what is fact and what is conjecture. The facts are retained and used to build knowledge. Opinions are compared with personal perspectives and beliefs and kept if consistent. At this phase, students may become frustrated when they find that previous learning strategies are not effective in their current classes or that the questions posed by their instructors are difficult to answer and often without a clear-cut answer. Unfamiliar with this ambiguity, students may struggle academically, which can lead to other psychosocial issues.

Multiplicity

Building on the learning that occurs in the first stage, students in the multiplicity stage begin perceiving knowledge as merely one person's opinion. From this perspective, the authority of external sources diminishes. Students no longer view instructors as the absolute word that must be accepted unconditionally. Instead, an attitude of acceptance, wherein diversity of opinion exists, emerges. In situations in which the definitive solution has yet to emerge, students acknowledge there might exist several different solutions, and it is up to them to select the solution they wish to believe. This phase includes students projecting their solutions as viable options. Fundamentally, students believe all opinions are equal, as they represent others' perspectives; therefore, they must trust themselves and make their own choices as to what is correct and what they believe.

The multiplicity stage includes two positions: *early multiplicity* and *late multiplicity.* In early multiplicity (Position 3), students acknowledge uncertainty in the world. For the first time, the realization sets in that some answers remain a mystery. When this happens, the student begins dividing known problems in the world into two categories: those with actual solutions and those whose solutions remain undiscovered. This uncertainty, however, is temporary. Students realize that new knowledge is continually being discovered, and solutions missing today may be known tomorrow. From this perspective, uncertainty is legitimized as the authority still looking to find the correct answer. At this level, students may wonder how their instructors evaluate their work at all when it is their opinion and not fact used to determine right and wrong.

In late multiplicity (Position 4), students begin coming to terms with the fact that most problems lack accurate identified solutions. They reason that either problems are unsolvable or, with a diversity of opinion, everyone has their own right way of doing something. Rampant legitimate uncertainty begins to overrule the theoretical perspective found in earlier positions. In an academic setting, students in the late multiplicity position may develop a "Do your own thing" mentality and seek to assert themselves and their solutions as correct. Feedback from instructors is then criticized as being unfair, biased, and off base. Successful development through this position occurs when students realize that although there may not be an identified solution to a problem, and their hypothesized solution may be correct, they are responsible for providing a logical rationale for how they came to accept their solution as fact.

Relativism

According to Perry (1970), the shift from multiplicity to relativism represents the most critical transition in his model. It is at this stage that students become accustomed to the notion that multiple truths exist, and many problems remain unsolved. By acknowledging there are many truths, students' approaches to learning evolve. Rather than accumulating truths, students look to accumulate data and evidence supporting these various truths. A diversity of belief, opinions, and values come from numerous sources, each with their logic, supporters, and sense of authority. Students who reach this stage, a feat few accomplish during their college years, understand knowledge as being contextual. The dual perspective found in earlier positions now exists only as a unique case scenario. What one knows to be true depends on several factors, including one's values, beliefs, assumptions, life experiences, and sources of inquiry used. Essentially, the view students have of the world they occupy becomes relativistic and context based, with few true black-or-white answers.

Relativism comprises two positions: *contextual relativism* and *precommitment*. In contextual relativism (Position 5), all proposed solutions to a problem are likely viable if applied in the correct context. For example, a solution to stay in one's room and read the assigned chapters for a class is a viable solution provided there is not a party going on in the hall outside the student's room. The merit of each solution does not reside in a vacuum. Instead, it fluctuates depending on time and place. Some solutions are better than others in given contexts. Students in this position are tasked with evaluating solutions and choosing the best option given the current circumstances.

In the precommitment position (Position 6), students begin to realize they are at a point in their lives at which they must begin making choices and commitments. Although college is hailed as a time of self-exploration and intellectual growth, students eventually will need to start developing the ability to apply the knowledge they are learning in school. At the precommitment position, students become active makers of meaning. According to Johnson (1981), any act of knowing, be it by thinking, talking, reading, or writing, requires individuals to take a point of view and acknowledge it as their own. By this point, intellectual development transforms into ethical development. Students know various truths and have had the opportunity to evaluate the merits of each. They must now assume one as their own and be able to defend their position going forward reliably. Challenges arise when students recognize others not at the same phase. They may find classes lacking in challenge or others clueless.

Commitment

The final stage is one in which the process of acquiring, evaluating, and synthesizing knowledge used in the academic setting is repurposed for use in everyday life. The way in which students went about learning in school is the way in which they now approach learning about their world and where they fit into it. This stage includes three positions, the first of which is *commitment* (Position 7). In the commitment position, students commit to a solution. When Perry talked about commitment, he was talking about more than just making a choice. For him, commitment occurs when individuals make choices in situations in which multiple viable options are available. The choices cause these individuals to experience doubt and uneasiness and ultimately require them to enter a period of deep thought and introspection. Only then can they commit to a solution consistent with who they are as persons in an ever-changing world.

The second of the three positions in this stage is the *challenges to commitment* position (Position 8). At this point, individuals have made a commitment and are beginning to realize the responsibility that comes with commitment. They may face challenges to their beliefs or encounter situations in which their point of view is not the favorite school of thought. In these situations, they must decide to adhere to their beliefs and remain true to themselves or compromise their values and succumb to popular thought. Commitment is a pledge to do something in the future. Students who make commitments allow themselves to be held accountable to others for their actions. Here, students are at a point when they are ready to make decisions and commitments in the real world (Evans et al., 2010).

The final position is *postcommitment* (Position 9). In this position, the personal identity students commit to is affirmed. Secure in their identity, they fully accept all the responsibilities associated with being committed. Furthermore, students begin understanding commitment as a continual, lifelong process. Making a choice is more than a static event. The real challenge is what follows when students must live with their commitment and fully integrate it into their complete identity. Students accept agency and relish the opportunity to be responsible for their choices be they related to their choice of career, political beliefs, values, or personal relationships. In doing so, they demonstrate the ability to merge the objective and rational learning approaches used in college with the empathic and experimental learning approaches used in other aspects of their lives.

Stages and Positions in Perry's Scheme of Intellectual and Ethical Development

In summary, the stages and positions in Perry's scheme of intellectual and ethical development are as follows:

Dualism
- Basic dualism (Position 1)
- Full dualism (Position 2)

Multiplicity
- Early multiplicity (Position 3)
- Late multiplicity (Position 4)

Relativism
- Contextual relativisim (Position 5)
- Precommitment (Position 6)

Commitment
- Commitment (Position 7)
- Challenges to commitment (Position 8)
- Postcommitment (Position 9)

General Applications of the Model

Perry's model provides a guide for understanding the transformation students make in how they learn and acquire knowledge. Early on (Positions 1–3), students perceive the world in purely absolutist terms. They cannot comprehend a world in which multiple truths exist. As they develop, and their learning strategies become more complex (Positions 4–6), students begin to acknowledge and embrace diversity and uncertainty in life. They see that there are many sides to an issue and many solutions to a problem.

Additionally, there may be problems to which no solution appears to exist. These situations emerge as opportunities for students to develop their own ideas and view of the world, becoming an authority themselves. Finally, with a mature way of learning (Positions 7–9), students perceive themselves as well-informed and sufficiently equipped to commit to forging their own identities through personal commitment in a relativistic world. According to Perry (1970), most traditional-age students enter college in Positions 3, 4, or 5 and eventually graduate in Positions 6, 7, or 8. He believed Position 9 to be elusive for most college students and a status not obtained until later in life. However, with the growing number of nontraditional students, community college transfers, and adult learners on college campuses, the likelihood that college counselors and student affairs professionals encounter students at this mature position is greater than it has been in the past. These individuals, for the most part, have families, careers, and responsibilities giving them experiences to better understand who they are and what their roles in life are. For all students, understanding their meaning-making processes and how they come to learn about themselves provides excellent insight into the problems and issues they might bring to a counseling session and guides the choice of intervention or treatment approach one might choose to use in the therapeutic relationship.

Applying Perry's Model to the Case of Lina

Using Perry's model as a lens, Lina would most likely be viewed as occupying a lower position on the basis of the information shared in her case study (refer to pages 186–187). Specifically, Lina exhibits a style of thinking and acting consistent with the full dualism position. Coming from a military family, she likely is familiar with discipline and organization. At college, she is now experiencing dissonance as her experiences are not matching her expectations. These mismatches include coursework being more challenging, faculty being less cordial, and her social group being less supportive. The lack of any evident truth has her doubting her abilities to be successful and whether she should even be in school. A counselor working with Lina should take time to help her see that there are many viable options for her in college. Her struggles in math do not mean she is bound to be a failure. Instead, they may provide the opportunity for her to explore other career options and see what a better fit for her might be. As she acclimates to the college environment and begins understanding how everything works, she may become more comfortable with the idea that there are multiple authorities—sometimes they will disagree, and that is not altogether bad.

Belenky, Clinchy, Goldberger, and Tarule's Women's Ways of Knowing

The study of cognitive development, as has been outlined here, was historically shaped by White male researchers and predominantly White male participants. Although it may seem obvious now that this would provide a partial or incomplete perspective on the issue at hand, it was broadly accepted until some female researchers stepped up and questioned what meaning these choices had for how the field of psychology was conceptualizing cognitive development. This was an important step but also points to further steps that need to be taken, in that the researchers were still coming from positions of social privilege (White, educated).

Nevertheless, in *Women's Ways of Knowing*, Belenky, Clinchy, Goldberger, and Tarule (1986) sought to shift the narrative away from this male-only landscape and "explore with the women their experience and problems as learners and knowers" (p. 11). They interviewed women who were recent college graduates, current college students, and participants in programs at community agencies. Their sample was diverse, representing women from rural and urban areas of various ages and educational backgrounds across class and ethnic backgrounds. Rhetorical questions such as *how are women supposed to claim power over their own minds, where can women seek knowledge that informs self-concepts, to what external authorities can women look for truth and rightness*, and *in what ways are women's ways of knowing intertwined* provided the structure for research questions. Through 135 interviews with questions concerning the background, self-descriptions, gender, relationships, real moral dilemmas, education, ways of knowing, and hypothetical moral dilemmas, five major themes were formulated. Like Perry's stages, these themes follow a progressive order from basic to complex.

Category and Characteristics

In the first category, *silence*, the researchers found that women did not see themselves as knowers, in that they often came from low socioeconomic statuses and/or carried histories of abuse. Because they had less social status and power, they did not seem to trust their own experiences; instead, they invested trust in authority figures they viewed as powerful and omniscient and, as such, remained without a voice.

In the second category, *received knowledge*, the interviews showed women defining themselves and their thoughts through the external opinions of others, such as parents, instructors, or peers. These women were characterized as listening to the voices of others and receiving those opinions as "truth." The application of being a received knower is insufficient self-confidence in oneself as capable of learning and knowing. As we consider the case study of Lina, we could make the argument that she has entered college as a received knower, one who trusts her instructors' evaluations of her appropriateness in her field of study or her peer's initial evaluations of her value as a friend. She does not question the authority of these individuals to pass judgment on her thoughts and behaviors, nor does she place higher value on her sense of her legitimacy as a college student.

In the third category, *subjective knowledge*, women have begun to value their knowledge as gained from experiences and come to doubt the "experts and authorities" that they had trusted in previous positions. This represents an important shift as women come to have more faith in their ability to generate knowledge and more trust in their personal perspectives. However, subjective knowledge is still limited in that "authority" has just shifted from being vested in the powerful men outside to the personal internal thoughts and intuitions of the individual. If we were to imagine Lina as a subjective knower, we could picture her pushing back on the ways her roommate or faculty members had constructed her as "insufficient or incapable," instead relying on her sense of personal value to decide how to proceed in college. However, as a subjective knower, Lina would be trusting her gut feelings about what knowledge and information to trust, but not consulting any further criteria.

Thus, in the fourth category, *procedural knowledge*, the critical shift is in considering the ways that knowledge can be generated and evaluated, not just its source. Knowledge is now considered to have a foundation in reason, beyond personal experience or a "gut feeling." Although this has some parallels to Perry's position of relativism, the women in Belenky et al.'s (1986) study appeared to describe two different strains of procedural knowledge. In one strain, which they characterized as "separated knowing," the women were detached and intellectually critical as they evaluated knowledge. They sought procedures, and that could establish the truth and a base of evidence or criteria to validate the truth. However, there were also some women who were characterized as "connected knowers." These women were seen as empathic and receptive to reciprocity in knowing. In seeking to be understood, they also wanted to understand others. Collaboration is a preferred learning approach, as knowledge can be built or constructed in a community of learners and thus validated. Women in this group tended to suspend judgment as they listened to others, and then they connected their thoughts to what had been expressed. In this way, the women in the Belenky et al. (1986) study described knowing in a way that was very distinct from the men in Perry's (1970) study.

Finally, *constructed knowledge* was the last category in *Women's Ways of Knowing* (Belenky et al., 1986). These women can integrate the voices and opinions of others while being analytical or connected. Knowledge building is viewed as a process and understanding as entirely constructed; therefore, it must be judged in its context. Women in this stage wanted to integrate the knowledge they had coconstructed back into their lives in a way that had implications for how they would live and act. In this way, it is like Perry's commitment position, which combines ways of knowing with being dedicated to living out one's life accordingly.

The Five Stages of Knowing

In summary, the five stages of knowing (Belenky et al., 1986) are as follows:

1. Silence
2. Received knowledge
3. Subjective knowledge
4. Procedural knowledge
   - Separate knowing
   - Connected knowing
5. Constructed knowledge

General Applications of the Model

The implications of this work for higher education environments is in the impact that the identities and learning styles of students (whether male or female) can have on their learning. Belenky et al. (1986) recommended a supportive but relatively impersonal approach. The challenge for the women in their study to be independent and active learners led them to the discovery of their voices. Rapport-building opportunities include modeling a trial-and-error process, wherein outcomes arise from imperfect attempts at solving problems. College counselors and student affairs professionals might use this approach to help clients understand their ways of knowing from a feminist perspective. Furthermore, this approach provides a framework in which students can begin to appreciate and understand knowledge as a socially constructed phenomenon and not an absolute truism. Working with students from this perspective, a focus on learning and how to gain knowledge would be front and center.

Applying Belenky et al.'s Model to the Case of Lina

With its distinct anchor point of silence drawing attention to the relationships and conditions causing oppression and the development processes involved in moving from silence to voice (Hartog, 2004), the *Women's Ways of Knowing* model is a helpful framework to use in working with Lina. From the case study, we learn that Lina feels alone and unable to communicate with others about how she is feeling or what she is experiencing at college. She is struggling academically and socially but does not want to be a burden on others, especially her family because they have sacrificed a lot for her to attend college. A counselor working from this approach could help Lina move from a state of received knowledge to subjective knowledge by helping her see that the way her roommate defines her, on the basis of her ethnic background, is not the absolute truth, and she can redefine how she views herself and others view her. The goal with Lina would be to reach a point at which she is in a state of constructed knowledge and is capable of successfully integrating the opinions of others with her own in a critical manner.

Kohlberg's Theory of Moral Development

Lawrence Kohlberg was trained as a psychologist in the 1950s, at a time when moral development was not seen to be an area of academic study as much as a cultural phenomenon whereby individuals absorb influences from their families, their communities, and their cultures to learn about right and wrong (Kuhmerker, 1991). Influenced by Jean Piaget's (1936) work in cognitive development, Kohlberg was one of the first theorists to connect moral development to the cognitive transitions through childhood, youth, and adulthood. He believed that there was an underlying structure that influenced how people engaged with moral dilemmas and tried to make sense of them and that the structure was linear and sequential. Kohlberg's stages focused on reasoning (not moral behavior) and were based on research in which he led participants through a structured interview process. One part of the interview was to pose a moral dilemma (such as the "Heinz dilemma," in which a man has to decide whether to steal a drug that will save his wife from a disease, because he does not have enough money to pay for it and the pharmacist is unwilling to lower the price) and to track the types of reasons individuals offered for their decisions. Thus, the Kohlberg stages are not about the content of moral reasoning but are focused on structures related to justice and fairness. One critique of Kohlberg, which will be addressed more fully later in the chapter, is that fairness is not the only way to approach a moral dilemma, but it was the sole focus of his stages.

The sequential stages in Kohlberg's theory are hierarchical, which means a person must start in Stage 1 and move forward into Stage 2 without skipping ahead. This linear approach carries two foundational implications: First, the highest level of awareness available must always be applied for decision-making, and second, insights gained at previous levels remain and are integrated into current thought processes. Kohlberg also believed that a person is not capable of comprehending more than one level above his or her current level of reasoning. He also asserted that the experience of cognitive dissonance promotes development, leading to the assimilation of higher levels of reasoning and fostering morality through role-playing and perspective exchanging.

Kohlberg's (1958) theory is organized into three major levels, with each level containing two stages. The first level, *preconventional,* is typically understood as a childhood developmental stage. Children have not yet learned the norms for behavior or right/wrong in their given societies, so their reasoning is "preconventional" in the sense that it is not yet reflective of awareness of conventions for behavior. Preconventional moral reasoning is focused on rules, obedience, and punishment; an example would be a child trying to follow his or her parents' rules for good behavior to avoid being scolded. The child does not yet have an internal compass guiding his or her moral reasoning, so he or she relies on adults and authorities to provide a framework. This is also related to a child's cognitive development, which is still predominantly egocentric (self-oriented) and concrete (not grasping abstractions).

The second level is, therefore, the *conventional* level, at which adolescents and traditional-age college students may be found. At this level, individuals have absorbed the rules, norms, and expectations of their social groups and are able to consider how other people may think or feel about a dilemma. Conventional reasoning focuses on living up to the expectations of others, whether those are one's peers, one's family members, or others in one's near environment. Some typical conventional statements could include "Act toward others as you would have them act toward you" or "We all have to live by the rules, or else it would be unfair." Adolescents often reference their friends' morality at this stage, along the lines of "Well, if he did it, it must be OK." Conformity to expectations is widely seen as the best approach to moral reasoning, such that Heinz would not be advised to steal the life-saving drug out of deference to the laws.

Finally, the third level in Kohlberg's stages is the *postconventional* level. This level is also referred to as *principled reasoning* by some, in that it moves beyond conformity to consider the idea that our values, moral reasoning, and ideas about right and wrong may not always align. A commonly offered example is civil disobedience in protest of an unjust law. Rather than conforming because "everyone else is," a postconventional thinker would be able to apply universal principles like equality, dignity, life, and liberty to a moral dilemma. In this line of reasoning, Heinz could conceivably be justified in stealing the drug, because his wife's right to a life-saving drug would be more compelling than a pharmacist's right to make a profit. Principled thinkers might also propose that the pharmacist could accept a payment plan or a reduced profit rather than stand by and watch Heinz's wife die. It is not a case of "majority rules" as much as it is an in-depth consideration of the moral and ethical dimensions of the dilemma and a decision to uphold ethical principles as the determining factors.

As you will see, each of the stages underlying Levels 1, 2, and 3 represent a slight movement forward in reasoning, often with the acknowledgment that moral dilemmas involve more than one party most of the time. The earlier stage is more often an individualistic stance toward the moral issue (e.g., the golden rule in Stage 3 is still generalizing to others what "I" would want to have done to me, whereas Stage 4 reasoning would move to consider the welfare of all, with the "I" just being one member of a community whose members have obligations to each other). Level 3 postconventional morality contains Stage 6 universal principles and Stage 5 social contract and individual rights, whereas Level 2 conventional morality contains Stage 4 social order and Stage 3 interpersonal relationships. Finally, Level 1 preconventional morality contains Stage 2 individualism and exchange and Stage 1 punishment and obedience.

In summary, Kohlberg's six stages of moral development (Kohlberg, 1958) are as follows:

Preconventional morality level
- Stage 1—Punishment and obedience
- Stage 2—Individualism and exchange

Conventional morality level
- Stage 3—Interpersonal relationships
- Stage 4—Social order

Postconventional morality level
- Stage 5—Social contract and individual rights
- Stage 6—Universal principles

General Applications of the Model

Recognizing the moral and ethical reasoning behind a person's decisions can be useful information to have when working with college students. In higher education settings, college counselors and student affairs professionals can use information such as this to assist students in understanding the importance of making ethical decisions on a higher level and can work with them to develop strategies for developing higher order ways of thinking (Kiser, Morrison, & Craven, 2009). Using Socratic questioning, counselors can help students reason their way through various ethical dilemmas (similar to the Heinz dilemma) and consider how they can apply lessons learned to their lives. Furthermore, the college years are a prime time for individuals' moral reasoning skills to develop. By design, college provides students with a level of intellectual stimulation that causes them to overhaul and rethink the fundamental ways in which they make moral judgments (Rest & Narvaez, 1991). A meta-analysis revealed that college attendance accounted for between 28% and 53% of the variance in the development of moral reasoning skills among young adults (Thoma & Rest, 1986). Given the importance of moral reasoning skills, college counselors should look for opportunities to integrate campus-wide programming into existing services (e.g., new student orientations, residence hall activities) to ensure students are exposed to knowledge and opportunity facilitating their moral development.

Applying Kohlberg's Model to the Case of Lina

A college counselor working with Lina could apply Kohlberg's theory to her moral development. Specifically, the counselor could help Lina clarify her ways of thinking about moral dilemmas and gently guide her to consider how that may influence her moral behavior. For example, if Lina felt that her roommate was not being "fair" to her by making assumptions about her religious orientation and spreading negative rumors about her, she might be reasoning through a conventional lens (e.g., "She should treat me fairly because I am trying to treat her fairly," which is perhaps a Stage 3 statement). The counselor could help Lina clarify her moral stance about this situation and perhaps help her practice what she might like to say to her roommate to reduce the impact of her behavior (e.g., "Please remember that we are both members of this campus and this residence hall, and I would like you to consider my welfare before you start spreading stories about me that are not actually true," which moves toward Stage 4). In doing so, Lina can feel heard, and the situation is managed in a nonconfrontational manner.

Critiques and Updates

The major criticism with respect to Perry's work is the relative homogeneity of the sample of participants whose data form the basis for his theoretical model. The student body at Harvard University was made up of predominantly affluent White males. The lack of diversity in participants calls into question the generalizability of his work. Counselors must make adaptations when using this approach with students from underrepresented populations.

Furthermore, the interview protocols he used were not in line with current best practices in research design. The lack of fidelity with which they were conducted further contributes to the questionable results obtained. Despite these limitations, which Perry himself noted, the model has proven a useful application in higher education settings by allowing professionals to understand better why students struggle and how best to help them.

Building on Perry's work and addressing its flaws was the work of Belenky and her colleagues. The timing of Belenky et al. (1986) was prime for empowering countless women, but the work is not without flaws (including a focus on gender to the exclusion of other essential identities and experiences). One criticism is that the research is biased because it is based solely on case studies of women, thus rendering it skewed in one direction. However, this research was in response to studies that had been skewed in the other direction and thus is corrective in some ways. Additionally, although Belenky et al. viewed their theory as nonlinear, the order of their five perspectives follows rational ascension (Brookes, 1988).

Finally, criticisms with respect to Kohlberg's moral development theory are tied to his research being done with all White men in a privileged educational space, making it essential to contextualize his findings and consider whether they remain applicable to today's college students. Many scholars have claimed limited applicability of these universal principles. For example, Carol Gilligan, a student of Kohlberg's, would go on to challenge his findings by conducting similar studies with female participants. Whereas Kohlberg claimed moral concerns involve justice and fairness, Gilligan asserted that a different set of moral principles, mediated through responsiveness and connection, was possible if one expanded the set of participants. The process of expanding our understanding of human cognitive and moral reasoning and behavior is not complete, as these foundational research studies are still mostly being narrated by and based on White voices.

Conclusion

The cognitive and moral theories of student development discussed in this chapter provide useful lenses through which college counselors and student affairs personnel can examine how students interpret, rationalize, and make meaning out of their lived experiences.

Knowing how students perceive and rationalize their experiences aids in understanding their motives for thinking and acting in certain ways. In addition to providing college counselors and student affairs professionals with a theoretical foundation for knowledge, expertise, and practice, these theories can aid in both program planning and policy development.

Consistent among the theories introduced in this chapter is the way in which learning occurs. Each of the theories views cognitive growth as a sequential process, with the mind's structures developing one at a time in a static fashion that is the same for everyone. In each subsequent stage, benchmarks for successful development are established, and information learned in previous stages is expanded and contextualized to a larger view of the world and human beings' place in it. Collectively, these theories allow helping professionals to address four key questions related to students' emerging belief systems. They included the following: (a) What interpersonal/intrapersonal changes occur while the student is in college? (b) What factors lead to this development? (c) What aspects of the college environment encourage or delay growth? (d) What developmental outcomes should we strive to achieve in college? Although a truly comprehensive model of student development does not exist, the models in this category can be a useful way to understand students and how they think.

Final Case Studies

Case 1

Marianna, a 27-year-old Hispanic woman, has spent most of her life in the geographic region of her birth, which is adjacent to Mexico. Her husband is in the Navy, and having been recently reassigned to a state on the eastern seaboard, Marianna enrolled in a nursing program. She is in her first semester and is struggling with feeling connected and significant. Specifically, she is shy about asking questions or expressing her ideas in class:

> I have always wanted to be a nurse, so I enjoy being back in school; but . . . I don't feel comfortable bringing attention to myself by asking or answering questions. It's not as bad when we do small group work, but even then, I don't feel I have anything to offer as far as knowledge like my classmates do.

Case 1 Exploration Questions

1. How might the five stages of knowing be applied to help Marianna?
2. What experiences would be helpful for Marianna to draw on in working through the stages?
3. How would these experiences affect her struggles with feeling connected and significant?
4. What could be done to help Marianna take the tenets of the five stages forward in her life to apply them in future situations?

Case 2

Jeremy is a master's counseling student who is currently completing practicum hours at a campus clinic that is free for enrolled college students. For the last several weeks, he has been seeing a female student named Emma as a client; she is going through a messy divorce involving custody of two small children. Emma has previously confided in Jeremy about her financial difficulties surrounding the divorce, including trouble with ensuring enough food is available at home for her children. In considering solutions, Jeremy and Emma discussed her seeking food assistance from the state.

At the following session, Jeremy follows up with Emma about this plan for assistance, and she updates him, saying that the agent she spoke with informed her that because she is not formally divorced yet, her husband's income disqualifies her for such state services. As a caveat, the agent told Emma that if she could provide residential proof of separation by giving another address, she and her kids would qualify for food assistance. Emma attempted to move on to another subject when Jeremy, thinking that he is practicing immediacy, asks her what she is going to do about state assistance. Emma thus informed Jeremy that she is going to use a friend's address to qualify for the needed help until her divorce is finalized. The session then proceeded as usual and concluded without incident.

Jeremy is writing his case notes and starts to hesitate about how to handle Emma's response of using an address other than her own to qualify for state assistance. He considers discussing this with his supervisor but questions how it may be handled because of the supervisor's reputation of being a stickler for rules. Jeremy also considers not saying anything to anyone for fear that it will cause more trouble for his client, as well as her innocent children.

Case 2 Exploration Questions

1. What is the moral/ethical dilemma in this situation? If there is more than one, how does Jeremy identify the main issue for which to identify a resolution?
2. What level and/or stage of Kohlberg's theory would ensure Jeremy follows the ethical guideline of do no harm? Is there more than one stage that allows adherence to this guideline?
3. How might Jeremy go about deciding on a course of action?
4. What, if any, additional information could be provided about this case to assist in making an easier decision?

References

Belenky, M. F., Clinchy, B. M., Goldberger, N. R., & Tarule, J. M. (1986). *Women's ways of knowing: The development of self, voice, and mind*. New York, NY: Basic Books.

Brookes, A. L. (1988). Reviewed work: Women's ways of knowing: The development of self, voice, and mind. *Curriculum Inquiry, 18,* 113–121. doi:10.2307/1179565

Evans, N. J., Forney, D. S., Guido, F. M., Patton, L. D., & Renn, K. A. (2010). *Student development in college: Theory, research, and practice* (2nd ed.). San Francisco, CA: Jossey-Bass.

Hartog, M. (2004). *Women's ways of knowing: A review and critique*. Retrieved from http://www.actionresearch.net/living/hartogphd/mhch3.pdf

Hofer, B. K., & Pintrich, P. R. (1997). The development of epistemological theories: Beliefs about knowledge and knowing and their relation to learning. *Review of Education Research, 67,* 88–140.

Johnson, M. H. (1981). Some new thoughts on the Perry scheme. *The Perry Newsletter,* Spring, 1–3.

Kiser, A. I. T., Morrison, E. E., & Craven, A. (2009). The application of Kohlberg's moral development model to college students' technology ethics decisions. *Journal of College Teaching and Learning, 6,* 89–96.

Kloss, R. J. (1994). A nudge is best: Helping students through the Perry scheme of intellectual development. *College Teaching, 42,* 151–158. Retrieved from http://www.jstor.org/stable/27558677

Kohlberg, L. (1958). *The development of modes of thinking and choices in years 10 to 16.* Chicago, IL: University of Chicago.

Kuhmerker, L. (1991). *The Kohlberg legacy for helping professions.* Birmingham, AL: Doxa Books.

Long, D. (2012). Theories and models of student development. In L. J. Hinchcliffe & M. A. Wong (Eds.), *Environments for student growth and development: Librarians and student affairs in collaboration* (pp. 41–55). Chicago, IL: Association of College and Research Libraries.

Perry, W. G. (1970). *Forms of intellectual and ethical development in the college years: A scheme.* Cambridge, MA: Harvard University.

Piaget, J. (1936). *Origins of intelligence in the child.* London, UK: Routledge & Kegan Paul.

Piaget, J. (1952). *The origins of intelligence in children.* New York, NY: Norton.

Piaget, J. (1958). *The growth of logical thinking from childhood to adolescence.* London, UK: Routledge & Kegan Paul.

Rest, J., & Narvaez, D. (1991). The college experience and moral development. In W. M. Kurtines & J. L. Gewirtz (Eds.), *Handbook of moral behavior and development: Vol. 2. Research* (pp. 229–245). Hillsdale, NJ: Erlbaum.

Thoma, S. J., & Rest, J. R. (1986). Moral judgment, behavior, decision making, and attitudes. In J. R. Rest (Ed.), *Moral development: Advances in research and theory* (pp. 133–175). New York, NY: Praeger.

Chapter 13

Experiential Theories of Student Development

Laura M. Gonzalez and Steven Mencarini

The purpose of life is to live it,
to taste experience to the utmost,
to reach out eagerly and without fear
for newer and richer experience.

—Eleanor Roosevelt

■ ■ ■

Reflection Exercise

If each of you as readers stopped for a moment to reflect on what your "college experience" meant to you, it is likely you would recall some pivotal moments. Take a moment to call to mind some of the key experiences that were part of your transition into college, and then some key experiences that were part of your transition out of college. You may be remembering some of the excitement and anxiety associated with a new experience that cannot be fully predicted, some of the people around you who helped provide the context or backdrop to your experience, or some critical moments that challenged or tested you to your maximum. We hope you will bring those vivid experiences from your own college days with you on the journey in this chapter, as we consider the developmental value and meaning of our experiences. Experience is quite unique to the beholder, so you may also take the opportunity to learn about the college experiences of some of your classmates as you move through this material. We consider the role of experience through the lens of three theories—David Kolb's (1984) learning theory, Nancy Schlossberg's (2008) transition theory, and Marcia Baxter Magolda's (2001) self-authorship theory. We will think about Lina Miller's (see pages 186–187) case again through the lens of these newer theories, will consider the limitations and critiques of the theories, and will then provide some opportunity for application to campus work.

■ ■ ■

At its best, college can be a transformative learning experience that broadens one's horizons in many ways. Ideally, it is a carefully structured environment that encourages students to have a broad set of experiences that will promote their cognitive, social/emotional, academic/career, and personal development (Chickering & Reisser, 1993). These experiences form a buffet of sorts—an amazing assortment of opportunities to learn in class (from faculty and other students in a variety of academic disciplines), outside of class (in student clubs and activities, campus events, leadership roles, athletics), and even in one's living space (e.g., in roommate situations—the educational value of having a roommate should never be underestimated). Student mental health and wellness also can be connected to students' lived experiences on campus. These vivid experiences add up to make college more than just a place to earn an academic credential—many people feel that they have developed and changed in important ways as a result of the interactions they have had with various aspects of campus life. For example, by engaging with others in a diverse campus community, students may feel themselves stretching to become more tolerant and accepting of worldviews that differ from their own.

Indeed, the theories that are presented in this chapter focus in some important way on the role of experience in the developmental gains that typically result from time spent in college. Experience in this educational sense is defined as something that is (a) active, direct, and engaging; (b) structured and purposeful; (c) unpredictable, in that the outcome (success, failure) cannot be guaranteed; and (d) supported by reflection to deepen the learning (Association for Experiential Education, n.d.). So, for example, sending text messages to friends or posting to social media accounts may qualify as virtual interactions but may not have some of the deeper educational qualities associated with a face-to-face experience (active and engaging, supported by reflection). Now, consider this academic example: Tutoring another student allows for active engagement both with scholarly material and another human being, is typically structured and purposeful, does not have a guaranteed outcome, and hopefully includes an opportunity to reflect. These are two small examples, but educational experience is a broad and varied category. Take a moment to jot down some of the key educational experiences you recall from your undergraduate days, and then look at Box 13.1 for a sample list of types of campus-based experiences that may provide meaningful experiences for today's undergraduates.

Campus-based experiences can provide college students with challenges and hopefully also with supports (Sanford, 1967). What is challenging to one person (e.g., a racial microaggression) may not feel challenging to another, so experience is also dependent on the perceiver. For example, if we think of Lina Miller and her early transition into college, we can see that her roommate's uninformed assumption that Lina is Muslim and Lina's

BOX 13.1

Types of Experiential Activities Available on Many Campuses

- Service learning with reflection
- Leadership roles with mentoring
- Athletic participation with coaching
- Membership in student organizations, including Greek life and many other types
- Practicums/internships with supervision
- Campus advocate for an issue
- Campus volunteer (admissions tours, orientation guide)
- Peer adviser/mentor/helper/educator/tutor with training
- Participation in student government
- Student conduct hearing officer
- Cultural exchanges (study abroad, service trips)
- Wilderness/outdoor exploration trips
- Creative/artistic presentations to others
- Research opportunities with faculty

discouraging start in a very large calculus class are challenging types of learning experiences. These perhaps exemplify the unpredictable aspect of experience, wherein the input is somewhat unstructured and the outcomes are not guaranteed. On the other hand, some supportive experiences (e.g., help in reflecting on and making meaning of the challenges, a greater sense of purpose in the challenges, strategies for engaging differently with the challenges) could be very useful to Lina in both the short and long term.

As you read through the three theories presented in this chapter, consider how you might encourage Lina to respond to these early discouraging experiences in a way that is resilient and adaptive. Reflection on experience is critical in that it can help turn a failure or a barrier into a lesson learned that informs an individual's efforts the next time around. Reflection can include both cognitive components ("I understand now that my high school calculus class was taught at a lower level and I will need to work harder here") and affective components ("I'm so scared that I might fail, what can I do?"), as the theories will show. Encouraging reflection is a basic and necessary helping skill for counselors but can also be taught and practiced in other areas of campus (i.e., student support services). Helping students/clients identify their purpose is another way to provide support, in that it can engage their motivation and help them become more persistent and resourceful problem solvers. Finally, there is usually more than one way to engage with the challenging experience, but students who are stuck in a discouraged and fearful place may not see that at first. Thus, counselors/helpers have a key role to play. As we turn to the theories, continue to look for ideas for engaging productively or creatively with experience to promote wellness and development in our student clients.

Experiential Learning Theory

In his seminal book *Experiential Learning*, D. A. Kolb (1984) introduced a fundamental shift in understanding the learning process. Rather than grounding the theory in behavioral theories or implicit theories that underlie traditional educational methods, D. A. Kolb's work was based on the work of social and developmental psychologists, such as Lewin, Dewey, and Piaget (D. A. Kolb, 1984). D. A. Kolb posited that "learning is the process whereby knowledge is created through the transformation of experience. Knowledge results from the combination of grasping and transforming experience" (p. 41). Additionally, experiential learning theory is intended to supplement other learning theories to provide a more holistic view of individuals' strengths as they engage in the learning process.

D. A. Kolb's (1984) experiential learning theory is outlined as a learning process that follows a cycle of differing modes of interaction. To be effective, a learner needs to function from four different kinds of perspectives or abilities: concrete experience abilities (CE), reflective observation abilities (RO), abstract conceptualization abilities (AC), and active experimentation (AE) abilities. The cycle may start with an experience that someone engages fully, openly, and without bias (CE). Individuals then must reflect on the experience and be able to observe their experience from multiple perspectives (RO). On the basis of their reflection, individuals integrate their observations into "logically sound theories" (AC). Finally, individuals use these theories in solving problems and initiating new concrete experiences (AE). This process is idealized as a cycle wherein the learner experiences, reflects, thinks, and acts in relation to what is being learned. Learners can theoretically enter the cycle at any point, so that some individuals prefer to start the learning in the abstract conceptualization stage, learning from reading or thinking, whereas others learn better when they can start with doing (experimentation). However, the fullest use of all of these learning capabilities occurs when individuals can move around the cycle and experience learning in several modalities.

Let's use the example of Lina to think our way around the learning cycle (see Figure 13.1). If we take her early experiences in her math class as concrete experience, how could we keep moving Lina around the cycle to help her process the failure in a different way? In reflective observation, we could encourage Lina to think reflectively about what she was doing well and what she could improve, perhaps identifying a role model with habits she could learn from. In abstract conceptualization, we could ask Lina to generate a new theory about herself as a math student (as in, are you doomed to fail, or did you just need some better study habits and test-taking strategies?). Finally, in active experimentation, Lina could start to apply some of those new study habits before the next test, and then see if her grade was higher as a result. Allowing Lina to experience these things for herself is much more powerful than simply telling her "I bet you just need a math tutor."

Research on experiential learning theory has focused on the concept of learning styles via the Learning Styles Inventory (A. Y. Kolb & Kolb, 2005). Four learning styles were determined by previous research: diverging, assimilating, converging, and accommodating (D. A. Kolb, 1984). A person who has a diverging approach scores high on CE and RO and is strong at brainstorming. An assimilating style has RO and AC as prevailing learning abilities. People with this style are strong at condensing information and putting it into a logical

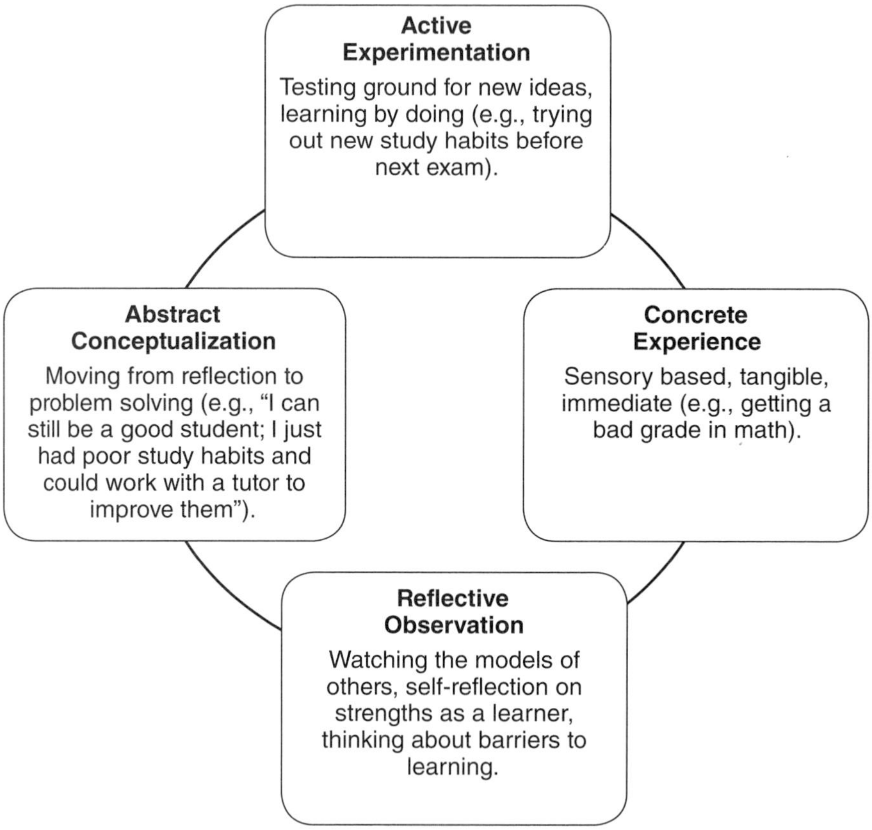

FIGURE 13.1

D. A. Kolb's (1984) Learning Cycle (Adapted) as Applied in the Case of Lina

Note. Refer to the case study of Lina on pages 186–187.

form. The third learning style is converging, which has dominant AC and AE learning abilities. Convergers find practical uses for ideas and theories. Finally, the accommodating learning style is characterized by having hands-on learning and is strong in AE and CE. Ultimately, all learning styles can be seen as helpful and adaptive, and students strong in one style can learn to use an additional style to strengthen their capabilities. For example, if Lina determined that she learned best by finding practical uses for information, but her instructor did not usually make those types of examples available in the classroom environment, she could search online for examples of "using calculus in the real world" or create such examples herself.

A variety of factors can affect students' learning styles, such as personality type, education specialization, professional career choice, and current job role (D. A. Kolb, Boyatzis, & Mainemelis, 2001). For example, accommodating styles are ideal for executive jobs in which decisions have to be made and tasks must be accomplished. Person-centered jobs, such as counseling or personnel administration, require a diverging learning orientation. Jobs revolving around information and data analysis have a need for an assimilating style preference. Convergent styles are ideal for technical jobs that require problem-solving skills.

D. A. Kolb's experiential learning model has been applied in a variety of ways within the field of counseling. Articles have used the model as a framework for the counseling process (Sugarman, 1985), the structuring of career exploration exercises and outreach (Atkinson & Murrell, 1988; Rakes 1994), the prediction of early career success (Hill & Wilson, 1996), goal setting that matches the client's preferred modalities (D. A. Kolb & Boyatzis, 1970), the processing of group activities and experiences (Glass & Benshoff, 1999), and supervision modalities (Abbey, Hunt, & Weiser, 1985). It also has many applications in student affairs work with college students, including academic advising and selection of major, tutoring/academic support for diverse learning styles, promotion of successful work in groups, considerations in program development, staff training and supervision, and problem-solving (Evans, Forney, & Guido-DiBrito, 1998).

Understanding and Coping With Transitions

Transitions are a particular type of experience that occur regularly in college students' lives. Schlossberg's (2008) theory of transitions is based in the adult development literature and includes understanding different types of transitions, the transition process, and what can influence transitions. A transition is defined as "any event or non-event that results in changed relationships, routines, assumptions, and roles" (Goodman, Schlossberg, & Anderson, 2006, p. 33). Transitions can have implications for individuals' mental health, wellness, and development, as well as for academic progress and success, so they are critical junctures to which college counselors and student support professionals must attend.

The first part of understanding transitions is to recognize that there are various types of transitions, such as planned, unanticipated, and nonevent (Schlossberg, 2011). For many college students, planned transitions occur as students start and end their college career. There are also unanticipated transitions such as an unexpected significant illness or the death of a parent or a friend. And there are expected events that never happen that are called nonevent transitions, such as never finding a life partner or not getting into graduate school. Often, it is not the transition itself that is the issue but how much the transition affects or does not affect one's roles, responsibilities, routines, and assumptions. For example, all first-year students are making some sort of transition to campus, but in Lina's case, this transition was complicated by her first-generation college student status, some microaggressions around religion and race, a difficult class, and financial worries. Although the transition may be a single event or nonevent, the influence of a transition extends over a period of time, and working through the transition is a process.

Schlossberg (2008) created a mnemonic to help individuals cope with transitions called the four *S*s: situation, self, supports, and strategies. The first *S*, *situation*, refers to what other stressors are happening at the time of the transition. Is the transition happening in a period in which many other aspects of life are stable and provide a foundation of strength and calm, or is the transition part of a larger crisis in which many aspects of life are destabilized? *Self* represents the person's inner strength for dealing with the transition. If the individual is optimistic, is resilient, and deals well with ambiguity, then he or she is more likely to be able to cope with the transition. If the individual already struggles with anxiety over change or has an avoidant coping style, then the transition may have a bigger impact. *Supports* implies what assistance is available at the time of the transition. A person with a strong support system (both on campus and at home) will be able to navigate a transition better than someone without support. Finally, *strategies* denotes the coping strategies used to manage the transition. A person who is able to use multiple coping strategies will be more successful in a transition experience than someone who is not able to manage that stress. The four *S*s provide a road map to college counselors and student support staff who wish to assist their student clients in improving their coping skills (see Table 13.1), as will be described in more detail later in the chapter.

Transitions also encompass the context in addition to the individual. For example, Lina's transition to college would have been more complicated if it had happened right around the time of the 9/11 attacks, when many people with ties to the Muslim community experienced hate crimes and felt under attack (Nassar-McMillan & Hakim-Larson, 2003). Some college transitions revolve around the environment (e.g., the transition from high school to college, the transition from college to the workforce), so these experiences can be embedded in particular campus ecologies and critical tasks. Picture what your college transition would have been like if you had started at a small women's college. A large public university far from home? A 2-year college in your hometown? A historically Black college or university? Support would likely differ depending on the specifics of the transition and whether it was wanted/anticipated or not.

Higher education institutions focus a lot of time and energy on a student's transition to college. Most universities have some sort of orientation program, and many have first-year experience programs to help students become acclimated to campus (Smith & Brackin, 2003). Starting college is a planned transition, and colleges and universities often use Schlossberg's (2008) transition model as a way to help frame initiatives tailored to first-year students. Counseling centers and advising offices frequently focus their resources on the first 6 weeks of the academic year, knowing that the early phase of the transition sets an important tone for the remainder of the student's experience (Woosley, 2003). Further-

TABLE 13.1

Suggestions for Applying the Four *S*s to College Counseling Clients

Situation	*Self*	*Supports*	*Strategies*
Is the situation temporary or permanent? Has this situation been experienced before? Is any aspect under the student's control? Is a change in role part of the situation?	What psychological strengths and assets can be utilized? How can the student show resilience in this situation? What demographic characteristics can be drawn upon (e.g., health, finances, age)?	Which relationships and networks can the student draw on? What resources or support structures are present on campus? What institutions and communities off campus can be called upon for support?	Can the student modify the situation? Can the student change how the situation is being interpreted? Can the student do better at managing stress reactions?

Note. Adapted from Schlossberg (2008).

more, a student moving from a community college to a 4-year institution or a student who is conditionally admitted to an institution may experience this change in a very different way than a "typical" student transitioning from high school.

There are a number of other hypothetical transitions a student may experience in college. A student studying abroad will encounter a transition to a new location and a new culture and may experience a separate transition as they reenter their home country and campus. Student athletes may experience an unexpected transition if they suffer a career-ending injury. Graduating seniors will also undergo a transition as they wrap up their studies from their undergraduate institution and decide on their next steps. What other student populations do you think may have specific needs surrounding their transition to campus and other transitions they may experience during their college years, and how could you structure a response? Thinking about transitions in a focused way can offer a helpful guide to intervention for counselors and student support staff members working on college campuses.

Self-Authorship

College can be a time of changing life roles and responsibilities for some, which can require a new way of making meaning of one's identity or life situation (Baxter Magolda, 2014). Indeed, the complexity of 21st-century life has meant that college students not only need to master an academic discipline to graduate and be successful but also need to become adept at solving problems, adapting to change, weighing the value of information or evidence, and living and working interdependently with others. Thus, students are required to navigate changing circumstances almost continually and need to be able to make meaning from new situations as they present themselves. One theory that describes that steady hand on the rudder that allows students to navigate change effectively is self-authorship (Baxter Magolda, 2014). *Self-authorship* can be defined as a meaning-making process that helps students move from a place of (a) accepting external definitions of themselves; to (b) actively wrestling with the discrepancies between others' definitions and their growing sense of their own, called *crossroads*; to (c) choosing one's own views about self; and (d) clearly stating their internal definitions related to identity and purpose. Self-authorship is a constructivist process that encourages making meaning of one's experiences in the social environment and generating the sense of identity required to keep moving forward into new experiences with confidence.

Self-authorship theory also is holistic in that it considers cognitive development ("How do I know what I know?"), psychological or intrapersonal development ("Who am I becoming?"), and social or interpersonal development ("How do I relate to others?"; Baxter Magolda, 2001; Baxter Magolda & King, 2007). Whereas some of the earlier theories presented would compartmentalize these areas of student development into silos, self-authorship is more flexible and complex in that it encompasses all three at once. If we think of the example of Lina, part of her early struggle at college may be described as accepting external definitions of herself as a knower ("you can't pass this math class"), as an individual ("I can't let my family down"), and as a social being ("she told everyone I was a Muslim").

For traditional-age college students, the early phases of college are typically characterized by trust in external authorities (adults at home or in college), but these students gradually shift to a more independent, and then interdependent, spirit (Baxter Magolda, 2014). In the most difficult moments in the process, the crossroads phases, students may be uncertain whose voice to listen to. Those are key moments for counselors and helpers to be present to assist with the meaning-making and self-authorship journey (Baxter Magolda, 2014). For example, students may begin on one side of the continuum with the external voices of their family and friends guiding their decisions but may become unsure whom to trust when they have started to individuate from early caretakers. As students enter the crossroads, they may need help discerning which relationships are mutual and healthy or which decisions fit them best, allowing them to sort out external expectations from internal direction. This represents movement toward the other end of the continuum, where students trust in their own ability to make meaning from their experiences and can direct themselves on the basis of their internal definitions of self. If we imagine Lina at graduation, we can hope that she has been able to generate a more self-authored sense of herself as a knower, of her psychological strengths and characteristics as a human being, and of her place of belonging in the social fabric of her university and her family.

Baxter Magolda (2014) did not conceptualize the self-authorship process as linear, straight and narrow, but instead visualized the possibility of many detours and direction changes as students learn to trust themselves and author their own experiences. Having a variety of interpersonal experiences, both good and bad, then permits for examination of the outcomes and movement in the direction preferred by the student. Again, the agency or authorship of students in their own lives is of critical importance as they grow to trust their own ability to make sound decisions and learn from their experiences.

To promote self-authorship, colleges can ask themselves, does our environment treat students like emerging adults and support their movement toward greater autonomy and interdependence? Are key support personnel present to help with meaning making at moments when students are at a crossroads (academically, socially, personally)? For example, Evans and Broido (1999) explored the dynamics at play that helped or hindered while lesbian, gay, bisexual, transgender, queer/questioning, intersex, and asexual students were coming out in the residential setting, which included the self-authorship questions. There are clear counseling applications of self-authorship (e.g., helping to stabilize students whose journey to self-authorship is more traumatic or contentious), classroom applications (e.g., clarifying personal stances or opinions), and extracurricular applications (e.g., taking on roles in student activities, student leadership, academic advising). Indeed, Baxter Magolda (2001) is a strong proponent of the learning partnerships model, wherein this meaning-making task is shared across campus units (Baxter Magolda & King, 2004).

In the example of Lina, her academic adviser has become a trusted adult on campus and may be able to help Lina sort through her early experiences to decide which are consistent with her goals for college. Is she here only to please her parents and be a role model to her brother, or does she have some internal motivation to "write the next chapter of her life"? What has she done in previous experiences when she was worried about the possibility of failure, and how can she draw on those lessons to help now? How can she make meaning around her bicultural identity to know its importance to her and how to respond to those who might criticize her? Some studies have found that minoritized students may be at risk for having their voices be discounted and marginalized (Pizzolato, 2004) or having additional developmental burdens related to discrimination (Torres & Hernandez, 2007), so Lina's sense of belonging and acceptance on campus will be important to explore. Lina might be encouraged to journal about these questions or be given help in finding a similar peer who has already navigated some of these challenges. To continue to develop and thrive at college, Lina will need to find her authentic internalized voice and learn to use it confidently.

Theory Critique

As responsible consumers of theory, we must always ask ourselves, for whom does this apply and when? For example, do students need a higher level of cognitive development to engage with the meaning-making and reflection parts of experience that are implicit in D. A. Kolb's and Baxter Magolda's theories? Do we trust and accept the conceptual parts of theories when there are few empirical studies to back them up (as in Schlossberg's theory)? Are there biases within the theories that preference certain social identities or groups?

One important question to ask about these experiential theories revolves around privilege and oppression (Jones & Stewart, 2016). Assuming that the hierarchy and power structures of our society are replicated in our colleges and universities, do they restrict the types of experiences that a particular student may have access to and therefore limit the student's opportunities for development? For example, if you are in a minoritized group on your campus, would you feel free to engage in genuine exploration, try out a variety of experiences, and create your own culturally authentic voice if those went against the norms on your campus? Would there be any retribution for doing so? We must be cognizant that some students will not feel that they have all possible options open to them, whether because of the limiting messages present in early discriminatory messages they received or current realities. However, a strength of these theories is that they rely in many ways on the individual's meaning-making or constructivist process, which does ideally allow for these questions about culture to be raised and taken seriously. It is our responsibility as counselors and student support staff to do so.

Guided Learning Applications

The experiential theories just reviewed can be used by a number of campus support offices to better understand a student's experience in various higher education environments. For example, offices and departments that foster leadership development within their students could consider D. A. Kolb's (1984) experiential learning theory and Baxter Magolda's (2001) self-authorship theory. In order for students to truly understand the concept of "leadership," they must go out and test-drive their leadership skills and capacities within various campus environments. Designing student experiences through the four phases of D. A. Kolb's experiential learning theory can help students to crystalize what they are learning about leadership and how to use their influence to create change on campus and within society. Leadership self-efficacy, or one's confidence in one's ability to lead (Komives & Dugan, 2010), frequently has an impact on whether one decides to lead. By using Baxter Magolda's self-authorship theory, a student can better understand why he or she may have decided to lead in a particular situation or step back in another.

Schlossberg's (2008) theory is grounded in counseling and is easily applicable to work with college student clients experiencing difficulty in transitions. Even students with diagnoses like depression or anxiety could be encouraged to cognitively reframe their difficulties using the four *S*s (see Table 13.1 for ideas). For example, strategies or coping responses that encourage students to change the aspects of the situation that are under their control could include reducing exposure to anxiety triggers or building in exercise for physiological stress release. Coping responses that modify the meaning of the problem could include changing self-blaming or catastrophizing thoughts. Finally, even for stressors that cannot be modified, we can help student clients manage the results or consequences of the situation to their best advantage (soliciting support, cultivating wellness practices, etc.).

Support staff and faculty within higher education who engage with service learning also can use these theories. Often, a process of preparation-action-reflection-evaluation, also known as the PARE model, is used to help students understand the important work being undertaken (Student Outreach Resource Center, n.d.). The PARE model is not attributed to D. A. Kolb but certainly follows a process similar to that of Kolb's experiential model of abstract conceptualization (preparation), active experimentation and concrete experience (action), and reflective observation (reflection and evaluation). Such a cycle could even be applied to career counseling or academic advising to help students explore their academic and career options in a more experiential way (e.g., identify some possible options of interest, find an internship or do an informational interview to gain experience, reflect on how well this experience matches the student's goals, and evaluate whether the option is a good fit).

Conclusion

The options for viewing campus work through an experiential lens are almost limitless. Almost any experience can be seen from the perspective of learning styles (e.g., campus conduct infractions are student actions in need of reflection and evaluation to arrive at the moment of preparation for a different set of actions the next time), transition (e.g., students in crisis are in need of both short-term support and longer term strategies), or self-authorship (e.g., self-authorship can be used to support students with disabilities in building agency and interdependence). Whether counselors and student support staff use these theories as conceptual aids, to help guide students toward more adaptive thoughts and behaviors, or as tools to share directly with students as they build their own capacity for responding, experiential theories are valuable for student development.

Final Case Study

In the functional area of residence life, there are a hundred kinds of experiences for students every day. For college students, "Who am I becoming?" and "How do I relate to others?" are pertinent questions that get expressed directly in living areas of campus. The answers to these questions change as students develop and mature but are also informed by the environments in which they live. First-year students not only have to adjust to potentially living away from home for the first time but also have to adapt to living in community with others.

One common challenge for residence life staff is to help students navigate differences with their roommates. Imagine two residents who have come to you with a request for a room change. It could be that the source of tension between them is that one student is gay and one is not, it could be that one student is religiously observant and one is not, or it could be that one is focusing on the academic side of college life and the other is focusing on the social transitions to college. Whatever the relevant difference may be, emotions can become involved in the conflict, and students may feel their identities or priorities are being called into question. Walking away from the experience of conflict may seem like the easiest way to resolve it, but what meaning is made then? You value the educational aspects of all experiences, even difficult experiences, so you sit down with these two residents with the intention to help them engage productively with their differences.

Case Exploration Questions

1. Which theory or theories might guide your thinking as you seek to reframe this conflict experience into something less threatening? Explain your choice.
2. If the conflict is connected to the identities of the roommates, how can you draw from these theories to help the students interact with each other in a more respectful or accepting way? Said another way, show how these theories have application to practice in the 21st century.

3. Could any of these theories be used to inform programming in the residence hall even before roommate conflicts start to be reported? What skills would you like all students to learn that might make for less conflict and better transitions for your residents?

References

Abbey, D. S., Hunt, D. E., & Weiser, J. C. (1985). Variations on a theme by Kolb: A new perspective for understanding counseling and supervision. *The Counseling Psychologist, 13,* 477–501.

Association for Experiential Education. (n.d.). *What is experiential education?* Retrieved from http://www.aee.org/what-is-ee

Atkinson, G., & Murrell, P. H. (1988). Kolb's experiential learning theory: A meta-model for career exploration. *Journal of Counseling & Development, 66,* 374–377. doi:10.1002/j.1556-6676.1988.tb00890.x

Baxter Magolda, M. B. (2001). *Making their own way: Narratives for transforming higher education to promote self-development.* Sterling, VA: Stylus.

Baxter Magolda, M. B. (2014). Self-authorship. *New directions for higher education, 166,* 25–33.

Baxter Magolda, M. B., & King, P. M. (2004). *Learning partnerships: Theory and models of practice to educate for self-authorship.* Sterling, VA: Stylus.

Baxter Magolda, M. B., & King, P. M. (2007). Interview strategies for assessing self-authorship: Constructing conversations to assess meaning making. *Journal of College Student Development, 48,* 491–508.

Chickering, A. W., & Reisser, L. (1993). *Education and identity* (2nd ed.). San Francisco, CA: Jossey-Bass.

Evans, N. J., & Broido, E. M. (1999). Coming out in college residence halls: Negotiation, meaning making, challenges, supports. *Journal of College Student Development, 40,* 658–668.

Evans, N. J., Forney, D. S., & Guido-DiBrito, F. (1998). *Student development in college: Theory, research, and practice.* San Francisco, CA: Jossey-Bass.

Glass, J. S., & Benshoff, J. M. (1999). PARS: A processing model for beginning group leaders. *Journal for Specialists in Group Work, 24,* 15–26.

Goodman, J., Schlossberg, N. K., & Anderson, M. L. (2006). *Counseling adults in transition* (3rd ed.). New York, NY: Springer.

Hill, A. P., & Wilson, R. M. S. (1996). Professional forum: Using the Learning Styles Questionnaire to predict early career success in accounting. *International Journal of Selection and Assessment, 4,* 228–233. doi:10.1111/j.1468-2389.1996.tb00056.x

Jones, S. R., & Stewart, D. L. (2016). Evolution of student development theory. *New Directions for Student Services, 2016,* 17–28.

Kolb, A. Y., & Kolb, D. A. (2005). Learning styles and learning spaces: Enhancing experiential learning in higher education. *Academy of Management Learning & Education, 4,* 193–212. doi:10.5465/amle.2005.17268566

Kolb, D. A. (1984). *Experiential learning: Experience as the source of learning and development.* Englewood Cliffs, NJ: Prentice Hall.

Kolb, D. A., & Boyatzis, R. E. (1970). Goal-setting and self-directed behavior change. *Human Relations, 23,* 439–457.

Kolb, D. A., Boyatzis, R., & Mainemelis, C. (2001). Experiential learning theory: Previous research and new directions. In R. Sternberg & L. Zhang (Eds.), *Perspectives on thinking, learning, and cognitive styles* (pp. 228–247). Mahwah, NJ: Erlbaum.

Komives, S. K., & Dugan, J. P. (2010). Influences on college students' capacities for socially responsible leadership. *Journal of College Student Development, 51,* 525–549. doi:10.1353/csd.2010.0009

Nassar-McMillan, S. C., & Hakim-Larson, J. (2003). Counseling considerations among Arab Americans. *Journal of Counseling & Development, 81,* 150–159. doi:10.1002/j.1556-6678.2003.tb00236.x

Pizzolato, J. E. (2004). Coping with conflict: Self-authorship, coping, and adaptation to college in first-year, high-risk students. *Journal of College Student Development, 45,* 425–442.

Rakes, T. D. (1994). Career outreach on the college campus. *Journal of Career Development, 21,* 155–159.

Sanford, N. (1967). *Where colleges fail: The study of the student as a person.* San Francisco, CA: Jossey-Bass.

Schlossberg, N. K. (2008). *Overwhelmed: Coping with life's ups and downs* (2nd ed.). Lanham, MD: Evans.

Schlossberg, N. K. (2011). The challenge of change: The transition model and its applications. *Journal of Employment Counseling, 48,* 159–162. doi:10.1002/j.2161-1920.2011.tb01102.x

Smith, B. F., & Brackin, R. (2003). Components of a comprehensive orientation program. In J. A. Ward-Roof & C. Hatch (Eds.), *Designing successful transitions: A guide for orienting students to college* (2nd ed., pp. 39–53). Columbia: University of South Carolina, National Resource Center for the First-Year Experience and Students in Transition.

Student Outreach Resource Center. (n.d.). *Service-learning models.* Retrieved from http://source.jhu.edu/publications-and-resources/service-learning-toolkit/service-learning-models.html

Sugarman, L. (1985). Kolb's model of experiential learning: Touchstone for trainers, students, counselors, and clients. *Journal of Counseling & Development, 64,* 264–268. doi:10.1002/j.1556-6676.1985.tb01097.x

Torres, V., & Hernandez, E. (2007). The influence of ethnic identity on self-authorship: A longitudinal study of Latino/a college students. *Journal of College Student Development, 48,* 558–573.

Woosley, S. A. (2003). How important are the first few weeks of college? The long term effects of initial college experiences. *College Student Journal, 37,* 201–208.

Chapter 14

Social Constructivism and Identity in Student Development

Laura M. Gonzalez and Christopher C. Graham

We may not be responsible for the world that created our minds, but we can take responsibility for the mind with which we create our world.

—Gabor Maté, Holocaust survivor, physician, author

■ ■ ■

Reflection Exercise

One young girl is told "You'll never be a doctor—people like you can't do that," and she reluctantly lets go of her dream. Another young girl receives the same message and thinks, "I'll show you what I can and can't do!" Why is this message received so differently? It is because we interact with our environments as human beings in a way that is bidirectional, or allows for us to express our ideas, behaviors, and strengths (agency) and also to be shaped in some ways by the environment around us (influence). This is at the core of social constructivism and is also at the core of the college student experience. In this chapter, we will explore how a social constructivist point of view differs from other student development theories you have studied. We will explore three theories that come from this perspective—social cognitive career theory (SCCT; Lent, Brown, & Hackett, 1994), the multiple dimensions of identity model first described by Jones and McEwen (2000), and the ecological model of multiracial identity development characterized by Renn (2003, 2004). As you read, think about students you may have worked with who have rich and complex social identities, whose realities may not be captured by a unidimensional or static theory of student development. Consider how these theories could help you as a counselor or a support person to engage students more fully around their multilayered realities or to help them construct meaning out of their situations and their identities.

■ ■ ■

As you have seen in the preceding chapters in this part, student development theory is rooted in some foundational work done in the 1960s but has continued to evolve since that time (Jones & Stewart, 2016). Much of the early student development theory, sometimes called "Wave 1," came from a psychological point of view, drawing from studies of individual child, adolescent, or human development with roots in the work of Erik Erikson. A psychological perspective has some important strengths (e.g., an understanding of a person's cognitive processes, social relationships, inner sense of self, and personality profile), but it also may miss an understanding of the context in which all of this development is taking place. Newer student development theories have borrowed more from sociology in an attempt to remedy this imbalance (Jones & Stewart, 2016). Thus, contemporary theories have tried to answer questions such as "How do social structures (family, community, campus, region/country) influence a student's subsequent development," and "In what ways are individualistic theories of psychology too narrow and restrictive to adequately describe today's diverse campus constituents?" In this chapter, we want to advance the argument made by Winkle-Wagner (2012), among others, that the field needs both psychological and sociological points of view to fully describe the development of college students, the importance of their social context, and the influence that individuals and social systems exert on each other.

This is especially important because college students today are demographically much different than they were in the 1960s when Perry, Chickering, Sanford, and Marcia were postulating some early college student development theory (as you have read in the preceding chapters). According to data available from the National Center for Education Statistics (1998), almost 95% of college students in 1960 were White, whereas 58% of college students at public 4-year institutions would describe themselves as White in 2016 (National Center for Education Statistics, 2018). Community colleges are even more diverse, with 24% of students enrolled for credit describing themselves as Latino/a; 13%, African American; 6%, Asian/Pacific Islander; 3%, two or more races; 1%, Native American; 4%, other/unknown, in addition to 47% White students (American Association of Community Colleges, 2018). Indeed, today's college campuses are more diverse not only in terms of race/ethnicity but also in terms of gender and gender identity, ability status, age, sexual orientation, religion, nationality, socioeconomic status, and many other social identity categories (Jones & Stewart, 2016). Community colleges, which have the broadest mission of educational access in the postsecondary arena, enrolled 36% students who were the first in their families to go to college, 17% students who were also single parents, 12% students with disabilities, and 58% students who were receiving some sort of financial aid (American Association of Community Colleges, 2018).

Thus, the earlier psychological theories that described a narrow slice of the individuals who were college students in 1960 (e.g., White, male, middle to upper class, heterosexual) are even less likely to match the lived experiences of today's students. It is important to recognize that students who have experienced oppression and discrimination due to their race, ethnicity, or nationality, for example, also are likely to approach the tasks of identity development differently, or that students with disabilities or students in the lesbian, gay, bisexual, transgender, queer/questioning, intersex, and asexual community, for example, may have different stressors as they seek to develop mature and healthy relationships.

Finally, it is also important to think of college students in a holistic manner that encompasses their race/ethnicity, gender, and socioeconomic class, in addition to other salient aspects of identity and social location (Jones & McEwen, 2000). None of us will wake up tomorrow and say, "Today, I am only my gendered self." As human beings, we simultaneously inhabit all of our identities, so we need theories that can take an integrated view as well. Students who have just failed a class and come to consult with counselors or student affairs personnel will not be displaying only their cognitive processes but they will also be displaying their fears about how this failing grade will affect their relationships, their sense of purpose/autonomy, their worries about their own competence and ability (with some possible stereotype threat or imposter syndrome in the background), and maybe their concerns about continuing to finance their education. We must always seek to view and work with college students in a holistic way that honors all parts of their experience.

Social Constructivism

How does the lens of social constructivism help us with some of these limitations and dilemmas? Social constructivism brings attention to both the individual and the context. As defined by Gergen (1985), this theoretical viewpoint posits that the world is not just an objective "given" but is something we have helped to create by our interactions with each other. Stated more formally, the assumptions of this perspective include (a) that we build our sense of social identity as we interact with others; (b) that we become more complex and adaptive as we develop over time; and (c) that we are the authors and meaning makers of our own experiences, the experts on our own lives (Jones & Stewart, 2016). To restate that more pointedly, we can say that individuals are making sense of their experiences in a way that is consistent with their own worldview and embedded in their lived history, not answering to an external set of standards. For example, the coauthors of this chapter (a fifth-generation European American woman who grew up in the North and an African American man who grew up in the South) have each endeavored to construct their identities in a way that honors their culture and gender, but those pathways to meaning have been distinctly different. We will also think about the ways that Lina Miller (see pages 186–187) has constructed her identity from her lived experiences and interaction with the ecological world in this chapter.

Social constructivism can also include periods of deconstruction, whereby a person resituates his or her learning and identity processes in a space that is supportive and consistent with who he or she is and may reject social influences that are inconsistent with that centered identity. For example, the historical "objective" understanding of gender as binary (male/female) has been deconstructed by queer theorists and human beings whose experience and understanding of their identity is nonbinary (Bilodeau & Renn, 2005). A constructive process is an active process, whereby we negotiate an understanding or interpretation of the world around us. Knowledge or understanding of a situation is not static, but is built between persons (Abes, Jones, & McEwen, 2007). Social constructivism helps us as counselors and student support providers to think about the subjective narrative the student is sharing with us and how that narrative incorporates not only the various aspects of the student's social identities but also the student's understanding of the context or situation in which the student finds himself or herself. It is social in that it is a collaborative process and in that it acknowledges the ways that social systems have influenced the individual (and vice versa). If our student Lina Miller (who failed a test) was a female student in an engineering major, her dilemma would have to be understood both in terms of her individual traits and qualities (e.g., good at math, slightly anxious, unsure of her identity or purpose) and her social environment (e.g., being the first in her family to attend college, seeing all male professors in her classes, working in addition to attending school to help pay her expenses). However, the student herself would be the expert in terms of generating meaning about her current situation and the next steps she wanted to take, with consultation from her adviser.

Social Cognitive Career Theory

If you have taken a career counseling course, you may have learned about SCCT (Lent et al., 1994). SCCT is very different from the older trait and factor theories in that it focuses on a person's learning experiences in social contexts and how those experiences help to form self-efficacy beliefs for tasks related to goals. Through this theory, we seek to understand (a) a person's given abilities and strengths, (b) the supports and barriers in the environment that may help or hinder a person's progress toward a goal, and (c) a person's agency to interact with the environment in a way that is bidirectional (both influencing and being influenced by the environment). In particular, personal agency is understood in terms of individuals' self-efficacy beliefs (i.e., "I am sure I can succeed at this math test"), individuals' outcome expectations (i.e., "When I do pass my math test, I will be on my way to my goal of majoring in accounting"), and individuals' goal-directed behaviors (i.e., "I will study every day and go to tutoring when I need to"). In this way, SCCT provides specific pathways to support student/client success.

For example, if Lina wanted to be a doctor when she grows up, she may have supportive parents who buy her a microscope or help her volunteer at the local hospital (positive learning experiences that bolster self-efficacy beliefs). She may also hear from others that "only boys are doctors," or "science is too hard for you," which would be negative learning experiences that can undermine self-efficacy beliefs. The key is that we, as counselors and student support providers, can continue to construct these experiences for and with our students/clients, and that students can have corrective learning experiences even when they have not been supported for their goal-related behaviors in the past. SCCT (Lent et al., 1994) can help to highlight, for example, the ways in which discrimination and oppression have placed barriers in the way of many individuals who were striving to reach their goals, and the ways that skilled helpers can provide support for those goals or diminish the impact of the barriers. Think of how meaningful it can be for a young student to see a near peer (someone who looks/acts like him or her) who is experiencing success or to have positive and encouraging voices to counteract the biased messages heard in other places. By helping students see models of success and wellness, we give them a map to move in that direction as well (i.e., social learning). This is how SCCT fits into the family of social constructivist theories—it focuses on the way students build their own sense of self-efficacy and meaning and move purposefully toward their own goals, with an acknowledgement of the influences that can emerge in the environment.

Multiple Dimensions of Identity

We now move on to even more contemporary theories in the constructivist family. The study of multiple identities (e.g., race, ethnicity, gender, sexual orientation, age, social class, religion, ability) emerged within multicultural counseling and student affairs in the last several decades and continues to expand rapidly. Consider the Multicultural and Social Justice Counseling competencies (Ratts, Singh, Nassar-McMillan, Butler, & McCullough, 2015) or the American College Personnel Association Strategic Imperative for Racial Justice and Decolonization (http://www.myacpa.org/sirjd), for example. The ways in which college students' many social identities intersect and overlap affect how they show up on colleges' campuses and the services, requests, accommodations, and expectations that come with them. As we have seen with the other theories in this chapter, multiple dimensions of identity are socially constructed, contextual phenomena enacted every day on a college campus (Abes et al., 2007). These multiple dimensions of identity are often at the crux of practice within the contemporary counseling and student affairs community, inspiring action for a more just and inclusive college campus. The waves of student development theory have evolved over time, as you have read, but we must keep interrogating and improving the theories to provide a more holistic view of students with multiple dimensions of identity.

One of the best examples of progress in this field is the model of multiple dimensions of identity, which is the work of Abes, Jones, and McEwen (Abes et al., 2007; Jones & McEwen, 2000). The final model integrates three key elements—a conceptualization of how our many social identities are interrelated, the influence of the context and the messages we are receiving about our social identities, and a meaning-making filter whereby we consider the salience and importance of those identities and how we wish to continue to construct or embody them (see Figure 14.1 for an adapted diagram of the model). Jones and McEwen (2000) first clarified how young adults may be understanding, developing, and navigating their identities along several key dimensions. Through gathering and coding qualitative interview data, they proposed a model that resembles the nucleus of an atom with electrons orbiting around it. The nucleus represents the core of our personal identities—the characteristics and attributes that genuinely make us who we are. The orbiting aspects of our social identities are dimensions that might become more or less salient depending on the circumstances (class, gender, race, ethnicity, religion, sexual orientation, etc.). For example, being the only woman in a meeting could cause gender to feel more salient than it might in an all-female setting like a sorority meeting. Being the only student of color in

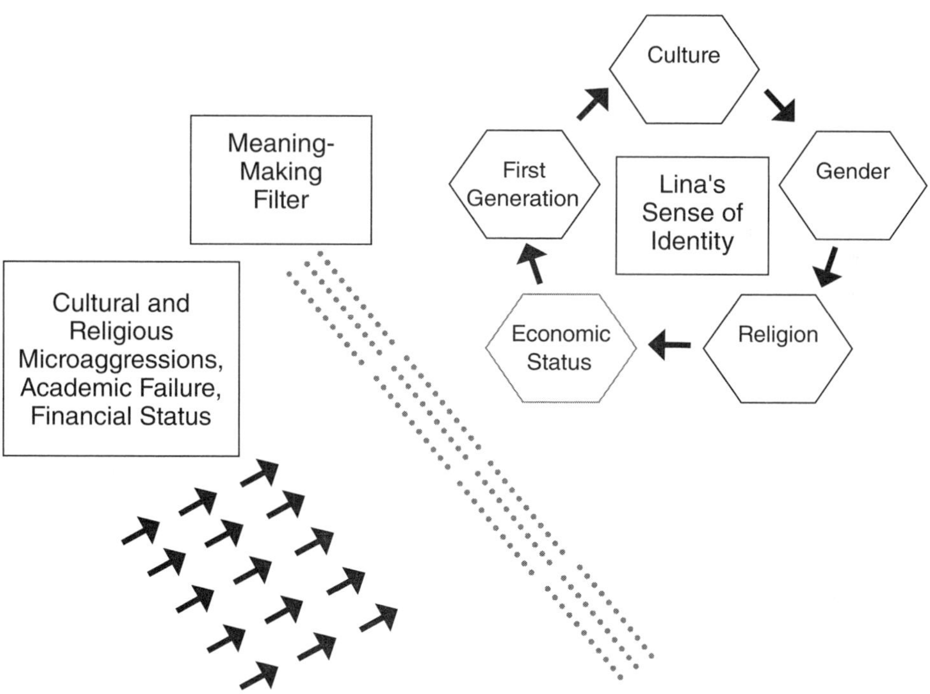

FIGURE 14.1

An Adapted Model of Multiple Dimensions of Identity for Lina

Note. Adapted from Abes, Jones, and McEwen (2007). The arrows indicate social context/social input. The dotted lines indicate the meaning-making filter between social inputs and the individual's core sense of self and multiple social identities.

a class can heighten one's awareness of racial/ethnic identity, or being asked to speak "for your group" can bring salience to that particular aspect of identity. This model also helps us, as counselors and student support providers, to understand how the parts of our identities that match the majority culture may be relatively unexamined—we may not think about our "Whiteness" if we are surrounded by other White people most of the time and are not prompted to think of our race or ethnicity as salient. However, it is clear from the ethics and competency statements of our professional organizations that we need to attend to our self-awareness to serve our student clients more effectively; if our students do not have the privilege to rest in their unexamined identities, then neither do we. It is typical that we "feel" more aware of various aspects of our social identities as we move through our days, experiencing ourselves in comparison with our settings. However, we always embody all of those aspects of our social identities.

A revision of the multiple dimensions of identity theory was completed by Abes et al. (2007). In addition to the nucleus model, the coauthors described the influence of social context more directly, as a set of arrows that were aimed toward the nucleus. Both supportive and destructive social opinions (e.g., arrows) could be aimed at our students by their peers, their families, their professors, the media, and many other sources (see Figure 14.1). Take a moment to think about any messages you may have received that told you that you did or did not belong in college; that you were valued and important; or that you were marginal, unacceptable, or invisible. What sense did you make of that input?

The most important part of the revised model (Abes et al., 2007) was the meaning-making filter that was placed between the arrows (social input) and the nucleus (core sense of self and social identities). Essentially, whether students allow those arrows to pierce them and influence the meaning they make of their own identities depends to a degree on their filtering processes. Students with wide open filters will tend to believe whatever they hear about their group without critically considering the origin or whether it matches other examples they have observed. They may take in negative or destructive comments and incorporate them as they construct their sense of self. Students with more fine-grained filters may question whether a statement seems relevant, true, or helpful to them before deciding to admit the statement or discard it. Thus, we can help college students think more critically about how they filter or interpret influences to maintain a positive process as they construct their own identity.

For example, in one study, Mexican American male college students provided perspective on how their working-class family backgrounds influenced their feelings of belonging and experiences on campus (Schwartz, Donovan, & Guido-DiBrito, 2009). The participants in this study shared how salient perceived differences in economic class were to them from the moment they stepped onto campus, in that they immediately felt a chasm between themselves and their peers with greater wealth. Social class also provided a strong level of motivation to these students, as a way to tie their college experience to a larger purpose for their families and communities. In particular, the students articulated how their male gender roles made it salient to them to complete a degree and be able to provide for family in the future. Finally, the participants in the study also identified at least one person on campus whom they could trust to help them decode the norms of middle-class or upper class America, thus learning how to present themselves on campus in a way that was more likely to be accepted. Their cultural identities and values were unchanged by the experience, but they learned a new set of habits that would help them adapt.

In a parallel example, Lina Miller is simultaneously a first-generation college student, a woman, a bicultural young adult with blended religious and ethnic traditions, someone who may be difficult to categorize with traditional racial labels, a student from a middle to lower socioeconomic background, and much more (see Figure 14.1). Per the multiple dimensions of identity theory (Abes et al., 2007), all of these aspects of her social identity may come in and out of salience, depending on the setting and tasks at hand, but they are all a part of Lina's identity, and she cannot be understood effectively as less than her whole self. Part of the challenge of the transition to college is that her setting and the tasks at hand have changed dramatically, so the contextual influences from peers and faculty are new, as are the norms and tasks of college life. Thus, the environmental messages that Lina is receiving about her multiple identity dimensions have likely changed as well, and not for the better. The power of understanding Lina's dilemma through this theoretical lens, however, is that it helps explain the overwhelmed feelings she is having by accounting for all of the identity-based stressors and microaggressions she is experiencing (see Figure 14.1).

At the same time, the model helps college counselors and student development staff to think about how Lina is making meaning out of these inputs and how she could be supported in that constructivist process. Right now, Lina seems to be letting all of the negative influences (i.e., arrows) through her meaning-making filter and questioning whether it is possible for her to even be at college as a result. One could imagine exploring with Lina the possibility that her roommate's opinion of her is not the only one that matters and encouraging her to identify a niche in the campus community where she could experience support and belonging. Lina could also be reminded that if she is feeling alienated on the topic of perceived religious identity, she could try to connect around a different identity dimension, finding common ground with other children of military service members or other first-generation college students. She could try to find allies in her calculus class to shift her meaning making around that difficult weed-out class from "impossible" to "challenging, but manageable with help."

Thus, the multiple dimensions of identity model (Abes et al., 2007) is a better fit than the older Wave 1 theories for complex social realities such as Lina's. It makes space for our many intersecting identities, helping us think more holistically and adaptively about today's college students. It also helps us consider the role of context and environment, which may or may not feel fully supportive to students and can be important to name. Finally, it suggests that we can intervene by helping students with their meaning-making process, which may mean changing their filter to screen out harmful input or refocusing them on their strengths and assets.

Multiracial and Multiethnic Identity Processes

We now turn to a particular subset of multiple identities, which pertain to students from multiple heritage or racially and culturally blended families. Some of the terms you may hear people use to describe these identities include *biracial* (involving the combination of two or more racial groups), *interracial* or *multiracial* (involving two or more groups), *multiple heritage* (including many cultures, ethnicities, or national origins as well as multiple races), *mixed race*, or *multiethnic* (Paladino, Rodriguez, & Long, 2018). The U.S. Census Bureau recognizes five racial categories currently (White, Black, Asian, Hawaiian/Pacific Islander, and Native American/Alaskan; Pew Research Center, 2015) and only permitted respondents to select multiple races starting with the 2000 census form. Thus, we do not have a long history of data to draw from, but it is estimated that there were over 9 million multiracial individuals in the United States as of 2010, including 7% to 10% of current college students who self-identify with these terms (Pew Research Center, 2015).

To clarify, we note that racial categories are social constructions themselves but have been used for many years in this country to describe or separate people. Ethnicity is related to culture, so there can be people who consider themselves to be Latina/o culturally, for example, but are also White, Black, Asian, or Native in terms of racial categories. Think of

Sammy Sosa, Pitbull, Sonia Sotomayor, Zoe Saldana, Rigoberta Menchú, George Lopez, Roberto Clemente, and Alberto Fujimori for some examples. Thus, multiracial or multiethnic combinations are various, going beyond the Black-White dynamic that has been historically prevalent in the United States.

Older theories about developing racial or ethnic identities (which typically considered students in a binary of majority- or minority-group members) do not fully express the identity processes of multiple heritage students. Indeed, rather than focusing on a linear process of "becoming" one's racial/ethnic identity amid culturally racist biases (e.g., Cross, 1995; Helms, 1995), more contemporary theories suggest a strengths-based and integrative view of being multiracial (e.g., Poston, 1990; Root, 1990) and then a focus on the ecological systems that surround the student (Renn, 2000). What are the patterns of how multiple-heritage individuals identify, given that those patterns may not be the same across all circumstances? For example, who is Lina Miller (or how does she describe herself) when she is at home with her mother participating in Iraqi traditions? Who is she when she is with her father or on her predominantly White college campus? Which aspects of her identity will feel most salient to her as she starts to make friends in this new environment? Each context of Lina's life will most likely draw out aspects of her multiple identities, and a fluid process for constructing and understanding that sense of identity is normative and healthy.

In today's world, more and more college students are coming from blended families, in which the racial/ethnic/cultural heritages of their parents are varied (Paladino & Davis, 2006). In counseling and educational literature about multiracial college students (Paladino & Davis, 2006; Renn, 2003, 2004; Root, 1994), several themes have emerged over time. In general, those include a sense of uniqueness, the challenge of formulating identity and then finding acceptance and belonging, and questions related to physical appearance and identity. We will spend some time describing each of these themes further.

In the most optimistic view, every human being is unique and those differences should be celebrated for how they enrich our world. However, in the daily lives of multiracial or multiethnic children, adolescents, and young adults, coming to understand and value the unique contributions of their racial and cultural backgrounds amid a society that wants to put them in one little checkbox can be a trial. Youth are still developing in many of the ways we have described in this book, so it is not always easy for them to feel comfortable and confident in their own skins while they are still forming a sense of identity. Multiple heritage children often have the experience of being asked "What are you?" or "Why don't you look like your parent?" Such microaggressions can make an individual feel like an oddity, rather than a beautiful example of unique cultural heritage, and can generate a sense of defensiveness or inadequacy (Henriksen & Paladino, 2009). They may also emphasize for a multiple heritage child the ways in which he or she is dissimilar from others or cause feelings of isolation and being misunderstood. However, it is also true that multiple heritage youth have the flexibility to participate in more than one culture, to appreciate the variety of traditions and experiences that are present in their families, and to be more culturally skilled and open to exchanges with other groups (Henriksen & Paladino, 2009). Their lives can be strengthened by their additional cultural heritages.

A part of the difference between feeling isolated and appreciating the strengths of a multiple heritage background is the process of formulating a strong and healthy identity and thus generating self-acceptance (Henriksen & Paladino, 2009). This process can be complicated, depending on the context, and can shift and change as individuals move throughout periods of transition in their lives (e.g., from high school to college, from college to work, from old friend groups to new ones). Because multiple heritage students are faced with a more complicated set of variables for identity construction, it is not uncommon for them to experience some sense of identity confusion, microaggressions from several quarters, difficult social interactions, and the pressure to choose one heritage culture over another (Paladino et al., 2018). Counselors and student support staff must not only be aware of these possibilities as they interact with multiracial and multiethnic students but also must listen carefully for each student's own needs and experiences. Rather than following a formula for accepting one's identity, multiple heritage youth may follow a more individual and fluid pattern. For example, a student may have grown up around her mother's family and their culture and may only have come to know her father's family and their culture later in life. One model, the multiple heritage identity development model (Henriksen & Paladino, 2009), suggests a flexible progression through six periods, including (a) neutrality, or lack of awareness of differences; (b) acceptance, or recognition of basic differences among people; (c) awareness of multiple heritages and identities; (d) experimentation regarding which group identity seems most fitting; (e) transition to a more internal definition of identity; and (f) recognition of what it means to identify with all of one's multiple heritages.

Depending on the particulars of the multiple heritages, individuals may physically resemble members of the majority racial/ethnic culture in their area, or they may trigger the stereotypes of "other" and be targets of microaggressions. Renn (2003) postulated that physical appearance has a strong influence on how students identify themselves and how others identify them, so this outward appearance may be internalized in important ways. It can also expose multiple-heritage youth to race-based discrimination and bias. We have not described what Lina's physical appearance might be like in this book, but each of you can imagine how her skin tone, eye and hair color, and other physical features may influence which groups on campus offer her acceptance ("You seem like one of us!") or rejection. Most likely, she heard comments growing up about which parent she looked like or which groups people guessed she belonged to, which could have molded how she started to make meaning of her own identity. Renn also affirmed that cultural knowledge or exposure to one's heritage communities helps a student feel legitimate or fit in with that group, regardless of what their physical features may communicate. For college students in particular, the cultural context of peers on the college campus can support or work against multiracial students' identity development as well.

For example, a student such as Lina, with one immigrant parent, who is growing up with little to no contact with that cultural heritage group, will know more about and feel more comfort in the heritage group that typifies his or her growing-up experience (in this case, the U.S. White culture of Lina's father and her home community in California). So, although Lina's roommate has been telling other students that Lina is from the Middle East, Lina does not have a deep or consistent exposure to her Iraqi heritage community. How then will she construct her sense of identity as a multiple heritage individual at the predominantly White institution where she has enrolled?

One way for Lina to start would be to explore the context to see where she can find a social niche to meet her belonging needs on campus (e.g., a classroom, a residence hall, a student organization, a friend group). Her interactions with those campus environments and the level of acceptance she finds will help to shape her sense of identity, potentially. Campus climate for students of color or multiracial students can be critically important in this process, especially given the potential for social isolation and microaggressions from more than one source. It is important to note that these interactions with peers will not determine Lina's identity but will have influence over which parts are encouraged, which parts feel most salient, and which parts are de-emphasized while she is enacting her student role.

Summarizing Lina: A Review and Integration

This will be the last chapter in which Lina's case is discussed, so we invite you to take a moment to reflect—which theoretical perspectives were most helpful to you in understanding Lina's adjustment challenges or providing a strategy to support her? We have covered neuro-informed counseling, psychosocial theories, cognitive/moral development, experiential theories, and social constructivism. Which perspectives addressed some of her concerns versus all of her concerns? The theories discussed in this chapter are perhaps the most holistic, but you can also think of ways to combine several theories in your work with college students. For example, you might opt to use cognitive theories to evaluate Lina's structural reasoning around her dilemmas but also include the multiple dimensions of identity model as a way to view her social situation in context and help her consider how her environment is influencing her meaning-making processes. In addition, hold Lina in your mind as you read Part IV, "Clinical Issues in the College Context." How might you work with Lina if she is living with any of the clinical issues that are being discussed, and what theory or theories are important for outreach, consultation, and clinical work?

Critique and Future Directions

In many ways, social constructivism represents a more adaptive theoretical stance than early theories from which to think about and work with college students in many social identity categories. It includes both student and environment, it allows for flexible learning and change, it focuses on the students' choices and agency, and it is holistic. However, there are still criticisms of social constructivism that are valid and should be given due consideration (Jones & Stewart, 2016). One key problem is that students with socially stigmatized identities may very well be interacting with negative reflections of themselves in the "social mirror" and thus constructing their identities in ways that include introjected racism, sexism, heterosexism, ableism, and so forth. Unless they have a guide to socialize them and help them separate their healthy sense of self from the hate speech and stereotypes (i.e., deconstructing before constructing), younger students could internalize these biased beliefs about who they are, what they are capable of doing, and how they are valued by those around them.

Critical theorists point out that oppressive "isms" are all around us and that we must assume all social structures (including 2- and 4-year colleges and universities) are built upon these damaging belief systems and must be interrogated (Jones & Stewart, 2016). These theorists would question whether a student from a marginalized group could have a positive experience (healthy, productive) in an educational structure that is oppressive at its foundations, which is an important question for counselors and support staff to wrestle with. As Abes (2012) eloquently stated, constructivism "only reveals how [students] make sense of their identities within the structures rather than challenging the structures" (p. 188). This is a call to advocacy for those in helping professions.

A second problem is that identity construction or development may differ from identity expression. Students who belong to marginalized social identity groups have had to learn to code switch, to express their genuine selves in contexts in which it is safe to do so and to express a more socially approved identity in spaces where their genuine selves may not be welcomed (Guiffrida, 2003). For example, if a particular campus allows homophobic incidents to occur without addressing them publicly or moving to stop them, would lesbian, gay, bisexual, transgender, queer/questioning, intersex, and asexual students feel that they have the agency to act freely and express themselves genuinely in all campus spaces? When we also consider the multiple identities model, we know that students simultaneously can be representatives of marginalized groups and privileged groups (Jones, 2009). Thus, they must learn to interpret campus spaces for safety or belonging along many vectors of identity.

There are many ways that student development theory is continuing to adapt and become a better lens for considering college students. Some of the newer theories have a more critical lens on reality, underscoring the ways that power and privilege are salient features of our context in higher education (Jones & Stewart, 2016). Intersectionality theory, for example, focuses our attention not on the individual student primarily, but on the systems of power that constrain or oppress them because of racial identity, ethnic/cultural identity, gender identity, sexual orientation, socioeconomic status, and many other intersecting social systems (Crenshaw, 1994/2005). How would our daily practice look different if we asked ourselves how we could transform unequal social systems on campus rather than try to meet one student's needs? We continue to strive to improve our theory, our conceptualization, and our practice.

For example, Baxter Magolda's description of self-authorship was reviewed in Chapter 13. As a way to update the theory, Torres and Hernandez (2007) asked a group of Latino/a college students to reflect over time on their holistic development, which paralleled the journey toward self-authorship. However, the authors noted that "In addition to having the same developmental characteristics as the majority White students in Baxter Magolda's study, the Latino/a students in this study had additional developmental tasks that are not included in the study of all White students" (p. 561). Torres and Hernandez highlighted how intrapersonal development ("Who am I?") revolved around a different set of questions for their Latino/a participants, as they sought to resolve both positive and negative images of their group portrayed in the world and how interpersonal development included solidifying one's ethnic identity to relate effectively and interdependently with other groups on campus. This point cannot be overemphasized—students with minoritized identities will often be doing the basic or normative developmental work appropriate to their age and stage and will have another set of tasks that are unique to their social identities and uncharted by previous theories.

Thus, if we, as counselors and student support providers, are to update our knowledge and permit a constructivist orientation, we will need to build a new set of understandings about how college students approach their cognitive tasks, their interpersonal tasks, and their intrapersonal development. We ask each of you to take a moment to consider a theory of development or counseling that has made sense to you and then consider how it might need to be updated to include pathways or constructs relevant to minoritized social identities. What new questions might you need to ask to elicit new knowledge from students, or how might you need to tune your ear differently to hear their answers if they are not part of your theory map?

Approaches to Practice

How could college counselors use these theories to guide their thinking and practice more effectively with today's college students? How might student support staff in other offices contribute to the network of support, especially if there is any stigma for students about going to counseling but willingness to seek help in other places? Do we know if there are students on our campuses who may not feel 100% comfortable presenting for services because of an aspect of their social identities? Are we aware of the culturally grounded attitudes and beliefs held by various groups on our campus, or how our own attitudes and beliefs may intersect with them? These questions compel us to consider all the identities students may have, both visible and invisible. This translation to practice is incredibly challenging, yet important in today's college environment. A commitment to social justice means developing a systemic approach to meeting all students where they are; developing relationships to deepen knowledge about them; designing the campus in a way that puts their needs at the center; and developing programs and services to ensure that all students, regardless of identity, have a space and staff to support them. This is no easy task but is necessary to the emotional, physical, and cognitive development of students.

In some cases, students may need a listening ear to reflect back their concerns and help them with the meaning-making process, as discussed in the Multiple Dimensions of Identity section (i.e., helping skills). In some cases, they may benefit from our knowledge of campus resources and networks, to assist them in finding social support and connection, in relieving some of their stressors, or in challenging the inequities that are presenting barriers to their progress (i.e., systems-level advocacy actions). In some cases, students are looking for new skills, such as the ability to code switch in a new context, the ability to form a healthy sense of self in an oppressive environment, or the ability to engage in meaningful dialogue across differences (Nagda & Zúñiga, 2003).

Most important, sometimes students need an advocate to help them navigate the systems of the university. Ask yourself how welcoming the campus climate is where you are in regard to a variety of social identities—what would it feel like to exist there as a multiracial student, a student with a disability, a student from a low-income family? Even better, rather than only imagining, ask someone for whom that is the daily reality, and then think carefully about how you could work in partnership with that student to create more visibility, more access, and more acceptance. What norms or policies would have to change, what symbols could be taken down and replaced, and what barriers could be removed? We cannot view our mission as only working within the therapeutic relationship (e.g., by supporting students using our helping skills)—we must consider ourselves as part of the institution and work to generate a healthier environment where all students can thrive (e.g., by engaging in advocacy actions).

We do have models to learn from in our advocacy efforts—students who embody these complex and intersecting identities are no longer just settling for a small room near the back of the student union or on the periphery of campus. They are literally standing up and protesting with lists of demands. They desire and seek acceptance and inclusion into the fabric of the institution. Not only do they want to see faculty and staff who look like them but they also are demanding the removal of signs and symbols that recall a previous time when their group may not have been welcome on campus. We have seen these protests recently at the University of Missouri; the University of California, Berkeley; the University of North Carolina at Chapel Hill; and many more. These examples of activism are helping campus-based professionals stay in touch with the needs and realities of 21st-century student lives, so we need to turn our active listening skills toward student protesters as well as toward our individual clients. That is to say, the students are helping our profession to develop the awareness we need to do this work, but it is up to us to address our knowledge base and develop appropriate skills to work with students who have multiple and layered identities. It is important to assess when appropriate self-awareness of our attitudes/beliefs, knowledge, and skills are present and when they are missing across the divisions of student affairs and counseling services that are designed to support and enhance the student experience. We also need to be mindful of our actions and to try to align them with our attitudes, knowledge, and skills in this area.

Conclusion

We hope this chapter has helped you think about social constructivism as a way to acknowledge the context of college students and also their agency and ability to make meaning about that context. We started with the assumption that the foundational or Wave 1 theories of student development were written in the 1960s, when social identities of students were not central to the theory in any meaningful way. Thus, to update our knowledge of student development, one critical step is to bring race/ethnicity, gender and gender identity, ability status, age, sexual orientation, religion, nationality, socioeconomic status, and other identities back into the picture to interrogate the original frameworks. From the perspective of SCCT (Lent et al., 1994), we can think about both the supports and the barriers that might exist in the present campus context as well as the previous home context. From the perspective of the model of multiple dimensions of identity (Abes et al., 2007), we can look at the messages that students are receiving from their contexts and how they might be making meaning from those inputs as they consider the multiple aspects of their own identities. Finally, thinking about models for multiracial and multiethnic student development reminds us that students are complex and nonbinary, and that who they are in context is something that can shift through time, acquiring more or less salience. However, in all of these models, students are constructing their lives, making sense of themselves and the world around them, and actively choosing how to be.

We hope that you, as future practitioners, will spend time thinking about the campus influences (context) and meaning-making filter (process) of the students you will see every day. For contextual influences, this means looking at their peers; residence living; stereotypes that the campus presents, both spoken and unspoken; sociopolitical conditions on campus and in society; and institutional efforts to engage or involve students. As it relates to the meaning-making filter, this endeavor will require a deep analysis of involvement, community, or agency that students develop, as well as campus programming, both in the academic and student affairs realms of campus. Oftentimes students create community in physical, emotional, academic, and living spaces that are intentional on their part but unintentional on the part of the campus. In the true sense of constructivism, such agency should be honored when it creates a healthy outlet for development. We encourage you to continue to explore social constructivism more generally (e.g., McAuliffe & Eriksen, 1999; Sexton & Griffin, 1997), as a stance to approach your future work with students in a way that honors their subjective experience of themselves, is flexible enough to incorporate multiple or intersecting identities, provides tools to help students construct more adaptive meaning in their worlds, and reduces the gap between yesterday's theories and today's college students.

Final Case Study

Rafael is a community college transfer student who is just starting his studies at the 4-year college where you work. As you interact with him during new student orientation, you ask about the hat he is wearing that says "Canto Construction Company." You learn this is his father's business, where Rafa has also worked during high school and throughout his time at the community college. He is proud of the ways he was able to support his family, and also worried about how they will get along now that he is farther away at college.

Rafa mentions that his parents grew up in El Salvador and are still more comfortable communicating in Spanish, so, while growing up, he was a key translator between them and the English-speaking world. Rafa tells you with a quiet sense of pride about his daily schedule of getting up at 5:00 a.m. to be ready to go to a work site with his father's crew, putting in 6 hours before lunch, and then coming home to change and make it to classes in the afternoon and evening. You admire his dedication and work ethic. You also wonder when he had time to study or utilize support services if he needed them. You are thinking about how best to support Rafa's transition to your campus, on the basis of the limited information you have about his goals, his identities, and how he might be received within this particular campus climate.

Case Exploration Questions

1. How would you describe some of the multilayered identities that Rafa embodies?
2. What are the supports and barriers that may have been present in Rafa's home and community college environment? How might that affect his transition to a 4-year college?
3. How has Rafa demonstrated his agency in moving toward his educational goals?
4. How might you learn more about his meaning-making filter in his past environments as you try to help him find a space for connection and belonging at this campus? What are the messages you are aware of for students from immigrant families on your campus?

References

Abes, E. S. (2012). Constructivist and intersectional interpretations of a lesbian college student's multiple social identities. *The Journal of Higher Education, 83,* 186–216.

Abes, E. S., Jones, S. R., & McEwen, M. K. (2007). Reconceptualizing the model of multiple dimensions of identity: The role of meaning-making capacity in the construction of multiple identities. *Journal of College Student Development, 48,* 1–22.

American Association of Community Colleges. (2018). Fast Facts 2018. Retrieved from https://www.aacc.nche.edu/wp-content/uploads/2018/04/2018-Fast-Facts.pdf

Bilodeau, B. L., & Renn, K. A. (2005). Analysis of LGBT identity development models and implications for practice. *New Directions for Student Services, 2005,* 25–39.

Crenshaw, K. W. (1994/2005). Mapping the margins: Intersectionality, identity politics, and violence against women of color. In M. A. Fineman & R. Mykitiuk (Eds.), *The public nature of private violence* (pp. 93–118). New York, NY: Routledge.

Cross, W. E., Jr. (1995). The psychology of Nigrescence: Revising the Cross model. In J. G. Ponterotto, J. M. Casas, L. A. Suzuki, & C. M. Alexander (Eds.), *Handbook of multicultural counseling* (pp. 93–122). Thousand Oaks, CA: Sage.

Gergen, K. J. (1985). The social constructionist movement in modern psychology. *American Psychologist, 40,* 266–275.

Guiffrida, D. A. (2003). African American student organizations as agents of social integration. *Journal of College Student Development, 44,* 304–319.

Helms, J. E. (1995). An update of Helm's White and people of color racial identity models. In J. G. Ponterotto, J. M. Casas, L. A. Suzuki, & C. M. Alexander (Eds.), *Handbook of multicultural counseling* (pp. 181–198). Thousand Oaks, CA: Sage.

Henriksen, R. C., Jr., & Paladino, D. A. (2009). *Counseling multiple heritage individuals, couples, and families.* Alexandria, VA: American Counseling Association.

Jones, S. R. (2009). Constructing identities at the intersections: An autoethnographic exploration of multiple dimensions of identity. *Journal of College Student Development, 50,* 287–304.

Jones, S. R., & McEwen, M. K. (2000). A conceptual model of multiple dimensions of identity. *Journal of College Student Development, 41,* 405–414.

Jones, S. R., & Stewart, D. L. (2016). Evolution of student development theory. *New Directions for Student Services, 154,* 17–28.

Lent, R. W., Brown, S. D., & Hackett, G. (1994). Toward a unifying social cognitive theory of career and academic interest, choice, and performance. *Journal of Vocational Behavior, 45,* 79–122.

McAuliffe, G. J., & Eriksen, K. P. (1999). Toward a constructivist and developmental identity for the counseling profession: The context-phase-stage-style model. *Journal of Counseling & Development, 77,* 267–280. doi:10.1002/j.1556-6676.1999.tb02450.x

Nagda, B. A., & Zúñiga, X. (2003). Fostering meaningful racial engagement through intergroup dialogues. *Group Processes and Intergroup Relations, 6,* 111–128.

National Center for Education Statistics. (1998). College enrollment rates of high school graduates, by race/ethnicity: 1960–1997. Retrieved from https://nces.ed.gov/programs/digest/d98/d98t183.asp

National Center for Education Statistics. (2018). *The condition of education.* Retrieved from https://nces.ed.gov/programs/coe/index.asp

Paladino, D. A., & Davis, H., Jr. (2006). Counseling and outreach strategies for assisting multiracial college students. *Journal of College Student Psychotherapy, 20,* 19–31.

Paladino, D. A., Rodriguez, E., & Long, P. (2018, February). *Counseling and advocacy with multiracial clients.* Presentation at the Cross-Cultural Counseling and Education Conference for Research, Action, and Change, Savannah, GA.

Pew Research Center. (2015). *Multiracial in America: Proud, diverse, and growing in numbers.* Retrieved from http://www.pewsocialtrends.org/2015/06/11/multiracial-in-america/

Poston, W. S. C. (1990). The biracial identity development model: A needed addition. *Journal of Counseling & Development, 69,* 152–155. doi:10.1002/j.1556-6676.1990.tb01477.x

Ratts, M. J., Singh, A. A., Nassar-McMillan, S., Butler, S. K., & McCullough, J. R. (2015). *Multicultural and social justice counseling competencies.* Retrieved from http://www.counseling.org/docs/default-source/competencies/multicultural-and-social-justice-counseling-competencies.pdf?sfvrsn=20

Renn, K. A. (2000). Patterns of situational identity among biracial and multiracial college students. *The Review of Higher Education, 23,* 399–420.

Renn, K. A. (2003). Understanding the identities of mixed race college students through a developmental ecology lens. *Journal of College Student Development, 44,* 383–403.

Renn, K. A. (2004). *Mixed race students in college: The ecology of race, identity, and community on campus.* Albany: State University of New York Press.

Root, M. P. P. (1990). Resolving "other" status: Identity development of biracial individuals. In L. S. Brown & M. P. P. Root (Eds.), *Diversity and complexity in feminist therapy* (pp. 185–205). New York, NY: Haworth Press.

Root, M. P. P. (1994). Mixed-race women. In L. Comez-Diaz & B. Green (Eds.), *Women of color: Integrating ethnic and gender identities in psychotherapy* (pp. 455–478). New York, NY: Guilford Press.

Schwartz, J. L., Donovan, J., & Guido-DiBrito, F. (2009). Stories of social class: Self-identified Mexican male college students crack the silence. *Journal of College Student Development, 50,* 50–66.

Sexton, T. L., & Griffin, B. L. (1997). *Constructivist thinking in counseling practice, research, and training.* New York, NY: Teachers College Press.

Torres, V., & Hernandez, E. (2007). The influence of ethnic identity on self-authorship: A longitudinal study of Latino/a college students. *Journal of College Student Development, 48,* 558–573.

Winkle-Wagner, R. (2012). Self, college experiences, and society: Rethinking the theoretical foundations of student development theory. *College Student Affairs Journal, 30,* 45–60.

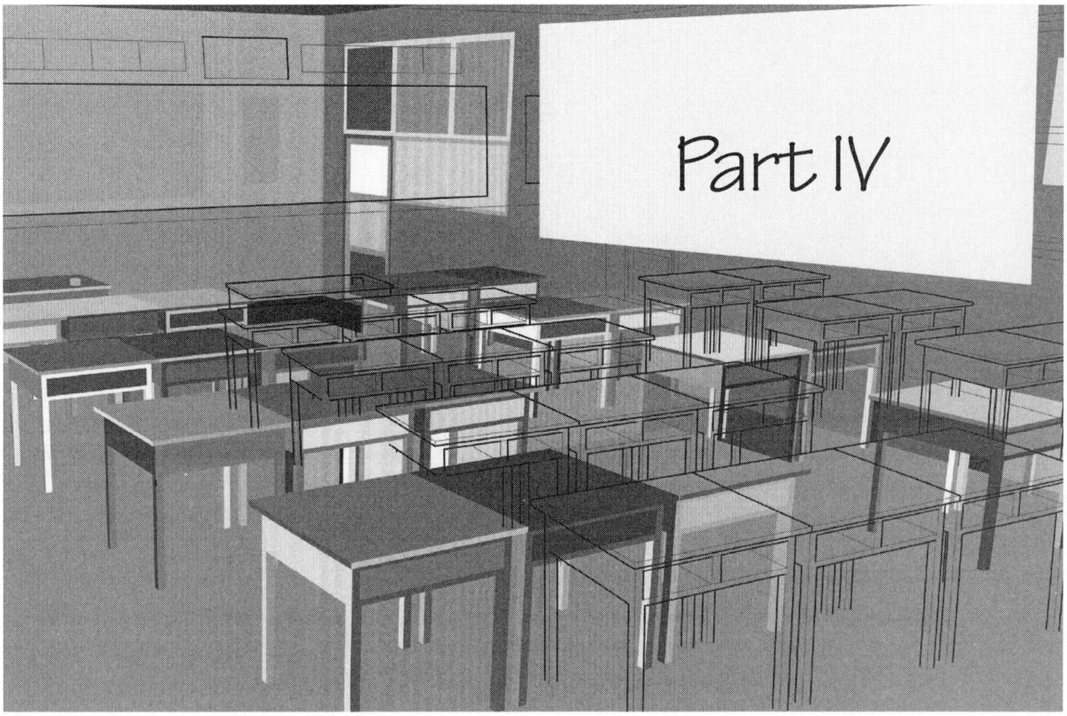

Clinical Issues in the College Context

Chapter 15

Family and Relationships

Lesley Casarez, Amy Murphy, and Brian Van Brunt

I also believe that parents, if they love you, will hold you up safely, above their swirling waters, and sometimes that means you'll never know what they endured, and you may treat them unkindly, in a way you otherwise wouldn't.

—Mitch Albom, *For One More Day*

■ ■ ■

Reflection Exercise

Think for a moment about your relationships during college.

1. What relationships were helpful and supportive of your college goals?
2. What relationships created obstacles and difficulties for you?
3. What role did friends and family play in your college experience?
4. How did your relationships shift and change over the course of your time in college?

The most successful people, the happiest and often healthiest among one's friends, students, patients, and colleagues, have invested in rich and deep social connections with others. Whether this be through their given families or chosen ones, formal or informal social networks, individuals are more supported, successful, resilient, and prosperous when they are able to connect and learn with others, reach beyond themselves for help, and offer themselves as assistance for others (Berkman, Glass, Brissette, & Seeman, 2000; Kuh, Kinzie, Schuh, & Whitt, 2005; Layard, 2005). This chapter explores the various types of relationships important to college students and the prevalence of relationship issues occurring during the college experience. From parents, guardians, and family members to peers, friends, and roommates to romantic partners, and finally to professors and staff, each type of relationship and its influence on students are examined. We also discuss the growing implications of social media for relationships and consider how relationships intersect with other issues of student development. We end the chapter with a review of clinical, outreach, and prevention implications.

■ ■ ■

Individuals experience a rich tapestry of relationships. Friends, romantic partners, early childhood relationships, mentors, health care providers and therapists, and college faculty and staff can all play a part in this tapestry. There is no set formula for which relationships are essential for any given individual, but rather there is an awareness that college students are more successful in their social, academic, and psychological development when they are able to lean on others for support in an interdependent way (Chickering & Reisser, 1993). Cultivating positive and diverse relationships in their educational environment also contributes to students spending time and energy being academically engaged (Kuh et al., 2005).

Although relationships can be helpful for college students, there are also some cautions. Relationships should feel supportive, offer a sense of balance and equanimity, and not be exploitative as described in more detail in Chickering and Reisser's (1993) vector of "developing mature interpersonal relationships" (p. 145). Relationships may be challenging on occasion, but they should never be abusive or exploit power differentials. Whether the relationships be with friends, family, peers, professors, student affairs staff, health care providers, therapists, or clergy, they should be caring, be encouraging, and inspire hope and growth. Although there are many types of relationships a college student can benefit from, it is critical these relationships be healthy and uplifting.

We have included three case examples at the start to the chapter to help the reader better understand some of the range of relationship events counseling staff may be called in to assist with on campus. In reading these case examples, ask yourself how you would describe the strengths and weaknesses of how each of these students is trying to forge relationships on campus. We will return to these cases throughout this chapter.

Case Examples

The Case of Arty

Arty is a freshman from a larger city attending a smaller college campus. Arty was very involved in high school theater, was the president of the gay-straight alliance, and was an outspoken advocate on social justice issues. During his first weeks at school, he has had several intimate sexual relationships with other students, and he has often been in the dean's office discussing changes that need to be made on the campus related to accessible bathrooms and the combating of microaggressions. He has signed up for leadership on the gay-straight alliance and Black Lives Matter, has talked to his sociology professor about becoming a Safe Zone trainer (http://thesafezoneproject.com/), and stays late talking to his professor about drafting plans for a new club on campus to push forward more social justice and advocacy ideas.

The Case of Tessa

Tessa is a second-semester junior who has trouble making friends. She struggles with depression and sees a therapist at the counseling center. Her depression significantly worsens when her boyfriend, Jacob, breaks up with her suddenly, stating, "I just can't see myself with you. You are sad all the time." Tessa doesn't have many friends, and her therapist worries about her suicidality being so bad that she might need to be hospitalized. Tessa is falling behind in her classes and comes to the attention of the Behavioral Intervention Team.

The Case of Dexter

Dexter would be the first to tell you that he lives his life on the computer. He is very much into his social media platforms and often responds to people in a snarky and abrupt manner. He would estimate he is online at least 8 hours a night. He frequently communicates in memes and "trolls" other students to get a reaction. He has few friends on campus. In one of his posts, he makes a veiled threat against another student in his class. This student makes a report to the campus Behavioral Intervention Team, and Dexter is required to complete a threat assessment within the Counseling and Psychological Services Center.

■ ■ ■

Prevalence of Family and Relationship Issues for College Students

Connections, social support, belonging, and acceptance are seen as basic human needs, drivers of attitudes and behaviors, and critical contributors to college students' success (Strayhorn, 2019). A study of the current generation of college students confirms that Generation Z students are motivated by relationships in their learning, career, and future opportunities (Seemiller, 2017). These relationships can be with family and friends, faculty and staff, or others in the campus community. Although cultural factors, generational differences, and other background characteristics influence students' experiences at home and in educational environments, the need for a sense of belonging remains a common element important to student success. This sense of belonging is driven by social supports, connection, acceptance, respect, and the experience of being valued and feeling important to the campus community (Strayhorn, 2019).

In a similar form, when relationship or family concerns arise, students can find themselves lost and confused. Issues of loneliness and homesickness have emerged as critical concerns for college students that can relate to more complex issues of psychological adjustment, depression, and suicide (Centers for Disease Control and Prevention, n.d.; Chang et al., 2017). Students may find themselves in the company of their cell phone more often than that of friends or family and may be unable to find connections in their new college environment. When romantic relationships turn unhealthy and abusive, students can feel additional isolation and seclusion, which can be the beginning of a pattern of escalating violent behaviors (Murphy & Van Brunt, 2017). Also, as distance education and online learning grow at greater rates than traditional college enrollment (Allen & Seaman, 2013), the impact on student-faculty interaction and engagement has not been positive. In fact, some reports indicate disproportionate negative impacts for students in lower socioeconomic groups (Protopsaltis & Baum, 2019). Students like Dexter (introduced in our case studies) can find the consistency and anonymity of the online environment to be more comfortable than face-to-face interactions, which may affect his ability to form and sustain relationships outside of the online environment.

Relationships also shape college student attitudes and behaviors in a variety of areas. Student perceptions of their peers, family, and even college staff relate to how they view the college environment. The power of social norms, a student's perception of normal attitudes and behaviors around them, highlights the influence of group and peer relationships on many students' beliefs about themselves and others (Cialdini, Kallgren, & Reno, 1991). Peers and family, for example, influence a college student's understanding of alcohol and substance use as well as sexual relationships. Students are less likely to binge drink or abstain from alcohol use if parents discussed alcohol use and its consequences early in the college experience (National Institute on Alcohol Abuse and Alcoholism, n.d.). Research also highlights the power of group relationships. For example, members of all-male fraternities or athletic organizations have comparatively less healthy attitudes about alcohol, sex, and sexual assault (Forbes, Adams-Curtis, Pakalka, & White, 2006; Zapp, 2014). Now more than ever, college student social identity is also influenced by the relationships built using Facebook and other social media tools (Young & Jordan, 2013). On the other hand, positive relationships with faculty and peers can support student learning and success by helping students to find assistance when needed and encouraging learning from those who are different (Kuh et al., 2005). These findings indicate that college students are influenced by those they have relationships with and interact with regularly in both positive and negative ways. This chapter continues with an examination of multiple aspects of student relationships and their influence on college success and the college experience.

Parents/Guardians/Family

Counselors will interact with college students who find their relationships with their parents and family to be supportive and inspirational as well as those who struggle with emerging perspectives different from how they were raised. Parent and family members have an impact on students' college choice and often remain influential well into the college experience (National Center for Education Statistics, 2018). For example, first-generation college students may be particularly interested in the past experiences of their parents with college and work. "In fact, nearly half (46.0%) of first-generation college students reported wanting to please their family as a 'very important' motivation for their decision to pursue a college degree" (Eagan et al., 2016). In the same 2016 national survey of American freshmen, students were choosing to enroll in colleges closer to home, often living with parents or family, and even sacrificing their first college choice for those opportunities.

This pattern of parental influence continues well beyond college choice and enrollment with parental and family involvement influencing a student's development and providing support throughout the college experience (Carney-Hall, 2008; Harper, Sax, & Wolf, 2012). If we consider the role of parental involvement in K–12 institutions, it lends perspective and insight to what we may expect in the college environment. In Chapter 1, you read about "helicopter parents" as those who are ready to swoop in to help their students in an overprotective and overinvolved way (Howe & Strauss, 2003). There is a dominant negative stereotype about parental involvement in higher education. Thinking about how K–12 institutions involve parents in schools helps explain why parental expectations of their involvement in higher education may differ from the college's or university's expectations. Others add that the characteristic of helicopter parents represents a small proportion of parents and are not representative of the diversity of college parents and families (Kiyama & Harper, 2018).

First, consider the role of parents in K–12 institutions. The National Education Association (2008) indicates a correlation between academic performance, school improvement, and parental involvement. Specifically, students need broad-based support that considers their social service needs as well as their academic ones. The National Education Association's guidance to K–12 institutions includes how to encourage the involvement of parents in education. They highlight the different models of parental involvement in the classroom from historically volunteer "room mothers" assisting with chaperoning and fundraising to a new, preferred model of family involvement shifting beyond the parents to extended family and aligned with other support and partnerships in the community.

As students transition into college, it is helpful to appreciate that K–12 institutions are asking parents to be involved in a variety of ways different from what they will now experience. Parents arrive to the college environment with expectations from K–12 of teachers and administrators asking them for information about their family background and culture to improve their student's learning experience. They were often asked to be part of two-way communication about the school and their student; to assist with homework and other learning activities outside of school; and to participate in school governance, advocacy, and other volunteer activities. Parental involvement was an integral part of the K–12 curriculum goal for teachers and schools. One professional development text for teachers explains how to help parents play three roles for their students: supporting their education, monitoring their progress, and advocating when necessary (Santana, Rothstein, & Bain, 2016). In college environments, parents will often experience a dramatic change in the communications from the school about their students, the requests for involvement, and structures for them to participate in their student's educational experience. Counselors should appreciate this shift in expectations about involvement for both parents and college students. A new student like Arty should be asked about whether it would be helpful to have his parents involved in his transition to school, how they have been supportive (or not supportive) in the past, and what might help him in moving forward with his adjustment to college.

There are a variety of reasons relationships with parents are critical to college students. The cost of higher education and past financial support has many parents contributing to financial support for students, and shifts in technology use make it easier and more likely that parents can stay in close communication with students from a distance (Savage, n.d.). College students may bring patterns of experiences from high school ranging from coordinated treatment teams, individualized education plans, coordinated activities, and strong parental involvement within each of those experiences. This past experience can give rise to expectations for service delivery in and outside of the classroom from financial aid to course selection and especially during times of crisis. These expectations can create a dilemma for college faculty and student affairs staff in balancing an attitude of care with provision of too much support that inhibits students' opportunities to learn and develop from typical college challenges, transitions, and adjustments. Understanding what students have experienced previously is helpful in understanding how to support them moving forward. College counselors can help students explore new patterns of independence and yet encourage the involvement of parents during times of crisis if helpful for the student.

It is equally important to remember that student experiences of parental and family involvement vary greatly. Some students will not have positive histories with parents and family members; may be in a different stage of their life entering college; or may experience differences based on gender, race, socioeconomic status, national origin, and parental educational level (Kiyama & Harper, 2018). In some families, the family unit is prioritized over individuals, and competing family responsibilities can have an impact on student success. Many students explore new values and perspectives different from those of their parents in the college environment, whether it be experimenting with alcohol and substances, sexual relationships and identities, or new spiritual and religious ideas. College campuses are also seeing a growth in the number of former foster care youth enrolling in college (Eagan et al., 2016). Adult learners and military veterans may also have unique relationships with parents that must be evaluated differently. Recent studies have confirmed striking differences based on socioeconomic status and how parents interact with their students in the college experience (Bauer-Wolf, 2018). When we fail to consider both the positive and the negative aspects of parental and family involvement, we disregard that for some students this could be the difference in succeeding or failing in the college experience.

If we consider a student such as Tessa, introduced earlier, exploring the potential for parental support as helpful for her should be part of a counselor's consideration. Good treatment providers know the importance of a diverse community of support for students, and this can include parents and family members. In this case, it would be important to recognize that Tessa may be embarrassed about certain aspects of her relationship with Jacob and worried about her parents' reaction. The depression and suicidality may be new to Tessa, or it may be that she has worked with her parents in the past on similar issues. The role of the counselor is to discuss with Tessa how her parents can be supportive and the best way to involve them in a helpful manner to assist her.

Peers/Friendships/Roommates

Friendships at college come in a wide variety of shapes and sizes. Some friendships may be continued from high school or a student's hometown. Others may be new, based on shared interests (like working at the college radio station or being members of the campus soccer club). Some have an intense intimacy and shared space, such as roommates or the other students who live on a floor or in a suite where there are shared bathroom and shower facilities. Other relationships may be more content based, that is, based on academic pursuits, hobbies, an honor society, or a fraternity or a sorority. Students on smaller campuses or in more intimate college environments may find that relationships across contexts (classroom, student activity, work, residence hall) blend and cross over, whereas students on larger campuses may compartmentalize relationships and have very different experiences depending on the situation. In the end, there are numerous types of friendships, peer relationships, study buddies, and teammates. These relationships may last for a few days, weeks, months, or years or remain important to students for the rest of their lives.

Although there may be a variety of social connections available, finding some larger sense of belonging with others helps mitigate feelings of marginalization and disenfranchisement. This is particularly important in populations of students who feel separated from others and lack a voice to share their perspectives (Van Brunt, Murphy, & Zedginidze, 2017). Students without some larger relationship with others who share their viewpoints are at risk of aggravating hopelessness; depression; and hardened, inflexible perspectives. Social groups, peer connections, clubs, and organizations that offer the opportunity for such a relationship can be numerous or limited, depending on the needs of each student in terms of desire to interact with others.

Roommates and floor mates are some of the more intimate and challenging relationships to maintain. Unlike college students in the United States, most college students in the United Kingdom have their own room. This difference is surprising, in that most residential university students in the United States share frequent stories of negotiating study times, room cleanliness, temperature, privacy, socks on doors, music types and volume, shared microwave usage, and phone and cable bills with roommates. As with most close relationships, these bring with them wonderful opportunities to get to know and share with other people in a close, confined space as well as upsetting and nerve-racking experiences wherein these relationships become overwhelming. In many ways, residential life programs, orientation events, intramural sports, student activities programs, and academic clubs and organizations all share a common mission of assisting students in forging and maintaining these social connections and learning to develop frustration tolerance, critical thinking, and interpersonal growth. This is often central to student conduct and Behavioral Intervention Team work as well through early identification of at-risk behaviors and use of case management and mediation services (Van Brunt, 2012).

College itself is full of stressful challenges and routine sources of annoyance or aggravation that can have a negative impact on health (Lazarus, 1966). Stress can accumulate over time, life changes can become increasingly overwhelming, and the environmental stressors of our culture can lead to decreased production and increased stress and worry. Friendship and social supports can be an important way to help offset these daily hassles and frustrations. Everyone has different preferences when it comes to choosing friends. Each of us has different desires for alone time versus outgoing social time, thinking things through quietly versus having a passionate debate, or carefully weighing options versus engaging in a more intuitive way of thinking (Clifton, Anderson, & Schreiner, 2006; Keirsey, 1998; Keirsey & Bates, 1978; Rath, 2007; Rath & Conchie, 2009). When one is selecting friends in terms of quality, quantity, and what connection they have to different areas in a person's life, taking into account these preferences for interaction, decision-making, and communication is important as well. Three tools to further explore these questions are the Myers-Briggs Type Indicator, the Keirsey Temperament Sorter, and the Gallup StrengthsFinder 2.0 (which can be found at www.myersbriggs.org, www.keirsey.com, and www.gallupstrengthscenter.com). Counselors can use these tools when working with students on improving relationships, managing conflict in relationships, and identifying the characteristics important to them in relationships.

Striking a balance in these relationships is critical. It can take time for a college student to master the delicate balancing among peers, school obligations, family, work pressure, and sometimes also adjustment to a new environment, food, geographic location, and climate. Glasser (1975, 1999) talked about the way we all have needs for survival, love and belonging, achievement/power, freedom, and fun. Imagine that each of these five basic needs has a slider switch ranging from 0 to 10. Successful individuals see these on a spectrum over the course of their lifetime and realize that these levels change depending on where they find themselves. In college, intimacy and friendship may be easier to come by than power/achievement. Although there may be time for fun and increased freedom, money may be lacking and survival (such as paying rent, having extra money for fun trips, or eating out) could be more challenging.

A student like Arty, highlighted at the beginning of the chapter, may experience some challenges coming to college. He may have expectations based on his friendships and social justice involvement in the city but struggle to adjust in a smaller town. Although Arty is within his rights to have as many consensual sexual relationships as he likes, starting college with multiple relationships such as these may have some impact on how he is seen on campus. Student affairs staff and faculty are wonderful resources for students and often share the passions and desires of students related to political, religious, or social justice issues. Again, the challenge for a student like Arty might be finding a slower balance to getting comfortable at the school before rushing into many things at once.

Romantic Partners and Breakups

As with friendships, romantic connections can be some of the most amazing and most challenging tasks to balance when at college. In a healthy relationship, one's partner is supportive to one's needs and desires (Chickering & Reisser, 1993). There is creation of a gestalt; both become greater than the sum of the parts. There is a sense of play, ease, and humor when things get tough. There is a respect for private times and times with outside friends and family. Sexual relationships can occur briefly, be part of a longer commitment, exist between same-sex individuals, or exist between multiple partners (either in a committed polyamorous relationship, such as a triad or V, or in a less committed way where the main goal is to have friends-with-benefits or hookup relationships).

Developmental changes, societal pressures, religious admonitions, geographical influences, and parental expectations may all influence the type of relationship, number of partners, and feelings of satisfaction or dissatisfaction with an individual's choices. College is often seen as a period of exploration related to sexual orientation and understanding what aspects of a relationship are most important. These challenges are heightened for students considering transitioning from male to female or female to male, for those involved in interracial or intercultural dating, for those who are exploring their sexual orientation and how they understand themselves, and for gay and lesbian students. Relationships that occur within a marginalized population often exacerbate typical dating stress, suicide risk, potential acts of violence, and increased challenges related to simple tasks nonmarginalized couples or individuals may take for granted (such as sharing a meal, holding hands in public, displaying affection, etc.). These populations may include gay and lesbian students, students involved in mixed race/ethnicity dating, and transgender students in relationships or dating. Each of these groups may experience increased pressure, discrimination, and marginalization in some college environments, geographical areas, or religious setting. This, in turn, can lead to depression, anxiety, and an increase in suicide risk (Centers for Disease Control and Prevention, 2016; James et al., 2016).

As a guide, Sternberg (1986) suggested that dating and marriage relationships have three distinct facets: commitment, intimacy, and passion. Commitment is the thinking or cognitive aspect of love. It is the conscious decision to love another and to maintain a relationship over time despite difficulties. Intimacy is the sense of being bonded to another person. It is the emotional component of love and includes feelings of warmth, sharing, and emotional closeness. Passion is the romantic feelings, physical attraction, desire, and sex. It includes the intense stimulation and pleasure that can create a powerful craving; passion is like an addiction.

Romantic love often possesses a strong mixture of intimacy and passion yet lacks a fuller commitment. Compassionate love may have a sense of intimacy and commitment yet lacks any passion. Fatuous love may have passion and commitment yet lacks any sense of intimacy. Consummate love balances all three facets: passion, commitment, and intimacy. A challenge for students is coming to know themselves, understanding what they are looking for in a loving relationship, and cementing that with their partner.

Bad relationships can start out well and then subtly move toward difficulty (Murphy & Van Brunt, 2017). Problems that once were small and cute differences can change into more serious control issues. It may be that a partner is always there to correct mistakes and tell the other partner when he or she is wrong. Such partners may judge physical appearance (e.g., weight, hair, and clothes) or insult their partner's ability to hold a conversation or talk "intelligently" about topics. They may not let a partner spend time with friends or even have friends that they don't also know and control. They chip away at family and friends, trying to make them turn against the partner and make the other seek all self-esteem and confidence from them. They may pressure the partner for sex or destroy his or her possessions. Students can feel increasingly isolated from previous relationships and supports, finding it difficult to reach for help and get a different perspective. Counselors and student development staff should be informed of these escalating patterns of negative behaviors in relationships and help students to recognize them while also offering resources and support.

When two people are not able to work things out to arrive at a mutually agreeable arrangement, a relationship can end. These relationship losses should be explored within the subjective context of the student's experience. Counselors should be cautioned to attend to their bias in terms of how they might view a "relationship" and where the value and importance may be different for the student than it might be for the therapist. For example, areas in which differences in perception may arise include online connections, short-term intimate hookups, polyamorous groups, or, in attitudes to family. Assessing the student's value in what has been lost is critical prior to moving to intervention or advice.

Many times, these relationships can have an abrupt end, bringing with it depression, sadness, or a lack of meaning and purpose. It can create feelings of betrayal, frustration toward a partner for failing to live up to expectations, jealousy, obsession, and rage. These intense reactions can parallel trauma experiences and spiral a person into thoughts of suicide. The answer here, as unsatisfying as it is, is the old saying that time heals all wounds—which really is about the person in question finding some perspective for his or her feelings and giving himself or herself time to adjust. In the college setting, talking to friends, a counselor, a professor, family members, and/or religious or spiritual mentors can greatly help in the process of gaining perspective. Again, counselors should be cautioned to attend to their own implicit and explicit biases that may value certain relationships over others when it comes time for the student to look for assistance. Connections to counseling, spiritual support, parental outreach, or online resources should be assessed for their helpfulness given the perspective of the student, not merely that of the therapist. Offering various suggestions for support could be helpful, but this depends highly on the perspective of the student. Imagine that a student asks for a restaurant recommendation when he or she is visiting a new city. Although it may be tempting to give a quick answer informed by our perspective, asking some additional questions about fancy or casual, cheap or expensive, the type of food (say, vegetarian, vegan, Italian, Chinese, or bar food), and the geographic location would make it more likely that the advice would be applied.

When a friend is going through a difficult time, one of the best things a helper can do is listen. The process of active listening is a bit of a lost art and is something that trained helpers can model effectively for students. It is rare to have a friend simply listen to what the other person is saying without immediately jumping in to give advice or tell his or her own story. A better approach is to encourage people to reach out (offer options, not advice) without telling them what to do (giving people options allows them to make their own decisions and empower themselves). Provide them with the resources, so they can follow up if they choose to. When the breakup or bad relationship involves abuse, it is helpful to know the signs of abuse and be able to listen and refer them to help when they are ready to take some steps. The National Domestic Violence Hotline offers tips and resources about abusive relationships (https://www.thehotline.org/). A helper should make sure he or she understands that no one deserves abuse and it's not their fault.

In the second case example of Tessa, we see a student with a history of depression that becomes worse when her boyfriend breaks up with her. We don't know much about the relationship beyond that he became frustrated with her state of mind. It could be that Tessa was leaning too heavily on her boyfriend and the relationship became untenable. It could be that Tessa and Jacob weren't meant to be and the depression became an excuse. In this scenario, it would be reasonable to have Tessa assessed more deeply at the counseling center for suicide risk along with establishing some additional social supports and broadening her friend circle.

Professors/University Staff

In the United States, the use of the term *faculty* often refers to academic or teaching staff—namely, professors and instructors. University staff often consist of the nonteaching members of the institutions. These range from maintenance and information technology staff to a range of student support staff. The organizational charts of many collegiate communities are primarily broken down into two main divisions: academic affairs (the teaching side) and student affairs (the support side). The counseling services or counseling centers are typically housed within the student affairs division, many times within the same branch of the chart as student health and wellness. It is imperative not only that students are aware of resources available to them on campus but also that faculty and staff know of these resources and know how to refer students to them as needed. Students quickly realize which individuals on campus are healthy support for them and where they can turn and which individuals may not be the best option.

In a collegiate community, the relationships between university faculty and students often entail the most crucial connection. That connection helps students feel as though they belong at the university. Sohail and Shaikh (2004) found that in the higher education industry, the most important determinant of students' evaluation of service quality is "contact personnel" (p. 63). When professors create rapport with students, they can enhance learning, encourage students to work harder, help students challenge themselves, support the educational process, and increase student engagement (Granitz, Koernig, & Harich, 2009).

However, student learning doesn't only happen in a classroom. One well-known concept in college student development is Astin's (1999) student involvement theory. Astin proposed that meaningful educational engagement in college leads to learning and development: "The amount of student learning and personal development associated with any educational program is directly proportional to the quality and quantity of student involvement in that program" (p. 519). Chickering and Reisser (1993) also underscored that educationally powerful environments are ones that include friendships in student communities, positive connections between students and faculty, and the opportunity to participate in the larger campus community through programs or activities. Student affairs staff can be key in facilitating these opportunities and programs for student participation.

However, part of the challenge is the initiation of a relationship between university employees and students. Students may not always seek out university faculty and staff for interaction beyond the classroom (Pingree, 2012). The many reasons for their not doing so may include being first-generation students who have no frame of reference for protocol in this situation or being students who feel intimidated and do not feel comfortable reaching out to their professors or other university employees. Encouraging interaction with students at the university or departmental level may help students to overcome these challenges. For instance, a Living Learning Community for first-generation students gives them the opportunity to interact with university staff and faculty in an informal manner that can promote interaction in other environments as well. These students can also ask questions of one another to see which employees are approachable or specifically able to help in particular situations. Astin (1999) emphasized the significant role postsecondary educators play in creating opportunities for students to be involved in experiences both inside and outside the classroom, helping to set the foundation for students to make developmental strides.

In addition to the beneficial relationships that can occur between postsecondary employees and students, there can also be relationships that are not so healthy. Faculty hold a great deal of power over students that, when misused, can result in threats and ultimatums. Consider for a moment an international graduate student whose resources and opportunities are tied to a research position, scholarship, grades, thesis project, and visa status. Romantic relationships that appear consensual between a faculty member and a student often have vast power differentials and are problematic (Murphy & Van Brunt, 2017). Many institutions of higher education have operating policies regarding the conduct between employees and students. In addition, Title IX requires institutions to quickly and competently investigate and adjudicate claims of sexual harassment and assault. "Title IX prohibits sex-based harassment by peers, employees, or third parties that is sufficiently serious to deny or limit a student's ability to participate in or benefit from the recipient's education programs and activities" (U.S. Department of Education, Office for Civil Rights, 2015). It is important that faculty members and staff set boundaries with students that determine what is appropriate and what is not appropriate in these relationships. Attending ongoing training related to bias awareness and mitigation is essential to address preconceived notions that may lead to bad advice and support. For example, all relationships between students and faculty may not be supportive or appropriate, as with family members.

In the example of Arty, we see that he has already initiated discussions with the dean's office in discussing changes that need to be made on campus, has talked to his sociology professor about becoming a Safe Zone trainer, and is working with his sociology professor to draft plans on a new club. Arty has made several beneficial connections on campus and has become actively involved. He seems to be thriving in his postsecondary education based on these relationships.

The Therapeutic Relationship

A therapeutic relationship is one in which one person, the therapist, is helping an individual, the client or student, change. Egan and Reese (2019), Corey and Corey (2016), Hackney and Cormier (2013), and Gladding (2012), as well as others, have provided models of the developmental nature of stages of the helping relationship. Terms used to describe these stages differ, but what is consistent is that the client or student moves from initiation of the relationship through a working phase into a termination stage. One of these models includes the orientation phase, identification phase, working phase, and resolution phase (Peplau, 1997). The orientation phase typically consists of completing necessary paperwork and getting to know one another on a surface level. The identification phase goes into more specific details regarding the problem that the client (student) came into counseling to address. This phase may include psychological testing or other paperwork to help if a diagnosis is needed, as well as guiding the student in goal setting. The working phase involves implementation of a treatment plan for the student to start working toward his or her goals. The resolution phase is where the therapist begins the termination process with the client to help the client find independence outside of therapy.

Boundaries within a therapeutic relationship help keep the relationship on a professional level. Many times, students will trust counselors on the basis of their being authority figures. Because of this trust, counselors should take steps to let students know how they will not take advantage of them and how they can help them feel safe. Healthy boundaries help the student to feel good after the session and are based on Kitchener's (1984) five moral principles:

- *Beneficence*—contribute to the welfare of the client and be proactive
- *Nonmaleficence*—not causing harm to others
- *Autonomy*—allow the individual the freedom of choice and action to make his or her own decisions
- *Justice*—formal meaning is "treating equals equally and unequally but in proportion to their relevant differences" (Kitchener, 1984, p. 49)
- *Fidelity*—loyalty, faithfulness, and honoring commitments

Additionally, the *ACA Code of Ethics*'s (American Counseling Association [ACA], 2014) principles of professional ethical behavior include all of the abovementioned moral principles and add veracity and define it as "dealing truthfully with individuals with whom counselors come into professional contact" (p. 3; see also Section A, The Counseling Relationship).

On the other side of the spectrum are boundary violations, which typically include major ethical violations. This may include the counselor overly disclosing personal information, the counselor violating confidentiality (unless the client threatens self or others), the counselor having countertransference feelings toward a student, or even more serious violations such as going too far in the relationship with the student. Boundaries exist to protect the student and to protect the counseling center from liability.

One of the trickier boundaries may be the relationship with the family of the student. Parents may wish to know what the student is discussing during therapy. Even if a student signs off on a Family Educational Rights and Privacy Act of 1974 (FERPA) waiver giving permission for parents to have access to records, that does not mean the parents should have access to the counseling records. Treatment records should be held to the strictest levels of confidentiality and generally should not be shared. The student should work through an informed consent process with the counselor to know how the records will be maintained and who will have access to those records. The one exception to FERPA is if a student is in danger of harming self or others; then information can be shared with appropriate parties, including the student's parents. Counselors can also help connect parents to others in student affairs who can share more general information about college processes and resources. It may not be possible to discuss the specific student, but often a parent's questions can be answered by talking about standard processes and options. Many campuses also have student affairs offices designated to assist and support parents in how to be appropriately involved in the college experience of their student.

There may also be concern from parents who are overinvolved with their children and may consistently try to cross those boundaries, even with FERPA and confidentiality in place. When this happens, it is important for the student to work with the counselor on ways to work with the parent. Encouraging the student to share "just enough" information with this type of overinvolved parent may alleviate some of the parental concern and allow the student to continue to work on the deeper concerns with the counselor. This information may include strategies the student is using, progress on a goal, or successes achieved.

Tessa has already tapped into a therapeutic relationship with a therapist at the counseling center on campus. Tessa and her therapist are currently in the working phase, as the therapist worries about suicidality and hospitalization. They are at the point of developing an intervention plan to help Tessa. Because of falling behind in her classes, Tessa has been brought to the attention of the Behavioral Intervention Team. It is important that the therapist maintain professional boundaries and confidentiality in her communication with the team.

The Impact of Social Media on Relationships

Albert Bandura's (1977) social learning theory describes how people observe, imitate, and model the behavior of others. In an age of constant social media, this theory allows people to digitize their human experience on platforms such as Facebook, Twitter, Snapchat, and Instagram. Communication on these platforms is a "two-way, three-way, and hundred-way tool that is interactive, immersive, and omnipresent" (Deaton, 2015). People tend to use these sites because they meet a basic need of connecting with others through making friends, following friends as they post about their lives, and updating friends with the status of life.

Although social media has some positives, such as the ability to connect with others at a distance, there are also additional pressures on relationships, such as pressure to be "perfect" to your friends or an increase in jealousy. Some millennials and beyond even have a sense of failure if they do not portray themselves as picture-perfect. Jealousy on social media can stem from who has more friends, what people are posting, who messaged or tagged whom, who commented on a status, and more. This jealousy can occur in romantic and nonromantic relationships alike. Pressure to prove a relationship is going well can be portrayed through highly visible messages about another person, but it may not be indicative of the relationship's true reality. Ridgway and Clayton (2016) revealed that the more selfies posted on social media platforms, the higher the likelihood of relationship conflicts and jealousy, especially if those posts get significant attention.

Another issue that has been broached recently (see Kavitha & Bhuvaneswari, 2016) is that millennials and others who were raised in the digital age have a hard time in face-to-face situations. Social media has created an environment in which it is easier for people to do things online than in person. This could include situations where people have anxiety about speaking aloud or having conversations in "real life." These direct communication skills are needed as students begin to interview for jobs and navigate romantic relationships. Career development offices can help role-play interview situations, and the counseling services centers can help with some of the communication skills needed for navigating those romantic encounters. However, the more opportunities provided for students to connect face-to-face through campus activities that student service organizations provide, the more practice they will have with using direct communication skills.

Dexter is a perfect example of a student who has used social media to meet his need to connect with others. He admits to living his life on the computer. His online behavior isn't necessarily positive (snarky communications, trolling, memes, threats, etc.), and Dexter has a hard time making friends on campus. Social media has ultimately led him to the Behavioral Intervention Team for assessment within the counseling services department.

Developmental Stage Impact on Relationships

Erik Erikson's (1950) developmental theory is one of the most well-known in describing the stages of human development. As mentioned in Chapter 9, there are two stages of this theory that are most relevant to the traditional and even some nontraditional college students: adolescence and early adulthood.

Erikson termed the adolescence stage as identity versus role confusion. In this stage, adolescents are crossing into adulthood. Individuals struggle with how others see them and how they view themselves. This stage includes career choices, romantic relationships, and many other choices to help them figure out who they are and who they want to be. As these adolescents transition into the postsecondary realm, they will continue to struggle with identity while participating in various activities, choosing a major, and participating in close relationships with friends or romantic partners. The adjustment for these first-year students is a difficult task and can set the tone for their entire postsecondary success or failure.

In describing the stage of early adulthood, Erikson used the terminology intimacy versus isolation. This is apt for those in postsecondary education because this stage may be the first time that real commitments are made to someone other than a family member. Adults at this stage work toward establishing committed relationships and friendships and may also sever unhealthy relationships. Finding close relationships during this stage can provide satisfaction to the young adult, whereas avoiding intimacy could result in the young adult feeling isolated or depressed.

As Tessa's boyfriend recently broke up with her and Tessa doesn't have many friends, she is on the isolation side of this stage of early adulthood. She is already being treated for depression at the counseling center and is falling behind in her classes.

One of the most influential theories of developmental issues faced by college students is Chickering's (1969) vectors of development. This theory builds on Erikson's ideals of identity and intimacy. In contrast to Erikson's stages, Chickering's vectors entail students moving at different rates and that they may deal with issues from more than one vector at the same time. These vectors do build on each other. Although there are seven vectors, two relate directly to development and relationships: moving through autonomy toward interdependence and developing mature interpersonal relationships. In the first, development comes through an increase in emotional dependence, and individuals recognize the importance of their interconnectedness with others. In the second, individuals develop the capacity for healthy and lasting relationships with close friends and intimate partners.

Arty recognizes the importance of his interconnectedness with others. He is actively involved on campus and is an outspoken advocate on social justice issues. He has made connections with university faculty and aims to increase relationships with others through his proposed club on campus, indicating that his development is moving through autonomy toward interdependence. Also, although Arty has had several intimate sexual relationships with other students, there is nothing to indicate that these are lasting partners, which indicates he has not moved through the vector of developing mature interpersonal relationships.

Clinical Implications (Assessment and Treatment)

A central factor in relationships that have a hierarchy, those with a power differential, is abusing, harming, or manipulating, either intentionally or accidentally, the person in the lesser power position. A more straightforward way of saying this is that professionalism should be central in the assessment and treatment relationship. It demands attendance to proper boundaries and guidelines to avoid breaches in trust, harm, or abuse.

Boundaries are the general rules, guidelines, or limits one uses to govern one's behavior on the basis of moral, spiritual, ethical, and legal expectations in relationships. These boundaries occur in two directions, affecting both the incoming and outgoing interactions between a therapist, counselor, or psychologist and a student. Good boundaries create clear expectations for behavior, can build a sense of community, set standards for interactions, and reduce anxiety and increase trust. For those students who have experienced boundary problems in the past, good healthy boundaries can correct past negative experiences, maximize the mentor/student relationship, and teach important skills for future classes and work environments (Haas & Malouf, 2005).

In both assessment and treatment, it is essential the therapist, counselor, or psychologist remain genuine, authentic, and congruent. The creation of inflexible limits with an authoritarian delivery creates conflict, makes communication less transparent, amplifies past problems with conflict, and dilutes the utility of the positive working relationship. Being clear about your expectations allows others to rise to the level of your expectations. Students may have had confusing or conflicting messages about what might be appropriate in the past, so clarifying expectations becomes important to developing clear and consistent communication. There is also an element of a good-boundary and limit-setting discussion that allows the person in the power position to be more proactive and get out in front of larger conflicts.

For both counselors and student affairs staff, setting limits and boundaries works best when the professional is being authentic and genuine, has built a rapport with the student, and articulates why he or she cares about this issue and how this conversation promotes success. Sharing yourself and your emotions with students can be a tricky task. There are risks and rewards. The key is finding a balance. A professional who strives to be a friend to the student may overshare, use inappropriate jokes, lack respect, and have difficulty establishing professionalism or authority. A professional who strives to be above reproach may come off as distant and overly professorial, conveying an unwillingness to get to know students and being more focused on the task over the person. The Goldilocks position offers the student a present, genuine, engaging professional who shares his or her point of view appropriately and sees the student as a partner and stakeholder in the task at hand. Table 15.1 highlights some common areas in assessment and treatment that require good communication and boundary discussion (Van Brunt, 2015).

With students like Dexter and Tessa who are required to complete an assessment for suicide or threat, it is important for the clinical staff to clearly spell out the nature of the assessment, where the records are kept, who sees the results, and what happens if they are a no-show for an appointment or disagree with the findings. With a student like Dexter, an additional challenge will be forming a rapport with a student who is more at home with his computer than in face-to-face interactions and thrives on snarky communication. However, to obtain an accurate assessment, addressing this potential defensiveness is key for the clinical staff doing the assessment.

Outreach and Prevention Implications

As with any prevention and outreach effort from the counseling unit, those related to family and relationship issues will be improved when informed by the specific campus and

TABLE 15.1

Assessment and Treatment Examples Showing Differing Approaches

Task	*Good Approach*	*Bad Approach*
Limits of confidentiality	A clear informed consent document that explains the limits and exceptions to confidentiality and when, how, and with whom information can be shared.	A vague discussion of the relationship being private without any detailed expectations. Or avoiding the conversation completely.
Communication	A discussion of how and when to connect with each other over phone, email, text with expectations about a response time.	Only allowing one way to communicate, offering vague or no clear advice about communication.
Meeting outside	A clear discussion of how you will communicate if you meet each other in a public setting. This is a back-and-forth discussion with the development of a shared plan.	No discussion about meeting outside or a comment like "I will just ignore you" without feedback or development of a plan.
Timeliness	A discussion about missed appointments, communication about canceling, and how long appointments will typically be.	Avoiding any of these discussions until they come up as a problem or listing them in the fine print of an intake document.
Cost	An open and clear discussion of any cost or payment for services, when payment is due, and what happens with late payments.	No discussion of cost or small mention of it in the fine print. Overly harsh policy on collection.
Sharing of raw test data	A clear discussion about second opinions, whom raw testing data can be released to (often only other clinical staff), and perhaps a list of providers who could offer other opinions.	No mention of the policy until it comes up as a problem.
Talking to parents/dean	Although this was discussed previously under limits of confidentiality, having a more detailed discussion about when parents can/will be notified and where the results of the assessment go (to the dean or referral agent).	Waiting until a crisis occurs and then sharing information or telling the student "they have no choice" or "should have read the informed consent closer."
Crisis	Discussion of how to access care during an emergency (both after-hours and during business hours).	A vague discussion or "call 911" advice when dealing with an emergency.

student population and when designed to embrace the broad diversity of relationships present on the college campus. Early, and even prior to a student's enrollment in college during orientation or admissions presentations, counseling units can provide education and information to parent and family members. Many 4-year institutions now have departments dedicated to parental and family involvement. Marjorie Savage, Parent Program director at the University of Minnesota, makes a case for parental involvement as a positive element when parents understand resources on campus and know how to balance helping their student with empowering their student. She said, "Parents can play a valuable role in their student's success when they understand and reinforce the messages we give students." Counselors can help to decrease parental anxiety about the college experience but also give them realistic information to help them talk with their students. One powerful tool can be teaching them the art of empowering their students and making good referrals for their students to resources and services on the campus. By helping to reinforce healthy boundaries and set expectations related to parental involvement early on, parents will be better prepared for knowing how to assist their students during times of crisis.

Counselors can also play an important role in teaching students about the warning signs of unhealthy relationships and teaching them how to build healthy relationships. Negative warning signs in relationships can include threats, manipulation, pressure, and isolation as well as other precursors and forms of sexual violence. Often, students may find themselves involved with partners who exhibit these negative characteristics or behaviors, but the student does not recognize them as unhealthy or violent. Prevention strategies should address the dangers of unhealthy relationships as well as aspects of healthy relationships. In the 2017 book *Uprooting Sexual Violence in Higher Education,* Murphy and Van Brunt identify six specific characteristics of healthy relationships to teach to students: communication, active listening/empathy, focus on the other's happiness, equanimity, social connection, and mutual respect. Strategies related to bystander intervention can also be useful to teach students to help recognize unhealthy relationships and help their friends, but it is important to remember the powerful draw of peer pressure and group belonging when teaching students to confront difficult situations that may go against the norms of those around them.

Finally, the case studies allude to various opportunities for prevention and outreach measures to better support positive student relationships. Arty's case reminds us of the importance of providing accurate and open information related to positive and healthy sexual relationships for all sexual orientations and gender identities. It also highlights the importance of having counselors who are well versed in issues of microaggressions and diversity and other social justice issues. Tessa's story prompts us to identify multiple ways of identifying students struggling with loneliness, depression, and suicidality. Exploring the implementation of gatekeeper programs that teach the warning signs and red flags for these concerns as well as how to help friends and students with good referrals and support is a critical function for counseling units. Finally, Dexter reminds us that our professional development and outreach programs must consider the influence of technology on campus relationships and how technology shifts the way we engage students in our programs and shifts how students interact throughout their various relationships. Because family and relationship issues span such a broad array of college student experiences, any prevention or outreach effort should consider the influence of relationships on college student attitudes and behaviors and how this affects our ability to engage them around the various prevention and outreach topics.

Conclusion

Relationships have the potential to provide positive, supportive, and encouraging aspects to college students' experiences as well as the ability to create obstacles to success and hinder students' belief in themselves and their access to educational opportunities. No one relationship is alike, and helping students navigate these experiences requires learning about each unique interaction and association affecting students and influencing their attitudes and behaviors. This chapter has attempted to help you understand these different types of relationships and leverage the positive aspects for students, while also watching for those red-flag indicators that a student may be experiencing harm or difficulty in a relationship. Our hope for students is that they form healthy, lasting relationships during college both in and outside of the classroom and that these positively affect how they think about their own contributions to relationships as friends, parents, partners, family members, and colleagues.

Final Case Study

Kara is entering her junior year and is in a poly relationship with Jack and Lisa. The relationship has Jack as a pivot rather than being a triad (Jack is sexual with Kara and Lisa individually at different times, but there is no sexual relationship between Lisa and Kara).

Kara's mother recently found out about her relationship when Kara explained she was going to rent an apartment off campus with Lisa and Jack. Even though they have been dating for over a year and get along very well, Kara's mother feels protective and worries her daughter is being taken advantage of by Jack and Lisa. She also has concerns about how a polyamorous relationship is against the faith in which Kara was raised.

Kara's father has a harder time with this and has threatened to cut her off from financial support. Kara feels trapped and struggles with her emotions and the lack of acceptance from her family. Kara also is beginning to struggle with her academics. She comes in to counseling to talk.

Case Exploration Questions

1. Where are some places to start the conversation with Kara?
2. When assessing risks for depression, suicide, and protective factors, how would you assess Kara's risk and support her?
3. Is there a point at which you have Jack and Lisa in for a conversation? How would you know? What would the intention be?
4. If Kara was willing to sign a release of information, what are the pros and cons of offering to talk to her mother.

References

Allen, E. I., & Seaman, J. (2013). *Changing course: Ten years of tracking online education.* Babson Park, MA: Babson Survey Research Group.

American Counseling Association. (2014). *ACA code of ethics*. Alexandria, VA: Author.

Astin, A. (1999). Student involvement: A developmental theory for higher education. *Journal of College Student Development, 40,* 518–529.

Bandura, A. (1977). *Social learning theory.* Englewood Cliffs, NJ: Prentice Hall.

Bauer-Wolf, J. (2018). Silver spoons. *Inside Higher Education.* Retrieved from https://www.insidehighered.com/news/2018/02/28/parental-involvement-drastically-changes-students-college-experience-study-shows

Berkman, L. F., Glass, T., Brissette, I., & Seeman, T. E. (2000). From social integration to health: Durkheim in the new millennium. *Social Science & Medicine, 51,* 843–857.

Carney-Hall, K. C. (2008). Understanding current trends in family involvement. *New Directions for Student Services, 2008,* 3–14. doi:10.1002/ss.271

Centers for Disease Control and Prevention. (n.d.). Strategic direction for the prevention of suicidal behavior: Promoting individual, family, and community connectedness to prevent suicidal behavior. Atlanta, GA: U.S. Department of Health and Human Services. Retrieved from https://www.cdc.gov/violenceprevention/pdf/Suicide_Strategic_Direction_Full_Version-a.pdf

Centers for Disease Control and Prevention. (2016). Sexual identity, sex of sexual contacts, and health-risk behaviors among students in Grades 9–12: Youth risk behavior surveillance. Atlanta, GA: U.S. Department of Health and Human Services.

Chang, E. C., Diaz, L., Lucas, A. G., Lee, J., Powell, N. J., Kafelghazal, S., . . . Jeglic, E. L. (2017). Ethnic identity and loneliness in predicting suicide risk in Latino college students. *Hispanic Journal of Behavioral Sciences, 39,* 470–485.

Chickering, A. W. (1969). *Education and identity.* San Francisco, CA: Jossey-Bass.

Chickering, A. W., & Reisser, L. (1993). *Education and identity* (2nd ed.). San Francisco, CA: Jossey-Bass.

Cialdini, R. B., Kallgren, C. A., & Reno, R. R. (1991). A focus theory of normative conduct: A theoretical refinement and reevaluation of the role of norms in human behavior. *Advances in Experimental Social Psychology, 24,* 201–234.

Clifton, D., Anderson, E., & Schreiner, L. (2006). StrengthsQuest: Discover and develop your strengths in academics, career, and beyond. New York, NY: Gallup Press.

Corey, M. S., & Corey, G. (2016). *Becoming a helper* (7th ed.). Boston, MA: Cengage Learning.

Deaton, S. (2015). Social learning theory in the age of social media: Implications for educational practitioners. *I-manager's Journal of Educational Technology, 12,* 1–5.

Eagan, K., Stolzenberg, E. B., Zimmerman, H. B., Aragon, M. C., Sayson, H. W., & Rios-Aguilar, C. (2016). *The American freshman: National norms Fall 2016.* Los Angeles: University of California, Higher Education Research Institute.

Egan, G., & Reese, R. J. (2019). *The skilled helper: A problem-management and opportunity-development approach to helping* (10th ed.). Boston, MA: Cengage Learning.

Erikson, E. H. (1950). *Childhood and society.* New York, NY: Norton.

Family Educational Rights and Privacy Act of 1974, 20 U.S.C. § 1232g (1974).

Forbes, G. B., Adams-Curtis, L. E., Pakalka, A. H., & White, K. B. (2006). Dating aggression, sexual coercion, and aggression-supporting attitudes among college men as a function of participation in aggressive high school sports. *Violence Against Women, 12,* 441–455.

Gladding, S. T. (2012). *Counseling: A comprehensive profession* (7th ed.). New York, NY: Pearson.

Glasser, W. (1975). *Reality therapy: A new approach to psychiatry.* New York, NY: Colophon Books.

Glasser, W. (1999). *Choice theory: A new psychology of personal freedom.* New York, NY: HarperPerennial.

Granitz, N. A., Koernig, S. K., & Harich, K. R. (2009). Now it's personal—Antecedents and outcomes of rapport between business faculty and their students. *Journal of Marketing Education, 31,* 52–65.

Haas, L., & Malouf, J. (2005). *Keeping up the good work: A practitioner's guide to mental health ethics* (4th ed.). Sarasota, FL: Professional Resources Press.

Hackney, H. L., & Cormier, S. (2013). *Professional counseling: A process guide to helping* (7th ed.). Boston, MA: Pearson.

Harper, C. E., Sax, L. J., & Wolf, D. S. (2012). The role of parents in college students' sociopolitical awareness, academic, and social development. *Journal of Student Affairs Research and Practice, 49,* 137–156.

Howe, N., & Strauss, W. (2003). *Millennials go to college.* Great Falls, VA: American Association of Registrars and Admissions Officers.

James, S., Herman, J., Rankin, S., Keisling, M., Mottet, L., & Anafi, M. (2016). *The report of the 2015 U.S. Transgender Survey.* Washington, DC: National Center for Transgender Equality.

Kavitha, S., & Bhuvaneswari, R. (2016). Impact of social media on millennials—A conceptual study. *Apeejay-Journal of Management Sciences and Technology, 4,* 80–86.

Keirsey, D. (1998). *Please understand me II: Temperament character intelligence.* Del Mar, CA: Prometheus Nemesis.

Keirsey, D., & Bates, M. (1978). *Please understand me: Character and temperament types.* Del Mar, CA: Prometheus Nemesis.

Kitchener, K. S. (1984). Intuition, critical evaluation and ethical principles: The foundation for ethical decisions in counseling psychology. *Counseling Psychologist, 12,* 43–55.

Kiyama, J. M., & Harper, C. E. (2018). Beyond hovering: A conceptual argument for an inclusive model of family engagement in higher education. *The Review of Higher Education, 41,* 365–385.

Kuh, G. D., Kinzie, J., Schuh, J. H., & Whitt, E. J. (2005). *Student success in college: Creating conditions that matter.* San Francisco, CA: Jossey-Bass.

Layard, R. (2005). *Happiness: Lessons from a new science.* New York, NY: Penguin Press.

Lazarus, R. (1966). *Psychological stress and the coping process.* New York, NY: McGraw-Hill.

Murphy, A., & Van Brunt, B. (2017). *Uprooting sexual violence in higher education: A guide for practitioners and faculty.* New York, NY: Routledge.

National Center for Education Statistics. (2018). *Factors that influence student college choice.* Washington, DC: U.S. Department of Education.

National Education Association. (2008). *Parent, family, community involvement in education: An NEA policy brief.* Washington, DC: NEA Education Policy and Practice Department.

National Institute on Alcohol Abuse and Alcoholism. (n.d.). *Fall semester—A time for parents to discuss the risks of college drinking.* Bethesda, MD: Author.

Peplau, H. E. (1997). Peplau's theory of interpersonal relations. *Nursing Science Quarterly, 10,* 162–167.

Pingree, A. (2012). *Encouraging student-faculty interaction outside of class.* Professional and Organizational Development Network. Retrieved from https://tomprof.stanford.edu/posting/1238

Protopsaltis, S., & Baum, S. (2019). *Does online education live up to its promise? A look at the evidence and implications for federal policy.* Houston, TX: Laura and John Arnold Foundation. Retrieved from https://mason.gmu.edu/~sprotops/OnlineEd.pdf

Rath, T. (2007). *StrengthsFinder 2.0.* New York, NY: Gallup Press.

Rath, T., & Conchie, B. (2009). *Strengths based leadership.* New York, NY: Gallup Press.

Ridgway, J. L., & Clayton, R. B. (2016). Instagram unfiltered: Exploring associations of body image satisfaction, Instagram #Selfie posting, and negative romantic relationship outcomes. *Cyberpsychology, Behavior, and Social Networking, 19,* 2–7.

Santana, L., Rothstein, D., & Bain, A. (2016). *Partnering with parents to ask the right questions: A powerful strategy for strengthening school-family partnerships.* Alexandria, VA: ASCD.

Savage, M. (n.d.). *The case for parental involvement during the college years.* Retrieved from http://www.stetson.edu/law/conferences/highered/archive/media/higher-ed-archives-2009/document/i-savage-case-for-parental-involvement.pdf

Seemiller, C. (2017). Motivation, learning, and communication preferences of Generation Z students. *eHearsay, 7,* 4–9.

Sohail, M., & Shaikh, N. (2004). Quest for excellence in business education: A study of student impressions of service quality. *International Journal of Educational Management, 18,* 58–65.

Sternberg, R. J. (1986). A triangular theory of love. *Psychological Review, 93,* 119–135.

Strayhorn, T. L. (2019). *College students' sense of belonging: A key to educational success for all students.* New York, NY: Routledge.

U.S. Department of Education, Office for Civil Rights. (2015, April). *Title IX resource guide.* Washington, DC: Author.

Van Brunt, B. (2012). *Ending campus violence: New approaches to prevention.* New York, NY: Routledge.

Van Brunt, B. (2015). *Harm to others: The assessment and treatment of dangerousness.* Alexandria, VA: American Counseling Association.

Van Brunt, B., Murphy, A., & Zedginidze, A. (2017). An exploration of the risk, protective, and mobilization factors related to violent extremism in college populations. *Violence and Gender, 4,* 81–101.

Young, S. D., & Jordan, A. H. (2013). The influence of social networking photos on social norms and sexual health behaviors. *Cyberpsychology, Behavior, and Social Networking, 16,* 243–247.

Zapp, D. (2014). *What have we learned about sexual assault from over half a million incoming college students?* Washington, DC: EverFi Coalition.

Chapter 16

Academic and Career Issues

Mark B. Scholl, Christy M. Buchanan, and Esther Suess

Instruction does much, but encouragement everything.
—Johann Wolfgang von Goethe

■ ■ ■

Reflection Exercise

Many students, when asked, will say that academic and career goals are central to their reasons for attending college. However, the way students think about or interpret academic and career issues will vary depending on other aspects of their identities. Think for a moment about transfer students from community colleges, international students, adult students with families, student athletes, students with learning disabilities or mental health issues that reduce academic functioning, students seeking to enter very competitive majors, students seeking to enter majors in which they will be underrepresented, and so forth. Student identities and life circumstances will intersect with their academic and career goals in many ways that will occasionally require extra support or assistance. We will not be able to cover all of these situations in the chapter but would like for you to think about how this chapter information may apply to all of these student populations. You may also reflect on your own experiences of finding your academic and career direction as an undergraduate, if that is helpful.

■ ■ ■

In this chapter, we focus on the nature of academic advising and career counseling services offered on college campuses, including basic definitions of roles and functions. After a general overview, we will use the examples of two special populations of college students (those from a lower socioeconomic background and those who do not have at least one parent who completed a college degree) to help you think further about applications to practice.

Academic Counseling

Overview of the Services and Roles of Academic Counselors and Advisers

For the purposes of this chapter, *academic counseling* and *academic advising* are used interchangeably. Although students may or may not present for services at the academic counseling center, every student is assigned an academic adviser at some point in his or her college career, so it is a common touchpoint for students. The Council for the Advancement of Standards in Higher Education (2015) articulated the mission of academic advising programs as follows: "to assist students as they define, plan, and achieve their educational goals" (p. 5). The National Academic Advising Association (https://www.nacada.ksu.edu/) is another key resource for learning about the work of academic advising. A primary responsibility of academic counselors (also known as academic advisers) is to provide the guidance and support students need to make successful academic progress toward graduation. One obvious component of this guidance pertains to helping students choose courses that allow them to successfully fulfill transfer requirements or graduation requirements and that build in a developmentally meaningful way from their first experiences in college through graduation (e.g., completing important entry-level prerequisites, upper level classes, or preprofessional tracks). When events of students' lives cause breaks in schooling along the way, advisers are often in the position of helping students consider alternative options for completing requirements as efficiently as possible, so as to minimize additional tuition or loss of financial aid.

Successfully defining, planning, and achieving educational goals, however, goes beyond identifying and taking all required courses in a developmentally appropriate sequence leading to graduation. Meeting this academic advising mission requires taking a broad view of the student as a whole person, being attuned to the multiple and complex facets of students' functioning that affect their ability to plan and achieve educational goals (e.g., understanding the culture of higher education and how to negotiate this culture, personal and communal experience and well-being; NACADA, 2006). Academic counselors should be well positioned to recognize these multiple facets and to support students across these facets. However, there is no set credential for becoming an academic adviser, and thus, the quality and style of service provision can vary quite a bit.

By and large, academic success will depend on making a positive transition to the college classroom (e.g., see Schlossberg's transition theory in Chapter 13). Many new college students—even some of the most successful in high school attending some of the most prestigious universities—do not, in fact, enter college having the requisite skills and knowledge of how to succeed in the college classroom (Archambault, 2017). They can learn, but they need guidance on how things will differ from high school. For example, many highly successful high school students have never had to study over the course of several days for an exam, or spend more than a day writing a major paper. Academic success in most colleges will require quite different work habits. A few examples of these habits include starting earlier, spending more hours studying or writing, and learning how to evaluate and revise one's own work (Schauss Fergueson, 2017). Academic counselors can help students recognize and anticipate these differences and remind students about them when students are faced with disappointing academic outcomes. They can also communicate confidence in students' capacity for learning, resilience, and growth in the face of transitional challenges.

Because academic success also depends heavily on personal health and well-being, academic advisers will often find themselves helping students identify or remedy physical or mental health challenges that affect academic success. At this point we should mention the caveat that academic counselors should remain mindful of the importance of role fidelity. On most campuses, although not all, counselors who are employed in the student affairs division do not specialize in the provision of mental health counseling. For this reason, generally speaking, we are not suggesting that academic counselors provide mental health counseling to the students they serve. Instead we are referring to supportive responses such as providing advice on good sleep habits (e.g., "Getting good sleep the night before an exam is likely to help your performance more than staying up all night to cram") or connecting a student showing signs of excessive anxiety or depression with the counseling center. Moreover, academic advisers must be attuned to personal well-being if they are to promote academic success in students.

Another important facet of academic success is relational: Students are more likely to succeed when they feel they belong in their college community. Belonging is a basic human need (e.g., Baumeister & Leary, 1995), and feelings of belonging are related to college students' personal and academic success (e.g., Tomasiewicz, 2017; Walton & Cohen, 2011). Academic advisers must be attuned to this aspect of academic success and understand how students may struggle or succeed in connecting on their particular campus (i.e. , is the college large or small, residential or commuter, or online or traditional, and does it serve a particular population?). Advisers can help by normalizing struggles to belong (e.g., Walton & Cohen, 2011); articulating their confidence in each student's belonging; exploring students' interests with them; and connecting students with people, offices, and student organizations that can help the student establish social connections. Work by Steve Asher and others has shown that belonging can come from many sources, including academic (e.g., Asher & Weeks, 2014). One student might, therefore, find belonging through working in a professor's research lab, whereas another might find it by joining a group that cheers for the school's sports teams, or participating in a musical group, or living in a theme house with other students who share an interest (e.g., theater or sustainability). Although these are nonacademic "extracurricular" opportunities, it is important for academic counselors to be aware of such opportunities or be well connected with campus partners who can help guide students toward them.

Academic counselors also play a vital role in educating and encouraging their advisees to communicate well and respectfully with professors and other adults on campus who can help them. One common regret expressed by students during and after academic crises is that as academic struggles developed and magnified, they tried to cope on their own. For any of a plethora of reasons—denial, feelings of shame or embarrassment, fear of being exposed as an imposter, fear of judgment—students often hesitate to admit or avoid admitting a need for help. We recommend that academic counselors normalize academic and other struggles during college, as well as the need to rely on others for help at times. It can be useful for academic counselors to characterize seeking help as a sign of strength, intelligence, and resilience, not weakness.

Academic Success and Jeopardy as Developmental Opportunities

The developmental opportunities for students who are experiencing good academic progress and success seem self-evident. Given that emerging adulthood is a time of important identity development, academic success can contribute positively to affirmation of intellectual competence and skills. The developmental opportunities in situations of academic jeopardy might be less obvious but, as the earlier discussion illustrates, are many. Learning from disappointment or even failure or crisis, and building resilience through those challenges, is one of the hallmarks of successful development (e.g., Bain, 2012). With respect to identity development, crises, in the sense of events that lead young adults to question aspects of their identity that they have either taken for granted or ignored, are in fact considered essential to mature identity achievement (see the discussion of Marcia's identity statuses in Chapter 11). Academic counselors are well-placed to help students experiencing academic jeopardy see that they are not alone in their challenges; that such jeopardy can be a source of insight about self that can lead to future growth and success; and that life challenges can be faced and overcome with effort, determination, patience, and use of the proper resources. Offering advice and counsel on topics ranging from study skills to well-being in college to development of a sense of belonging to communication (including asking for help) to personal responsibility to challenges as learning opportunities is a way that academic counselors can help students achieve developmental growth as a result of academic jeopardy.

Career Counseling: Overview of the Services and Roles of Career Counselors

Academic counseling and career counseling are interdependent and complementary. For example, an academic counselor may encourage a student who is having difficulty selecting a major to meet with a career counselor. In addition, careful academic planning is essential for ensuring that students are able to take advantage of important career opportunities after completing their degree requirements. Recognizing the interdependent nature of these two sets of services, some college career centers employ counselors who are uniquely qualified to assist students majoring in specific areas (e.g., business and accounting, education, social sciences, arts and entertainment).

As you read in Chapter 1, vocational guidance (or career counseling) was a foundational part of the counseling profession and one of the early services provided on college campuses. Most students in counseling programs will have an entire class on career theory and career development and will be familiar with a range of approaches, so we will not duplicate that material here. Those who want further reading and resources can access the National Career Development Association's website (ncda.org). Today's career counselors on a college campus provide students with a variety of services, which can be placed in three primary categories: (a) assistance with early career development and decision-making, (b) assistance in developing career-entry skills, and (c) assistance with networking.

With regard to career decision-making, career counselors administer and interpret instruments that help students better understand their interests, values, and strengths. The information from these instruments—for example, the Strong Interest Inventory (Harmon, Hansen, Borgen, & Hammer, 1994) or the StrengthsFinder 2.0 (Rath, 2007)—is then used to assist the student with relevant decisions such as choosing a major or an occupational field. The individual's self-concept is a key factor in deciding on an appropriate occupation and career setting (Gottfredson, 2005). There are also clear connections to psychosocial development, such as the vectors for developing intellectual competence and clarifying purpose (see Chapter 11). For this reason, career counselors are trained to assist students in gaining a better understanding of their self-concepts (e.g., values, personality, abilities, aspirations) through the use of assessment instruments as well as through conversations with students.

With regard to helping students develop career-entry skills, career counselors help students learn to write effective résumés and cover letters. When well crafted, these documents have the potential to open doors to career opportunities. Career counselors also help students prepare for common interview questions (e.g., "What is your greatest strength?") and to anticipate and prepare for questions that employers are likely to ask based on a job applicant's unique characteristics (e.g., questions about gaps in an individual's work history). In a *mock interview,* the career counselor videotapes a practice employment interview with a college student and then provides the student with constructive feedback.

Finally, career counselors also organize career fairs and employer interviews on campus or assist students in finding internships or part-time work that helps them develop job-related skills. Depending on the campus, career services centers may also organize workshops about online career networking, applying to graduate programs, or making a good transition into the world of work. These events provide students with networking and employment opportunities in a relatively familiar and comfortable environment.

The majority of these services are delivered from a career services center and provided in one-to-one counseling sessions. Sometimes career counselors provide information in a group format, and they may also deliver services through outreach (e.g., visiting an academic class and critiquing the students' résumés) or web-based formats (e.g., instructional videos, brief Q and A chats with a staff person, an exchange of ideas about a cover letter via email). Career services may also be tailored depending on the campus type, including such services as decoding what "professional dress" means at an etiquette event or focusing on how to complete an associate's degree at a community college and then transfer to achieve a credential that will open doors to a desired career field. A high number of the services described in this section (e.g., personality assessment, help with selection of a major, job search activities) may also be addressed through online services, and college campus career centers commonly include computers for accessing these services. Where online assessments are concerned, we believe it is essential for a career counselor to meet with the client to aid her or him in understanding the assessment results (e.g., the results of an interest inventory).

Special Populations: Students From Low-Income Families and First-Generation Students

Imagine entering a community or setting that is unfamiliar (e.g., a neighborhood where the majority of residents are from a different culture than your own). Add the fact that you are visiting for an extended period and your successful adaptation to that setting is essential for achieving a personally meaningful goal. You might find yourself comparing yourself with individuals who are approximately your age and realizing that these peers possess special knowledge and social contacts that you do not possess. In comparison with these individuals, you feel uncertain and less informed. Perhaps you do not have to imagine what this would be like because you have actually had an experience like this. Once you have identified a specific experience with an unfamiliar culture, actual or imagined, reflect upon the following questions:

1. How would/did you approach the task of learning unwritten, informal rules for succeeding in your new environment?
2. How comfortable would/did you feel asking others for help in this unfamiliar cultural setting?
3. What feelings would/did you experience on realizing that you lacked knowledge and resources the majority possessed and took for granted? How would/did you cope with these feelings?
4. How would/did you determine whom to turn to for advice, guidance, or access to resources?
5. What qualities or characteristics would/did you look for in the people you approached for help?

As a result of reflecting on these questions, the authors hope you will find it easier to understand and empathize with the experiences of many undergraduates from special populations. For these students, the college campus is an unfamiliar culture that can be frustrating and perplexing.

The National Center for Education Statistics defines *low-income* families as those whose incomes fall in the lowest quintile of all family incomes (DeSilver, 2014), and low socioeconomic status (SES) has also been defined as the lowest income quartile (Doyle, 2011).

On the basis of DeSilver's definition, the National Center for Education Statistics reported in 2012 that 50.9% of low-income recent high school graduates (a category that includes both graduates and people who completed equivalency degrees and are ages 16 to 24) were enrolled in a 2-year or 4-year college. That percentage is considerably less than the 64.7% and 80.7% enrollment rates reported by the National Center for Education Statistics for middle-income and high-income students, respectively, for the same year (DeSilver, 2014). Furthermore, once enrolled in college, a lower percentage of students from low-income families complete the requirements for a bachelor's degree relative to students from middle-income and upper income families (Chapman, Laird, & Remani, 2011; Long, 2007; Rumberger, 2010). Low SES is associated with low academic achievement and school dropout, due to factors including but not limited to family resources, low-quality schools, and discrimination (American Psychological Association, 2017).

First-generation college students (FGCSs) are defined as those who do not have at least one parent who completed a college degree (DeAngelo, Franke, Hurtado, Pryor, & Tran, 2011). UCLA's Higher Education Research Institute reported that FGCSs graduated at a rate 14 percentage points below that of other students (DeAngelo et al., 2011). Because the parents of FGCSs are less familiar with college than other parents, these students are potentially at a disadvantage when it comes to college adaptation (Longwell-Grice, Adsitt, Mullins, & Serrata, 2016; Wheeler, 2016). This transition, as a result, commonly entails more difficulty (e.g., locating resources and required services), anxiety, confusion, and cultural discontinuity (Ishitani, 2006). Recently, researchers (Sun, Hagedorn, & Zhang, 2016) found that FGCSs are more likely to experience *intense homesickness* entailing feelings of distress detrimental to students' ability to concentrate and to their academic performance (Stroebe, Vliet, Hewstone, & Willis, 2002). Sun et al. also found that higher levels of *sense of belonging* at college (e.g., as a result of forming one or more quality relationships or membership in social groups) predicted lower levels of distress associated with intense homesickness. Wheeler (2016) described students as commonly experiencing a "pull to home" (p. 115) that compels them to want to visit family frequently.

From the preceding, it is evident that both lower SES and FGCSs face special challenges with regard to persisting to degree completion. Furthermore, many students from these special populations are part of other marginalized groups. For example, in the United States, individuals from African American or Latino backgrounds are more than twice as likely to live in poverty compared with their European American counterparts. Thus, many low-SES students and FGCSs face multiple oppressions. It is critically important not to stereotype any individual from these groups with respect to challenges typical of the group, yet it is equally important for academic advisers and career counselors to be sensitive to their possibility (see Tomasiewicz, 2017, for an excellent chapter on advising special populations in the first year of college). For all students, but particularly underrepresented students, academic and career issues are intertwined with issues of identity, wellness, purpose/aspirations, and self-concept. For these reasons, and because perceptions of a college's level and quality of support for underrepresented students is related to their self-concept and academic motivation (e.g., Browman & Destin, 2016), it is critical for academic advisers and career counselors to be highly intentional with regard to their interpersonal responses and the services they provide.

Academic Advising With Lower SES Students

Low-SES students are, on average, likely to arrive at college with less adequate preparation and support. Robert Putnam (2016) documented the many opportunity gaps between rich and poor that exist in the United States, including large and growing gaps in degree of family stability; access to quality day care; overall life stability and predictability; neighborhood social capital and safety; educational opportunities in school (e.g., excellent teachers, available Advanced Placement classes, well-stocked science labs); cocurricular opportunities; and frequency of "rich verbal interaction[s]" (p. 116). More than ever before, low-income students in the United States are at a disadvantage with respect to these predictors of educational and personal success. On average, low-income students have also experienced parenting styles that put more emphasis on obedience to authority figures and less emphasis on verbal interaction with them (Putnam, 2016). Together with a lower sense of trust in others and institutions (Putnam, 2016), this socialization history might create some challenges in college. For example, it might be more difficult for students from such backgrounds to ask questions that might be seen as challenging authority in class, or it could be more difficult to ask authority figures for help.

Low-income students do not arrive entirely at a disadvantage, however. Experience with a more authoritarian parenting style might be a source of strength with respect to well-being and success if it potentially fosters greater adherence to college rules and a decreased tendency to engage in high-risk behaviors. Data show, for example, that low-income adolescents and young adults are less likely to drink alcohol and use marijuana than are affluent students (e.g., Luthar, 2003; Patrick, Wightman, Schoeni, & Schulenberg, 2012).

Nonetheless, once on campus, low-income students face unique direct and indirect threats to their academic success. Direct threats include potential difficulties paying for all course materials in a timely manner or avoiding courses or other academic opportunities that have fees or extra expenses (e.g., study abroad). They might not have extra cash to avail themselves of the "extra" resources available to more affluent students (e.g., psychoeducational testing for learning disabilities, mental health services, or intensive tutoring). It is not uncommon for students to share financial aid for nontuition expenses at home with their family, even though it means they forgo the textbooks or food that the aid was intended to purchase. When facing significant academic challenges (e.g., failing a class or struggling to maintain a full course load during a regular semester), a low-income student might not be able to afford the tuition or time away from employment to retake a class or make up work during a summer or extended session; they would be severely challenged to consider extra semesters of enrollment once financial aid packages end. Indirect threats include inability to engage in social activities that other students might take for granted: going out for dinner, participating in a campus fundraiser that requires an entry fee; joining fraternities or sororities that have joining fees and expectations for participation in activities (e.g., beach weekends) that are costly. These latter threats are threats to belonging, which affects academic success. It is important to note that low-income students are already more likely than others to interpret the normal challenges, frustrations, and disappointments of college as signs that they do not belong (e.g., Tough, 2014); additional barriers to belonging resulting from lack of money to participate in clubs or social activities might exacerbate this problem.

Another threat is the chronic stress created by financial strain, stress that has been shown to directly affect the brain and cognitive functioning (e.g., Badger, 2013; Mullainathan & Shafir, 2013). As previously mentioned, availability of financial aid is positively associated with lower SES students' perceptions of a college as supportive (Browman & Destin, 2016). Accordingly, having paid employment while in school, while reducing time available to study or participate in college extra- and cocurricular activities, might also promote students' academic motivation. Given these many threats and obstacles, it should come as no surprise that students from low-income families are at significantly higher risk of college dropout, even when factors such as SAT scores (as rough measures of ability; e.g., Tough, 2014) are held constant.

Implications for Academic Advising With Lower SES Students

Clearly, academic advisers must attend to far more than simply course schedules and grades for low-income students. Advisers must be sensitive to the many threats to academic success and personal well-being experienced by low-income students, while recognizing the strengths that such students might bring (e.g., resilience in the face of adversity and gratitude for opportunities that are not taken for granted). Effective advising would include empathy and understanding of the many pressures and needs these students are likely to have, as well as strategies for tackling those challenges and information about campus resources that might be available to address needs (e.g., emergency financial funds, free online academic resources through the college library, and textbook rentals).

Career Counseling With Lower SES Students

Doyle (2011) reported that individuals from low-SES backgrounds tend to find it more difficult to transition to college life and may intentionally choose less prestigious institutions, believing they will fit in better. Abrahamsen and Drange (2014) found that ethnic minority students from a low-SES background had higher career ambitions than middle-class students from the majority culture but that their career expectations did not match their high aspirations. A major contributing factor to this aspiration-expectation gap, which is well-documented in the literature, is perceived career barriers due to structural racism and/or classism (Diemer & Hsieh, 2008).

Low-SES college graduates of color have an unemployment rate of 12.4%, which is more than double the general unemployment rate among young college graduates, and are more prone to accruing high student debts (Houle, 2014; Jones & Schmitt, 2014). Thus, low-SES students may feel that there is not a sufficient payoff for completing college.

Implications for Career Counselors With Lower SES Students

For career counselors, it is important to be aware of these trends, while acknowledging that each individual's experiences, strengths, and challenges are unique. For career counselors who belong to a middle-SES or an upper SES group, a stance of *cultural humility* is appropriate when working with lower SES students. Cultural humility is characterized by respect and an egalitarian attitude toward a client's cultural experience and background and is positively associated with the quality of the counselor-client alliance (Hook, Davis, Owen, Worthington, & Utsey, 2013).

Assuming that the reader has had a course in career theory, we will emphasize only one theory that is relevant for the special populations under consideration in this chapter. Gottfredson's (2005) theory of circumscription and compromise emphasizes the processes of circumscription and compromise as influencing career development. *Circumscription* refers to students' elimination of occupations that conflict with their self-concept or their social space. Through this process, lower SES individuals may rule out occupations that they associate with a middle-class or upper class background, limiting their zone of acceptable alternatives. In addition, individuals may rule out occupations that are inconsistent with their personal view of their sex role (e.g., occupations that are viewed as too masculine or too feminine). *Compromise* refers to students' relinquishing their most preferred alternatives for more accessible ones. This factor may be particularly related to the aspiration-expectation gap mentioned earlier, in that lower SES individuals may eliminate prestigious occupations because of perceived structural barriers.

Career counselors should be familiar with Gottfredson's (2005) theory when working with low-SES individuals. Gottfredson recommended that formal assessments of ability, interests, values, and personality, as well as an analysis of past activities, support, barriers, and effect on others, can serve to address circumscription through self-insight. Gottfredson identified several strategies that can address compromise through increasing self-investment. Among them are training in résumé writing, interviewing, skills building, and anxiety management; job banks and placement services; and assistance in identifying preferred occupations and backups. Diemer and Hsieh (2008) found that sociopolitical development in low-SES students of color led to recognizing, managing, and overcoming structural barriers and attaining career aspirations. Career counselors can promote this form of development by providing "systematic exposure to occupational alternatives and nonstereotypic workers [to] reduce" students' overreliance on stereotypes about race, gender, and SES (Gottfredson, 2005, p. 91). Thus, counselors can act as facilitators for students' sociopolitical development to narrow the aspiration-expectation gap.

Counselors can focus on several areas to increase the employment chances of low-SES college graduates. Doyle (2011) reported that low-SES students engaged in fewer activities related to employability skills and invested most of their time in studying to get a good degree. This was not related to financial resources. Students often simply did not realize that employers valued engagement in activities that demonstrate and build skills such as communication and teamwork. Many low-SES students showed a lack of awareness of the importance of career planning activities and often completed tasks one at a time, pushing career activities down the priority list of short-term "to-do" items and pushing more immediate course deadlines up this list (Doyle, 2011). Thus, career counselors may focus on activities related to employability skills and career planning with low-SES students who fail to prioritize them.

Despite a higher risk of experiencing additional challenges, low-SES students are less likely to utilize college career counseling services (Doyle, 2011). Thus, outreach services are crucial to reach low-SES students who may benefit from career assistance. Career counselors should also be aware of the increased risk of emotional difficulties (e.g., anxiety, depression) among this population and refer students to mental health counseling services as needed. In general, encouraging students to utilize appropriate services (for instance, academic resource centers on campus, the financial aid office, etc.) may be a key aspect of career counseling with low-SES college students. Castleman, Page, and Schooley (2014) identified the summer after high school as a major time of attrition among college-bound students from lower SES backgrounds because of limited supports, confusing forms and strict deadlines, and unanticipated fees such as student health insurance. Career counselors could reach out to incoming students during this period to provide additional information and assistance with these issues and tasks.

In conclusion, low-SES students tend to face additional challenges such as discrimination, financial concerns, and difficulty adjusting to college life. Career counselors should keep in mind that each student's experience is unique, while being aware of these potential struggles. Topics that may be explored in career counseling are overcoming structural barriers, utilizing services, and engaging in career planning activities.

Case Study of a Student From a Lower SES Family

The Case of Sam

Sam is a 21-year-old, African American junior at a small private college. He grew up in a low-SES urban neighborhood with his mother, his grandmother, and his three younger siblings. He was consistently at the top of his class in high school and has always had an incredible drive to do well in school. A lot of his friends chose to start work after high school, because they thought there was no point in even applying to college. Sam received a full-tuition scholarship to go to a small, prestigious liberal arts college with a largely middle-class and upper class student body. Although low-SES students are a minority of the student population, even fewer students are African American.

Before reading further, hearken back to the Reflection Exercise wherein you thought about your own encounter with an unfamiliar culture and reflect on the following questions:

1. How comfortable do you think it would be for Sam to ask others (e.g., peers, professors, advisers, counselors) for help?
2. What feelings do you imagine he might be experiencing when he compares himself with his college student peers? How might he be attempting to cope with these feelings in lieu of seeking help from student support personnel?
3. In addition to academic and career counseling, what other student support offices and personnel might be integrated into a comprehensive approach to helping Sam?
4. Imagine you are Sam's academic counselor. What qualities, knowledge, and behaviors would increase the likelihood that Sam would view you as a trusted and valuable resource?

Sam's high school counselor helped him with his application, but the summer before he started, he had little support with the enrollment process. It included a lot of paperwork, confusing forms, deadlines, and unanticipated costs such as required student health insurance that his family found difficult to produce. Sam felt uncomfortable asking for help and did not know to whom to turn. In the end, he managed to get a loan to pay for these fees.

When Sam arrived at his new college, he felt like he did not fit in with the other students, and it was difficult for him to make friends. He often felt that he had to "prove" his academic abilities to his peers, which was a lot of pressure. On top of this, his classes were more difficult than his high school classes, and he felt overwhelmed with the amount of coursework. He was aware of the career center, the learning assistance center, and the counseling center on campus but felt uncomfortable asking strangers for help, thinking that they might judge him—thus reinforcing his belief that he did not belong there. Furthermore, he had so many assignments and readings to do that he did not have time to attend any appointments. Sam had enjoyed being a part of the debating team in high school and had always had an interest in law. However, he knew that law school was expensive and did not believe that it would be realistic for him to become a lawyer.

Although Sam has a financial aid package that covers all tuition and fees, Sam runs into difficulty paying for textbooks at the start of the semester, either because actual text and course material costs exceed the estimates used for financial aid or because all of his aid has not arrived at the very start of the semester when textbooks and materials are first needed. His academic counselor has connected him with the university's emergency fund to pay for extra costs, but because those material needs are not always settled until classes start, it is often difficult to get started on coursework in a timely manner. His adviser therefore tries to help Sam find online or library resources that can tide him over and reminds Sam to communicate with his professors about these challenges so that professors understand he is not being irresponsible if he has difficulty keeping up. Sam's adviser also advises Sam against sending aid provided for textbooks and food home to his family, reminding Sam that using the aid as intended will ultimately help his family the most because it will help Sam be academically successful.

Sam has often doubted whether he really belongs at the university. Classes are much more difficult than his high school classes were, and especially at the start, he really struggled to get good grades. Thanks to support from his academic adviser and the resource centers, and general adjustment, he is doing better with each semester, but it still seems to him that he has to work much harder than his peers. Unlike many of them, he works a job 15 hours per week, which leaves less time for studying or socializing. Although he is aware of and has used many resources (e.g., the office of academic advising, the career center, the learning assistance center, and the counseling center), he still feels uncomfortable about asking for help. Furthermore, he has so many assignments and readings to do that he does not have time to attend any appointments.

He also continues to feel like he does not fit in and that it is difficult for him to make friends, as well as continuing to experience the pressure associated with feeling a need to prove himself academically to his peers. When hall mates decide to go off campus to dinner, a movie, or a concert, they sometimes invite him, but he always declines because of the costs. He hates to use money as an excuse, so he worries they think he is unfriendly.

Sam's academic adviser has helped Sam by expressing confidence in Sam's ability to succeed and thrive at the university and helping him to understand that his challenges and struggles are normal. The adviser reaches out regularly to see how Sam is doing and consciously aims to convey the caring and empathy he realizes is required for Sam to be willing to share his story, his doubts, and his needs. The adviser has been careful to connect Sam with the learning assistance center, where he can learn specific time management and study strategies that he did not need to excel in high school. He looks for ways to connect Sam to offices and programs where he can meet other students who can normalize his struggles, as well as individual academic advising that expresses caring and empathy.

In addition, Sam met Regina at an outreach program he attended. Regina was a counselor who worked in the career center at his university. She encouraged him to make an appointment, and together, they explored his career aspirations in more detail, looking at his reasoning behind thinking it is unrealistic to plan to attend law school. Together, they found that perceived discrimination was a main reason Sam did not believe he would be able to become a lawyer. Regina facilitated Sam's exploration of his preferred possible selves (Markus & Nurius, 1986) and through this process discovered that in order of preference Sam desired, sociocultural and socioeconomic barriers aside, to become—a lawyer, a politician, or a history professor.

Regina expressed empathy regarding Sam's past experiences of perceived discrimination and was careful to encourage Sam to maintain an aspirational attitude in spite of these discouraging experiences. At the same time, she made a concerted effort to reinforce the salient factors such as Sam's academic aptitude (e.g., his high school grade point average and SAT scores), interests, and transferable skills. She asked Sam to complete several assessment instruments, including the Strong Interest Inventory, the StrengthsFinder 2.0, a values scale, and a transferable skills inventory. Once Sam completed these instruments, Regina scheduled two subsequent sessions to interpret the results. During these subsequent sessions, Regina emphasized how the results were consistent with his stated possible occupational selves, and she further established the greater importance of his strengths and attributes (relative to sociopolitical factors) with regard to his decision-making process. She also encouraged Sam to become involved in potentially related cocurricular activities such as the Debate Club. Finally, she connected him with law school students and student government leaders who were also from a lower SES background and/or African American.

Regina assisted Sam in exploring financial aid and scholarship options. She provided him with a document detailing the appropriate timing of academic events such as registering for the Law School Admission Test and the Graduate Record Exam, requesting letters of recommendation, and submitting applications for postgraduate programs. During his senior year, Regina assisted Sam in scheduling and conducted a mock interview to help him prepare for his law school admission interviews.

■ ■ ■

Academic Advising With First-Generation College Students

Many, although not all, FGCSs are also low income, so many FGCSs face the challenges already described. Additionally, first-generation students, by definition, have parents without firsthand knowledge of the college environment. As a result, despite the best of intentions, parental support and guidance might be lacking or misguided. FGCSs might, of course, have other family members, including siblings, with college experience; nonetheless, on average, FGCSs will have less familiarity with the college context and less access to individuals who can help them understand and interpret this new context and culture. When normal college difficulties arise, parents of FGCSs will not be as equipped as other parents to support and guide their student in important ways (e.g., normalizing such difficulties and encouraging communication with professors). In fact, parents, like their students, might be quick to conclude that the student is out of his or her element and does not really belong (e.g., Tough, 2014), reinforcing the "imposter syndrome" that is all too common. Parents and other family members might also send mixed messages about college, at times expressing pride in the unique achievements and potential of the student but at other times expressing fear of emotional distancing or even resentment or disdain for the student's absence or growing intellectual identity (e.g., Longwell-Grice et al., 2016; Schauer, 2005; Sickles, 2004). FGCSs at 2-year as well as 4-year institutions can experience high levels of obligation to succeed so as to help their families and to make them proud because of their unique opportunity (e.g., Kirkner & Levinson, 2017).

Implications for Academic Advising With First-Generation College Students

It is critical that academic advisers be conscious of these special needs and circumstances. Advisers can help promote success for FGCSs by expressing confidence in the student's belonging and ability to succeed and by normalizing academic and other challenges. As with all students, but perhaps even more so with FGCSs, behavioral and verbal messages of care and concern are critical for creating trust (e.g., Longwell-Grice et al., 2016). *Intrusive advising* that anticipates the challenges described, that reaches out actively and often to students, and that provides direct and explicit guidance and encouragement on academic and nonacademic matters is recommended (Longwell-Grice et al., 2016). Furthermore, the design of advising programs can draw on research-based practices to help students at higher risk of college dropout. In particular, these students appear to benefit in multiple ways from hearing stories from other students who have overcome challenges (e.g., Walton & Cohen, 2011), and perhaps especially from other students who share stories specifically related to generational or economic background (e.g., Stephens, Townsend, Hamedani, Destin, & Manzo, 2015).

With respect to both income and generational status, it is important for advisers to be conscious of getting to know students as individuals. Although there are tendencies for low-income or FGCSs to face the challenges delineated, inclusive advising means recognizing that every student has his or her own story, and taking the time to hear that story.

Career Counseling With First-Generation College Students

Although FGCSs may come from any SES, authors have reported that they most typically come from the working class (Lippincott & German, 2007). The working class comprises laborers who work for wages rather than owning their own business or the means for production. FGCSs commonly report that their reasons for attending college include gaining respect and social standing (Bui, 2002; Wheeler, 2016), making their families proud (Bui, 2002), and obtaining a better occupational position than would be possible without a college degree (Gibbons & Woodside, 2014; Wheeler, 2016). A particularly troubling psychological characteristic is the common experience of *achievement guilt* because these students are commonly confronted with the reality of close family members who are working hard and making sacrifices to make their success possible (Longwell-Grice et al., 2016). In addition, parents and other family members may experience feelings ranging from resentment to lack of understanding regarding the FGCS's need to separate and become better acculturated to the college environment. For these reasons, it should come as no surprise that FGCSs have a lower rate of persistence to degree completion (Ishitani, 2006; Seidman, 2005).

An important point to recognize is that FGCSs have unique strengths and potential strengths that career counselors can use to promote their adjustment and success. One unique strength is that in some families, the FGCS is a source of family pride (Wheeler, 2016). Being considered a source of pride, and viewing the family as an extension of one's identity, can engender strong feelings of family identification and responsibility to succeed. These feelings can increase the likelihood that the student will persist to degree completion. Another potential strength is that FGCSs tend to be receptive to advisers and counselors who take care to cultivate a good working alliance. As a result, career counselors are encouraged to seek ways to enhance students' sense of belonging in the college community.

Implications for Career Counseling Practice With First-Generation College Students

We recommend that career counselors remain mindful of the unique difficulties FGCSs are facing during their transitions to college and during their undergraduate years. For example, the "pull to home" that Wheeler (2016, p. 115) described might lead FGCSs to prioritize living close to family in their career decisions more so than would other students.

Understandably, many college students are autonomy oriented and prefer to complete interest inventories online, and they may even be resistant to meeting with a career counselor to discuss the results. However, in working with an FGCS, it might be advantageous to take a more conversational approach to assessment. For example, a career counselor might discuss the six occupational themes composing Holland's (1985) hexagonal model (e.g., Realistic, Investigative, Artistic, etc.) and ask the student to relate his or her impressions and work experiences vis-à-vis each of the themes, one at a time. The student might arrange in rank order the relative strength of his or her liking for each of the six occupational themes. The career counselor should emphasize that an individual's interests are subject to change as he or she gains additional firsthand experience with activities congruent with any given Holland theme and encourage the student to seek opportunities (e.g., volunteer or part-time work, participation in campus organizations) to enhance his or her self-understanding. A primary objective is to use the conversation to promote a good relationship, which is particularly important for the success of FGCSs.

Another significant consideration is the fact that FGCSs are less familiar with the college experience (e.g., personnel, locations of resources) and the process of completing a degree. They may also be less familiar with the relationships among college majors and related occupations. In addition, they may lack an appreciation of the importance of becoming active in campus organizations and how cocurricular activities potentially complement academics and career development. Some FGCSs may mistakenly believe that campus activities are unimportant and may underestimate their relevance to developing a sense of belonging that can foster career development and academic performance. For this reason, we recommend that career counselors take particular care in educating FGCSs in the importance of involvement in campus activities. Career counselors should also familiarize FGCSs with the content of a résumé and the value placed on cocurricular participation by employers and company recruiters, so that they can better anticipate the road ahead when they are making decisions in the first year of college.

Conclusion

Academic counselors and career counselors are prime examples of college support personnel who, through the provision of a quality relationship, can promote a sense of belonging for students from any and all populations. However, we spent time exploring the additional needs of both lower SES students and FGCSs, who may face unique direct and indirect threats to developing a sense of belonging in college, which can affect academic progress and career development. These students' perceptions of the college environment as warm and supportive is of key importance with regard to enhancing their self-confidence and academic motivation. We believe that an integral component of such a relationship is a stance of cultural humility. We have provided specific recommendations for approaches and services to meet the unique needs of students, which can be tailored for use on particular campuses or with particular populations in the future. Ultimately, we recommend that academic and career counselors adopt a relationship-oriented approach that is at once warm, empathic, and developmentally appropriate.

Final Case Study

Laura is a 19-year-old FGCS who is White. She is attending a state university located approximately 170 miles from her parents' hometown of 15,000 people. Her mother and father both completed high school. Her mother is a claims representative for the Social Security Administration, and her father is a mechanic. Laura also has a 15-year-old brother, Eric, who is a sophomore in high school, and she considers herself to be an important role model for him. Laura is now in the first month of her second semester of college. She is very close to her parents and brother. Every week, on Friday afternoon, she completes the 4-hour drive home to see her family, and every Sunday afternoon, she completes the 4-hour drive back to arrive at her residence hall by about 8 p.m.

At the beginning of the preceding fall semester, Laura had decided she wanted to be a biology major and that after receiving her bachelor's degree, she would enroll in medical school. She enrolled in biology, calculus, and chemistry courses, and although she was able to attain a cumulative grade point average of 3.3, she now questions her original decision to attend medical school. However, she also worries that her parents would never understand if she switched to a nonscience major.

Recognizing the potential challenges Laura might face being an FGCS, her academic adviser invited her in for a brief chat after the first few weeks of the first semester, expressing interest in how the transition was going for Laura. At that time, Laura shared that she was somewhat discouraged by the difficulty of the work and by some of her early grades on quizzes and homework assignments. It seemed that all of the students around her were so much more confident and self-assured. She did not feel comfortable sharing her discouragement with her parents because she did not want them to have doubts about whether she should be at the university (even though she was having such doubts). She also knew they would not feel confident giving her relevant advice. Laura's adviser reminded her that regardless of how it appeared, doubts and struggles in the transition to college are common and normal. The adviser also reassured her that asking for help is a sign of strength, and that she should not feel embarrassed or ashamed to ask professors or teaching assistants for help. The adviser gave her some tips for approaching the conversation with her professors. Her adviser also reminded her of other resources, such as the Chemistry Center and the Math Center.

Taking advantage of these resources helped, and by the end of the semester, Laura was doing much better. Ultimately, she did well in the courses she took to fulfill premedical requirements. However, she began to have second thoughts regarding whether she wanted to become a medical doctor. Her academic adviser encouraged her to take the classes in which she is most interested, because this is most likely to keep her motivated and successful. The adviser pointed out that there are a lot of satisfying careers in the health professions and that Laura could benefit from meeting with a career counselor. Laura shared that she worried her parents would never understand if she decided not to attend medical school. She decided to continue to major in biology and to explore other options besides going to medical school.

Case Exploration Questions

1. If you were in Laura's shoes, how do you think you could start asking others (e.g., peers, professors, advisers, counselors) for help? What would make it easier or harder?
2. What feelings might she be experiencing when she compares herself with her college student peers? What are some ways she might be attempting to cope with these feelings?
3. In addition to academic counseling, what other student support offices and personnel might be integrated into a comprehensive approach to helping Laura? How could those offices help specifically?
4. Imagine you are Laura's academic counselor. What qualities, knowledge, and behaviors on your part would increase the likelihood that Laura would view you as a trusted and valuable resource?

5. Imagine you are a career counselor whom Laura has come to see. What approach would you use in your work with Laura? What might you do first?
6. Describe your approach to career assessment (formal, informal, etc.). What would be your goals for assessment?
7. How would you provide Laura with feedback resulting from the assessment process? Consider how you would ensure that your feedback is developmentally appropriate and culturally responsive.

References

Abrahamsen, B., & Drange, I. (2014). Ethnic minority students' career expectations in prospective professions: Navigating between ambitions and discrimination. *Sociology, 49,* 252–269. doi:10.1177/0038038514542494

American Psychological Association. (2017). Education and socioeconomic status factsheet. Retrieved from http://www.apa.org/pi/ses/resources/publications/education.aspx

Archambault, K. L. (2017). Emerging concerns. In J. R. Fox & H. E. Martin (Eds.), *Academic advising and the first college year* (pp. 3–18). Columbia: University of South Carolina, National Resource Center for the First-Year Experience and Students in Transition and NACADA: The Global Community for Academic Advising.

Asher, S. R., & Weeks, M. W. (2014). Loneliness and belongingness in the college years. In R. J. Coplan & J. C. Bowker (Eds.), *The handbook of solitude: Psychological perspectives on social isolation, social withdrawal, and being alone* (pp. 283–301). Hoboken, NJ: Wiley-Blackwell. doi:10.1037/t37005-000

Badger, E. (2013, August 29). How poverty taxes the brain. *The Atlantic*. Retrieved from https://www.citylab.com/life/2013/08/how-poverty-taxes-brain/6716/

Bain, K. (2012). *What the best college students do.* Boston, MA: Harvard University Press.

Baumeister, R. F., & Leary, M. R. (1995). The need to belong: Desire for interpersonal attachments as a fundamental human motivation. *Psychological Bulletin, 117,* 497–529.

Browman, A. S., & Destin, M. (2016). The effects of a warm or chilly climate toward socioeconomic diversity on academic motivation and self-concept. *Personality and Social Psychology Bulletin, 42,* 172–187.

Bui, K. T. (2002). First-generation college students at a four-year university: Background characteristics, reasons for pursuing higher education, and first-year experiences. *College Student Journal, 36,* 3–11.

Castleman, B. L., Page, L. C., & Schooley, K. (2014). The forgotten summer: Does the offer of college counseling after high school mitigate summer melt among college-intending, low-income high school graduates? *Journal of Policy Analysis and Management, 33,* 320–344.

Chapman, C., Laird, J., & Remani, A. K. (2011). *Trends in high school dropout and completion rates in the United States: 1972–2009.* Washington, DC: National Center for Education Statistics.

Council for the Advancement of Standards in Higher Education. (2015). *CAS professional standards for higher education* (9th ed.). Washington, DC: Author. Retrieved from https://www.nacada.ksu.edu/Resources/Pillars/CASstandards.aspx

DeAngelo, L., Franke, R., Hurtado, S., Pryor, J. H., & Tran, S. (2011). *Completing college: Assessing graduation rates at four-year institutions.* Los Angeles, CA: Higher Education Research Institute.

DeSilver, D. (2014, January 15). College enrollment among low-income students still trails richer groups. Retrieved from www.pewresearch.org/fact-tank/2014/01/15/college-enrollment-among-low-income-students-still-trails-richer-groups/

Diemer, M. A., & Hsieh, C. (2008). Sociopolitical development and vocational expectations among lower socioeconomic status adolescents of color. *The Career Development Quarterly, 56,* 257–267. doi:10.1002/j.2161-0045.2008.tb00040.x

Doyle, E. (2011). Career development needs of low socio-economic status university students. *Australian Journal of Career Development, 20,* 56–65. doi:10.1177/103841621102000309

Gibbons, M. M., & Woodside, M. (2014). Addressing the needs of first-generation college students: Lessons learned from adults from low-education families. *Journal of College Counseling, 17,* 21–36. doi:10.1002/j.2161-1882.2014.00045.x

Gottfredson, L. S. (2005). Applying Gottfredson's theory of circumscription and compromise. In S. D. Brown & R. W. Lent (Eds.), *Career development and counseling: Putting theory and research to work* (pp. 71–98). Hoboken, NJ: Wiley.

Harmon, L. W., Hansen, J. C., Borgen, F. H., & Hammer, A. L. (1994). *Strong Interest Inventory: Applications and technical guide.* Stanford, CA: Stanford University Press.

Holland, J. L. (1985). *Making vocational choices: A theory of vocational personalities and work environments* (2nd ed.). Englewood Cliffs, NJ: Prentice-Hall.

Hook, J. N., Davis, D. E., Owen, J., Worthington, E. L., & Utsey, S. O. (2013). Cultural humility: Measuring openness to culturally diverse clients. *Journal of Counseling Psychology, 60,* 353–367.

Houle, J. N. (2014). Disparities in debt: Parents' socioeconomic resources and young adult student loan debt. *Sociology of Education, 87,* 53–69. doi:10.1177/0038040713512213

Ishitani, T. T. (2006). Studying attrition and degree completion behavior among first generation college students in the United States. *The Journal of Higher Education, 77,* 861–885.

Jones, J., & Schmitt, J. (2014). *A college degree is no guarantee* (No. 2014-08). Retrieved from http://cepr.net/publications/reports/a-college-degree-is-no-guarantee

Kirkner, T., & Levinson, J. (2017). Unique transitions at two-year colleges. In J. R. Fox & H. E. Martin (Eds.), *Academic advising and the first college year* (pp. 63–84). Columbia: University of South Carolina, National Resource Center for the First-Year Experience and Students in Transition and NACADA: The Global Community for Academic Advising.

Lippincott, J. A., & German, N. (2007). From blue collar to ivory tower: Counseling first-generation, working class students. In J. A. Lippincott & R. B. Lippincott (Eds.), *Special populations in college counseling: A handbook for mental health professionals* (pp. 89–98). Alexandria, VA: American Counseling Association.

Long, B. T. (2007). The contributions of economics to the study of college access and success. *Teachers College Record, 109,* 2367–2443.

Longwell-Grice, R., Adsitt, N. Z., Mullins, K., & Serrata, W. (2016). The first ones: Three studies on first-generation college students. *NACADA Journal, 36,* 34–46.

Luthar, S. S. (2003). The culture of affluence: Psychological costs of material wealth. *Child Development, 74,* 1581–1593. doi:10.1046/j.1467-8624.2003.00625.x

Markus, H., & Nurius, P. (1986). Possible selves. *American Psychologist, 41,* 954–969.

Mullainathan, S., & Shafir, E. (2013). *Scarcity: Why having too little means so much.* New York, NY: Times Books.

NACADA: The Global Community for Academic Advising. (2006). *NACADA concept of academic advising.* Retrieved from https://www.nacada.ksu.edu/Resources/Pillars/Concept.aspx

Patrick, M. E., Wightman, P., Schoeni, R. F., & Schulenberg, J. E., (2012). Socioeconomic status and substance use among young adults: A comparison across constructs and drugs. *Journal of Studies on Alcohol and Drugs, 73,* 772–782. doi:10.15288/jsad.2012.73.772

Putnam, R. D. (2016). *Our kids: The American dream in crisis.* New York, NY: Simon & Schuster.

Rath, T. (2007). *StrengthsFinder 2.0.* New York, NY: Gallup Press.

Rumberger, R. W. (2010). Education and the reproduction of economic inequality in the United States: An empirical investigation. *Economics of Education Review, 29,* 246–254. doi:10.1016/j.econedurev.2009.07.006

Schauer, I. (2005, February). Issues facing first generation college students. *Academic Advising Today, 28*(1). Retrieved from https://www.nacada.ksu.edu/Resources/Academic-Advising-Today/View-Articles/Issues-Facing-First-Generation-College-Students.aspx

Schauss Fergueson, N. (2017). Academic recovery in the first year. In J. R. Fox & H. E. Martin (Eds.), *Academic advising and the first college year* (pp. 107–126). Columbia: University of South Carolina, National Resource Center for the First-Year Experience and Students in Transition and NACADA: The Global Community for Academic Advising.

Seidman, A. (Ed.). (2005). *College student retention: Formula for student success.* Westport, CT: American Council on Education and Praeger.

Sickles, A. R. (2004). *Advising first-generation students.* Retrieved from the NACADA Clearinghouse of Academic Advising Resources website: http://www.nacada.ksu.edu/Clearinghouse/AdvisingIssues/1st_Generation.htm

Stephens, N. M., Townsend, S. S. M., Hamedani, M. G., Destin, M., & Manzo, V. (2015). A difference-education intervention equips first-generation college students to thrive in the face of stressful college situations. *Psychological Science, 26,* 1556–1566. doi:10.1177/0956797615593501

Stroebe, M., Vliet, T., Hewstone, M., & Willis, H. (2002). Homesickness among students in two cultures: Antecedents and consequences. *British Journal of Psychology, 93,* 147–168. doi:10.1348/000712602162508

Sun, J., Hagedorn, L. S., & Zhang, Y. (2016). Homesickness at college: Its impact on academic performance and retention. *Journal of College Student Development, 57,* 943–957.

Tomasiewicz, R. (2017). Advising special populations in the first year. In J. R. Fox & H. E. Martin (Eds.), *Academic advising and the first college year* (pp. 127–150). Columbia: University of South Carolina, National Resource Center for the First-Year Experience and Students in Transition and NACADA: The Global Community for Academic Advising.

Tough, P. (2014, May 15). Who gets to graduate? *The New York Times.* Retrieved from http://nyti.ms/1gjJOoU

Walton, G. M., & Cohen, G. L. (2011). A brief social-belonging intervention improves academic and health outcomes of minority students. *Science, 331,* 1447–1451. doi:10.1126/science.1198364

Wheeler, M. (2016). Potential family and mental health considerations for working with first generation college students exploring careers. *Career Planning and Adult Development Journal, 32,* 112–119.

Chapter 17

Substance Use and Addiction

Elizabeth Likis-Werle

An over-indulgence of anything,
even something as pure as water,
can intoxicate.

—Criss Jami

■ ■ ■

Reflection Exercise

Jeremy is a 19-year-old sophomore who came to college to play baseball. His father had played when he was younger but eventually settled down to a 9-to-5 factory job. He remembers his dad losing his job and drinking heavily for a few years, but Jeremy felt bad for him and didn't think much of it. He tried alcohol in high school and smoked marijuana a couple of times to relax but didn't like the way it affected his breathing for his sports workouts. In college, Jeremy got decent grades. He drank on the weekends but mostly stayed out of trouble. His family expected him to succeed and graduate in 4 years, but recently, he was injured in practice and was not able to play much.

He became depressed being on the bench and his grades suffered; he lost sleep trying to stay up and study after practice, and the energy drinks were not helping. He was exhausted and frustrated with this cycle that was getting him nowhere. One of his teammates suggested he take some pain pills, train harder, and prove to the coach he could get back in the lineup. One weekend night, Jeremy and the guys were out drinking to celebrate a victory, and Jeremy tripped, reinjuring his knee. His buddy gave him some more pain pills just to get through the night, and the next thing he knew, he woke up in the emergency room, having wrecked his car. Now he has been sent by the Student Affairs Conduct Office for a substance use assessment in the counseling center. He is scared that he will get kicked off the team and fail his classes.

Many students like Jeremy are unaware of their risk factors for developing an addiction and do not ever see themselves as someone who could be affected by substance use. College students often share prescription medications and mix them without understanding the risky implications. With the perfect storm of genetic predispositions, injuries, life stressors, and situational factors, one choice can escalate into a horror story with lasting consequences. How would you answer the following questions?

1. What are your beliefs about what is typical or the "norm" for college student substance use?
2. Do you think it is okay to share one's medications?
3. Have you ever found yourself in a situation that snowballed in a way that you didn't intend?
4. How would you, as a campus professional, address and intervene effectively with Jeremy?

■ ■ ■

Substance use is one of the costliest behaviors for college students and the campuses that serve them in terms of academic, health, wellness, and physical and mental health impacts. Ask a student affairs administrator what his or her top concerns are for maintaining safety on campus, and substance use will likely be a top issue. College counseling center directors have reported substance abuse as one of the top six most prevalent issues among students who use their services for several years in a row (Reetz, Bershad, LeViness, & Whitlock, 2016). The American College Health Association (ACHA) has been administering a survey twice a year since 2000 to college students, inquiring about several different health domains. In a recent survey of the National College Health Assessment from Fall 2016, 64.2% of participants reported using alcohol in the last 30 days and 18.4% used marijuana (ACHA, 2016). Additionally, 11.7% said they had used prescription drugs in the last year that were not prescribed to them. This represents an upward trend from recent years, compared with 59.5% who reported using alcohol and 15% using marijuana the previous year in Fall 2015 and 61.3% using alcohol and 14.1% using marijuana in Fall 2013. Dennhardt and Murphy's (2013) findings were even more alarming; 36% of college students surveyed reported using drugs in the past year. In a time of increased education, mandated assessments, comprehensive prevention programs, and grant money available to address collegiate substance abuse, many practitioners are puzzled as to why these numbers continue to rise. Clearly, the information provided and required has not translated into consistent behavioral change. In this chapter I will provide an overview of both legal and illegal substance use rates, trends, and unique factors in the college population that span the continuum of experimentation, regular use, and addiction as well as review assessment, treatment, prevention, and intervention strategies for college students.

Research has been conducted on those enrolled in college versus those of the same age group not enrolled. Dawson, Grant, Stinson, and Chou (2004) examined drinking rates in college versus noncollege peers and found that college students were more likely to engage in heavy drinking than those of similar age not in college. Timberlake et al. (2007) also studied longitudinal drinking rates and patterns between those attending college and not attending college for young adults and concluded those who had never enrolled in college were less likely to drink in a risky fashion than those who attended college. Even those who initially had not engaged in high-risk drinking prior to entering college and then later attended college surpassed their noncollege peers in high-risk drinking rates once they were students.

The National Institute on Drug Abuse (NIDA) oversees the yearly Monitoring the Future data collection. The 2017 Monitoring the Future report (Schulenberg et al., 2017) trends illustrate that differences in use between college students and their noncollege peers vary by substance, with alcohol and amphetamine use higher among college students whereas opiates and marijuana are higher among those not enrolled but college age. Although prescription opioid use is slightly less in college students than in their noncollege peers, researchers concluded that students experiencing depression and distress may initiate nonmedical use of prescription painkillers (Morioka, Howard, Caldeira, Wang, & Arria, 2018). Another pertinent finding is that drinking rates peak in the 18- to 24-year-old category and then steadily decline. For example, in an earlier Monitoring the Future report by the NIDA in 2011, one of the findings is that heavy drinking rates peaked at age 24, and "then there is a falloff at each subsequent age level above age 24, dropping to 18% by age 50" (as cited in Johnston, O'Malley, Bachman, & Schulenberg, 2011, p. 87). All of these studies support the idea that factors in the college culture and environment seem to create a unique time frame of substance abuse. However, even with these substance abuse rates increasing, fewer than 2% of college students surveyed reported that they were treated or diagnosed with an addiction or substance issue (ACHA, 2016).

Continuum of Use: Abstinence to Addiction

It is important for a college counselor to discriminate where on the continuum of use a student may be when assessing risk, developing prevention programs, and planning treatment. Each level of use necessitates its own unique tailored approach: In college substance use, one size definitely does not fit all. The continuum of abstinence, experimentation, social/regular use, abuse, and addiction must be acknowledged. It is essential to recognize the college students who do not engage in substance misuse because focusing only on high-risk users could inadvertently perpetuate the common misperception that all students drink and do drugs and ignore the healthy majority who use responsibly.

Abstinence

A significant number of students who attend college report not using substances at all (ACHA, 2016). Students who choose abstinence may do so for a variety of reasons including religious and faith traditions, family history of addiction, their own recovery, and so forth. According to the most recent National College Health Assessment survey, 21.4 % reported that they had never used alcohol with an additional 14.4% not using in the last 30 days; 62.6 % said they had never used marijuana with an additional 19% saying they had not used in the last month (ACHA, 2016).

Experimentation

Most students come to college already having tried or experimented with alcohol or drugs on some level. Because younger age of exposure correlates with higher risk of dependency, gathering a history of first use is vital for assessment. If an individual begins to use regularly before the age of 15, he or she is 4 times more likely to develop a substance addiction. Additionally, college is often viewed as a time for exploring new behaviors as students are spreading their wings and testing independent decision-making without parents around. Occasional use may be developmentally appropriate or at least typical.

Social/Regular Use

Many students fall into the broad middle group of use, reporting that they only use in certain groups, occasionally for social events like holidays and parties, and students may use responsibly without much long-term impact. Many students form habits of regular use—for example, only on the weekends, every Saturday at the game, or during tailgating. These two categories of use (social and regular) vary greatly by frequency and amount being used, so it is imperative to help students understand their personal risk factors and make safer, healthier choices, lessening consequences. It is certainly possible to use infrequently and still engage in dangerous or risky behaviors such as drinking heavily, mixing alcohol with other substances, driving under the influence, or getting in fights.

Abuse and Dependence

With the change in diagnostic categories and criteria in the *Diagnostic and Statistical Manual of Mental Disorders* (*DSM*) from *DSM IV-TR* (American Psychiatric Association, 2000) to *DSM-5* (American Psychiatric Association, 2013), clinically distinguishing abuse and dependence has altered somewhat (American Psychiatric Association, 2013). Previously, abuse was characterized by varying consequences associated with use—regret, sexual and physical assault, work and relationship impact, legal issues—whereas dependence focused on tolerance; withdrawal; and time spent obtaining, using, and recovering from the substance. Now the criteria have been collapsed into one group, and a substance use disorder is given specifiers for mild, moderate, and severe on the basis of the number of criteria the client meets. Specifically, meeting two to three criteria is categorized as mild, meeting four to five criteria is categorized as moderate, and meeting six or more criteria is categorized as severe (American Psychiatric Association, 2013).

Drugs Versus Alcohol

Although alcohol remains the most widely used substance among the college population, legal and illegal drug use has also been on the rise, and certain trends have surfaced in the last decade. According to U.S. state data, marijuana use has been increasing in the last several years, and legalization in some form has occurred in more than two dozen states (Governing, 2018). The literature on risks of ongoing marijuana use is critical and contentious. However, in one study comparing two distinct college groups from 2005 and 2013, authors examined how cannabis affected grade point averages (Martinez, Roth, Johnson, & Jones, 2015). After other student identity measures, engagement, and perceptions of campus were accounted for, it was evident that grade point averages were negatively affected by marijuana use. These connections cannot be ignored by college counselors and student affairs staff, and specific attention must be paid to effective interventions for those whose college success, retention, and subsequent employability are affected by marijuana. Additional implications for those students who come from states where marijuana may be legal for recreational use and then attend college in a state where marijuana is illegal or has legalized medical use may affect outreach and treatment focus.

The rising rates of stimulant misuse have been noted in the college population, with motives, demographic variables, academic interactions, and co-occurring substance use being examined (Benson, Flory, Humphreys, & Lee, 2015). In a meta-analysis of college student misuse of stimulant medications, the authors reviewed 30 peer-reviewed studies to determine the nature and scope of this issue. Overwhelmingly, college students named academic performance as the main motivator for use, and stimulant misusers tended to be Greek affiliated, Caucasian, male, and have a lower grade point average than nonusers (Benson et al., 2015).

An emerging trend that bears further exploration is college students who enroll and attend a higher education institution already in recovery from addiction. In a survey of Collegiate Recovery Programs across the country, of 486 students who participated in Collegiate Recovery Programs, 52% reported drug addiction as their lifetime primary issue, 40% smoke, and most reported co-occurring mental health issues (Laudet, Harris, Kimball, Winters, & Moberg, 2015). Their average age at treatment was 20.6, and they had 3 years of sobriety at enrollment. Because recovery requires structure and support, these college students who are still learning discipline, organization, and time management need access to additional services to address relapse prevention. Counselors and student affairs staff may provide care through substance-free residential options, support groups, activities, and advocacy.

The Influence of Developmental Stage

The minimum legal drinking age comprises about half of most traditional-age college populations, and some argue that underage use has become less taboo and more a rite of passage in college. Indeed, the culture of college drinking has been documented in popular culture, documentaries, and dozens of studies. In a qualitative study in which college women were interviewed about their drinking experiences, a theme of maturation and development surfaced (Likis-Werle & Borders, 2017). Specifically, 18- and 19-year-old students stated they drank as much as they could at each sitting compared with juniors and seniors, who said as they got older and had more responsibilities such as work and internships, their drinking amounts and frequencies decreased (Likis-Werle & Borders, 2017). Additionally, the authors noted that younger college students did not have as much success in regulating their drinking as did older students. Older student drinkers felt they had matured and had grown more responsible across their college career (Likis-Werle & Borders, 2017).

College student identity development models identify several prominent tasks during this time—gaining peer social approval; navigating interdependent relationships, acceptance, identity, and belonging; exploring values and crisis resolution; coping with stress and new freedoms; and managing emotions (Chickering & Reisser, 1993; Erikson, 1968; Josselson, 1991). Because of the significance of peer social approval during this developmental time frame, social norms marketing campaigns may be especially effective for increasing awareness of the difference between perceptions of alcohol and other drug use versus actual alcohol and other drug use. Social norms theory postulates that students base their behavior on what they think peers are doing, but they misperceive and overestimate use. If counselors and other student affairs staff can point out the discrepancy and publicize the actual rate of use, students may change their substance use behaviors to align with the real rates, thus decreasing overall use (Perkins & Berkowitz, 1986).

Men Versus Women

Differences have been noted in drinking behaviors between college men and college women; college men's rates of dangerous drinking are consistently higher than college women's rates, but college women experience serious consequences at lower amounts and frequencies of use because of hormones, enzymes that break down alcohol, body mass, and metabolism (Pedrelli, Collado, Shapero, Brill, & MacPherson, 2016; W. B. Smith & Weisner, 2000). Substance-related sexual assault, unplanned sexual activity, and sexually transmitted infections put college women at higher risk when using substances. In fact, experiences of perceived sexual objectification were correlated with women's substance issues (Carr & Szymanski, 2011). Understandably, then, college women and men may view safety and prepare for drinking differently before going out. For example, women tend to use more protective strategies like staying in groups, eating beforehand, and consuming the same kind of alcohol when they socialize. The majority of men tend to drink five or more drinks at a sitting whereas 67% of college women report drinking four or fewer drinks (ACHA 2016). Likewise, college stimulant misuse tends to be higher for men than for women (Benson et al., 2015).

Direction, Details, Defining the Territory

The 1990s and early 2000s were an era of more comprehensive education and outreach programs across campuses, more self-directed information available on the internet, and funding aimed at reducing substance-related issues for college students (Wechsler et al., 2002). However, the time and resources have not translated into consistent sustainable behavior change. The National Institute on Alcohol Abuse and Alcoholism (2007) suggested three levels of intervention—(a) individual, (b) campus, and (c) community. However, subsequent literature examined factors associated with more specific groups to increase effectiveness—targeted assessment, prevention, and intervention based on peer groups: sororities; fraternities; athletes; residence hall groups; small groups of women and men; and lesbian, gay, bisexual, transgender, and queer/questioning (LGBTQ) groups (Lewis & Neighbors, 2007; M. A. Smith & Berger, 2010).

Clinical Implications (Assessment and Treatment)

Screening and Assessment

The Alcohol Use Disorders Identification Test is the most commonly used measure of collegiate drinking (Devos-Comby & Lange, 2008) that assesses points on the basis of frequency and amount of use, consequences experienced, and others' concern about use. It is based on a 40-point scale, and DeMartini and Carey (2012) further extended the use of the Alcohol Use Disorders Identification Test by distinguishing between high-risk cutoff scores for men (8+ points) and women (7) on the basis of physiological differences of alcohol effects. Because it is free, easy to administer, and brief, it is commonly used at campus-wide National Alcohol Screening Day events (retrieved from http://auditscreen.org/). Other tools often used in college counseling centers are the Substance Abuse Subtle Screening Inventory (Miller, Roberts, Brooks, & Lazowski, 1997), the Michigan Alcohol Screening Test (Seltzer, 1971), and the CAGE questionnaire (Ewing, 1986). A comprehensive substance assessment addresses biopsychosocial factors, exploring a student's history of use, family history of addiction and mental health issues, exposure to use, parental and peer models, and beliefs about alcohol and drugs.

Treatment should be based on risk level, personality traits, social groups, sex and gender, and any other issues the student is experiencing such as traumatic events (Dennhardt & Murphy, 2013).

Gender Responsive Programs and Services

Some of the unique issues for college women that interact with substance use are body image and weight concerns (Giles, Champion, Sutfin, McCoy, & Wagoner, 2009). These are prominent issues for college women more so than the general population, and women who use substances report that initial use of certain drugs is motivated by weight management. Additionally, on the other end of the continuum, fear of weight gain when abstaining from use can inhibit recovery (Warren, Lindsay, White, Claudat, & Velasquez, 2013). Warren and colleagues (2013) studied women in treatment for a variety of addictions and found that women who smoked and used stimulants prior to treatment experienced weight gain in recovery, and this weight gain acted as a disincentive to abstain and maintain sobriety.

Likewise, in a study of more than 1,400 college students, calorie counting/cutting on drinking days was reported by 45% of women and 29% of men. This was alarming specifically because these women also were more likely to experience memory loss, injury, assault, and unplanned sexual activity (Giles et al., 2009). As a result, college counselors and student affairs staff who are working with female substance users may need to consider these factors in assessment, treatment planning, support, and relapse prevention.

Mandated Versus Volunteer Counseling

Many students find their way to college counseling centers by way of a substance citation or violation issued from the student affairs conduct office or dean of students. This necessitates collaboration among various campus offices to ensure student success and follow-through. In a study comparing mandated students with voluntary students, "the addition of a BMI [brief motivational intervention] to disciplinary proceedings appeared to produce larger decrease in alcohol consumption than did disciplinary action alone" (Terlecki, Larimer, & Copeland, 2010, p. 58). Additionally, results were similar across both groups, suggesting BMIs were successful with both mandated and voluntary students.

Risk Level

There are several categories of higher risk users within college populations that bear consideration: those affiliated with Greek life, those involved with athletics, those identifying as LBGTQ, and those with co-occurring mental health issues. High-risk users tend to report greater frequency and higher amounts of using or using despite experiencing consequences. Student affairs staff in the various campus offices working with the aforementioned populations have an opportunity for targeted education and outreach.

LGBTQ Populations

The higher risk for substance abuse is not from being gay but from the associated stressors, trauma, and added discrimination that LGBTQ college students may face with being ostracized by the community, isolated in the coming out process, and estranged from family relationships. College students identifying as LGBTQ may feel isolated, depressed, and anxious and may be more likely to use substances to cope. Green and Feinstein (2012) further found differences within the LBG population; that lesbians are more likely to abuse alcohol whereas gay men are more susceptible to drug use; bisexuals had higher risk than either of the former two categories. In a study of LGBT youth, Kelly, Davis, and Schlesinger (2014) found "gender diverse young people reported the highest rates of alcohol consumption, the highest prevalence of tobacco and illicit substance use and were more likely to engage in polysubstance use" (p. 5) compared with gay and bisexual youth or the general population. College counselors need to plan inclusive programming and services that recognize the compounded effects of being a sexual minority on a college campus.

Co-Occurring Issues

Those with co-occurring issues such as depression, anxiety, identity issues, and addiction in their family may be at higher risk for abusing or misusing substances to self-medicate and to cope with and escape from emotional dysregulation, family tensions, and confusion. Many researchers have found correlations among misuse of one substance and misuse of another such as alcohol, marijuana, energy drinks, and stimulants (Benson et al., 2015; Woolsey et al., 2015). Traumatic experiences such as those assessed in the Adverse Childhood Experiences scale (Felitti et al., 1998) are also linked to substance use and could also be explored for effective treatment (LeTendre & Reed, 2017).

Emerging Issues and Trends

Process and Behavioral Addictions

An area that deserves attention in the collegiate addiction field is process addictions. A *process addiction*, also known as a *behavioral addiction*, is defined as the group of non–substance related compulsive or problematic behaviors such as gambling, gaming, sex addiction, and disordered eating that have an impact on functioning and well-being. The International Association of Addiction and Offender Counselors, a division of the American Counseling Association, has a Process Addictions Committee that emphasizes how to assess and intervene with college students who may be exhibiting addictive behaviors that affect academic, health, and social domains. Their Process Addictions Committee website states, "We hope to undertake research and develop resources that provide ongoing continuing education to the counseling profession to improve competency in assessment, diagnosis, and treatment of these issues" (Process Addictions Committee, International Association of Addiction and Offender Counselors, n.d., Mission Statement, para. 1). There are some co-occurring issues between process addictions and substance use, possibly due to impulsivity, lowered inhibition, risk-taking, and sensation seeking, that are motivators and effects of each (Geisner et al., 2016). Specifically, researchers have linked stimulant use and gambling in college students, noting that after other substance-related variables were controlled for, "recent stimulant use remained significantly associated with problem gambling, predicting a 74% greater likelihood of problem gambling in the last six months" (p. 1011).

Energy Drinks

Energy drinks with added caffeine and other stimulants are very popular among college students, particularly for enhancing academic performance, staying awake, and remaining alert. Brands such as Red Bull, Monster Energy, Rockstar, and 5-hour Energy are highly accessible and unregulated and are used alone and often with alcohol to prolong drinking. According to a recent NIDA report (NIDA, 2017), college students who regularly consumed energy drinks were at higher risk of misusing stimulants, cocaine, and alcohol than were those who did not consume energy drinks. Authors suggested that because the brain is still developing, essential neural pathways can be primed for risk-taking sensations related to future drug use. Additional risks for mixing these substances included cardiac issues, anxiety, insomnia, and co-occurring mental health issues (Woolsey et al., 2015). The ACHA (2016) reported a spike in stimulant use for high-stress situations, academic rigor, attention, and alertness. In another survey by Woolsey et al. (2015), the relationship between stimulant misuse and energy drinks was examined, with 48.9% of college students reporting using energy drinks in the last 30 days. Of these students, there was a predictive relationship between those who misused stimulants. Other substances that may need to be monitored in college student populations include heroin, possibly because of the opioid prescription use rise and the availability of inexpensive opiates.

Outreach and Prevention Implications

There has been a trend to provide online screenings, assessment, and education for incoming first-year college students, that is, a basic alcohol and drug education training. Some campuses require the completion of this program for registration, whereas other campuses use online programs for first-time offenders who violate campus substance policies. Either of these approaches can be administered by professionals in housing, conduct, or student life, so familiarity with the material is prudent. The more common programs designed specifically for college use include the Brief Alcohol Screening and Intervention for College Students (Dimeff, Baer, Kivlahan, & Marlatt, 1999); brief motivational interviewing; and web-based programs such as eCHECKUP TO GO (http://echeckuptogo.com/), MyStudentBody, and Alc 101. In a meta-analysis of interventions for mandated alcohol violators, four intervention protocols (i.e., Brief Alcohol Screening and Intervention for College Students, e-CHUG, Alcohol 101, and Alcohol Skills Training Program) were associated with risk reduction (Carey, Scott-Sheldon, Garey, Elliott, & Carey, 2016).

Although disciplinary action should remain the domain of the dean of students office, other prevention and outreach strategies more appropriate for counseling center staff include small group facilitation and family involvement. Regarding marijuana use in college students, adding parents in the intervention as a part of a brief motivational interviewing intervention may be worth examining because Grossbard and colleagues (2010) found that "students who received the combined intervention used marijuana significantly less frequently compared with those receiving BASICS [Brief Alcohol Screening and Intervention for College Students] alone or the control group" (p. 387). This suggests involving parents could have a possible preventive effect with respect to continued use. Researchers studying the prevalence of stimulant use in the college population have suggested that a wider and more comprehensive substance use assessment be completed as a routine part of health or counseling services that asks about all substances (Benson et al., 2015).

There are numerous ways to include prevention and intervention on college campuses, such as infusing substance abuse risk and protective strategies in curricula and outreach programs in Health and Wellness courses, University Life 101, and orientation programs. Also many campuses have reported implementing harm-reduction programs like Safe Ride shuttles to reduce drinking and driving.

Another model for college addiction treatment is the collegiate recovery model. DePue and Hagedorn (2015) discussed and outlined components of successful Collegiate Recovery Programs specifically designed to meet the unique social and academic needs of those college students who have already been in treatment for addiction. Several exemplary models included individual counseling, weekly group circles, 12-step programs, peer support, and academic and life mentoring (DePue & Hagedorn, 2015).

Most counselors focus on individual-level or group interventions, and progress has been limited. However, the National Institute on Alcohol Abuse and Alcoholism (2007) proposed best practices in which college student substance use also can be greatly affected by changing the culture of use on campus. This environmental approach entails stakeholders at all levels of staff, faculty, and administration assessing the attitudes, policies, enforcement, and environmental messages that may unintentionally promote substance use and working to correct misperceptions and implement more uniform policies that focus on safety and health. For example, offering substance-free housing and clearly educating students about and enforcing laws regarding illicit drug use and underage drinking creates an atmosphere in which wellness takes priority (Harding et al., 2016).

Conclusion

The world of today's college student is more complex than that of any previous generation—access to massive volumes of information, identity formation on several dimensions, and the pressures to keep up with global trends as well as peer social cultures all confound the college experience. Addiction is one of multiple arenas that some college students will find themselves navigating, and our roles as counselors and student affairs professionals are to help them do so successfully. Assessing risk and protective factors, developing and implementing targeted and tailored prevention and intervention initiatives, and making referrals to specialists all fall within our scope, and this chapter is meant to highlight just a few of the essential pieces of the puzzle.

Final Case Study

Cory, a female college student, 21 years old, came to the College Counseling Center of a midsize university because she was written up by a residence assistant for being "on something" in the residence hall and stating she wanted to kill herself. She identified as a lesbian; she said she just broke up with her first girlfriend and had been in the process of coming out to her family about her sexual identity and had been contemplating introducing her partner to them. She is from a small town and a fairly religious background and experienced a sexual assault by a male student as a first-year college student under the influence of alcohol. You administered the Alcohol Use Disorders Identification Test, and she scored a 10, which indicates high risk for alcohol use and consequences. She also admitted to occasionally smoking weed and had used some club drugs when she was out with her friends "just to loosen up" a few times. She denied using any "harder drugs." Upon further probing, she says she had been on antidepressants 2 years ago through the University Health Services after her assault and felt she could not trust people on her campus.

Case Exploration Questions

1. What are the biopsychosocial components of assessment and risk factors you would want to know more about?
2. Are there any safety concerns for her on campus related to her perpetrator?
3. How is her sexual identity process affecting her coping currently?
4. How would you develop a treatment plan for her, and what are some possible immediate, short-term, and long-term goals?
5. What psychoeducational material may be useful to discuss with her?
6. To which student affairs offices and additional resources would it be appropriate to connect her?
7. What ethical and confidentiality issues arise with this case?

References

American College Health Association. (2016). *American College Health Association–National College Health Assessment II: Reference Group Executive Summary Spring 2016*. Hanover, MD: Author.

American Psychiatric Association. (2000). *Diagnostic and statistical manual of mental disorders* (4th ed., text rev.). Arlington, VA: Author.

American Psychiatric Association. (2013). *Diagnostic and statistical manual of mental disorders* (5th ed.). Washington DC: Author.

Benson, K., Flory, K., Humphreys, K. L., & Lee, S. S. (2015). Misuse of stimulant medication among college students: A comprehensive review and meta-analysis. *Clinical Child and Family Psychology Review, 18*, 50–76. doi:10.1007/s10567-014-0177-z

Carey, K. B., Scott-Sheldon, L. J., Garey, L., Elliott, J. C., & Carey, M. P. (2016). Alcohol interventions for mandated college students: A meta-analytic review. *Journal of Consulting and Clinical Psychology, 84*, 619–632. doi:10.1037/a0040275

Carr, E. R., & Szymanski, D. M. (2011). Sexual objectification and substance abuse in young adult women. *The Counseling Psychologist, 39,* 39–66.

Chickering, A. W., & Reisser, L. (1993). *Education and identity* (2nd ed.). San Francisco, CA: Jossey-Bass.

Dawson, D. A., Grant, B. F., Stinson, F. S., & Chou, P. S. (2004). Another look at heavy episodic drinking and alcohol use disorders among college and noncollege youth. *Journal of Studies on Alcohol, 65,* 477–488.

DeMartini, K. S., & Carey, K. B. (2012). Optimizing the use of the AUDIT for alcohol screening in college students. *Psychological Assessment, 24,* 954–963. doi:10.1037/a0028519

Dennhardt, A. A., & Murphy, J. G. (2013). Prevention and treatment of college student drug use: A review of the literature. *Addictive Behaviors, 38,* 2607–2618.

DePue, M. K., & Hagedorn, W. B. (2015). Facilitating college students' recovery through the use of collegiate recovery programs. *Journal of College Counseling, 18,* 66–81. doi:10.1002/j.2161-1882.2015.00069.x

Devos-Comby, L., & Lange, J. E. (2008). Standardized measures of alcohol-related problems: A review of their use among college students. *Psychology of Addictive Behaviors, 22,* 349–361.

Dimeff, L. A., Baer, J. S., Kivlahan, D. R., & Marlatt, G. A. (1999). *Brief Alcohol Screening and Intervention for College Students (BASICS): A harm reduction approach.* New York, NY: Guilford Press.

Erikson, E. (1968). *Identity: Youth and crisis.* New York, NY: Norton.

Ewing, J. A. (1986). Detecting alcoholism: The CAGE questionnaire. *Journal of the American Medical Association, 52,* 1905–1907.

Felitti, V. J., Anda, R. F., Nordenberg, D., Williamson, D. F., Spitz, A. M., Edwards, V., . . . Marks, J. S. (1998). Relationship of childhood abuse and household dysfunction to many of the leading causes of death in adults: The Adverse Childhood Experiences (ACE) Study. *American Journal of Preventive Medicine, 14,* 245–258.

Geisner, I. M., Huh, D., Cronce, J. M., Lostutter, T. W., Kilmer, J., & Larimer, M. E. (2016). Exploring the relationship between stimulant use and gambling in college students. *Journal of Gambling Studies, 32,* 1001–1016. doi:10.1007/s10899-015-9586-2

Giles, S. M., Champion, H., Sutfin, E. F., McCoy, T. P., & Wagoner, K. (2009). Calorie restriction on drinking days: An examination of drinking consequences among college students. *Journal of American College Health, 57,* 603–609.

Governing. (2018, January 8). State marijuana laws map. Retrieved from http://www.governing.com/gov-data/state-marijuana-laws-map-medical-recreational.html

Green, K. E, & Feinstein, B. A. (2012). Substance use in lesbian, gay, and bisexual populations: An update on empirical research and implications for treatment. *Psychology of Addictive Behaviors, 26,* 265–278. doi:10.1037/a0025424

Grossbard, J. R., Mastroleo, N. R., Kilmer, J. R., Lee, C. M., Turrisi, R., Larimer, M. E., & May, A. (2010). Substance use patterns among first-year college students: Secondary effects of a combined alcohol intervention. *Journal of Substance Abuse Treatment, 39,* 384–390. doi:10.1016/j.jsat.2010.07.001

Harding, F. M., Hingson, R. W., Klitzner, M., Mosher, J. F., Brown, J., Vincent, R. M., . . . Cannon, C. L. (2016). Underage drinking: A review of trends and prevention strategies. *American Journal of Preventive Medicine, 58,* 148–157. doi:10.1016/j.amepre.2016.05.020

Johnston, L. D., O'Malley, P. M., Bachman, J. G., & Schulenberg, J. E. (2011). *Monitoring the Future national survey results on drug use, 1975–2010: Vol. 2. College students and adults ages 19–50.* Ann Arbor: University of Michigan, Institute for Social Research.

Josselson, R. E. (1991). *Finding herself: Pathways to identity development in women.* San Francisco, CA: Jossey-Bass.

Kelly, J., Davis, C., & Schlesinger, C. (2014). Substance use by same sex attracted young people: Prevalence, perceptions, and homophobia. *Australasian Professional Society on Alcohol and Other Drugs: Drug and Alcohol Review,* 1–8. doi:10.1111/dar.12158

Laudet, A. B., Harris, K., Kimball, T., Winters, K. C., & Moberg, P. (2015). Characteristics of students participating in collegiate recovery programs: A national survey. *Journal of Substance Abuse Treatment, 51,* 38–46.

LeTendre, M. L., & Reed, M. B. (2017). The effect of adverse childhood experiences on clinical diagnosis of a substance use disorder: Results of a nationally representative study. *Substance Use & Misuse, 52,* 689–697. doi:e10.1080/10826084.2016.1253746

Lewis, M. A., & Neighbors, C. (2007). Optimizing personalized normative feedback: The use of gender-specific referents. *Journal of Studies on Alcohol and Drugs, 68,* 228–237.

Likis-Werle, E., & Borders, L. D. (2017). College women's experiences and perceptions of drinking: A phenomenological exploration. *Journal of College Counseling, 20,* 99–112. doi:10.1002/jocc.12063

Martinez, J. A., Roth, M. G., Johnson, D. N., & Jones, J. A. (2015). How robustly does cannabis use associate to college grades? Findings from two cohorts. *Journal of Drug Education, 45,* 56–67. doi:10.1177/0047237915596606

Miller, F. G., Roberts, J., Brooks, M. K., & Lazowski, L. E. (1997). *SASSI-3 user's guide.* Bloomington, IN: Baugh Enterprises.

Morioka, C. M., Howard, D. E., Caldeira, K. M., Wang, M. Q., & Arria, A. M. (2018). Affective dysregulation predicts incident nonmedical prescription analgesic use among college students. *Addictive Behaviors, 76,* 328–334. doi:10.1016/j.addbeh.2017.08.034

National Institute on Alcohol Abuse and Alcoholism. (2007). *What colleges need to know now: An update.* Rockville, MD: Author.

National Institute on Drug Abuse. (2017, August 8). Energy drinks and risk to future substance use. Retrieved from https://www.drugabuse.gov/news-events/news-releases/2017 /08/energy-drinks-risk-to-future-substance-use

Pedrelli, P., Collado, A., Shapero, B. G., Brill, C., & MacPherson, L. (2016). Different pathways explain alcohol-related problems in female and male college students. *Journal of American College Health, 64,* 535–544.

Perkins, H. W., & Berkowitz, A. (1986). Perceiving the community norms of alcohol use among students: Some research implications for campus alcohol education programming. *International Journal of the Addictions, 21,* 961–976.

Process Addictions Committee, International Association of Addiction and Offender Counselors. (n.d.). Mission statement. Retrieved from processaddictions.weebly.com/

Reetz, D. R., Bershad, C., LeViness, P., & Whitlock, M. (2016). *The Association for University and College Counseling Center Directors annual survey.* Retrieved from https://www.aucccd.org/assets/documents/aucccd%202016%20monograph%20-%20public.pdf

Schulenberg, J. E., Johnston, L. D., O'Malley, P. M., Bachman, J. G., Miech, R. A., & Patrick, M. E. (2017). *Monitoring the Future national survey results on drug use, 1975–2016: Vol. 2. College students and adults ages 19–55.* Ann Arbor: University of Michigan, Institute for Social Research. Retrieved from http://monitoringthefuture.org/pubs.html#monographs

Seltzer, M. L. (1971). The Michigan Alcoholism Screening Test: The quest for a new diagnostic instrument. *American Journal of Psychiatry, 127,* 1653–1658.

Smith, M. A., & Berger, J. B. (2010). Women's ways of drinking: College women, high-risk alcohol use, and negative consequences. *Journal of College Student Development, 51,* 35–49.

Smith, W. B., & Weisner, C. (2000). Women and alcohol problems: A critical analysis of the literature and unanswered questions. *Alcoholism: Clinical and Experimental Research, 24,* 1320–1321. doi:10.1111/j.1530-0277.2000.tb02098

Terlecki, M. A., Larimer, M. E., & Copeland, A. L. (2010). Clinical outcomes of a brief motivational intervention for heavy drinking mandated college students: A pilot study. *Journal of Studies on Alcohol and Drugs, 71,* 54–60. Retrieved from https://iris.etsu.edu:3443/login?url=http://go.galegroup.com.iris.etsu.edu:2048/ps/i.do?pAONE&sw=w&u=tel_a_etsul&v=2.1&it=r&id=GALE%7CA218598593&asid=3c25da53a2bc02aa25bc5cbd3e9d60e

Timberlake, D. S., Hopfer, C. J., Rhee, S. H., Friedman, N. P., Haberstick, B. C., Lessem, J. M., & Hewitt, J. K. (2007). College attendance and its effects on drinking behaviors in a longitudinal study of adolescents. *Alcoholism: Clinical and Experimental Research, 31,* 1020–1030. doi:10.1111/j.1530-0277.2007.00383.x

Warren, C. S., Lindsay, A. R., White, E. K., Claudat, K., & Velasquez, S. C. (2013). Weight-related concerns related to drug use for women in substance abuse treatment: Prevalence and relationships with eating pathology. *Journal of Substance Abuse Treatment, 44,* 494–501.

Wechsler, H., Lee, J. E., Kuo, M., Seibring, M., Nelson, T. F., & Lee, H. (2002). Trends in college binge drinking during a period of increased prevention efforts. *Journal of American College Health, 50,* 203–217. doi:10.1080/07448480209595713

Woolsey, C. L., Williams, R. D., Jacobson, B. H., Housman, J. M., McDonald, J. D., Swartz, J. H., . . . Davidson, R. T. (2015). Increased energy drink use as a predictor of illicit prescription stimulant use. *Substance Abuse, 36,* 413–419. doi:10.1080/08897077.2014.969470

Chapter 18

Stress and Anxiety

Joshua C. Watson and Amanda Faucher

Anxiety does not empty tomorrow of its sorrows,
but only empties today of its strength.
—Charles Spurgeon

■ ■ ■

Reflection Exercise

Life is full of stress for college students. According to "5 Main Causes of Stress for College Students" (College Parents of America, 2019), the most common causes of stress among college students include (a) unhealthy competition, (b) parental expectation and style, (c) homesickness, (d) social anxiety, and (e) financial burden. Take a moment and think about these issues:

1. Were they sources of stress for you as an undergraduate student?
2. How did you manage these stressors?
3. What coping strategies did you use?
4. Who were the individuals most helpful to you in overcoming these stressors on campus?

Although these stressors may have seemed overwhelming at the time, you got through them. Unfortunately, not all college students have a similar success story to share. For some students, the stress and anxiety they experience prevents them from having an enriching college experience. As you are beginning your career as a campus support provider for students like these, and considering your own experiences as a stressed college student, what advice would you have for someone who came to you feeling overwhelmed and unable to function? The likelihood you work with students like these is high.

■ ■ ■

In this chapter we will explore stress and anxiety, particularly as they are experienced on college campuses. Although stress and anxiety are often used synonymously, we will examine how they are separate constructs referencing different experiences. After helping you understand how to identify someone who is experiencing overwhelming stress or anxiety, we will introduce a variety of assessment and treatment approaches to help students. Finally, we conclude the chapter by looking at outreach implications and how college counseling center staff can work cooperatively with other campus offices and programs to help students succeed.

At some point in your life you likely have experienced feeling stressed. Maybe you have upcoming assignments requiring a great deal of time and effort. Perhaps you are trying to find time to balance being a student and an employee, spouse, or parent. If so, you are not alone. Most people experience stress from time to time. In fact, scientists believe a certain amount of stress to be a normal part of everyday life. But what is stress? In simple terms, stress is your body's reaction to a real or perceived challenge. In small, manageable doses, stress can be quite beneficial. When individuals become stressed, their bodies release several hormones, including adrenaline, norepinephrine, and cortisol, producing a wide range of physical and mental reactions (Holsboer & Ising, 2010). These chemical messengers engage the fight-flight-or-freeze response and are responsible for the immediate reactions to experienced stressors. Their primary role is to induce arousal, making individuals more alert and responsive. Of the three, it takes a little longer to experience the effects of cortisol release. Cortisol helps maintain fluid levels, stabilizes blood pressure, and regulates body functions, readying the body for protective action. In optimal amounts, these hormones help individuals meet daily challenges and achieve their goals. However, at elevated levels negative effects can occur. According to Lazarus and Folkman (1984), stress originates in our perceptions that a situation or event exceeds our available coping resources. When stress becomes too much to handle, and is not handled effectively, it can cause anxiety.

Anxiety disorders—defined by excess worry, hyperarousal, and fear that is counterproductive and debilitating—are the most common category of mental disorders present in the general population (Simpson, Neria, Lewis-Fernandez, & Schneier, 2010), with estimated lifetime prevalence rates of up to 33.7% noted across large, population-based studies (Bandelow & Michaelis, 2015). Within the United States, researchers have estimated the 12-month prevalence rate among adults to be 18.1% (Kessler, Chiu, Demler, Merikangas, & Walters, 2005), meaning in any given year over 40 million Americans age 18 and older are experiencing anxiety disorders. When one considers that there are individuals who are experiencing symptoms but do not meet diagnostic criteria, this number grows exponentially. In a study conducted by the Anxiety and Depression Association of America (n.d.), 70% of adults surveyed reported experiencing daily anxiety or stress at least moderately interfering with their daily living. With the average age of onset for many mental health disorders occurring during the traditional college age range (18–24 years of age), it is likely these percentages are higher on college campuses.

Stress and anxiety have many symptoms in common, so it is important to discuss their similarities and differences. According to the U.S. National Library of Medicine (2019), stress is a feeling of emotional or physical tension, coming from any event that can make one feel frustrated, whereas anxiety is something that continues after the stress is gone. Although *stress* is a term that often carries a negative connotation, it is worth noting that some short-term (acute) stress can be a good thing! For example, it is a good thing when you must suddenly hit the brakes while driving to avoid hitting something, or when you experience the exciting but stressful feeling you might get on your wedding day. Stress also can help heighten your ability to think quickly and avoid danger. Anxiety is more pervasive, its symptoms lasting long after the stressful and anxiety-provoking event ends; the symptoms of anxiety often are more debilitating than is the response to stress. College students likely are exposed to many stressors during their time in school. In most instances, these stressors eventually pass. However, for some students, these stressors can develop into greater problems, and issues with anxiety arise.

Prevalence of Anxiety Disorders on College and University Campuses

The college years have always been viewed as one of the most stressful periods in a person's life (Hales, 2009). Although anxiety always has ranked as one of the most common presenting concerns for college students, a noted increase in the number of college students seeking services at college and university counseling centers for anxiety-related concerns has been seen in recent years (Bamber & Kraenzle Schneider, 2016; Beiter et al., 2015; Mackenzie et al., 2011). Recent data collected from over 3,000 counselors at 139 college and university counseling centers show anxiety being identified as a presenting concern for 61% of the students seeking mental health treatment during the 2015–2016 academic year, surpassing depression as the leading mental health issue addressed by college counselors nationwide (Association for University and College Counseling Center Directors, 2017; Center for Collegiate Mental Health, 2017). According to the American College Health Association's annual National College Health Assessment survey, nearly one in five college students (22.1%) reported being diagnosed with or treated for an anxiety disorder in the past 12 months (American College Health Association, 2018). Among women, the statistic is one in four students (25.1%), more than double the percentage for men (11.7%).

However, recent findings are not specific to U.S. college campuses. Evidence suggests the mental health of college and university students is becoming a global epidemic. According to researchers, stress and anxiety are common experiences for college students worldwide, significantly affecting their quality of life and academic attainment (January, Madhombiro, Chipamaunga, Ray, Chingono, & Abas, 2018). In the past, scholars estimated that at any given time, 20% to 25% of college students globally are stressed (Kumaraswamy, 2013). It appears the trend is continuing. Initial results from the World Health Organization's World Mental Health International College Student project indicate anxiety to be a common problem for college students on a global level (https://www.hcp.med.harvard.edu/wmh/college_student_survey.php). Among data collected from nearly 14,000 students at 19 colleges and universities in eight countries, anxiety-related symptoms were the second most prevalent disorder (depression being the first), noted (Auerbach et al., 2018). Across countries, prevalence rates for generalized anxiety disorder ranged between 16.7% and 18.6%. As prevalence rates continue rising, both researchers and practitioners have focused attention on identifying potential factors associated with the increasing morbidity of anxiety and anxiety-related symptomatology.

Common Stressors for College Students

Students face many challenges throughout their college careers. As such, stress is a major issue for college students (Bland, Melton, Welle, & Bigham, 2012). Scholars have noted that students are exposed to a wide range of psychosocial stressors unique to the collegiate experience that increase their vulnerability to a variety of mental health issues including anxiety (Farrer, Gulliver, Bennett, Fassnacht, & Griffiths, 2016). In a study of 374 undergraduate students between the ages of 18 and 24, Beiter et al. (2015) sought to understand how prevalent a series of common stressors identified through a comprehensive review of the college counseling literature were in the lives of these students. Their results suggest academics being the biggest cause for concern among students. The top 10 stressors that students rate as either a moderate or an extreme concern are as follows: academics (84.5%), success (69.8%), postgraduation plans (54.8%), finances (54.0%), sleep (36.9%), friends (35.6%), family (35.2%), overall health (33.7%), body image (32.4%), and self-esteem (32.4%; Beiter et al., 2015).

Studies like this one are important, because identifying stressors allows counselors to more effectively target those students at risk for developing mental health problems and intervene appropriately (Jones, Park, & Lefevor, 2018). Some of the more common experiences students report as stress-inducing and anxiety-provoking are discussed below. As you review some of these common stressors, remember that mental health outcomes are not usually the result of a single factor but rather are the result of multiple factors operating in concert across multiple levels (e.g., individual, interpersonal, and institutional). Therefore, it is important for counselors to examine the entire ecological system of the anxious student to fully understand where stress emerges from and how it is sustained (Byrd & McKinney, 2012).

College Adjustment

The transition from high school to college can be stressful for any traditional-age student. Going off to college is simultaneously one of the most exciting yet one of the most challenging developmental milestones associated with young adulthood. Although most students report positive adjustment and for the most part enjoy the college experience (Kenney, Lac, Hummer, Grimaldi, & LaBrie, 2015), there are a growing number of students who report being adversely affected and feeling overwhelmed by this transitional period (Crede & Niehorster, 2012). Specifically, researchers have linked adjustment stress to a host of socioemotional problems including isolation, loneliness, anxiety, and depression (Horgan, Sweeney, Behan, & McCarthy, 2016; Puff et al., 2016; Quan, Zhen, Yao, & Zhou, 2014).

For many traditional-age students, going away to college marks the first time they will be living away from home. Along with experiencing increased personal freedom, students quickly realize they also must manage increased responsibilities, increased demands for time management, and an increased need to self-motivate. For returning adult students, adding a new set of responsibilities (taking classes, paying tuition, and navigating a new system) on top of existing responsibilities (which may include doing paid work, caring for dependents, and performing upkeep on their home) can cause adjustment stress.

Because it entails having to make multiple changes in a relatively short amount of time, the adjustment period could present challenges that eclipse the coping skills students have at their disposal. In these situations, stress compounds and students begin feeling trapped in a cycle they cannot exit. With attrition being a major concern for colleges and universities, researchers have posited stress overload as a key warning sign among first-year students at risk for failure and attrition (Amirkhan & Kofman, 2018). For counselors tasked with assisting students in successfully acclimating to college, it is important to be aware that outside of involuntary events, most variables causing students distress and affecting their perseverance toward degree completion are preventable when addressed early (Pritchard & Wilson, 2003).

Academic Stress

Academic stress refers to a condition in which a student's bodily response to academic-related demands exceeds the adaptive capabilities of the student (Wilks, 2008). Multiple elements of students' academic experiences can cause stress. Specifically, academic stress can be generated by having to perform assignments within tight time frames with rigid deadlines, managing heavier workloads than previously encountered, balancing multiple assignments being due at the same time, studying for examinations, and having trouble interacting with faculty (Dixon Rayle & Chung, 2007). Researchers have identified academic stress as a contributing factor in both mental and physical health problems faced on college campuses. These problems, in turn, have been linked to poorer academic outcomes and a diminished level of degree persistence (Macgeorge, Samter, & Gillihan, 2004). In fact, when reviewing the Center for Collegiate Mental Health 2013–2014 client database, Jones et al. (2018) found that academic stress accounted for the largest amount of variance in anxiety across various student subgroups.

Academic stress experiences vary across students. What may be stressful for one student may not be viewed in a similar fashion by another. As counselors, it is helpful for us to learn more about the stress students are experiencing around their academics and where that stress may be originating. For some students the stress may be related to a lack of ability or perceived incompetence in an area of study. Feeling unable to complete assigned tasks or projects can be stressful. Similarly, feeling inadequate in relation to others can be a source of stress. In today's competitive culture students may become stressed when they perceive their performance as not matching that of their peers. Constant comparisons with others can put an unsustainable amount of academic pressure on students that is bound to result in negative outcomes (Uno, Mortimer, Kim, & Vuolo, 2010).

Interpersonal Stress

Establishing positive peer relationships is important to the successful collegiate experience (Shim & Ryan, 2012). Students enter school looking to make friends and form lasting bonds. When they are successful, they tend to perform better academically, graduate, and generally report a more positive experience in school. In addition, having a strong social support network helps to mitigate the negative effects of stress and worry. However, conflicted or negative relationships can be a source of significant amounts of stress in the lives of college students. According to Riddell (2017), toxic friends can emotionally and psychologically damage an individual in multiple ways including criticism, competition, deception, exclusion, gossip, bullying, resentment, manipulation, inconsistency, and use of insults. These negative experiences can be face to face and, increasingly, in virtual spaces as well. When students find their interpersonal relationships bring more negativity than positivity to their lives, their stress increases, and anxiety builds. Counselors may be tasked with helping these students critically evaluate their existing peer relationships and transition out of those deemed negative and harmful.

Romantic relationships can also be a cause of stress and anxiety. Previous researchers have identified romantic relationship concerns as one of the more common reasons college students seek counseling services (Price, Hides, Cockshaw, Staneva, & Stoyanov, 2016). In fact, it has been argued that stress experienced within a romantic relationship has a more severe impact on the psychological well-being of college students than the stress experienced in any other relationship (Liu, 2016). Because most romantic relationships are still in their nascent stages during the college years, partners remain highly susceptible to the strains associated with the early development stages of a mature adult relationship. Nontraditional students may also experience concerns in romantic relationships—for example, they may be married or living with a long-term partner, and going back to school later in life can disrupt the normal daily flow they may have established and alter the roles of each partner. As a result, students are likely to experience both highs and lows in their romantic relationships and may seek the services of college counselors for help and guidance.

Counselors should also note the role that social media could play in anxiety. Social media is a focal point in the lives of many adults and is used by about 90% of adults (Vannucci, Flannery, & Ohannessian, 2017). Studies have shown a positive association between addictive social media use and increased anxiety disorders; some reasons for this connection are as follows: receiving negative feedback, experiencing cyberbullying, being exposed to stress in the lives of others, and experiencing pressure to maintain updates (Schou Andreassen et al., 2016; Vannucci et al., 2017). The fear of missing out, commonly referred to as FOMO, is anxiety associated with social media use when users do not know the happenings of fellow social media users (Syahniar et al., 2018). Although social media has benefits, such as access to social support, it can also be used as an escape of real-world stressors and/or increase rumination related to problems (stalking, excessive posting, etc.; Vannucci et al., 2017).

Homesickness

Homesickness, defined as distress or impairment resulting from an actual or anticipated separation from the home (Thurber & Walton, 2012), is a natural experience for younger students as they work through the abrupt shift from their previous familiar environments to their new lives as college and university students. Overall, a mild sense of homesickness can have a positive impact on the college experience because it motivates students to develop their personal coping skills and establish new and healthy relationships (Sun, Hagedorn, & Zhang, 2016). Typically, as students begin feeling more comfortable on campus and focus shifts to academic studies, making friends, and getting involved in campus activities, feelings of homesickness begin to wane.

However, when felt more intensely, and persistently, homesickness can be far more debilitating. As such, homesickness is a real and present concern for some students living away from home for the first time (English, Davis, Wei, & Gross, 2017). English and colleagues stated, in their review of the literature, that previous researchers have estimated 19% to 70% of college students will experience homesickness distressing enough to interfere with their daily functioning depending on how the construct is measured. In fact, the sudden departure from normality and familiarity may prove challenging to even the most independent young adults (Longo & Kim-Spoon, 2013). Counselors would be wise to assess for symptoms of homesickness among students, especially first-year students, because unaddressed feelings can have deleterious effects. Additionally, counselors should ensure they remain mindful of family values and level of support because this will play a major role in the therapeutic process.

Financial Stress

Financial stress is another major contributor both directly and indirectly affecting student anxiety (Jones et al., 2018). Across the country, the cost of higher education continues to rise. During the 2018–2019 academic year, the average cost of attendance for an undergraduate student (tuition and fees only) ranged from $9,716 (public, in-state institution) and $35,676 (private institution) per year. Over 4 years, students could end up paying north of $35,000 or $140,000 for a baccalaureate degree at a public or private institution, respectively (Powell, 2018). This amount is nearly four times what students paid for the same 4-year degree in 1989, or twice as much when adjusted for inflation (Maldonado, 2018). At an annual growth rate of 2.6%, the higher education costs have risen five times more than wages have increased. Skyrocketing costs have resulted in students taking out increasingly more loan debt to finance their education or starting a postsecondary degree and not being able to finish it. According to the U.S. Federal Reserve, as of the spring of 2018 there were 44.5 million student loan borrowers with a collective debt of over $1.5 trillion (as cited in Friedman, 2019).

The repercussions of financial stress are felt by students in many ways. Researchers have found financial stress to be a significant contributor to lower retention rates (Engle & Tinto, 2008) and an increased likelihood of discontinuing college (Britt, Ammerman, Barrett, & Jones, 2017). Among low-income and first-generation college students, researchers have identified financial stress and lack of financial support as robust stressors strongly related to probability of graduating (Adams, Meyers, & Beidas, 2016). Although each student is unique in his or her situation, consider the following examples and speculate on the different types of stress these students might be experiencing:

1. Traditional or nontraditional students who are working full-time as well as going to school full-time.
2. Younger students who have parents paying for their education, but with expectations, such as selecting the major that the parents prefer, going to a specific school, maintaining certain grades, and so forth.
3. An older student going back to school to make a career change and being in classes with much younger students.
4. A student attending a university that has a majority population of students from different cultural backgrounds.

Gender Differences

The Anxiety and Depression Association of America (2018) noted that females, from the age of puberty until about the age of 50, are twice as likely to experience anxiety disorders as males. They are also more likely to have multiple psychiatric disorders in their lifetime, with the most common co-occurring disorder being depression (discussed in further detail in Chapter 19). Women have higher rates of generalized anxiety disorder and in those who have panic disorder, experience greater vulnerability to experiencing panic attacks over their male counterparts. They are twice as likely to develop posttraumatic stress disorder after a traumatic event, as well as having more severe, debilitating, and persistent symptoms (Maeng & Milad, 2015). Reasons for the large gender disparity continue to be studied, but there are likely both social and biological reasons for this difference.

Some social factors that might account for this difference is the role women often play within their family system. For example, women are often caregivers for children, older adults, and/or disabled family members. They might be juggling these caregiving responsibilities with taking care of themselves, careers, or school. Women are also more likely to be experiencing lower income and part-time employment, which leads to financial stress. Finally, rates of abuse are higher among women, which can lead to a long-term impact on their own mental health (Recovery Across Mental Health, 2019). However, males are less likely to report symptoms, possibly skewing reported numbers (Hosseini & Khazali, 2013).

In addition to social factors, biological factors may play a role in these higher rates of anxiety, although specifics of this neurobiological phenomenon remain unclear. A meta-analysis of 12 psychophysiological studies found that women had higher heart rates than men, subsequently remaining higher during stressful events, whereas men had higher levels of systolic blood pressure (Stoney, Davis, & Matthews, 1987). Although hormones may not directly affect anxiety, different hormonal phases, such as puberty, menses, pregnancy, postpartum, and menopause, place women at higher levels of vulnerability for experiencing stress and anxiety during these hormonal fluctuations (Maeng & Milad, 2015). Testosterone, a hormone far more abundant in men, may help ease anxiety, whereas estrogen in women can contribute to an easier activation of stress hormones (McHenry, Carrier, Hull, & Kabbaj, 2014; Premier Health, 2017). Men with lower levels of testosterone experience higher levels of anxiety and depression, which one study suggests is because testosterone has anxiolytic and antidepressant benefits. This, along with testosterone therapy in women, continues to be studied (McHenry et al., 2014).

Normative and Clinical Anxiety as Presenting Concerns

Anxiety is a natural part of life and something we all experience from time to time. As human beings, we may not like feeling anxious and look to quickly remove ourselves from situations that cause our anxiety to rise. Or, we may try, when possible, to avoid certain people, places, and situations we believe will cause our stress levels to rise or make us feel anxious. But the truth is, we all need some degree of anxiety in our lives. A small amount of anxiety is necessary for survival because it is a natural reaction to stress and an evolutionary protective mechanism. Anxiety helps us avoid potentially dangerous situations and motivates us to escape such situations should we find ourselves engulfed in one. In other words, anxiety is the force that keeps us from acting recklessly and engaging in hazardous behaviors. It also is the force that causes us to rise to the occasion and overcome challenges in our lives. Despite its benefits, anxiety also can be perceived negatively. When anxiety persists, and exceeds our coping abilities, it can become a debilitating force.

Further complicating the issue is the fact that anxiety presentations vary by individual and potentially can include a variety of physical, cognitive, or behavioral symptoms. Physical symptoms might include things like sweating, tension, nausea, or rapid heartbeat. Cognitive symptoms might include racing thoughts, the inability to focus on the task at hand, or a preoccupation with the situation causing anxiety. Behavioral symptoms might include expressions of anger, foot/hand tapping, alcohol consumption, or pacing. As counselors, identifying the symptoms your clients are experiencing as well as the frequency and extent to which they affect their daily lives is important in assessing severity.

So, what constitutes a normal amount of anxiety? A. D. Brown (2010) suggested that symptoms cross the line from normal to toxic anxiety when they begin to impede functioning at work or at school. For example, is the student nervous about a midterm exam and motivated to study harder, or is the student rattled with fear of failure and no longer wanting to go to class or socialize with friends? The line between normal and toxic anxiety is different for everyone. Some students may have strong coping skills and be able to handle considerable adversity and stress in their lives. Other students may have less developed coping skills and begin stressing out over even the most minor stressors. The following section provides information that is helpful in differentiating the experiences of normal stressors and anxiety disorders in college students. Assessing the situation and talking with students should help you better understand what is going on and the best way to proceed in the counseling relationship.

Healthy Versus Unhealthy Anxiety

In general, healthy anxiety does not get in the way of daily activities and responsibilities, can be controlled with conscious effort, may be unpleasant but does not cause significant distress, is limited to a specific issue or small series of realistic concerns, and lasts for only a short period of time when a stressor is present or there is a perceived imminent threat. Unhealthy anxiety, however, is uncontrollable, is extremely upsetting and severe symptoms manifest, becomes more generalized in nature, and becomes a pervasive part of every day for a substantial period of time (usually 6 months or more).

When a counselor is working with college students, educating them on the differences between normative and clinical anxiety is a useful endeavor. Although it is important to stress that students should seek help when needed and that avoiding available campus resources is never a good option, talking about ways to self-manage normative stress can be helpful as well. For example, counselors can help students see that normative stress tends to center on a specific situation or event, is time-limited, and often does not include physiological distress, whereas clinical anxiety generally is more pervasive, covers a broad range of topics and issues, often lasts for longer periods of time, and produces both psychological and physiological symptoms. Identifying triggering events, developing a set of effective coping strategies, and being proactive in avoiding potentially worrisome situations all are helpful skills for students to learn. For example, the student who worries about finances at the end of the month could be directed to learn more about budgeting and be educated about various job opportunities available on campus. Similarly, students who deal with issues of food insecurity may need to be made aware of campus resources (e.g., a food pantry) that might be available for them to use in times of need. The key is helping ensure worry does not go unaddressed, pile up, and eventually lead to a more problematic situation in which students begin experiencing clinical symptoms requiring a more intensive level of treatment. Counselors should be mindful of common areas of concern and be aware of available resources to present. Some common resources might include, among others, a career counseling center; organizations for lesbian, gay, bisexual, transgender, and queer/questioning students; the Newman Center or other religious groups; a disability department; or a financial aid office. The following section describes some of the current practices used in addressing stress and anxiety on college campuses.

Management Versus Prevention

The proliferation of mental disorders on college campuses is on the rise. In many cases, the demand for mental health services far exceeds the available resources most colleges and universities provide to their students (Auerbach et al., 2018). In response to this national shortage of qualified mental health providers, campus health care models are shifting. Traditional approaches aimed at treating and managing mental health issues gradually are being supplemented with a new focus on preventive models. In this section we examine the difference between the two foci, how they support one another, and what they mean for the work you likely will do as a college counselor.

Health management treatment approaches are based on the chronic care model and are responsive in nature. Students present for mental health services, are assessed and triaged, and are provided with appropriate treatment options. The efficacy of each largely depends on the individual student and the initial cause for seeking help. For example, a psychiatric referral might be warranted to assess for candidacy for antianxiety medications. However, antianxiety medications often mask symptoms and do not treat the underlying cause of those symptoms. In other cases, referral to a counselor may be the best option because it often is easier to manage behaviors and emotions than it is to remove an underlying stressor. A more effective approach incorporates both medical and behavioral health services in an integrated manner as part of a cohesive team program (Pedrelli, Nyer, Yeung, Zulauf, & Wilens, 2014). Additionally, several institutions have begun the process of implementing new stepped-care service delivery models aimed at addressing the specific needs of individual students using a variety of services and treatment options (Cornish et al., 2017).

As a college counselor, you will play an important role in the management of mental health issues on your campus. Becoming familiar with the various treatment approaches used in college counseling centers will be to your advantage. For many students, a brief cognitive behavioral therapy (CBT) program can be effective at managing emotions (J. Brown, 2016). These types of programs teach students to identify cognitive distortions and avoid thinking that might contribute to anxiety while learning how to react differently in stressful or anxiety-provoking situations. The specific interventions used might vary on the basis of what the student needs but might include relaxation techniques, assessment of lifestyle versus goals, identification of faulty thinking, or slow exposure to reduce fears or decrease symptoms of an obsessive-compulsive disorder. Several well-established, evidence-based CBT models exist and are being used on college campuses nationwide (Regehr, Glancy, & Pitts, 2013). Although literature supports the efficacy of CBT models, researchers found that most mental health professionals who report following a CBT model in their clinical work actually drift from using proven techniques and that their stated theoretical orientation may not be a reliable indicator of the type of therapy they actually are providing (Waller, Stringer, & Meyer, 2012).

Prevention-based models address student mental health in an alternative manner. Preventive efforts focus on early identification and curbing of an issue before it becomes a problem and interferes with normal functioning. From a preventive perspective, counselors work with students to help identify triggers to anxiety. Identifying triggers and recognizing when symptoms might start is the first step toward helping the students use their identified coping skills before symptoms continue to get worse. In addition, a study done by Bland et al. (2012) helped identify lifestyle habits that act as risk and protective factors against anxiety. Consistent with prior research, the study's authors indicated the factor most commonly associated with a high stress tolerance is "feeling supported by family, friends, and teachers." They also identified eight other factors associated with a high stress tolerance, including cleaning the living quarters, talking to a friend, praying, using social media networks, calling parents, shopping, eating, and using substances. Each of these nine coping skills relies on an external source and may include distraction or disengagement from the stressor (Bland et al., 2012). Counselors could benefit from this knowledge by identifying these factors and assessing for opportunities to increase social support as much as possible.

Assessing and Treating Anxiety-Related Disorders

The term *anxiety* is a blanket term that covers multiple disorders, including generalized anxiety disorder, social anxiety disorder, panic disorder, agoraphobia, phobias, separation anxiety disorder, illness anxiety disorder, obsessive-compulsive disorder, and posttraumatic stress disorder. Each disorder has a different set of criteria that varies by symptoms, timing, or severity, but they all have one thing in common—anxiety. The most common variations you likely will see on college campuses include generalized anxiety disorder, social anxiety disorder, panic disorder, obsessive-compulsive disorder, and separation anxiety disorder. Additionally, several potentially stressful situations and conditions are addressed as Z codes in the International Classification of Diseases (10th rev.; World Health Organization, 1992). It is important to consider these diagnoses as well, because students may be at a subthreshold level for *Diagnostic and Statistical Manual of Mental Disorders* (5th ed. [*DSM-5*]; American Psychiatric Association, 2013) diagnoses but still be dealing with tangible stressful and anxiety-provoking issues.

Generalized Anxiety Disorder

Generalized anxiety disorder is characterized by persistent and excessive worry about several different issues. Individuals with generalized anxiety disorder become anxious over situations both current and anticipated. Their worry becomes difficult to control and often interferes with daily living. Among a sample of over 14,000 students across 26 campuses, researchers found a prevalence rate of 7% for generalized anxiety disorder in U.S. college and university students (Eisenberg, Hunt, & Speer, 2013). Students with generalized anxiety disorder may find the transition to college challenging and stressful as they are forced to deal with a new environment, new schedule, and the need to build new relationships.

Social Anxiety Disorder

Social anxiety disorder is a condition wherein social interactions cause irrational anxiety for an individual. Students with social anxiety disorder experience a persistent fear of being watched, judged, or scrutinized by others. The thought of failure, rejection, and negative evaluation is always on their mind and deters them from getting close to others. Students with a social anxiety disorder may struggle to make friends and acclimate to the college environment. In treatment, these individuals often work with a counselor to develop their self-presentation skills (National Institute of Mental Health, n.d.).

Anxiety can present as a variety of physical, cognitive, or behavioral symptoms. Physical symptoms might include things like sweating, tension, nausea, or rapid heartbeat. Cognitive symptoms might include racing thoughts, the inability to focus on the task at hand, or a preoccupation with the situation causing anxiety. Behavioral symptoms might include anger, foot/hand tapping, alcohol consumption, or pacing. As counselors, it is important for us to identify the symptoms the client is experiencing as well as how often they affect his or her daily life and to what extent.

Panic Disorder

Panic disorder is diagnosed when individuals experience spontaneous panic attacks. These attacks are characterized by an intense fear that manifests in multiple physiological symptoms including increased heart rate, sweating, shaking or trembling, shortness of breath and chest tightness, dizziness, nausea, and hot flashes. Panic attacks vary in length, with most lasting only a few minutes. After a panic attack, the individual feels tired and worn out. Panic attacks themselves are not life-threatening; however, the intense fear associated with them significantly impairs daily living. According to the World Health Organization (Auerbach et al., 2018), prevalence rates for panic disorder on campus are like those of young adults (ages 18–22) across the general population.

Obsessive-Compulsive Disorder

Obsessive-compulsive disorder involves excessive thoughts that lead to uncontrollable and repetitive behaviors. Obsessions are the unwanted and intrusive thoughts that trigger the experiencing of negative and distressing emotions. Compulsions are the urges or impulses to complete a behavioral ritual. The median age of onset for obsessive-compulsive disorder is 19, with 25% of all diagnosed cases occurring by age 14 (Anxiety and Depression Association of America, n.d.). Consequently, it is not surprising that researchers have found clinically significant levels of obsessive-compulsive disorder symptoms to be relatively common on college campuses (Sulkowski, Mariaskin, & Storch, 2011). For college students, much planning and effort are needed to identify triggers, arrange schedules, and develop contingency plans to deal with unwanted thoughts and potentially debilitating behavioral rituals.

Separation Anxiety Disorder

Separation anxiety disorder is a disorder commonly diagnosed in children. It is characterized by an excessive fear associated with separation from parents or caregivers. To be diagnosed with a separation anxiety disorder, individuals must exhibit an irrational level of distress incongruent with their developmental level. Although common in young children, the removal of the age onset stipulation in *DSM-5* (American Psychiatric Association, 2013) has led to an increase in diagnoses of adult-onset separation anxiety disorders (Baldwin, Gordon, Abelli, & Pini, 2016). For many college students, especially those who have not lived away from home before, separation from their secure attachment figures could cause intense anxiety and fear.

Assessment

Symptoms often overlap, making diagnosing challenging at times. Using a screening tool can help determine whether symptoms are appropriate for receiving a formal diagnosis. Counselors should be mindful of the ethical implications of using various screening tools. Specifically, counselors should ensure they are properly trained and qualified to administer the screening tool they plan to use. They also need to be aware of age, developmental level, or language barriers that may exist. Although there are a multitude of screening tools for the various anxiety disorders, some common ones are the following:

- Generalized Anxiety Disorder Scale (GAD-7; Spitzer, Kroenke, Williams, & Lowe, 2006)
- Social Phobia Inventory (Connor et al., 2000)
- Patient Health Questionnaire (PHQ-4; Kroenke, Spitzer, Williams, & Lowe, 2009)
- Beck Anxiety Inventory (Beck & Steer, 1993)
- Hamilton Anxiety Rating Scale (HAM-A; Hamilton, 1959)
- Penn State Worry Questionnaire (Meyer, Miller, Metzger, & Borkovec, 1990)

Stress assessment tools also are available. A common measure used is the Perceived Stress Scale (PSS; Cohen, Kamarck, & Mermelstein, 1983). The PSS is a brief 10-item instrument in which individuals rate the frequency with which they have dealt with a stressor in the past month. Scores on the PSS range from 0 to 40, with higher scores indicating higher perceptions of stress. The PSS is a free tool to use and is supported by its use across many research studies.

Outreach Implications

Although college counseling centers might be fully prepared to handle the needs of students, and anxiety is a treatable issue, many students continue to resist the idea of getting help and/or recognize that an issue is present (J. Brown, 2016). For this reason, outreach becomes an important task in that it can increase awareness of what counseling centers have to offer, help educate the campus community on symptoms, and reduce the stigma of reaching out for assistance. One option suggested by J. Brown (2016) is to offer free screenings on a day on which no appointment is needed. Everyone who is screened could be given information on the services that are available and receive answers to any questions he or she may have. In addition, counseling staff could address students with higher scores on the screenings and simply ask them how they can be helped. Appointments and appropriate referrals can be made at that time. To include nontraditional students, counseling centers should consider extended or flexible hours because some of these students might be out in the workforce (Pedrelli et al., 2014).

Although stress and anxiety can arise at any time, there may be certain periods during which students are more at risk on the basis of how higher education institutions operate. Counseling at a college or university usually means having breaks throughout the year that align with the academic calendar. Although this is often viewed as a perk, counselors should be mindful about the need for continuity of care during these breaks. It is always advisable to consult with a supervisor if there are any questions, but some things to consider are the following: Is this student stable? Is there any suspicion of potential harm over the break? Should a referral be issued? Should homework be given? Counselors must also think ahead regarding events that may be stressful to the student. For example, holidays might be stressful if there is family discord, a lot of travel, or financial constraints. Finals could also be a stressful time of the semester or quarter. If there are major events coming up, counselors should plan ahead and address coping skills and emergency backup plans with their students that might need to be used over a break or during a particularly hectic time. If a counselor feels a referral is necessary, he or she should also consider any potential barriers (such as lack of insurance, lack of transportation, providers who are not in town for holidays, etc.) and plan for them as much as possible. An extensive list of local community referrals and campus resources is a tool that all counseling centers should have (Pedrelli et al., 2014).

Population-Specific Case Studies

The Case of Donald

Donald is an 18-year-old, African American, first-year college student at a local community college. He chose to attend a 2-year institution because he felt intimidated going away to a larger school, where there would be thousands of people he did not know, and wanted to remain living at home with his parents. Additionally, he would be saving money and not having to take on as much student loan debt to pay tuition. During his first semester, Donald began realizing he was feeling anxious more and more of the time. In fact, he describes how he now finds himself worrying constantly about anything and everything. Furthermore, he reports feeling more tired and fatigued than usual and reports tension in his shoulders and neck. He wants to do well in school, but persistent stress makes it hard for him to focus or concentrate. He fears failing and is beginning to worry that college may not be for him. Without a degree, he worries that he may not find a job and be able to help his family financially. Worse, he stresses over the idea of having to pay back student loans with no degree to show for the expenses he has incurred. Unsure where to turn or what to do, he presents at the community college counseling center for help. The three-step process discussed below can be used to guide you through the treatment process.

■ ■ ■

Step 1: Assessment

The first step for the counselor to perform is to assess the situation. Donald obviously is experiencing a great deal of anxiety, and it is beginning to interfere with his daily functioning. As Donald's counselor, you will need to identify the specific symptoms he is experiencing, when they occur, how often they occur, and what precipitates their occurrence. Gathering this information will assist you in narrowing down what may be the root problem for Donald. One of the screening tools mentioned earlier in this chapter might be a good way to gather the information needed to proceed with Donald. A psychosocial interview is another good intervention you could begin with in your relationship. Psychosocial interviews are designed to obtain comprehensive information on a client's beliefs, values, history, and family situation. It may take up the entire first session, but you'll be able to find out a lot of relevant information that will likely be useful in the counseling process, as well as the rapport-building stage, such as Donald's religion, sexual orientation, living situation, social supports, employment status, previous counseling history/diagnosis, history of traumas, and so forth. Be sure to create a safe place to discuss such personal information. It can be a good idea to let Donald (or any student) know that although you are asking these questions to better understand his situation, he does not have to answer any questions he is uncomfortable with. Keep in mind that as trained counselors, we may be comfortable hearing this information, but the student in front of us might not always be comfortable sharing such personal information with a stranger. Some questions are simply easier to answer than others.

Step 2: Diagnosis

The second step for the counselor is to aggregate the data collected and arrive at a diagnosis for the client. On the basis of the information presented, Donald appears to be experiencing a generalized anxiety disorder. Identification of the disorder only begins the process. Effective treatment options should emerge out of the symptoms present and not solely the label affixed to a client. At this step in the process, communication with the client is key. Donald should be apprised of the results of the assessment and how they will be used to inform a counseling process to follow.

Step 3: Treatment

With a diagnosis of generalized anxiety disorder confirmed, the counselor begins treatment planning with input from Donald. A process of active monitoring should ensue for a period to get a better idea of the scope of the problem. Donald would be asked to self-monitor and record his experiences for 2 to 3 weeks and document what happens. Because Donald does not live on campus, recording his experiences can help the counselor understand some of the events or situations causing him to feel anxious. Active monitoring may help diminish the occurrence of symptoms in individuals with less severe presentations, thereby reducing the need for further intervention, and guide future treatment. Individuals with generalized anxiety disorder respond well to therapy, and short-term approaches, particularly using a CBT-type treatment, have been shown to be very effective in reducing symptoms and improving overall functioning (Covin, Ouimet, Seeds, & Dozois, 2008). On campuses where session limits may be in place, the community college counselor may resort to referring Donald to a local mental health provider where extended therapy can occur. Finally, the counselor may devote time to helping Donald explore his academic options should the course load in his current major remain a source of stress for him. Together, Donald and his counselor could investigate all his options. Community colleges offer vocational programs, certificates, and transfer options. Checking them all out carefully may help Donald find an alternative to dropping out.

Conclusion

Although students often are told college represents the best 4 years of their lives, the reality is the time spent in college can be a stressful period that many students struggle to address daily. For most students, this stress leads to feeling anxious and worried.

Anxiety among college students can occur for a variety of reasons. Sometimes a specific event becomes a stressor significant enough to cause anxious thinking. Other times anxiety emerges in response to a building up of stressors until an individual's coping abilities are exceeded. When this happens, the need for mental health services rises. Indeed, college counseling centers are reporting a dramatic increase in the number of students seeking services, with anxiety often the leading reason given for their decision to seek help. As an emerging professional likely to be tasked with working among students who are feeling stressed and anxious, understanding how stress and anxiety occur on the college campus and what can be done to assist those being adversely affected by supporting their mental health is important.

Throughout this chapter, we sought to improve your understanding of the various anxiety-related disorders and how they look among a college student population. Armed with this knowledge, you are in a better position to help students and improve their quality of life.

Final Case Studies

Case 1

Melanie is a 19-year-old college sophomore attending a state university in a different state than the one in which she grew up. She lives in a sorority dorm that she had become part of in her freshman year. She has average grades and misses class on occasion because of oversleeping. She often stays up late and enjoys partying with her friends. Last year, she began dating Mark, a popular athlete and member of a fraternity with whom her sorority often socializes. About a month ago, Melanie and Mark broke up after he became interested in someone else. Melanie finds herself "cyberstalking" Mark on social media to see what he has been doing. Because her sorority sisters often socialize with Mark's fraternity, Melanie has not been wanting to hang out as often, causing a rift in her friendships. She fears her sorority sisters may not want her to be a part of things anymore, causing her to ruminate about who her friends will be and where she will live if that happens. In addition, she is facing pressure from her parents, who are paying her tuition and dorm fees, to take school more seriously and get her grades up. They are giving her this year to improve or will cut her off financially.

Melanie is familiar with the counseling center but wants to be sure no one will find out that she is there because she does not want to damage her image. During her initial assessment, she tells you that twice since her breakup, she may have had a panic attack, endorsing symptoms of elevated heart rate, shortness of breath, and shaking. She states she is embarrassed by this and is looking for ways to cope with stress.

Case 1 Exploration Questions

1. What, if any, additional information would you need to know about Melanie?
2. What are her presenting concerns?
3. What might be your initial diagnosis and treatment plan?
4. What specific interventions and/or coping skills might be beneficial for her?

Case 2

Jason is a 48-year-old Caucasian man working full-time while taking night classes to earn his MBA. His current job requires him to work 50 plus hours per week. He has a wife and two children at home (Stacy, 12, and Conner, 16). He states it is important to show his kids that education is important and that goals can be reached at any age. Although he is struggling to find work-life balance, he fears that dropping out of the program will teach his children the wrong lesson. He is maintaining above-average grades so far, although he has only completed one semester, and is still performing well at work, but he describes himself as "having no life" and being "always on the go." He says he has never been under this level of stress before.

He is worried about many things. He worries his kids will regret his not being around. He worries he will not be able to teach his son to drive or go to his daughter's dance competitions. He worries his wife will get overwhelmed and leave him. He doesn't want his grades to drop or his work performance to suffer. During class last week, Jason rushed in about 20 minutes late because he was caught up at work. He stayed after class to explain what happened. The professor suggested he explore the counseling center to help manage his stress, worry, and good intentions. He has not sought counseling before and is skeptical it will help. He fears ongoing sessions will make his schedule even tighter but did not want his professor to think he didn't take the suggestion seriously.

Case 2 Exploration Questions

1. What, if any, additional information would you need to know about Jason?
2. What are his presenting concerns?
3. What might be your initial diagnosis and treatment plan?
4. What specific interventions and/or coping skills might be beneficial for him?

References

Adams, D. R., Meyers, S. A., & Beidas, R. S. (2016). The relationship between financial strain, perceived stress, psychological symptoms, and academic and social integration in undergraduate students. *Journal of American College Health, 64,* 362–370. doi:10.1080/07448481.2016.1154559

American College Health Association. (2018). *American College Health Association–National College Health Assessment II: Reference group executive summary Spring 2018.* Silver Spring, MD: American College Health Association.

American Psychiatric Association. (2013). *Diagnostic and statistical manual of mental disorders* (5th ed.). Arlington, VA: Author.

Amirkhan, J. H., & Kofman, Y. B. (2018). Stress overload as a red flag for freshman failure and attrition. *Contemporary Educational Psychology, 54,* 297–308. doi:10.1016/j.cedpsych.2018.07.004

Anxiety and Depression Association of America. (n.d.). Physical activity reduces stress. Retrieved from https://www.adaa.org/understanding-anxiety/related-illnesses/other-related-conditions/stress/physical-activity-reduces-st

Anxiety and Depression Association of America. (2018). Facts. Retrieved from https://adaa.org/living-with-anxiety/women/facts

Association for University and College Counseling Center Directors. (2017). *The Association for University and College Counseling Center Directors annual survey*. Retrieved from https://www.aucccd.org/assets/documents/Governance/2017%20aucccd%20survey-public-apr26.pdf

Auerbach, R. P., Mortier, P., Bruffaerts, R., Alonso, J., Benjet, C., Cuijpers, P., . . . WHO WMH-ICS Collaborators. (2018). WHO World Mental Health Surveys International College Student Project: Prevalence and distribution of mental disorders. *Journal of Abnormal Psychology*. Advance online publication. doi:10.1037/abn0000362

Baldwin, D., Gordon, R., Abelli, M., & Pini, S. (2016). The separation of adult separation anxiety disorder. *CNS Spectrums, 21*, 289–294. doi:10.1017/S1092852916000080

Bamber, M. D., & Kraenzle Schneider, J. (2016). Mindfulness-based meditation to decrease stress and anxiety in college students: A narrative synthesis of the research. *Educational Research Review, 18*, 1–32. doi:10.1016/j.edurev.2015.12.004

Bandelow, B., & Michaelis, S. (2015). Epidemiology of anxiety disorders in the 21st century. *Dialogues in Clinical Neuroscience, 17*, 327–335.

Beck, A. T., & Steer, R. A. (1993). *Beck Anxiety Inventory Manual*. San Antonio, TX: Psychological Corporation.

Beiter, R., Nash, R., McCrady, M., Rhoades, D., Linscomb, M., Clarahan, M., & Sammut, S. (2015). The prevalence and correlates of depression, anxiety, and stress in a sample of college students. *Journal of Affective Disorders, 173*, 90–96. doi:10.1016/j.jad.2014.10.054

Bland, H. W., Melton, B. F., Welle, P., & Bigham, L. (2012). Stress tolerance: New challenges for millennial college students. *College Student Journal, 46*, 362–375.

Britt, S. L., Ammerman, D. A., Barrett, S. F., & Jones, S. (2017). Student loans, financial stress, and college student retention. *Journal of Student Financial Aid, 47*, 25–37.

Brown, A. D. (2010). *Waiting to live*. Bloomington, IN: iUniverse.

Brown, J. (2016). Anxiety: The most common mental health diagnosis in college students. *BU Today*. Boston University. Retrieved from http://www.bu.edu/today/2016/college-students-anxiety-and-depression

Byrd, D. R., & McKinney, K. J. (2012). Individual, interpersonal, and institutional level factors associated with the mental health of college students. *Journal of American College Health, 60*, 185–193. doi:10.1080/07448481.2011.584334

Center for Collegiate Mental Health. (2017, January). *2017 annual report* (Publication No. STA 17–74). University Park, PA: Author.

Cohen, S., Kamarck, T., & Mermelstein, R. (1983). A global measure of perceived stress. *Journal of Health and Social Behavior, 24*, 385–396. doi:10.2307/2136404

College Parents of America. (2019, January 3). *5 main causes of stress for college students*. Retrieved from https://collegeparents.org/2019/01/03/5-main-causes-of-stress-for-college-students%EF%BB%BF/

Connor, K. M., Davidson, J. R., Churchill, L. E., Sherwood, A., Foa, E., & Weisler, R. H. (2000). Psychometric properties of the Social Phobia Inventory (SPIN): New self-rating scale. *The British Journal of Psychiatry, 176*, 379–386. doi:10.1192/bjp.176.4.379

Cornish, P. A., Berry, G., Benton, S., Barros-Gomes, P., Johnson, D., Ginsburg, R., . . . Romano, V. (2017). Meeting the mental health needs of today's college student: Reinventing services through Stepped Care 2.0. *Psychological Services, 14*, 428–442. doi:10.1037/ser0000158

Covin, R., Ouimet, A. J., Seeds, P. M., & Dozois, D. J. A. (2008). A meta-analysis of CBT for pathological worry among clients with GAD. *Journal of Anxiety Disorders, 22*, 108–116. doi:10.1016/j.janxdis.2007.01.002

Crede, M., & Niehorster, S. (2012). Adjustment to college as measured by the Student Adaptation to College Questionnaire: A quantitative review of its structure and relationships with correlates and consequences. *Educational Psychology Review, 24,* 133–165. doi:10.1007/s10648-011-9184-5

Dixon Rayle, A., & Chung, K. Y. (2007). Revisiting first-year college students' mattering: Social support, academic stress, and the mattering experience. *Journal of College Student Retention, 9,* 21–37.

Eisenberg, D., Hunt, J., & Speer, N. (2013). Mental health in American colleges and universities: Variation across student subgroups and across campuses. *Journal of Nervous and Mental Disease, 201,* 60–67. doi:10.1097/NMD.0b013e31827ab077

Engle, J., & Tinto, V. (2008). *Moving beyond access: College success for low-income, first-generation students.* Pell Institute for the Study of Opportunity in Higher Education. Retrieved from https://files.eric.ed.gov/fulltext/ED504448.pdf

English, T., Davis, J., Wei, M., & Gross, J. J. (2017). Homesickness and adjustment across the first year of college: A longitudinal study. *Emotion, 17,* 1–5. doi:10.1037/emo0000235

Farrer, L. M., Gulliver, A., Bennett, K., Fassnacht, D. B., & Griffiths, K. M. (2016). Demographic and psychosocial predictors of major depression and generalized anxiety disorder in Australian university students. *BMC Psychiatry, 15,* 241. doi:10.1186/s12888-016-0961-z

Friedman, Z. (2019, February 25). Student loan debt statistics in 2019: A $1.5 trillion crisis. Retrieved from https://www.forbes.com/sites/zackfriedman/2019/02/25/student-loan-debt-statistics-2019/#41e80cd7133f

Hales, D. (2009). *An invitation to health* (13th ed.). Belmont, CA: Wadsworth/Cengage Learning.

Hamilton, M. (1959). The assessment of anxiety states by rating. *British Journal of Medical Psychology, 32,* 50–55. doi:10.1111/j.2044-8341.1959.tb00467.x

Holsboer, F., & Ising, M. (2010). Stress hormone regulation: Biological role and translation into therapy. *Annual Review of Psychology, 61,* C101–C111.

Horgan, A., Sweeney, J., Behan, L., & McCarthy, G. (2016). Depressive symptoms, college adjustment and peer support among undergraduate nursing and midwifery students. *Journal of Advanced Nursing, 72,* 3081–3092. doi:10.1111/jan.13074

Hosseini, L., & Khazali, H. (2013). Comparing the level of anxiety in male & female school students. *Procedia - Social and Behavioral Sciences, 84,* 41–46. doi:10.1016/j.sbspro.2013.06.506

January, J., Madhombiro, M., Chipamaunga, S., Ray, S., Chingono, A., & Abas, M. (2018). Prevalence of depression and anxiety among undergraduate university students in low- and middle-income countries: A systematic review protocol. *Systematic Reviews, 7,* 57. doi:10.1186/s13643-018-0723-8

Jones, P. J., Park, S. Y., & Lefevor, G. T. (2018). Contemporary college student anxiety: The role of academic distress, financial stress, and support. *Journal of College Counseling, 21,* 252–264. doi:10.1002/jocc.12107

Kenney, S. R., Lac, A., Hummer, J. F., Grimaldi, E. M., & LaBrie, J. W. (2015). Pathways of parenting style on adolescents' college adjustment, academic achievement, and alcohol risk. *Journal of College Student Retention: Research, Theory & Practice, 17,* 186–203. doi:10.1177/1521025115578232

Kessler, R. C., Chiu, W. T., Demler, O., Merikangas, K. R., & Walters, E. E. (2005). Prevalence, severity, and comorbidity of 12-month *DSM-IV* disorders in the National Comorbidity Survey replication. *Archives of General Psychiatry, 62,* 617–627. doi:10.1001/archpsyc.62.6.617

Kroenke, K., Spitzer, R. L., Williams, J. B., & Lowe, B. (2009). An ultra-brief screening scale for anxiety and depression: The PHQ-4. *Psychosomatics, 50,* 613–621. doi:10.1176/appi.psy.50.6.613

Kumaraswamy, N. (2013). Academic stress, anxiety, and depression among college students—A brief review. *International Review of Social Sciences and Humanities, 5,* 135–143.

Lazarus, R. S., & Folkman, S. (1984). *Stress, appraisal, and coping.* New York, NY: Springer.

Liu, B. L. (2016). *The impact of interpersonal stress in romantic relationships on college students' mental health and academic performance* (Doctoral dissertation). Retrieved from https://repositories.lib.utexas.edu/handle/2152/41572

Longo, G. S., & Kim-Spoon, J. (2013). Homesickness in college students: The role of religion in combatting depression. *Mental Health, Religion, & Culture, 16,* 489–500. doi:10.1080/13674676.2012.696600

Macgeorge, E. L., Samter, W., & Gillihan, S. J. (2004). Academic stress, supportive communication, and health. *Communication Education, 54,* 365–372. doi:10.1080/03634520500442236

Mackenzie, S., Wiegel, J. R., Mundt, M., Brown, D., Saewyc, E., Heiligenstein, E., . . . Fleming, M. (2011). Depression and suicide ideation among students accessing campus health care. *American Journal of Orthopsychiatry, 81,* 101–107. doi:10.1111/j.1939-0025.2010.01077.x

Maeng, L. Y., & Milad, M. R. (2015). Sex differences in anxiety disorders: Interactions between fear, stress, and gonadal hormones. *Hormones and Behavior, 76,* 106–117. doi:10.1016/j.yhbeh.2015.04.002

Maldonado, C. (2018). Price of college increasing almost 8 times faster than wages. Retrieved from https://static1.squarespace.com/static/5901f7e759cc6865e5b69297/t/5b7dce7c40ec9a44bf0443cc/1534971517362/Price+Of+College+Increasing+Almost+8+Times+Faster+Than+Wages.pdf

McHenry, J., Carrier, N., Hull, E., & Kabbaj, M. (2014). Sex differences in anxiety and depression: Role of testosterone. *Frontiers in Neuroendocrinology, 35,* 42–57. doi:10.1016/j.yfrne.2013.09.001

Meyer, T. J., Miller, M. L., Metzger, R. L., & Borkovec, T. D. (1990). Development and validation of the Penn State Worry Questionnaire. *Behavior Research and Therapy, 28,* 487–495. doi:10.1016/0005-7967(90)90135-6

National Institute of Mental Health. (n.d.). *Social anxiety disorder: More than just shyness.* Retrieved from https://www.nimh.nih.gov/health/publications/social-anxiety-disorder-more-than-just-shyness/index.shtml

Pedrelli, P., Nyer, M., Yeung, A., Zulauf, C., & Wilens, T. (2014). College students: Mental health problems and treatment considerations. *Academic Psychiatry: The Journal of the American Association of Directors of Psychiatric Residency Training and the Association for Academic Psychiatry, 39,* 503–511. doi:10.1007/s40596-014-0205-9

Powell, F. (2018). See the average costs of attending college in 2018–2019. Retrieved from https://www.usnews.com/education/best-colleges/paying-for-college/articles/paying-for-college-infographic

Premier Health. (2017). *Your gender may be causing your worries.* Retrieved from https://www.premierhealth.com/Women-Wisdom-Wellness/Content/Your-Gender-May-Be-Causing-Your-Worries/

Price, M., Hides, L., Cockshaw, W., Staneva, A. A., & Stoyanov, S. R. (2016). Young love: Romantic concerns and associated mental health issues among adolescent help-seekers. *Behavioral Sciences, 6,* 9. doi:10.3390/bs6020009

Pritchard, M. E., & Wilson, G. S. (2003). Using emotional and social factors to predict student success. *Journal of College Student Development, 44,* 18–28.

Puff, J., Kolomeyer, E., McSwiggan, M., Pearte, C., Lauer, B. A., & Renk, K. (2016). Depression as a mediator in the relationship between perceived familial criticism and college adaptation. *Journal of American College Health, 64,* 604–612. doi:10.1080/07448484.2016.1210612

Quan, L., Zhen, R., Yao, B., & Zhou, X. (2014). The effects of loneliness and coping style on academic adjustment among college freshman. *Social Behavior and Personality, 42,* 969–978. doi:10.2224/sbp.2014.42.6.969

Recovery Across Mental Health. (2019). *Gender differences in mental health.* Retrieved from https://ramh.org/guide/gender-differences-in-mental-health

Regehr, C., Glancy, D., & Pitts, A. (2013). Interventions to reduce stress in university students: A review and meta-analysis. *Journal of Affective Disorders, 148,* 1–11. doi:10.1016/j.jad.2012.11.16

Riddell, K. (2017). End that friendship! Some friendships are bad for you. Retrieved from https://www.psychologytoday.com/us/blog/friendship-observation/201707/end-friendship

Schou Andreassen, C., Billieux, J., Griffiths, M. D., Kuss, D. J., Demetrovics, Z., Mazzoni, E., & Pallesen, S. (2016). The relationship between addictive use of social media and video games and symptoms of psychiatric disorders: A large-scale cross-sectional study. *Psychology of Addictive Behaviors: Journal of the Society of Psychologists in Addictive Behaviors, 30,* 252–262.

Shim, S. S., & Ryan, A. M. (2012). What do students want socially when they arrive at college? Implications of social achievement goals for social behaviors and adjustment during the first semester of college. *Motivation and Emotion, 36,* 504–515. doi:10.1007/s11031-011-9272-3

Simpson, H. B., Neria, Y., Lewis-Fernandez, R., & Schneier, F. (2010). *Anxiety disorders: Theory, research, and clinical perspectives.* Cambridge, UK: Cambridge University Press.

Spitzer, R. L., Kroenke, K., Williams, J. B. W., & Lowe, B. (2006). A brief measure for assessing generalized anxiety disorder. *The Archives of Internal Medicine, 166,* 1092–1097. doi:10.1001/archinte.166.10.1092

Stoney, C. M., Davis, M. C., & Matthews, K. A. (1987). Sex differences in physiological responses to stress and in coronary heart disease: A causal link? *Psychophysiology, 24,* 127–131. doi:10.1111/j.1469-8986.1987.tb00264.x

Sulkowski, M. L., Mariaskin, A., & Storch, E. A. (2011). Obsessive-compulsive spectrum disorder symptoms in college students. *Journal of American College Health, 59,* 342–348. doi:10.1080/07448481.2010.511365

Sun, J., Hagedorn, L. S., & Zhang, Y. (2016). Homesickness at college: Its impact on academic performance and retention. *Journal of College Student Development, 57,* 943–957.

Syahniar, S., Maysitoh, M., Ifdil, I., Ardi, Z., Yendi, F. M., Rangka, I. B., . . . Churnia, E. (2018). Social media fear of missing out: Psychometrics evaluation based on Indonesian evidence. *Journal of Physics: Conference Series, 1114,* 12095. doi:10.1088/1742-6596/1114/1/012095

Thurber, C. A., & Walton, E. A. (2012). Homesickness and adjustment in university students. *Journal of American College Health, 60,* 415–419.

Uno, M., Mortimer, J. T., Kim, M., & Vuolo, M. (2010). "Holding on" or "coming to terms" with educational underachievement: A longitudinal study of ambition and attainment. In S. Shulman & J. Nurmi (Eds.), *The role of goals in navigating individual lives during emerging adulthood* (pp. 41–56). San Francisco, CA: Jossey-Bass.

U.S. National Library of Medicine. (2019). *Stress and your health.* Retrieved from https://medlineplus.gov/ency/article/003211.htm

Vannucci, A., Flannery, K. M., & Ohannessian, C. M. (2017). Social media use and anxiety in emerging adults. *Journal of Affective Disorders, 207,* 163–166. doi:10.1016/j.jad.2016.08.040

Waller, G., Stringer, H., & Meyer, C. (2012). What cognitive behavioral techniques do therapists report using when delivering cognitive behavioral therapy for the eating disorders? *Journal of Consulting and Clinical Psychology, 80,* 171–175. doi:10.1037/a0026559

Wilks, S. E. (2008). Resilience amid academic stress: The moderating impact of social support among social work students. *Advanced Social Work, 9,* 106–125.

World Health Organization. (1992). *The ICD-10 classification of mental and behavioural disorders: Clinical descriptions and diagnostic guidelines.* Geneva, Switzerland: Author.

Chapter 19

Depression and Suicide

Joshua C. Watson and Amanda Faucher

Depression is being colorblind and constantly told how colorful the world is.

—Atticus

■ ■ ■

Reflection Exercise

College is the best 4 years of your life! We all have likely heard this saying. Perhaps for you, this was (or has been) true. College really was a great experience, producing memories you will cherish for a lifetime. Unfortunately, this is not a universal experience. Others may struggle through college for a variety of reasons. Imagine what it would have been like if your college experience had made it difficult for you to function. Imagine that it was hard for you to get out of bed each day, and you dreaded the thought of having to leave your room and interact with others. No matter how hard you tried to "feel happy," you could not get yourself to see any positives in your life. The image you have is likely not one you would associate with a positive experience. However, the image you have is a reality for students experiencing depression. Now ask yourself the following questions:

1. Would you tell anyone what you were experiencing?
2. Would you seek help through the campus counseling center or another campus office/organization?
3. Would you worry what others would say about you or whether you would be labeled?
4. What would you do if you began having thoughts of harming yourself?

These are questions students dealing with depression face every day. They also speak to the reason why many students forgo seeking help when depression starts taking over their lives. In this chapter, we examine issues of depression and suicide and how college students experience them every day. In addition to highlighting the prevalence of these issues on college campuses, we include information to help you identify and treat individuals who may be depressed and at risk for self-harm, specifically addressing issues related to screening for suicidal ideation and intent. Finally, we discuss outreach and campus collaborations that can be implemented to help address issues of depression and suicide from a more holistic perspective. Case studies conclude the chapter to provide readers with an opportunity to apply what they have learned.

■ ■ ■

At various times, as human beings, we all have felt sad, blue, or down in the dumps. These emotions often are triggered by a specific situation (e.g., final exam week), person (e.g., argument with a significant other), event (e.g., loss of a loved one), or environmental condition (e.g., dealing with daily microaggressions across campus as an undocumented student). Although it is natural to feel down from time to time, when these episodes of low mood continue for an extended period, it could indicate the onset of depression. *Depression* is an umbrella term used to cover several different experiences. Otherwise referred to as *clinical depression* or *major depressive disorder* (MDD), it is a serious medical illness (American Psychiatric Association, 2017). Recent estimates indicated MDDs affecting 16.2 million American adults over the age of 18 in any given year, making it one of the most common mental disorders in the United States (National Institute of Mental Health, 2017). According to a Columbia University (2017) study, this figure represents a rise in the MDD prevalence rate. Between 2005 and 2015, the number of American adults affected by MDD rose from 6.6% to 7.3%. Additionally, the economic burden associated with MDD also is on the rise. When considering both direct and indirect costs, MDD-related expenses surpassed $210 billion in 2010, representing a 21% increase from 2005 statistics (Greenberg, Fournier, Sisitsky, Pike, & Kessler, 2015).

Although MDD is on the rise among Americans from all age groups, its growth appears most pronounced in teens and young adults. Among adolescents and young adults between the ages of 18 and 25, the 12-month prevalence of major depressive episodes increased from 8.7% and 8.8% in 2005 to 11.3% and 9.6% in 2014, respectively (Mojtabai, Olfson, & Han, 2016). Additionally, researchers identified the college years as a peak age period for depression to manifest, especially first episodes (Cuijpers, Cristea, Karyotaki, Reijnders, & Huibers, 2016). Potentially exacerbating the situation is the multiple challenges, pressures, and anxieties associated with college, causing students to feel overwhelmed and hopeless. These feelings are strongly related to mental health problems, including the emergence of suicidal thoughts. According to researchers, over 20% of college students surveyed reported having thoughts of harming themselves (Liu, Stevens, Wong, Yasui, & Chen, 2019). Furthermore, those diagnosed with depression have been shown to be 5 times more likely to attempt suicide (Borchard, 2018). With nearly 20 million students attending U.S. colleges and universities in Fall 2018 (National Center for Education Statistics, 2019), it is likely that college counselors will work with students experiencing MDD and potentially having thoughts of harming themselves or attempting suicide. The strong relationship between depression and suicide, especially on college and university campuses, compelled us to include discussions of both phenomena in this chapter.

Prevalence of Depression Among College Students

Researchers have been confirming marked increases in the number of college students experiencing mental health issues for the better part of the past decade (Daddona, 2011; Fier & Brzezinski, 2010; MacKean, 2011). Specifically, depressive disorders were identified as one of the most common diagnoses made by mental health professionals working on college campuses (Kirsch, Doerfler, & Truong, 2014). In a systematic review of the professional literature, Ibrahim, Kelly, Adams, and Glazebrook (2013) found prevalence rates of MDD to be substantially higher among college students than what was found in the general population. According to data collected through the National College Health Assessment of the American College Health Association (ACHA), 18.1% of students surveyed reported being diagnosed with MDD or treated by a mental health professional at some point in the past year (ACHA, 2018). However, although many students may experience MDD symptoms for the first time during their college years, the clear majority of them do not seek the help they need. Nearly 42% of students in the ACHA study reported feeling so depressed at some point in the last 12 months that it was difficult for them to function (ACHA, 2018). On community college campuses, depression also ranks as the number one mental health issue faced by students (Gallagher, 2014). Figure 19.1 illustrates the rise in the number of students experiencing depression.

The increased prevalence of depression among college-age students is alarming because depression can have deleterious effects on many aspects of college students' lives, including self-esteem, academic performance, social relationships, and physical health (Bell, Barclay, & Stoltz, 2014). If left untreated, depressive symptoms can lead to additional mental health crises among college students (Gruttadaro & Crudo, 2012). As noted in the most recent ACHA National College Health Assessment survey, 11.3% of more than 26,000 students surveyed reported they had been seriously considering suicide at least once in the past year (ACHA, 2018). Therefore, the ability to recognize the signs and symptoms of depression is an important skill for college counselors to develop when working with students at risk.

Symptoms of Depression

Depression is a highly treatable mental health condition. Therefore, being able to recognize the signs and symptoms of depression is key to helping individuals gain access to effec-

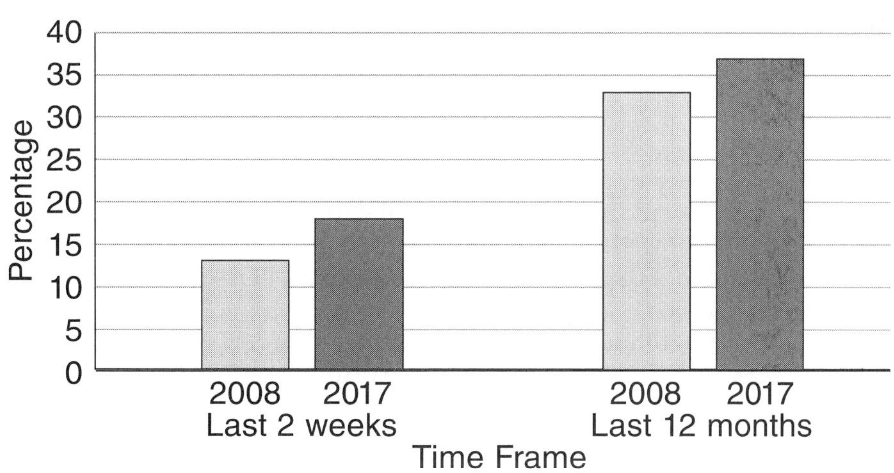

FIGURE 19.1

Comparison of Student Data From 2008 to 2017

Note. Graph shows percentages of students experiencing depressive symptoms (within the last 2 weeks or within the last 12 months) that make it difficult to engage in daily functioning.

tive treatment. A review of the professional literature indicates a high number of depressive symptoms. In a recent study, a researcher performed a content analysis of clinical instruments used to screen for depression. Among the seven most common screening instruments, he found 52 unique symptoms of depression (Fried, 2017). Clearly, not everyone experiences all 52 of the symptoms identified. Instead, depression varies from person to person. Individuals may report experiencing emotional symptoms, cognitive symptoms, physiological symptoms, or some combination of all three. Some experience a few symptoms; others report experiencing many. Which symptoms are reported may also differ slightly depending on cultural or gender-based norms (e.g., masculine norms may allow for discussing physiological symptoms but may restrict discussion of emotional symptoms). Furthermore, several of the symptoms of depression differ in important properties such as biological markers, risk factors, and impact on impairment of functioning, affecting how they are experienced and reported on by individuals, making depression a very heterogeneous disorder (Fried & Nesse, 2015). However, there are some symptoms common to most experiences of depression that you should get to know. Some of the most common symptoms reported in association with a major depressive episode include the following (Holland, 2018):

- Persistent sadness, anxiety, and emptiness
- Hopelessness and pessimism
- Feelings of guilt, worthlessness, and helplessness
- Loss of interest in and inability to derive pleasure from hobbies and activities
- Decreased energy, fatigue, and feeling like one is functioning in slow motion
- Difficulty concentrating, remembering, and making decisions
- Insomnia or irregular sleep patterns
- Changes in appetite coupled with unintentional weight gain or loss
- Restlessness and irritability
- Thoughts of self-harm or suicide
- Persistent physical symptoms that persist despite treatment (headaches, stomach pains)

Being able to identify these symptoms and talk with students regarding their frequency and severity will help you provide effective treatment. Furthermore, it may provide you with the opportunity to lend support during a bleak time in a student's life and possibly prevent something disastrous from happening.

College counselors might consider screening for MDD if a client appears to have depressed mood nearly every day and/or a loss of interest in things that would typically bring him or her pleasure. Additional symptoms that might indicate MDD include significant changes in weight, slowed thought, fatigue, feelings of worthlessness, inappropriate guilt, poorer than usual concentration, or suicidal ideations. Please refer to your diagnostic manual for specific criteria.

Additionally, there are different types of depressive disorders. In addition to MDD, individuals might present with persistent depressive disorder or psychotic depression. Each disorder is characterized by a set of symptoms that vary in their presentation. Depression may also manifest as a co-occurring disorder. A co-occurring disorder is one in which two disorders are experienced simultaneously. For example, depression often is diagnosed in individuals who are experiencing an anxiety disorder or who are abusing drugs or alcohol. Considering that the prevalence of abusive drinking and depression is higher in the college population, it is not surprising that a high rate of comorbidity has been noted between the two issues (Geisner, Mallett, & Kilmer, 2012). Although not an issue for most students, depression also has been shown to co-occur with medical illnesses such as heart disease, stroke, cancer, and diabetes (Mental Health America, n.d.). For nontraditional and returning students, this might become an issue to monitor.

Among college students, recognizing the signs and symptoms of depression can be tricky. College is filled with normal developmental challenges for students, regardless of their age and past experiences. Common challenges students face include being away from home for the first time, having to be personally responsible, encountering increased academic difficulty, experiencing financial stress, and managing a new social environment and relationships. Each of these challenges can result in students experiencing some of the symptoms associated with depression. Displaying these symptoms does not mean a student automatically meets criteria for a diagnosis of depression. Life is complicated, and experiencing some of the symptoms of depression is considered a part of everyday life. In college, students juggle assignments from multiple classes, work, friends, and relationships every day. Managing the present while preparing for the future can become overwhelming and lead to symptoms of depression. When these symptoms are experienced more frequently, their intensity increases, and it becomes harder to shake them off, this is when concern should set in. Because most students who deal with these unpleasant symptoms refuse to seek help (Eisenberg, Golberstein, & Gollust, 2007), college counselors should educate students in how to assess themselves and their friends before symptoms increase and situations worsen. The top five warning signs students should look for as an indication that depression may be reaching a point where professional help is needed include the following:

- Students are no longer enjoying activities they used to find pleasurable and relaxing.
- Students are no longer attending class or participating in regular social activities.
- Students are experiencing extreme anger or sadness over a close relationship.
- Students are reacting negatively or with extreme apathy to everyday events.
- Students begin talking about death or suicide.

At a growing number of colleges and universities, programs training students to recognize and respond to signs of mental distress among their peers are being implemented by or in collaboration with campus counseling centers. A current campaign called StigmaFree campus, sponsored by the National Alliance on Mental Illness, promotes the elimination of demeaning stereotypes and misinformation regarding mental illness and encourages those struggling with depression to seek help rather than remain in silence. Campuses participating in this initiative encourage their students to pledge to do the following (National Alliance on Mental Illness, 2019, "Join us in creating a StigmaFree campus!"):

- Be educated on mental illness.
- See the person, not the illness.
- Act against negative stigma.

College counselors interested in additional information on the StigmaFree campus initiative can visit the National Alliance on Mental Illness website (https://www.nami.org/Get-Involved/StigmaFree/StigmaFree-Community/StigmaFree-on-Campus) for more details.

Situational or Normative Depression: The Experience of Loss

As we have discussed, everyone experiences symptoms of depression from time to time in their lives. The experience of these symptoms alone does not equate to being diagnosed with a mental illness. Often, depression can be situational and a part of the normative developmental process for college students. Situational depression, also known as adjustment disorder with depressed mood, can look very much like clinical depression, so accurate assessment is essential (see diagnostic criteria below). Attempting to differentiate between these diagnoses, counselors should focus on two key aspects: origin and duration.

Situational depression is a stress-related form of depression whose onset occurs after experiencing a traumatic event or series of events. Sometimes, the traumatic event does not even have to be experienced firsthand. For African American students, the racial trauma inflicted by the increased number of police shootings of African Americans can lead to feelings of depression (Turner, 2016). These events can be positive or negative, as you learned in the previous chapter that even joyous events can be a source of great stress for individuals. Common stressful events, both positive and negative, that many college students experience include the following:

- Arriving on campus for the first time
- Living away from home
- Academic struggles (failing an examination)
- Establishing a new social network
- Experiencing concerns in romantic relationships
- Experiencing changes in financial situation

Furthermore, as student populations become increasingly diverse, counselors will need to broaden their understanding of some of the events that can precipitate situational depression. For example, for a military veteran returning to school, acclimating to an environment structured differently than the environment that was experienced in the service may be challenging. For the nontraditional student, unemployment or childcare issues may bring on symptoms of stress. Regardless of the precipitating event or series of events, their presence makes it difficult to manage daily living. Although these individuals do not meet criteria for a major depressive episode, their experiences clearly are troubling. As the stress they experience begins to exceed their coping abilities, a temporary state of depression sets in.

This leads to the other distinguishing feature of situation depression, duration. Unlike clinical depression, situational depression is a short-term condition. Once the traumatic event has passed, symptoms usually begin dissipating. Although individual experiences may vary, on average situational depression will subside when the stressful event ends or within 6 months of the event occurring. Helping students recognize that the experience is only temporary is often the first step in working on a plan to recover.

Symptoms Associated With Situational Depression

In addition to assessing for origin and duration, several behavioral and emotional symptoms may emerge. There is no uniform constellation of symptoms, and everyone will have his or her own unique experience. Common symptoms reported by individuals diagnosed with situational depression include the following:

- Listlessness
- Feelings of hopelessness and sadness
- Difficulty sleeping (fall asleep and staying asleep)
- Changes in appetite
- Frequent episodes of crying
- Headaches or stomachaches
- Unfocused anxiety and worry

- New and uncharacteristic engagement in risky behaviors
- Inability to focus or concentrate
- Increased alcohol or drug use
- Withdrawal from family and friends
- Loss of interest in normal activities and hobbies
- Suicidal ideation

Among children and adolescents, behavioral symptoms typically are most prevalent. In adults, emotional symptoms are more common. As most college students are in the stage of young adulthood, which bridges childhood and adulthood, assessment of both behavioral and emotional symptoms is recommended. Complicating the situation for counselors is the fact that adjustment disorders (including situational depression) remain a subthreshold disorder and so cannot be diagnosed when the threshold for another condition has been reached (Casey, 2014). When counselors assess clients, a diagnosis of adjustment disorder with depressed mood might be applicable when symptoms of depression are in response to a recent stressor and are not aligned with the severity of said stressor. Symptoms include a decrease in social, occupational, and other areas of functioning that does not last for more than 6 months. These symptoms are not representative of normal grief or loss but instead are related to a recent life change. Consult with your diagnostic manual for specific criteria.

Although situational depression is a response to an extreme stressor or traumatic event, students should not expect to ignore it or "tough it out" until things get better. To lessen the chance of its developing into a more serious case of depression, treatment should be sought. When students present to the campus counseling center with symptoms of situational depression, treatment options exist. The most common approach to treating situational depression is counseling. Through working with a counselor, students may be able to uncover the root causes of their distress and develop a new way of coping with them. Although situational depression does not stem from a chemical imbalance, medications may be the recommended course of action for some students depending on their symptom severity. In cases where medication represents the best option, selective serotonin reuptake inhibitors often are prescribed (Hameed, Schwartz, Malhotra, West, & Bertone, 2005). However, medications take time for their full therapeutic effect to be realized. Depending on the medication and its composition, the client may not realize symptom relief for 4 to 6 weeks. Given the brevity of situational depression, medications may take too long to be impactful. Finally, students can make changes in their lifestyle to help combat situational depression. Performing mindfulness exercises, adhering to a healthier eating regimen, exercising more, finding meaningful support, and exploring new hobbies or leisure activities all can be ways to help alleviate situational depression symptoms naturally.

Clinical Depression and Risk for Suicidal Ideation

Depression and suicide are significant public health concerns affecting a large percentage of the population (Rao & Hong, 2016). On the basis of statistics reported by officials at the Centers for Disease Control and Prevention (CDC), in 2016 suicide was the 10th leading cause of death overall in the United States. That year, there were twice as many deaths by suicide as there were homicides. For young people, the situation appears to be more dangerous. Among individuals between the ages of 15 and 34, suicide skyrockets to the second leading cause of death following unintentional injury. Every year, approximately 1,100 traditional-age college students (18–24 years of age) die by suicide, with another

23,000 students attempting suicide (Appelbaum, 2006). Among sexual and gender minority students, the risk increases exponentially (Woodford et al., 2018). For example, in recent surveys 41% of transgender adults report having attempted suicide. That number increases to 61% for transgender adults who were victims of physical assault. Lesbian, gay, and bisexual young adults coming from families that do not accept them are 8 times more likely to attempt suicide than those with accepting families (CDC, 2017; Suicide Awareness Voices of Education, 2019).

Additionally, there is a gender gap in terms of experiences with symptoms of depression. Before the age of 15, boys are more likely to be depressed. However, between ages 15 and 54, women become twice as likely to experience depression, with declining percentages as women approach and surpass menopause. A factor potentially contributing to this disparity is hormonal changes beginning with the onset of puberty. From that point, females experience drastic hormonal changes during menstrual cycles and pregnancy and have a much higher rate of hormone fluctuation than men throughout their lives. Researchers continue studying these changes, especially their potential effects on brain chemistry and stress hormones due to the inability of estrogens to neutralize the effects of glucocorticoids released during stress (Faravelli, Scarpato, Castellini, & LoSauro, 2013; Oldehinkel & Bouma, 2011). Furthermore, some researchers have hypothesized that personality and environmental factors, such as neuroticism (Goodwin & Gotlib, 2004), physical health, rumination style, perceived interpersonal and employment problems, physical activity, stressful life events, childhood abuse, and trouble with social support, play a role in the gender differences (Leach, Christensen, Mackinnon, Windsor, & Butterworth, 2008).

Just as suicide attempts are more common among particular demographic groups (e.g., among females, racial/ethnic minorities, and sexual minorities), prevalence of death by suicide is also more common in particular demographic groups. Caucasian males accounted for 69.67% of suicide deaths in 2017, followed by Alaska natives, with the highest rates occurring among White, middle-age males. Rates of death by suicide are significantly lower for Black Americans and Asian/Pacific Islanders (CDC, 2017). As a result, effectively addressing suicide and suicidal behaviors has become a major concern for college and university personnel (Suicide Prevention Resource Center [SPRC], 2014).

As college counselors, the likelihood you will engage in both direct clinical service as well as outreach and prevention programming targeting suicide prevention and intervention efforts is great. To help you in these endeavors, we believe it important to clarify the terminology you may see used. *Suicide* refers to a death caused by injuring oneself with the intent to die (CDC, 2019). When individuals begin having thoughts of killing themselves, they engage in a cognitive process known as *suicidal ideation. Suicidal behavior* refers to the range of activities associated with suicidal thoughts and behaviors, including preparatory acts (National Suicide Prevention Lifeline, 2017). Collectively, these thoughts and behaviors constitute a *suicide plan*. In a suicide plan, ideation is accompanied by a defined idea as to how to kill oneself and immediate access to the means necessary to carry out the act. Accurate understanding of the terminology used will aid in assessing clients and communicating with other health care professionals.

Suicidal Behavior Risk Factors

Now that you are familiar with terminology, we can turn our attention to the question of what leads a person to ponder or choose suicide as a solution to his or her problems. Suicidal behavior is complex because it is influenced by several factors. One such factor is the presence of a mood disorder. According to researchers, clinical depression is the most common psychiatric disorder in people who die by suicide (Hawton, Comabella, Haw, & Saunders, 2013). However, although most people who commit suicide experience depression, fewer than 4% of those who experience depression eventually end up taking their own lives. Clearly, there are more issues involved causing someone to choose death by suicide. Indeed, previous researchers have uncovered several risk factors associated with suicide (SPRC, 2014, pp. 2–3). Although the presence of these risk factors in a student's life may be an indication that the student is contemplating suicide, there is not a causal relationship. Counselors should further assess and work with their clients to better understand what might be going on in their lives.

Behavioral Health Issues/Disorders
- Depressive disorders
- Substance abuse or dependence
- Conduct disorders
- Anxiety disorders
- Eating disorders
- Previous suicide attempts
- Nonsuicidal self-injury

Individual Characteristics
- Hopelessness
- Loneliness
- Social isolation or lack of belonging/mattering
- Anger, hostility
- Engaging in risky behaviors
- Impulsivity
- Low stress and/or frustration tolerance
- Poor coping skills

Adverse/Stressful Life Circumstances
- Interpersonal relationship issues
- School or work problems
- Financial problems
- Physical, sexual, and/or psychological abuse
- Chronic physical illness or disability
- Insomnia

Family Characteristics
- Family history of suicide or suicidal behavior
- Parental mental health problems
- Family violence or abuse
- Family instability
- Lack of parental support
- Loss of a family member

School and Community Factors
- Limited access to effective care options
- Stigma associated with seeking help
- Negative social and emotional environment
- Victim of discrimination, bullying, or harassment
- Access to lethal means
- Exposure to media normalizing or glamorizing suicide

Students dealing with any of the issues mentioned in this list may have the ability to cope with any associated stress and not think about or attempt suicide. Statistics do show that the more risk factors affecting a student, the greater the probability of that student resorting to suicidal behavior (SPRC, 2014). Recognizing warning signs is essential to intervention (Juhnke, Granello, & Granello, 2012).

Even when counselors are armed with an understanding of the risk factors and warning signs associated with suicide, the assessment, management, and treatment of suicidal clients is still one of the most stressful and anxiety-provoking tasks counselors face (Fowler, 2012). Fortunately, there are good resources available for you to use when assessing clients. These resources allow you to gather information related to the two fundamental aspects of sound suicide assessment: (a) the presence of risk factors and (b) the lethality of means.

Suicide Assessment

Depression is strongly associated with suicide and nonfatal suicidal behavior, and ongoing assessment of suicide risk should be integral to the management of patients with this disorder (Hawton et al., 2013). Additionally, suicide assessment helps counselors identify at-risk individuals and direct them to an appropriate level of treatment. The SAMHSA-HRSA [Substance Abuse and Mental Health Services Administration/Health Resources and Services Administration] Center for Integrated Health Solutions provides information concerning valuable screening and assessment tools for counselors. Related to suicide, the Columbia-Suicide Severity Rating Scale (Posner et al., 2008) and the Suicide Assessment Five-step Evaluation and Triage (Jacobs, 2007) instruments represent brief measures that can be used to effectively assess the severity of a client's suicide risk. The Columbia-Suicide Severity Rating Scale (https://www.integration.samhsa.gov/clinical-practice/Columbia_Suicide_Severity_Rating_Scale.pdf) is a 6-item instrument. All clients are asked two questions related to ideation. Their responses dictate which follow-up questions are asked. Using the Suicide Assessment Five-Step Evaluation and Triage instrument (https://www.integration.samhsa.gov/images/res/SAFE_T.pdf), counselors identify risk factors (Step 1), identify protective factors (Step 2), conduct a suicide inquiry (Step 3), determine risk level/intervention (Step 4), and document (Step 5).

Another approach you might encounter in your work as a college counselor is the Collaborative Assessment and Management of Suicidality. More than a singular assessment, the Collaborative Assessment and Management of Suicidality provides counselors with a framework through which counselor and client collaboratively manage suicidal thoughts and behaviors. The approach requires active participation on the part of the client. Typically used by licensed professionals, the Collaborative Assessment and Management of Suicidality framework also can be used by trained paraprofessionals (SPRC, 2017). The implementation flexibility makes it a popular choice for many campus counseling centers.

Clinical Implications

Assessment

Treatment of depression has been shown to be effective, both in alleviating symptoms, reducing mortality from comorbid medical conditions, and preventing suicide. As such, accurate identification of clients with depression is an important step toward being able to deliver an appropriate level of care (Maurer, 2012). In fact, the U.S. Preventive Services Task Force (2009) recommended screening when appropriate treatment and follow-up care options are readily available. The following screening tools are commonly used by college counselors to identify individuals who are at risk and assess for depression.

Patient Health Questionnaire-9

The Patient Health Questionnaire (PHQ) scales are some of the more validated tools in mental health. The PHQ-9 scale (Spitzer, Williams, Kroenke, & Colleagues, n.d.) is a self-administered survey that can be used to objectify and assess degree of depression severity. In addition to serving as a screening tool, the PHQ-9 can aid in diagnosis and symptom tracking. The nine items of the PHQ-9 directly relate to the nine diagnostic criteria for MDD as listed in the *Diagnostic and Statistical Manual of Mental Disorders* (4th ed.; *DSM-IV*; American Psychiatric Association, 1994). Higher scores represent greater symptom severity. Advantages associated with using the PHQ-9 scale include the following (AIMS Center, n.d., "Advantages of the PHQ-9"):

- Is shorter than other established depression rating scales
- Allows for multiple administration methods (clinician or self, in-person, or online)
- Facilitates diagnosis of major depression
- Provides assessment of symptom severity
- Has strong psychometric properties when used across diverse populations
- Is useful for a wide range of clients, including as young as age 12

A shorter version, the PHQ-2, also is available. This version is used when clients do not have a current diagnosis of depression. The PHQ-2 consists of the first two questions of the PHQ-9. An affirmative response on either of these questions triggers the use of the remaining seven questions that make up the PHQ-9.

Beck Depression Inventory–II

The Beck Depression Inventory–II (BDI-II; Beck, Steer, & Brown, 1996), published in 1996, represents a revised version of the BDI first appearing in the 1960s. Revisions were made to more closely align the questions with the diagnostic criteria appearing in the *DSM-IV*. The BDI-II contains 21 multiple-choice items addressing various symptoms of depression. Each item features four statements representing increased levels of symptom severity. Total scores range from 0 to 63, with the following score ranges established: 0 to 13 (minimal depression), 14 to 19 (mild depression), 20 to 28 (moderate depression), and 29 to 63 (severe depression). The BDI-II demonstrates strong psychometric properties and has been shown to correlate highly with counselor assessment of depression severity (Beck et al., 1996). The BDI-II is copyrighted and a license must be purchased to use it.

Center for Epidemiologic Studies Depression Scale–Revised

The Center for Epidemiologic Studies Depression Scale–Revised (Eaton, Smith, Ybarra, Muntaner, & Tien, 2004) is a commonly used self-report measure of depressive symptoms college counselors might consider using. The Center for Epidemiologic Studies Depression Scale–Revised is a 20-item measure assessing symptoms of depression with items phrased as self-statements (e.g., "My sleep was restless"). Respondents are asked to rate how frequently each item applies to them over the course of the past 2 weeks. Their subjective ratings are based on a 5-point Likert-type scale with response options ranging from 0 (*not at all* or *less than 1 day*) to 4 (*nearly every day for 2 weeks*). Higher scores equate to a greater risk for depression and elevated symptom severity. The revised version was created to reflect current diagnostic criteria included in the *DSM-5* (American Psychiatric Association, 2013).

Treatment

According to the National Alliance on Mental Illness (2017), several options are available for treating depression. Current best practices call for counselors to select treatment approaches whose efficacy and utility is supported by the research literature. The practice of using such approaches is referred to as evidence-based practice. Applying evidence-based principles ensures that counselors use the best existing evidence as a starting framework, while simultaneously affording them flexibility to individualize treatment (Cook, Schwartz, & Kaslow, 2017). However, counselors should always be mindful of current client dynamics and choose the approach that best fits the client in question as well as his or her presenting issue. Examples of evidence-based treatments for depression are mentioned below.

Cognitive Behavioral Therapy

Cognitive behavioral therapy (CBT) refers to a classification of cognitive and behavioral interventions and techniques that draw on the ideology of unwellness maintained by maladaptive cognitions (Hofmann, Asnaani, Vonk, Sawyer, & Fang, 2012). Originally used in reference to a specific therapeutic approach, CBT is now recognized as an umbrella term used to classify similar therapeutic approaches such as acceptance and commitment therapy, rational emotive behavior therapy, cognitive therapy, dialectical behavior therapy, trauma-focused cognitive behavioral therapy, and mindfulness-based cognitive therapy. According to Watson and Schmit (2019), CBT-based treatment tends to be structured or manualized, empirically supported, goal oriented, brief, cost-effective, and adaptable to a wide variety of mental health issues, including depression.

Interpersonal Psychotherapy

Interpersonal psychotherapy (IPT) is a brief, focused approach used to treat clients diagnosed with mood disorders. The primary treatment goal when using IPT is to improve the quality of a client's interpersonal relationships and social functioning to help reduce personal distress. IPT helps the client develop strategies for resolving problems in four key areas: interpersonal deficits, unresolved grief, difficult life transitions, and interpersonal disputes. Originally designed to treat clients with MDD, IPT may be a particularly useful treatment option for college counselors because interpersonal conflict, difficulty with role transitions, and experiences of loss are all well-known as risk factors in the development of depressive disorder in young people (Lipsitz & Markowitz, 2013; McCauley, Pavlidis, & Kendall, 2001).

Outreach and Prevention Implications

As discussed earlier in Chapter 7, college counselors are uniquely positioned to make a positive impact on mental health–based outreach and prevention initiatives on their campuses. In terms of depression and suicide, campus counseling centers and their staff can facilitate several activities for presenting clients as well as the entire campus community. Examples of outreach initiatives include partnering with residence life or student affairs personnel to provide programming to student groups on the warning signs of depression and where and how to seek help. Using technology, online assessments can be used to quickly triage students and point them in the right direction for care and treatment. Additionally, campus counseling centers can participate in campus wellness events, offered during orientation events or other campus activities, where large groups of students will be available.

Depression and suicide prevention programs also can be implemented on college campuses. When designing such prevention programs, especially for suicide prevention, there are three main strategies that can be used: universal strategies, targeted strategies, and selected strategies. Universal strategies are designed for implementation with an entire population. Campus-wide prevention programs are examples of a universal strategy. At this level, a systematic approach supported by broad campus-wide cooperation is needed (SPRC, 2004). The JED Foundation provides a thorough suicide prevention strategic planning guide counselors can access (http://www.jedfoundation.org/wp-content/uploads/2016/06/Framework_color.pdf). Targeted strategies are designed to be implemented within a population in which there are individuals known to be at risk. For example, environmental microaggressions can be a source of stress for underrepresented students because they feel marginalized or that their experiences are not important. As a result, researchers have reported higher rates of suicidality among sexual minorities and multiracial students (Peter, Edkins, Watson, Adjei, Homma, & Saewyc, 2017; Wong, Sugimoto-Matsuda, Chang, & Hishinuma, 2012). Armed with this knowledge, counselors can develop prevention programs tailored to these groups to boost effectiveness. Finally, selected strategies are designed for specific students. For example, transfer students have been found to be more likely to endorse suicidal ideation or to attempt suicide than non–transfer students (Beiter et al., 2015). College counselors could work with admissions personnel to flag transfer students and incorporate depression or suicide screening in their orientation to the institution as a standard operating procedure.

Conclusion

Through this chapter our goal was to help you see that depression is a common health problem faced by most students. The stress and challenges of college leave students susceptible to depression and its negative effects. Despite mental health services on college campuses being more abundant now than ever, students largely continue to not seek help for their problems. As symptoms progress from feeling sad or blue to having difficulty functioning in day-to-day life, a student's coping abilities may become overwhelmed and thoughts of self-harm or suicide materialize as a viable alternative. Aware of the warning signs and risk factors associated with depression (both situational and clinical), and knowledgeable of various assessment and treatment strategies, college counselors can positively contribute to helping students dealing with depression and thoughts of suicide get the help they need.

Final Case Studies

Case 1

Sarah is an 18-year-old, heterosexual woman who is away from home for the first time, attending an out-of-state university. She is a freshman studying psychology and is able to complete her first semester but remains unsure about her major. She is experiencing some anxiety due to her course workload being a little more than she had anticipated. Sarah comes from a stable, middle-class home with supportive parents, whom she misses. She has a history of mild depression related to being bullied in high school because of being slightly overweight. She never sought treatment nor told anyone of her feelings of sadness because she did not want her parents to worry about her. There is no known mental illness on either side of the family. She was raised Roman Catholic but is not currently attending church anywhere.

Sarah presents with concerns of having "so many unknowns." She is concerned about her major because it is turning out to be different than she thought it would be. She has also heard from others that there isn't much that can be done with a bachelor's in psychology and does not want to have to go to graduate school. She has not researched the field much on her own but rather just found the subject to be of interest. As a result, she is considering changing her major, but she is not sure what else to pick. In addition, she is from a small, suburban town, and is now living on campus in a large city. Not being used to this many people, she struggles to make friends and is trying to find a place where she fits in. Her dorm participates in intramural sports, but she is not athletic and does not enjoy sports. When asked if she has looked into any clubs or social groups, she replied, "I'm not really the sorority type." She has a roommate who enjoys going out and partying. Sarah has found that she does not have much in common with her roommate, but they get along and respect each other.

Sarah is experiencing feelings of loneliness and sadness and states she feels she's "different" from the other students. Although she has always felt different on some level, her close-knit and loyal group of friends was a support system for her and made high school enjoyable. She misses her hometown and her parents. When she looks through her social media accounts, she sees what she perceives as "all the fun" her friends and family are having back home and exactly what she is missing out on. When she's alone, she often cries and wonders if going off to college was a mistake. She denies any current suicidal thoughts but states she is struggling to find her purpose and comfort zone.

Case 1 Exploration Questions

1. What are Sarah's risk factors? What are her protective factors?
2. What are your initial diagnostic impressions? What do you need to know to confirm the impressions?
3. How might you proceed with Sarah? Is there anything you would assess for?

Case 2

Aryan is a 20-year-old, premed, molecular biology major, about to enter his junior year of college. He is heterosexual and a practicing Hindu. His family moved to the United States from India when he was 10, seeking a more successful life for him. His parents, who came from a lower socioeconomic class, wanted to see their son succeed and become a doctor. He had always done well in school and had an aptitude for science. They saved up money and applied for their visa. When it finally came through, they made the move to the United States and worked toward achieving the "American Dream." He is an only child and will be expected to be successful, help the family, get married, and carry on the family name. He has never attended counseling before, because it is generally preferred in his culture to keep issues within the family. There is no known mental illness on either side of his family (likely because of its being uncommon to seek professional help), but he suspects that his mother and several members of his extended family have experienced depression.

Aryan is an only child and feels a great deal of pressure to make his family proud and not disappoint them after they worked so hard and gave up their friends, family, and life in India to start over in another country. Since the move, his parents have owned and operated a business that does well. Although money is not plentiful, the business is stable, and they have all they need. They are also able to pay his tuition without having to take out any loans. Aryan describes himself as "adapted to American life" but states his parents remain very traditional with their Indian heritage. He is living at home still and has only a short commute to the university. He does not love his major and is unhappy with his classes, despite making straight *A*s. He finds it to be stressful and not very interesting but continues to work extremely hard to make perfect grades. He has made many friends, and he observes them having a great time in college while Aryan spends most of his spare time either studying or with family. If he takes too long of a break, his mother reminds him how challenging medical school will be and encourages him to do some reading. As a perfectionist who has always gone above and beyond in school, this frustrates him. He would like to change his major but fears disappointing his parents after all the sacrifices they have made for him. As he gets closer to his senior year, he knows medical school interviews will be approaching, and he states he really has no interest embarking on such a long journey. He has an interest in working with children and has thought that he would love to be a teacher. Although he has not mentioned teaching to his parents, he did mention a desire to work with children. His parents informed him that they would be okay if he wanted to become a pediatrician instead of a cardiologist. Aryan states he feels stuck because there is no other option besides becoming a physician.

Aryan has friends and social support, but he does not get to spend as much time with them as he would like because he needs to study. He states he feels as though his life has been planned out for him. He has experienced fleeting thoughts of suicide and has stated that his parents might not have to work as hard if he wasn't around. He also feels that if he changes his career path, it would bring shame to the family, leaving the extended family and his parents to be upset since they left India, when they did not want to, just to seek a better opportunity for him.

Aryan has not dated but has an interest in starting to date. His parents look forward to him finding "a nice Indian girl" of whom they could approve. Aryan has met a girl he really likes but knows his parents will disapprove of her because she is not of Indian descent. As a result, he keeps the relationship hidden and never brings her to his house. He is experiencing feelings of guilt from hiding this relationship and lying to his parents about where he is at. He also finds he spends less time studying because some of the time that he is supposed to be at the library is actually spent with his girlfriend. In addition, she is starting to get upset because she does not understand why he is so hard on himself or why he cannot just be honest with his parents.

Case 2 Exploration Questions

1. What are Aryan's risk factors? What are his protective factors?
2. What are your initial diagnostic impressions? What do you need to know to confirm the impressions?
3. How might you proceed with Aryan? Is there anything you would assess for?

References

American College Health Association. (2018). *American College Health Association–National College Health Assessment II: Reference group executive summary Spring 2018.* Silver Spring, MD: American College Health Association.

American Psychiatric Association. (1994). *Diagnostic and statistical manual of mental disorders* (4th ed.). Washington, DC: Author.

American Psychiatric Association. (2013). *Diagnostic and statistical manual of mental disorders* (5th ed.). Arlington, VA: Author.

American Psychiatric Association. (2017). What is depression? Retrieved from https://www.psychiatry.org/patients-families/depression/what-is-depression

AIMS Center. (n.d.). *PHQ-9 Depression Scale*. Retrieved from https://aims.uw.edu/resource-library/phq-9-depression-scale

Applebaum, P. S. (2006). Law and psychiatry: "Depressed? Get out!": Dealing with suicidal students on college campuses. *Psychiatric Services, 57*, 914–916.

Beck, A. T., Steer, R. A., & Brown, G. K. (1996). *Manual for the Beck Depression Inventory–II*. San Antonio, TX: Psychological Corporation.

Beiter, R., Nash, R., Mccrady, M., Rhoades, D., Linscomb, M., Clarahan, M., & Sammut, S. (2015). The prevalence and correlates of depression, anxiety, and stress in a sample of college students. *Journal of Affective Disorders, 173*, 90–96. doi:10.1016/j.jad.2014.10.054

Bell, S. C., Barclay, S. R., & Stoltz, K. B. (2014). Depression in college students: Diagnosis, treatment, and campus planning. In S. Degges-White & C. Borzumato-Gainey (Eds.), *College student mental health counseling* (pp. 219–236). New York, NY: Springer.

Borchard, T. J. (2018). Statistics about college depression. Retrieved from https://psychcentral.com/blog/statistics-about-college-depression/

Casey, P. (2014). Adjustment disorder: New developments. *Current Psychiatry Reports, 16*, 451. doi:10.1007/s11920-014-0451-2

Centers for Disease Control and Prevention. (2017). *Ten leading causes of death and injury*. Retrieved from https://www.cdc.gov/injury/wisqars/leadingcauses.html.

Centers for Disease Control and Prevention. (2019). *Preventing suicide*. Retrieved from https://www.cdc.gov/violenceprevention/suicide/fastfact.html

Columbia University. (2017). Depression is on the rise in the U.S., especially among young teens. Retrieved from https://www.mailman.columbia.edu/public-health-now/news/depression-rise-us-especially-among-young-teens

Cook, S. C., Schwartz, A. C., & Kaslow, N. J. (2017). Evidence-based psychotherapy: Advantages and challenges. *Neurotherapeutics, 14*, 537–545. doi:10.1007/s13311-017-0549-4

Cuijpers, P., Cristea, I. A., Karyotaki, E., Reijnders, M., & Huibers, M. J. H. (2016). How effective are cognitive behavior therapies for major depression and anxiety disorders? A meta-analytic update of the evidence. *World Psychiatry, 15*, 245–258. doi:10.1002/wps.20346

Daddona, M. F. (2011). Peer educators responding to students with mental health issues. *New Directions for Student Services, 2011*, 29–39. doi:10.1002/ss.382

Eaton, W. W., Smith, C., Ybarra, M., Muntaner, C., & Tien, A. (2004). Center for Epidemiologic Studies Depression Scale: Review and revision (CESD and CESD-R). In M. E. Maruish (Ed.), *The use of psychological testing for treatment planning and outcomes assessment: Vol. 3. Instruments for adults* (3rd ed., pp. 363–377). Mahwah, NJ: Erlbaum.

Eisenberg, D., Golberstein, E., & Gollust, S. E. (2007). Help-seeking and access to mental health care in a university student population. *Med Care, 45*, 594–601.

Faravelli, C., Scarpato, M. A., Castellini, G., & Lo Sauro, C. (2013). Gender differences in depression and anxiety: The role of age. *Psychiatry Research, 210*, 1301–1303. doi:10.1016/j.psychres.2013.09.027

Fier, S. M., & Brzezinski, L. G. (2010). Facilitating the high school-to-college transition for students with psychiatric disabilities: Information and strategies for school counselors. *Journal of School Counseling, 8*, 1–40.

Fowler, J. C. (2012). Suicide risk assessment in clinical practice: Pragmatic guidelines for imperfect assessments. *Psychotherapy, 49*, 81–90. doi:10.1037/a0026148

Fried, E. (2017). Moving forward: How depression heterogeneity hinders progress in treatment and research. *Expert Review of Neurotherapeutics, 17*, 423–425. doi:10.1080/14737175.2017.1307737

Fried, E. I., & Nesse, R. M. (2015). Depression is not a consistent syndrome: An investigation of unique symptom patterns in the STAR*D study. *Journal of Affective Disorders, 172,* 96–102. doi:10.1016/j.jad.2014.10.010

Gallagher, R. P. (2014). *National Survey of Counseling Center Directors*. Alexandria, VA: International Association of Counseling Services.

Geisner, I. M., Mallett, K., & Kilmer, J. R. (2012). An examination of depressive symptoms and drinking patterns in first year college students. *Issues in Mental Health Nursing, 33,* 280–287. doi:10.3109./01612840.2011.653036

Goodwin, R. D., & Gotlib, I. H. (2004). Gender differences in depression: The role of personality factors. *Psychiatry Research, 126,* 135–142. doi:10.1016/j.psychres.2003.12.024

Greenberg, P. E., Fournier, A. A., Sisitsky, T., Pike, C. T., & Kessler, R. C. (2015). The economic burden of adults with major depressive disorder in the United States (2005 and 2010). *Journal of Clinical Psychiatry, 76,* 155–162.

Gruttadaro, D., & Crudo, D. (2012). *College students speak: A survey on mental health.* National Alliance on Mental Illness. Retrieved from www.nami.org/namioncampus

Hameed, U., Schwartz, T. L., Malhotra, K., West, R. L., & Bertone, F. (2005). Antidepressant treatment in the primary care office: Outcomes for adjustment disorder versus major depression. *Annals of Clinical Psychiatry, 17,* 77–81. doi:10.1080/10401230590932344

Hawton, K., Comabella, C. C., Haw, C., & Saunders, K. (2013). Risk factors for suicide in individuals with depression: A systematic review. *Journal of Affective Disorders, 147,* 17–28. doi:10.1016/j.jad2013.01.004

Hofmann, S. G., Asnaani, A., Vonk, I. J., Sawyer, A. T., & Fang, A. (2012). The efficacy of cognitive behavioral therapy: A review of meta-analyses. *Cognitive Therapy and Research, 36,* 427–440. doi:10.1007/s10608-012-9476-1

Holland, K. (2018). Depression and anxiety: How to identify and treat coexisting symptoms. Retrieved from https://www.healthline.com/health/mental-health/depression-and-anxiety#signs-and-symptoms

Ibrahim, A. K., Kelly, S. J., Adams, C. E., & Glazebrook, C. (2013). A systematic review of studies of depression prevalence in university students. *Journal of Psychiatric Research, 47,* 391–400.

Jacobs, D. (2007). *Suicide Assessment Five-step Evaluation and Triage for mental health professionals (SAFE-T).* Retrieved from https://www.integration.samhsa.gov/images/res/SAFE_T.pdf

Juhnke, G. A., Granello, D. H., & Granello, P. F. (2012). *Suicide, self-injury, and violence in the schools: Assessment, prevention, and intervention strategies.* Hoboken, NJ: Wiley.

Kirsch, D. J., Doerfler, L. A., & Truong, D. (2014). Mental health issues among college students: Who gets referred for psychopharmacology evaluation? *Journal of American College Health, 63,* 50–56. doi:10.1080/07448481.2014.960423

Leach, L. S., Christensen, H., Mackinnon, A. J., Windsor, T. D., & Butterworth, P. (2008). Gender differences in depression and anxiety across the adult lifespan: The role of psychosocial mediators. *Social Psychiatry and Psychiatric Epidemiology, 43,* 983–998. doi:10.1007/s00127-008-0388-z

Lipsitz, J. D., & Markowitz, J. C. (2013). Mechanisms of change in interpersonal therapy (IPT). *Clinical Psychology Review, 33,* 1134–1147.

Liu, C. H., Stevens, C., Wong, S. H. M., Yasui, M., & Chen, J. A. (2019). The prevalence and predictors of mental health diagnoses and suicide among U.S. college students: Implications for addressing disparities in service use. *Depression & Anxiety, 36,* 8–17. doi:10.1002/da.22830

MacKean, G. (2011). *Mental health and well-being in postsecondary education settings: A literature and environmental scan to support planning and action in Canada*. Canadian Association of College and University Student Services preconference workshop Student Mental Health: A Call to Action, Toronto, Ontario, Canada.
Maurer, D. M. (2012). *Screening for depression.* Retrieved from http://www.usafp.org/wp-content/uploads/2013/12/Screening-for-Depression.pdf
McCauley, E., Pavlidis, K., & Kendall, K. (2001). Developmental precursors of depression: The child and the social environment. In I. M. Goodyer (Ed.), *The depressed child and adolescent* (2nd ed., pp. 46–78). Cambridge, UK: Cambridge University Press.
Mental Health America. (n.d.). Co-occurring disorders and depression. Retrieved from https://www.mhanational.org/co-occurring-disorders-and-depression
Mojtabai, R., Olfson, M., & Han, B. (2016). National trends in the prevalence and treatment of depression in adolescents and young adults. *Pediatrics, 138*(6). E20161878
National Alliance on Mental Illness. (2017). Depression. Retrieved from https://www.nami.org/Learn-More/Mental-Health-Conditions/Depression
National Alliance on Mental Illness. (2019). StigmaFree on campus. Retrieved from https://www.nami.org/Get-Involved/StigmaFree/StigmaFree-Community/StigmaFree-on-Campus
National Center for Education Statistics. (2019). College enrollment rates. Retrieved from https://nces.ed.gov/programs/coe/indicator_cpb.asp
National Institute of Mental Health. (2017). Major depression. Retrieved from https://www.nimh.nih.gov/health/statistics/major-depression.shtml
National Suicide Prevention Lifeline. (2017). Mental health & suicide prevention glossary. Retrieved from https://suicidepreventionlifeline.org/mental-health-suicide-prevention-glossary/
Oldehinkel, A. J., & Bouma, E. M. C. (2011). Sensitivity to the depressogenic effect of stress and HPA-axis reactivity in adolescence: A review of gender differences. *Neuroscience and Biobehavioral Reviews, 35,* 1757–1770. doi:10.1016/j.neubiorev.2010.10.013
Peter, T., Edkins, T., Watson, R., Adjei, J., Homma, Y., & Saewyc, E. (2017). Trends in suicidality among sexual minority and heterosexual students in a Canadian population-based cohort study. *Psychology of Sexual Orientation and Gender Diversity, 4,* 115–123. doi:10.1037/sgd0000211
Posner, K., Brent, D., Lucas, C., Gould, M., Stanley, B., Brown, G., . . . Mann, J. (2008). *Columbia-Suicide Severity Rating Scale.* Retrieved from https://cssrs.columbia.edu/wp-content/uploads/C-SSRS_Pediatric-SLC_11.14.16.pdf
Rao, A. L., & Hong, E. S. (2016). Understanding depression and suicide in college athletes: Emerging concepts and future directions. *British Journal of Sports Medicine, 50,* 136–137. doi:10.1136/bjsports-2015-095658
Spitzer, R. L., Williams, J. B. W., Kroenke, K., & Colleagues (n.d.). *Patient Health Questionnaire–9 (PHQ-9).* Retrieved from https://www.phqscreeners.com/sites/g/files/g10049256/f/201412/PHQ-9_English.pdf
Suicide Awareness Voices of Education. (2019). Suicide facts. Retrieved from https://save.org/about-suicide/suicide-facts/
Suicide Prevention Resource Center. (2004). *Promoting mental health and preventing suicide in college and university settings.* Waltham, MA: Education Development Center.
Suicide Prevention Resource Center. (2014). *Suicide among college and university students in the United States.* Waltham, MA: Education Development Center.
Suicide Prevention Resource Center. (2017). *Collaborative Assessment and Management of Suicidality (CAMS).* Retrieved from https://www.sprc.org/resources-programs/collaborative-assessment-management-suicidality-cams

Turner, E. A. (2016). Racial trauma is a real thing: The impact of police shootings on African Americans. Retrieved from https://psychologybenefits.org/2016/07/14/racial-trauma-police-shootings-on-african-americans/

U.S. Preventive Services Task Force. (2009). Screening for depression in adults: U.S. preventive services task force recommendation statement. *Annals of Internal Medicine, 151,* 784–792.

Watson, J. C., & Schmit, M. K. (2019). *Introduction to clinical mental health counseling: Contemporary issues.* Thousand Oaks, CA: Sage.

Wong, S. S., Sugimoto-Matsuda, J. J., Chang, J. Y., & Hishinuma, E. S. (2012). Ethnic differences in risk factors for suicide among American high school students, 2009: The vulnerability of multiracial and Pacific Islander adolescents. *Archives of Suicide Research, 16,* 159–173. doi:10.1080/13811118.2012.667334

Woodford, M. R., Weber, G., Nicolazzo, Z., Hunt, R., Kulick, A., Coleman, T., . . . Renn, K. A. (2018). Depression and attempted suicide among LGBTQ college students: Fostering resilience to the effects of heterosexism and cisgenderism on campus. *Journal of College Student Development, 59,* 421–438.

Chapter 20

Continuum of Disordered Eating in College

Natalie Arce Indelicato and Brianna Kane

Listen to me, your body is not a temple.
Temples can be destroyed and desecrated.
Your body is a forest. Thick canopies of maple trees and
sweet scented wildflowers sprouting in the underwood.
You will grow back, over and over,
no matter how badly you are devastated.

—Beau Taplin, *Temples*

■ ■ ■

Reflection Exercise

Think about your relationship with food. How would you describe it? Would you describe it as healthy and balanced, or controlled and preoccupying? Being concerned about what you put into your body is common in our culture, but at what point does this attention become a fixation or be considered a disorder? Consider what you know about disordered eating and eating disorders in the following case and dialogue.

Sarah is a sophomore at a large university and is in a popular sorority. She comes to the university counseling center to address symptoms of anxiety. Upon meeting, you notice that she appears lethargic and her hair and nails look dull and brittle. She is dressed in workout attire and carries an extra sweater, despite the hot summer weather. Sarah reported that her anxiety makes her strive for perfection and act controlling in various aspects of her life. After gathering some background information and beginning to ask Sarah about her daily activities, you want to address what might be symptoms of an eating disorder:

Counselor (CO): So, Sarah, tell me more about what you eat and drink in a typical day.

Sarah (S): Well, I'll have an iced coffee when I wake up, maybe a protein shake, and then I have my meals at the sorority house.

CO: What kind of food do they have at your sorority? Do you enjoy it?
S: It's alright, I guess. Sometimes the food is gross, so I'll just make a salad. If they don't have the salad bar set up, I'll make a shake or just wait for the next meal.
CO: So, when the food isn't appetizing, you'll substitute it with one of your shakes? Or just wait and see if the next meal looks any better?
S: Yeah, basically.
CO: What constitutes the food being gross?
S: If it's like super greasy or I can't tell what's in it by looking at it.
CO: Have you been observant of your food throughout your childhood?
S: Not in my childhood but probably since I was like 13 or so.
CO: What were the attitudes toward food in your household?
S: Well, my mom was always on a diet and would gain and lose weight pretty regularly. My dad has always been pretty thin and enjoys exercise and sports. I would say that both my parents have high expectations when it comes to eating healthy and staying fit.
CO: How have those attitudes influenced your own relationship with food and body image?

What is your initial impression of Sarah? Explore some of the preconceived notions about her age, gender, location, and campus involvement that may have occurred to you as you were reading. On the basis of the preceding brief exchange and her physical appearance, would you feel comfortable diagnosing her with an eating disorder? Although some signs indicate that she might fit the criteria for anorexia nervosa, it is important to continue to explore other risk factors and emotional and behavioral symptoms for accurate conceptualization, as explained throughout this chapter.

■ ■ ■

Continuum of Disordered Eating in College

Although eating disorders can develop in children, adolescents, and older adults, college students, particularly college-age women, are at the most risk for developing them because of the academic, social, and familial pressures that often are newly experienced in college (Feibelman & Turner, 2015; Lipson et al., 2017). Furthermore, late adolescence and early adulthood is the developmental period when underlying mental health issues typically appear. Increased anxiety, learning differences, poor self-esteem, substance use, and relational challenges often intersect with increased workload, financial responsibilities, less structure, and more peer pressure in college (Allen, Byrne, Oddy, & Crosby, 2013; Merikangas et al., 2010). Mixed messages about food, dieting, and healthy eating and a culturally rigid definition of beauty and which body types are acceptable make disordered eating pervasive on college campuses. These standards are often proliferated by social media. Eating disorders are complex mental health disorders that arise from a combination of biological, psychological, interpersonal, and social factors (American Psychiatric Association [APA], 2013).

The prevention and treatment of disordered eating on college campuses continue to be a significant challenge for college counseling professionals. Most college counseling services operate on a brief, time-limited treatment model, which makes it more difficult to provide the interdisciplinary, coordinated, and often longer term services needed. Furthermore, disordered eating exists on a spectrum from disordered eating behaviors that do not meet diagnostic criteria, like orthorexia and diabulimia, to severe anorexia, bulimia, and binge-eating disorders. Defining the boundary between treating disordered eating within the context of an outpatient college counseling center and asking students to withdraw to get more intensive treatment can be complicated, especially given the often conflicted feelings of the student and parents, along with the academic pressure to graduate on time. Prevention and early intervention strategies, even when symptoms are minimal, should be prioritized, given that anorexia nervosa has the highest mortality rate of any psychiatric disorder (Arcelus, Mitchell, Wales, & Nielsen, 2011; Smink, van Hoeken, & Hoek, 2012) and prognosis is related to duration of illness.

In this chapter, we will provide a differentiation between disordered eating versus eating disorders along with the prevalence, risk factors, and protective factors for disordered eating. We will outline symptoms and characteristics of eating disorders, contextual influences, and considerations for assessment and treatment planning, outreach, and prevention. Finally, we will offer specific case studies with guided applications.

Disordered Eating Versus Eating Disorders

Approximately 35% of "normal dieters" develop a pattern of behaviors that can be diagnosed as eating disorders (National Eating Disorders Association [NEDA], 2013); however, the continuum of disordered eating is much broader than the diagnostic categories found in the *Diagnostic and Statistical Manual of Mental Disorders* (5th ed.; *DSM-5*; APA, 2013; Shisslak, Crago, & Estes, 1995). Disordered eating is present when an individual engages in abnormal eating patterns or food behaviors on a regular basis. Not all individuals with disordered eating behaviors meet criteria for a diagnosable disorder, and it "by no means indicates that all who engage in disordered eating will have an eating disorder" (Zucker, 2017). The difference lies in the frequency and severity of behaviors and how much distress is caused in the individual's social, occupational, or other important areas of functioning.

On the continuum of those with disordered eating, individuals who meet the diagnostic criteria for anorexia, bulimia, and binge-eating disorder are considered to have the most severe form and have the most potential physical and emotional consequences (Mental Health America, 2018; National Alliance on Mental Illness, 2018). At the other end of the continuum are individuals who exhibit disordered eating patterns as a way to cope with difficult emotions and/or manage their weight. Disordered eating behaviors range from overly restrictive behaviors that follow "fad diets" (i.e., no-carbohydrate or "clean" eating regimens) to more severe behaviors such as extreme anxiety around food, overexercising, abusing laxatives or diuretics, binging/purging, or extreme calorie monitoring. Although these behaviors can be serious, in isolation, they do not yet meet the criteria for an eating disorder. However, it is important to note that disordered eating behaviors such as binge eating, restraint, emotional eating, eating disinhibition, strict eating, and controlling body weight and shape through inappropriate compensatory behaviors are all risk factors for eating disorders (Jacobi et al., 2011; Quick & Byrd-Bredbenner, 2013) and should be addressed within the counseling setting and through outreach efforts.

At least 30 million people of all ages and genders in the United States struggle with an eating disorder (Hudson, Hiripi, Pope, & Kessler, 2007; Le Grange, Swanson, Crow, & Merikangas, 2012). Approximately 20% of college students report that they have had disordered eating at some point in their lives (Tillman, Arbaugh, & Balaban, 2012). The prevalence of eating disorders among college students varies depending on the source; however, the range most often identified is between 8% and 20% (Eisenberg, Nicklett, Roeder, & Kirz, 2011; NEDA, 2013), with 10% to 20% of college women and 4% to 10% of college men having an eating disorder. According to NEDA (2013), there is an unmet need for the identification and referral of college students with eating disorders. The 2017 Association for University and College Counseling Center Directors Annual Survey found that of the 621 participating schools, 187 centers identified "eating" within the client's presenting problem, with a mean percentage of 10.6% (LeViness, Bershad, & Gorman, 2017).

Eating disorders affect individuals across gender, age, race, ethnicity, culture, size, socioeconomic status, and sexual orientation (NEDA, 2019), although people of color are significantly less likely to receive help for their eating issues (Marques et al., 2011). The exact prevalence of eating disorders among college students is uncertain because of the high number of unreported cases of eating disorders and disordered eating behaviors in both males and females. Yu and Tan (2016) found that a significant portion of students who display signs of eating disorders have not been diagnosed or sought treatment. Another study found that the prevalence of diagnosable eating disorders is more than 3 times higher than rates of treatment, and that 80% of students with clinically significant symptoms do not receive care (Lipson et al., 2017). Even with ambiguous prevalence levels, researchers have consistently shown that certain groups—college-age, females, and athletes—are at a higher risk for developing an eating disorder than the general population (McLester, Hardin, & Hoppe, 2014).

Risk Factors for Disordered Eating and Eating Disorders

In the United States, disordered eating and body image concerns are pervasive, they affect all races and ethnic groups (Marques et al., 2011), and it is often difficult to predict who will progress from disordered eating to an eating disorder; however, there are some risk factors that may increase this likelihood. For any disorder, understanding the risk factors, or variables that predict the development of the disorder, is vital to prevention efforts (Evans et al., 2012). Scientists and researchers are still learning about the underlying causes of disordered eating; however, there is knowledge about some of the general issues that can contribute to their development. General risk factors for disordered eating include genetic factors, hormonal (biological) changes, and environmental influences. Environmental influences, specifically sociocultural influences, such as media, family, and peers, contribute to increased risk (Choate, 2013). Additionally, risk factors include a history of dieting or a family history of dieting or eating disorders, difficulty coping with stress, the experience of being bullied about weight, feelings of shame or dissatisfaction with body shape and size, perfectionism, and feeling the need to please others. Dieting is a significant risk factor for developing an eating disorder (Grigg, Bowman, & Redman, 1996; Patton, Selzer, Coffey, Carlin, & Wolfe, 1999). Researchers found that adolescent girls who dieted moderately were five times more likely to develop an eating disorder than those who did not engage in dieting behaviors, and those who dieted at a severe level were 18 times more likely to develop an eating disorder compared with those who did not diet (Patton et al., 1999).

Mass media sources, such as magazines and television shows, have portrayed the "ideal" body for both men and women for years. In recent years, social networks such as Facebook, Instagram, and Pinterest have promoted these body image ideas. Social comparisons across platforms, as well as "body challenges" and pro-anorexia websites, are at the fingertips of the college population. In a systematic review of 20 articles related to social media and body image, researchers found evidence that social networking site use is associated with increased body dissatisfaction and disordered eating across genders (Holland & Tiggemann, 2016). Asking your clients about their social media usage is increasingly important to holistically understand concerns of body image and disordered eating.

College students are at an increased risk of developing an eating disorder or disordered eating behaviors for several reasons. Although eating disordered behaviors can occur throughout the life span, the age at which individuals generally enter college, late adolescence and early adulthood, coincides with the typical age of onset for eating disorders (Feibelman & Turner, 2015; Lipson et al., 2017). The transition into college also increases the risk of developing an eating disorder. Dramatic lifestyle changes from high school to college produce stressors that have been shown to influence the risk of weight gain, disrupt eating patterns, and change social support in college students (Blair et al., 2017). Unfortunately, many individuals across the spectrum of disordered eating remain undiagnosed and untreated across campuses. College counselors may observe clients' anxieties, low self-esteem, and academic challenges intersect with unhealthy coping behaviors such as food restriction, overexercise, and increased focus on weight. Also, a counselor might see additional sociocultural influences from campus organizations and athletics that place specific attention on appearance and performance. Given examples of factors that may contribute to disordered eating, it is difficult to definitively identify which may "*cause* body image problems versus those that *maintain* or *intensify* body image concerns" (Worell & Goodheart, 2006, p. 71).

Cultural pressures, especially in Western societies, encourage individuals to achieve a certain level of thinness or "fitness," which results in normative discontent with their bodies. This discontentment and dissatisfaction with one's body is often an antecedent to overevaluating one's weight and shape in relation to self-worth and becomes a key component of disordered eating behaviors (Choate, 2013). Media (e.g., social media, movies, television, magazines, the internet) are one of the strongest conveyors of the perceived importance of body image. Family is another source of influence on body image development and subsequent disordered eating. Parental influence can either involve modeling maladaptive attitudes and behaviors around eating and/or parents making explicit or implicit comments about their child's body and/or appearance (Choate, 2013). Peers also contribute to the development of eating disorders by either influencing an individual by their own disordered eating or by teasing and bullying, leading to dissatisfaction of the individual.

Eating disorders are seen in male, female, and transgender college students, yet women remain at higher risk (Garner, 2004; West & Barrack, 2016). In addition to gender, predisposing factors include having low self-esteem and falling between the ages of adolescence and young adulthood (Garner, 2004). Between 4% and 22% of college-age women engage in eating disorder behaviors (McLester et al., 2014), whereas overall estimates of eating disorders on college campuses range from 8% to 17%, and 20% of students said that they suspected that they have had an eating disorder at some point in their lives (Eisenberg et al., 2011). Some estimates report that roughly 14% of female and 4% of male students screen positive for clinically significant eating disorders (Lipson et al., 2017). Sixteen percent of transgender college students reported having an eating disorder (Diemer, Grant, Munn-Chernoff, Patterson, & Duncan, 2015). The low rates of eating disorders in men likely have influenced Western society's view of disordered eating as a women's issue, but evidence suggests that men, including college men, who are diagnosed with an eating disorder exhibit maladaptive eating-related behaviors and attitudes similar to those found in women (Ousley, Cordero, & White, 2008). Eating disorders may also present differently in some males, where they are trying to attain muscles or definition rather than achieve a thinner ideal body size or shape (Ousley et al., 2008). In addition to gender considerations, sexual orientation has to be examined as a risk factor given that 3.5% of college women and 2.1% of college men who identify as a sexual minority reported having an eating disorder (Diemer et al., 2015), and culturally appropriate interventions are needed.

The following websites include helpful information outlining risk factors for eating disorders and eating disorders in the college population:

https://www.eatingdisorderhope.com/information/eating-disorder/college-trigger-eating-disorder
https://eatingdisorder.org/eating-disorder-information/underlying-causes/
https://www.nationaleatingdisorders.org/risk-factors
https://www.ncbi.nlm.nih.gov/pmc/articles/PMC2719561/

Protective Factors

Research on protective factors, as they relate to the development of disordered eating, is fairly limited. In addition, they are not universal, and they vary depending on gender, social class, ethnicity, age, and other variables (Langdon-Daly & Serpell, 2017). However, some research has shown that higher levels of social support are associated with a weaker relationship between eating disturbances and a variety of risk factors (Ferreiro, Seoane, & Senra, 2012). Known protective factors can be categorized into three groups: individual, family, and sociocultural.

Individual factors include having high self-esteem and a positive body image. They also include being self-directive and assertive and having appropriate problem-solving and coping skills (National Eating Disorders Collaboration, 2019). Family factors include belonging to a family that does not overemphasize weight and physical attractiveness. Langdon-Daly and Serpell (2017) found that factors in the family environment around food, eating, and weight, such as frequent family meals and avoiding comments about weight, may be beneficial to protect young children from developing maladaptive eating behaviors. Additional sociocultural factors include belonging to a less Westernized culture, being involved with a sport or an industry that does not place emphasis on thinness, and having peer or social support wherein weight and physical appearance are not of high concern (National Eating Disorders Collaboration, 2019). Exposure to media sources that provide a non-appearance-related source of self-esteem and avoid focusing on the thin ideal may also be protective (Worell & Goodheart, 2006). One study indicated that elementary school girls who actively rejected the media ideal of thinness showed lower internalization of this ideal and had better body esteem, compared with girls who were uncertain about the images that were shown (Worell & Goodheart, 2006).

Symptoms and Characteristics of Disordered Eating

According to the *DSM-5*, eating disorders are classified into four major categories: anorexia nervosa, bulimia nervosa, binge-eating disorder, and other specified feeding or eating disorders. Disordered eating is a subtype of these categories and has no formal diagnostic process. These disorders are all characterized by "a persistent disturbance of eating or eating-related behavior that results in the altered consumption or absorption of food that significantly impairs physical health or psychosocial functioning" (APA, 2013, p. 329). Diagnoses of eating disorders are mutually exclusive, meaning only one diagnosis can be assigned, although they may co-occur with other mental disorders.

A summary of each of the eating disorders referenced in the *DSM-5* is provided below; however, it is often difficult for clinicians to distinguish between the groups of symptoms and define clear diagnostic categories. For example, many students present with all the symptoms of bulimia nervosa, except that their compensatory behaviors occur less than once a week for several months. Other common disordered eating behaviors that are not found in the *DSM* and are common for clinicians to experience with clients are also described.

Anorexia Nervosa

For a clinician to diagnose an individual with anorexia nervosa, the *DSM-5* requires that three essential features be met. First, there must be a persistent restriction of energy intake relative to requirements, leading to a significantly low body weight in the context of age, sex, developmental trajectory, and physical health (Criterion A). The individual's body mass index also determines the severity of the disorder, which may indicate the intensity of the symptoms of the illness, degree of functional impairment, and the need for medical or clinical supervision (APA, 2013). Ideally, the measure of severity would provide an index of the intensity of defining psychopathological features of the illness, as well as the level of functional impairment and the need for treatment services (Gianini et al., 2017).

Second, an individual typically displays an intense fear of gaining weight or of becoming fat or a persistent behavior that interferes with weight gain (Criterion B). This fear is usually not alleviated by weight loss. Finally, there typically is a disturbance in the way in which one's body weight/shape influences body weight or shape on self-evaluation, or there is a persistent lack of recognition of the seriousness of the current low body weight (Criterion C). Some individuals feel overweight, and others realize that they are thin but are still concerned by certain body parts. Self-esteem of individuals with anorexia nervosa is highly dependent on their opinion of their body.

When diagnosing a student with anorexia nervosa, it is also important to specify whether it is a restricting type or a binge-eating/purging type. *Restricting type* is defined as, within the past 3 months, the individual has not engaged in recurrent episodes of binge-eating or purging behaviors. In this subtype, weight loss is accomplished mainly through dieting, fasting, and/or excessive exercise. *Binge-eating/purging type* is defined as, within the past 3 months, the individual has engaged in recurrent episodes of binge-eating or purging behaviors. Purging behaviors include self-induced vomiting or the misuse of laxatives, diuretics, or enemas.

It is common that anorexia nervosa can co-occur with bipolar, depressive, and anxiety disorders. Obsessive-compulsion disorder may be present in some individuals, especially those with restricting type.

Bulimia Nervosa

Bulimia nervosa commonly begins in adolescence or young adulthood (APA, 2013). There are also three essential features to diagnose an individual with bulimia nervosa listed in the *DSM-5*. There must be recurrent episodes of binge eating (Criterion A). An episode of binge eating is described by both eating a significantly larger amount of food in a discrete period of time and feeling lack of control over eating during the episode (APA, 2013). A discrete period of time is usually less than 2 hours.

There must also be recurrent inappropriate compensatory behaviors to prevent weight gain (Criterion B). Compensatory behaviors include self-induced vomiting; misuse of laxatives, diuretics, or other medication; fasting; or excessive exercise. Vomiting is the most common of compensatory behaviors for individuals with bulimia nervosa because there is an immediate relief from the physical discomfort caused by binge eating. Exercise is considered excessive when the behavior significantly interferes with daily functioning or the individual continues to exercise despite injury or medical complications.

Finally, self-evaluation is excessively influenced by body shape and weight (Criterion D). Individuals may resemble those with anorexia nervosa in their fear of gaining weight, desire to lose weight, and level of dissatisfaction related to their bodies. However, the disturbance does not occur exclusively during episodes of anorexia nervosa (Criterion E; APA, 2013).

For an individual to be diagnosed with bulimia nervosa, binge eating and inappropriate compensatory behaviors must occur, approximately at least once a week for three months. The type of food consumed in a binge episode varies across individuals, but individuals typically eat food they otherwise would avoid. The type of food eaten is less important to the diagnosis than the abnormality in the amount consumed. Individuals with bulimia nervosa are typically ashamed of their behaviors and try to cover up their symptoms. Binge episodes usually occur in secrecy and will continue until the individual is uncomfortably or painfully full. Triggers for binge eating include interpersonal stressors; dietary restraint; negative feelings toward body weight, shape, and food; and boredom.

Individuals with bulimia nervosa typically are within normal weight or overweight range; the disorder is uncommon among obese individuals. Menstrual irregularity or amenorrhea, the absence of menstruation, often occurs among females with bulimia nervosa. There are disturbances of fluids and electrolytes, resulting from the purge behaviors, that sometimes cause severe medical problems. Bulimia nervosa is more common in females than males. There is an approximate 10:1 female-to-male ratio of individuals diagnosed with bulimia nervosa.

Binge-Eating Disorder

Binge-eating disorder occurs in individuals who are normal weight, who are overweight, and who are classified as obese. Binge-eating disorder is often associated with obesity and being overweight in treatment-seeking individuals. Those with this disorder consume more calories, have greater impairments in daily functioning, have lower quality of life, and have more subjective distress and greater psychiatric comorbidity. Binge-eating disorder is the most common eating disorder, and the gender ratio is far less skewed than for individuals with other eating disorders (Striegel-Moore & Franko, 2003). Binge-eating disorder is seen more predominantly among individuals seeking weight-loss treatment than in the general population (APA, 2013), and there is a trend toward a higher prevalence of binge-eating disorder in all minority groups (Swanson, Crow, Le Grange, Swendsen, & Merikangas, 2011).

Diagnostic criteria include recurrent episodes of binge eating (same classification of binge eating in bulimia nervosa) and binge-eating episodes associated with at least three of the following: eating much more rapidly than normal; eating until feeling uncomfortably full; eating large amounts of food when not feeling physically hungry; eating alone because of feeling embarrassed by how much one is eating; and feeling disgusted with oneself, depressed, or guilty after engaging in a binge-eating episode (APA, 2013). There must also be marked distress related to binge eating, with binge eating occurring, on average, at least once a week for 3 months and the eating is not associated with recurrent use of inappropriate compensatory behaviors as noted with bulimia nervosa, and it does not occur exclusively during bulimia nervosa or anorexia nervosa.

Other Specified Feeding or Eating Disorder

This grouping of eating disorders does not meet full criteria for anorexia nervosa, bulimia nervosa, or binge-eating disorder but entails symptoms characteristic of a disorder that cause significant distress or impairment in either social, occupational, or other important areas of functioning. For college students, this may include not attending class, withdrawing from social groups, and avoiding eating in front of other people. The following indicates diagnosis of an "other specified feeding or eating disorder": atypical anorexia nervosa, bulimia nervosa (of low frequency and/or limited duration), binge-eating disorder (of low frequency and/or limited duration), purging disorder, or night eating syndrome (APA, 2013). It is important to monitor clients with this diagnosis and provide intervention as early as possible to decrease the likelihood of the increase in symptom severity.

Atypical anorexia nervosa is characterized by meeting all of the criteria for anorexia nervosa, except that despite weight loss, the individual's weight is within or above the normal range (NEDA, 2019). A specifier of bulimia nervosa meets the requirements for bulimia nervosa, but inappropriate compensatory behaviors occur less than once a week and/or for less than 3 months. Similar specifications for bulimia nervosa (of low frequency and/or limited duration) apply to binge-eating disorder (of low frequency and/or limited duration) with the exception that episodes are of binge eating, rather than inappropriate compensatory behaviors. Purging disorder is characterized by the recurrent purging to influence weight or shape in the absence of binge eating (NEDA, 2019). Night eating syndrome is classified as recurrent episodes of night eating, as established by eating after waking from sleep or by excessive food consumption after the evening meal. An individual with night eating syndrome is aware of his or her eating, he or she can recall the night eating episode, and it occurs without a better explanation like changes in the individual's sleep cycle or social norms.

Food Addiction

Some individuals report eating-related symptoms that resemble characteristics of substance use disorders, such as the cravings and patterns of compulsive use (APA, 2013). The scientific acceptance of the term *food addiction* has been controversial, and it is not a recognized diagnosis; however, the APA (2013) has formally recognized the existence of behavioral addictions in the *DSM-5* chapter on "Substance Related and Addictive Disorders," and symptom variability across all substance use disorders has been acknowledged in the *DSM-5* where each specific substance has been listed as its own disorder. Food addiction is a term first introduced by Randolph (1956) to describe the compulsive consumption of certain types of foods such as those high in sugar, fat, and/or salt (Corwin & Grigson, 2009; Gearhardt, Corbin, & Brownell, 2009; Hebebrand et al., 2014; Randolph, 1956).

Food addiction highlights both the addictive potential of palatable foods and changes to the reward system in at-risk individuals (Gearhardt, Boswell, & White, 2014). There are commonalities among food addiction and disordered eating behaviors in that both reflect a compulsive overeating psychopathology; however, binge-eating disorder is conceptualized as a psychobehavioral pathology and a culture-bound symptom whereas food addiction is conceptualized as an addiction disorder that has an etiology tied to the pleasure/reward system of specific eating patterns (Davis, 2017; Yu et al., 2018). Food addiction has been reported to be more prevalent in populations with disordered eating than those without (57.6% vs. 16.2%; Pursey, Stanwell, Gearhardt, Collins, & Burrows , 2014).

Other Common Nonprofessional Disordered Eating Definitions

There are several terms that are used among professionals and nonprofessionals to describe disordered eating behaviors. Some recognized terms include orthorexia, diabulimia, drunkorexia, and bigorexia.

NEDA defines *orthorexia* as the obsession with "healthy" eating (NEDA, 2019). This term was coined in 1998, and people who experience orthorexia typically become fixated on ingredients, spend hours a day thinking about what food might be served at upcoming events, and can obsessively follow health blogs on social media. Some individuals with orthorexia may also experience symptoms of obsessive-compulsive disorder (NEDA, 2019).

Diabulimia refers to an eating disorder in which a person with diabetes purposefully restricts insulin intake to lose weight (NEDA, 2019). The *DSM* does address the omission of insulin as a purging behavior, and it may be coded as bulimia nervosa if the person binges and then restricts insulin. If the individual is severely restricting both food and insulin intake, he or she may follow criteria for anorexia nervosa. Common behaviors associated with diabulimia include neglect of diabetes management, fear that insulin will make the individual fat, and a discomfort testing or injecting in front of others (NEDA, 2019).

NEDA defines *drunkorexia* as a struggle with an eating disorder and alcohol abuse. Individuals who experience drunkorexia will often undereat during the day and binge drink at night (NEDA, 2019). Binge drinking, the rapid consumption of alcohol in a short period of time, is common among college students, making it imperative to assess for both alcohol use and eating behaviors.

Bigorexia, or what is clinically known as *muscle dysmorphia*, is becoming more commonly recognized in men. This term refers to the societal pressure for men, and particular athletes, to reach an extreme level of muscularity and leanness. Males who present with bigorexia may be involved in sports such as football, wrestling, or competitive weight lifting. Behaviors associated with bigorexia include a preoccupation with working out, often at the expense of social commitments; training despite injuries; and abuse of dietary agents or steroids (Leone, Sedory, & Gray, 2005).

Assessment and Treatment

Assessment

Many students do not initially present to counseling center services with an identified eating disorder or body image issues. Instead, the presenting issue may be anxiety, homesickness, relationship issues, low self-esteem, or other issues that are easier to initially discuss for students. All intake assessments should include at least several questions about potential eating issues, such as "How much do you go on diets or worry about your weight?" or "How often have you had a sense of loss of control over eating and you also ate what most people would regard as more than most people would eat under similar circumstances?" Ask for a sample of a typical day's intake and whether the student's eating patterns have changed over the past few months.

If the client identifies eating issues as a part of the presenting problem(s), a careful assessment should move forward to include weight history; medical concerns; restricting, binging, or purging behaviors and frequency; preoccupation with food and body image; degree of distress related to body size, weight, and shape; and exercise patterns. Additionally, the following are all relevant aspects to an assessment for eating disorders: family history of eating disorders or other mental health disorders; family history of obesity; and family dynamics and attitudes related to eating, body image, and exercise. Finally, from a strengths-based perspective, it is important to assess for client and family strengths, relational support, and times in the client's life when disordered eating was not an issue. Online screening tools, such as the Eating Disorders Screening Tool (NEDA, 2018) and the Eating Attitudes Test self-test (EAT-26, 2017), provide a valid and reliable means to identify individuals with eating disorders who might need to seek professional attention.

Clients with eating disorders should also be assessed for co-occurring disorders, including depression and suicide risk, anxiety disorders, and substance use disorders given their frequency of co-occurrence (Ulfvebrand, Birgegard, Norring, Hogdahl, & von Hausswolff-

Juhlin, 2015). Ulfvebrand et al. (2015) found that among individuals with bulimia nervosa, binge-eating disorder, and other specified feeding or eating disorder, almost 1 in 10 have a comorbid substance abuse disorder and more than half have a comorbid mood disorder and anxiety disorder. They also found that 33% to 50% of individuals with anorexia nervosa have a comorbid mood disorder and about half have comorbid anxiety disorders, including obsessive-compulsive disorder and social phobia.

Treatment

Importance of a Team Approach

Because of the physical and psychological nature of disordered eating symptoms and consequences, a multidisciplinary team approach is widely recognized as the best practice. Team members often include mental health professionals (i.e., counselors and psychiatrists or mental health nurse practitioners), nutrition counselors, and general practice or family medicine physicians. All should be experienced in the care of individuals with eating disorders. Clinicians need to communicate regularly with one another regarding their assessments, impressions, treatment plans, interventions, and the tasks of each team member. This is essential to monitoring client progress and ensuring that splitting or mixed messages do not occur.

The APA work group on Eating Disorders developed practice guidelines for the treatment of eating disorders on the basis of extensive interviews with clinicians along with a comprehensive literature review (APA, 2006). Strategies for treatment should be informed by these original guidelines (http://psychiatryonline.org/pb/assets/raw/sitewide/practice_guidelines/guidelines/eatingdisorders.pdf), as well as the updated guideline watch (https://psychiatryonline.org/pb/assets/raw/sitewide/practice_guidelines/guidelines/eatingdisorders-watch.pdf), which provide level-of-care recommendations based on physical and psychological status.

Individual Counseling

Most treatment for eating disorders begins with individual counseling. At the beginning, it is important for the counselor to build trust and rapport, establish mutual respect, and develop a therapeutic alliance to serve as the foundation for ongoing treatment. Research supports the efficacy of using cognitive behavioral approaches, which focus on learning to identify and change thoughts and behaviors related to maintaining the eating disorder behavior, and interpersonal psychotherapy, which focuses on interpersonal/relational issues in the client's life, as the two primary counseling approaches (Evans et al., 2012). Other approaches that have shown promise in treating eating disorders include dialectical behavior therapy, expressive arts therapies (e.g., art therapy, dance/movement therapy, equine therapy), acceptance and commitment therapy, and the Maudsley method family therapy (Eisenberg et al., 2011; Evans et al., 2012; Lipson et al., 2017; NEDA, 2019). Family-based treatment is typically used in intensive outpatient treatment programs wherein parents are integrated into their child's recovery process (APA, 2006). There are three phases of the Maudsley family approach, which include restoring weight, returning control over eating to the individual, and establishing a healthy identity (Evans et al., 2012).

Group Counseling

Male and female students with eating disorders may isolate themselves by not leaving their residence hall room and by withdrawing from extracurricular activities (organized or intramural sports, Greek life, etc.) because of shame, guilt, low self-esteem, or fear of judgment. Their lack of social interaction and support tend to exacerbate symptoms, so increasing social support, as a part of treatment, is critical. Some research has shown that eating disorder support groups can be a helpful and supportive supplement to individual counseling for those in recovery (Lázaro et al., 2011). However, screening for appropriateness for group becomes important because if a person is too early in his or her recovery, he or she may not be prepared for the internal reactions of others in the group or may not yet be able to behave in ways that maintain group safety. Eating disorder groups can be self-help support groups, wherein the members of the group are the organizers and consist of men or women who have personal experience with eating disorders or groups led by professional counselors. There are groups that focus on the psychoeducational aspects of eating disorders; some focus on specific skills such as mindful eating, whereas others are process oriented—members give and receive empathic feedback and increase their social support networks. Other groups work on advocacy and public policy issues related to eating disorders awareness, access to treatment, and research funding.

Medical Evaluation

When a client is diagnosed with an eating disorder, he or she should be referred to a primary care or family medicine practitioner to determine whether additional medical conditions exist that should be treated. The practitioner may complete a physical; order additional blood work or an electrocardiogram; and check electrolyte levels, liver functioning, and other vital signs including heart rate, weight, and blood pressure. Many individuals who are being treated for an eating disorder can benefit from psychotropic medication, which is prescribed by either their physician, their psychiatrist, or their mental health nurse practitioner. Because many clients who are diagnosed with an eating disorder also struggle with symptoms of anxiety, obsessive-compulsive disorder, and depressive disorders, antidepressants are often prescribed to help with these symptoms.

Nutrition Counseling

Nutrition counseling is a critical part of the eating disorder treatment and recovery process to help individuals learn their body's internal cues for hunger and fullness, improve the relationship an individual has between food and thinking, decrease myths regarding certain foods or categories of foods, and eat adequately to meet the individual's daily nutritional needs. Disordered eating is often characterized by an unhealthy focus on food and nutrition. The goal of nutrition counseling is to replace disordered, unhealthy eating patterns with healthy, nutritious eating patterns. Although most students can be seen in an outpatient college counseling center setting, there may be a time when outpatient treatment is insufficient because of the severity of the eating disorder—for example, if clients are not able to sustain basic nutritional needs and/or need supervision during all meals.

Outreach and Prevention

Although not specifically mentioned in the guidelines for treatment, many campuses have outreach and prevention teams that should be considered an important part of the treatment model and multidisciplinary approach. Campus outreach programs, like the Body Project (NEDA, https://www.nationaleatingdisorders.org/school-community) and Be Body Positive (The Body Positive, https://www.thebodypositive.org/campus-leadership), use a prevention framework to provide education and awareness of local resources, including campus counseling, nutrition, and health promotion services. National outreach and advocacy programs, such as NEDA (https://www.nationaleatingdisorders.org/), promote events across campus to raise awareness and provide education on eating disorders. National Eating Disorder Awareness Week is the largest eating disorders outreach effort in the United States. Campus volunteers, including eating disorder professionals, students, health care providers, and educators, work collaboratively to educate others on the need for early intervention and treatment. Other advocacy programs and events include toll-free information and referral help lines, patient navigators, media literacy campaigns, organized walks and runs, and national and international conferences. Toll-free information and help lines range from ones that can cover general issues, such as the Hopeline Network, 1-800-442-4673, which assists with any crisis, to those that have a focus on specific eating issues like Overeaters Anonymous, 1-505-891-2664; the National Association of Anorexia Nervosa and Associated Disorders, 1-630-577-1330; and the NEDA Helpline, 1-800-931-2237. Additional information about these help lines and more can be found online (https://www.bulimia.com/topics/eating-disorder-hotline/).

Conclusion

Identifying and providing counseling for students on the continuum of disordered eating continues to be a challenge for college counseling professionals. Collaboration among various campus and community health service providers is vital to providing a coordinated, comprehensive, culturally competent, and strengths-based approach. Demonstrating awareness of risk and protective factors; providing nonjudgmental respect and empathy; increasing awareness and consequences of disordered eating; and incorporating recognition of the unique developmental academic, social, and familial pressures facing students can help students make significant gains toward recovery and wellness.

Final Case Studies

Case 1

Laney, a 19-year-old African American soccer player, came to the counseling center after an injury ended her soccer career and she felt that she had lost a major part of her identity. Initially, she indicated symptoms of depression and anxiety; however, it became clear that she was underweight, was significantly restricting her food intake, had an intense fear of gaining weight, and perceived herself as "flabby" and out of shape. Because she was not playing soccer anymore, Laney spent a significant amount of time thinking about food, her body, and how to exercise despite her injury. Laney's preoccupation with her weight and body began to interfere with her academic performance and her relationships as well. Typically an outgoing, friendly person, Laney became more and more isolated.

Case 2

Jessica, an 18-year-old Latina first-year student, came to counseling at the encouragement of her roommate, who overheard her purging in their dorm bathroom several times. Jessica stated that these were isolated incidents after drinking too much alcohol. However, after several sessions, she stated that she had a history of binging and purging in high school. Jessica shared that following the stress of moving to college and starting classes, she periodically would purge after binging in the cafeteria on campus.

Case 3

Paul, a 32-year-old White graduate student who identified as bisexual, initiated counseling after a Counseling Center outreach presentation in his class. Paul came back to school to get his master's degree in architecture and was overwhelmed with juggling a full-time job and the pressures of graduate school. He also stated that he was confused about his sexual identity and feeling pressure from his gay friends to "decide" whether he was gay or straight. Paul struggled with weight from an early age and began dieting in the fourth grade. He found that when he binged, he did not think about the stress of school, work, or his sexual identity. After gaining 30 pounds his first year, he felt guilty and ashamed but could not control his binging.

Case Exploration Questions

For the preceding case studies, answer the following case exploration questions and begin to develop a conceptualization for each client. We will provide responses for the first case study to guide you.

1. What other information would you want to know about the clients?

   For example, with Laney, a counselor would want to know how long her symptoms have been present, whether her medical doctor is aware of her weight loss and that she is exercising despite her injury, and to what degree her preoccupation is interfering with her academic performance and relationships. The counselor would also want to inquire about her mental health history, including past issues with anxiety, depression, and disordered eating, among other family and contextual factors that could be contributing to her presenting issues.

2. Is there a provisional diagnosis you would choose and/or other potential co-occurring diagnoses that should be ruled out prior to specifying a provisional diagnosis?

   Depending on her weight, a provisional diagnosis for Laney would be anorexia nervosa or other specified feeding or eating disorder. Prior to making a formal diagnosis, the counselor would need to know Laney's weight and rule out a mood disorder such as major depressive disorder or an anxiety disorder such as generalized anxiety disorder.

3. Identify the clients' risk and protective factors.

   Laney's risk factors for an eating disorder include being female, college-age, an athlete, and experiencing a major loss of identity after her career-ending injury. Her protective factors include that she has sought out counseling and seemingly has an intact social support network.

4. Using a cognitive behavioral approach, what types of interventions would you implement and why? Using a relational/interpersonal approach, what types of interventions would you implement and why?

   A cognitive behavioral approach with Laney would include the use of interventions such as identifying cognitive distortions, engaging in cognitive restructuring, increasing healthy coping strategies, identifying triggers, and assigning homework to practice new behaviors. A relational/interpersonal approach would focus on gaining an increased understanding of interpersonal difficulties (i.e., role disputes, role transitions, unresolved grief, and interpersonal disconnections), increasing social support, and working to improve self-esteem and self-evaluation.

5. What other professionals and/or support resources would you involve in care for each client?

   In Laney's case, the counselor should involve her medical doctor and a nutrition therapist. In addition, it may be helpful for her to engage in group therapy focused on body image and/or eating disorder recovery.

References

Allen, K. L., Byrne, S. M., Oddy, W. H., & Crosby, R. D. (2013). Early onset binge eating and purging eating disorders: Course and outcome in a population-based study of adolescents. *Journal of Abnormal Child Psychology, 41,* 1083–1096.

American Psychiatric Association. (2006). *Practice guideline for the treatment of patients with eating disorders* (3rd ed.). Arlington, VA: American Psychiatric Association.

American Psychiatric Association. (2013). *Diagnostic and statistical manual of mental disorders* (5th ed.). Arlington, VA: Author.

Arcelus, J., Mitchell, A. J., Wales, J., & Nielsen, S. (2011). Mortality rates in patients with anorexia nervosa and other eating disorders. *Archives of General Psychiatry, 68,* 724–731.

Blair, L., Aloia, C. R., Valliant, M. W., Knight, K. B., Garner, J. C., & Nahar, V. K. (2017). Association between athletic participation and the risk of eating disorder and body dissatisfaction in college students. *International Journal of Health Sciences, 11,* 8–12.

Choate, L. H. (2013). *Eating disorders and obesity: A counselor's guide to prevention and treatment*. Alexandria, VA: American Counseling Association.

Corwin, R. L., & Grigson, P. S. (2009). Symposium overview—Food addiction: Fact or fiction? *Journal of Nutrition, 139,* 617–619.

Davis, C. (2017). A commentary on the associations among 'food addiction', binge eating disorder, and obesity: Overlapping conditions with idiosyncratic clinical features. *Appetite, 115,* 3–8.

Diemer, E. W., Grant, J. D., Munn-Chernoff, M. A., Patterson, D., & Duncan, A. E. (2015). Gender identity, sexual orientation, and eating-related pathology in a national sample of college students. *Journal of Adolescent Health, 57,* 144–149.

Eating Attitudes Test. (2017). The Eating Attitudes Test. Retrieved from https://www.eat-26.com/

Eisenberg, D., Nicklett, E. J., Roeder, K., & Kirz, N. E. (2011). Eating disorders symptoms among college students: Prevalence, persistence, correlates, and treatment-seeking. *Journal of American College Health, 59,* 700–707. doi:10.1080/07448481.2010.546461

Evans, D., Foa, E., Gur, R., Hendin, H., O'Brien, C., Seligman, M., & Walsh, B. (2012). *Treating and preventing adolescent mental health disorders: What we know and what we don't know. A research agenda for improving the mental health of our youth.* Oxford, UK: Oxford University Press. Retrieved from http://oxfordmedicine.com/view/10.1093/9780195173642.001.0001/med-9780195173642-chapter-16

Feibelman, J. L., & Turner, L. A. (2015). Relationships between eating disorder symptomology and forgiveness among college students. *Current Psychology, 34,* 121–129.

Ferreiro, F., Seoane, G., & Senra, C. (2012). Gender-related risk and protective factors for depressive symptoms and disordered eating in adolescence: A 4-year longitudinal study. *Journal of Youth and Adolescence, 41,* 607–622. doi:10.1007/s10964-011-9718-7

Garner, D. (2004). *EDI-3: Eating Disorder Inventory–3: Referral form (RF) manual.* Lutz, FL: Psychological Assessment Resources.

Gearhardt, A. N., Boswell, R. G., & White, M. A. (2014). The association of "food addiction" with disordered eating and body mass index. *Eating Behaviors, 15,* 427–433.

Gearhardt, A. N., Corbin, W. R., & Brownell, K. D. (2009). Preliminary validation of the Yale Food Addiction Scale. *Appetite, 52,* 430–436.

Gianini, L., Roberto, C. A., Attia, E., Walsh, B. T., Thomas, J. J., Eddy, K. T., . . . Sysko, R. (2017). Mild, moderate, meaningful? Examining the psychological and functional correlates of *DSM-5* eating disorder severity specifiers. *International Journal of Eating Disorders, 50,* 909–916. doi: 10.1002/eat.22728

Grigg, M., Bowman, J., & Redman, S. (1996). Disordered eating and unhealthy weight reduction practices among adolescent females. *Preventive Medicine, 25,* 748–756.

Hebebrand, J., Albayrak, O., Adan, R., Antel, J., Dieguez, C., de Jong, J., . . . Dickson, S. L. (2014). "Eating addiction", rather than "food addiction", better captures addictive-like eating behavior. *Neuroscience & Biobehavioral Reviews, 47*, 295–306.

Holland, G., & Tiggemann, M. (2016). A systematic review of the impact of the use of social networking sites on body image and disordered eating outcomes. *Body Image, 17*, 100–110. doi:10.1016/j.bodyim.2016.02.008

Hudson, J. I., Hiripi, E., Pope, H. G., & Kessler, R. C. (2007). The prevalence and correlates of eating disorders in the National Comorbidity Survey Replication. *Biological Psychiatry, 61*, 348–358.

Jacobi, C., Fittig, E., Bryson, S. W., Wilfley, D., Kraemer, H. C., & Taylor, C. B. (2011). Who is really at risk? Identifying risk factors for subthreshold and full syndrome eating disorders in a high-risk sample. *Psychological Medicine, 41*, 1939–1949.

Langdon-Daly, J., & Serpell, L. (2017). Protective factors against disordered eating in family systems: A systematic review of research. *Journal of Eating Disorders, 5*, 12. doi:10.1186/s40337-017-0141-7

Lázaro, L., Font, E., Moreno, E., Calvo, R., Vila, M., Andrés-Perpiñá, S., . . . Castro-Fornieles, J. (2011). Effectiveness of self-esteem and social skills group therapy in adolescent eating disorder patients attending a day hospital treatment programme. *European Eating Disorders Review, 19*, 398–406. doi:10.1002/erv.1054

Le Grange, D., Swanson, S. A., Crow, S. J., & Merikangas, K. R. (2012). Eating disorder not otherwise specified presentation in the US population. *International Journal of Eating Disorders, 45*, 711–718.

Leone, J. E., Sedory, E. J., & Gray, K. A. (2005). Recognition and treatment of muscle dysmorphia and related body image disorders. *Journal of Athletic Training, 40*, 352–359.

LeViness, P., Bershad, C., & Gorman, K. (2017). *The Association for University and College Counseling Center Directors annual survey*. Retrieved from https://www.aucccd.org/public

Lipson, S. K., Jones, M., Taylor, C. B., Wilfley, D. E., Fitzsimmons-Craft, E. F., & Eisenberg, D. (2017). Understanding and promoting treatment-seeking for eating disorders and body image concern on college campuses through online screening, prevention, and intervention. *Eating Behaviors, 25*, 68–73.

Marques, L., Alegria, M., Becker, A. E., Chen, C., Fang, A., Chosak, A., & Diniz, J. B. (2011). Comparative prevalence, correlates of impairment, and service utilization for eating disorders across US ethnic groups: Implications for reducing ethnic disparities in health care access for eating disorders. *International Journal of Eating Disorders, 44*, 412–420.

McLester, C. N., Hardin, R., & Hoppe, S. (2014). Susceptibility to eating disorders among collegiate female student-athletes. *Journal of Athletic Training, 49*, 406–410.

Mental Health America. (2018). Eating disorders. Retrieved from http://www.mentalhealthamerica.net/conditions/eating-disorders

Merikangas, K. R., He, J., Burstein, M., Swanson, S. A., Avenevoli, S., Cui, L., . . . Swendsen, J. (2010). Lifetime prevalence of mental disorders in US adolescents: Results from the national comorbidity study-adolescent supplement (NCS-A). *Journal of the American Academy of Child and Adolescent Psychiatry, 49*, 980–989. doi:10.1016/j.jaac.2010.05.017

National Alliance on Mental Illness. (2018). Eating disorders. Retrieved from https://www.nami.org/Learn-More/Mental-Health-Conditions/Eating-Disorders

National Eating Disorders Association. (2013). *Eating disorders on the college campus: A national survey of programs and resources*. Retrieved from https://www.nationaleatingdisorders.org/CollegiateSurveyProject.

National Eating Disorders Association. (2018). *Eating Disorders Screening Tool*. Retrieved from https://www.nationaleatingdisorders.org/screening-tool

National Eating Disorders Association. (2019). Orthorexia. Retrieved from https://www.nationaleatingdisorders.org/learn/by-eating-disorder/other/orthorexia

National Eating Disorders Collaboration. (2019). Risk and protective factors. Retrieved from https://nedc.com.au/eating-disorders/eating-disorders-explained/risk-and-protective-factors/

Ousley, L., Cordero, E. D., & White, S. (2008). Eating disorders and body image of undergraduate men. *Journal of American College Health, 56,* 617–622.

Patton, G. C., Selzer, R., Coffey, C., Carlin, J. B., & Wolfe, R. (1999). Onset of adolescent eating disorders: Population based cohort study over 3 years. *BMJ, 318,* 765–768. doi:10.1136/bmj.318.7186.765

Pursey, K. M., Stanwell, P., Gearhardt, A. N., Collins, C. E., & Burrows, T. L. (2014). The prevalence of food addiction as assessed by the Yale food addiction scale: A systematic review. *Nutrients, 6,* 4552–4590. doi: 10.3390/nu6104552

Quick, V. M., & Byrd-Bredbenner, C. (2013). Disturbed eating behaviours and associated psychographic characteristics of college students. *Journal of Human Nutrition and Dietetics, 26*(Suppl. 1), 53–63.

Randolph, T. G. (1956). The descriptive features of food addiction; addictive eating and drinking. *Quarterly Journal of Studies on Alcohol, 17,* 198–224.

Shisslak, C. M., Crago, M., & Estes, L. S. (1995). The spectrum of eating disturbances. *International Journal of Eating Disorders, 18,* 209–219.

Smink, F. E., van Hoeken, D., & Hoek, H. W. (2012). Epidemiology of eating disorders: Incidence, prevalence and mortality rates. *Current Psychiatry Reports, 14,* 406–414.

Striegel-Moore, R. H., & Franko, D. L. (2003). Epidemiology of binge eating disorder. *International Journal of Eating Disorders, 34*(Suppl. 1), S19–S29. doi:10.1002/eat.10202

Swanson, S. A., Crow, S. J., Le Grange, D., Swendsen, J., & Merikangas, K. R. (2011). Prevalence and correlates of eating disorders in adolescents: Results from the National Comorbidity Survey Replication Adolescent Supplement. *Archives of General Psychiatry, 68,* 714–723.

Tillman, K. S., Arbaugh, T., & Balaban, M. S. (2012). Campus programming for National Eating Disorders Awareness Week: An investigation of stigma, help-seeking, and resource knowledge. *Eating Behaviors, 13,* 281–284. doi:10.1016/j.eatbeh.2012.03.010

Ulfvebrand, S., Birgegard, A., Norring, C., Hogdahl, L., & von Hausswolff-Juhlin, Y. (2015). Psychiatric comorbidity in women and men with eating disorders results from a large clinical database. *Psychiatry Research, 230,* 294–299.

West, J., & Barrack, M. (2016). Prevalence and predictors of disordered eating among a diverse sample of college freshman. *Journal of the Academy of Nutrition and Dietetics, 116,* A57. doi:10.1016/j.jand.2016.06.196

Worell, J., & Goodheart, C. D. (2006). *Handbook of girls' and women's psychological health.* New York, NY: Oxford University Press.

Yu, Z., Indelicato, N. A., Fuglestad, P., Tan, M., Bane, L., & Stice, C. (2018). Sex differences in disordered eating and food addiction among college students. *Appetite, 129,* 12–18.

Yu, Z., & Tan, M. (2016). Disordered eating behaviors and food addiction among nutrition major college students. *Nutrients, 8,* 673. doi:10.3390/nu8110673

Zucker, T. (2017). Eating disorders vs. disordered eating: What's the difference? National Eating Disorders Association. Retrieved from https://www.nationaleatingdisorders.org/blog/eating-disorders-versus-disordered-eating

Chapter 21

Understanding and Responding to Self-Injury

Julia L. Whisenhunt

I can tell you that our bodies sometimes serve as
the symbolic ground where order and disorder fight for supremacy,
an uneasy divide that to some of us feels as porous and
inconstant as a frayed tatter of gauze. . . .
At any given moment, life is falling apart
as fast as we're shoring it up.

—Kettlewell, *Skin Game: A Memoir*

■ ■ ■

Reflection Exercise

Imagine for a moment that you are an 18-year-old female international student. You are in an unfamiliar country, surrounded by new people and learning to acclimate to a different set of cultural norms. You have always been an intelligent and resilient person, but this experience is proving overwhelming.

Following the birth of your younger brother, you and your family went through some major emotional challenges. Your brother's medical condition has been a consistent source of concern and financial stress for your family for several years. When your brother was first diagnosed, your parents were particularly preoccupied with him and with their own grief. As such, you felt a need to "handle" your emotions on your own. Everything built up for a while, and your old coping skills were not working any longer. One day, you discovered that physical pain distracted you from the emotional pain. That is when you started burning your skin. Your parents eventually found the burn marks and sent you to a mental health professional. Things improved, and you eventually stopped burning. However, the past few months have been more than you can take, and, knowing no other viable option, you start burning your skin again. This time, after 3 months of self-injury, you decide to seek help. The catalyst for your own help seeking was when you began having thoughts of suicide.

You have always known that self-injury has a high correlation with suicide, but burning has always been a coping skill for you. This change startled and concerned you. So, you scheduled an appointment with the counselor at your college counseling center.

The intake was a little uncomfortable, but you basically knew what to expect because of your previous experience in counseling. Now, you are meeting with your counselor for the first time, and he is asking several questions that are difficult to answer. He wants to know why you self-injure—what purpose it serves for you—and why other coping skills do not work. He is asking if you want to die. He is telling you that you have to stop burning yourself, or else he cannot work with you. He is telling you that you are smart and capable, and that there is no reason to self-injure.

1. How might you answer the first question and explain the coping function(s) of self-injury?
2. What can you tell your counselor about the relationship between self-injury and suicide?
3. What are your thoughts and feelings about the prospect of being unable to burn your skin to cope with your intense emotional pain? How might giving up burning right now affect your overall functioning?
4. What affective and cognitive reactions do you have to your counselor's compliments and attempts to reason with you regarding your self-injury?
5. Step out of your role as the client. As a college counselor or counselor-in-training, what is the counselor failing to do in the context of this therapeutic relationship? What are the risks of the counselor's current approach to the client? Are there any potential benefits to the counselor's current approach?

■ ■ ■

Most people reading this book are probably familiar with the concept of *nonsuicidal self-injury*, defined by the International Society for the Study of Self-Injury (n.d.) as "the deliberate, self-inflicted destruction of body tissue without suicidal intent and for purposes not socially sanctioned" (What Is Nonsuicidal Self-Injury?, para. 1). Nonsuicidal self-injury has gone by many different names across time and countries. Some of these terms have included *self-injury* (SI), *self-harm*, *deliberate self-harm*, *self-cutting*, and *self-mutilation*. In my professional work, I prefer to use the term SI, rather than nonsuicidal self-injury, because I assume that SI is neither suicidal nor nonsuicidal; I believe the comorbid presence of suicide risk is a fluid matter that has to be continually assessed within a clinical context, and that it is ill-advised to assume either the presence or absence of suicide risk in clients who self-injure. As such, throughout this chapter, I will use the term SI. As you can readily imagine, then, one limitation with the research and literature on SI is the lack of consensus in the terminology and what that terminology indicates. For instance, in many research studies, the term *self-harm* indicates both SI and suicide attempts. It is important to remember this key fact about terminology because, as counselors consume the literature, we must be aware of the ways researchers define SI so that we can understand the applicability of their findings to our own work. In other words, if researchers are referring to factors that elevate risk in people who self-harm (and those researchers combine both SI and suicide attempts into their category of self-harm), the applicability of those findings to our work with nonsuicidal clients who self-injure may be limited.

Prevalence of Self-Injury Among College Students

More times than I can count, counselors have told me that they have never worked with a client who self-injures. In reality, most counselors will eventually work with clients who self-injure, even if they do not realize it. In fact, there is an approximate lifetime prevalence of 18.0% for SI (Muehlenkamp, Claes, Havertape, & Plener, 2012), with research indicating a rate of 15% (Kakhnovets, Young, Purnell, Huebner, & Bishop, 2010) to 17% (Whitlock, Eckenrode, & Silverman, 2006) in college student samples. Not everyone who self-injures once will continue to self-injure. In fact, Kakhnovets and colleagues (2010) found that approximately 4% of their sample self-injured once, whereas 11% self-injured multiple times. Not surprisingly, people who self-injure multiple times tend to have higher rates of suicidal ideation, trauma, and drug and alcohol misuse (Kakhnovets et al., 2010). In addition, it appears that people who self-injure more often and use more methods may be at higher risk for suicide (Wester, Ivers, Villalba, Trepal, & Henson, 2016). It is easy to see, then, that SI is relatively common in the college setting and, as such, all college counselors should be equipped to therapeutically address SI and monitor for its associated risks.

Although there are certain groups of people who are most at-risk for SI, clients of any gender, race, ethnicity, age, or sexual orientation may self-injure. At one time, SI was thought to occur largely in White females, but more recent researchers have reported similar prevalence rates for males and females (e.g., Andover, Pepper, & Gibb, 2007; Lloyd-Richardson, Perrine, Dierker, & Kelley, 2007) and relatively high rates among African American (Hankin & Abela, 2011), Latina/o, Native American, and multiracial (Wester & Trepal, 2015) adolescents. Age is another important factor. SI tends to be most common in adolescents, with a typical age of onset of around 13 to 14 years old (see Klonsky, Victor, & Saffer, 2014). Additionally, adolescents who identify as a lesbian, gay, bisexual, transgender, queer, or intersex minority tend to have elevated rates of SI (Reisner, Biello, Perry, Gamarel, & Mimiaga, 2014). Although many students may begin self-injuring during high school, a large portion of them may continue self-injuring into college.

Types and Functions of Self-Injury

The reasons people first turn to SI are unclear. Some clients may talk about having the spontaneous idea to harm themselves without fatal intent. Others may say that they heard about it somewhere and decided to see if it would work for them. Still, some clients report that they accidentally injured themselves while in a distressed state and found that it helped them. As counselors, we may not know the reasons clients turn to SI, but we can seek to understand what SI means for our individual clients. In so doing, it is important to consider the many ways in which people self-injure. For some people, SI is very ritualistic and controlled. For others, SI is impulsive, or perhaps addictive.

The most common type of SI is cutting (Chapman & Dixon-Gordon, 2007; Muehlenkamp & Gutierrez, 2004; Trepal & Wester, 2007), but people who self-injure may also hit themselves (Chapman & Dixon-Gordon, 2007; Muehlenkamp & Gutierrez, 2004; Trepal & Wester, 2007), burn themselves, scratch or pick at their skin, interfere with the healing of their wounds (Muehlenkamp & Gutierrez, 2004), swallow objects, or bang their head (Trepal & Wester, 2007; Whitlock et al., 2006). There are many other, albeit less common, ways to self-injure. People who self-injure may do so on any part of the body, although areas that are easy to cover and disguise, such as the arms, hands, wrists, thighs, stomach, calves, head, and fingers, tend to be most common (Whitlock et al., 2006). Many people who self-injure use more than one method. If one method does not effectively work to regulate their emotional distress, they may transition to another method. In a sample of almost 37,000 students across eight universities in the United States, Whitlock and colleagues (2011) found that 63% of participants who self-injured used more than one form of SI, with two forms of SI being the most common.

Although there do not appear to be any definitive gender differences in SI methods, gender should be considered when discussing SI with clients. Some self-injurious behaviors may be considered more socially accepted for males than for females (e.g., carving images and letters into the skin, burning skin, hitting walls) and, thereby, less likely to be identified as problematic or self-injurious in nature. As such, counselors should be clear and provide examples when screening for and discussing SI. Remember, however, that ways in which people self-injure are very unique to them individually and, as such, counselors should avoid making assumptions about a student's SI without talking directly to that student in a respectful manner.

Some counselors tend to ask clients to show their wounds. Although there may be some settings and situations in which this is advisable (e.g., counselors working in patient advocate roles within a campus-based medical facility; counselors who hold appropriate medical training to evaluate medical severity), I generally advise against this for a number of reasons. First, if the counselor is not trained in medicine, any assessment that counselor makes about the wound could be considered outside of the counselor's bounds of competence. Second, SI is typically a very private experience for clients, and asking them to reveal their wounds can feel invasive and shameful. Third, some of the parts of the body on which clients self-injure are inappropriate for counselors to see. Rather than asking students to put their wounds on display, it is more advisable to ask them to describe their wounds, the locations on which they self-injure, their wound care practices, and the instruments they use for self-injuring. This information is important to collect so that counselors can know how deeply students are injuring themselves and in what locations, so they can get a better idea about the risk of unintentional severe SI. Counselors also need to know how carefully they care for their wounds and what types of instruments they use to wound their skin, so that counselors can determine the need for medical referral and psychoeducation about disinfection of instruments and wound care. When collecting this information, counselors should avoid allowing students to romanticize their SI or go into unnecessary detail that could retrigger them to self-injure. Just as in trauma therapy, there is a fine line between gathering necessary information and triggering or retraumatizing a client.

SI can, in many ways, be considered a coping skill. This may be difficult for people who have never self-injured to understand, but it remains that people who self-injure often report feeling better—calmer, relieved, more in control—after they self-injure. In fact, although SI was once conceptualized as an addictive process, researchers have indicated that SI is more related to emotion regulation than to addiction (Victor, Glenn, & Klonsky, 2012). Chapman and Dixon-Gordon (2007) conducted research on the emotional antecedents and consequences of both SI and suicide attempts. They found that anger tends to precede, but diminishes following, SI, and that relief is a common emotional consequence of self-injuring. Their research exemplifies the emotion regulation function of SI—that SI helps some people to cope with intense emotional distress. Although it is true that many people injure themselves to help regulate their emotions, there are other functions of SI. David Klonsky is a leader in the field of SI research. He reviewed the available research on SI and found six most common functions of SI. These include the following: (a) emotion regulation, (b) self-punishment, (c) anti-suicide/life preserving, (d) feeling generation/anti-dissociation, (e) interpersonal influence and communication, and (f) sensation seeking (Klonsky, 2014). Let's explore each of these in a little more detail.

It is sometimes the case that people who self-injure experience alexithymia—difficulty identifying and describing their emotions (Norman & Borrill, 2015). Therefore, it stands to reason that people who self-injure may struggle to express their emotions when they feel hurt, scared, anxious, or out of control. For reasons that we do not yet entirely understand, reasons that may be neurophysiological in nature, hurting one's own body helps some people to regulate those intense emotions and feel calmer, relieved, or in control. In fact, Nock, Prinstein, and Sterba (2010) found that a large portion of adolescents may self-injure to help them manage anxiety, sadness, anger, bad thoughts, and painful memories. This is the basis for the most common function of SI—*emotion regulation*. Similarly, when people who self-injure become upset with themselves, they may use SI as a form of *self-punishment*. It may be that they punish themselves for large trespasses, but it is common for people who self-injure to be very self-critical and self-persecutory (Gilbert et al., 2010). So, they feel particularly upset with themselves over very small mistakes or even perceived mistakes. To this point, Nock et al. (2010) found that anger toward self and self-hatred were significantly connected to self-injurious behavior for adolescents. *Anti-suicide* is a function that may, on the surface, be difficult to understand. Because SI is so effective in helping some people cope with intense feelings, it can actually be life preserving in that it helps them to manage painful feelings without resorting to suicide. SI may, in fact, be the only coping skill that helps them to make it through challenging life experiences. When I first learned about SI, I often heard from students and clients about the *feeling generation* or *anti-dissociation* effects. Indeed, this is a relatively common function of SI, albeit less common than the three we have already covered. For some people who feel disconnected from the world (i.e., derealization) or from their own body (i.e., depersonalization), the pain inflicted during SI or the sight of their own blood can help them feel "real" or "connected" again. Research conducted by Nock et al. (2010) yielded support for this function of SI in adolescents, specifically in that feelings of numbness or feeling nothing tended to trigger SI behavior within their participant sample. Although SI has often been conceptualized as manipulative in nature, most people who self-injure do not seek to hurt or manipulate others. Rather, the *interpersonal influence and communication* function of SI is largely related to the person's attempts to help others understand their distress—to say through their body what they cannot say through their words. For adolescents, feelings of social rejection and anger toward other people may trigger self-injurious thoughts and behaviors (Nock et al., 2010). It is important to remember that many, if not most, people who self-injure do so privately and do not seek to use their SI as a means of interpersonal influence or communication. Finally, some people who self-injure may feel exhilarated or some other type of positive physical or psychological sensation—like a thrill. In these cases, we consider the function of SI to be *sensation seeking*. This is a relatively uncommon function of SI. It is important to note, however, that SI can serve more than one function for a single person, and that the functions may change over time. That is why it is very important to talk candidly with clients who self-injure and conduct what we call a *functional analysis of SI*. We will talk more about that later.

Suicide and Self-Injury: Similarities and Differences

Approximately 61% of people who self-injure also engage in suicide behavior (Whitlock et al., 2013). Accordingly, there appears to be some type of connection between SI and suicide, the nature of which remains largely unclear. In short, there are three primary hypotheses. Hamza, Stewart, and Willoughby (2012) provided a nice summary of these three explanatory models for the high risk of suicide in people who self-injure, all three of which are well-grounded in the research and literature.

The first model is the *gateway model*, which basically states that SI and suicide exist on a continuum, and SI is a precursor to suicide. Consider a person who experiences high levels of emotional distress. As those levels of distress continue to rise or fail to dissipate, the person may eventually feel that SI is no longer helping him or her to cope and may determine that suicide is the only pathway out of distress. Hamza et al. (2012) pointed to the elevated risk of suicide among people who self-injure, particularly among people who frequently self-injure, as possible support for this model.

The second model is the *third-variable theory.* This model assumes that there is some third variable that accounts for the high correlation between SI and suicide. Rather than SI and suicide being related, this model basically states that there is something else (a third variable) that SI and suicide have in common. According to the model, it is this third variable or common factor that actually increases the risk for suicide in people who self-injure, rather than the SI itself being the cause of the increased suicide risk. Rather than SI and suicide being related, it may be that they are simply both strong indicators of psychological distress.

The third model, *acquired capability for suicide,* is based on Joiner's (2005) interpersonal-psychological theory of suicidal behavior. In short, Joiner's theory states that the highest risk for suicide occurs when a person simultaneously feels like a burden to others, feels socially alienated or lacks a sense of belongingness, and has the acquired capability to inflict fatal harm to himself or herself. Joiner's theory further posits that, when people engage in self-injurious acts or are repeatedly exposed to pain and death, those people build a tolerance to physical pain and the idea of harming themselves. This tolerance thereby develops into a capability for inflicting fatal harm to self (Joiner, 2005). As such, people who self-injure and experience a perceived sense of burdensomeness and lack of belonging are, according to this model, those individuals who are most at risk for suicide. However, not all individuals who self-injure may feel like a burden or feel isolated and, according to the model, may not be at present risk for suicide. For each of these models, there are confirmatory or supportive research findings, limitations, and contradictory research findings, which Hamza et al. (2012) summarized.

So, although we have three promising models that help us, as counselors, to conceptualize the reason for high rates of suicide in people who self-injure, we have yet to identify a single model that fully explains the nature of this relationship. Nonetheless, the research conducted in pursuit of a single model has yielded some very important findings that can help professional counselors to better understand the experience of SI and the suffering that precedes suicide. Table 21.1 provides a summary of some notable distinctions between

TABLE 21.1

Comparisons of Self-Injury and Suicide

Self-Injury	*Suicide*
Nonlethal intent (Klonsky, Muehlenkamp, Lewis, & Walsh, 2011)	Lethal intent (Klonsky et al., 2011)
Typically less severe physical damage (Klonsky et al., 2011)	Typically more severe physical damage (Klonsky et al., 2011)
Typically frequent (Klonsky et al., 2011)	Typically infrequent (Klonsky et al., 2011)
Typically less repulsed by life—more positive outlook on life (Muehlenkamp & Gutierrez, 2004)	Typically more repulsed by life—less positive outlook on life (Muehlenkamp & Gutierrez, 2004)
Anger precedes but diminishes following self-injury; relief is a common emotional consequence (Chapman & Dixon-Gordon, 2007)	Anger precedes and increases following suicide attempt; guilt is a common emotional consequence (Chapman & Dixon-Gordon, 2007)
Can often identify reasons for living (Muehlenkamp & Gutierrez, 2007)	May be unable to identify reasons for living, or may identify few reasons for living (Muehlenkamp & Gutierrez, 2007)
Self-injury thoughts may be more intense and briefer (Nock, Prinstein, & Sterba, 2010)	Suicide thoughts may be less intense but pervasive (Nock et al., 2010)

SI and suicide. Although this table is not comprehensive, it demonstrates some of the major conceptual and practical distinctions between these two phenomena (see Table 21.1).

Researchers have uncovered a number of factors that can increase the risk for suicide in people who self-injure. These include, but are not limited to, the following: (a) the use of websites that encourage SI (Mitchell, Wells, Priebe, & Ybarra, 2014; see Lewis, Heath, Michal, & Duggan, 2012); (b) a sense of hopelessness (Chapman, Gratz, & Turner, 2014); (c) critical self-talk (Gilbert et al., 2010); (d) distorted self-image (Kerr & Muehlenkamp, 2010); (e) repeated SI (Kakhnovets et al., 2010); (f) childhood sexual abuse (Chapman et al., 2014); (g) use of multiple SI methods (Wester et al., 2016); (h) history of alcohol use, alongside current depression (Jenkins, Singer, Conner, Calhoun, & Diamond, 2014); and (i) for adolescents, peer victimization (see Heilbron & Prinstein, 2010). Another factor to remember when considering the relationship between SI and suicide is unintentional fatal or severe SI. For some people who self-injure, unintentionally severe SI occurs. In fact, unintentional severe SI may occur in as much as 31% of people who self-injure (Buser, Buser, & Rutt, 2017). Factors that tend to increase unintentional severe SI include the addictive properties of SI and possibly, to a lesser degree, impulsivity (Buser et al., 2017). Taking all of this into consideration, it is critically important that professional counselors talk openly and honestly with their clients about SI, factors that trigger self-injurious thoughts, past events and habits that may perpetuate SI, and indications that their level of distress is rising above that which SI can help them to manage.

Signs and Symptoms of Self-Injury

Although every college counselor should screen for SI at intake, it is also helpful to pay attention to possible indications of SI. Janis Whitlock is one of the founders of the International Society for the Study of Self-Injury and is also a key leader in the field of SI research. Her team at Cornell University has created a website, Self-Injury and Recovery Research and Resources, which contains a wealth of information regarding SI, including resources for people who self-injure, parents, and mental health professionals. Among those resources is information about possible signs of SI. Ernhout and Whitlock (2014) suggested that mental health professionals and parents consider the possibility of SI when they observe the following: (a) having cuts, burns, or other unexplained injuries to the skin; (b) having supplies of cutting instruments and rubber bands; (c) spending long times alone, particularly in bedroom and bathroom; and (d) wearing clothing that is inappropriate for the weather. In addition, Ernhout and Whitlock (2014) suggested the following as possible indicators of SI: (a) refusing to participate in events or activities wherein others could observe their skin, (b) frequently using bandages and/or accessories that can hide wounds, (c) consistently using wristbands or other accessories that could hide injuries, and (d) talking about friends who self-injure. When college counselors notice these possible signs, they should talk with their student or client openly and respectfully about SI. However, in so doing, it is critically important that counselors appreciate the often private and sensitive nature of SI. We must approach these conversations with care, patience, and understanding. The Self-Injury and Recovery Research and Resources website provides video accounts from clients and parents about the ways in which these conversations can be done well and the common pitfalls to having a successful conversation about SI.

Clinical Implications: Assessment and Treatment

Given the often private nature of SI, the intense distress that underlies it, and the social stigma of SI, it is no surprise that building therapeutic rapport with students who self-injure can be challenging. Students who self-injure may be reticent to seek professional support (Whitlock et al., 2006). As such, college counselors are tasked with approaching treatment with students who self-injure in a way that is sensitive and nonjudgmental (see Whisenhunt et al., 2014, 2015). It is from the context of that therapeutic relationship that assessment and treatment can take place.

Assessment of Self-Injury

Assessment of SI should begin at intake with a screening for SI with each client. One instrument that can be helpful to achieve this is the Deliberate Self-Harm Inventory (Gratz, 2001). The Deliberate Self-Harm Inventory is a 17-item self-report measure that screens for the presence of SI, age of onset, duration, frequency, and severity. The Deliberate Self-Harm Inventory begins with a question to address the presence of SI: "Have you ever intentionally (i.e., on purpose) cut your wrist, arms, or other area(s) of your body (without intending to kill yourself)?" (Gratz, 2001, p. 262). If clients respond affirmatively to this item, they are asked to respond to an additional 16 questions that address the types of SI in which they have engaged. Once SI is indicated, college counselors can then pursue the process of learning more about the client's unique experience of SI and the function(s) SI serves for that client. I recommend beginning with a functional analysis. Klonsky et al. (2011) described a functional analysis/assessment as a means of "identifying factors that motivate and reinforce" SI (p. 41). To accomplish this, counselors can talk with clients about the feelings, thoughts, and events that precede, accompany, and follow their self-injurious episodes. Because SI can serve multiple functions for any given client, it is important to talk about different self-injurious episodes. Walsh (2014) recommended a similar process. The components of his informal SI assessment include the following: (a) environmental antecedents/triggers, (b) biological antecedents, (c) intrapersonal antecedents, (d) strength of urges, (e) number of wounds, (f) start and end time of each SI episode, (g) physical pain, (h) extent of physical damage, and (i) locations of SI. These informal approaches to understanding the client's SI are helpful, but there are also formal assessment tools that evaluate functions. The Inventory of Statements About Self-Injury (Klonsky & Glenn, 2009) is a well-regarded SI assessment tool. It is 46 items and includes 13 function scales. The Non-Suicidal Self-Injury–Assessment Tool (Whitlock, Exner-Cortens, & Purington, 2014) is an online assessment tool that consists of 12 modules that cover various factors related to motivations and functions, recency and frequency, onset, wounds, patterns or rituals, severity, habituation, treatment history, disclosures, and reflections and advice. It is vitally important to understand the functions of SI, so that counseling can address ways to mitigate SI triggers, resolve or diminish underlying motivations, and align positive coping skills to eventually replace SI. See Box 21.1 for an example of functional analysis questions.

In consideration of the elevated risk of suicide in people who self-injure (Toprak, Cetin, Guven, Can, & Demircan, 2011; Whitlock et al., 2013), assessment of suicide should be a standard practice when working with all clients who self-injure—both at intake and as indicated throughout the therapeutic process. As with all clients, suicide risk assessment should occur at standard intervals and as indications of risk arise. However, counselors should avoid assuming that all clients who self-injure are suicidal, in that this assumption can be inaccurate and potentially interfere with treatment for some clients. When one is assessing for suicide with clients who self-injure, there are a few helpful instruments. The Brief Severity Index for Nonsuicidal Self-Injury (Buser, Peterson, & Hill, 2016) is a newer tool that is early in the validation process. However, it shows promise for assessing the severity of SI. Although not directly related to suicide, this instrument may help counselors ascertain severity, which we know is related to unintentional severe SI and

BOX 21.1

Functional Analysis Questions

I am going to ask you some questions about your self-injury (SI) to help us gain a better understanding of the functions SI serves for you. These questions may be uncomfortable; we can go at a pace that works for you. If, during our conversation, you begin feeling the need to self-injure, please tell me. We will practice some grounding skills to help you reorient to the present moment, and we will slow down to help avoid you feeling overwhelmed by this process.

Think about the last time you self-injured; what happened prior to the SI that may have led you to want to self-injure?

Pretend as if you are describing for me a scene in a movie; in other words, we will stick to what happened, rather than your judgments about what happened. Tell me about your last self-injurious episode by explaining the things that happened before, during, and after the SI. Include information about anything that happened in your environment, physical sensations you had, and your feelings and thoughts. It can sometimes be difficult to label your feelings. If so, help me understand what sensations you had in your body (e.g., racing heart, sweating, clammy skin, numbness) and what you were doing physically (e.g., pacing, clinching your wrist, crying, staring into space). We will do these one at a time, starting with the time prior to the SI, then we will talk about during the SI, followed by the time after the SI.

Now, we will do this again with another self-injurious episode. Sometimes, the experience is different for various episodes of SI. Therefore, I want to make sure that we have a full picture of what you are experiencing.

What do you notice that is different for you after you self-injure? Consider the things you think and feel, as well as the way you interact with others and the way they interact with you.

suicide. The Self-Injurious Thoughts and Behaviors Interview (Nock, Holmberg, Photos, & Michel, 2007) is well-known in the SI literature. The Self-Injurious Thoughts and Behaviors Interview is a 169-item structured interview (also available in a 72-item short-form) that measures suicidal ideation, suicide plans, suicide gestures, suicide attempts, and SI. It also asks participants to identify their means of SI. The Suicide Attempt Self-Injury Interview (Linehan, Comtois, Brown, Heard, & Wagner, 2006) was developed, in part, by the originator of dialectical behavior therapy—Dr. Marsha Linehan. The Suicide Attempt Self-Injury Interview is a 37-item structured interview that includes six scales: Suicide Intent, Interpersonal Influence, Emotion Relief, Suicide Communication, Lethality, and Rescue Likelihood. Additionally, counselors may choose to use traditional suicide screening and assessment tools, such as the Columbia Suicide Severity Rating Scale (Posner et al., 2011), the Suicidal Behaviors Questionnaire–Revised (Osman et al., 2001), the Beck Scale for Suicide Ideation (Beck, 1991), or the Suicide Probability Scale (Cull & Gill,1982).

Treatment of Self-Injury

There are no well-established treatments for SI at this time (Flaherty, 2018; Glenn, Franklin, & Nock, 2015). However, specific variations of the following treatments show promise: Cognitive behavioral therapy, family-based therapy, interpersonal psychotherapy, and psychodynamic therapy (see Glenn et al., 2015). There is competing evidence surrounding the efficacy of dialectical behavior therapy in treating SI (see Glenn et al., 2015; Hunnicutt Hollenbaugh & Lenz, 2018). However, some research supports dialectical behavior therapy as potentially effective for addressing SI (see Barley et al., 1993; Harned, Jackson, Comtois,

& Linehan, 2010; Harned, Korslund, Foa, & Linehan, 2011; Muehlenkamp, 2006; Pistorello, Fruzzetti, MacLane, Gallop, & Iverson, 2012; Shearin & Linehan, 1994; Van Goethem, Mulders, Muris, Artnz, & Egger, 2012). In general, Glenn et al. (2015) stated that efficacious treatments for SI in adolescents should (a) focus on relationships and interpersonal functioning, (b) involve skills training, (c) address other maladaptive behaviors, and (d) be intensive. In addition, I suggest working to address underlying risk factors and enhance protective factors.

As with any therapeutic approach, when working with clients who self-injure, it is important to begin the therapeutic process by conducting a comprehensive psychosocial intake, using appropriate risk assessments and identifying relevant treatment goals (Flaherty, 2018). Perhaps one of the most important goals of therapy should surround helping clients who self-injure to develop or enhance their support system. We know that poor family relationships increase the risk for SI (Toprak et al., 2011; Wester et al., 2016) and that certain variations of family therapy, or involving family in the treatment of SI, can yield positive results (see Glenn et al., 2015). Moreover, it can be difficult for some clients who self-injure to use social supports as a means of coping (Andover et al., 2007). As such, when possible, therapeutic goals may address helping the client to develop a positive and healthy support system. This may involve building a new support system or enhancing the client's present relationships. When appropriate, it may be helpful to use a family systems approach to address the underlying contributors to SI and support a healthy family dynamic (Miner, Love, & Paik, 2016). Other practical ways this exploration of potential interpersonal factors related to SI and work to enhance the client's support system could manifest might include the following: (a) using a genogram to identify individuals and patterns in the client's support system (including trusted friends, professors, and student support staff on campus), (b) teaching the client assertiveness skills and conflict resolution skills, (c) teaching the client reflective listening skills, (d) role-playing difficult anticipated conversations, (e) conducting family sessions or sessions with trusted loved ones, (f) and providing psychoeducational content on SI to family members and people within the student's support system. Students who do not have a supportive biological family may prefer to involve or focus their attention on their "chosen family." College counselors may need to acquire additional consent to work with nonbiological loved ones but can integrate trusted support persons into the therapeutic process as a means of promoting healthy relationships and a sense of belonging within their students.

In addition to helping the client to develop healthy interpersonal skills, training for other skills may help to address SI. For instance, we know that SI is a coping skill for many people. As such, working with clients to develop or enhance active coping skills may be helpful, as active coping appears to be inversely related to SI (Andover et al., 2007; Chapman et al., 2014). Oftentimes, it is useful to try to match coping skills to the functions SI serves for the client. So, for instance, if SI helps the person to avoid depersonalization, exercise might be useful to help the client feel real again. Likewise, if SI helps the person to regulate emotions, mindful breathing or visualization techniques might be useful substitutes. Kilburn and Whitlock (2009) of the Cornell Research Program on Self-Injury and Recovery suggested a number of active coping strategies that can be used to match the functions of SI, such as coping strategies for feelings of anger, depression or sadness, self-blame or guilt, and emptiness or feeling unreal.

It is important to remember, however, that SI may be the client's only effective coping skill. In fact, many people who self-injure report that they have tried multiple means of coping, and none of them have been as effective as SI. I have even had people tell me that SI is the way they manage suicidal ideation and avoid taking their life. For this reason, it can be risky to ask clients to cease self-injuring entirely prior to developing other skills that help them manage intense thoughts and/or feelings. Naturally, when clients engage in severe or dangerous SI methods, counselors should not endorse the continuation of those SI methods. However, they may work with clients to identify ways to minimize risk and harm and explore other methods that do not result in tissue damage. Altering SI methods is not the end goal of counseling, however; this approach should only be considered a temporary means of reducing risk while the client works to develop non-self-injurious coping skills. This can be a challenging process that can involve both risk to the client and professional risk, because the client continues to self-injure. Counselors must weigh the risk of taking away SI, compared with the risk of using SI methods that are nonsevere for a time-limited period. Oftentimes, the latter is the preferred option, as ceasing SI in the absence of other means of coping can escalate distress and potentially increase suicide risk. However, an additional approach that may help to reduce the frequency and/or severity of SI involves teaching clients emotion regulation strategies to delay SI. This approach does not take SI entirely away from the client prior to his or her developing other coping skills, but it teaches the client to use other methods to manage intense emotions, rather than relying solely on SI. Although clients may continue to self-injure using this approach, they may find that the intensity of their distress preceding SI is somewhat diminished, which could lower the risk of accidental severe SI. As with all professional counseling issues that involve significant risk to client and counselor, supervision and consultation are advised. Indeed, this is perhaps one of the most important lessons for counselors to learn about working with clients who self-injure: Use supervision and consultation to help support an appropriate, respectful, and evidence-based approach to treating clients who self-injure.

People who self-injure may struggle to use problem-solving as a means of coping with emotional distress (Andover et al., 2007). As such, it may also be helpful to help clients who self-injure to develop problem-solving skills (Andover et al., 2007) and learn to enhance positive emotions (Morris, Simpson, Sampson, & Beesley, 2014). Problem-solving therapy is a form of cognitive behavioral therapy that has demonstrated utility in the treatment of SI (Hatcher, Sharon, Parag, & Collins, 2011; Muehlenkamp, 2006) and may be one approach for helping clients to develop problem-solving skills.

Some other factors that might influence SI include, but certainly are not limited to, having a high external locus of control (Wester et al., 2016), having maladaptive cognitive patterns that contribute to hopelessness (Chapman et al., 2014) and distorted self-image, and using websites that encourage SI (see Lewis et al., 2012; Mitchell et al., 2014). Cognitive behavioral therapy can be useful in addressing locus of control, maladaptive cognitive patterns, and body image. Positive affirmations and thought substitution are two means of working to address distorted self-image. Related to self-image, counselors may work to support clients' identity exploration beyond SI, given that SI may be one means that adolescents use to manage identity confusion (Claes, Luyckx, & Bijttebier, 2014). For some clients who self-injure, SI may become an integral part of their identity and the prospect of ceasing SI can, therefore, evoke anxiety. Additionally, it might be helpful to explore with clients ways that they can minimize their exposure to triggers, such as those that are environmental, inter- and intrapersonal, and physiological (Walsh, 2014). Using the findings of a functional analysis of SI (Klonsky et al., 2011) can help clients develop plans for minimizing exposure to SI triggers. With adolescents, it is particularly important to also address contextual and social factors surrounding SI (Voon, Hasking, & Martin, 2014) because those factors may trigger and/or exacerbate SI. There are multiple ways to manage these therapeutic issues, and I have already discussed a few of those, but I also want to suggest creative counseling interventions as one means of addressing SI (see Whisenhunt & Kress, 2013). I believe that creative counseling interventions have great utility with clients who self-injure, in part because those clients may experience alexithymia and, therefore, have difficulty expressing their internal state through words. However, creative counseling must be approached with competence and care; recreational arts are not equivalent to the therapeutic application of art and creativity.

A relatively new concern in the treatment of SI surrounds clients' consumption of popular media and/or use of websites that encourage and glamorize SI, and even instruct people in how to self-injure. In recent years, SI has entered, at least in part, into mainstream culture and is being talked about with increasing frequency. Research is not yet available on the effects of media portrayals of SI. However, research reveals that websites that encourage SI can exacerbate both SI and suicidal thoughts (Mitchell et al., 2014). Mitchell and colleagues (2014) found that approximately 16% of adolescents who reported past self-injurious thoughts visit SI/suicide websites. This subgroup of adolescents was also more likely to experience depressive symptoms, abuse, and sexual trauma. Moreover, they were more likely to engage in delinquent behavior, substance use, and SI behavior (Mitchell et al., 2014). Lewis and Seko (2015) reviewed the literature on the topic of online SI activity to identify risks and benefits of this behavior. They found evidence of three potential risks of engaging in online SI activities. These include the following: (a) reinforcing SI (e.g., normalizing SI as a viable coping skill, minimizing the risks of SI, encouraging SI, discouraging professional help seeking, characterizing SI as a helpless struggle or addiction, portraying competition between people who self-injure, encouraging more SI to be considered a legitimate self-injurer, teaching strategies that maintain SI), (b) triggering SI (e.g., viewing videos or written content, resulting in increased urges and/or actual SI; intentionally searching for graphic content), and (c) perpetuating SI stigma (e.g., making harassing, demeaning, and hateful comments about people who self-injure; minimizing distress associated with SI; promoting misinformation about SI; Lewis & Seko, 2015). Conversely, they found that the research supports four potential benefits to engaging in online SI activities. These include the following: (a) reducing isolation and enhancing social support (e.g., disclosing their SI to others, rather than keeping it private; sharing a common experience with nonjudgmental others; mitigating feelings of aloneness), (b) supporting healing and recovery (e.g., serving as a support in the absence of counseling/therapy, providing encouragement to diminish or cease SI, providing encouragement to seek professional help, providing accurate information about SI), (c) fostering emotional expression (e.g., cathartic expressions, disinhibited disclosure of thoughts and feelings), and (d) minimizing urges to self-injure (e.g., distraction from SI urges, self-soothing function of viewing others' SI photos). The role of media and SI websites in the initiation and maintenance of SI is still unclear and probably varies for each client. There are, however, some marked risks and potential benefits that certainly need to be explored with each client.

In consideration of these findings, college counselors should be knowledgeable of SI websites and prepared to talk with students about the potential benefits and risks associated with using the websites. Specifically, counselors may seek to help clients address the needs they have related to engaging in online SI activities. For instance, on the basis of the results of their methodical review of the literature, Lewis and Seko (2015) advised that counselors work with clients who self-injure to identify other means of establishing social support and provide clients with psychoeducation about SI or access to accurate information about SI. College counselors may also help clients identify strategies for expression of their emotions, outside of counseling sessions, without fear of judgment or hurting others. Moreover, counselors can work with students to minimize the negative effects of engaging in online SI activities through using sites that do not minimize SI, include triggering content, or promote stereotypes or derogation of people who self-injure. Being able to work with students who use SI websites requires that college counselors be familiar with the websites and sufficiently versed in ways that technology can be adapted to enhance the therapeutic functions and minimize the challenges. This is particularly important on college campuses, in a time during which 88% of 18- to 29-year-olds report the regular use of some form of social media (Pew Research Center, 2018).

There are a number of risk factors for SI, but a few stand out as most appropriate for therapeutic intervention. Trauma is often correlated with SI (see Kakhnovets et al., 2010), and, as such, it is advisable to both screen for trauma and address it therapeutically when present. In consideration of the link between alexithymia and SI (Norman & Borrill, 2015) and the fact that emotion regulation is the most common function of SI (Klonsky, 2014), college counselors may seek to help clients who self-injure develop their ability to identify, express, and regulate their emotions. Dialectical behavior therapy is well-known for its emphasis on emotion regulation, particularly related to treating clients who are diagnosed with borderline personality disorder and who self-injure (see Rizvi, Hughes, & Thomas, 2016; Van Goethem et al., 2012). Additionally, given that substance misuse tends to increase risk for suicide (Toprak et al., 2011), it is important to work with clients who self-injure to address issues of substance misuse or abuse. These are only a few risk factors that might be relevant to treatment. As college counselors uncover clients' unique risk factors, they may consider incorporating strengths-based therapeutic interventions to help counter the potentially harmful effects of these risk factors. This could include developing a safety plan to help the client identify strategies for countering distress at the different levels, from first thoughts of SI to suicide impulses.

The standard components of a safety plan include identification of the following: (a) warning signs of deteriorated functioning or increased suicide risk, (b) internal coping strategies that can be used to manage distress, (c) people and social situations that can help distract from the distress, (d) people who can help, (e) professionals and agencies that can assist during times of emotional distress or crisis (see Stanley & Brown, 2012), and (f) ways to make the environment safer or otherwise limit access to lethal means. Stanley and Brown (2012) and the Suicide Prevention Resource Center have provided useful outlines for the content that should be included in a safety plan. In a college counseling context, sources of support may include staff, counseling center and medical personnel, and the student's social support system. Use of a collaborative approach between campus partners can help to insulate students from risk and improve treatment efficacy.

Additionally, the wellness approach to counseling offers a means of helping clients to enhance their protective factors and, thereby, diminish their reliance on SI. Juhnke, Granello, and Granello (2011) identified a number of protective factors for SI. These include being able to identify and express negative emotions, having supportive parents, having parent engagement in treatment, having appropriate adult role models, engaging in healthy social outlets and having a positive social support system, and having access to mental health assistance. Relatedly, Toprak et al. (2011) found that having a romantic partner can serve as a protective factor to SI. Largely, these protective factors center around positive and supportive relationships, a sense of belonging, and the ability to identify and express negative or painful thoughts and feelings. Naturally, the therapeutic process can be a means of enhancing these protective factors, perhaps in conjunction with addressing the aforementioned risk factors.

Finally, the topic of group counseling with clients who self-injure is important to address. There are mixed opinions about social contagion as it relates to SI. Generally speaking, SI researchers and clinicians advise against using a group format for the treatment of SI (Bubrick, Goodman, & Whitlock, n.d.; Walsh & Muehlenkamp, 2013). One major exception to this rule is in regard to skills training groups (Richardson, Surmitis, & Hyldahl, 2012; Walsh & Muehlenkamp, 2013). However, counseling centers that choose to organize an SI support group may want to consider the following recommendations. First, the counselor leading the group should be well trained in SI and fully competent to address both SI and contagion (Richardson et al., 2012). The group should be closed, so as to encourage the establishment of trust and safety (Richardson et al., 2012). Group members should avoid detailed conversations about their self-injurious episodes and should bandage their wounds (Bubrick et al., n.d.; Richardson et al., 2012). Additionally, counseling centers may choose to prescreen participants to control for factors that may make group therapy an inappropriate therapeutic intervention for the student's unique treatment issues. Examples of these factors could include things like severe psychopathology, attention seeking, repetitive manipulative behavior, high suicide risk, or therapeutic noncompliance. Although groups may provide a unique context through which to establish universality and interpersonal skills, groups can prove challenging when used for the purpose of treating SI.

Outreach and Prevention Implications

Outreach and prevention begin with competence. Therefore, it is critically important that the college counseling center staff are appropriately trained in the areas of SI identification, therapeutic intervention, differentiation of SI from suicide, and suicide risk assessment. Moreover, each counseling center should have a clear protocol for assessing and responding to suicide. Similar to SI protocols for secondary schools, it is advantageous for college counseling centers to establish a framework for assisting students who self-injure, so that all students are provided an appropriate level of care and intervention, and so that risk to the student is minimized through adherence to evidence-based protocols. Although the literature is somewhat limited in this area, there are a few articles that can help guide college counseling centers in their development of SI policy: Berger, Hasking, and Reupert (2015); Bubrick et al. (n.d.); and Walsh and Muehlenkamp (2013).

We have already addressed the stigma associated with SI and the reluctance of students who self-injure to seek professional assistance. It should be no surprise, then, that college counselors may need to get out of their offices and into the campus community to make contact with people who self-injure. Working with student groups (e.g., sororities, fraternities, athletics, band), counselors can help to promote awareness and help seeking while destigmatizing SI. It may also be helpful to train college student affairs professionals who have direct contact with students (e.g., resident assistants and directors, advisers, mentors) to notice the signs and symptoms of both general emotional distress and SI, so that they can make appropriate referrals to the counseling center. Through incorporating SI into their mental health awareness programming, college counselors can affirm their understanding of and sensitivity toward people who self-injure, while helping to bring awareness of SI to the lay community. However, it is important that, when college counselors discuss SI in a public forum, they do not glamorize or romanticize SI (Jarvi, Jackson, Swenson, & Crawford, 2013). Rather, they can speak about the emotional distress that underlies SI, helping students to understand and be able to identify the common indications of emotional distress, and emphasize the importance of active coping. This may help students to notice when their peers are in distress, regardless of the specific nature of that distress, and refer their peers to counseling when they have concerns. College counselors may also work with students to identify and practice healthy coping skills for various types of emotions, as well as develop skills related to assertiveness, conflict resolution, and problem-solving. Prevention programming that not only familiarizes students with the signs of distress but also helps them to understand available resources and identify health alternatives can be particularly valuable for cultivating a healthy campus community.

Conclusion

SI is prominent on college campuses and, as such, counselors in college settings are sure to work with clients who self-injure. SI treatment can be challenging, even to experienced counselors. However, the ability to address SI therapeutically is particularly important for college counselors in consideration of the prevalence of SI among college-age students. College counselors must be prepared to identify the indicators of SI, use established assessment inventories and procedures, adapt therapeutic intervention to address SI and the underlying factors that contribute to SI, and manage suicide risk with clients who self-injure. The potentially lethal nature of SI necessitates a thoughtful and comprehensive therapeutic approach that is guided by a thorough understanding of SI. Although there is no single proven method for treating SI, counselors should use the available research base to develop appropriate treatment goals and implement relevant therapeutic interventions. Counseling may address the underlying factors that have contributed to the client's distress, but counselors may also help clients to build their healthy support system, improve their interpersonal skills, develop active coping skills, enhance their emotion regulation skills, expand their problem-solving skills, and address cognitive distortions that contribute to SI. Moreover, college counselors must be prepared to address social and contextual factors that contribute to SI, including the media and websites that encourage SI. However, perhaps most importantly, college counselors should collaborate with campus partners to promote awareness of campus mental health resources and support help seeking. It is important to remember these two things: (a) Students who self-injure are in pain and deserve to be treated with dignity, and (b) SI is a symptom of underlying distress.

Final Case Study

At the conclusion of the case study you will find questions for your reflection as a college counselor. Because of the complexity of SI, guiding answers are included among the questions. However, prior to reading the answers, you are encouraged to pause and think about how you might conceptualize this case yourself, applying the material you have read in this chapter.

The Case of Rosalia

You have been working as a college counselor at a small midwestern university for approximately a year. A colleague performs an intake on a female freshman and believes that you and this client would be a good therapeutic match, given your interest and training in intimate partner violence and Rosalia's recent dissolution of an abusive relationship.

Rosalia self-identifies as an 18-year-old Latina American who is a first-generation college student. You can see from her intake paperwork that Rosalia excels academically and wishes to enroll in the nursing program. The first time you meet Rosalia, you are struck by how quiet and calm she is. The intake counselor described Rosalia as being highly emotional and "sobbing through the intake session." When you ask Rosalia essential questions about the reasons she sought counseling, she is very factual and concrete—showing little emotion. You ask her about coping, and she says that she has not really been coping; she cannot sleep well, is not eating or drinking much, and struggles to control the intense emotional pain. You ask about the pain, and she states, "It's just a lot of stuff. I can't really describe it. This has been going on for years, but since the breakup, everything just feels out of control." As you do with all students, you talk with Rosalia about her support network. She tells you that she does not really have many friends and she is not particularly close with her family members. She has one little sister about whom she cares but does not often see her. In consideration of her limited support and heightened emotional distress, you ask about suicide. Rosalia denies suicide intent but tells you that she thinks about death and "just feel[s] numb."

You ask her what she does to cope with the suicide thoughts and numbness, but she refuses to speak. You notice that she is wearing a thin long-sleeved shirt, but it is July—the middle of summer. You also notice that she is wearing a combination of large woven bracelets and athletic wristbands. You begin to wonder about the possibility that Rosalia self-injures.

Case Exploration Questions

1. What signs of SI do you notice?

   You have only just met Rosalia, and this is a sensitive topic. So, you decide that it is important to normalize the pain that follows a breakup and the confusing feelings and thoughts that one can experience after surviving intimate partner violence. You also want to let her know that, if she self-injures, that is something she can feel safe talking about with you.

2. What could you say or do next to help Rosalia feel safe and understood?
3. What types of statements and behaviors from you do you think might make Rosalia feel threatened or hesitant to talk about her distress and, if present, her SI?

   You address the topic of SI sensitively with Rosalia and she acknowledges that she has been scratching her wrists with a paper clip since she was 13 years old. Over the past few months, as the relationship became particularly emotionally abusive, she has found that scratching has not worked to help her manage the pain and numbness. So, she has started burning her wrists with matches. Rosalia says that the smell of her skin burning reminds her that she is alive, and then pressing on her burn wounds throughout the day helps when she begins to "feel like [she is] falling apart and losing control." Rosalia is relatively forthcoming when discussing her SI, and you suspect that you can continue the conversation, as long as you remain respectful of her SI and demonstrate an absence of judgment. At this juncture, it is important to talk with Rosalia about the functions SI serves for her. She has given you some of this information, but more is needed for you to better understand her experience of SI.

4. What three elements do you need to discuss when performing a functional assessment of SI?
5. How will you ask Rosalia about these three elements, so that she understands the type of information you need and why you need it?

   Now that you have a better understanding of the functions SI serves for Rosalia, and how those functions can change for her across time and situations, it is time to have a conversation with Rosalia about the severity and risks associated with SI. However, it is important for Rosalia to know that you are not trying to shame or judge her for self-injuring, and that you understand she relies on SI at this time to help her manage her distress.

6. How will you evaluate the level of severity of Rosalia's SI and her level of risk for accidental severe SI and/or suicide? What formal and informal assessments could you use?
7. What type of psychoeducation about SI do you think might be helpful and appropriate for Rosalia?

   Through your conversations and use of formal assessments, you and Rosalia determine that her SI and suicide risk are minimal to moderate. Her self-injurious episodes are planned and habitual—not impulsive—and she has never used particularly lethal means, such as deep cutting or cutting in dangerous locations. Furthermore, her religious beliefs do not condone suicide, and, although she is not very close to her family, she would not want to leave her little sister. She tells you that "I am all my sister has. Our parents don't understand us and are too busy with work to really care about us." You have quite a bit of information to inform a safety plan. As with all clients who experience suicidal ideation, it is helpful to develop a safety plan.

8. How will you adapt the safety plan to include SI, rather than focusing solely on suicidal thoughts and behaviors?
9. What are some strategies Rosalia might be able to use at different levels of distress that trigger her self-injurious thoughts and behaviors?
10. Who can Rosalia include as her sources of support on her safety plan, considering that she does not feel connected to her parents?

    You work with Rosalia to develop a safety plan, and even practice using some of the techniques that are included in the safety plan. This seems like a good time to start identifying goals for counseling and determining Rosalia's openness to learning new ways of coping.

11. What types of goals do you think might be appropriate for you and Rosalia to work toward in your therapeutic relationship?
12. What types of goals do you think would be inappropriate or might minimize Rosalia's distress?
13. What can you say to Rosalia to gauge her openness to learning new coping skills that do not cause harm to her body?

    You and Rosalia work together to identify three primary goals for counseling. You reconfirm her understanding of the safety plan and willingness to use it. The session is drawing to an end, but you want Rosalia to know that you and she will explore her SI more in the next session and in the future. However, you want her to know that her SI will not be the entire focus of your work together. In fact, you will need to ask some more questions about her history to get an understanding of how her history might be contributing to her SI.

14. In addition to the recent abusive relationship, what information would be helpful for you to collect to inform your treatment planning with Rosalia?
15. When you meet with your supervisor later this week, what questions and concerns do you need to address with your supervisor? Are there any legal or ethical concerns that you need to address related to your work with Rosalia?

Resources

Brown and Stanley Safety Planning website (http://www.suicidesafetyplan.com/Home_Page.html)

Cornell University Self-Injury and Recovery Research and Resources (http://www.selfinjury.bctr.cornell.edu/index.html).

International Society for the Study of Self-Injury (http://itriples.org/)
Klonsky's Non-Suicidal Self-Injury: Description, Motivations, and Relationship to Suicide webinar (SPRC) (https://www.youtube.com/watch?feature=player_embedded&v=hjEEYL1gboY)
Suicide Prevention Resource Center (SPRC) (http://www.sprc.org/)
Walsh's Understanding and Treating the Complex Puzzle of Non-Suicidal Self-Injury webinar (ICRC-S) (http://suicideprevention-icrc-s.org/understanding-and-treating-complex-puzzle-non-suicidal-self-injury)
Wester, K. L. & Trepal, H. C. (2017). *Nonsuicidal self-injury: Wellness perspectives on behaviors, symptoms, and diagnosis*. New York, NY: Routledge.

References

Andover, M. S., Pepper, C. M., & Gibb, B. E. (2007). Self-mutilation and coping strategies in a college sample. *Suicide & Life-Threatening Behavior, 37*, 238–243.

Barley, W. D., Buie, S. E., Peterson, E. W., Hollingsworth, A. S., Griva, M., Hickerson, S. C., & Bailey, B. J. (1993). Development of an inpatient cognitive-behavioral treatment program for borderline personality disorder. *Journal of Personality Disorders, 7*, 232–240.

Beck, A. (1991). Beck Scale for Suicide Ideation (BSS) [Measurement instrument]. Pearson. Retrieved from https://www.pearsonassessments.com/store/usassessments/en/Store/Professional-Assessments/Personality-%26-Biopsychosocial/Beck-Scale-for-Suicide-Ideation/p/100000157.html

Berger, E., Hasking, P., & Reupert, A. (2015). Developing a policy to address nonsuicidal self-injury in schools. *The Journal of School Health, 85*, 629–647. doi:10.1111/josh.12292

Bubrick, K., Goodman, J., & Whitlock, J. (n.d.). *Non-suicidal self-injury in schools: Developing & implementing school protocol.* Cornell Research Program on Self-Injury and Recovery. Retrieved from http://www.selfinjury.bctr.cornell.edu/documents/schools.pdf

Buser, T. J., Buser, J. K., & Rutt, C. C. (2017). Predictors of unintentionally severe harm during nonsuicidal self-injury. *Journal of Counseling & Development, 95*, 14–23.

Buser, T. J., Peterson, C. H., & Hill, T. M. (2016). Brief Severity Index for Nonsuicidal Self-Injury: Initial validation of a self-report measure. *Journal of Mental Health Counseling, 38*, 28–46.

Chapman, A. L., & Dixon-Gordon, K. L. (2007). Emotional antecedents and consequences of deliberate self-harm and suicide attempts. *Suicide and Life-Threatening Behavior, 37*, 543–552.

Chapman, A. L., Gratz, K. L., & Turner, B. J. (2014). Risk-related and protective correlates of nonsuicidal self-injury and co-occurring suicide attempts among incarcerated women. *Suicide & Life-Threatening Behavior, 44*, 139–154. doi:10.1111/sltb.12058

Claes, L., Luyckx, K., & Bijttebier, P. (2014). Non-suicidal self-injury in adolescents: Prevalence and associations with identity formation above and beyond depression. *Personality and Individual Differences, 61–62*, 101–104. doi:10.1016/j.paid.2013.12.019

Cull, J. G., & Gill, W. S. (1982). Suicide Probability Scale (SPS) [Measurement instrument]. Los Angeles, CA: WPS.

Ernhout, C., & Whitlock, J. (2014). *Bringing up self-injury with your clients.* The Practical Matters Series, Cornell Research Program on Self-Injury and Recovery. Retrieved from http://www.selfinjury.bctr.cornell.edu/perch/resources/bringing-up-self-injury-with-clients-pm-1.pdf

Flaherty, H. B. (2018). Treating adolescent nonsuicidal self-injury: A review of psychosocial interventions to guide clinical practice. *Child & Adolescent Social Work Journal, 35*, 85–95. doi:10.1007/s10560-017-0505-5

Gilbert, P., McEwan, K., Irons, C., Bhundia, R., Christie, R., Broomhead, C., & Rockliff, H. (2010). Self-harm in a mixed clinical population: The roles of self-criticism, shame, and social rank. *British Journal of Clinical Psychology, 49,* 563–576.

Glenn, C. R., Franklin, J. C., & Nock, M. K. (2015). Evidence-based psychosocial treatments for self-injurious thoughts and behaviors in youth. *Journal of Clinical Child and Adolescent Psychology, 44,* 1–29. doi:10.1080/15374416.2014.945211

Gratz, K. L. (2001). Measurement of deliberate self-harm: Preliminary data on the Deliberate Self-Harm Inventory. *Journal of Psychopathology and Behavioral Assessment, 23,* 253–263.

Hamza, C. A., Stewart, S. L., & Willoughby, T. (2012). Examining the link between non-suicidal self-injury and suicidal behavior: A review of the literature and an integrated model. *Clinical Psychology Review, 32,* 482–495. doi:10.1016/j.cpr.2012.05.003

Hankin, B. L., & Abela, J. R. (2011). Nonsuicidal self-injury in adolescence: Prospective rates and risk factors in a 2 ½ year longitudinal study. *Psychiatry Research, 186,* 65–70. doi:10.1016/j.psychres.2010.07.056

Harned, M. S., Jackson, S. C., Comtois, K. A., & Linehan, M. M. (2010). Dialectical behavior therapy as a precursor to PTSD treatment for suicidal and/or self-injuring women with borderline personality disorder. *Journal of Traumatic Stress, 23,* 421–429.

Harned, M. S., Korslund, K. E., Foa, E. B., & Linehan, M. M. (2011). Treating PTSD in suicidal and self-injuring women with borderline personality disorder: Development and preliminary evaluation of a dialectical behavior therapy prolonged exposure protocol. *Behaviour Research and Therapy, 50,* 381–386. doi:10.1016/j.brat.2012.02.011

Hatcher, S., Sharon, C., Parag, V., & Collins, N. (2011). Problem-solving therapy for people who present to hospital with self-harm: Zelen randomised controlled trial. *The British Journal of Psychiatry, 199,* 310–316. doi:10.1192/bjp.bp.110.090126

Heilbron, N., & Prinstein, M. J. (2010). Adolescent peer victimization, peer status, suicidal ideation, and nonsuicidal self-injury: Examining concurrent and longitudinal associations. *Merrill-Palmer Quarterly, 56,* 388–419.

Hunnicutt Hollenbaugh, K. M., & Lenz, A. S. (2018). Preliminary evidence for the effectiveness of dialectical behavior therapy for adolescents. *Journal of Counseling & Development, 96,* 119–131. doi:10.1002/jcad.12186

International Society for the Study of Self-Injury. (n.d.). Fast facts. Retrieved from https://itriples.org/category/about-self-injury/

Jarvi, S., Jackson, B., Swenson, L., & Crawford, H. (2013). The impact of social contagion on non-suicidal self-injury: A review of the literature. *Archives of Suicide Research, 17,* 1–19. doi:10.1080/13811118.2013.748404

Jenkins, A. L., Singer, J., Conner, B. T., Calhoun, S., & Diamond, G. (2014). Risk for suicidal ideation and attempt among a primary care sample of adolescents engaging in nonsuicidal self-injury. *Suicide and Life-Threatening Behavior, 44,* 616–628. doi:10.1111/sltb.12094

Joiner, T. (2005). *Why people die by suicide*. Cambridge, MA: Harvard University Press.

Juhnke, G. A., Granello, D. H., & Granello. P. F. (2011). *Suicide, self-injury, and violence in the schools: Assessment, prevention, and intervention strategies*. Hoboken, NJ: Wiley.

Kakhnovets, R., Young, H. L., Purnell, A., Huebner, E., & Bishop, C. (2010). Self-reported experience of self-injurious behavior in college students. *Journal of Mental Health Counseling, 32,* 309–323.

Kerr, P. L., & Muehlenkamp, J. (2010). Features of psychopathology in self-injuring female college students. *Journal of Mental Health Counseling, 32,* 290–308.

Kilburn, E., & Whitlock, J. L. (2009). *Distraction techniques and alternative coping strategies.* The Fact Sheet Series, Cornell Research Program on Self-Injury and Recovery. Ithaca, NY: Cornell University.

Klonsky, E. D. (2014, September 12). *Non-suicidal self-injury: Description, motivations, and relationship to suicide* [Webinar]. Retrieved from https://www.youtube.com/watch?feature=player_embedded&v=hjEEYL1gboY

Klonsky, E. D., & Glenn, C. R. (2009). Assessing the functions of non-suicidal self-injury: Psychometric properties of the Inventory of Statements About Self-injury (ISAS). *Journal of Psychopathology and Behavioral Assessment, 31,* 215–219. doi:10.1007/s10862-008-9107-z

Klonsky, E. D., Muehlenkamp, J. J., Lewis, S. P., & Walsh, B. (2011). *Nonsuicidal self-injury: Advances in psychotherapy evidence-based practice.* Cambridge, MA: Hogrefe.

Klonsky, E. D., Victor, S. E., & Saffer, B. Y. (2014). Nonsuicidal self-injury: What we know, and what we need to know. *Canadian Journal of Psychiatry, 59,* 565–568.

Lewis, S. P., Heath, N. L., Michal, N. J., & Duggan, J. M. (2012). Non-suicidal self-injury, youth, and the internet: What mental health professionals need to know. *Child and Adolescent Psychiatry and Mental Health, 6.* doi:10.1186/1753-2000-6-13

Lewis, S. P., & Seko, Y. (2015). A double-edged sword: A review of benefits and risks of online non-suicidal self-injury activities. *Journal of Clinical Psychology, 72,* 249–262. doi:10.1002/jclp.22242

Linehan, M. M., Comtois, K. A., Brown, Z. M., Heard, H. L., & Wagner, A. (2006). Suicide Attempt Self-Injury Interview (SASSI): Development, reliability, and validity of a scale to assess suicide attempts and intentional self-injury. *Psychological Assessment, 18,* 303–312.

Lloyd-Richardson, E. E., Perrine, N., Dierker, L., & Kelley, M. L. (2007). Characteristics and functions of non-suicidal self-injury in a community sample of adolescents. *Psychological Medicine, 37,* 1183–1192. doi:10.1017/S003329170700027X

Miner, C. L., Love, H. A., & Paik, S. E. (2016). Non-suicidal self-injury in adolescents: Addressing the function and the family from the perspective of systemic family therapies. *American Journal of Family Therapy, 44,* 211–220. doi:10.1080/01926187.2016.1150798

Mitchell, K. J., Wells, M., Priebe, G., & Ybarra, M. L. (2014). Exposure to websites that encourage self-harm and suicide: Prevalence rates and association with actual thoughts of self-harm and thoughts of suicide in the United States. *Journal of Adolescence, 37,* 1335–1344. doi:10.1016/j.adolescence.2014.09.011

Morris, C., Simpson, J., Sampson, M., & Beesley, F. (2014). Cultivating positive emotions: A useful adjunct when working with people who self-harm? *Clinical Psychology & Psychotherapy, 21,* 352–362.

Muehlenkamp, J. J. (2006). Empirically supported treatments and general therapy guidelines for non-suicidal self-injury. *Journal of Mental Health Counseling, 28,* 166–185.

Muehlenkamp, J. J., Claes, L., Havertape, L., & Plener, P. L. (2012). International prevalence of adolescent non-suicidal self-injury and deliberate self-harm. *Child and Adolescent Psychiatry and Mental Health, 6.* doi:10.1186/1753-2000-6-10

Muehlenkamp, J. J., & Gutierrez, P. M. (2004). An investigation of differences between self-injurious behavior and suicide attempts in a sample of adolescents. *Suicide and Life-Threatening Behavior, 34,* 12–23.

Muehlenkamp, J. J., & Gutierrez, P. M. (2007). Risk for suicide attempts among adolescents who engage in non-suicidal self-injury. *Archives of Suicide Research, 11,* 69–82. doi:10.1080/13811110600992902

Nock, M. K., Holmberg, E. B., Photos, V. I., & Michel, B. D. (2007). Self-Injurious Thoughts and Behaviors Interview: Development, reliability, and validity in an adolescent sample. *Psychological Assessment, 19,* 309–317. doi:10.1037/1040-3590.19.3.309

Nock, M. K., Prinstein, M. J., & Sterba, S. K. (2010). Revealing the form and function of self-injurious thoughts and behaviors: A real-time ecological assessment study among adolescents and young adults. *Psychology of Violence, 1*(Suppl.), 36–52. doi:10.1037/2152-0828.1.S.36

Norman, H., & Borrill, J. (2015). The relationship between self-harm and alexithymia. *Scandinavian Journal of Psychology, 56,* 405–419. doi:10.1111/sjop.12217

Osman, A., Bagge, C. L., Guitierrez, P. M., Konick, L. C., Kooper, B. A., & Barrios, F. X. (2001). The Suicidal Behaviors Questionnaire–Revised (SBQ-R): Validation with clinical and nonclinical samples. *Assessment, 8,* 443–454.

Pew Research Center. (2018, March 1). *Social media use in 2018*. Retrieved from http://www.pewinternet.org/2018/03/01/social-media-use-in-2018/

Pistorello, J., Fruzzetti, A. E., MacLane, C., Gallop, R., & Iverson, K. M. (2012). Dialectical behavior therapy (DBT) applied to college students: A randomized clinical trial. *Journal of Consulting and Clinical Psychology*. Advance online publication. doi:10.1037/a0029096

Posner, K., Brown, G. K., Stanley, B., Brent, D. A., Yershova, K. V., Oquendo, M. A., . . . Mann, J. J. (2011). Columbia-Suicide Severity Rating Scale: Initial validity and internal consistency findings from three multiple studies with adolescents and adults. *The American Journal of Psychiatry, 168,* 1266–1277.

Reisner, S. L., Biello, K., Perry, N. S., Gamarel, K. E., & Mimiaga, M. J. (2014). A compensatory model of risk and resilience applied to adolescent sexual orientation disparities in nonsuicidal self-injury and suicide attempts. *American Journal of Orthopsychiatry, 84,* 545–556. doi:10.1037/ort0000008

Richardson, B. G., Surmitis, K. A., & Hyldahl, R. S. (2012). Minimizing social contagion in adolescents who self-injure: Considerations for group work, residential treatment, and the internet. *Journal of Mental Health Counseling, 34,* 121–132.

Rizvi, S. L., Hughes, C. D., & Thomas, M. C. (2016). The DBT Coach mobile application as an adjunct to treatment for suicidal and self-injuring individuals with borderline personality disorder: A preliminary evaluation and challenges to client utilization. *Psychological Services, 13,* 380–388. doi:10.1037/ser0000100

Shearin, E. N., & Linehan, M. M. (1994). Dialectical behavior therapy for borderline personality disorder: Theoretical and empirical foundations. *Acta Psychiatrica Scandinavica, 89,* 61–68.

Stanley, B., & Brown, G. K. (2012). Safety planning intervention: A brief intervention to mitigate suicide risk. *Cognitive and Behavioral Practice, 19,* 256–264.

Toprak, S., Cetin, I., Guven, T., Can, G., & Demircan, C. (2011). Self-harm, suicidal ideation and suicide attempts among college students. *Psychiatric Research, 187,* 140–144.

Trepal, H. C., & Wester, K. L. (2007). Self-injurious behaviors, diagnoses, and treatment methods: What mental health professionals are reporting. *Journal of Mental Health Counseling, 29,* 363–375. doi:10.17744/mehc.29.4.d277t298667q5367

Van Goethem, A., Mulders, D., Muris, M., Artnz, A., & Egger, J. (2012). Reduction of self-injury and improvement of coping behavior during dialectical behaviour therapy (DBT) of patients with borderline personality disorder. *International Journal of Psychology and Psychological Therapy, 12,* 21–34.

Victor, S. E., Glenn, C. R., & Klonsky, E. D. (2012). Is non-suicidal self-injury an "addiction"? A comparison of craving in substance use and non-suicidal self-injury. *Psychiatry Research, 197,* 73–77. doi:10.1016/j.psychres.2011.12.011

Voon, D., Hasking, P., & Martin, G. (2014). The roles of emotion regulation and ruminative thoughts in non-suicidal self-injury. *British Journal of Clinical Psychology, 53,* 95–113. doi:10.1111/bjc.12030

Walsh, B. (2014, February 12). *Understanding and treating the complex puzzle of non-suicidal self-injury* [Webinar]. Retrieved from http://suicideprevention-icrc-s.org/understanding-and-treating-complex-puzzle-non-suicidal-self-injury

Walsh, B., & Muehlenkamp, J. J. (2013). Managing nonsuicidal self-injury in schools: Use of a structured protocol to manage the behavior and prevent social contagion. *School Psychology Forum, 7,* 161–171.

Wester, K. L., Ivers, N., Villalba, J. A., Trepal, H. C., & Henson, R. (2016). The relationship between nonsuicidal self-injury and suicidal ideation. *Journal of Counseling & Development, 94,* 3–12. doi:10.1002/jcad.12057

Wester, K. L., & Trepal, H. C. (2015). Nonsuicidal self-injury: Exploring the connection among race, ethnic identity, and ethnic belonging. *Journal of College Student Development, 56,* 127–139.

Whisenhunt, J. L., Chang, C. Y., Brack, G. L., Orr, J., Adams, L. G., Paige, M. R., . . . O'Hara, C. (2015). Self-injury and suicide: Practical information for college counselors. *Journal of College Counseling, 18,* 275–288. doi:10.1002/jocc.12020

Whisenhunt, J. L., Chang, C. Y., Flowers, L. R., Brack, G. L., O'Hara, C., & Raines, T. C. (2014). Working with clients who self-injure: A grounded theory approach. *Journal of Counseling & Development, 92,* 387–397. doi:10.1002/j.1556-6676.2014.00165.x

Whisenhunt, J. L., & Kress, V. E. (2013). The use of visual arts in counseling clients who engage in non-suicidal self-injury. *Journal of Creativity in Mental Health, 8,* 120–135.

Whitlock, J., Eckenrode, J., & Silverman, D. (2006). Self-injurious behaviors in a college population. *Pediatrics, 117,* 1939–1948. doi:10.1542/peds.2005-2543

Whitlock, J., Exner-Cortens, D., & Purington, A. (2014). Assessment of nonsuicidal self-injury: Development and initial validation of the Non-Suicidal Self-Injury–Assessment Tool (NSSI-AT). *Psychological Assessment, 26,* 935–946. doi:10.1037/a0036611

Whitlock, J., Muehlenkamp, J., Eckenrode, J., Purington, A., Baral Abrams, G., Barreira, P., & Kress, V. (2013). Nonsuicidal self-injury as a gateway to suicide in young adults. *Journal of Adolescent Health, 52,* 486–492. doi:10.1016/j.jadohealth.2012.09.010

Whitlock, J., Muehlenkamp, J., Purington, A., Eckenrode, J., Barreira, P., Baral Abrams, G., . . . Knox, K. (2011). Nonsuicidal self-injury in a college population: General trends and sex differences. *Journal of American College Health, 59,* 691–698. Retrieved from https://articles.westga.edu:2116/10.1080/07448481.2010.529626

Chapter 22

Sexual Issues and Concerns

Meghan K. Root

When it comes to sex, the most important six inches are the ones between the ears.

—Ruth K. Westheimer

■ ■ ■

Reflection Exercise

Take a few moments to recall your best consensual sexual experience. Maybe it was with a partner, maybe with yourself. Maybe it was passionate, or loving, romantic, or relaxing. What were the sensations, sounds, tastes, and smells involved? What were the surrounding circumstances that contributed to making those moments and feelings pleasurable? What details of the memory stand out the most to you? How did you feel at the time? How do you feel now recalling the event?

On a scale of 0 to 10, with 0 being not comfortable at all and 10 being 100% comfortable, how comfortable would you be writing down the detailed story of your sexual experience? How comfortable would you be sharing that written story with a friend? With a stranger? With a therapist? Would you be willing to read that story out loud to a group?

Reflect on what the factors are that affect your level of comfort. How might your age, race, gender, career, spirituality, community, culture, and/or relationships affect your comfort? If you were asked to share a sexual experience that you identify as negative, shameful, or traumatic, does that have an impact on your comfort sharing level, and why? As you read through this chapter, it is important to keep in mind what influences your comfort with human sexuality and sexual experiences, including any biases (conscious or implicit) that exist.

■ ■ ■

Students often find college a time to explore their sexuality in new ways, perhaps triggered by the freedom of being outside the home, the opportunities to step away from the stigmas/scripts they may have had in their life before college, the new perspectives they are receiving in the classroom and from peers, the developmental changes that are occurring at the tail end of puberty, and the new opportunities college provides. As counselors, how do you prepare to provide an empathetic response to students as they explore their natural sexual development, sexual identities, and sexual feelings (both emotional and physical) that may be unfamiliar, stressful, or problematic? It is your role to help them find a healthy balance between sexual empowerment and risk reduction.

This chapter will cover the prevalence of sexuality-related issues among college men and women, followed by a discussion on human sexuality education and the Circles of Sexuality, which provides a comprehensive framework for understanding the many ways sexuality affects one's life. Following this is an exploration of assessing sexual issues, including intake tools, the process of obtaining a sexual history, and a model to help determine the appropriate level of intervention for a client presenting with sexual issues. Next is an exploration of the diagnosis and treatment options for both nonclinical issues (dating/hookup problems, masturbating, sexual fantasies, etc.) and the sexual dysfunctions that are found in the *Diagnostic and Statistical Manual of Mental Disorders* (5th ed.; *DSM-5*; American Psychiatric Association [APA], 2013). The chapter concludes with a few case studies for applying this new information.

It is vital that counselors acknowledge the diversity of backgrounds that students come from and the huge range of sexuality-related issues they may present with at a college counseling center. In the same week, students may present to the center with the following range of sexual concerns:

- Student A has lost all interest in sex with their new partner; the student is trying to balance classes, support a child, and maintain a single-income home.
- Student B wants advice on whether to stay with their high school partner and explore having an open long-distance relationship or break up.
- Student C has fears concerning having reached orgasm/ejaculated quickly (possibly too quickly) during sexual activity with casual sex partners.
- Student D was referred by student housing because their roommate is uncomfortable with Student D watching graphic pornography in the shared residence hall room.

Did you make any assumptions while reading the preceding scenarios about the students? About their age? Race? Sexual orientation? Gender? Are counselors prepared to provide a nonjudgmental, bias-aware response to the students they are supporting and not contribute to the shame frequently associated with human sexuality? We will return to these students at the end of the chapter.

Before moving forward into the depths of this chapter, it is important to bring awareness to the stage of sexual development that the majority of college students are in. Although every body has its own process, and there are countless biological, societal, and environmental factors that affect the individual, most college students can be categorized into the "late adolescence" (ages 17–19) phase of sexual development (Kar, Choudhury, & Singh, 2015). During this phase, they are learning through their freedom and social identity development to recognize that choices have consequences, to connect self-respect with the feeling of empowerment, and to balance safety/health with pleasure/experimentation. This experience provides the framework for many of the sexual choices today's students make.

Prevalence of Sexual Issues Among College Students

Our sexuality is an essential part of who we are as humans, whether we are sexually active or not. Counseling may be the only place a client feels safe to discuss a problem or ask a sexuality-related question. Sexual satisfaction and related problems are based on the client's subjective perception and experience. One student may see a lack of interest in sexual activity as unproblematic and identify as asexual, whereas to another it may be a source of intense worry. This subjectivity, as well as the taboo around sexuality, has made it challenging to establish the prevalence of sexual issues. A Canadian study of 16- to 21-year-old males and females found that 51.1% reported a sexual problem (mostly in relationship contexts) and 50% reported clinically significant levels of distress associated with the sexual problems (O'Sullivan, Brotto, Byers, Majerovich, & Wuest, 2014).

Prevalence Among Women

The National Health and Social Life Survey found that about 43% of women experienced some sexual difficulties (Laumann, Paik, & Rosen, 1999). McCabe et al. (2016) echoed a similar prevalence following their literature review of sexual dysfunction, estimating that between 40% and 50% of women, irrespective of age, report at least one sexual dysfunction. The National Health and Social Life Survey found that the dominant difficulties that women reported were a lack of interest and being unable to achieve orgasm (Laumann et al., 1999). McCabe et al. found lack of interest/desire disorders ranging from 17% to 55%, arousal/lubrication difficulties ranging from 12% to 49% depending on the population of women studied, and orgasmic disorders ranging from approximately 16% to 25% in American women.

For women, *DSM-5* estimated that 15% report recurrent pain during intercourse and about 10% do not experience orgasm throughout their lifetime (APA, 2013). However, women tend to report less persistent distress about the lack of orgasm, so it is challenging to obtain accurate data.

Prevalence Among Men

A significantly higher amount of research has been done on the prevalence of male sexual dysfunctions compared with those of women, but establishing an overall prevalence for men's sexual dysfunctions is challenging because it varies so greatly by study and type of dysfunction, with erectile dysfunction and premature ejaculation being the disorders primarily researched (McCabe et al., 2016). The National Health and Social Life Survey found that about 31% of men experienced some sexual difficulties, and that in the past 12 months, the most common issue was climaxing too early (Laumann et al., 1999). McCabe et al. (2016) estimated that for men, 15% to 25% of the population experienced lack of interest or desire, 1% to 10% (for males below age 40) experienced erectile dysfunction, 8% to 30% experienced premature ejaculation, and 2% to 8% were unable to achieve orgasm; limited research indicated that about 17% have experienced pain with erection or ejaculation. Specific to the college-age population, Wilcox, Redmond, and Hassan (2014) found that erectile dysfunction was present in 33% of U.S. military men ages 21 to 40.

DSM-5 estimated that 2% of males younger than age 40 complain of frequent problems with erections but that 8% experienced erectile problems that hindered penetration during the first sexual experience. *DSM-5* estimated that 1.8% of men ages 16 to 44 will meet the criteria for hypoactive sexual desire disorder and 1% to 3% of men will be diagnosed with premature ejaculation (APA, 2013). Some students may worry that they aren't lasting "long enough," and educating them on the diagnostic criteria (ejaculation within 1 minute of penetration) may provide them with some reassurance and reduce their anxiety.

Prevalence of Paraphilic Disorders

Regarding the prevalence of paraphilic disorders, the true prevalence is unknown. The data that do exist are typically based on those who have broken a law related to paraphilia or sought out clinical treatment. Many individuals have attractions or fetishes that are not causing distress or harm and actually increase sexual satisfaction and pleasure. It is very important to delineate between these and the paraphilias, which are sexual desires or behaviors that produce significant physical, emotional, or social consequences for an individual or those around them (Schwartz & Masters, 1983).

According to *DSM-5*, it is estimated that 3% to 5% of males have a pedophilic disorder, up to 30% of adult men have engaged in a frotteuristic act, and 2% to 4% of males meet the criteria for an exhibitionistic disorder (APA, 2013). All of the paraphilic disorders are seen with much less frequency in women than men.

Human Sexuality Education

College counselors are in a unique situation because many students who present are really seeking education on, or the normalization of, human sexuality issues. As a society, we do not (typically) teach our elementary, middle, or high school students comprehensive sexuality, only reproduction, how to prevent sexually transmitted infections (STIs), and how to prevent pregnancy. Although the internet has made sexuality information much more accessible, it can also be a challenge for students to recognize what is reliable or accurate information. It is important to collaborate with your institution's wellness center and be aware of what programming is offered around healthy sexuality, often through the women's center, feminist clubs, or peer health educators.

As a college counselor, you will be asked about human sexuality issues. Too often, when talking about sex, one defaults to thinking about "intercourse" and, in doing so, focuses on the physical and leaves out the psychological, mental, relational, biological, spiritual, and cultural aspects. One way to comprehensively approach human sexuality is through the five Circles of Sexuality model created by Dennis Dailey (Dailey, 1981); Advocates for Youth (2007) has a great handout for this model in their sexual education curriculum that is a useful tool (https://www.advocatesforyouth.org/wp-content/uploads/storage//advfy/lesson-plans/Session-4.pdf, p. 85). The circles include sensuality, intimacy, sexual identity, sexual health and reproduction, and sexualization.

The first circle is our *sensuality*, the awareness and feelings about our own bodies and others (Advocates for Youth, 2007). It includes body image, the experience of pleasure, the desire and need to touch and be touched (skin hunger), physical attractions to other humans, and fantasy. Students may be struggling to feel confident in their own body, feeling shame regarding what and whom they find attractive, or feeling confusion around the meaning of their sexual fantasies. They may seek advice concerning whether cuddle parties with their friends are healthy or "normal." The paraphilic dysfunctions would fall under this circle as sexual urges that are acted on without consent or cause significant distress or impairment.

The second circle is *sexual intimacy*, or the ability to be emotionally close and accept closeness with another human (Advocates for Youth, 2007). Students struggling with intimacy may have trouble opening up or being vulnerable. They may seek help on creating connections with others, feeling safe while taking emotional risks, or recovering from the loss and hurt of an intimate relationship. A student may identify as asexual but still have a desire for intimacy.

The third circle, *sexual identity*, is our understanding, as human beings, of who we are as sexual beings (Advocates for Youth, 2007). This includes sexual orientation (whom we are attracted to), gender identity (femininity, masculinity, androgyny), and gender presentation (perceived maleness and/or femaleness). Students may desire to explore and seek acceptance regarding one or all of these areas in counseling. They may also be deeply affected by bias, phobias, or hatred from society and need to find physical and emotional safety on campus. If a student seeks counseling because of getting harassed for identifying as a furry (a person who is a fan of animal characters with human attributes), are you prepared to provide support for that student? Is your intake paperwork gender neutral? Does it allow students to self-identify their sex and orientation? If a student is trans (does not identify as the biological sex assigned at birth), is it important to assess whether the student will feel supported in the counseling space?

The fourth circle is *reproduction and sexual health* (Advocates for Youth, 2007). This circle includes understanding factual information about reproduction, sexual anatomy, STIs, and sexual behaviors. A student who has an unplanned pregnancy may seek counseling to explore their options. Or students may seek your help because they have tested positive for HIV or are navigating a new relationship with an intersex person.

Included in this circle is the basis for the *DSM-5* sexual dysfunctions: Masters and Johnson's (1966) sexual response cycle. This is the sequence of physical and emotional changes that occur as a person becomes sexually aroused and participates in sexually stimulating activities. Having an understanding of this theory is essential to providing effective sexual counseling and education. You will need to assess whether the student is experiencing problems with the excitement, the plateau, or the orgasm phase. Many students think (because of the portrayal of sexual acts in the media, including pornography) that men and women engaging in intercourse frequently reach orgasm at the same time. It may be your role to educate them that it is unlikely that both orgasm at the same time because of how men and women move through the sexual response cycle differently.

The final circle is *sexualization* and covers when people behave sexually to influence, manipulate, control, or harm other people (Advocates for Youth, 2007). This includes flirting, seduction, sexual harassment, and sexual violence. Students may seek assistance in recovering from sexual trauma during or prior to college or coping with feeling objectified.

A sixth circle, added by Satterly and Dyson (2010), is our *values* and interconnects the original five circles. It is the lens through which we understand and perceive all of the other circles. This circle encompasses our beliefs about abortion; premarital relationships; lesbian, gay, bisexual, transgender, and queer rights; consent; gender roles; body shaming; and other issues. Students may seek counseling to help understand where their values came from and explore what they want their values to be moving forward.

In clinical work with college students, you can use the Circles of Sexuality to collect a student's sexual history, use it as a framework to help understand the roots of a sexual problem, or normalize a desire or behavior. In addition to understanding human sexuality comprehensively for the individual students you counsel, it is important to be aware of the college culture around sexuality. Wellness educators and student clubs have done a lot in recent years to increase sexuality education, including hosting sex fair events; creating accessibility to condoms and birth control; providing free STI screenings; and bringing in guest speakers on consent, orgasms, or kink. That said, many students who are struggling with sexuality issues are not reaching out to student clubs, wellness educators, professors, or peers with their questions. They may not be comfortable in those settings, so they reach out to a counselor for answers. It is your role to be prepared.

It is also part of your job as a college counselor to be well-informed about the efficacy and side effects of birth control and emergency contraception; have reliable medical resources and knowledge regarding STIs, and normalize regular testing; work with the health center staff and local medical professionals to understand the impact of medications (from antibiotics to antidepressants) on sexual desire and functioning; know the college policy on consent; and have trustworthy and sex-positive referrals for gynecological and urological issues that may be affecting clients' sexual functioning. Your center should have a plan to provide medical treatment, advocacy, and support specific to trans students, including legal advocate referrals to help students navigate legal name changes, medical support for hormone injections, clinical letters of approval to provide to insurance companies, and referrals to clinicians who specialize in working with trans folk.

The good news is that there are many great resources that you can consult to help educate yourself and your clients:

- *Advocates for Youth:* Comprehensive sexuality education tools, lessons plans, and resources (www.advocatesforyouth.org).
- *American Association of Sexuality Educators, Counselors and Therapists* (www.aasect.org).
- Fetlife: BDSM/kink social networking and information (www.fetlife.com).
- Go Ask Alice at Columbia University: Excellent source of expert answers to a huge range of sexuality-related questions (www.goaskalice.columbia.edu).
- "The Guide to Getting It On" by Paul Joannides: Well researched, detailed, and funny book for most sex-related questions (www.guide2getting.com).
- The Kinsey Institute at Indiana University: Resources and evidence-based information (www.kinseyinstitute.org).
- Planned Parenthood: Resource on pregnancy, STIs, and reproductive health (www.plannedparenthood.org).
- Sexuality Information and Education Council of the United States: Comprehensive sexuality education clearinghouse (www.siecus.org).
- The Society for the Scientific Study of Sexuality: Evidence-based sexuality research (www.sexscience.org).

Clinical Assessment of Sexuality Issues

We should start from a place of openness and positive sexuality. Many students are using this time to explore new sexual behaviors like polyamorous relationships or fetishes (including bondage, dominance, submission, sadism, or masochism, which is referred to as BDSM). They may be free for the first time to engage in behaviors that align with their sexual orientation or dress in ways that align with their sexual identity. It is important to not "yuck someone else's yum" in your assessment and practice. We may think pineapple on pizza is gross, but that doesn't mean someone else should be ashamed because they love pineapple on pizza. Our implicit biases have a huge impact on our work, so take the time to self-evaluate, monitor, and control your initial reactions, and have appropriate ethical referrals for when a sexual issue is outside of your scope. If a counselor does "yuck" a student's "yum," they risk causing significant damage and shame for that student, possibly driving the student back into the proverbial closet or putting others at risk if the student is engaging in harmful behaviors.

Along a similar line, it is also imperative to assess that no one is getting harmed or engaging in sexual acts without implicit consent. Are all parties agreeing to the sexual acts involved? Is everyone well-informed and of a clear state of mind to consent? It is our clinical obligation to assess for harm and help our students engage in risk-reducing behaviors like wearing condoms, asking for consent, setting clear boundaries, and not breaking laws.

For example, some students may engage in the practice of "stealthing," or removing a condom during intercourse without their partner knowing. The individual removing the condom may be doing so thinking that it causes no harm to the partner and helps increase their sexual satisfaction and not be aware that they do not have consent and the act may have legal or student conduct implications.

Assessment of sexual problems can be challenging because people are uncomfortable discussing the topic. Creating a safe place, embracing the awkwardness, and modeling language to discuss sexuality issues can increase the student's comfort (Wincze & Carey, 2001). Being nonjudgmental, asking open-ended questions, gradually moving from less sensitive to more sensitive material, and ensuring privacy and confidentiality all help comfort the student (Long, Burnett, & Thomas, 2006). Sometimes saying the words "penis, "vagina," or "sex" in the assessment will help the student provide more details about the issue instead of using vague euphemisms.

Each college counseling center has a different intake process, and it is the counselor's role to ensure that sexuality issues are assessed for with each student. A combination of clinical interviewing and self-report questionnaires is recommended, but any tool(s) the counselor uses should take a comprehensive biopsychosocial approach (Wincze & Carey, 2001). Even if a client is seeking help for depression and they have more significant pressing concerns than their sexual satisfaction, it is useful to know how the depression has affected their sexuality and how their sexual functioning may be a factor in the depression. Assessment should be ongoing throughout treatment, not just at the start of counseling. The aforementioned student may feel less depressed through counseling and pharmacological interventions but feel a significant decline in sexual desire.

The clinical interview should include a psychosexual history, asking about the student's childhood, adolescence, trauma, any unwanted sexual acts, and current sexual functioning (Wincze & Carey, 2001). A combination of structured and unstructured questions is recommended, allowing for the counselor to guide the assessment conversation to areas that the student may avoid because of discomfort. You can also use this as an opportunity for the student to create a sexual genogram: creating a physical representation of their and their partner's family of origin messages, generational patterns of sexual behaviors, and significant events in their sexual development (Long et al., 2006). Hof and Berman (1986) offer a deep dive into the sexual genogram process and its usefulness in creating a generational assessment.

There are many sexuality self-report questionnaires available to counselors. The *Handbook of Sexuality-Related Measures* is a comprehensive collection of assessments (Fisher, Davis, Yarber, & Davis, 2011), including assessments of sexual functioning, sexual satisfaction, attitudes, and behaviors. Self-reports are also useful in helping students identify relational strengths or areas of resilience but should be reviewed with the student (Long et al., 2006).

The assessment of sexuality issues has to include a medical component (Leiblum, 2007). What medical treatments, if any, have been sought prior to seeking counseling? Should you refer the student for a sexual medical exam (conducted by a gynecologist or urologist) to assess for medical conditions that may be affecting the student's sexual functioning? Medications (prescribed, over the counter, illegally obtained), hormones, alcohol and/or tobacco use, surgeries, and medical conditions can all affect sexual functioning. One example of why the medical assessment is important is that some men, and a few women, in college may take Viagra or an herbal performance-enhancing supplement to treat a self-diagnosed dysfunction, or just to see what happens. The impact of these chemicals is important to your assessment of the sexual problem. Or if you have a client who is worried about pregnancy, it may be useful to advise that student on pregnancy-testing options.

Some students may present for couples counseling around sexual issues in their relationship. Communication, or lack of, is a central theme for couple's counseling, and this is no different for sexual dysfunctions. When a counselor is completing an intake assessment with a couple, it is recommended that the counselor interview them as a couple around the sexual issues as well as taking individual sexual histories (Long et al., 2006; Wincze & Carey, 2001).

Tangible goal setting is key for treating sexual problems. Clients' goals for counseling and their measures of success should help guide the therapeutic way forward and determine whether a referral is appropriate (Long et al., 2006). Especially with couples, goals should meet everyone's desired outcomes. Facilitating the conversation around sex therapy goals can provide valuable insight into a couple's dynamics. It is important to externalize the problem (not "her" orgasm problem but "the" orgasm problem), use joining language ("we" instead of "you"), and be realistic.

Assessment and goal setting are key to using the permission, limited information, specific suggestions, intensive therapy (P-LI-SS-IT) model of sex therapy (Annon, 1974). This model is foundational to the field of sex therapy. It helps counselors decide what level of intervention is appropriate and whether the counselor has the skills/training needed to help the student (Long et al., 2006). Most college counselors who are not specifically training in sex therapy should provide appropriate referrals to problems reaching the third or fourth stages of the P-LI-SS-IT model but are well equipped to support students in the first and second stages of the model (Mason, 1991). See Table 22.1.

Diagnosis and Treatment of Sexual Issues

This section breaks down the range of sexual issues that students may present with into three categories. The Nonclinical Sexuality Issues section covers areas of sexuality that are the most common for students to seek counseling for but that do not meet a *DSM-5* clinical diagnosis covered in the two sections that follow it. Most of these issues can be treated using the first two stages of the P-LI-SS-IT model. The Sexual Dysfunctions section explores the *DSM-5* diagnoses related to problems with the human response cycle and pain disorders. The Paraphilic Disorders and Sexual Addiction section addresses problematic sexual behaviors or attractions that involve potential harm to others.

Nonclinical Sexuality Issues

Relationships, Dating, Hookups, and One-Night Stands

One issue that is prominent in everyone's lives is navigating romantic relationships. Students are constantly struggling with how to ask someone out, online dating, rejection of

TABLE 22.1

The Permission, Limited Information, Specific Suggestions, Intensive Therapy (P-LI-SS-IT) Model of Sex Therapy

Permission	*Limited Information*	*Specific Suggestions*	*Intensive Therapy*
Talk about sexual issues, contextualize experience, provide empathy and support	Provide sex/psycho-education, teach communication skills, challenge myths/biases, direct to reliable resources	Referral to trained sex therapist to provide interventions like Kegel exercises, sensate focused practice, cognitive restructuring, relaxation skills, empathy building, harm reduction	Referral to trained sex therapist for treatment of complex sexuality issues including CBT, systematic desensitization, stop/start or squeeze techniques, physical therapy, aversion techniques, hormonal or psychotropic medications

Note. From Long, Burnett, and Thomas (2006) and Wincze and Carey (2001). CBT = cognitive behavioral therapy.

someone whom they are not interested in (or running into the person they ghosted last year). Students may be married, engaged, divorced (or in the process of divorcing), single, dating, or exploring polyamorous relationships. Hookups and one-night stands may be commonplace for some students but a source of distress for others. Your role as counselors is to help students explore what they want, learn to communicate their desires, listen to the desires of their partners, and empower them. Counselors need to be familiar with the college's hookups and dating cultures (you should know what Tinder is) as well as the role alcohol plays as a contributing factor (see Chapter 17 on substance use and addiction). You will need to evaluate for abusive or unhealthy relationships and help students learn to give and get consent.

Virginity, Chastity, and Abstinence

Some students may choose not to engage in sexual behaviors, and it is important to normalize this. There is a huge range of reasons why folks don't engage in sexual behaviors or engage in some sexual behaviors but not others. Counseling may focus on boundary setting, communication, empowerment, or support. There can be a lot of cultural beliefs around the value of one's virginity. Generally, men feel pressured to have sex for the first time and women are pressured to wait, but this varies greatly between cultural and social groups. Students may experience shame, guilt, or pressure around their "virginity status." They may engage in other sexual behaviors such as anal or oral sex because they believe it preserves their virginal status. Counselors should create space for them to explore what values they hold around their virginity.

On the flip side, other students may come in to the counseling center because they want to have sex but are not sure how to go about obtaining it. An online support group, self-identified as "incels" (involuntarily celibate), gained attention in the media after multiple mass murderers self-identified as members of the inceldom (online community). Some incels have strong misogynistic beliefs, and the community is mostly made up of White, heterosexual males. The counselor's role is to help students who want to have sex/relationships learn realistic ways of obtaining consensual sexual interactions and create a relationship wherein the students can be challenged on their misperceptions.

Pregnancy, Birth Control, Abortion, and STIs

A nontraditional student may seek counseling because they are experiencing infertility while another may have an unplanned pregnancy and need a neutral space to explore their desires to keep the pregnancy, adopt, or terminate. Be equipped with appropriate referrals for all possibilities including adoption agencies, abortion providers, and new parents support. Does the college offer daycare for students? Are there local resources to help with the financial burden of a child? Some colleges may not have a local provider of pregnancy termination options, so work with your colleagues to develop a plan for students. It is important to be aware that some "crisis pregnancy" centers may not provide a student with abortion as an option or can be misleading as to the services offered.

Therapy may also include education about birth control, the efficacy of pulling out compared with wearing a condom, or exploration of which type of hormonal birth control a student should select. We should encourage students to be well-informed, balanced with risk-reduction, and counselors who work the medical providers and wellness centers on campus for efficacy information. Students also need to know the risks of obtaining an STI and how to reduce this risk. Counselors should inform students that they should stop having intercourse with a condom only if they are in a committed relationship in which both partners have been tested after 6 months of true monogamy, they are both found to not have any STIs, and (if heterosexual) that another method of birth control is being used (correctly).

Students with STIs may come to counseling because they need help telling a partner or exploring the long-term impact of an incurable STI.

Self-Pleasure

College may be a time of sexual freedom for some, but it may also be the first time a student has had to share a room, and so the student may feel more sexually restrained than ever before (at least some moms knock). Some may be exploring self-pleasuring for the first time, whereas others may arrive with their bag of sex toys and lube. Your role may include negotiating between two roommates how they will set boundaries with each other around self-pleasure or partnered sexual activity. Self-pleasure can also be used as a coping technique for stress and students should explore what is a "normal" or "healthy" amount.

If students masturbate to the point of injuring themselves, if masturbation prevents them from completing assignments on time or going to classes/things they want to attend, or if they are doing it in risky situations/facing legal or student conduct action related to the self-stimulation, then the behavior may require a higher level of intervention or referral. Counselors may need to explore healthier ways for the student to engage in self-care or whether the masturbation is a coping mechanism for delaying anxiety.

Sexual Fantasies/Kink

Most sexual fantasies and behaviors are indicators of healthy sexuality (Crooks & Baur, 2011). Students will present frequently asking if what they desire or do is "normal," and providing a nonjudgmental response will assist them in the exploration of *their* answer to this question. As long as no one is getting hurt, they are engaging in behaviors with everyone's explicit consent, and the desire or behavior is not causing significant distress or harm to themselves or others, then our role as counselors is to encourage the safe exploration of their sexuality. Colleges have seen an increase in students exploring bondage, discipline, submission, and dominance following the recent popular books and movies about the topic. Counselors can take this as an opportunity to educate clients about boundaries, sexual limits, safe words, explicit consent, and the requirement of complete sobriety as tenets of the BDSM community.

Although you do not need to be an expert in BDSM or other kink behaviors, giving students permission to talk freely about their desires and fantasies and knowing the best resources is the best practice (Long et al., 2006). Being honest with your clients that you are not an expert on a particular topic, be it a fantasy, birth control, STIs, dating in the online world, and so forth is imperative to having a trusting relationship with them; as is having reliable, accurate, and unbiased resources.

Sexual Dysfunctions

This category is broken down into groups of dysfunctions on the basis of the human sexual response cycle (Masters & Johnson, 1966). Students may need to be evaluated for substance/medication-induced sexual dysfunctions in which the symptoms developed during or shortly after substance intoxication, withdrawal, or exposure to a medication that is capable of causing the sexual symptoms and is causing significant distress (APA, 2013). Treatment varies on the basis of the substance inducing the dysfunction. Helping one student reduce their alcohol use may be sufficient, whereas another may need a supervised detox and inpatient treatment for their alcohol addiction and resulting sexual dysfunction. A counselor should seek a psychiatric consult if an antidepressant could be a trigger. Alcohol has a significant effect on both men's and women's sexual response cycle, but experiencing sexual side effects such as not being able to obtain an erection following a binge-drinking session is to be expected and does not meet the criteria for a dysfunction.

DSM-5 also has coding for "Other Specified Sexual Dysfunction" and "Unspecified Sexual Dysfunction." The first is to be used if a client meets most, but not all, of the criteria for a diagnosis of a specific disorder. The second can be used when a student does not meet the criteria for any of the disorders but is experiencing significant distress. An example of the latter may be a male with the medical condition called Peyronie's disease, in which the penile scar tissue creates significant clinical pain and distress (Crooks & Baur, 2011). There is no pain disorder diagnosis for males, so this may be the only diagnostic fit.

Desire

The two disorders that address problems with sexual desire are male hypoactive sexual desire disorder and female sexual interest/arousal disorder (APA, 2013). Female sexual interest/arousal disorder includes dysfunction in the desire and/or the arousal phase of the sexual response cycle. Desire disorders are marked by a deficiency or absence of sexual/erotic thoughts or fantasies and desire for sexual activity for a period of at least 6 months and causing significant distress in the individual. The female disorder can also include a lack or reduction of sexual excitement or pleasure in response to physical stimulation/erotic cues or the absence of/reduction in genital or nongenital sensations during most sexual encounters.

Researchers have suggested that a woman's subjective sexual arousal is key over the physical stimulation or feelings of desire (Basson et al., 2003). Improving overall mental health or addressing depression, increasing the emotional intimacy in the relationship, and changing the context of sexual behaviors can be effective alongside assessing for biological factors (Basson et al., 2003). For male clients, treatment tends to focus on increasing relationship satisfaction and achieving arousal rather than actually increasing desire (Maurice, 2005). Counselors should also explore whether the lack of desire is a result of performance anxiety, trauma, or attitudinal factors, and whether it is a lifelong issue or acquired. Erotica or self-stimulation can be used to increase desire, as well as desensitization, cognitive restructuring, and/or sensate focus. For women, sometimes introducing external stimulation via sex toys, fantasies, or lubrication can help in triggering desire or arousal.

Arousal

Female arousal disorder was addressed in the preceding section. Male arousal disorder in *DSM-5* is perhaps the best researched and famous of the sexual dysfunctions: erectile disorder. This is an uncommon diagnosis among the traditional college population, and it is recommended that a counselor ensure a medical assessment is completed to rule out injuries or conditions that may be triggers. It is diagnosed on the basis of having difficulty in obtaining or maintain an erection most or all of the time for at least 6 months and the symptoms causing significant distress to the individual (APA, 2013). Not being able to maintain an erection to ejaculation when drunk is not sufficient to meet diagnostic criteria. Although some may default to medical treatment for this, understanding the psychological barriers to the client's arousal, including performance anxiety or pressure to perform sex, is often effective treatment (Long et al., 2006).

Orgasm

The three orgasm-related dysfunctions are delayed ejaculation (delayed, infrequent, or absence of orgasm in males), premature (early) ejaculation (occurring during partnered activity within approximately 1 minute or less following or before penetration), and female orgasmic disorder (delay, infrequent, absence of, or reduced intensity of orgasmic sensations). These criteria must occur almost or all of the time for at least the past 6 months and be a source of significant distress (APA, 2013).

Treatments for delayed ejaculation and orgasmic disorder include sensate focus, cognitive therapy, medical interventions, and introduction of relaxation training into sex play to reduce anxiety (Masters & Johnson, 1970). Female college students may present with orgasmic disorder but would benefit from exploring their sexual pleasure and learning what stimulates them prior to diagnosis. Teaching that women can experience orgasms from a variety of ways (clitoral, penetration, combination) and encouraging self- or partnered exploration can reduce the need for more complicated treatments. Delayed ejaculation is often a perpetuated anxiety in college men; they were unable to ejaculate once, and the fear of not being able to do so again triggers a self-fulfilling cycle (Wincze & Carey, 2001). This disorder is perceived to be common among younger college men, but rarely does it meet the diagnostic criteria requiring ejaculation to occur less than 1 minute after penetration. More often, a counselor can use this as an opportunity to educate the student about the perception of male sexual performance versus the reality and explore the relational dynamics and sexual misunderstandings and teach relaxation skills.

Pain

Genito-pelvic pain/penetration disorder is specific to females and is marked by the persistent or recurrent difficulty with either vaginal penetration, vulvovaginal or pelvic pain during penetration attempts, fear/anxiety about the pain, or tensing/tightening of the pelvic floor during attempts at penetration (APA, 2013). This diagnosis is often associated with sexual violence and/or physical trauma to the genitals and frequently has an anxiety-based component. Any treatment of pain should be done with the consultation of medical professionals and be focused on avoiding further trauma to the student.

Treatment varies depending on which criteria of the diagnosis are met. A gynecological exam is important but should also be trauma informed to avoid the triggering of pain. Cognitive behavioral therapy, trauma-based treatments, relaxation skills, desensitization, vaginal dilation, and surgery are all treatment options. For some, the regular practice of Kegel exercises (strengthening and restoring vaginal muscle tone) may decrease the pain (Long et al., 2006). More intensive physical treatment can be conducted by a pelvic floor physical therapist (Rosenbaum, 2007).

Paraphilic Disorders and Sexual Addiction

Paraphilias are sexual desires or behaviors that produce significant physical, emotional, or social consequences for an individual or those around them (Schwartz & Masters, 1983). Again, these are different than sexual fantasies, fetishes, or kink in that they may lack consent; break the law; are deemed harmful to self, others, or society; or are causing significant distress or impairment in social, occupational, or other areas of functioning. Often these students are only brought to the counselor's attention following student conduct or legal problems. It is important to provide an empathetic response; it can be challenging to build rapport with students who have been referred as a consequence of their behaviors.

The paraphilic disorders are diagnosed on the basis of intense and persistent sexual fantasies, urges, or behaviors that cause significant distress, impair functioning, or potentially cause harm to oneself or others (APA, 2013). They include the following: voyeuristic disorder, which is observing or fantasizing about watching people disrobe, be naked, or engage in sexual activity without their consent; exhibitionistic disorder, which is flashing or otherwise exposing one's genitals to another, nonconsenting, person(s); frotteuristic disorder, which is touching or rubbing against people without their consent; sexual masochism disorder, which is sexual arousal from being humiliated, beaten, bound, or otherwise made to suffer; sexual sadism disorder, which is sexual arousal from making someone else suffer, either psychologically or physically nonconsensually; pedophilic disorder, which is sexual attraction/activity of an adult with a child or children, typically age 13 years or younger; fetishistic disorder, which is engaging in sexual activities with a nonliving object (excluding sex toys) or nongenital body parts (e.g., feet); transvestic disorder, which is cross-dressing for sexual arousal derived from the fabric, materials, or garments or arousal by the thoughts/images of oneself as that gender (typically male to female). All other named paraphilias fall under the category other paraphilic disorder, which includes zoophilia (sexual attraction to animals), necrophilia (corpses), coprophilia (feces), or urophilia (urine); and nonspecified paraphilic disorder, which includes possible dependency on cybersex, compulsive masturbation, prolonged promiscuity, and/or pornography dependence as well as any other sexual behaviors if the behavior has been occurring over a long period of time and is causing significant distress.

Sexual addiction is a controversial topic in the field of therapy. In 2016, the American Association of Sexuality Educators, Counselors and Therapists published a position paper stating it does not find sufficient empirical evidence to support sex/porn addiction as a mental health disorder and that sexual addiction training and treatment are not adequately informed by accurate knowledge of human sexuality (American Association of Sexuality Educators, Counselors and Therapists, 2016). On the other side of the conversation is the International Institute for Trauma and Addiction Professionals, which provides the Certified Sex Addiction Therapist program founded by Dr. Patrick Carnes (International Institute for Trauma and Addiction Professionals, 2017), which recommends that the treatment of sexual addiction involves participation in a 12-step program, cognitive behavioral therapy, family therapy, and trauma treatment. This controversy and conversation around whether a person can be addicted to sex continues, but all sides agree that the behaviors are underpinned by an anxiety-based compulsion, so a comprehensive assessment is essential.

If a student is self-presenting with sex addiction, your response as a counselor should start with assessing the problematic behaviors and beliefs associated with those behaviors. It may be useful to have the student attend a 12-step sex addiction meeting or refer the student out for addiction treatment once the student is well-informed about sex addiction/compulsion and if they think that treatment model will be useful. Some students, particularly men, have a sexual script that they cannot control their sexual desires, so learning to abstain for a time period may shift perspective.

Conclusion

Addressing sexuality-related issues and concerns among the college population can be both exciting and challenging for counselors. If we, as counselors, create a welcoming, sex-positive environment, students will have a place to safely explore their sexuality and discuss very intimate problems, and we get to witness their incredible resilience and growth. If counselors are not aware of their own biases and beliefs within the different Circles of Sexuality, we can cause significant harm or reinforce shame in our clients. Counselors are encouraged to make use of regular supervision, engage in peer feedback, seek counseling as needed, and invest in continuing education around the topic of human sexuality. If counselors would like to learn more and explore becoming a credentialed sexuality therapist, educator, or counselor, information is available online (www.aasect.org).

Final Case Study

Consider the following case studies and begin to develop a conceptualization for each client. At the conclusion of these case studies you will find questions for your reflection as a college counselor.

Case 1

Dominic was introduced earlier in this chapter with this description: "Student A has lost all interest in sex with their new partner; the student is trying to balance classes, support a child, and maintain a single-income home." Dominic is a divorced, Hispanic, straight, male student, age 30, who is in his first year at a small private liberal arts college in rural Pennsylvania, attending full time after being separated from the Air Force for medical reasons after serving for 8 years. His child is 7 years old, and his ex-wife lives nearby and struggles with opioid addiction. He has been dating his current partner for 2 years, but they have not had sex in 3 months, and she has talked about ending the relationship because of his lack of desire for her.

Case 2

Joan was introduced earlier in this chapter with this description: "Student B wants advice on whether to stay with their high school partner and explore having an open long-distance relationship or break up." Joan is a 23-year-old, straight, Chinese, female international graduate student in art history from London, attending a university in New York City. She has been with her partner, Chris, for 3 years, and they were living together before she moved to New York City. He has plans to move to New York City within the year. She has found a supportive and stable friend group in her graduate cohort and does not plan on moving back after graduation.

Case 3

Marcia was introduced earlier in this chapter with this description: "Student C has fears concerning having reached orgasm/ejaculated quickly (possibly too quickly) during sexual activity with casual sex partners." Marcia is a 19-year-old, second-year, Black, gender queer, pansexual student attending a historically Black college in Virginia for computer science. She enjoys having sex at least daily and is feeling guilty for frequently not leaving her partners sexually satisfied. Following her orgasms, it is too painful for penetrative activities to continue. She struggled with severe depression in middle and high school but has not felt depressed since coming to college.

Case 4

Jamie was introduced earlier in this chapter with this description: "Student D was referred by student housing because their roommate is uncomfortable with Student D watching graphic pornography in the shared residence hall room." Jamie is a 21-year-old, White, straight, male, third-year student attending a state college in California on a math scholarship. He completed his associate's degree in math prior to transferring, and this is the first roommate he has had. He has a diagnosis of autism spectrum disorder and is on anti-anxiety medications. He was sexually assaulted in middle school by a group of male classmates at a sleepover, and the assault made national headlines because of the lack of support from the community and the school. His mother and father have requested to meet with you as well.

Case Exploration Questions

For the preceding case studies, answer the following case exploration questions. Responses have been provided for the first case study to guide you.

1. What additional information would you want to know about this student?

   With Dominic, a counselor would explore his medical history; what was his medical reason for separation from the Air Force, and may that be affecting his sexual desire levels? A counselor should also explore what he has done on his own to try to address his lack of sexual desire prior to coming into counseling. How may the many stressors he is coping with be affecting him? Is he able to self-pleasure? What are his feelings around his current partner?

2. What might be some biases you have related to this student's presentation that you should be aware of?

   Did you assume when you read the scenario at the beginning of the chapter that the student was female? Were you surprised that he was a former member of the military or Hispanic? Although everyone's biases are different, one should consider one's beliefs about gender, race, age, and ethnicity while also checking the stereotypes one holds.

3. What area(s) of the Circles of Sexuality would you prioritize exploring with this student, and why?

   The counselor working with Dominic should start with discussing the sensuality and intimacy circles of his sexuality because he is presenting with a sexual desire problem. What does he think a "normal" amount of sexual desire should look like? How does he communicate a desire for intimacy with his partner, and how would she like him to communicate sexual desire for her? When in the past did he feel sexual desire, and what is different now?

4. Is there a provisional diagnosis you would choose and/or other potential co-occurring diagnoses that should be ruled out prior to specifying a provisional diagnosis?

   Dominic's counselor should consider male hypoactive sexual desire disorder as a provisional diagnosis, depending on how long the lack of desire has been occurring. The counselor should also evaluate whether an arousal disorder predicated the desire disorder, because often a lack of desire is a manifestation of difficulty obtaining/maintaining an erection for men. One should also rule out the role anxiety/stress and trauma may be playing. Although not explicitly mentioned in the scenario, one should also assess for indicators of posttraumatic stress disorder because he is former military and spent significant time with an addict.

5. Using the P-LI-SS-IT model, what would your first treatment steps cover with the student?

   Dominic's counselor should start with permission giving, validating the courage it took to seek counseling for this issue and normalizing that experiencing a lack of desire does not make him "less" of a man, partner, Airman, or father. For the limited information stage, a counselor may educate Dominic about the human sexual response cycle and explore where the breakdown is occurring—for example, maybe he is obtaining erections and experiencing desire in the mornings but has to get his child ready before he can engage in sexual activity with his partner. Dominic's counselor might also provide some education on communication skills—for example, having him and his partner explore their love languages or experimenting with a date night.

6. What additional resources and referrals would you consider?

   Potential resources for Dominic to explore include the following: additional low-cost childcare options (on and off campus); financial resources for veterans (Veterans Affairs or a person on campus who specializes in working with veterans); support groups for veterans or those coping with someone in their life having an addiction; a medical evaluation/assessment; and stress management/self-care resources, including trauma-informed yoga. If the desire disorder persists, one should consider a referral to an American Association of Sexuality Educators, Counselors and Therapists–credentialed sexuality therapist.

References

Advocates for Youth. (2007). The circles of human sexuality. Retrieved from https://www.advocatesforyouth.org/wp-content/uploads/storage//advfy/lesson-plans/Session-4.pdf

American Association of Sexuality Educators, Counselors and Therapists. (2016). AASECT position on sex addiction. Retrieved from https://www.aasect.org/position-sex-addiction

American Psychiatric Association. (2013). *Diagnostic and statistical manual of mental disorders* (5th ed.). Arlington, VA: Author.

Annon, J. S. (1974). *The behavioral treatment of sexual problems* (Vol. 1). Honolulu, HI: Enabling Systems.

Basson, R., Leiblum, S. R., Brotto, L., Derogatis. L., Fourcroy, J., Fugl-Meyer, K., . . . Schulz, W. W. (2003). Definitions of women's sexual dysfunction reconsidered: Advocating expansion and revision. *Journal of Psychosomatic Obstetrics and Gynaecology, 24*, 221–229.

Crooks, R., & Baur, K. (2011). *Our sexuality.* Belmont, CA: Wadsworth/Cengage Learning.

Dailey, D. (1981). Sexual expression and ageing. In F. Berghorn & D. Schafer (Eds.), *The dynamics of ageing: Original essays on the process and experiences of growing old* (pp. 311–330). Boulder, CO: Westview Press.

Fisher, T. D., Davis, C. M., Yarber, W. L., & Davis, S. L. (2011). *Handbook of sexuality-related measures* (3rd ed.). New York, NY: Routledge.

Hof, L., & Berman, E. (1986). The sexual genogram. *Journal of Marital and Family Therapy, 12*, 39–47.

International Institute for Trauma and Addiction Professionals. (2017). About CSAT certification and training. Retrieved from https://iitap.com/

Kar, S. K., Choudhury, A., & Singh, A. P. (2015). Understanding normal development of adolescent sexuality: A bumpy ride. *Journal of Human Reproductive Sciences, 8*, 70–74. doi:10.4103/0974-1208.158594

Laumann, E. O., Paik, A., & Rosen, R. C. (1999). Sexual dysfunction in the United States: Prevalence and predictors. *Journal of the American Medical Association, 281,* 537–544.

Leiblum, S. R. (Ed.). (2007). *Principles and practice of sex therapy* (4th ed.). New York, NY: Guilford Press.

Long, L. L., Burnett, J. A., & Thomas, R. V. (2006). *Sexuality counseling: An integrative approach.* Hoboken, NJ: Pearson.

Mason, M. J. (1991). Family therapy as the merging context for sex therapy. In A. S. Gurman & D. P. Kniskern (Eds.), *Handbook of family therapy* (Vol. 2, pp. 479–507). New York, NY: Brunner/Mazel.

Masters, W. H., & Johnson, V. E. (1966). *Human sexual response.* Boston, MA: Little, Brown.

Masters, W. H., & Johnson, V. E. (1970). *Human sexual inadequacy.* Boston, MA: Little, Brown.

Maurice, W. L. (2005). Male hypoactive sexual desire disorder. In R. Balon & R. T. Segraves (Eds.), *Handbook of sexual dysfunction* (pp. 67–109). Boca Raton, FL: Taylor & Francis.

McCabe, M. P., Sharlip, I. D., Lewis, R., Atalla, E., Balon, R., Fisher, A. D., . . . Segraves, R. T. (2016). Incidence and prevalence of sexual dysfunction in women and men: A consensus statement from the Fourth International Consultation on Sexual Medicine 2015. *Journal of Sexual Medicine, 13,* 144–152. doi:10.1016/J.JSXM.2015.12.034

O'Sullivan, L. F., Brotto, L. A., Byers, E. S., Majerovich, J. A., & Wuest, J. A. (2014). Prevalence and characteristics of sexual functioning among sexually experienced middle to late adolescents. *Journal of Sexual Medicine, 11,* 630–641. doi:10.1111/jsm.12419

Rosenbaum, T. Y. (2007). Physical therapy management and treatment of sexual pain disorders. In S. R. Leiblum (Ed.), *Principles and practice of sex therapy* (4th ed., pp. 157–177). New York, NY: Guilford Press.

Satterly, B., & Dyson, D. (2010). Social work practice with gay, lesbian, bisexual, and transgendered persons. In J. Poulin (Ed.), *Collaborative social work: Strengths-based generalist practice* (3rd ed.). Belmont, CA: Wadsworth.

Schwartz, M. F., & Masters, W. H. (1983). Conceptual factors in the treatment of paraphilias: A preliminary report. *Journal of Sex & Marital Therapy, 9,* 3–18.

Wilcox, S. L., Redmond S., & Hassan, A. M. (2014). Sexual functioning in military personnel: Preliminary estimates and predictors. *Journal of Sexual Medicine, 11,* 2537–2545. doi:10.1111/jsm.12643

Wincze, J. P., & Carey, M. P. (2001). *Sexual dysfunction: A guide for assessment and treatment* (2nd ed.). New York, NY: Guilford Press.

Chapter 23

Sexual Victimization

Kristin Bruns

Today in science class I learned that
every cell in our entire body is replaced every 7 years.
How lovely it is to know one day I will have a body
you will have never touched.

—Anonymous survivor

Reflection Exercise

1. What assumptions do I hold about those who have been sexually assaulted?
2. How might my own experiences of sexual assault (or experiences of those I am close with) affect my work with college students?
3. What do I know about intimate partner violence (IPV)? What do I need to learn more about?
4. Do I know my university expectations/protocol if a student tells me he or she has been sexually harassed or sexually assaulted?

Sexual victimization affects students on college campuses across the country. This chapter will discuss the prevalence of sexual victimization among college students to provide context on the severity of this experience for students. Critical terms (*rape, sexual assault, intimate partner violence*, etc.) are defined to ensure that professionals on the college campus are aware of correct terminology and information for each respective topic. Stalking and tracking via technology will also be discussed, given the rise of access to and the use of technology. Clinical implications for college counselors will be discussed. Finally, federal guidelines and prevention resources will be provided.

Prevalence of Sexual Victimization (and Reporting) Among College Students

Sexual violence, stalking, and IPV are public health problems that affect millions of Americans each year. Sexual violence can happen to anyone regardless of race, gender, sexual orientation, class, or profession. Nationally, one in five women and one in 71 men will be raped at some point in their lives (Black et al., 2011). For college students, one in five women and one in 20 men experience sexual assault while enrolled in college (Krebs et al., 2016). Whereas the statistics for women stay the same, the drastic increase in likelihood of a male college student experiencing sexual assault is worth noting, as sexual assault is at times stereotyped as something that only happens to women.

Many sexual assaults on college campuses fall under the definition of "incapacitated sexual assault," which describes assaults that take place while the victim is "drunk, under the influence of drugs, passed out, asleep, or otherwise incapacitated" (Pact5, n.d.). About half of sexual assaults involve victims consuming alcohol before the assault (Orchowski & Gidycz, 2012; Orchowski, Untied, & Gidycz, 2013). Although alcohol does not directly cause sexual assault, perpetrators can use alcohol as a tool for committing the sexual violence, and an intoxicated person is more vulnerable to sexual violence. Another important factor is the relationship between the perpetrator and the victim of the sexual assault. Research has shown that for seven out of 10 people experiencing sexual assault, the perpetrator is someone known to the victim (Department of Justice, Office of Justice Programs, Bureau of Justice Statistics, 2015b).

College counselors need to be aware of many factors surrounding sexual assault, including the reporting rates of college students who have experienced sexual violence. In 2015, the *Report on the AAU* [Association for American Universities] *Campus Climate Survey on Sexual Assault and Sexual Misconduct* surveyed more than 150,000 students at 27 universities (Cantor et al., 2017). The AAU study found that overall rates of reporting to campus officials and law enforcement or others were low, with university reporting percentages ranging from 5% to 28%, depending on the specific type of sexual violence behavior. When participants were asked about reasons for not reporting, the most common response for not reporting incidents of sexual assault and sexual misconduct was that "it was not considered serious enough"; other participant reasons included statements sharing that they were "too embarrassed, ashamed or that it would be too emotionally difficult," and they "did not think anything would be done about it" (Cantor et al., 2017, p. 36). These findings help to demonstrate not only the significant number of students that choose not to report but also the potential emotional impact that prevents students from feeling safe to report.

Rape and Sexual Assault

When talking about sexual assault and sexual victimization with clients, counselors must be knowledgeable of current terms and their definitions. Counselors must also be able to have an appropriate dialogue using accurate definitions. This will create a safe space that gives clients permission to engage in dialogue about their experiences if they so choose. *Rape* is defined as "penetration, no matter how slight, of the vagina or anus with any body part or object, or oral penetration by a sex organ of another person, without the consent of the victim" (Department of Justice, 2012). This definition provides clarification, in that the victim and perpetrator can be of any gender. This updated definition shows progression in addressing the misperception that sexual assault only happens to women (by men). The current definition provides clarity in that there is no change in the meaning of rape whether a person experiences rape with an object or penile/vaginal rape. Furthermore, this definition recognizes the importance of consent.

Another area for counselors to be knowledgeable in is consent. Physical resistance is not required on the part of the victim to demonstrate lack of consent. Furthermore, the use of substances can have an impact on consent. As stated earlier, many incidences of sexual violence are facilitated by drugs or alcohol. *Drug-facilitated sexual assault* occurs when drugs or alcohol are used to compromise an individual's ability to consent. Alcohol is most commonly used to facilitate sexual assault; however, other drugs such as Rohypnol (roofies), gamma hydroxybutyrate (known as GHB), and gamma Butyrolactone (known as GBL) also are used in reducing a person's ability to consent to sexual activity (Sexual and Relationship Violence Support Services, n.d.). In addition, drugs and alcohol can reduce the resistance, memory, and credibility of the victim. The current definition of rape recognizes that a victim can be incapacitated and thus unable to consent because of ingestion of drugs or alcohol. Counselors need to be aware that each state holds their own individual statutes to provide additional clarification for legal purposes. Counselors can search for applicable laws in their state online (https://apps.rainn.org/policy/).

Sexual assault is defined as any type of sexual contact or behavior that occurs without the explicit consent of the recipient (Department of Justice, Office of Justice Programs, Bureau of Justice Statistics, 2014). Although different from rape, an important component that remains in this definition is the term *explicit consent*. Consenting for sexual activities includes an agreement (verbal or nonverbal) between participants to engage in the decided upon sexual activity. Although consent does not have to be verbal, communicating verbally can provide additional clarity with respect to each person's boundaries. The following are examples of consent: (a) explicitly agreeing to a sexual activity (e.g., saying "yes") or another affirmative statement (e.g., "I'm open to trying") and (b) using physical cues to communicate comfort in continuing a sexual activity. Communicating consent for sexual activity should happen every time. If a person gives consent for one activity, one time, this does not automatically mean he or she is giving consent for increased or recurring sexual contact. For example, agreeing to kiss someone does not give a person permission to remove their clothes, without additional consent.

Sexual assaults, including rape, are criminal and university offenses, and there are options for pursuing these charges should a client choose to do so. Clients may decide to pursue legal action for one, both, or neither of these charges. Deciding to press criminal charges and involve the police is solely the client's decision. Initially, the counselor's role includes being aware of additional resources on campus and within the local community; connecting the client to resources (if the client wants this); allowing time and space in the counseling office for the client to weigh his or her options; and most important, providing the client with a place to process his or her experience. To be clear, it is not the counselor's role to persuade clients into a decision to report or not report. Many professionals on campus will have a role that makes them a mandatory reporter of sexual assault. Counselors can protect a client's privacy through confidentiality as defined in the American Counseling Association's (ACA's) *ACA Code of Ethics* (ACA, 2014). Protection under the *ACA Code of Ethics* (Standards A.2.b., B.1.d., B.5.a., and F.1.c.) gives students a safe place to process their experiences of sexual victimization without worries of mandated reporting. However, other student affairs professionals may be mandated reporters. Title IX guidelines state, "responsible employees" with authority to take action to redress sexual violence, or who have been deemed mandated reporters by their institutions, or who students reasonably could believe have authority or responsibility over such matters, are required to report discrimination (Department of Education, 2015). Therefore, it is critical for all student affairs professionals to understand who their campus deems a "responsible employee."

Sexual Harassment

Sexual harassment is defined as unwelcome sexual advances, requests for sexual favors, or other conduct (verbal or physical) of a sexual nature (U.S. Equal Employment Opportunity Commission, n.d.). Examples of sexual harassment include sharing sexually inappropriate images or videos, such as pornography, with coworkers; making sexual comments about appearance, clothing, or body parts; inappropriately touching another person, including pinching, patting, rubbing, or purposefully brushing up against another person; asking sexual questions, such as questions about someone's sexual history or their sexual orientation; or making offensive comments about someone's sexual orientation or gender identity. This is not an all-inclusive list; sexual harassment can take form in any sexual action that creates a hostile work environment. Sexual harassment can have an impact on not only the victim of the harassment (or target of offense) but also anyone who is affected by the inappropriate behavior. The person engaging in harassing behavior typically has some form of power or authority over the victim; however, the harasser can be a peer or a subordinate of the victim of harassment (e.g., a colleague, supervisee, student employee).

Legally, sexual harassment happens when "(1) submission is either explicitly or implicitly a condition affecting academic or employment decisions; (2) the behavior is sufficiently severe or pervasive as to create an intimidating, hostile or repugnant environment; or (3) the behavior persists despite objection by the person to whom the conduct is directed" (Sexual Assault Prevention and Awareness Center, n.d.). Universities consider any of these categories of behavior, whether physical or verbal, to be a breach of its standards of conduct. According to Title IX (defined below), universities have a responsibility to prevent incidents of sexual harassment and take corrective action when sexual harassment occurs.

Two types of sexual harassment are quid pro quo and hostile environment. *Quid pro quo* (meaning "this for that") occurs when an academic or employment decision about a student or employee depends upon whether the student or employee submits to conduct of a sexual nature. This can be directly stated or implied. For example, a student employee is offered a promotion if he or she goes on a date with his or her supervisor. *Hostile environment* occurs when unwelcome conduct of a sexual nature creates an intimidating, threatening, or abusive working or learning environment. When a person's conduct is so severe, persistent, or pervasive that it affects another's ability to participate in or benefit from a university program or activity, this would likely meet the criteria for a hostile work environment. As stated earlier, sexual harassment can be reported by the target of the offense or any individuals who feel it has directly and negatively affected them.

If a university is receiving federal funding, it must designate at least one employee to coordinate its efforts to comply with and carry out its responsibilities under Title IX (discussed in the Federal Guidelines and Prevention section) and must notify all students and employees of that employee's contact information. This employee is generally referred to as the Title IX coordinator. Also under federal law, all institutions of higher education must designate members of their staff with significant responsibility for student and campus activities as "responsible employees." Responsible employees have an obligation to report immediately any information they come to learn regarding suspected sexual misconduct. Furthermore, these individuals cannot agree to maintain privacy or confidentiality with respect to such matters. Many times, a majority of student affairs professionals are identified as "responsible employees." However, because of the *ACA Code of Ethics* (ACA, 2014), college counselors are not identified as people who need to report to the Title IX coordinator or other institutional officials if a client discloses experiences with sexual misconduct. Confidentiality, as identified by the *ACA Code of Ethics* (ACA, 2014, Standards A.2.b., B.1.d., B.5.a., and F.1.c.), protects the disclosure of sexual misconduct within the counseling setting. However, if a person is trained as a counselor, but is working in a student affairs role (e.g., academic adviser), he or she would need to comply with the university guidelines on who is considered a "responsible employee." The *ACA Code of Ethics* is only applicable if you are working in the role of a counselor, not as a student affairs professional.

Intimate Partner Violence

IPV is a serious, preventable public health problem that affects millions of Americans and occurs across the life span. Women ages 18 to 24 and 25 to 34 generally experience the highest rates of IPV (Department of Justice, Office of Justice Programs, Bureau of Justice Statistics, 2015a). Because many college students fall into these age ranges, college counselors need increased awareness and knowledge in this area. IPV is also referred to as *domestic violence*, which includes physical violence, sexual violence, stalking, and psychological aggression (including coercive tactics) by a current or former intimate partner (i.e., spouse, boyfriend/girlfriend, dating partner, or ongoing sexual partner). Victims of IPV experience a variety of negative health issues, including posttraumatic stress disorder, depression, anxiety, and loss of self-esteem (Posick, 2014; Posick, Agnich, Policastro, & Hatfield, 2016). Studies of sexual and IPV victimization have suggested that victims often disclose their victimization to, and seek help from, informal sources, including friends (Sabina & Ho, 2014; Sylaska & Edwards, 2014). Knowing this, university administrators can increase efforts to raise general awareness among students about IPV and available resources, as well as providing peer gatekeeper training that encourages students to direct their peers to counseling resources when needed. Overall, this may lead to increased levels of counseling services utilization among victims. As a standard, universities should provide information not only about counseling services but also about other available services specific to victims of IPV (Posick et al., 2016).

IPV occurs in all types of intimate relationships; however, the distribution of IPV among groups is not shared equally. There is a disproportionate effect of IPV on racial/ethnic and sexual minority groups. Data from the National Intimate Partner and Sexual Violence Survey (Black et al., 2011) indicated that the lifetime prevalence of experiencing contact sexual violence, physical violence, or stalking by an intimate partner for women is as follows: 57% among multiracial women, 48% among American Indian/Alaska Native women, 45% among non-Hispanic Black women, 37% among non-Hispanic White women, 34% among Hispanic women, and 18% among Asian-Pacific Islander women. The lifetime prevalence for men is as follows: 42% among multiracial men, 41% among American Indian/Alaska Native men, 40% among non-Hispanic Black men, 30% among non-Hispanic White men, 30% among Hispanic men, and 14% among Asian-Pacific Islander men. Additionally, the National Intimate Partner and Sexual Violence Survey (Smith et al., 2017) report on victimization shows IPV disproportionately affecting minorities of sexual orientation as well, with lifetime IPV prevalence rates reports of 61% of bisexual women, 37% of bisexual men, 44% of lesbian women, 26% of gay men, 35% of heterosexual women, and 29% of heterosexual men.

Stalking and Monitoring via Technology

IPV can include threats or stalking in person or through mobile devices, email, and social media sites. While legal definitions of stalking vary from one state to another, one definition of stalking is "a course of conduct directed at a specific person that would cause a reasonable person to feel fear" (Stalking Resource Center, 2012). Common behaviors that stalkers may engage in are following the victim and showing up to places uninvited; sending unwanted gifts, emails, or texts; monitoring a person's phone calls or computer use; or threatening to hurt the victim or their family and friends (emotionally or physically). Regarding prevalence of stalking on college campuses, individuals ages 18 to 24 experience the highest rate of stalking (Breiding et al., 2014). Cantor et al. (2017) found that 4.2% of students reported having experienced stalking since entering college. As with rates of perpetrators of sexual assault being known to the victim, many times victims of stalking know the perpetrator too. In a study by Breiding et al. (2014), 61% of female victims and 44% of male victims of stalking reported being stalked by a current or former intimate partner, whereas only 25% of female victims and 32% of male victims reported being stalked by an acquaintance. Knowing the statistics of stalking helps to provide a strong rationale for counselors assessing stalking behaviors when assessing for IPV.

Clinical Implications (Assessment and Treatment)

Assessment Tools for IPV

The most studied tools for assessing IPV are the Hurt, Insult, Threaten, and Scream (Sherin, Sinacore, Li, Zitter, & Shakil, 1998); the Woman Abuse Screening Tool (Brown, Lent, Brett, Sas, & Pederson, 1996); the Partner Violence Screen (Feldhaus et al., 1997); and the Abuse Assessment Screen (Rabin, Jennings, Campbell, & Bair-Merritt, 2009). A brief description for each of the inventories is provided. Hurt, Insult, Threaten, and Scream is a screening tool that uses four questions and a simple rating scale to assess for IPV. Each question uses a severity scale (e.g., 1 = *never*, 2 = *rarely*, 3 = *sometimes*, 4 = *fairly often*, and 5 = *frequently*) to determine an overall severity score, with a maximum of 20. The screening tool may be completed via self-report or during an interview with the client. Any score over 10 warrants further examination for IPV risk. The Woman Abuse Screening Tool is a screening instrument that consists of seven questions that assess for IPV, specifically looking for symptoms of physical and emotional violence. The tool is meant to be used as a self-report instrument for the individual. There is also a shortened version that consists of two questions. Both are set up using a rating scale (e.g., *often*, *sometimes*, or *never*) to determine frequency of incidents. The Partner Violence Screen is a screening tool that is administered by the clinician. The clinician asks three questions; if any are answered with a "yes," the tool is considered positive for IPV. The Abuse Assessment Screen is an assessment instrument that uses five questions administered by a clinician. If any of the five questions are answered with a "yes," the screen is considered positive in terms of IPV. If the individual answers "yes" to any of the abuse questions, the clinician then asks the individual to use a pencil to specifically mark the areas of their body (on the given diagram within the screening tool) in which the abuse occurred. All of these assessment tools can be found online (https://www.cdc.gov/violenceprevention/pdf/ipv/ipvandsvscreening.pdf).

Regarding the aforementioned inventories/screening tools, it is important to understand that overall, there is a lack of consensus about the most appropriate measure for IPV. Because IPV includes many facets, which complicates the sensitivity and specificity of inventories, there is currently no benchmark for a chosen inventory. However, to strengthen an assessment for IPV, a counselor can use the noted inventories in conjunction with a verbal assessment. Regardless of whether a college counseling center has a specific inventory for IPV, counselors should be verbally assessing for IPV with every client at the time of the intake assessment, as well as any time a client shares information that may suggest there is any level of IPV in their relationship.

Assessment of IPV

If a client discloses IPV, the counselor should, at a minimum, assess for the client's immediate safety, provide brief counseling, and link the client to campus and community support services and resources. Counselors should consider identifying local resources and contacting domestic violence and sexual violence support services ahead of time to best understand the services provided. More than 27% of women and 11% of men have experienced IPV and experienced an IPV-related impact (Smith et al., 2017). Some of the negative impacts reported were feeling fearful (62%, women; 18%, men), feeling concern for their safety (57%, women; 17%, men), and experiencing symptoms of posttraumatic stress disorder (52%, women; 17%, men; National Intimate Partner and Sexual Violence Survey (Smith et al., 2017). Clients may also present with guilt and shame, loss of control, mistrust, self-blame, anger, avoidance, and numbness. These symptoms would indicate a clinician might consider doing further assessment for a diagnosis of posttraumatic stress disorder. Regarding long-term work with clients who have experienced IPV and meet criteria for trauma-related disorder, there are evidence-based modalities of counseling that should be considered. The following have shown efficacy in working with clients who have experienced trauma: cognitive behavioral therapy, cognitive processing therapy, prolonged exposure, and eye-movement desensitization and reprocessing therapy (Simiola, Neilson, Thompson, & Cook, 2015).

Counselors engaged in treatment with clients reporting any level of IPV need to be aware of how their professional code of ethics guides them, and what differences exist on campus for expectations of reporting. As mentioned earlier, counselors do not fall under the category of a mandated reporter for Title IX, as most student affairs professionals do. Counselors do, however, have a duty not only to uphold confidentiality (directly stated in *ACA Code of Ethics*, Standards A.2.b., B.1.d., B.5.a., and F.1.c.; ACA, 2014) but also to make sure the client understands what falls under protected information (it should be written into the informed consent). College counselors can engage in a trusted relationship with clients (with exceptions of limits of confidentiality) because of the protection from the professional guidelines provided by the *ACA Code of Ethics* (Standards A.2.b., B.1.d., B.5.a., F.1.c.). The counselor has a responsibility to define these components when reviewing the informed consent with clients at the time of intake and any other appropriate time during treatment.

Assessment and Treatment of Sexual Assault and Rape

If a student were to report a sexual assault or rape to a counselor or a student affairs professional, both parties would offer the resource of the identified Title IX coordinator. To clarify (as discussed earlier), the counselor (working in a counseling setting) would not be a mandatory reporter, but depending on the university guidelines, the student affairs professional may be. Either way, students should be made aware of this resource. Counselors and student affairs professionals are not in a place to investigate/assess a sexual assault or rape reported by a student. That is the role of the identified Title IX coordinator on each campus. Rather, both college counselors and student affairs professionals can provide a safe space and nonjudgmental approach to hearing the student's story. The following tips may be helpful when one is listening to a student recount his or her experience: (a) present and engage with a calm demeanor; (b) do not rush the process—give the student time; (c) do not overwhelm the student with questions about the incident; and (d) be empathic in your reflections/statements.

Following a student's report of sexual assault or rape, college counselors will be engaged in the treatment process with the client (as long as the client is seeking treatment) and would treat a client who has experienced this type of traumatic incident in a way similar to the way in which they would treat those who have experienced other traumas. For example, trauma-focused cognitive behavioral therapy, eye-movement desensitization and reprocessing, and somatic experiencing have been identified as evidence-based practices for trauma and would be appropriate for victims of sexual assault or rape. Counselors should be using an overall trauma-informed care approach when working with students who have experienced sexual assault or rape.

Federal Guidelines and Prevention

Universities receiving federal funding must comply with and follow all federal requirements. Employees on college campuses (including college counselors) need to know about the following policies that give professionals guidance when responding to reports of sexual violence:

- Jeanne Clery Disclosure of Campus Security Policy and Campus Crime Statistics Act of 1990
  https://clerycenter.org/
- Title IX
  https://www2.ed.gov/about/offices/list/ocr/docs/dcl-title-ix-coordinators-guide-201504.pdf
- Violence Against Women Reauthorization Act of 2019
  https://www.leahy.senate.gov/imo/media/doc/VAWA_Reauth2013.pdf

For example, under Title IX, schools must follow a three-part protocol, which includes (a) distributing a notice of nondiscrimination policy to students, employees, and other campus personnel; (b) designating a Title IX coordinator to manage and respond to complaints; and (c) developing and publishing grievance procedures that provide practices to prevent, investigate, and remediate complaints in a timely manner (Department of Education, 2015). Beyond this, universities are required to provide education and prevention programs on sexual assault, sexual violence, dating violence, domestic violence, and stalking. As sexual assault can affect the lives of many college students, it is imperative for college campus personnel to focus on prevention and identify evidence-based strategies that reduce violence. Listed in the next section are resources to better understand Title IX, as well as sexual violence prevention and programming.

Additional Resources for Title IX and Sexual Violence Programming/Prevention

- American Association of University Women: Ending Campus Sexual Assault Tool Kit
  http://www.aauw.org/resource/campus-sexual-assault-tool-kit/
- Information and an overview of Title IX
  http://www.justice.gov/crt/title-ix-education-amendments-1972
- Know Your IX/Empowering Students to Stop Sexual Violence
  http://knowyourix.org
- The Red Flag Campaign
  http://www.theredflagcampaign.org/
- Relationship and Sexual Violence Prevention office and programming, University of Georgia
  https://www.uhs.uga.edu/rsvp/
- *Sexual Violence on Campus: Strategies for Prevention*
  https://www.cdc.gov/violenceprevention/pdf/campussvprevention.pdf

Conclusion

Sexual victimization affects students and campuses nationwide; therefore, the response of professionals on campuses is critical to students' safety, health, and development. Because instances of sexual victimization can affect a student's academic performance and retention, it is imperative that counselors and student affairs professionals respond appropriately when faced with a student experiencing distress. Counselors and student affairs professionals play a critical role in providing students with access to appropriate resources. Whereas counselors have guidance from their professional code of ethics regarding confidentiality, student affairs professionals need to be mindful of federal guidelines and university expectations to best understand what is expected of them when it comes to reporting. Although much of the chapter has focused on how to respond after finding out about an incident of sexual victimization, prevention is a critical step for campuses creating a safe and supportive atmosphere. Being proactive versus reactive helps demonstrate the significance of the issue and stance of the university.

Final Case Studies

Case 1

Heather is a first-year, first-generation student attending University ABC, pursuing a bachelor's degree in economics. University ABC has a student population of 14,000 students and is a traditional, residential campus in the Midwest. Heather identifies as a 19-year-old, Native American, bisexual, cisgender, female student. Before coming to University ABC, Heather took a year off between high school and college to be with her family after both of her maternal grandparents passed away in a car accident. Heather has not received any formal mental health counseling to address the grief she recently experienced but did seek out spiritual guidance from a well-respected elder within her tribal community. Heather is required to live on campus in residential housing because the university policy states all first- and second-year students must reside on campus unless their home residence is within a 50-mile radius. Heather grew up in a tribal community located more than 3 hours from campus.

Heather presents to the college counseling center, noting her primary concern as "relationship concerns." As you (the assigned college counselor) meet with Heather for the first time to complete the intake assessment, she provides information indicating she may be experiencing IPV. Heather shared the following when describing the relationship with her significant other: "I think it is just his way of showing me he loves me. I mean . . . if I don't answer my phone, he will call or text me repeatedly or sometimes he'll even show up at the end of my chemistry class. Sometimes he says he will share intimate photos that we have taken or tell my family that we are having sex, but I think it is just because he wants me to know how important I am to him. Once, he told me that he would send his friends nude pictures of me if I wouldn't have sex with him. He just . . . always wants to hook up . . . which is kind of cool. No one has ever wanted me so much." When Heather was asked who else she has shared her "relationship concerns" with, she stated, "No one, really. I don't want my family to worry."

Case 1 Exploration Questions

1. What are the cultural/contextual issues you need to pay attention to?
2. What do you believe is a "healthy relationship"? How might these beliefs affect your work with this client?
3. What are the resources within your campus/university that may be beneficial for Heather?
4. How would the role of a counselor be different than the role of a student affairs professional in this case study?

Case 2

Joe is a sophomore attending a large public institution in the Midwest. Joe is proud to be a member of a fraternity and was very excited to move into the fraternity house in his sophomore year. Last week, while the fraternity was hosting an event, Joe passed out from alcohol use. When Joe woke up, he was receiving oral sex from a woman whom he did not know. Joe felt uncomfortable and asked the woman to stop. Joe has shared this experience with only one friend, who responded, "Dude, are you kidding me? Why are you even upset?"

Joe has come to your office to "catch up," as he hasn't seen you since living in the residence halls. You (a residence hall director) happily invite Joe into your office to talk. Joe asks you to close the door and shares his experience.

Case 2 Exploration Questions

1. What thoughts came to mind as you read the case study? Are there any biases that came through?
2. How would you respond to Joe? What would be the first thing you would say?
3. What are your campus's policies for mandated reporting? Whom do you report to on your campus if you are a mandated reporter?
4. What boundaries would be important to keep in mind when talking with/supporting Joe?

References

American Counseling Association. (2014). *ACA code of ethics*. Alexandria, VA: Author.

Black, M. C., Basile, K. C., Breiding, M. J., Walters, M. L., Merrick, M. T., . . . Stevens, M. R. (2011). *National Intimate Partner and Sexual Violence Survey: 2010 summary report.* Centers for Disease Control and Prevention, National Center for Injury Prevention and Control. Retrieved from http://www.cdc.gov/ViolencePrevention/pdf/NISVS_Report2010-a.pdf

Breiding, M. J., Smith, S. G., Basile, K. C., Walters, M. L., Chen, J., & Merrick, M. T. (2014). Prevalence and characteristics of sexual violence, stalking, and intimate partner violence victimization—National Intimate Partner and Sexual Violence Survey, United States, 2011. *Morbidity and Mortality Weekly Report, Surveillance Summaries, 63*(8). Retrieved from http://www.cdc.gov/mmwr/preview/mmwrhtml/ss6308a1.htm?s_cid=ss6308a1_e

Brown, J. B., Lent, B., Brett, P. J., Sas, G., & Pederson, L. L. (1996). Development of the Woman Abuse Screening Tool for use in family practice. *Family Medicine, 28*, 422–428.

Cantor, D., Fisher, B., Chibnall, S., Townsend, R., Lee, H., Bruce, C., & Thomas, G. (2017). *Report on the AAU Campus Climate Survey on Sexual Assault and Sexual Misconduct.* Association of American Universities (AAU). Retrieved from https://www.aau.edu/sites/default/files/AAU-Files/Key-Issues/Campus-Safety/AAU-Campus-Climate-Survey-FINAL-10-20-17.pdf

Department of Education. (2015). Sexual harassment guidance. Retrieved from https://www2.ed.gov/about/offices/list/ocr/docs/sexhar01.html

Department of Justice. (2012). The Department of Justice Archives. Retrieved from https://www.justice.gov/archives/opa/blog/updated-definition-rape

Department of Justice, Office of Justice Programs, Bureau of Justice Statistics. (2014). Rape and sexual assault victimization among college-age females, 1995–2013. Retrieved from https://www.bjs.gov/content/pub/pdf/rsavcaf9513.pdf

Department of Justice, Office of Justice Programs, Bureau of Justice Statistics. (2015a). Intimate partner violence, 1993–2010. (Original work published 2012). Retrieved from http://www.bjs.gov/content/pub/pdf/ipv9310.pdf

Department of Justice, Office of Justice Programs, Bureau of Justice Statistics. (2015b). National Crime Victimization Survey (NCVS), 2010–2014. Retrieved from https://www.bjs.gov/index.cfm?ty=dcdetail&iid=245

Feldhaus, K. M., Koziol-McLain, J., Amsbury, H. L., Norton, I. M., Lowenstein, S. R., & Abbot, J. T. (1997). Accuracy of 3 brief screening questions for detecting partner violence in the emergency department. *Journal of the American Medical Association, 277,* 1357–1361.

Jeanne Clery Disclosure of Campus Security Policy and Campus Crime Statistics Act of 1990, 20 U.S.C. § 1092(f) (2019).

Krebs, C., Lindquist, C., Berzofsky, M., Shook-Sa, B., Peterson, K., Planty, M., . . . Stroop, J. (2016). Campus Climate Survey validation study: Final technical report. Washington, DC: Department of Justice, Bureau of Justice Statistics.

Orchowski, L. M., & Gidycz, C. A. (2012). To whom do college women confide following sexual assault? A prospective study of predictors of sexual assault disclosure and social reactions. *Violence Against Women, 18,* 264–288. doi:10.1177/1077801212442917

Orchowski, L. M., Untied, A. S., & Gidycz, C. A. (2013). Social reactions to disclosure of sexual victimization and adjustment among survivors of sexual assault. *Journal of Interpersonal Violence, 28,* 2005–2023. doi:10.1177/0886260512471085

Pact5. (n.d.). Substance use and sexual assault. Retrieved from http://pactfive.nextmp.net/resources/prevention-and-readiness/substance-use-and-sexual-assault/

Posick, C. (2014). Victimization and reporting to the police: The role of negative emotionality. *Psychology of Violence, 4,* 210–223.

Posick, C., Agnich, L. E., Policastro, C., & Hatfield, H. (2016). Who seeks counseling for intimate partner violence? The role of emotional distress. *Criminal Justice Review, 41,* 159–172. doi:10.1177/0734016816635249

Rabin, R. F., Jennings, J. M., Campbell, J. C., & Blair-Merritt, M. H. (2009). Intimate partner violence screening tools. *American Journal of Preventive Medicine, 36,* 439–445. doi:10.1016/j.amepre.2009.01.024

Sabina, C., & Ho, L. (2014). Campus and college victim responses to sexual assault and dating violence: Disclosure, service utilization, and service provision. *Trauma Violence Abuse, 15,* 201–226.

Sexual and Relationship Violence Support Services. (n.d.). Alcohol, drugs and sexual assault. Retrieved from https://www.kent.edu/srvss/alcohol-drugs-and-sexual-assault

Sexual Assault Prevention and Awareness Center. (n.d.). What is sexual harassment? Retrieved from https://sapac.umich.edu/article/63

Sherin, K. M., Sinacore, J. M., Li, X. Q., Zitter, R. E., & Shakil, A. (1998). HITS: A short domestic violence screening tool for use in a family practice setting. *Family Medicine, 30,* 508–512.

Simiola, V., Neilson, E., Thompson, R., & Cook, J. (2015). Preferences for trauma treatment: A systematic review of the empirical literature. *Psychological Trauma: Theory, Research, Practice, and Policy, 7,* 516–524. doi:10.1037/tra0000038.supp

Smith, S. G., Chen, J., Basile, K. C., Gilbert, L. K., Merrick, M. T., Patel, N., . . . Jain, A. (2017). *The National Intimate Partner and Sexual Violence Survey (NISVS): 2010–2012 state report.* Atlanta, GA: Centers for Disease Control and Prevention, National Center for Injury Prevention and Control.

Stalking Resource Center. (2012). What is stalking? Retrieved from https://victimsofcrime.org/our-programs/past-programs/stalking-resource-center

Sylaska, K., & Edwards, K. M. (2014). Disclosure of intimate partner violence to informal social support network members: A review of the literature. *Trauma Violence Abuse, 15,* 3–21. doi:10.1177/1524838013496335
U.S. Equal Employment Opportunity Commission. (n.d.). Sexual harassment. Retrieved from https://www.eeoc.gov/laws/types/sexual_harassment.cfm
Violence Against Women Reauthorization Act of 2019, 42 U.S.C. §§ 13701 (2019).

Index

Boxes, figures, and tables are indicated by b, f, and t following the page numbers.

A

Abes, E. S., 191, 194–196, 265–266, 270
Abortion, 421–422
Abrahamsen, B., 306
Abstinence, 421
Abuse Assessment Screen, 436
ACA. *See* American Counseling Association
ACA Code of Ethics
  on advocacy, 87
  on assessments, 88–89
  on autonomy, 87–88, 91
  on confidentiality, 85–86, 433–434, 437
  on diversity and multiculturalism, 79
  on informed consent, 82, 84, 88–89
  on minors as clients, 80
  on multicultural competence, 52, 56
  overview, 78
  principles of professional ethical behavior, 289
  on social media use, 91–92
Academic adjustment, 112–113
Academic and career counseling, 299–316
  academic counseling, 83, 299–302, 304–306, 310–311
  career counseling, 4, 264, 302–303, 306–307, 311–312
  case studies, 307–308
  first-generation students and, 310–312
  lower SES students and, 304–310
  reflection exercise, 299
  special populations and, 303–312
Academic stress, 334–335
ACCA. *See* American College Counseling Association
Accessibility Guidelines for Buildings and Facilities (ADA), 8
Access to higher education, 7–9, 109*b*, 262
Accommodations, 89–90, 147, 234
Accreditation, 15–16, 28–29, 80
Acculturation, 117
ACHA. *See* American College Health Association
Achievement guilt, 311
ACPA. *See* American College Personnel Association–College Student Educators International
Active listening, 170, 287
Active Minds, 157
Activism, 272
ADA (Americans With Disabilities Act of 1990), 8, 48, 89
Adams, C. E., 355
Adams, S. D., 131
Adaptation, 234
Addictions. *See also* Substance use and addiction
  behavioral, 324, 381
  food, 381
  sexual, 424–425
Adjustment of students. *See also* Homesickness
  coping skills for, 254, 257
  first-generation college students and, 304
  situational depression and, 357–360
  stress and, 134, 334
  student affairs and support for, 111–114, 111–112*b*
Adrenaline, 332
Adult ADHD Self-Report Scale, 35
Adult nontraditional students, 18
Adverse Childhood Experiences scale, 323
Advocacy, 66–68, 87, 93–94
Advocates for Youth, 416, 418
African American students, 114–115*b*, 304. *See also* Historically black colleges and universities
Agency, 264
Age under 18 of clients, 80–81
Agricultural College Act of 1890, 103
Alamuddin, R., 149
Albom, Mitch, 279
Alcohol use. *See* Substance use and addiction
Alcohol Use Disorders Identification Test, 322
Alessandria, Kathryn P. "Tina," 3
Alexithymia, 394, 403
American Association of Sexuality Educators, Counselors and Therapists, 418, 425

American College Counseling Association (ACCA)
ACA Code of Ethics and, 78
as advocacy resource for counselors, 93
collaborative relationships and, 126
community college counseling survey, 37–38, 189
on outreach and prevention services, 149
overview, 11–12
personal/mental health counseling survey, 21
American College Health Association (ACHA)
history of, 5
on mental health issues and trends, 21
National College Health Assessment, 318, 319, 333, 355
overview, 11, 13
Recommended Standards and Practices for a College Health Program, 7
on stimulant use, 324
on substance use and abuse, 318
Task Force on Students and College Health, 7
American College Personnel Association–College Student Educators International (ACPA)
as advocacy resource for counselors, 94
on collaborative relationships, 126
College Counseling and Psychological Services Knowledge Base, 114
Commission for Counseling and Psychological Services, 11, 12–13
crisis management trainings, 179
history of, 10
multicultural ethical considerations, 56
The Professional Competency Areas for Student Affairs Educators, 54
professional competency areas of, 193
task force for future of student affairs profession, 104
American Council on Education, 5, 103, 104, 189
American Counseling Association (ACA). *See also* *ACA Code of Ethics;* American College Counseling Association
on crisis and emergency management, 178
crisis management trainings of, 180
International Association of Addiction and Offender Counselors, 324
multicultural competencies of, 52
multicultural ethical considerations of, 56
American Psychiatric Association, 7, 381, 383
American Psychological Association (APA), 11, 16, 53–54
American Student Health Association, 5
Americans With Disabilities Act of 1990 (ADA), 8, 48, 89
Amygdala, 204, 206, 211
Anorexia nervosa, 379, 381. *See also* Disordered eating
Anti-suicide, 395
Anxiety. *See* Stress and anxiety
Anxiety and Depression Association of America, 332, 337
Archer, J. A., Jr., 8, 144
Arnold, K., 57–59, 65
Arousal disorders, 423
Arredondo, P., 52
ASCA (Association for Student Conduct Administration), 179
Asher, Steve, 301
Asidao, C., 150
Assessments and evaluations. *See also* Intake interviews; *specific assessment tools*
for career counseling, 302, 306–307
collaborative relationships for, 128
for depression, 362–363
for disordered eating, 382–383
for families and relationship issues, 292–293, 293*t*
mandatory assessment and counseling, 87–91, 111–112*b*, 323, 325
psychological testing, 34–35
for self-injury, 398–399, 399*b*
for sexual issues and concerns, 418–419, 420*t*
for sexual victimization, 436–437
for stress and anxiety, 340–344
for substance use and abuse, 322
for suicidal ideation, 362, 398–399
in triage model, 131–132
Assimilation, 234
Association for American Universities, 432
Association for Student Conduct Administration (ASCA), 179
Association for University and College Counseling Center Directors (AUCCCD)
on anxiety and depression of students, 129
on client concerns, 50
on clinical staff demographics, 31
on crisis and emergency management, 173
on demographics of directors of counseling clinics, 30–31
on disordered eating, 376
on group counseling, 32
history of, 12
on mental health issues and trends, 21, 29
on need for services, 146
overview, 11
on psychiatric care availability, 34
on teletherapy, 32
Association for University and College Counseling Center Outreach (AUCCCO), 142, 146, 148, 155
Association of Threat Assessment Professionals (ATAP), 179
Associations and organizations, 10–14
Astin, A., 288
Atticus (poet), 353
Autonomy, 87–88, 90–91, 92, 132, 219*t*, 221, 289
Awareness outreach activities, 149*b*, 150

B

Baby boomers, 19
Balancing Safety and Support on Campus (HEMHA), 14
Bandura, Albert, 290
Banning, J. H., 104
Barnes, A. C., 222

Barriers to counseling services
during holidays, 343
lack of awareness of service availability, 134, 147
in outreach and prevention services, 147, 147*t*, 151–152, 155, 157
waiting lists and low staffing, 146–147
BASICS (Brief Alcohol Screening and Intervention for College Students), 325
Baxter Magolda, Marcia, 255–256, 257, 271
Be Body Positive, 384
Beck Depression Inventory–II (BDI-II), 363
Beck Scale for Suicide Ideation, 399
Behavioral addictions, 324, 381
Behavioral intervention teams (BITs)
collaborative relationships for, 126, 134
counselor role in, 36–37, 174–177, 176*t*
defined, 164
legal and ethical issues, 85–87
overview, 172–174
privacy and confidentiality issues, 174–177
red flags and warning signs for further investigation by, 167–168
Behavior management skills, 170
Behaviors that cause disruption, 166–167*b*
Beiter, R., 333
Belenky, M. F., 239–241, 244
Belonging, 301, 304
Bender, M., 149
Beneficence, 289
Berger, E., 403
Berman, E., 419
Bias, social. *See* Discrimination; Race and racism
Bias awareness of counselors, 195, 289
Bigorexia, 382
Binge-eating disorder, 379–381. *See also* Disordered eating
Biopsychosocial approach to counseling, 202
Birth control, 418–419, 421–422
BITs. *See* Behavioral intervention teams
Bland, H. W., 340
Blended families, 267–269
BMIs (brief motivational interventions), 323, 325
Body image, 374, 376–377
Body mass index, 379
Body Project, 384
Booker Ammah, B., 65
Boundaries
between faculty and students, 289
in relationships with hierarchy, 292–293
in therapeutic relationships, 289–290
Brain. *See* Neuro-informed college counseling
Brain stem, 203–204
Breiding, M. J., 436
Brief Alcohol Screening and Intervention for College Students (BASICS), 325
Brief motivational interventions (BMIs), 323, 325
Brief Severity Index for Nonsuicidal Self-Injury, 398
Broaching behavior, 65
Broido, E. M., 256
Bronfenbrenner, U., 57–59, 66
Brown, A. D., 338
Brown, Brené, 125
Brown, G. K., 403
Brown, J., 342
Brunner, J., 21
Bruns, Kristin, 431
Bubrick, K., 403
Buchanan, Christy M., 299
Budget requirements, 143
Bulimia nervosa, 379–380, 381. *See also* Disordered eating
Burnett, Dana, 101, 125

C

CACREP (Council for Accreditation of Counseling and Related Educational Programs), 16, 17, 145, 188
CAGE questionnaire, 322
Campbell, A., 151
Campus-based experiences. *See* Experiential theories of student development
Campus Care and Counseling Act of 2003, 146–147
Campus climate
multiculturalism and, 46, 52
outreach and prevention services and, 142, 152
social identity and, 272
social justice and, 67
substance abuse and, 325
Campus Climate Framework, 52
Campus Climate Survey on Sexual Assault and Sexual Misconduct (AAU), 432
Campus safety or campus police staff, 166
Cantor, D., 435
Career counseling. *See* Academic and career counseling
Career-entry skills, 302
Career fairs, 302
CARE teams, 172–174
Carey, K. B., 322
Carnegie Classification of Institutions of Higher Education, 108–109, 109*b*
Carnes, Patrick, 425
CAS (Council for the Advancement of Standards in Higher Education), 15, 28–29, 146, 300
Casarez, Lesley, 279
Case study of Lina Miller, 186–187, 188, 190–191, 195–197, 203–206, 208–213, 218, 220–224, 226, 228, 234, 239–241, 243–244, 249–256, 263–270
Castleman, B. L., 307
CBT (cognitive-behavioral therapies), 33, 170, 340, 364, 401
CCAPS (Counseling Center Assessment of Psychological Symptoms), 34
CCCs. *See* College counseling centers
Center for Collegiate Mental Health, 21, 335
Center for Epidemiologic Studies Depression Scale–Revised, 363
Cerebellum, 204
Cerebrum, 204–205
Certificate programs, 188

Certification and licensure of counselors, 16–17, 29
Chambers, Judith, 102
Chang, C. Y., 67
Chapman, A. L., 394
Chastity, 421
Chickering, Arthur W., 132, 218–223, 219*t*, 280, 288, 291
Child development, 242
Children as clients, 80–81
Chou, P. S., 318
Chronic care model, 339
Cilente, K., 191
Circles of Sexuality model (Dailey), 416–417
Circumscription, 306
Civil rights movement, 6–7
Clayton, R. B., 291
Clinchy, B. M., 239–241, 244
Clinical depression, 354. *See also* Depression
Clinical interviews. *See* Intake interviews
Codes of ethics, 80. *See also ACA Code of Ethics*
Code switching, 270
Cogan, G., 63
Cognitive and moral theories of student development, 233–247
    case studies, 245–246
    critiques and updates, 244
    Kholberg's theory of moral development, 241–244
    Perry's scheme of intellectual and ethical development, 234–239
    reflection exercise, 233
    women and, 239–241
Cognitive-behavioral therapies (CBT), 33, 170, 340, 364, 401
Collaborative Assessment and Management of Suicidality, 362
Collaborative campus relationships, 125–139
    case studies, 135–137
    crisis and emergency management, 131, 133–134, 166, 170, 178–179
    defined, 126
    diverse roles of counselors and, 127
    equity, diversity, and inclusion roles, 128
    leadership and assessment roles, 128
    for outreach and prevention services, 9, 157
    physical and mental health resources, 9
    professors and university staff, 288
    rationale for, 128–129
    reflection exercise, 125
    for social justice, 67
    student affairs professionals, 9, 126–129, 189
    student needs and service utilization, 130–135
Collectivist traditions, 56
College admissions scandal (2019), 47–48
College Counseling and Psychological Services Knowledge Base, 114
College counseling centers (CCCs), 27–42
    barriers to accessing. *See* Barriers to counseling services
    case studies, 38–39
    directors of, 29–31
    history of, 3–26. *See also* History and evolution of college counseling
    missions and goals of, 29–30, 45, 109
    outreach of, 35–38, 148–149, 148*t*
    promoting awareness of, 149*b*, 150, 288
    reflection exercise, 27
    roles of, 29–31
    services of, 32–35
    staff of, 29–31, 85, 146–147
    triage framework for, 131–132
College Counseling from a Distance (HEMHA), 14
College Students Speak: A Survey Report on Mental Health (National Alliance on Mental Illness), 147, 147*t*
Collegiate Recovery Programs, 320–321, 325
Columbia-Suicide Severity Rating Scale, 362, 399
Communication skills, 291
Community colleges
    combined offices and roles, 83
    counseling centers of, 37–38
    diversity in, 262
    life-span development theories and, 189
    missions of, 109*b*, 262
    multiple dimensions of counseling in, 119*b*
    outreach and prevention services at, 149
    psychological disorders of students, 118*b*
    student affairs and, 105*b*
Competence of counselors
    in assessment instruments, 89
    in leadership and assessment, 128
    multicultural, 51–56, 53*f*, 128
    in social justice and inclusion, 128
    in student learning and development, 127, 193
Competence of students, development of, 219–220, 219*t*
Competition, 335
Compromise, 306
Confidentiality
    ACA Code of Ethics on, 85–86, 433–434, 437
    academic advising and, 83
    BITs and, 174–177
    boundary violations and, 290
    consultation and, 35
    counseling center staff and, 85
    limits of, 84, 175, 177, 290
    mandated counseling and, 91
    multicultural competence and, 52, 56
    privacy vs., 174–175
    sexual victimization and, 433–434, 437
    student affairs and, 129
Conners Continuous Performance Test, 35
Consent for sexual activity, 418–419, 432–433
Consultation, 35, 126
Continuity of care, 343
Contraceptives, 418–419, 421–422
Co-occurring issues, 323, 356, 382–383
Cooper, D. L., 67, 68
Cooper, S., 144, 155
Coping skills
    self-harm and, 394–395, 400–401
    stress and anxiety, 207, 336, 338–340
    transitions and, 254, 257

Corey, M. S., & Corey, G., 289
Cormier, S., 289
Cortisol, 204, 211, 332
Cost of higher education, 336–337
Council for Accreditation of Counseling and Related Educational Programs (CACREP), 16, 17, 145, 188
Council for the Advancement of Standards in Higher Education (CAS), 15, 28–29, 146, 300
Counseling Center Assessment of Psychological Symptoms (CCAPS), 34
Counseling center directors, 29–31
Counseling centers. *See* College counseling centers
Counseling center staff, 29–31, 85, 146–147
Counseling relationships, 79–80, 209–210
Counseling theory, 187–188
Counselors-in-residence, 135
Countertransference, 290
Couples counseling, 419–420
Cover letters, 302
Credentials, 16–17, 29
Crime, 416, 424–425. *See also* Sexual victimization
Crisis and emergency management, 163–181
- behavioral intervention and CARE teams, 172–177. *See also* Behavioral intervention teams
- campus models for, 168–170
- case examples, 164–165, 178–179
- collaborative campus relationships and, 131, 133–134, 166, 170, 178–179
- counselor role on BIT, 174–177, 176*t*
- crisis intervention, 170–171
- crisis recovery and trauma-informed care, 171–172
- reflection exercise, 163
- settings limitations and, 82–83
- social media monitoring and, 92
- types of crises, 165–168, 166–167*b*
- violence risk assessments, 177–178

Critical race theory, 192
Cultural competence, 51–56, 53*f*, 128
Cultural humility, 306
Cultural identity development, 59–60
Cultural theory, 57–61
Culture. *See* Multiculturalism and social justice
Curling parents, 20

D

Dailey, Dennis, 416
Dali Lama, 141
Davis, C., 323
Davis, C. M., 419
Davis, S. L., 419
Dawson, D. A., 318
Day-Vines, N., 65
Dean, L. A., 4, 31
Decision-making trees, 131
De-escalation skills, 166–167
Deliberate Self-Harm Inventory, 398
Demand for services
- outreach and, 9, 142–143, 146–147, 147*t*, 148*b*
- stress management and, 339

DeMartini, K. S., 322
Demographics of clients and counselors, 50–51, 51*t*
Denino, David J., 3
Dennhardt, A. A., 318
Department of Homeland Security, 169, 178
Depression, 353–371
- assessment of, 362–363
- as most common mental health issue, 21
- outreach and prevention, 364–365
- prevalence among college students, 129, 354–355, 355*f*
- reflection exercise, 353–354
- suicidal ideation risk and, 354, 359–362
- symptoms of, 355–359
- treatment for, 363–364

DePue, M. K., 325
DeSilver, D., 304
Desire disorders, 423
Developmental plasticity, 206–207
Diabetes, 382
Diabulimia, 382
Diagnosis. *See* Assessments and evaluations
Diagnostic and Statistical Manual of Mental Disorders (3rd ed. *DSM-3*), 7
Diagnostic and Statistical Manual of Mental Disorders (4th ed. *DSM IV*), 363
Diagnostic and Statistical Manual of Mental Disorders (4th ed., text revision, *DSM IV-TR*), 320
Diagnostic and Statistical Manual of Mental Disorders (5th ed. *DSM-5*)
- on anxiety, 340, 342
- on behavioral addictions, 381
- on depression, 363
- on eating disorders, 378–379, 381
- on sexual issues and concerns, 415–417, 423
- on substance abuse and dependence, 320

Dialectical behavior therapy, 399, 403
Diemer, M. A., 307
Dieting, 375, 376. *See also* Disordered eating
Direct counseling services, 32–33
Directors of counseling centers, 29–31
Disciplinary actions, 323, 325
Discrimination. *See also* Race and racism
- ADA and, 8
- assessments and, 89
- ethics and, 52
- intersectionality and, 47
- multiracial and multiethnic identity and, 269
- sexual identity and, 417

Disordered eating, 373–389
- assessment of, 382–383
- case studies, 385–386
- continuum of, 374–375
- eating disorders vs., 375–376
- preventive interventions for, 130
- protective factors, 378

(Continued)

Disordered eating *(continued)*
reflection exercise, 373–374
risk factors for, 376–378
symptoms and characteristics, 378–382
treatment for, 383–385
Disruptive behaviors, 166–167*b*
Distance learning, 93, 118*b*, 281
Distractibility problems, 118*b*
Diversity, 47, 79–80, 151–152, 262. *See also* Multiculturalism and social justice
Dixon-Gordon, K. L., 394
Dixon v. Alabama State Board of Education (5th Cir. 1961), 6–7
Doerfler, L. A., 34
Domestic violence, 157*b*, 287, 435–437
Dopamine, 206
Downtime, 214
Doyle, E., 306
Drange, I., 306
Drug use. *See* Substance use and addiction
Drunkorexia, 382
DSM. *See Diagnostic and Statistical Manual of Mental Disorders*
Due process, 6–7, 89, 90
Durham, J. C., 68
Dyson, D., 417

E

Eating Attitudes Test, 382
Eating disorders. *See also* Disordered eating
categories of, 378
disordered eating vs., 375–376
outreach and preventions, 384–385
risk factors for, 376–378
Eating Disorders Screening Tool, 382
Ecological systems theory (Bronfenbrenner), 57–59, 66
Ecomaps, 62–66, 63*f*
Educational records, 83–84
Education-career outreach programming, 153
Edwards, Jon, 37, 149
Eells, G. T., 33
Egan, G., 289
Eisenberg, D., 8
Electronic medical records system, 44
Embedded counselors, 134–135
Emergency management. *See* Crisis and emergency management
Emergency preparedness activities, 168
Emotions, management of, 220, 395, 403
Empathy, 49, 170–171, 194–195
Employment. *See* Academic and career counseling
Empowerment, 209
Ending Campus Violence (Van Brunt), 167
Energy drinks, 324
English, T., 336
Enrollment trends, 79
Environments and student development, 190–191
Epigenesis, 210
Epinephrine, 206
Epstein, B., 37
Equilibrium, 234
Erectile disorder, 423
Erikson, Erik, 188, 217, 218, 224, 262, 291–292
Ernhout, C., 397
Ethical development, Perry's framework for, 234–239
Ethical issues. *See also ACA Code of Ethics;* Legal and ethical issues
boundary violations and, 290
consultation services and, 35
level of care and, 131
multicultural competence, 52, 56, 79
Ethnic identity processes, 267–269
Ethnicity. *See* Diversity; Multiculturalism and social justice; Race and racism
Evaluations. *See* Assessments and evaluations
Evans, N. J., 58, 193, 196, 256
Evidence-based practice, 33, 113–114, 145, 363–364
Excitatory neurotransmitters, 206
Executive functioning, 205
Exercise and physical activity, 213
Existential crisis, 227
Experiential Learning (Kolb), 251
Experiential learning theory (Kolb), 251–253, 252*f*, 257–258
Experiential theories of student development, 249–260
case study, 258–259
critique of, 256–257
experiential learning theory, 251–253, 252*f*
guided learning applications, 257–258
reflection exercise, 249
self-authorship and, 255–256
transitions, understanding and coping with, 253–255, 254*t*
types of activities on campuses, 250*b*

F

Facebook, 92
Face-to-face situations, 291
Faculty, 287–288
boundaries with students, 289
as colleagues to student affairs offices, 106–107
Fairness and justice, 242, 244, 289
Family and relationships, 279–298. *See also* Parents; Social support
assessment of, 292–293, 293*t*
case examples, 280–281
case study, 295
coping skills for stress and, 340
developmental stage impact on, 291–292
disordered eating and, 377, 378
gender roles and, 337
homesickness and, 281, 304, 311, 336
interpersonal stress and, 335–336
outreach and prevention implications, 293–294
parents, guardians, and families, 282–284
peers, friends, and roommates, 284–285

prevalence of issues, 281–282
professors and university staff, 287–289
reflection exercise, 279
romantic partners and breakups, 285–287, 288, 335, 420–421
self-injury and, 400
social media and, 290–291
therapeutic relationships, 289–290
treatment for issues with, 292–293, 293*t*
Family Assistance Centers, 169
Family Educational Rights and Privacy Act of 1974 (FERPA), 83–84, 174–175, 177, 290
Faucher, Amanda, 331, 353
Federal Bureau of Investigation (FBI), 47–48, 178
Federal Emergency Management Agency (FEMA), 169
Feinstein, B. A., 323
Female sexual interest/arousal disorder, 423
Fetlife, 418
Fidelity, 289, 300–301
Financial aid, 112*b*, 305, 336–337
Financial stress, 336–337
First-generation college students (FGCSs)
academic advising with, 310–311
career counseling with, 311–312
collaborative college relationships and, 134
defined, 18, 304
family relationships and, 282
financial stress and, 337
professors and university staff relations, 288
Fisher, T. D., 419
Focus, 213
Folkman, S., 332
Food addiction, 381
Forms of Intellectual and Ethical Development in the College Years: A Scheme (Perry), 235
Foubert, J. D., 222
Francis, Perry C., 77
Fraternities, 116
Frey, L. L., 61
Friends. *See* Family and relationships; Peers
Frontal lobe of brain, 205, 211
Functional analysis questions, 398, 399*b*
Functional magnetic resonance imaging, 202

G

Gallup StrengthsFinder 2.0, 285
Garfield, James, 103
Gender. *See also* Males; Women
depression and anxiety and, 337, 356, 360
disordered eating and, 374, 377, 380, 382
identity and, 417
intimate partner violence and, 435, 437
masculinity norms, 116
self-harm and, 394
sexual dysfunction and, 423–424
sexual issues and concerns, 415–416
sexual victimization and, 432
stalking and, 436
stress and anxiety prevalence and, 337–338
substance use and addiction, 321–323
suicide and, 360
virginity and, 421
Generalized anxiety disorder, 341
Generational influences on students, 18–20
Generation Alpha, 20
Generation Google, 20
Generation X, 19
Generation Y, 19–20
Generation Z, 20, 281
Genito-pelvic pain/penetration disorder, 424
Gergen, K. J., 263
G.I. Bill (1944), 5–6
Giftedness evaluation, 35
Gilligan, Carol, 244
Gladding, S. T., 289
Glasser, W., 285
Glazebrook, C., 355
Glenn, C. R., 400
Glosoff, H. L., 68
Gnilka, P. B., 67
Goals. *See* Missions and goals
Go Ask Alice (Columbia University), 418
Goethe, Johann Wolfgang von, 264
Goldberger, N. R., 239–241, 244
Golightly, T., 158
Gonzalez, Laura M., 125, 135, 233, 249, 261
Google, 92
Gottfredson, L. S., 306–307
Grace, M., 20
Graduation rates, 105, 142, 304, 305, 334
Graham, Christopher C., 261
Granello, D. H., & Granello, P. F., 403
Grant, B. F., 318
Greek organizations, 116
Green, K. E., 323
Grief, 129, 172, 359
Griffin, K., 47, 52
Group counseling services, 32, 383–384, 403–404
Group relationships, 282
The Guide to Getting It On (Joannides), 418
Guiffrida, D. A., 119–120

H

Hackney, H. L., 289
Hagedorn, W. B., 325
Hallisey, B. J., 144
Hamza, C. A., 395–396
Handbook of Sexuality-Related Measures (Fisher, Davis, Yarber, & Davis), 419
Hardy, J. A., 33
Hasking, P., 403
Hassan, A. M., 415
Hayden, B., 131
Hazelwood, S., 131
HBCUs (historically black colleges and universities), 46–47, 103, 109

Health insurance, 34, 82, 177, 308, 343
Health Insurance Portability and Accountability Act of 1996 (HIPAA), 174, 175
Health-related outreach programming, 153
Health relationship characteristics, 294
Health Resources and Services Administration (HRSA), 362
Healthy mind platter (Rock & Siegel), 213
Heenan, C., 155
Helicopter parenting, 20
HEMHA (Higher Education Mental Health Alliance), 11, 13–14, 14*f*, 172
Hemispheres of brain, 205, 212
Hernández, E., 192, 271
Higher Education Act of 1965, 103, 146
Higher Education Mental Health Alliance (HEMHA), 11, 13–14, 14*f*, 172
HIPAA (Health Insurance Portability and Accountability Act of 1996), 174, 175
Hippocampus, 204
Hispanic-serving institutions (HSIs), 46, 103
Hispanic students, 103, 304
Historically black colleges and universities (HBCUs), 46–47, 103, 109
History and evolution of college counseling, 3–26
- 1800s, 4
- 1900–1939, 5
- 1940s and 1950s, 5–6
- 1960s and 1970s, 6–7
- 2000s, 8–10
- case study, 22–23
- college counselor preparation, 16–17
- college populations defined, 17–20
- mental health issues and trends, 21–22
- professional organizations and associations, 10–14
- professional standards and accreditation, 15–16
- reflection exercise, 3
- student affairs and, 102–103

Hitchcock, Edward, 4
Hof, L., 419
Hoff, L. A., & Hoff, M., 144
Holidays, 343
Holland, J. L., 312
Homeland Security Department, 169, 178
Homesickness, 281, 304, 311, 336
Hook, J. N., 55
hooks, bell, 43
Hope, 209
Hopeline Network, 385
Hopkins, Mark, 103
Hostile environment sexual harassment, 434
Hougaard, Bent, 20
How to Counsel Students (Williamson), 5
HRSA (Health Resources and Services Administration), 362
Hsieh, C., 307
HSIs (Hispanic-serving institutions), 103
Hubbard, S. M., 193
Humility, 55, 62, 306
Hunt, J., 8
Hurst, J. C., 7
Hurt, Insult, Threaten, and Scream assessment tool, 436
Hypothalamus, 204

I

IACS (International Association of Counseling Services), 15–16, 28–29, 35, 145
Ibrahim, A. K., 355
ICS (Incident Command System), 168
Identity. *See also* Intersectionality; Social constructivism and identity in student development
- development models for, 59–60
- life-span development and, 188
- male, 116
- multiple dimensions of, 264–267, 265*f*
- multiracial and multiethnic identity processes, 267–269
- privilege and, 47–49
- self-injury and, 401
- seven vectors of identity development theory (Chickering), 132, 218–223, 219*t*, 291–292
- sexual, 417
- substance use and abuse, 321

Identity achievement, 227
Identity diffusion, 226
Identity foreclosure, 226
Identity status theory (Marcia), 224–228
iGen/Generation Z, 20
Implicit bias, 49
Imposter syndrome, 263, 310
Incapacitated sexual assault, 432
Incels (involuntarily celibate), 421
Incident Command System (ICS), 168
Inclusivity, 128, 194–195
Indelicato, Natalie Arce, 373
Indigenous populations, 44–46
Individual direct counseling services, 32, 383
Informal consultations, 148*b*
Informal theory, 185, 191, 195
Informed consent
- confidentiality and, 175
- distance learning and, 93
- mandated assessments and, 88–89
- ongoing process of, 82
- social media use, 92
- treatment records and, 84

Inhibitory neurotransmitters, 206
Institutional adjustment, 113
Institution-specific roles and responsibilities, 37–38
Insurance. *See* Health insurance
Intake interviews
- disordered eating and, 382
- forms for, 68, 417
- intimate partner violence, 436
- self-injury and, 397, 398, 400
- sexual issues and concerns, 419–420
- triage services and, 33

Integrated care, 9
Integrative theory, 212–213
Integrity and identity development, 219*t*, 222–223
Interdependence, 221
Intermediate interventions, 111, 129–130
International Association of Addiction and Offender Counselors, 324
International Association of Counseling Services (IACS), 15–16, 28–29, 35, 145
International Classification of Diseases, 340
International Institute for Trauma and Addiction Professionals, 425
International Society for the Study of Self-Injury, 392, 397
Internet. *See also* Social media
  iGen/Generation Z and, 20
  searching, 92
Internships, 93, 302
Interpersonal psychotherapy (IPT), 364
Interpersonal relationships, 219*t*, 221
Interpersonal stress, 335–336
Intersectionality
  adjustment of students and, 114
  discrimination and, 47
  identity development models and, 60
  social constructivism and, 264–265, 271
  training in, 51
Interventions. *See also* Behavioral intervention teams
  for crisis and emergency management, 170–171
  culturally appropriate, 61–66, 63*f*
  intermediate, 111, 129–130
  prevention, 110–111, 129–130
  psychotherapeutic, 111, 118*b*, 130
  for student development, 116, 129–130, 132
Interview preparation, 302, 307
Intimacy, 416–417
Intimate partner violence (IPV), 157*b*, 287, 435–437
Intrusive advising, 310
Inventory of Statements About Self-Injury, 398
IPT (interpersonal psychotherapy), 364
Isolation, 214, 383

J

Jami, Criss, 317
Jane Doe v. University of Oregon (D. Or. 2015), 84
Jealousy, 290–291
Jeanne Clery Disclosure of Campus Security Policy and Campus Crime Statistics Act of 1990, 438
Joannides, Paul, 418
Johnson, M. H., 237
Johnson, V. E., 417
Joiner, T., 396
Jones, P. J., 335
Jones, S. R., 191, 192, 194–196, 265
Jordan, J. V., 61
Jordan, T. A., 55
Journals on college counseling and student affairs, 11
Juhnke, G. A., 403
Justice and fairness, 242, 244, 289

K

Kakhnovets, R., 393
Kane, Brianna, 373
Kearney, L., 50
Keirsey Temperament Sorter, 285
Kelly, J., 323
Kelly, S. J., 355
Kern, C. W., 152, 153
Kettlewell, Caroline, 391
Kilburn, E., 400
King, Martin Luther, Jr., 3
King Lyn, M. M., 149
King-Toler, E., 147
Kinsey Institute, 418
Kiracofe, N. M., 90
Kirsch, D. J., 34
Kitchener, K. S., 289
Klonsky, David, 394, 398
Kloss, Robert J., 233
Knefelkamp, L., 101
Kocet, Michael M., 43, 54
Kohlberg, Lawrence, 241–244
Kolb, David A., 251–253, 252*f*, 257–258
Kraft, D. P., 6
Kuk, L., 104

L

Langdon-Daly, J., 378
Language learning, 207
Lannon, P., 90
Latino students, 103, 304
Law enforcement personnel, 166, 169, 178
Lawnmower parenting, 20
Lazarus, R. S., 332
Leach, M. M., 54
Learning obstacles, 118*b*
Learning Reconsidered (NASPA), 104
Learning Styles Inventory, 252–253, 252*f*
Lee, C., 49
Lee, P, 4
Legal and ethical issues, 77–98
  advocacy and care, 87
  advocacy resources, 93–94
  behavioral intervention teams, 85–86
  case studies, 81, 86–87, 94
  combined offices and roles, 83–84
  complex cases and treatment limitations, 81–83
  diverse student populations and, 79–80
  mandated assessments, 88–90
  mandated counseling, 90–91
  minors as clients, 80–81
  multiple roles in college community, 84–85
  reflection exercise, 77–78
  social media and internet, 91–92
  student affairs colleagues and Title IX, 87

(Continued)

Legal and ethical issues *(continued)*
telehealth and distance counseling, 92–93
Lenhart, Amy, 37, 149
Lepeau, L. A., 194, 195
Lewin, Kurt, 57, 190, 191
Lewis, S. P., 402
Lewis, W., 166
LGBTQ people, 323, 360, 365, 377, 435
Licensure and certification of college counselors, 16–17, 29
Life-span development, 188–189, 218, 224, 291
Likis-Werle, Elizabeth, 125, 135, 317
Limbic system, 204
Linder, C., 67, 68
Linehan, Marsha, 399
Lipson, Sarah, 27
Living Learning Community, 288
Locke, B., 21
Loneliness, 281
Lower SES students, 303–310, 337

M

Major depressive disorder (MDD), 354
Males. *See also* Gender
bigorexia and, 382
eating disorders, manifestation of, 377
erectile disorder, 423
history of American higher education aimed at white males of higher socioeconomic background, 103
as incels (involuntarily celibate), 421
male hypoactive sexual desire disorder, 423
male identity and alcohol use expectations, 116
paraphilic disorders and, 416
Perry's model based on white males at Harvard University, 235, 244
self-injuries and, 394
Manchester, R. A., 113
Mandatory assessment and counseling, 87–91, 111–112*b*, 323, 325
Mandatory reporters, 87, 176–177, 433, 437
Mann, Horace, 103
Marcia, James, 224–228
Marginalized students. *See also* Multiculturalism and social justice
diversity and, 47
low SES and first-generation college students, 304
outreach and, 152
romantic relationships and, 286
student development theory and, 194
suicide and, 365
Marijuana use, 320. *See also* Substance use and addiction
Masculinity norms, 116
Masters, W. H., 417
Masturbation, 422
Maté, Gabor, 261
MBIs (mindfulness-based interventions), 211–212, 214
McCabe, M. P., 415
McCarthy, T., 6
McDavis, R., 52
McEwen, M., 191, 265
McIntosh, Peggy, 48
MCO (multicultural orientation), 54–56, 62
MDD (major depressive disorder), 354
Meadows, M. E., 4
Meaning making
multiple dimensions of identity and, 265–267
scheme of intellectual and ethical development and, 238
self-authorship theory and, 255–257
Media. *See also* Social media
self-injury and, 402
sexual concerns and, 417
Medical evaluations, 384
Medication services, 33–34, 339, 359, 422–423
Meditation, 211, 214
Medulla oblongata, 204
Mencarini, Steven, 249
Mental health issues and trends. *See also specific issues*
academic advisors and, 300–301
community colleges and, 105*b*
counseling centers and, 29–30
legal issues and, 89
mental wellness vs. illness, 211
most common, 117, 129
outreach services and, 142–143, 146–147, 147*t*
prevalence of stress and anxiety, 333
stereotypes, 357
stigma associated with, 4, 51, 147, 147*t*, 342, 357
studies and reports on, 21–22
Mental wellness outreach programs, 213–214
Meyers, A., 64
Michigan Alcohol Screening Test, 322
Microaggressions, 48, 49–50, 268–269, 365
Microgenerations, 19
Midbrain, 204
Millennials, 19–20, 290–291
Miller, W., 171
Mindfulness-based interventions (MBIs), 211–212, 214
Mini-Mental State Examination, 35
Minorities. *See* Multiculturalism and social justice
Minors as clients, 80–81
Missions and goals
of academic advising programs, 300
of community colleges, 109*b*, 262
of counseling centers, 29–30, 45, 109
of institutions, 104–105, 105*b*, 109
of outreach programs, 150–151
Mitchell, K. J., 402
Mitchell, S. L., 9
Mock interviews, 302
Monitoring the Future data collection, 318–319
Moral principles (Kitchener), 289
Moral theories of student development, 234, 241–244
Moratorium stage of identity status, 227
Morrill, W. H., 7

Morrill Act of 1890, 103
Moving away from home
 homesickness. *See* Homesickness
 separation anxiety disorder, 342
Muehlenkamp, J. J., 403
Multicultural and Social Justice Counseling Competencies (MSJCC), 52
Multicultural Guidelines: An Ecological Approach to Context, Identity, and Intersectionality (APA), 53–54
Multiculturalism and social justice, 43–76
 applying multicultural lens to practice, 57–66, 63*f*
 competence and ethical practice, 51–56, 53*f*
 competence in, 128, 264
 ethics and, 52, 56, 79
 example of college counseling center, 44–46
 multiracial and multiethnic identity processes, 267–269
 outreach programming and, 151–152
 reflection exercise, 43–44
 role of social justice and advocacy, 66–68
 student development theory and, 192
 suicide and, 365
 understanding, 46–51, 51*t*
Multicultural orientation (MCO), 54–56, 62
Multiple dimensions of identity model (Abes, Jones, & McEwen), 264–267, 265*f*
Multiracial and multiethnic identity processes, 267–269
Murdock, N. L., 195–196
Murphy, Amy, 163, 166, 167, 279, 294
Murphy, J. G., 318
Muscle dysmorphia, 382
Myelin, 208
Myers-Briggs Type Indicator, 285

N

Naglieri Nonverbal Ability Test, 35
Narrative therapy, 211
National Academic Advising Association, 300
National Alcohol Screening Day, 322
National Alliance on Mental Illness, 147, 147*t*, 357, 363
National Association of Student Personnel Administrators (NASPA), 10, 11, 13, 54, 104, 179, 193
National Behavioral Intervention Team Association (NaBITA), 85, 173, 179
National Career Development Association, 302
National Center for Education Statistics, 262, 303–304
National Child Welfare Workforce Institute, 66
National College Health Assessment (ACHA), 318, 319, 333, 355
National Domestic Violence Hotline, 287
National Eating Disorder Awareness Week, 384
National Eating Disorders Association (NEDA), 375–376, 381, 382, 384
National Education Association, 282
National Health and Social Life Survey, 415
National Incident Management System (NIMS), 168
National Institute on Alcohol Abuse and Alcoholism, 322, 325
National Institute on Drug Abuse (NIDA), 318–319, 324
National Intimate Partner and Sexual Violence Survey, 435
National Library of Medicine, 332
National Response Framework, 168
Native Hawaiian and Pacific Islander, 44–46
NEDA (National Eating Disorders Association), 375–376, 381, 382, 384
Neurogenesis, 210
Neuro-informed college counseling, 201–216
 brain areas, 203–205
 brain development stages, 207–208
 brain processing, description of, 203
 counseling advancements, 202
 developmental plasticity, 206–207
 neurons and neurotransmitters, 206
 neuroscience and counseling, 208–213
 outreach, promoting mental wellness through, 213–214
 practitioners and, 202–203
 reflection exercise, 201–202
 student development theories and, 196
Neurons and neurotransmitters, 203, 206
Neuroplasticity, 206–207
Neuropsychological evaluation, 35
Neville, H. A., 59
NIDA (National Institute on Drug Abuse), 318–319, 324
NIMS (National Incident Management System), 168
Nixon, M. L., 222
Nock, M. K., 395
Nonclinical sexuality issues, 420–421
Nonmaleficence, 289
Nonsuicidal self-injury. *See* Self-injury
Non-Suicidal Self-Injury–Assessment Tool, 398
Nontraditional students, 18
Norepinephrine, 206, 332
Normative depression, 357–359
Nutrition counseling, 384

O

Obsessive-compulsive disorder, 341–342
Occipital lobe of brain, 205
Oetting, E. R., 7
O'Hara, C., 67
Online communities, 155. *See also* Social media
Onset of mental health disorders during college years, 332, 354–355, 374, 377
Operation Varsity Blues (2019), 47–48
Oppression, 67, 89, 192, 270
Organizations and associations, 10–14
Orgasm, 417, 423–424
Orientation programs, 254, 325
Orthorexia, 381–382
Outcome Questionnaire-45, 34
Outreach and preventative services, 141–161
 for career counseling, 307
 case study, 158

(Continued)

Outreach and preventative services *(continued)*
client demographics and, 51
creating programming for, 149–157, 149*b*, 154*t*, 156*t*, 157*b*
crisis and emergency management, 169
definitions and standards, 142, 144–146, 145*b*
for depression, 364–365
for disordered eating, 384–385
for family and relationship issues, 293–294
as function of counseling center, 148–149, 148*t*
impact of, 142–143, 143*b*
mental wellness promotion through, 213–214
need for, 146–147, 147*t*, 148*b*
to reduce demand for direct services, 9
reflection exercise, 141
roles and responsibilities of, 35–38
satellite counselors for, 134–135
for sexual victimization, 438
for stress and anxiety, 339–340, 342–343
for substance use and addiction, 324–325
for suicidal ideation, 364–365
Owen, J., 54, 55, 152

P

Page, L. C., 307
Paladino, Derrick A., 3, 27, 43, 141, 185
Panic disorder, 341
Paraphilic disorders, 416, 424–425
Parcover, J., 154
PARE (process of preparation-action-reflection-evaluation) model, 257–258
Parents, 20, 282–284, 290, 294, 305. *See also* Family and relationships
Parietal lobe of brain, 205
Parker, C. A., 101, 185, 188
Partner Violence Screen, 436
Part-time nontraditional students, 18
Pascarella, E., 18
Paternalism, 4–7
Pathways (therapeutic skills seminar), 35
Patient Health Questionnaire (PHQ) scales, 362–363
Paton, Stewart, 5
Peer counselors, 35
Peer mentoring, 114–115*b*
Peers, 284–285, 321, 335–336, 377
People with disabilities, 8, 48, 89. *See also* Accommodations
Perceived Stress Scale (PSS), 342
Permission, limited information, specific suggestions, intensive therapy (P-LI-SS-IT) model of sex therapy, 420
Perry, William, 234–239, 240, 244
Personal-emotional adjustment, 113
Personal-social outreach programming, 153
Personal values, 87
Peyronie's disease, 423
Phobias, 417
PHQ (Patient Health Questionnaire) scales, 362–363
Physical activity, 213
Physical health, 9, 213–214, 300, 356–357
Piaget, Jean, 234, 241
Planned Parenthood, 418
Plasticity, 206–207
Playtime, 213
Pons, 204
Positive-focused therapies, 211
Posttraumatic stress disorder (PTSD), 337
Postvention, 172
Postvention: A Guide for Response to Suicide on College Campuses (HEMHA), 14
Poverty, 303–310
Power differentials, 288, 292
Predominantly White institutions (PWIs), 46–47
Pregnancy, 421–422
Preventative services. *See* Outreach and preventative services
Prevention interventions, 110–111, 129–130
Preventive Services Task Force, 362
Prinstein, M. J., 395
Privacy, 174–177. *See also* Confidentiality
social media accounts and, 92
Privilege, 47–49
Privileged communication, 175
Problem-solving skills, 401
Process addictions, 324
Process of preparation-action-reflection-evaluation (PARE) model, 257–258
The Professional Competency Areas for Student Affairs Educators (ACPA & NASPA), 54, 193
Professional organizations and associations, 10–14
Professional standards and accreditation, 15–16, 28–29, 80
Professors. *See* Faculty
Protests, 272
PSS (Perceived Stress Scale), 342
Psychiatry services, 33–34, 38
Psychoeducational evaluations, 35
Psychoeducational materials, 91, 116, 130, 149, 155
Psychological testing, 34–35
Psychology Today's therapist finder, 92
Psychosocial development model (Sanford), 191
Psychosocial theories of student development, 217–231
case studies, 229–230
Chickering's seven vectors of identity development theory, 218–223, 219*t*
guided learning application, 223–224, 228
identity status theory, 224–228, 225*f*
reflection exercises, 217
Psychotherapeutic interventions, 111, 130
PTSD (posttraumatic stress disorder), 337
Public speaking, 291
Purging as eating disorder, 379. *See also* Disordered eating
Purpose, student's development of, 219*t*, 222
Putnam, Robert, 304
PWIs (predominantly White institutions), 46–47

Q

Quid pro quo sexual harassment, 434

R

Race and racism. *See also* Diversity; Multiculturalism and social justice
African American students, 46–47, 103, 109, 114–115*b*, 304
career counseling and, 306
Hispanic students, 103, 304
intimate partner violence and, 435
microaggressions, 48, 49–50, 268–269, 365
multiracial and multiethnic identity processes, 267–269
student development theory and, 192
trauma and, 358
Racial identity development, 59–60
Randolph, T. G., 381
Rape, 432–433, 437
Rapport, 288
RCT (relational-cultural theory), 60–61
Recommended Standards and Practices for a College Health Program (ACHA), 7
Records
educational, 83–84
electronic medical records system, 44
informed consent and, 84
parental access to, 290
treatment, 83–84, 290
Redmond, S., 415
Reese, R. J., 289
Referrals
campus-based services and, 131
collaborative campus relationships and, 133
for holidays and breaks, 343
peer counselors and, 35
session limitations and, 82
settings limitations and, 82–83
Reflection, 214, 250–251, 257–258
Reflection exercises
academic and career counseling, 299
cognitive and moral theories of student development, 233
collaborative campus relationships, 125
college counseling centers, 27
crisis and emergency management, 163
depression, 353–354
disordered eating, 373–374
experiential theories of student development, 249
family and relationships, 279
history and evolution of college counseling, 3
legal and ethical issues, 77–78
multiculturalism and social justice, 43–44
neuro-informed college counseling, 201–202
outreach and preventative services, 141
psychosocial theories of student development, 217
self-injury, 391–392
sexual issues and concerns, 413
sexual victimization, 431
social constructivism and identity in student development, 261
stress and anxiety, 331
student affairs, 101
student development theory, 185–186
substance use and addiction, 317–318
Reisser, Linda, 132, 219, 221–223, 280, 288
Relational-cultural theory (RCT), 60–61
Relationships. *See* Family and relationships
Release of information forms, 175
Renn, K., 57–59, 269
Renoir, Pierre-Auguste, 185
Report on the AAU (AAU), 432
Reproduction and sexual health, 417
Responsible employees, 433–434
Résumés, 302, 307
Retention rates, 105, 112*b*, 114–115*b*, 142, 334, 337
Reupert, A., 403
Riddell, K., 335
Ridgway, J. L., 291
Rifkin, Carolyn, 125
Risk assessments, 33, 173, 177–178
Risk-reducing behaviors, 418–419
Robertson, Benjamin, 217
Rock, David, 213
Rockland-Miller, H. S., 33
Rodolfa, E., 152
Rogers, Carl, 6
The Role of the Counselor on the Behavioral Intervention Team (Van Brunt & Sokolow), 175
Rollnick, S., 171
Romantic partners and breakups, 285–287, 288, 335, 420–421
Roommates, 284–285
Roosevelt, Eleanor, 249
Root, Meghan K., 413
Roper, Larry, 108
Rudd, M. D., 117

S

Safety plans, 403
SAMHSA (Substance Abuse and Mental Health Services Administration), 362
SAMHSA-HRSA Center for Integrated Health Solutions, 362
Sanabria, Samuel, 201
Sanchez, D., 147
Sanford, N., 191
Sanghavi, E., 90
Sasso, P. A., 116
Satellite counselors, 134–135
Satterly, B., 417
Savage, Marjorie, 294
SCCT (social cognitive career theory), 264

Scheme of intellectual and ethical development (Perry), 234–239, 244
Schlesinger, C., 323
Schlossberg, Nancy K., 132, 253–255, 254*t*, 257
Scholl, Mark B., 299
Schooley, K., 307
School shootings, 10, 85, 173
Schwitzer, Alan M., 101, 111*b*, 114*b*, 116, 118*b*, 125
Screening. *See* Assessments and evaluations
Seemiller, C., 20
Seko, Y., 402
Selective serotonin reuptake inhibitors (SSRIs), 359
Self-authorship theory (Baxter Magolda), 255–256, 257, 271
Self-efficacy, 264
Self-Injurious Thoughts and Behaviors Interview, 399
Self-injury, 391–412
  assessment of, 397–399, 399*b*
  case study, 405–407
  defined, 392
  depression and, 354
  outreach and prevention, 404
  prevalence of, 393
  protective factors, 403
  reflection exercise, 391–392
  signs and symptoms of, 397
  suicide and, 395–397, 396*t*
  treatment for, 399–404
  types and functions of, 393–395
Self-Injury and Recovery Research and Resources, 397
Self-pleasure, 422
Self-punishment, 395
Sensation-seeking behaviors, 395
Sensuality, 416
Separation anxiety disorder, 342
Serpell, L., 378
Servicemen's Readjustment Act of 1944, 5–6
Session limitations on student access, 82
Setting limitations on range of services offered, 82–83, 147*t*
Seven vectors of identity development theory (Chickering), 132, 218–223, 219*t*, 291–292
Sevig, T., 150
Sexual addiction, 424–425
Sexual assault, 432–433, 437
Sexual dysfunctions, 422–423
Sexual fantasies, 422
Sexual harassment, 433–434
Sexual identity, 417
Sexual intimacy, 416–417
Sexual issues and concerns, 413–429
  assessment of, 418–420, 420*t*
  case studies, 426–428
  diagnosis and treatment of, 420–425
  outreach programs for, 143*b*
  prevalence of, 415–416
  reflection exercise, 413
  sexuality education, 416–418
  substance use and abuse, 321
Sexuality Information and Education Council of the United States, 418
Sexualization, 417
Sexually transmitted infections (STIs), 418, 421–422
Sexual orientation, 417. *See also* LGBTQ people
Sexual relationships, 285–287, 288
Sexual response cycle (Masters & Johnson), 417
Sexual victimization, 431–442
  assessment of, 436–437
  case studies, 439–440
  federal guidelines and prevention, 438
  outreach and prevention services for, 157*b*
  prevalence of, 431–436
  reflection exercise, 431
  Title IX of the Education Code and, 87, 288–289, 438
  treatment for, 437
Shaffer, K. S., 33
Shaikh, N., 288
Shakin, Rachel, 233
Shapiro, C., 64
Sharkin, B. S., 8, 148
Siegel, Daniel J., 201, 213
Sisson, V. S., 222
Situational depression, 357–359
Sleep, 213
Smartphones, 9, 20
Smith, L., 59, 67
Snowplow parenting, 20
Social adjustment, 113
Social anxiety disorder, 341
Social cognitive career theory (SCCT), 264
Social constructivism and identity in student development, 261–275
  approaches to practice, 271–272
  case study, 273–274
  critique of, 270–271
  multiple dimensions of identity, 264–267, 265*f*
  multiracial and multiethnic identity processes, 267–269
  overview, 263
  reflection exercise, 261
  social cognitive career theory, 264
Social contagion, 403
Social justice, 12, 43–46, 128, 192, 271. *See also* Multiculturalism and social justice
Social learning theory (Bandura), 290
Social media
  ethical issues in counseling and, 91–92
  iGen/Generation Z and, 20
  relationships, impact on, 290–291
  social identity and, 282
  standards of beauty and, 374, 376
  stress and anxiety, 336
Social norms and pressures, 116, 321
Social support. *See also* Family and relationships
  academic success and, 301
  brain health and, 214
  disordered eating and, 378
  from peers and friends, 284–285

self-injury and, 400, 403
stress management and, 340
Society for the Scientific Study of Sexuality, 418
Sociopolitical student development, 307
Sohail, M., 288
Sokolow, B., 175
Solomon, Jeff, 163
Solution-focused therapy, 211
SPPV. *See The Student Personnel Point of View*
Spurgeon, Charles, 331
SSRIs (selective serotonin reuptake inhibitors), 359
Stalking, 435–436
Standards of practice, 15–16, 28–29
Stanley, B., 403
Steen, S., 65
Steenberger, B. N., 113
Sterba, S. K., 395
Stereotypes, 269, 357
Sternberg, R. J., 286
Stewart, D. L., 54, 192, 195
Stewart, S. L., 395–396
Stigma associated with counseling, 4, 51, 147, 147*t*, 342, 357
Stimulants, 320, 324. *See also* Substance use and addiction
Stinson, F. S., 318
STIs (sexually transmitted infections), 418, 421–422
Stone, G. L., 8
Strange, Carney, 189–190
Strength-based therapies, 211
StrengthsFinder 2.0, 302
Stress and anxiety, 331–351
academic stress, 334–335
animal therapy program for, 145*b*
anxiety disorders, defined, 332
assessment of, 340–344
case studies, 343–346
common stressors, 334–338
communication skills and, 291
coping skills for, 207, 336, 338–340
crisis and emergency management, 170
depression and, 356–359
disordered eating and, 377
exercise and, 213
friendships and social supports to offset, 285
gender and, 360
healthy vs. unhealthy, 338–339
interpersonal stress, 335–336
limbic system and, 204
low SES students and, 305
management vs. prevention, 339–340
as most common mental health issue, 21
neuroplasticity and, 207
normative and clinical anxiety, 338
outreach implications, 342–343
physiological effects of, 332
prevalence of anxiety disorders, 129, 332, 333–334
reflection exercise, 331
technology use and, 10, 336
treatment and therapies for, 211, 212, 339, 344
Strong Interest Inventory, 302
Student adjustment, 111–114, 111–112*b*
Student affairs, 101–124. *See also* Collaborative campus relationships
Carnegie Classification of Institutions of Higher Education and, 108–109, 109*b*
case illustration, 116
case study, 119–120
college counseling-related skills, adaptation for, 117, 119*b*
counseling, similarities and differences, 126–127
effective support and, 110
faculty and divisional colleagues, 106–107
history of, 102–103
institutional differences and, 107–108
institutional mission and, 104–105, 105*b*
modern divisions of, 104
organization of, 105–106, 107*t*
reflection exercise, 101
responsible employees and, 433–434, 437
student adjustment and, 111–114, 111–112*b*
student development and, 114–116, 114–115*b*, 193
student wellness and success, 116–117, 118*b*
training for career in, 16, 126–127
tripartite intervention model and, 110–111
Student development. *See also* Identity
academic success and jeopardy in, 301–302
competence in, 127, 193
defined, 116
family and relationships, stage of development's impact on, 291–292
interventions for, 116, 129–130, 132
outreach programming for, 144, 146
social norms and, 116
sociopolitical, 307
stressors in, 129
student affairs and, 114–116, 114–115*b*
substance use and addiction in, 321–322
Student development theory, 185–200
case example, 186–187
case study, 197–198
cognitive and moral, 233–247. *See also* Cognitive and moral theories of student development
emergence of, 189–191
exponential, 249–260. *See also* Experiential theories of student development
general groupings of, 191–193
importance of, 187–189
inclusiveness and, 194–195
neuro-informed, 201–216. *See also* Neuro-informed college counseling
psychosocial, 217–231. *See also* Psychosocial theories of student development
reflection exercise, 185–186
social constructivism and, 261–275. *See also* Social constructivism and identity in student development
student affairs profession and, 193–194
study of, 195–197
Student involvement theory (Astin), 288

Student loans, 112*b*, 305, 336–337
Student needs and service utilization, 130–135
Student organizations, 157
The Student Personnel Point of View (SPPV, American Council on Education), 5, 103, 104, 189
Student populations, defined, 17–18
Student rights, 6–7
Study abroad, 92–93
Study skills, 300
Substance Abuse and Mental Health Services Administration (SAMHSA), 362
Substance Abuse Subtle Screening Inventory, 322
Substance use and addiction, 317–329
  abstinence, 319
  abuse and dependence, 320
  alcohol use expectations, 116
  assessment of, 322
  case study, 326
  depression and, 356
  drug-facilitated sexual assault, 432–433
  drugs vs. alcohol, 320–321
  drunkorexia, 382
  energy drinks, 324
  experimentation, 319
  fraternities and, 116
  gender and, 321–323
  incapacitated sexual assault and, 432
  low SES students and, 305
  mandated assessment and, 88
  outreach and prevention, 324–325
  process and behavioral addictions, 324
  reflection exercise, 317–318
  sexual dysfunction and, 422–423
  social/regular use, 319–320
  student development and, 321–322
  treatment for, 322–323, 325
Sue, D. W., & Sue, D., 59, 60
Suess, Esther, 299
Suicidal Behaviors Questionnaire–Revised, 399
Suicidal ideation
  assessment of, 362, 398–399
  behavioral risk factors for, 360–362
  crisis and emergency management for, 172
  defined, 360
  depression and risk for, 354, 359–362
  mandated assessment and, 88
  outreach and prevention, 364–365
  rates of, 129
  self-injury and, 395–397, 396*t*
  treatment for, 362
Suicide Assessment Five-step Evaluation and Triage, 362
Suicide Attempt Self-Injury Interview, 399
Suicide Prevention Resource Center, 403
Suicide Probability Scale, 399
Sun, J., 304
Supervision roles, 36, 64, 68
Support groups, 383–384
Survey of Community/Two Year College Counseling Services (ACCA), 189

T

Tan, M., 376
TAO (Therapist Assisted Online), 32–33
Taplin, Beau, 373
Tarule, J. M., 239–241, 244
Technology. *See also* Social media
  depression outreach and prevention, 364
  distance learning, 93, 118*b*, 281
  electronic medical records system, 44
  family communication and, 283
  generational differences in use of, 19–20
  online communities for outreach services, 155
  sexual victimization and, 433–436
  social media use and guidance, 91–92
  student communication trends and, 9–10
  teletherapy, 32–33, 92–93
Telephone help lines, 385
Teletherapy and telehealth, 32–33, 92–93
Temporal lobe of brain, 205
Terenzini, P., 18
Terrorism, 10. *See also* Violence
Theory of challenge and support (Sanford), 191
Theory of circumscription and compromise (Gottfredson), 306–307
Therapeutic dialogue, 210–211
Therapeutic relationships, 289–290, 292
Therapist Aid, 155
Therapist Assisted Online (TAO), 32–33
Therapy dogs, 145*b*
Threat assessments, 177–178
Threat-to-self indicators, 9, 21
Timberlake, D. S., 318
Time-in activities, 214
Time management, 118*b*
Titanium (electronic medical records system), 44
Title IX, Education Amendments of 1972, 87, 157*b*, 288–289, 433–434, 438
Toner, C., 64
Toprak, S., 403
Torres, V., 194, 195, 271
Traditional students, 17
Training of college counselors
  in behavioral intervention teams, 86
  in college counseling centers, 36
  credentials and certifications, 16–17, 29
  in crisis and emergency management, 168, 170, 179–180
  in diversity and intersectionality, 51
  in life-span development, 188
  in prevention services, 145
  recent trends in, 8–9
  student affairs training, differences in, 126–127
Transfer students, 365, 377
Transgender people, 360
Transitions. *See* Adjustment of students
Transition theory (Schlossberg), 132, 253–255, 254*t*, 257
Trauma, 357–359, 403

Trauma-informed care, 171–172
Treatment. *See also* Assessments and evaluations; Interventions
for depression, 363–364
direct counseling for, 32–33
for disordered eating, 383–385
for family and relationship issues, 292–293, 293*t*
limitations of, 81–83
of minors, 80–81
psychological assessment, 34–35
for self-injury, 399–404
for sexual issues, 420–425
for sexual victimization, 437
for stress and anxiety, 211, 212, 339, 344
for substance use and addiction, 322–323, 325
for suicidal ideation, 362
triage for, 33–34
Treatment records, 83–84, 290
Triage services, 33–34, 131–134
Tribal Colleges, 103
Tripartite intervention model, 110–111, 112*b*, 114*b*, 118*b*, 130
Truman, Harry S., 6
Truong, D., 34
Turner, E. A., 51
Twenge, J. M., 20

U

Uhernik, J., 168, 170
Ulfvebrand, S., 383
Underrepresented students, 47, 152, 194. *See also* Multiculturalism and social justice
University of Hawai'i at Hilo (UHH), 44–46
Uprooting Sexual Violence in Higher Education (Murphy & Van Brunt), 294
U.S. National Response Framework, 168

V

Values, 417
Van Brunt, Brian, 163, 166, 167, 175, 177–178, 279, 294
Veterans, 5–6
Veterans Administration, 5–6
Violence
behaviors leading to, 167–168, 166–167*b*
domestic violence, 157*b*, 287, 435–437
mandated assessment and, 88
school shootings, 10, 85, 173
sexual assault, 432–433, 437
terrorism, 10
Violence Against Women Reauthorization Act of 2019, 438
Virginity, 421

W

Wallace, D., 21
Walsh, B., 398, 403
Warren, C. S., 322
Warren, G., 118*b*
Watson, Joshua C., 27, 217, 233, 331, 353
Web-based counseling services, 32–33, 92–93
Wechsler Adult Intelligence Scale–IV, 35
Weight gain and sobriety, 322–323
Wellness centers, 9, 416
Wells, L., 90
Westheimer, Ruth K., 413
Wheeler, M., 311
Whisenhunt, Julia L., 391
White matter (brain), 208
White privilege, 48–49
Whitlock, Janis, 394, 397, 400
Whitt, Elizabeth, 108
Whyte, A. K., 119–120
Widick, C., 101
Wilcox, S. L., 415
Williams, Frankwood, 5
Williamson, E. G., 5
Willoughby, T., 395–396
Winkle-Wagner, R., 192, 262
Woman Abuse Screening Tool, 436
Women. *See also* Sexual victimization
cognitive and moral theories of student development and, 239–241, 244
depression rates among, 360
disordered eating and, 374, 377
domestic violence and, 157*b*, 287, 435–437
sexual dysfunction and, 423–424
sexual issues and concerns among, 415
substance use and abuse, 321–323
Women's Ways of Knowing (Belenky, Clinchy, Goldberger, & Tarule), 239–241, 244
Woodcock-Johnson Tests of Cognitive Abilities, 35
Woolsey, C. L., 324
Workforce development, 109*b*
Working memory, 213
World Health Organization, 333, 341
World Mental Health International College Student project, 333
World War II, 5–6

X

Xennials, 19

Y

Yarber, W. L., 419
Yeung, S., 151
Yu, Z., 376